CONCORDIA POPULAR COMMENTARY

REVELATION

LOUIS A. BRIGHTON

CONCORDIA PUBLISHING HOUSE • SAINT LOUIS

Copyright © 2009 Concordia Publishing House
3558 S. Jefferson Ave., St. Louis, MO 63118-3968
1-800-325-3040 • www.cph.org

Concordia Publishing House thanks the Reverend Dr. Paul E. Deterding for editing this volume.

Unless otherwise indicated, Scripture quotations are the author's translation.

Quotations from the pseudepigrapha are taken from *The Old Testament Pseudepigrapha*, two vols., ed. James H. Charlesworth (New York: Doubleday, 1983–85).

Manufactured in the United States of America

Library of Congress Cataloging-in-Publication Data

1 2 3 4 5 6 7 8 9 10   18 17 16 15 14 13 12 11 10 09

CONTENTS

EDITORS' PREFACE — VI

AUTHOR'S PREFACE — X

PRINCIPAL ABBREVIATIONS — XII

INTRODUCTION

The Significance of Revelation — 1
  The Last Book of the Bible — 1
  The Christological Testimony of Revelation — 1
  Revelation: A Celebration of the Saints — 2

The Character of Revelation — 2
  Revelation, a Prophetic Apocalypse — 2
  The Purpose of Revelation — 4
  The Message of Revelation — 4
  The Structure of Revelation — 6

The Author and Writing of Revelation — 8
  The Author — 8
  The Writing of Revelation — 9
  John the Author: The Man for the Time and Place — 11
  The Acceptance of Revelation — 14
  The Gospel and Revelation: Literary Complements — 14
  Literary Style — 15

The Transmission and Interpretation of Revelation — 17
  The Greek Text of Revelation — 17
  Interpreting Revelation — 18

COMMENTARY

1:1–3:22 INTRODUCTION
  1:1–8 Prologue — 25
  1:9–20 Commissioning of John: Vision of the Son of Man — 32
    Excursus Son of Man — 38
  2:1–3:22 Letters of Preparation to the Seven Churches
    Excursus The Seven Letters of Preparation (2:1–3:22) — 42
      2:1–7 To the Angel of Ephesus — 47
      2:8–11 To the Angel of Smyrna — 50
      2:12–17 To the Angel of Pergamum — 52
      2:18–29 To the Angel of Thyatira — 55
      3:1–6 To the Angel of Sardis — 58
      3:7–13 To the Angel of Philadelphia — 61
      3:14–22 To the Angel of Laodicea — 65

4:1–22:5 THE PROPHETIC MESSAGE
  4:1–5:14 The Inaugural Vision of Heaven, Introducing
    the Message
    Excursus The Inaugural Vision of Heaven (4:1–5:14) — 75

4:1–11   The Throne of God and His Heavenly Court   77

5:1–14   The Coronation and Enthronement of the Lamb:
The Seven-Sealed Scroll   89

Excursus   *The Lamb of God*   101

6:1–16:21   **The Prophecy**

Excursus   *Three Prophetic Visions of History, Each from Christ's
Ascension to the End (6:1–16:21)*   106

6:1–8:5   **First Sevenfold Vision of History from the Cross
to the End (The Seven-Sealed Scroll Introduced
by the Lamb)**

6:1–17   The First Six Seals: Tribulations and the End   112

7:1–17   Interlude: The Church Militant and the
Church Triumphant   122

Excursus   *Angelic Mediators in Jewish Tradition and the
Book of Revelation*   143

8:1–5   The Seventh Seal Introduces the Second Sevenfold
Vision   147

8:6–11:19   **Second Sevenfold Vision of History from the
Cross to the End (The Seven Trumpet-Angels):
Disorders in Nature Accompanied by Sufferings
of Evil Afflict Humanity**

8:6–13   The First Four Trumpet-Angels: Upheavals in Nature   158

9:1–21   The Fifth and Sixth Trumpet-Angels: Demons
from the Abyss and the Last Battle   164

10:1–11   First Scene of the Interlude: The Mighty Angel
from Heaven Commissions John   176

Excursus   *The Identity and Function of the Mighty
Angel of Revelation 10*   191

Excursus   *The Mediators of Revelation: Guides to the Structure
of the Book*   193

Outline of the Mediating Structure of Revelation   194

11:1–14   Second Scene of the Interlude: The Temple
Measured and the Two Witnesses   197

11:15–19   The Seventh Trumpet-Angel: The End and Its Joy   211

Excursus   *The Missiology of Revelation*   216

12:1–14:20   **Interregnum: The Cosmic War between Christ and
Satan, between God's Saints and the Forces of Evil**

12:1–18   The Woman with Child and the Dragon   224

13:1–18   The Evil Forces of the Dragon: The Beast from
the Sea and the Beast from the Earth   238

14:1–5   The Conquering Lamb and the Victory Song
of the Saints   250

Excursus   *144,000*   255

14:6–13   The Defeat of the Dragon and His Beasts Announced   257

14:14–20   The Son of Man and the Harvest at the End   263

15:1–16:21   **Third Sevenfold Vision of History from the Cross
to the End (The Seven Censer-Angels): Plagues
of God's Wrath as God's Judgment Is Poured Out**

15:1–8	Preparation for the Last Plagues: Introduction of the Seven Censer-Angels	272
16:1–11	The First Five Censers of God's Wrath	279
16:12–16	The Sixth Censer of God's Wrath: Armageddon	285
16:17–21	The Seventh Censer of God's Wrath: The End	291
17:1–22:5	**The Conclusion: The End and the New Heaven and New Earth**	
17:1–18:24	**The Judgment and Overthrow of the Forces of the Dragon**	
17:1–18	The Judgment of the Harlot	298
18:1–24	The Fall of Babylon and the Rejoicing of the Saints	314
Excursus	*Is the Harlot the Antichrist?*	328
19:1–21	**Victorious Celebration**	
19:1–10	A Song of Victory and the Marriage Feast of the Lamb	334
19:11–21	The Second Coming of Christ at the End	345
Excursus	*The Use of the Definite Article with "God"*	358
Excursus	*The Great Te Deum of Praise in Revelation*	359
20:1–10	**The Judgment and Overthrow of the Dragon**	
Excursus	*The Millennium*	368
20:1–6	The Millennium: The New Testament Era, When the Dragon's Power Is Restricted	372
20:7–10	The Battle of Gog and Magog and the Final Doom of Satan	388
20:11–15	The Bodily Resurrection and the Last Judgment	394
21:1–22:5	**The New Heaven and New Earth Portrayed as the Heavenly City Jerusalem**	
21:1–8	The New Heaven and New Earth	402
21:9–27	The New Jerusalem	413
22:1–5	The Garden Restored	422
Excursus	*The Restored Physical Creation*	428
22:6–21	**EPILOGUE**	432
Excursus	*Summary of the Christology of Revelation*	447

LIST OF FIGURES

Figure 1	The Three Divine Titles in Revelation 22:13	439

EDITORS' PREFACE

What may a reader expect from the Concordia Popular Commentary?

This commentary series brings faithful Christian Bible scholarship to the people. Based on the Concordia Commentary series, its goals are similar: to help Christians understand and talk about God's Word with greater clarity, understanding, and faithfulness to the divine intent of the text.

The commentaries in this popular commentary series are designed for Christians that have an intermediate-level familiarity with Scripture and with the teachings of historic Christianity, especially those of the Lutheran Church. These volumes offer the insights of the scholarly Concordia Commentary series without the need to know foreign languages like Greek, Hebrew, and Aramaic. The central points from the scholarly series remain the same. Some differences include the removal of foreign-language textual notes. Footnote references and extensive interaction with certain technical, academic sources also have been removed. If the reader wishes to consult a list of sources, he or she is encouraged to look at the bibliography in the corresponding Concordia Commentary volume.

Jesus Christ is the content of the scriptural testimony. The Lord himself has said, "The Scriptures ... testify to me" (Jn 5:39). The message of the Scriptures is the Good News of God's work to reconcile the world to himself through the life, death, resurrection, ascension, and everlasting session of Jesus Christ at the right hand of God the Father. Under the guidance of the same Spirit who inspired the writing of the Scriptures, these commentaries seek to find in every passage of every canonical book "that which promotes Christ" (as Martin Luther's hermeneutic is often described). They are Christ-centered, "Christological" commentaries.

Even as the God of the Gospel came into this world in Jesus Christ (the Word in human flesh), the scriptural Gospel has been given to and through the people of God, for the benefit of all humanity. God did not intend his Scriptures to have a life separated from the church. He gave them through servants of his choosing: prophets, sages, evangelists, and apostles. He gave them to the church and through the church for admonition and comfort, for preaching and teaching. The living context of Scripture is always the church, where the Lord's ministry of preaching, baptizing, forgiving sins, teaching, and celebrating the Lord's Supper continues. This series remains aware of the close union of Scripture and church, of Word and Sacraments, a result of God taking up human flesh in Christ.

This Gospel Word of God creates a unity among all those in whom it works the obedience of faith and who confess the truth of God revealed in it. This is the unity of the one holy Christian and apostolic church, which extends through world history. The church is to be found wherever the marks of the church are present: the Gospel in the Word and the Sacraments. These have been proclaimed, confessed, and celebrated in many different cultures and are in no way limited or especially attached to any single culture or people. These commentaries seek to promote concord, in the best sense of the terms, to be confessional, ecumenical, and "catholic" (universally Christian).

All of those convictions and characteristics describe the theological heritage of Martin Luther and of the confessors who subscribe to the *Book of Concord* (1580)—those who have come to be known as Lutherans. The editors and authors forthrightly confess their subscription to the doctrinal exposition of Scripture in the *Book of Concord*. As the publishing arm of The Lutheran Church—Missouri Synod, Concordia Publishing House is bound to doctrinal agreement with the Scriptures and the Lutheran Confessions and seeks to herald the true Christian doctrine to the ends of the earth.

As they unfold the scriptural testimony to Jesus Christ, these commentaries talk about Law and Gospel. These are the overarching doctrines of the Bible. Understanding them in their proper distinction and relationship to one another is a key for understanding the self-revelation of God and his plan of salvation in Jesus Christ. God's Law condemns our sin, and his Gospel forgives our sin. However, Law and Gospel do not always appear simply labeled as such in Scripture. The language in Scripture is multicolored, with many and rich hues. A Bible passage may express Law and Gospel by the themes of the fallen creation and the new creation in Christ; darkness and light; death and life; wandering and the promised land; exile and return; ignorance and wisdom; demon possession and the kingdom of God; sickness and healing; being lost and then being found; guilt and righteousness; flesh and Spirit; fear and joy; hunger and feast; or Babylon and the new Jerusalem. But the common element is God's gracious work of restoring fallen humanity through the Gospel of his Son. This stress on the Gospel proclamation makes these commentaries, in the proper sense, evangelical.

Scripture is God's vehicle for communicating the Gospel. The editors and authors accept without reservation that the canonical books of the Old and New Testaments are, in their entirety, the inspired, infallible, and inerrant Word of God. The triune God is the ultimate author of the Bible, and the Holy Spirit breathed forth every word in the original Hebrew, Aramaic, and Greek through the holy authors in a supernatural process of divine inspiration. This is much more profound than the common use of "inspired" to describe a person who is moved by a poignant event in life, a great idea, a brilliant speaker, and so on. God is the one who inspired the authors of Scripture. He worked through those men and achieved his goal in every respect, so that the Scriptures are God's Word, without blemish, error, or falsehood.

Yet in the mysterious process by which the Scriptures were divinely inspired (e.g., 2 Tim 3:16; 2 Pet 1:21), God made use of the human faculties, knowledge, interests, and styles of the biblical writers, whose individual books surely are marked by distinctive features. At the same time, the canon of Scripture has its own inner unity, and each passage must be understood in harmony with the larger context of the whole. This commentary series pays heed to the smallest of textual details because of its acceptance of plenary and verbal inspiration.

Authors in this series interpret each text in accord with the analogy of faith, following the principle that Scripture interprets Scripture. Passages that are clearer, such as when Jesus explains a parable, guide the interpretation of passages that are not as transparent, such as the parable itself. One always looks first at the clear passages for the meaning and intent of the Lord. One then looks to related passages that have similar themes and language. Obscure passages should never be interpreted in a way that conflicts with well-understood passages. Doctrine is established by the plain sense of clear passages. Literal passages include Mt 28:19–20 and the Lord's Words instituting the Lord's Supper in Mt 26, Mk 14, Lk 22, and 1 Cor 11. Even though "this is my body" may not be captured by human reason, nevertheless, the passage has Jesus, the elements, and the congregation of disciples. That is as real as the pastor, the elements, and today's congregation.

Scripture passages do not exist in isolation. One can find the literal sense of a difficult passage in a clearer parallel text, a passage where prophecy is fulfilled, or the accumulated evidence concerning a topic in Scripture. The Bible is replete with passages covering all aspects of human life from before birth to after death, from the house of worship to the outhouse. No one can find a situation so unique or so bad into which a loving, forgiving God will not enter. God really means "all nations." God wants to save you, and his Word speaks to where you are in life.

Sometimes one can find both a literal meaning and an additional, spiritual meaning called the "mystical sense." This spiritual meaning always rests on and connects with the literal sense, as orthodox Lutheran theologians like Johann Gerhard describe. There may indeed be ways of applying Scripture to oneself, to cultural changes, and to political events. For example, a Christian identifies the sin of the prodigal son with his own and therefore hears the forgiveness of the gracious, loving father as God's forgiveness to him. The parable is more than a mere story. It plays a vital role in the application of Law and Gospel. Figures of speech, allegory, morality, and heavenly revelation all connect with this spiritual sense. Yet this sense can be abused, a caution that Lutheran biblical interpretation has always sounded.

Such application may be very helpful, for example, in cross-cultural communication. After the fall of Rome and the huge upheaval of migrant nations with different languages, the Church relied heavily on allegory to help Germanic and Slavic peoples to identify with the literal meaning of Scripture using ideas familiar to them. Allegory unfortunately became the dominant method of interpretation and got separated from the literal sense. People began to read all kinds of meaning into Scripture, which is contrary to God's intent.

In many passages one can see a moral sense where the literal meaning of a passage also establishes a universal moral principle revealed by God to curb the unrighteous, mirror brightly our sin, and guide our steps. Additionally, one may encounter a heavenly sense in some passages that speaks not only to how God literally deals with us here and now, but also to heavenly realities that pass beyond human understanding and to our eternal home with God. All these other senses, as Gerhard describes in Topic II, On the Interpretation of Scripture, in his 1610 *Loci Theologici* and in Topic IV, On Christ, in the 1625 *Exegesis*, rest on the fundamental, literal sense.

The authors and editors stand in the exegetical tradition of Martin Luther and the other Lutheran reformers, who in turn stand in continuity with faithful theologians of the early and medieval church. All remain rooted in the hermeneutics of the Scriptures themselves (evident, for example, by how the New Testament interprets the Old). This method, practiced also by many non-Lutherans, includes (1) interpreting Scripture with Scripture in harmony with the whole of Christian doctrine revealed in the Word; (2) giving utmost attention to the grammar of the original language of the text; (3) seeking to discern the intended meaning of the text, the "plain" or "literal" sense as it connects to different literary genres and figures of speech; (4) drawing on linguistics, archaeology, literature, philosophy, history, and other fields as they help one understand the text; (5) considering the history of the church's interpretation; (6) applying the text as authoritative also for today's interpreter, and (7) above all, seeing the present application and fulfillment of the text in terms of Jesus Christ and his corporate church; upholding the Word, Baptism, and the Supper as the means through which Christ imparts salvation today; and affirming the inauguration, already now, of the eternal benefits of that salvation that is yet to come.

AUTHOR'S PREFACE

The particular study of Revelation has been a lifelong vocation and pursuit. It began early in my pastoral ministry, in the 1950s in London, England, while ministering to a beloved adopted mother in Christ. On her deathbed she asked me to read to her the words of Rev 7:9–17. As I did so from the King James Version, she recited them along with me from memory. At the conclusion of saying together these beautiful words, she said that tonight or tomorrow she would be with those blessed saints in heaven, because "I also have washed myself in the blood of the Lamb." I had read those words before, but I had never focused my attention and faith on them. Nor had I given any careful attention to Revelation in my personal study of the Bible. But that aged saint of God, who closed her eyes in death by looking at her Savior through these words in Revelation, motivated me to begin a lifelong study of this last book of the Bible. For as these words of Revelation 7 were a fitting conclusion of comfort for this blessed saint as she waited for her Lord to come, they now became for me a beginning of an understanding that Revelation is the conclusion of the entire Bible. Thus began my earnest study of it.

Throughout the years, many people have been a part of my study of Revelation through guidance, encouragement, and prayers. I can mention only a few here by name, though there are many more. Those who have provided guidance in formal study in academia include Drs. Martin H. Franzmann, William F. Arndt, and Paul M. Bretscher, professors of exegetical theology at Concordia Seminary in St. Louis, Missouri, and Dr. Robert F. O'Toole, S.J., professor of New Testament in the School of Theological Studies at Saint Louis University. Those who have furnished encouragement and prayers include my beloved wife of over fifty years, Mary Belle, and colleagues in ministry in the parish such as Rev. E. George Pearce and Rev. Ralph F. Fischer, and colleagues in academic life such as Dr. L. Dean Hempelmann, and especially the students at Concordia Seminary, who, for over twenty-five years in the classroom, were an inspiration and a prayerful encouragement to continue in the awesome task of the study of Revelation and of applying its message to the pastoral ministry. It is to these students in particular that I dedicate this humble effort of a commentary on Revelation.

During the many years of study and preparation and all through the writing of this commentary, it has been my prayer that if, by the grace of God, this undertaking should be completed, it would be for the praise of God and for the continued witness to the glory of the exalted Jesus Christ, the Lamb of God. Now at its conclusion, my prayerful hope is that through this effort all the readers will experience what I received by way of that sainted lady as she waited for her Lord Christ: a purpose for the study of this last book of the Bible and a love of its message. For Revelation is the last word from Jesus Christ until he comes at the End to receive all who put their hope in him as their Savior and Lord.

PRINCIPAL ABBREVIATIONS

BOOKS OF THE BIBLE

Gen	2 Ki	Is	Nah	Rom	Titus
Ex	1 Chr	Jer	Hab	1 Cor	Philemon
Lev	2 Chr	Lam	Zeph	2 Cor	Heb
Num	Ezra	Ezek	Hag	Gal	James
Deut	Neh	Dan	Zech	Eph	1 Pet
Josh	Esth	Hos	Mal	Phil	2 Pet
Judg	Job	Joel	Mt	Col	1 Jn
Ruth	Ps (pl. Pss)	Amos	Mk	1 Thess	2 Jn
1 Sam	Prov	Obad	Lk	2 Thess	3 Jn
2 Sam	Eccl	Jonah	Jn	1 Tim	Jude
1 Ki	Song	Micah	Acts	2 Tim	Rev

BOOKS OF THE APOCRYPHA

1 Esdras	Judith	Sirach	Add Dan	Manasseh
2 Esdras	Add Esth	Bar	Sus	1 Macc
Tobit	Wisdom	Ep Jer	Bel	2 Macc

OTHER ABBREVIATIONS

ET   English translation (Shows differences in verse numbers between the Greek text and common English translations.)

INTRODUCTION

THE SIGNIFICANCE OF REVELATION

THE LAST BOOK OF THE BIBLE

Even if the book of Revelation was not written last, the church was led to place it at the end of the canon to show it as the completion of God's revelation. *Nothing further would be revealed* by God until the second coming of Jesus Christ. Revelation is thus the culmination of the entire story of salvation contained in the Bible, for it draws all of revelation, both prophetic and apostolic, to its final goal: the exalted reign of Jesus Christ as King of kings and Lord of lords (19:11–16) and the fulfillment of the promise of the new heaven and earth (21:1).

As the last book of the Bible and the completion of God's revelation to his church, the book of Revelation is the lens through which the entire Scripture is to be viewed. *Revelation reveals and confirms that Christ was prophetically promised and that his incarnation, death, and resurrection happened so that God's creation could be restored to its original glory and righteousness.* In addition, as the last book, Revelation serves as a *final confirmation* of the divine truth and origin of God's spoken and written Word. This points to the *urgency* of the last times, in which all things will be brought to an end—an urgency which reminds the Christian to hold fast to the faith (2:10) and which encourages the church to complete her mission (10:11).

THE CHRISTOLOGICAL TESTIMONY OF REVELATION

All of the Scriptures testify to Christ (Jn 5:39). The thesis and chief emphasis of this commentary's exposition is that the book of Revelation is a profound theological work whose heart and center is *Christology*.

The Christology of Revelation is surely based on the saving work of Christ. The saving work of Christ is implicit throughout Revelation as it focuses on the exalted reign of Christ, which exaltation resulted from his death and resurrection. Because of his death and resurrection and since his ascension, the Lord Christ, in his state of exaltation, is Lord over all. Revelation everywhere assumes that the meritorious work of Christ (his humiliation and vicarious atonement) has already taken place, and it assumes that the reader knows and trusts that work. While the four gospels narrate the incarnation, humiliation, and resurrection of Jesus, Revelation pictures the exaltation of Christ and what this exalted reign of Christ means for the church. Where the gospels end at the resurrection and ascension of Christ, Revelation picks up and continues the story from the ascension to the second coming of the Lord—and into eternity. Revelation also demonstrates (as does the Acts of the Apostles) how the church

1

carries on the mission of Christ in the world, for it was *the ascended and exalted Lord* who worked by the Spirit for and through the apostles (Acts 2:47).

The Christology of Revelation is rich and broad in its scope. Throughout the book Jesus Christ is presented as the exalted Son of Man (Revelation 1), the Lamb of God (Revelation 5), the Lord of the church (Revelation 2–3; 22), the Judge of the world (Revelation 19), the everlasting God (22:12–13), the Word of God (19:13), and the "source" of the creation of God, the new heaven and earth (3:14; cf. 21:1–22:5). Revelation presents a rich lode, the mining of which extends and deepens the Christology of the NT, and in particular that of John's gospel.

REVELATION: A CELEBRATION OF THE SAINTS

This revelation of the Lamb, slain and exalted, evokes from the saints in heaven (often joined by the angels) and the saints on earth a great hymn of praise to God and the Lamb. The great acclamation begins to swell in Revelation 4 and 5, "Worthy is the Lamb who was slain to receive [all] the power and wealth and wisdom and strength and honor and glory and blessing" (5:12). Such heavenly praise and worship is first given to God the Father (4:11), then to both God the Father and God the Son, the Lamb (5:13).

This celebrating worship is all the more striking when it is viewed in contrast to the terrible suffering and warfare that God's people on earth endure. In fact, it seems that the more the church on earth suffers, the more confidently and joyously do God's people sing in faith and hope of Jesus Christ (15:1–4). Throughout Revelation, interwoven with all the tribulations depicted, there is heard the hymn of victory. This celebration begins before the throne of God and before the Lamb in chapters 4 and 5 and continues throughout the prophecy, reaching its triumphant crescendo at the second coming of Jesus Christ (19:1–8). Surely part of the purpose and uplifting effect of Revelation is to move the Christian to voice the prayer, "Come now, Lord Jesus" (22:20), and to join all the saints in this celebration and worship of Jesus Christ.

THE CHARACTER OF REVELATION

REVELATION, A PROPHETIC APOCALYPSE

The name of the book comes from its first verse. The Greek word usually translated "revelation" has also been transliterated into English as "apocalypse," from which comes the name of a certain genre of literature, "apocalyptic literature." Having roots in the prophetic books of the OT, apocalyptic literature flourished (in both Jewish and Christian contexts) from around 200 BC to AD 300. It is generally agreed that apocalyptic is a kind of literature in which divine secrets are revealed, usually by heavenly angelic figures, to a human recipient in a historical setting. There is also general agreement as to the chief characteristics of apocalyptic literature, among which are the following. Apocalyptic deals mostly with *eschatology,* the end times. It often uses *symbolic language* to convey its message. Its view of life in this world (under God's ultimate sovereignty) pictures the human race and its history in a *warfare between good and evil* in which there is no neutrality. Most often the message is received by the author *through angelic, heavenly figures* who appeared in *visions*.

In the OT, Jacob (Genesis 28), Joseph (Genesis 40–41), Moses (Exodus 24) and the later prophets (e.g., Isaiah 6) were among those given to see heavenly and/or future things. Especially the visions described in Isaiah 24–27; Ezekiel 1–3; 38–39; Joel; Daniel 7–12; and Zechariah exhibit some of the characteristics prominent in the genre of apocalyptic literature. Important Jewish apocalypses outside the OT are 1 Enoch, the Book of Jubilees, 4 Ezra, the Assumption of Moses, 2 Baruch, the Apocalypse of Abraham, and the Testaments of the Twelve Patriarchs. Among Christian apocalypses are the Ascension of Isaiah (appended to the Jewish-Christian Martyrdom of Isaiah), the Shepherd of Hermas (not totally apocalyptic), the Apocalypse of Peter, and the Apocalypse of Paul. This body of literature is important for interpreting Revelation, because Revelation is composed in the apocalyptic literary genre and shares much common imagery and thought with these other works.

Revelation can be viewed in the tradition of apocalyptic literature and compared to other apocalypses—OT, Jewish, or Christian. But there are characteristics of Revelation that also set it apart. Most obviously, it is *a true revelation of the true God*. The author identifies himself quite clearly and does not hide under the assumed identity of a previously known person. He names himself John both at the beginning and at the end of his work (1:1, 4, 9; 22:8), and he takes for granted that his hearers know who he is (1:9–11). Secondly, the book is *Christocentric,* not just theocentric. The chief figure in Revelation, around whom everything revolves and from whom everything originates, is Jesus Christ. While the person of Christ acts under the authority of God the Father and frequently uses angels to mediate the revelation, it is quite clear that he dominates the entire prophetic message from beginning to end (1:1; 22:20). Third, Revelation pictures the people of God on earth playing an important role as they represent God and his Christ in the battle between righteousness and evil.

Above all, Revelation is *prophetic* in intention. The author of Revelation is conscious of his role as a prophet, for he calls his work a "prophecy" (1:3; 22:7, 10, 18, 19). He does so because he views his work, and his role in that work, in the OT prophetic tradition (22:6, 18–19). His purpose is not primarily to reveal secrets to God's people, but rather to call them to repentance and faith, and to worship—to the blessedness of faithful service in the confidence of God's love and care. The special emphases of Revelation within the apocalyptic tradition can be summed up in these words: "Blessed is the one who reads and [blessed are] those who hear the words of this prophecy and who keep the things written in it, for the time is near" (1:3; see also 22:12–21).

THE PURPOSE OF REVELATION

John would have his readers take to heart the words of the prophecy, for the time is near (1:3). The time is near for the fulfillment of what is described, because the Lord Christ is coming quickly (22:6–7). The purpose of the message of Revelation is therefore best summed up in this word: *preparation*. The hearer and reader are *to be ready* for what is to come to pass. It is a readiness that comes about through hearing the message. Such preparation consists of baptismal sealing (7:2–3), of being washed in the blood of the Lamb (1:5; 7:9, 13–14; 19:13; 22:14) and through such cleansing to stand ready for the coming of Christ (22:12). *As the Christian stands prepared for the coming Lord, he is encouraged in the hope of his faith (2:10) and is inspired for the mission that Christ has given to his church on earth (10:11).*

Revelation ends with the promise that the Lord Jesus is coming quickly, and with John's prayerful response, "Amen, come now, Lord Jesus" (22:20).. *Thus the explicit goal of Revelation is to lift up to God this prayer. The Spirit (through the message of Revelation) leads God's people to voice this prayer now and until it is answered.* This is the prayer that not only sums up all for which the church prays (see 6:9–11) but also testifies to the longing of the Christian heart to be in the presence of God's holiness and glory in heaven.

As the Spirit led Simeon to pray for departure into the presence of God after he had seen the Lord's Christ (Lk 2:28–32), so the Spirit now moves the believer to pray in response to all that he has witnessed through the biblical revelation of God—which revelation is now concluded in the last book of the Bible. Simeon, in the presence of the Word Incarnate, prayed the Nunc Dimittis, and was moved by the Spirit to witness to others about the Christ (Lk 2:33–35). So likewise the hearer of Revelation is given the full biblical revelation from above; hence, he prays this prayer, "Amen, come now, Lord Jesus" (Rev 22:20), and he is moved by the Spirit to witness.

In short, *the more the Christian is confident by faith—strengthened through Word and Sacrament—of going to heaven because of the merits of Christ, the more the Spirit moves the believer to desire to enter heaven. And the more the Christian desires the glory of God in heaven, the more the Spirit moves him to witness through this longing hope of faith.* This too is part of the purpose of Revelation: to comfort and encourage the worshiping Christian to pray this prayer of longing and to witness to the world.

THE MESSAGE OF REVELATION

The message of Revelation reveals two ongoing phenomena: the terrifying sufferings and horror on earth, and the reign of Jesus Christ as Lord in his heavenly exalted glory. As these two phenomena are described, God's people on earth are encouraged to cling in hopeful faith to the eternal heavenly glory that beckons them in Christ. In turn they also are strengthened and encouraged for the work of Christ's mission on earth. These tribulations and sufferings demonstrate God's wrath and judgment for the purpose of motivating the godless to repentance (16:1, 8–11). God's own people also experience these same sufferings and plagues, for the dragon, Satan, uses these sufferings and plagues in his attempt to destroy the church and her witness (12:13–13:18).

Thus an anomaly is set up. While mankind's sin and rebellion against God prompt all the tribulations and sufferings (6:1–11), the dragon uses them and adds to them as he tries to destroy the Gospel witness of the church (11:7–10). In his permissive will, God lets the dragon do this, so that all these sufferings work together to show his anger and judgment, which aim to bring the human race to repentance before it is too late. For the Christian the sufferings serve both as a reminder of God's judgment against all sin, but especially as opportunities to witness to the sufferings and death of Christ.

While much of the prophetic message of Revelation reflects a negative view of the human race and its history, interspersed throughout the book are beautiful pictures of God's glory in heaven and Christ's exalted glory, and of the saints before God's heavenly throne. In fact, the Bible's most beautiful pictures of heaven are in Revelation. Against the backdrop of all the doom and darkness and horror portrayed in Revelation, these visions of the heavenly glory stand out all the more in bold relief. Revelation uses the visions of doom and horror to show that all human history is heading to a certain and terrifying end in the judgment of God. Despite all human efforts and ambitions, human life here on earth in this present age will *not* improve into a happy state. Mankind can do nothing to avert this coming doom, the punishment of God.

Into this description of despair, which leads only to the abyss of hell (Revelation 17–18; 20:7–10), there are interjected the glorious pictures of God's hope and plan for the human race, the peace and righteousness of Christ which have come to believers already now and which will be consummated in the resurrection and the new heaven and earth (20:11–15; 21:1). Therefore the visions of heaven inspire Christians *to gaze steadily in faith at Christ and the glory that awaits them and to witness to the victory of Christ.* Indeed, sufferings can even facilitate witnessing to the Gospel (15:2–4). Meanwhile, through it all the Christian continually prays, "Amen, come now, Lord Jesus" (22:20) confident of the Lord's promise, "Yes, I am coming quickly" (22:20; see also 6:9–11).

Thus *the overarching and dominating theme of Revelation is the unveiling of Christ in his exalted glory as the reigning Lord. Before the eyes of the assembled worshiping Christians, the divine presence and the glory of the Savior and Lord is revealed.* The Lord Christ, because of his exalted enthronement at the right of God, by right of his death and resurrection (5:1–14), now rules everything for the sake of his church on earth. This is the faith and comfort of the church: her Lord rules over all history, all events, over sin and evil, the devil, suffering and death and hell. He governs everything so that the church can carry out the mission given to her by God (10:1–11:19). When that mission is completed, then the Lord Christ will come to claim his bride (19:5–16).

THE STRUCTURE OF REVELATION

Revelation is made up of three parts: an introduction (1:1–3:22), the prophetic message proper (4:1–22:5), and an epilogue (22:6–21).

The introduction consists of a prologue (1:1–8), a description of John's commissioning to write the book (1:9–20), and the seven letters to the seven churches (2:1–3:22). The seven letters are not a part of the prophetic message per se but rather serve to prepare the hearer for reception of the message by calling the churches to repentance.

The second part, the prophetic message, is by far the largest section of Revelation (4:1–22:5). The prophetic message is introduced by a vision of God's throne and glory in heaven, together with angels and the saints of God, and of the exaltation of the victorious Christ, depicted as a Lamb (4:1–5:14). *This vision of God's heavenly glory and of the exaltation of the Lamb not only introduces the prophetic message of Revelation but also dominates and controls it.* This vision establishes this truth in the context of which *everything* is to be seen and heard: Jesus Christ, the Lamb who was slain, is alive and reigns! *The victory has been won! Salvation has been accomplished!* Believers in heaven and on earth can join in the triumphal song. Everything in the book that follows is normed by the reassurance of this opening vision.

The prophecy itself contains three visions of events taking place on earth. Each vision covers the same time period: from the first advent of Christ (specifically, his ascension) up to his second coming at the end of this present world. Moreover, each vision has seven scenes.

The first sevenfold vision (6:1–8:5) is introduced by the opening of the seven seals of the scroll which Christ the Lamb had received in the heavenly vision of God's glory (5:6–7). The opening of the seals introduces the scenes of this vision. The first five scenes, the four horsemen and the martyred souls beneath God's altar (6:1–11), symbolize events happening concurrently from the ascension of Christ up to the End, and they refer to the sufferings that humankind perpetrates upon itself—from which also Christians suffer. The opening of the sixth seal pictures the End, with the destruction of the present universe and the terror that this instills (6:12–17). Before the seventh seal is opened, there is an interlude in which John sees God's people on earth (pictured as the 144,000) sealed for divine protection. They are the church militant (7:1–8). In this interlude John next sees the saints who are in heaven because of the blood of the Lamb, now at peace; they are the church triumphant (7:9–17). The opening of the seventh seal leads the hearer into the second sevenfold vision.

The second sevenfold vision is introduced by seven angels with trumpets. As each angel in turn blows a trumpet, a scene appears. The first four scenes display natural disasters which plague the human race all during the time period from the ascension of Jesus up to the End (8:6–13). The fifth trumpet-angel introduces the terrifying scene of demons from the abyss who afflict unbelieving mankind (9:1–12). The sixth scene shows the gathering of an evil host that will be unleashed on humanity just before the End (9:13–21). This is the first of three glimpses that John sees of what is called Armageddon in 16:16 and the battle of Gog and Magog in 20:8. As in the first sevenfold vision, there is an interlude between the sixth and seventh scenes. In this interlude (10:1–11:14) John sees a mighty angel from heaven commissioning him (and the church) to proclaim the message of God to all peoples (10:1–11), and then, by way of the two witnesses (11:1–14), John sees the church carrying out this mission. Then the seventh trumpet-angel introduces the last scene in this second vision. Like the sixth scene of the first sevenfold vision, this seventh scene displays again the end of this world, but this time not the world's destruction, but rather the joy that the End brings to God's people (11:15–19).

Before the third sevenfold vision of events on earth is ushered in, there is presented a vision of the cosmic war between God and the dragon (12:1–14:20). *This cosmic vision is the heart of Revelation, for it reveals the cause of all the tribulations and sufferings on earth and the final triumph of Christ's church.* The vision is made up of the symbols of the woman with Child and the dragon (12:1–18), the beasts of the dragon (13:1–18), and the defeat of the dragon and the beasts, together with the end of this world (14:1–20). When the Child of the woman is taken to heaven, the dragon (Satan) and his angels are cast out of heaven. Unable to destroy the woman (the church), the dragon conjures up the two beasts, which war against the woman throughout the time period from the ascension up to the present world's end. The cosmic vision concludes then with the defeat of the evil forces of the dragon and with the victory song of the 144,000 at the End, which this time is pictured as a great harvest.

The third and final sevenfold vision of events on earth is introduced by the seven censer-angels (15:1–16:21). As each angel pours out his censer on the earth, a scene is presented. The first five scenes refer to God's anger poured out on the human race in the form of various plagues (15:1–16:11). When John sees the sixth scene, introduced by the sixth censer-angel, he receives a second view of the last battle before the End, the battle now called Armageddon (16:12–16). The seventh scene again brings John to the End (16:17–21).

The remainder of the prophetic message is a lengthy conclusion which describes the end of this world in greater detail and the new heaven and earth (17:1–22:5). Chapters 17 and 18 describe the evil forces of the dragon (Babylon—the harlot and the beast) in graphic detail, and then their judgment and destruction. Chapter 19 depicts the second coming of Jesus Christ and the celebration of God's saints. Revelation 20 details the binding, overthrow, and final judgment of Satan by means of the depiction of the millennium and the battle of Gog and Magog—the last battle—together with reference to the two resurrections and the judgment of the human race. The prophecy climaxes with a description of the new heaven and earth and with the heavenly city Jerusalem (21:1–22:5).

Revelation then concludes with the epilogue (22:6–21). See further the outline which forms the table of contents.

THE AUTHOR AND WRITING OF REVELATION

THE AUTHOR

The author calls himself "John" (1:1, 4, 9; 22:8), but he nowhere indicates *which* John he might be. In the NT there are three well-known persons named John: John the Baptist, John Mark, and the apostle John, who was the son of Zebedee and the brother of James Conceivably the author of Revelation could be any of the first three, or even another John not mentioned in the NT. The author assumed that his hearers would know who he was.

The traditional view from the church fathers of the second and third centuries is that the author is John the son of Zebedee, one of the twelve disciples. Irenaeus, a Syrian father who was bishop of Lyons, testifies in his Greek work *Against Heresies* that John the Lord's disciple was the author of Revelation. He furthermore testifies that it was near the end of the reign of the Roman emperor Domitian that Revelation was written. Irenaeus most likely received this information from Polycarp, at whose feet he sat as a young man. Polycarp (ca. 60–ca. 155) was bishop of Smyrna and had sat at the feet of John in Ephesus. Thus Irenaeus himself may stand in the Johannine tradition. Clement of Alexandria (ca. 150–ca. 215) says that after the death of Domitian, "John the apostle" went back to Ephesus after his exile on Patmos. An earlier father who testifies to the Johannine authorship of Revelation is Justin Martyr (ca. 100–ca. 165), who, before moving on to Rome, taught for a time in Ephesus.

In the first two centuries the only possible witness against the Johannine authorship of Revelation is Papias (ca. 60–ca. 130), bishop of Hierapolis in Asia Minor. According to Irenaeus, Papias was a hearer of John and a companion of Polycarp. In a quotation preserved by Eusebius, Papias appears to speak of two distinct persons named John. However, it cannot be determined whether Papias was referring to two different Johns or twice to the same John. Even if one should conclude that Papias was referring to two different Johns, both of considerable stature and both residing at Ephesus (which is highly unlikely), this could not be used against the apostolic Johannine authorship of either the gospel or Revelation, for authorship is not the subject Papias is addressing in this excerpt.

It is not until the third century AD that there appears clear evidence of any father speaking against apostolic Johannine authorship. According to Eusebius, Caius (early third century), who was said to have been a Roman presbyter, rejected the Johannine authorship of Revelation, attributing it instead to Cerinthus, a Gnostic heretic (late first century). A more important witness against apostolic Johannine authorship is Dionysius (died ca. 264), bishop of Alexandria and a pupil of Origen. He believed that Revelation was written by a John, but not the apostle. He came to this conclusion primarily because of the difference between the literary styles of John's gospel and Revelation, though he accepted Revelation as inspired and canonical.

Later fathers who either rejected or had doubts about the Johannine authorship of Revelation are Cyril of Jerusalem (ca. 315–ca. 386), Gregory of Nazianzus (ca. 329–ca. 389), Chrysostom (ca. 347–407), and Theodoret (ca. 393–ca. 458). These later fathers all seemed to have been influenced by Dionysius. While some fathers of the third and fourth centuries followed Dionysius in doubting or rejecting the Johannine authorship of Revelation, most did not. Tertullian (ca. 160–ca. 225), Hippolytus of Rome (ca. 170–ca. 235), and Origen (ca. 185–ca. 254) accepted the apostolic Johannine authorship without question. The great fathers of the fourth century such as Athanasius, Jerome, and Augustine also accepted the apostolic Johannine authorship of this last book of the Bible.

The problem that Dionysius raised, that of the difference between the literary styles of John's gospel and of Revelation, will be addressed in the following section. That section will also offer a final conclusion about the authorship of Revelation.

THE WRITING OF REVELATION

It can be said with some certainty that the book of Revelation was not planned in the same sense that John must have planned his gospel. John wrote the gospel after long thought and maturity in his apostolic witness to Jesus Christ, but there was no way that he could have anticipated the visions he experienced and recorded in Revelation. It happened, under inspiration, through a visionary experience similar to those that came upon Paul (2 Cor 12:1–4) and Stephen (Acts 7:55–56). John experienced and wrote Revelation while he was "in the Spirit" (Rev 1:10; 4:2). As he was in the Spirit, he evidently not only saw the visions but also was caught up into them so as to experience them more immediately as well (see 4:1–2). This is beyond our ability to analyze. Perhaps even John himself, like Paul (2 Cor 12:1–4), could not tell whether he was in the body or out of the body when he saw and heard what he relates. What matters is that he was "in the Spirit," and he truly was given this Revelation by God. The finished product is a gift of God through his servant John, God's final word until the Lord's return at the End (Rev 1:3; 22:20).

As part of their investigation of the question of authorship, some scholars have compared the language and literary styles of John's gospel to those of Revelation. This comparison is inconclusive, however. Whatever decision one makes about the authorship of these two documents, some problems remain. If one concludes because of the dissimilarities in language and style that John and

Revelation must have been composed by two different authors, then how does one account for their pointed similarities? If, on the other hand, one concludes because of the similarities that both are products of the same author, then how does one account for the pointed dissimilarities? Certainly the many similarities point to some connection between the authorship of these two books.

One of the most noticeable dissimilarities in language is the increased presence in the Greek text of Revelation of grammatical irregularities and Semiticisms. Careful analysis of the Greek text reveals that it is not translation Greek. Rather the author wrote and thought in a Greek that was influenced by Semitic idioms and expression. It appears that he *wrote* in Greek while he was *thinking* in his original and native language, most likely Aramaic. *Unless he took the time to translate (in his mind) from the Semitic idiom to the Greek before he spoke or wrote, his Greek would be more Semitic, but if he first took the time to translate the Semitic idiom mentally into Greek, then his Greek would be less Semitic.*

The difference between the *extent* of the Semiticisms in John's gospel and Revelation is due to the fact that the gospel is a carefully planned theological *narrative,* while Revelation is a composition that may have been written *more quickly and with great urgency.* One can imagine that the author worked deliberately in the composition of his gospel, not only for clarity of thought and expression but also to screen out many of his natural Semitic idioms—though even the Greek of the gospel is more Semitic than Hellenistic literary Greek. When the same author came to write Revelation he did not, for whatever reason, screen out as carefully the Semitic idioms.

Was this because of his state of mind—highly emotional, even mystic? Or was it because of a concern to write quickly in order not to lose anything of what he had seen and experienced? Perhaps both are true. What is clear is that the author did *not* always translate in his mind from his native Semitic way of thinking into standard Greek idiom before he wrote the Greek text of Revelation. One might assume that he did not write several drafts, as might have been the case with his gospel. He left his written Revelation in the language in which he first described what he had seen—composed from the immediate impressions that were made on his mind by the visions and experiences he encountered. The quantity and kind of Semiticisms in Revelation, then, account for much of the difference between the language of John's gospel and Revelation. But one can detect the same mind, with similar Semitic influence, behind the Greek of both the gospel and Revelation.

On the other hand, certain grammatical anomalies in Revelation are not attributable to the author's Semitic way of thinking. Rather, they are intentional. The author, when he stops to think, knows standard, conventional Koine Greek grammar. But as a skilled artist he sometimes employs unconventional or anomalous grammar in order to make a point, either for emphasis or for theological impact. As one works with the Greek text and begins to notice that many of the grammatical irregularities are repeated in Revelation, it becomes clear that with them the author is *creating literary thought patterns that aid him in giving full expression and meaning to the subject matter at hand.* This author is a highly skilled, literary craftsman. He does not think or express himself as one following ordinary logic or common rhetoric. Rather, he thinks and expresses himself visually in inspired, artistic patterns of thought. Humanly speaking, while one could not imagine John writing Romans, one could also not conjecture that Paul could have written Revelation. In each case, the Holy Spirit moved a particular individual in a certain historical context to produce a unique writing.

Thus the chief dissimilarities in language and literary style between the gospel according to St. John and Revelation can be explained without resorting to the assumption that there were two different authors. All the evidence, when weighed, points to John the apostle and son of Zebedee as the author of Revelation—as well as of the gospel. Since there is no compelling evidence to the contrary, and there is persuasive supporting evidence, this commentary is written on the premise that the John mentioned in Rev 1:1, 4, 9; 22:8 is the John who was one of the twelve apostles and who was the brother of James.

JOHN THE AUTHOR: THE MAN FOR THE TIME AND PLACE

The character and personality and reputation of John play an important role in his authorship of Revelation—and also of his gospel. According to Athanasius, John was known as "the theologian" of the apostolic church. In the gospel he is referred to as the disciple "whom Jesus loved" (e.g., Jn 13:23; 20:2), the one who lay against Jesus' bosom in the Upper Room (Jn 13:23), and as "the other disciple" (Jn 20:2). Of this disciple Jesus says tantalizingly, "If I wish him to remain until I come …" (Jn 21:22; cf. 21:20). This disciple then acquired the reputation that he would not die until the Lord's second coming, although he himself protested that Jesus had not promised that (Jn 21:23). Finally, in the gospel the author says that he was an eyewitness of Jesus' death and resurrection, and that his witness is the truth (Jn 19:34–35; 21:24).

In Revelation the author uses his name, John, to identify himself (1:1, 4, 9; 22:8). In 22:8 he emphasizes that it was he, John, who heard and saw the things that are written in Revelation. There is a similar attestation in the gospel concerning the author and the validity of what he visually witnessed (19:35; 21:24). In 1 Jn 1:1–4 this same author again makes the claim that his testimony is that of an eyewitness of Jesus Christ. In 2 and 3 John he introduces himself as "the elder" (2 Jn 1; 3 Jn 1). By his use of the article ("the") he shows that he takes for granted that everyone knows who he is and that they will without question accept his authority because of his relationship to Christ (cf. also 1 Jn 5:13; 2 Jn 9; 3 Jn 9–10). In Revelation he refers to his writing as a "prophecy" (1:3; 22:7, 10, 18, 19), that is, a prophetic work in line with the ministry and writings of the

OT and NT prophets of God. *He thus understands that his apostolic witness to the ministry of Jesus Christ—his incarnation, death, resurrection, and exalted heavenly glory—is in harmony with and in succession to the prophetic ministry of old.*

In the latter part of the first century, when (to our present knowledge) John was the last remaining apostolic witness and voice yet on earth, he was known as *the* elder of the church, *the* theologian and teacher of the church. Certainly it can be said of him that the church could not neglect the word that was spoken by the Lord and witnessed by those who heard it (Heb 2:1–4). As the first century AD came to an end, John was the sole apostolic voice witnessing to what Jesus had done and said. He was the last living link between the church at the turn of the first century AD and the people among whom Jesus lived during his earthly ministry.

According to Irenaeus, John lived into the reign of the Roman emperor Trajan, who ruled from 98 to 117. This means that John not only witnessed the earthly life of Jesus Christ but also the life and ministry of the church up to the early part of the second century. For example, he was still living in Ephesus when Clement, the bishop of Rome, wrote an epistle to the church in Corinth (ca. AD 95) known today as 1 Clement. He died near the time that Ignatius was martyred under Trajan. In more than one of the letters of Ignatius, which are reckoned among the most famous documents of the early church, Ignatius seems to show that he knew Revelation. John lived through some seventy years of the formative history of the church before his own witness was finished!

What had John witnessed? It appears that the author of the gospel and Revelation was introduced to Jesus at Jesus' baptism by John the Baptist (Jn 1:35–42; Acts 1:21–22). Prior to meeting Jesus, John was a fisherman, together with his brother James and their father Zebedee. But after having been called by Jesus he became one of the twelve apostles (Mk 1:19–20). John, together with his brother James, and Peter, made up the inner circle and as such witnessed the raising of Jairus' daughter (Mk 5:37), the transfiguration of the Lord (Mk 9:2), and the agony of Jesus at Gethsemane (Mk 14:33). Most likely John witnessed most, and perhaps all of the miracles of Jesus and heard his public and private teachings (Jn 21:25). John is usually thought of as reserved, but he was not afraid to push himself forward, even when he should not have (Mt 20:20–21). He may have been the youngest of the Twelve, or at least among the younger disciples; he ran faster than Peter (Jn 20:4), and he is mentioned after his brother James (Mk 1:19). Given Jesus' fondness for the lowly, including children, it may have been partly in light of John's younger status that Jesus loved him and perhaps sheltered him (Jn 13:23). At any rate his youth did not prevent him from becoming one of the leaders of the Twelve (cf. Jer 1:5–7).

But what stands out most prominently about John is that *he was the only disciple to witness the entire passion of Jesus Christ.* With Peter he witnessed the trial of Jesus before the Jewish court (Jn 18:15–16). But after Peter left (Mt 26:75; Lk 22:62), through the trials of Pilate and Herod and on to Golgotha, John was the only disciple to witness the entire suffering, crucifixion, and death of Jesus. It was to John that Jesus entrusted the care of his mother (Jn 19:26–27). John saw the shameful treatment and bitter earthly end as Jesus died (Jn 19:31–37). And John saw with his own eyes the resurrected Lord and believed in his resurrection. This was crucial for his later witness to the truth.

John ends his gospel by relating not the ascension of Jesus but the commissioning of Peter and the foretelling of Peter's death, to which is attached Jesus' affirmation of the *possibility* that John could remain alive until the Lord's return (Jn 21:20–23). Whether the early Christians believed that John *would* remain alive until the return of Jesus, or whether they entertained the idea only as a *possibility* dependent on the Lord's will (Jn 21:23), certainly John's long life on this earth would have heightened the hope of the Lord's return within John's lifetime. His extended life also can be seen as a confirmation of the *possibility* about which Jesus spoke.

By ending his gospel with the foretelling of Peter's ministry and death, and the foretelling of the enduring witness of the beloved disciple, John prepares his readers to be introduced to the mission of the church under the apostolic ministry. This ministry would proclaim the words and actions of Jesus and would be sealed by suffering and death. This ministry would be confirmed by the ongoing eyewitness of the apostolic tradition, of which John was a part and also of which he would be the last (cf. Heb 2:1–4; 1 Jn 1:1–4). This ministry of the apostles, as exemplified by John, would continue until their proclamation concerning Christ was authoritatively established and codified for the church, that is, *their personal apostolic ministry would continue until their apostolic Word was set down in writing, so that it and it alone would remain authoritative for the church until the Lord's return.* The long apostolic ministry of John played an important role in the establishment of that authoritative apostolic legacy.

What all did John witness? After witnessing the Lord's ascension and the promise of his return (Acts 1:6–11) and receiving the fulfillment of Jesus' promise to send the Spirit (Acts 2:1–4), John became one of the leaders of the church in Jerusalem, together with Peter and James the brother of Jesus (Acts 12:17; Gal 2:9). How long John's ministry lasted in Jerusalem is not known. Church fathers testify that John was in Ephesus before and after his exile on the island of Patmos. It can be surmised that he became the bishop at Ephesus before the fall of Jerusalem in AD 70. The lack of precise knowledge as regards the date of his move to Ephesus notwithstanding, it seems that he was the pastor and bishop of the church there for many years. (That church had been founded by Paul together with Apollos, Aquila, and Priscilla [Acts 18:24–19:1].) During his long ministry at Ephesus, John witnessed the growth of the church throughout much of the Roman Empire. Certainly it can be said that before his death he saw the church well established, despite severe sufferings and persecutions.

While at Ephesus, and for many years, John was *the* theologian of the church, *the* elder and apostolic spokesman. His long apostolic witness and ministry was an affirmation of the oral tradition of Christ's words and actions. John did not die until after the apostolic tradition concerning the words, deeds, and message of Christ had been established in written form. John lived long enough for the writings of the NT not only to have been written but also to be in circulation. When his apostolic witness was no longer necessary to vouch for the authenticity of the apostolic tradition (now in literary form), the Lord Christ called his servant John to himself. While there is no direct evidence that John helped determine the NT canon, he was alive through the whole process of the writing and the circulation of those documents that came to be recognized as authoritative for the church. *In his wisdom, God left this servant of Christ alive to vouch for the veracity and faithfulness of those writings that would be accepted by the church. After that oral apostolic tradition was set in written form and after it was no longer necessary for a living voice to confirm that apostolic tradition, the prophecy was fulfilled, "If I wish him to remain until I come..." (Jn 21:22). Jesus came to his church in the written Scriptures and would continue to come to his people through the reading of those Scriptures.*

After John's death the church would not consider including in the canon a previously unknown writing lately brought to light, for there was no longer a living apostolic voice to vouch for its authenticity—though the church would for some time leave open the possibility of receiving or rejecting a writing that had been known during John's lifetime.

The Acceptance of Revelation

It might appear surprising that the early church received Revelation as authoritative and canonical, apparently with little question, for over a century. Whether or not it was used and understood as much as the other writings of the NT is not clear, but it was certainly accepted by the church. It would be difficult to understand today how it could have been accepted unless it was known to have been written by a recognized, authoritative teacher of the church. Perhaps even the young John could not have had the theological stature to motivate the church to accept a writing such as Revelation! But from a mature John, who was recognized as *the* elder and theologian, it would be received. When doubts arose in the third century about the canonicity of Revelation, it was because some thought that John the apostle perhaps was not the author. But where there was no doubt of the apostolic Johannine authorship, it was accepted.

The Gospel and Revelation: Literary Complements

One might ask, Why did not John include an account of Jesus' transfiguration in his gospel? After all, of the four gospel authors, he is the only one who actually witnessed it. This, together with the fact that John's gospel also does not have an account of or even a reference to Christ's ascension, may be *telling marks* in the gospel, directing John's readers to look to Revelation. In 1:9–20 there is a description of Jesus in his transfigured glory after he had come into it at his ascension. John on the mount of transfiguration saw a preview of this glory. Now in Revelation he sees this glory once again, *but after the Lord Christ had fully and permanently entered it.*

Could the fact that John in Revelation gives to the reader a description of Christ in his transfigured glory be the reason why he does not have an account of the transfiguration in his gospel? The same may be said for the absence of any account of the ascension in his gospel, since there is in Revelation 5 a beautiful description of Jesus' ascension, but as seen and understood from heaven's viewpoint. If this might be the explanation for the absence of any report of these important events in John's gospel, *then perhaps John wrote the gospel after Revelation.* The scenario might be this: first John experienced and wrote Revelation and then, after meditating on it, he undertook to write a gospel *as an introduction for Revelation.*

Whether the above conjecture is true or not, there is a strong probability that after he had written both the gospel and Revelation, John saw that *they went together and thus were two parts of one work.* Luke planned beforehand that his gospel and Acts were to be received as one work in two parts (Lk 1:1–4; Acts 1:1–5), but perhaps John did not begin with such a plan in mind. Yet after both his gospel and Revelation were finished, they stood out as one grand account of Christ's humiliation and exaltation, for the gospel leads into and finds its goal in Revelation, and Revelation has its foundation in the gospel. Revelation thus is not to be read and understood in isolation, but rather in relationship with John's gospel. What is seen and interpreted in Revelation is anchored in the incarnation of the Word (Jn 1:1, 14; Rev 19:13). Whatever is seen and interpreted in the gospel points to the exalted reign of Christ as depicted in Revelation. They are complementary.

LITERARY STYLE

The literary style of the author of Revelation is more that of an artist than of a technical writer (cf. 12:1–2). He thinks and writes in visual patterns rather than in logical axioms. His artistry is even evident in his use of grammar and syntax. For example, he is fond of parallelism (see 21:23), especially antithetical statements, where he first states the positive and then the negative (3:3; 10:4). All these oddities and irregularities, whether due to the author's Semitic background or to his own peculiar use of language, are used in a skilled, disciplined fashion which contributes to his artistic way of presenting the inspired message.

The literary artistry of the author finds expression in his use of the symbolic pictures which make up so much of his prophetic message. The experience of the author, and perhaps more importantly the content of his message from God, evidently demanded such images. For the hearer and reader of Revelation, this type of literary presentation poses certain questions. What do the various symbols mean? What do they represent? Once those questions have been answered for John's original historical context, we still must ask, What significance do they have for the reader and the church today?

Symbolic imagery is usually patterned after some known entity. Something served the creator of the symbol as a model. It could be a historical person, a historical event, or a noted geographical place. Once the symbol is created, it then is used by the author to suggest and evoke a meaning without any explicit explanation of it. The symbol, as used by the writer, no longer refers to the model after which it was patterned. Rather, it refers to something different or new. If the model can be identified, this can help to determine how the model was used by the author and so can help the reader arrive at a correct interpretation of the symbol. However, when one discovers and examines the model, he may fall prey to the danger of thinking that the symbol *refers* to the model. The interpreter should not equate the symbol with its model. The model is *only a pointer to clues* which will help the reader to discover the application of the symbol. The symbol is a metaphor, and so its meaning is metaphorical, not literal.

When an author creates a symbol as an image or metaphor for something that is common to human life and experience, the reader may be able to draw on that which is recognizable and known from his own experience in order to interpret the symbol. But when a symbol employs elements that are not drawn from common human experience and are not from human knowledge or nature, then the reader may conclude that the symbol is being used to picture something of the supernatural. An example of this is the dragon of Revelation 12. A dragon is not a real, natural creature known from common human experience. Rather, it is drawn from human imagination. The referent in Revelation 12 is Satan, a supernatural being.

In addition to literary symbols that are modeled after created things (the Lamb) or after the imagination (the dragon and beasts), other nonphysical realities from the realm of human thought—such as numbers—can be made to serve as symbols. Examples in Revelation are the numbers four, seven, ten, twelve, twenty-four, one thousand, and one hundred forty-four thousand.

Much of the symbolic imagery in Revelation is taken from the OT. The OT often uses symbols as a method of teaching especially in the later prophets. The body of this commentary will show how knowledge of the OT plays an important role in interpreting Revelation. Jewish writings of the Intertestamental period are also a rich source for the symbolism in Revelation. Another possible source of symbolic imagery is the mythological milieu of the Greco-Roman world. John at times seems to use this milieu—but for his own theological purposes.

Finally, the literary style of Revelation includes John's artistic appropriation of the OT, not only as a source for symbolism, but even more importantly as the basis for much of his theological insights and literary expressions. John's use of the OT can be subtle. On the one hand, he never formally introduces an OT quotation with a citation formula. Yet no writer in the apostolic age, including the NT authors, makes more use of the writings of the OT. John constantly uses OT imagery, phrases, thought patterns, and theological motifs. The OT furnishes the vocabulary, mode of expression, and theological mind-set with which Revelation was written.

John's quotations from and allusions to the OT are primarily from the Septuagint. This Greek translation of the Hebrew OT was John's Bible. It gave to John his theological vocabulary in the Greek language. He uses it as a skilled artist, for it is the palette which he employs to depict the images he saw in his vision. Often John will use the words and phrases and thought patterns of the Septuagint as an artist would inlay small pieces of various colored glass or tile to form a mosaic. For example, in 1:12–16, where John describes the appearance of the exalted Christ as the Son of Man, he uses Daniel 7 and 10 as his sources. He takes the words and phrases of Daniel and uses them to form his mosaic of the exalted Son of Man in Revelation 1. While Daniel serves as his source, the finished picture of Christ in Revelation 1 transcends that of the Son of Man in Daniel 7 and 10. John's portrait of the Son of Man is similar to that of Daniel, yet distinctly his own rendering. At various places throughout Revelation he demonstrates his literary artistry in other innovative uses of the OT. In this type of creativity he is paramount among the authors of the NT.

THE TRANSMISSION AND INTERPRETATION OF REVELATION

THE GREEK TEXT OF REVELATION

The earliest manuscript of Revelation is a papyrus fragment of 1:13–20 now located in Cairo in the French Institute of Oriental Archaeology and dated probably to the second century AD It is too brief to be of much significance for establishing the text of Revelation. Its importance lies rather in the fact that it is dated so close to the autograph of Revelation. There are six known Greek papyri manuscripts of Revelation, five of which are only small fragments. The sixth is by far the most important papyrus manuscript of Revelation. It is in the Chester Beatty Library collection in Dublin. It is dated in the third century and is of great use in helping to establish the text of Revelation. However, even this important witness is fragmentary, containing only 9:10–17:2 with some gaps.

There are eleven known uncial manuscripts of Revelation, dating from the fourth to the tenth centuries. Only four contain the whole of Revelation. In addition there are around 275 cursive/minuscule manuscripts dating from the tenth to the fifteenth centuries, the most important of which is codex 1 of the twelfth century.

Interpreting Revelation

Throughout the history of the church, Revelation has been interpreted in many different ways. In the final analysis, the variety of methods can be reduced to two basic ways of interpreting and understanding the book. One places the book on a linear scale, a straight line, so that each item related in the book follows or succeeds that which was related before, and the events unfold in an orderly, chronological way. This method is sometimes called the *millenarian* method. The other method is cyclic, today more commonly called the *recapitulation* approach. This method understands the prophecy of the book to be repetitive, so that the events are described several times, with each description covering the same time period.

Throughout most of the history of the church these two methods of interpreting Revelation have coexisted, but often with one, then the other dominating. While the linear or millenarian method is popular today, increasingly the recapitulation method is coming again into its own. At first glance, the linear way of understanding Revelation might seem more rational and plausible, but the repetition of many of the events makes it difficult to view the book as linear. For example, the end of this present world is depicted several times, though in different ways, throughout the book (6:12–17; 11:15–19; 14:14–20; 16:17–21; and 19:1–21). The repetition of events such as this suggests that Revelation cannot be interpreted on a linear, chronological scale. The visions of the seven seals (6:1–17; 8:1–5), the seven trumpet-angels (Revelation 8:6–9:21; 11:15–19), and the seven angels with censers (15:1–16:21) are all parallel and cover the same time period, namely, events on earth from Christ's ascension to his parousia. This suggests that the proper method of interpretation is that of the cyclic or recapitulation approach. It is with this method of interpreting and understanding the structure of Revelation that the present commentary is written.

COMMENTARY

REVELATION 1:1–3:22

INTRODUCTION

1:1–8 **Prologue**

1:9–20 **Commissioning of John:
Vision of the Son of Man**

Excursus   *Son of Man*

2:1–3:22 **Letters of Preparation to
the Seven Churches**

Excursus   *The Seven Letters of
Preparation (2:1–3:22)*

2:1–7   To the Angel of Ephesus

2:8–11   To the Angel of Smyrna

2:12–17   To the Angel of Pergamum

2:18–29   To the Angel of Thyatira

3:1–6   To the Angel of Sardis

3:7–13   To the Angel of
Philadelphia

3:14–22   To the Angel of Laodicea

REVELATION 1:1–8
PROLOGUE

TRANSLATION

1 ¹The revelatory-unveiling of Jesus Christ which God gave to him to show to his slaves what things are necessary to come about quickly, and he [Christ] communicated in visible signs these things as he sent them through his angel to his slave John, ²who witnessed to the word of God and to the witness [testimony] of Jesus Christ, what things he saw. ³Blessed is the one who reads and [blessed are] those who hear the words of this prophecy and who keep the things written in it, for the time is near. ⁴John, to the seven churches which are in Asia: Grace to you and peace from the One Who Is and Who Was and Who Is Coming, and from the seven Spirits that are before his throne, ⁵and from Jesus Christ, the witness, the faithful one, the firstborn of the dead and the ruler of the kings of the earth. To him who loves us and set us free from our sins by his blood, ⁶and he made us to be a kingdom, priests to his God and Father, to him be [all] the glory and the dominion forever and ever, amen. ⁷Behold, he is coming with the clouds,

and every eye will see him,

even those who pierced him,

and all the tribes of the earth will

mourn over him. Yes, amen!

⁸"I am the Alpha and the Omega," says Yahweh, the [only] God, the One Who Is and Who Was and Who Is Coming, the Almighty.

COMMENTARY

THE TITLE: REVELATION/ APOCALYPSE OF JOHN

Titles were not a part of the original texts of books of the NT, and so they were not considered an important and unchangeable part of the texts. In antiquity a title would be a strip or tag attached on the back of a roll; the title was also written inside the roll at the end of the text. Before such tags were attached, the first words of the document itself would have indicated its contents. The earliest manuscripts of Revelation have the title "apocalypse/revelation of John," taken from 1:1. As time went on, this title was sometimes expanded, such as "apocalypse/revelation of John the theologian and evangelist."

THE TITLE AND ITS EXPLANATION (1:1–3)

Within the original text, the first words, "the revelatory-unveiling of Jesus Christ," serve as a title for the whole book. The rest of the introduction (1:1–3) then serves as a brief commentary on the title.

The revelation is given to God's people ("his slaves") so that they might know what is to happen "quickly"—soon, immediately (1:1). The revelation comes from God to Jesus Christ, who in turn gives it to John through an angel, identified as "his angel" (1:1)—an angel of Jesus. In the epilogue, it is said that God through "his angel" gave the revelation to his people ("his slaves") concerning things that would happen "soon" (22:6). In 22:16, Jesus says that he was the one who gave the witness of this revelation to the churches, and he gave this witness by means of "my angel."

There is, then, a clear sequence of mediation through which John and his audience received the revelation: God, Jesus Christ, his angel, John, and the seven churches. The source of the revelation is God. The mediator of the revelation is Jesus Christ, who uses an angel to give it to John and the churches. Angels play an important role throughout the book of Revelation. They help in the mediation by leading or attending John through the visions, with the interpretation of the visions, in aiding John to focus on what is important in a particular vision, and by answering John's questions concerning something within a vision (5:2).

While the mediating agents of the revelation are Jesus Christ and his angel(s), the perceptible means by which John receives it are visions and/or visionary experiences. This is indicated by two verbs in 1:1, both done by Christ: "to show" and "communicated in visible signs." John also describes his reception in 1:2 with the verb "saw." At the very beginning John is alerted to the fact that the primary means of his perception of the revelation will be visions (1:1), and he tells the reader(s) and hearer(s) that he will describe for them what "he saw" (1:2). However, the audible word will also be used, as indicated by "word," "who hear," and "words" (1:2–3). Though visions will be used to convey the revelation to John, they only serve as visual aids in the revelation. The communication from John to the reader(s) and hearer(s) takes place through words. Of primary importance in the revelation is the word, the meaning and witness of the prophetic message which is portrayed by the visions (e.g., 7:13–17). *Thus the prophetic message of Revelation is the Word of God given in and with visual form.*

The revelatory message is called a "prophecy" (1:3). Revelation is the only book in the NT which is referred to in this way. Whether or not John consciously thought of his work as the climax of the prophetic writings of the OT, he certainly viewed his work as belonging to that prophetic tradition. He understands that the church, as it witnesses the message of Christ, is the heir and fulfillment of the OT prophetic message (see Revelation 11). The witness of Jesus in the message of Revelation is also equated with the Spirit of prophecy (19:10), and in the epilogue the message is again referred to several times as a prophecy (22:7, 10, 18, 19). The fact that John understood his Revelation to be a prophecy suggests that he believed this writing would be the last message of God to his people before the End (cf. "prophecy" in 22:18) and that he was the last prophet of the salvation story which had begun with the promise of old and now was concluded in the revelatory-unveiling of Jesus Christ (1:3; 10:7; 15:8; 22:6–7, 10–12).

Finally, these verses speak a blessing upon "the one who reads [aloud] and those who hear … and who keep" this prophetic message (1:3). The blessing is not here defined, but when the six other instances in Revelation of a pronounced blessing (14:13; 16:15; 19:9; 20:6; 22:7, 14) are examined, it becomes clear that the blessing bestowed is the *participation in the heavenly banquet of the bride and the Lamb (19:9).* It is a blessing which is also now received by *the washing of the Christians' robes (22:14) in the blood of the Lamb (7:13–14)* and is a *participation now in the first resurrection (20:6).* At both the beginning and the end of the prophecy this blessing is spoken upon the hearers (1:3; 22:7). It is also the present gift of God to the faithful recipients of the Gospel as it comes in the word of Christ's crucifixion and resurrection and in Holy Baptism and the Lord's Supper. Thus it is spoken over the Christians assembled for corporate worship, where the Holy Scriptures are read aloud to the assembly and the Sacraments instituted by the Lord Jesus are cherished and followed.

DIVINE CONFIRMATION OF THE MESSAGE (1:4–6)

These verses give a trinitarian stamp of approval by which God himself confirms the validity of the message of Revelation. It is given in the form of a greeting benediction in which John speaks the blessing of God's grace and peace to his recipients, the seven churches.

The trinitarian formula is presented in the words "the One Who Is and Who Was and Who Is Coming, and from the seven Spirits … and from Jesus

Christ" (1:4–5). In these words John names the triune God: Father, Spirit, and Jesus Christ. At first glance it would appear that already in the first phrase, "the One Who Is and Who Was and Who Is Coming," there is a representation of the triune God. However, it is better to hear 1:4–5 as naming three distinct persons: (1) "the One Who Is and Who Was and Who Is Coming"; (2) the seven Spirits; and (3) Jesus Christ. Each refers to one of the persons of the Trinity.

First, the revelation comes from God the Father. "The One Who Is" leads one to the holy name of God in Exodus 3. In the context of 1:4–6 "the One Who Is" then refers to God the Father.

John, in his own way, uses "the One Who Is and Who Was and Who Is Coming" for the holy name in Exodus 3. He takes "the One Who Is" from Ex 3:14 and then expands it by adding "and Who Was and Who Is Coming." By so doing he states that the ever present One is continually present now, as he was in the past and as he always will be in the future. *The entire three-part phrase, then, is really a rendition of "I Am" in Ex 3:14, which is God's own explanation for his holy name, Yahweh* (Ex 3:13–16).

John emphasizes "the One Who Is and Who Was and Who Is Coming" by having it in a grammatically unusual form, in the nominative after the preposition "from" instead of in the genitive that normally follows that preposition. Whether John did this consciously in deference to the holy name, because to have used an oblique case would have necessitated a vocalized change of that name, can only be surmised. Certainly John, because of his Jewish background, would be aware of Jewish practices in deference toward the holy name. But more likely, if not also in addition, John wanted to make and emphasize a theological truth: that the Father is the first among equals. The Father, while equal in essence with the Spirit and Jesus Christ, is nevertheless the primus of the three persons (cf. 1 Cor 15:28; Jn 14:16–17, 26). In deference to the holy name, that is, in deference to God the Father, through worship of Jesus Christ by means of the Spirit, John keeps this Greek rendering of the holy name in a grammatically unusual form.

Wherever this Greek form of the holy name ("the One Who Is") appears in Revelation, John keeps to this theological principle, namely, that the Father is the first among equals; he also keeps to this principle throughout the book whenever the heavenly court worships God and the Lamb (in that order; e.g., 4:8–11; 5:9–14). The One Who Is" appears a total of five times in Revelation, *all in reference to the Father.* In 1:4 and 1:8 the elements of the three-part title "the One Who Is and Who Was and Who Is Coming" appear in the same order, but in 4:8 "the One Who Was" comes first and then "and Who Is and Who Is Coming." In 11:17 and 16:5 only "the One Who Is and Who Was" is present. In each case where there is a difference, the author is making a theological statement—each will be treated in the commentary on the respective verses. Here in

1:4 this Greek rendering of the holy name points to the fact that the message of Revelation comes first of all from God the Father.

Second, the prophetic message of Revelation comes from "the seven Spirits" (1:4). Because of the number seven, commentators have wondered whether these are seven angels, corresponding to the seven archangels in Jewish tradition (see 1 Enoch 19:1; 20:1–7, where seven archangels are listed and named), or corresponding to the seven angels of the seven churches (and thus also to the seven angels with the trumpets [Rev 8:6–11:19] and censers [Revelation 15–16]). Against this identification is the fact that "the seven Spirits" (1:4) are on the same level of authority as God the Father and Jesus Christ. If these "Spirits" were angels, they would never be accorded the same status as God and Jesus Christ in Christian theology. (In Revelation angels are never worshiped, only God; cf. 19:10; 22:8–9.) Rather, these "seven Spirits" are a reference to the Holy Spirit.

In biblical thought, the number seven symbolizes God. It is the sum of the number three, which symbolizes God himself (cf. Gen 18:1–2; Is 6:3), and the number four, which symbolizes creation (cf., e.g., Ezek 37:9; 1 Chr 9:24). Seven thus symbolizes the God of creation. Because God rested on the seventh day (Gen 2:2–3), the number is also used to picture or refer to perfection, completion, and holiness, especially in reference to God's activities and creative works.

The seven lamps and seven eyes in Zech 3:9–4:10 represent the Spirit of God, by which God sees the whole earth. In Is 11:1–2 the sevenfold gifts of the Spirit from God will rest upon the Branch of Jesse, the Messiah. *The seven Spirits of Rev 1:4, therefore, represent the Holy Spirit. . Throughout Revelation the number seven represents God's presence by his Spirit.* Thus the church, when represented in Revelation by the seven churches (Revelation 2–3), is pictured as always under the Spirit of God. The heavenly hosts worship God by the presence of the seven Spirits before God's throne (4:5). The Lamb of God, with the seven horns and eyes (5:6), is he on whom the sevenfold Spirit rests (Is 11:1–2). And the exalted Christ, as the Son of Man, stands in the midst of the seven golden lampstands, which represent the church under the lordship of Christ by the Spirit (1:13).

Third, in addition to the Father and the Spirit (1:4), the revelation comes "from Jesus Christ," identified as the conqueror of death and as "the *ruler* of the kings of the earth" (1:5). Jesus Christ, the witness to the truth of God, was faithful in his messianic mission and went to his death. But he is the firstborn of the dead, raised on the third day. Thus, he is described as the one who set God's people free from their sins and as a result made them a kingdom for God, as well as priests to serve in the kingdom (the royal priesthood of all believers). The doxology voiced at the end of 1:6, while directly applied to Christ, is through him directed to God the Father by the Spirit.

Why is Jesus Christ spoken of last, after the Father and the Spirit? It is because of his saving work, by which he has redeemed God's people so that they can now worship God as his royal priests. This worship is directed through Christ to the Father and is inspired by the Spirit.

This is the only book in the Bible which has such a trinitarian stamp of approval (1:4–6), at least in this explicit form, by which the source and authority of God is placed upon a human's writing. Because Revelation is the culmination of all scriptural revelation, this seal of approval is also placed, by inference, on the entire Scripture, both the OT and the NT. This may also indicate that there will not be another word of God spoken until the Lord Christ comes at the End. God's people must listen, for "the time is near" (1:3)—the time of judgment, but in particular the time of blessing in the presence of the exalted Christ.

THE LORD'S RETURN (1:7–8)

The prologue concludes with a reference to the returning Lord: "Behold, he is coming with the clouds" (1:7). Jesus' words to Caiaphas were, "You will see the Son of Man ... coming on the clouds of heaven" (Mt 26:64; cf. 1 Thess 4:17). This suggests that the thought "the time is near" (Rev 1:3) refers to the coming of the Lord Christ at the End. The epilogue also leads to this interpretation (22:6–7, 12, 20).

The whole human race will witness his coming. No one will be exempt from this confrontation with Jesus Christ, not "even those who pierced him" (1:7). While this is not a direct quote of Zech 12:10, it brings to mind that prophecy that the Lord will pour out his Spirit of grace on the house of David, and, says Yahweh, "They will look upon me whom they have pierced." The reference to this verse brings to light again Christ's death (cf. Rev 1:5); note that John alone among the four evangelists recounts the piercing of Jesus on the cross (Jn 19:33–37; cf. 1 Jn 5:6). And this piercing will cause people to beat their breasts and wail over him. Here in Rev 1:7 John states that "all the tribes of the earth will mourn over him." While "those who pierced him" most probably refers to God's manifest enemies, "the tribes" who wail and mourn over him probably refers to God's own repentant people (Zech 12:12–14 suggests such an interpretation; see also Lk 2:35; 23:27; Jn 20:11). The fact that the Lord Christ at his second coming will be recognized as *the one who was pierced* is a witness and confirmation of the truth that *by his death and resurrection* he alone is the Savior and Judge of the human race (see Jn 19:33–35; 1 Jn 5:6–12).

The last verse of the prologue (Rev 1:8), while strange when compared to ordinary literary style, is characteristic of the style of both the prologue and epilogue of Revelation (22:7, 12). The divine voice (first person singular) breaks in to confirm the authority of God the Father as the prime source and originator of the revelatory-unveiling of Jesus Christ. It is the voice of God himself, by which he confirms the exalted status of his Son, Jesus Christ, as the Lord and Judge of all history, the human race and the world.

There is no consensus as to the identity of the speaker of 1:8. Some commentators take the speaker to be Jesus Christ, others God the Father. To take the voice to be that of Jesus Christ would break up the literary symmetry of the prologue, which begins with God the Father as the giver of the revelation and ends with the Father as the authenticator of it. While Jesus Christ is the subject and object of the message, only God the Father, who originates and gives it to Jesus, can also then be the one who authenticates it (cf. Mt 3:17). By these words God himself testifies to the position that his Son has earned and merited. The revelation of his Son's exalted position is now to commence and unfold in the prophetic message of Revelation. There is no greater witness, and the affirmation of the divine authority of the book calls for no less a witness (Jn 5:36–37; 8:18).

The title "the Alpha and the Omega" (1:8), the first and last letters of the Greek alphabet, expresses the eternity of God. In rabbinic theology the first and last letters of the Hebrew alphabet represented totality and entirety, and in particular they represented the Shekinah, that is, God's visible presence for the benefit of his people, as at the burning bush (Exodus 3). That rabbinic theology draws on OT passages such as Is 41:4; 43:10; 44:6; 48:12. The title "the Alpha and the Omega" appears again in 21:6, where it also is applied to God the Father, and in 22:13, where it is applied to Jesus Christ. Christ is the revealed glory of God (Jn 1:14, 18), the one through whom God graciously appears to his people. He is the eternal one who has entered human history and time. "The Alpha and the Omega" is one of the titles which God the Father and Jesus share in Revelation. In this case it is shared because the Son of God is eternal in the same absolute sense as is the Father.

God the Father speaks directly only in 1:8 and 21:5. God is further identified in 1:8 by "the One Who Is and Who Was and Who Is Coming" (first mentioned in 1:4), but now he is also called "the Almighty." While in Revelation God shares with Jesus Christ the title "the Alpha and the Omega," the titles "the One Who Is and Who Was and Who Is Coming" and "the Almighty" in Revelation are reserved for the Father alone. This is done so as to preserve the prime position of God the Father while at the same time displaying the equality of the Father and the Son.

Thus the Father's speaking of this word (1:8) here is analogous to the word at the transfiguration (with the added understanding here about the role of the Spirit from Jn 15:26–27; 16:13–15). At the transfiguration the Father confirms the Son, whom he has sent and on whom the Spirit rests: "This is my beloved Son; hear him" (Mk 9:7). Here in Rev 1:8 the Father confesses that this Spirit-given (Jn 15:26–27; 16:13–15) prophecy about the sent, crucified, and exalted Son (whose exaltation is the chief focus of the revelation) has its origin in himself, the Father, and so has his authority behind it.

REVELATION 1:9–20

COMMISSIONING OF JOHN: VISION OF THE SON OF MAN

TRANSLATION

1   [9]I John, your brother and partner in the suffering and kingdom and patience in Jesus, was on the island which is called Patmos on account of the Word of God and the witness of Jesus. [10]I was in the Spirit on the Lord's day when I heard behind me a great voice like that of a trumpet [11]saying, "What you see, write in a book and send [it] to the seven churches—to Ephesus and to Smyrna and to Pergamum and to Thyatira and to Sardis and to Philadelphia and to Laodicea." [12]And I turned about to look at the voice which was speaking with me, and when I had turned I saw seven golden lampstands. [13]And in the midst of the lampstands [I saw] someone like the Son of Man, clothed in a long flowing robe and tied around at the chest with a golden sash. [14]And his head and his hair were white as wool, white as snow, and his eyes were like a flame of fire, [15]and his feet were like burnished brass as if fired in a furnace, and his voice was like the sound of many waters. [16]And he had in his right hand seven stars, and there was coming out of his mouth a sharp two-edged sword, and his appearance was like the sun when it shines in its full power. [17]And when I looked at him, I fell at his feet as dead. And he placed his right hand on me, saying, "Stop being afraid; I am the First and the Last, [18]and the Living One. Indeed I was dead, but, behold, I am alive forever and ever, and I have the keys of death and the grave. [19]Write then what you see, both the things which are and those

which will come to pass after these things. ²⁰The
mystery of the seven stars which you see in my
right hand and the seven golden lampstands—the
seven stars are angels of the seven churches, and
the seven lampstands are seven churches."

COMMENTARY

JOHN ON PATMOS (1:9–11)

John was on the island of Patmos because of his proclaiming "the Word of
God" and because of his "witness" to Jesus Christ (1:9). Even as Jesus was "the
witness, the faithful one" (1:5), so also John was an eyewitness (1 Jn 1:1) who
testified faithfully to the truthfulness of Jesus' life, death, and resurrection.
Because he would not back down, he suffered exile. He was a "partner" with
Christ "in the *suffering*"—placed first for emphasis—and in the "kingdom" of
God and in the "patience" given to him by Christ (Rev 1:9). Others also were
suffering persecution in this time of affliction (cf. Mk 13:19), some even death
(Rev 2:9–10, 13).

Patmos, an island about forty miles west-southwest of Miletus, thus
became the locale where Revelation was written. It was during a moment of
worship and meditation "in the Spirit" (1:10) on the Lord's day that John heard
a loud, trumpet-like voice commissioning him to write the revelation and to
send it to the seven churches. In the midst of suffering (1:9), the affliction which
is part of the kingdom (Acts 14:22), John received the grace of the vision of the
exalted Christ through which he received the revelation.

No other person has been permitted to see and describe the exalted Christ
in such detail. Stephen saw the exalted Christ at the right of God and was thus
comforted and fortified for his death, but he gave no detailed description (Acts
7:55–56). Paul was met on the way to Damascus by the exalted Christ (Acts
9:1–9) through a light, and he was once taken up into the third heaven and given
revelations of the Lord (2 Cor 12:1–4), but in neither case does he give a description of Christ. John was given the grace not only to see the exalted Christ but
also to share his vision with the church.

THE EXALTED CHRIST (1:12–16)

In his description of the exalted Son of Man, John draws upon several
sources in the OT. These sources serve as a literary palette from which he creates
in artistic language the image of the one who commissioned him. But also he
draws from his own experience and memory of the event of the transfiguration.
He recognizes the one before him, but yet there is a difference. When John
saw the glorified Christ on the holy mount, he received a preview of the glory
into which Jesus would come as a result of his death and resurrection. Now in

Revelation 1 he sees the same Lord in that glory; the merited glory that John saw beforehand on the holy mount, he now sees in all its fulfillment. Daniel had prophetically seen this merited glory of the Son of Man long before (Dan 7:13), and, as Peter says about all the prophets (1 Pet 1:10–12), Daniel longed for the time when Christ would come into that glory. The prophetic promise, *seen prophetically by Daniel* and *momentarily experienced by John at the transfiguration shortly before the promise's fulfillment*, stands *now consummated* in all its everlasting beauty.

The Lord Christ appeared to John "like the Son of Man" (Rev 1:13). John had once before seen the heavenly glory of Jesus at his transfiguration, when Christ gave to the three disciples a *preview* of the heavenly glory that he would merit by his cross and resurrection and come into *fully* at his ascension (cf. 2 Pet 1:16–18). Here again John sees the Lord Christ in his heavenly glory, and as he sees Christ *he is reminded that his Lord is now in this glory because he has completed his mission through his death and resurrection* (Rev 1:18).

John gives a rather detailed description. As the Son of Man, the Lord Christ is clothed in a *long flowing robe*. In the Septuagint this word refers to the stately garment of the high priest. Here then we have a reminder of the high priestly role of the exalted Christ before the heavenly Father (Heb 4:14–16). A *golden belt or sash* is tied around his chest. Such a high tying of a sash, around the chest rather than around the waist, was usual with this robe. The seven censer-angels in Rev 15:6 are girded or tied about the chest with golden sashes or belts. According to 1 Macc 10:89 and 14:44, such a golden belt indicated royalty. In Dan 10:5 the heavenly figure dressed in fine linen has a golden belt tied around his waist. Thus noting the golden belt attached to the Son of Man (Rev 1:13), John deliberately links the heavenly figure of Daniel 10 with the Son of Man figure of Dan 7:13. The golden belt is indicative of the kingship of the exalted Christ and of his identification with the Son of Man figure of Daniel.

His head is *white like wool and snow*. In the OT the hoary or grey head of the aged commanded respect and was worthy of honor (Lev 19:32); it also symbolized a crown of splendor and righteous wisdom (Prov 16:31; 20:29). The Ancient of Days, to whom the heavenly court presents the Son of Man in Dan 7:9–14, has clothing white like snow and his head was white as wool. In Dan 7:13–14, when the Son of Man is presented to the Ancient Days, he is given authority to establish an everlasting kingdom. Here in Rev 1:14, the Son of Man now has this whiteness; glory and honor are now due him because he has successfully carried out his commission of establishing—through his "suffering" (1:9), death, and resurrection—this everlasting "kingdom" (1:9). *Ascended, he now reigns. The whiteness of the Ancient of Days has been transferred to the victorious Christ.* The glory and worship given to God the Father now is also fully given to God the Son (see 5:11–14).

The eyes of the Son of Man are *"like a flame of fire"* (1:14). In Dan 7:9 the throne of the Ancient of Days was flaming with fire. The eyes of the heavenly figure in Dan 10:6 were like lamps of fire. This is another hint that the Son of Man of Revelation is to be identified with the heavenly figure of Daniel 10 and is the same as the Son of Man of Daniel 7. In the OT fire symbolizes the holy purifying presence of God, before whom only those thus purified can stand. The corollary is that the holy presence of God destroys evil. In antiquity, Greek and Roman authors spoke of eyes like flaming fire. The penetrating glance of Jesus while here on earth held a foreboding of righteous anger for those upon whom it fell (Mk 3:5). John now sees these piercing, fiery eyes in the exalted Christ, the one whom God had authorized to destroy evil and purify his people.

The feet of the exalted Christ are like *fiery burnished brass* (Rev 1:15), reminiscent of the legs of the heavenly figure in Dan 10:6. Feet of brass represent a strength that conquers all enemies (Dan 2:33). The enemies of death and the grave now lie vanquished beneath his feet (Rev 1:17–18; 1 Cor 15:25–27). His voice was like the *roar of mighty waters* (Rev 1:15), similar to the voice of the heavenly figure in Dan 10:6, whose voice sounded like a great crowd of people. But Christ's voice suggests especially the mighty voice of God which attended the coming of his glory, which voice is like the roar of many waters (Ezek 43:2); compare the sound of the wings of the four winged creatures of God's glory in Ezek 1:24. *When John stands before the exalted Son of Man, he is standing before the very majesty and glory of God* (see Rev 10:3).

The Son of Man has *in his right hand seven stars,* which represent the angels of the seven churches (1:20). It is by his right hand of mercy (Mt 25:34; Rev 1:17) that the Lord Christ blesses and comforts his church through the sevenfold presence of the Spirit (Jn 14:15–17; 16:7). The angels are also a reminder that the church is represented before God's heavenly throne by angels, through whom God also protects his people on earth (Heb 1:14; Mt 18:10; 25:31). But in particular the angels represent the human messengers of Christ's Word to his church. The *"two-edged sword"* (Rev 1:16) indicates that the Son of Man will execute the judgment of God according to his Word (Heb 4:12).

Last of all John mentions how *the whole appearance* of the Son of Man is *like the sun in its most powerful brightness* (Rev 1:16). In the OT the sun is used as a metaphor for God, in particular for his glory, by which he blesses his people and bestows upon them the light which produces life, bringing them out from darkness. In Mal 4:2 the prophet declares that "the Sun of righteousness" will arise with healing in his wings, a heavenly figure which is associated with the Messiah because of Mal 3:1–4 and 4:1–2. The heavenly figure of Daniel 10 is pictured with a face like lightning (Dan 10:6). In Matthew's account of the transfiguration we are told that Jesus' face was like the sun (Mt 17:2). Here in Revelation 1 *the face and the whole person of Jesus show that the exalted Christ is*

the person through whom the glory and the life-giving light of God are now pres-
ent. Christ's face and person radiate God's glory, which brings light to a world of
darkness.

THE GRACIOUS HAND UPON
THE MESSENGER (1:17–20)

When John now sees the exalted Christ in all his glory, he falls down before
him as dead, as a corpse (1:17). Before the transfigured Christ, John (and Peter
and James) first stood (Mt 17:1–5) and then, when the voice spoke from the
cloud (Mt 17:6), fell on their faces (in a posture of worship) because of the fear
that the experience evoked. But now John is completely knocked down and out
as dead. While he could stand before the transfigured Christ and then in fear
willingly bow down, here he is completely overwhelmed and *unwillingly,* as it
were, forced down as when death strikes the body (cf. Jn 18:4–6). Perhaps when
Jesus displayed his glory on the holy mount, it was dimmed just enough so that
John could still remain standing. But here before the exalted Lord he is struck
by a full blast of that consummate majestic glory, and as a result he is knocked
down as a corpse. John could no more stand before the heavenly Christ than
he could approach the sun and touch it. Indeed, he could no more stand before
the glorified Christ than Moses could stand before God and see his face at Mt.
Sinai—unless given special grace and permission. It is similar to what Isaiah
said when he saw Yahweh on his throne:

> Woe to me,
>> for I am ruined,
>> for I am a man unclean of lips and in the midst
>>> of a people unclean of lips I am dwelling,
>> for my eyes have seen the King,
>>> Yahweh of hosts. (Is 6:5)

No human person can stand before the exalted Son of Man because of the
corruption of sin and God's own holiness. Not even John could stand before
Christ on his own ability and merit because of John's state of sinful corruption
and Christ's own holiness and glory. John's falling down as dead is like the
action of every proclaimer of the Word as he falls down in repentance before
the Word that comes to him. Every ministry of the Word begins with the repentance of the minister and Christ's forgiveness of his sin (cf. Rev 10:9–11).

But Jesus Christ gave John the grace and permission to stand before him.
Placing his right hand on John, Jesus tells John, "Stop being afraid," (1:17). This
word of gracious comfort empowers Christ's slave to stand up in his presence.

The Lord Christ identifies himself as "the First and the Last" (1:17). Like
"the Alpha and the Omega" (1:8), "the First and the Last" also denotes the
eternalness, but the titles are not synonymous. "The Alpha and the Omega"
refers to the eternalness of God (1:8) and Christ (22:13), an eternalness that

is far beyond creation, but "the First and the Last" refers to the eternalness of Christ *in relationship to his bride, the church.* It is a reflection and fulfillment of Is 44:6 and 48:12, where Yahweh says to the people of Israel as their King and Redeemer, "I am the first and I am the last." In using this title Jesus assures John that, as the Eternal One, he *is* his Savior; therefore John should not be afraid (see also Is 44:8, where Yahweh tells his people not to be afraid).

Furthermore, Jesus identifies himself as "the Living One" (Rev 1:18), a title used in the OT to contrast the true God with all idols, which are dead and thus have no existence. Jesus Christ was dead *but now lives forever.* Because of his death and resurrection Jesus Christ now has the keys of death and the grave. As the conqueror of death and the grave he demonstrates that there is only one true God, the God who now reaches out to all through Jesus Christ in order to bring life. All other gods are false and dead idols. The death *and resurrection* of Jesus Christ validate the truth that the God ("the first and … the last," Is 44:6) who is now present in the exalted Christ is the only true God (Is 44:8–10), Creator (Is 48:12–13) and Judge/Redeemer (Is 48:14–22).

Having revived John with the gracious and life-giving touch of his hand, Jesus now commissions John to "write" (Rev 1:19) to the seven churches in order that they might receive and know the prophetic message of the unveiling of the Lord's majesty.

SON OF MAN AND LAMB OF GOD

The book of Revelation generally presents the Lord Christ as either the Son of Man or the Lamb of God. When he appears as the Son of Man, it is fearful to contemplate him, for as such he is the judge of all the human race on behalf of God the Father (Rev 19:11–16; cf. Jn 5:22–23, 27). When he appears as such, it strikes fear and terror in the hearts of all people (Rev 6:12–17), even momentarily in the hearts of God's own people (1:17). *He has the authority to carry out God's judgment as the Son of Man because as the Lamb of God he suffered God's judgment in place of the human race* (5:6–10; 6:15–17; 19:13–15). When, however, he appears as the Lamb, it is to his own people only, and there is no fear. God's people can stand before him in his love as ones washed in his blood (7:9–17). They have no fear, no uncertainty, only the love that assures them that they are God's people (19:5–9). In the final appearance of Jesus Christ in Revelation, the grand vision of his second coming as the Son of Man in judgment (19:11–21), God's people are not to fear. He is coming not as their judge, but as their deliverer. This is demonstrated in the first vision of Christ's second coming in Revelation 14, where the two pictures, the Son of Man and the Lamb of God, coalesce. As he comes as the Son of Man to judge (14:14–20), God's people are to view him as the Lamb (14:1–5). At his coming they will see him as the Son of Man and will (momentarily) be afraid, but they are to look upon him not as judge but as the Lamb, the Savior. All fear then disappears as he says, "Come, you blessed, into the kingdom that has been prepared for you."

EXCURSUS

SON OF MAN

Though the title "son of man" is used in Ezekiel as an appellation of the prophet, identifying him as a spokesman for God, it is chiefly the use of the term in Daniel that gives the theological background for its usage in the NT. Already in the intertestamental period a theology of the Son of Man developed. For example, 1 Enoch comments on and interprets the Son of Man described in Dan 7:13–14. The Son of Man *represents* the Ancient of Days and *rules* God's people on his behalf (1 Enoch 46:1–8; 48:1–10). The Son of Man's preexistence is affirmed, he is identified as the Anointed One (Messiah), and he will be the light of the Gentiles (1 Enoch 48:1–10). He is also identified with Wisdom and will be in charge of the resurrection and the judgment (1 Enoch 49:1–4; 51:1–5).

When Jesus began to call himself the "Son of Man," the term already had a theological meaning within Judaism. It was the favorite title that Jesus used when speaking of himself in the third person. It appears some eighty-eight times in the NT, eighty-four of which appear in the four gospels and two in Revelation (1:13 and 14:14). In the gospels it is used in connection with all of Christ's ministry, but in particular in connection with statements that say that *because of his death and resurrection he will come again in judgment* (Mt 24:30; 26:64; cf. Ps 8:3–9). Jesus' use of this title to identify himself and his ministry expresses that he is the fulfillment of the prophetic picture and word of the Son of Man in the OT (Dan 7:13–14; Ps 8:3–9; cf. also Ps 2:12). It also invites hearers to recognize him as such. He is *the* man whom God had chosen (Is 42:1; 49:7) to take Israel's place (Is 49:3), and also that of the Gentiles (Is 49:6), and to represent them before God (Is 53:12). He is the one who established God's kingdom (Rev 1:6), incorporating into it both Jews and Gentiles, and he did this by his own death and resurrection (Mk 8:31; Rev 1:5–6).

The Bible bestows on Jesus the son of Mary three great titles: "Christ," "Lord," and "Son of Man." There are of course many other descriptive names and terms that are applied to Jesus which help to explain the fullness of those three great titles, such as Savior, Holy One, Redeemer. In addition there are terms that describe his essence and person, such as Son of God, son of Joseph. To these can be added terms that describe the mystery of his being, such as Logos ("Word"), light, truth. But the three great titles conferred upon Jesus of Nazareth *identify and encapsulate all that the Son of God became and did on behalf of the human race.*

The title *"Christ"* ("Messiah") designates Jesus of Nazareth as the chosen one, the anointed Redeemer of the world. As a result of his redemptive activity he became the *"Lord"* of God's people, the church. And furthermore, as a result of his being the Christ and the Lord of God's people, he is also the *"Son of Man,"* that is, the master of all history, of the human race and of the final judgment of God. The title "Son of Man" is bestowed upon Jesus because, as *the* man who represents God's people before the heavenly Father, he reconciled them to the Father by his being the Christ. Now, as the Lord of the church, this same Son of Man will also be the Lord and Judge of the whole human race and of the world.

This title, "Son of Man," not only identifies Jesus, the Son of God, as the true man who came to take the place of the human race in his life and death and resurrection. It also emphasizes the fact that Jesus Christ, as *the* human being, was elevated to the high and unique status of being *the* Man to rule everything on behalf of God the Father.

The OT roots, the intertestamental Jewish development, and the self-revelation of Jesus testified to in the NT all lead one to see that when the title "Son of Man" is applied to Jesus, the God-man, it emphasizes how he *represents* God's people as he establishes for them God's kingdom, and he also *rules* God's people (and judges the whole world) by the authority of and on behalf of God the Father. These are the very emphases of Dan 7:13–14, the seminal passage that narrates how "one like a Son of Man" approached "the Ancient of Days" and received from him "authority, glory, and kingship" to the end that those from all peoples of the earth who are brought into his eternal kingdom will worship him forever and ever.

2:1–3:22

LETTERS OF PREPARATION TO THE SEVEN CHURCHES

EXCURSUS

THE SEVEN LETTERS OF PREPARATION

(2:1–3:22)

THE SEVEN LETTERS WITHIN THE BOOK OF REVELATION

The letters to the seven churches form a distinct literary unit within Revelation. Because there are *seven* letters, some commentators have suggested that they are to be interpreted as part of the prophetic, visionary message, which is presented in a sevenfold literary structure. Each of the other sevenfold sections of Revelation (the seven seals, the seven trumpets, and the seven censers) speaks of and/or portrays events taking place on earth over certain periods of time. This would mean, then, that in the opinion of interpreters who consider Revelation to be historically sequential, the seven letters would give information about the period of time from Christ's first coming up to the time in history when the sufferings pictured from 6:1 to 18:24 take place. Interpreters who view Revelation as cyclical would say that the seven letters give parallel information about the same period of suffering that is described in each sevenfold section (that is, the seven letters, the seven seals, the seven trumpets, and the seven censers all would describe the same general time period).

This commentary's view is that the structure of the three sevenfold sections of Revelation (the seven seals, trumpets, and censers) is indeed cyclical, meaning that each of those sections covers the time period between Christ's first and second advents. But the seven letters are different. They do not give information about periods of time as do the seven seals, trumpets, and censers. Rather, these letters, while not part of the prophetic message, nevertheless fulfill an important role in the book of Revelation. *Their intent and purpose is to prepare the recipients for receiving and applying the message in the visions that begin in 4:1.* They are thus *preparatory* in character and *call for repentance.*

Each of the seven letters has a similar literary pattern. First, the addressee or recipient is mentioned, "to the angel of the church in [city]," followed by a descriptive phrase that identifies Christ as the author and sender. Each letter then continues with an acknowledgment of the particular historical circumstances of the church addressed and of the work that the church is doing for Christ. The sender then also mentions and describes a danger or dangers that the particular church faces because of the sin of its members and some flaw or weakness in their Christian faith and character. The author of the letter then urges the recipient to repent lest the sender take away the recipient's place with him. This is followed by a promised blessing to the one who repents, trusts, and conquers. Each letter concludes with an urgent appeal to whomever has an ear to "listen to what the Spirit says to the churches." That plural ("churches") implies that these are "open letters" since their author intends all hearers (or readers) to listen to all seven of the letters.

THE SEVEN CHURCHES AND THE CHURCH

The letters indicate that the Lord Christ knows all about his churches, his people. The contents and messages, addressed to specific historical congregations, have a generalizing tendency within them. They are relevant for Christians of all time, from the Lord's ascension until his return at the End. They intimately reveal the Lord Christ's love and concern for his church. The heart of each letter is the danger that each church faces, and these are dangers that any member of Christ's entire church may face at any given moment. The most imminent danger to the church's faith may be, at any given time and place, a particular sin or failing. Whatever it is, it is a real threat to the Christians' faith; unless they repent, it can destroy their fellowship with Christ. The end result of each letter is to direct the Christians' attention and faith to a promised blessing. Through these messages, the Spirit enables the hearers to repent, to stand firm, and to take comfort in the promised blessing and hope of victory. In this way, the Spirit prepares the recipients of these letters to receive the prophetic message of Revelation (4:1–22:5).

The seven churches which received the letters are historical congregations that existed at the time of John's exile on Patmos. Each of the letters is, however, intended for the entire church throughout the world, at that time and of all time until the Lord's return. Thus the seven letters indicate that the *entire church* is under the care of Christ through the *sevenfold presence of the Spirit.* The seven churches thus model how the entire church is always under the grace, forgiveness, renewal, guidance, motivation, and power of the Spirit.

"THE ANGEL OF THE CHURCH"

In 1:11 the trumpet-like voice of the Lord Christ tells John to send the revelation to the *seven churches,* but in Revelation 2–3, each letter is addressed to the *angel* of the particular church. These angels, first mentioned in 1:20, are represented by the seven stars in the right hand of Christ. Commentators past and present have disagreed about the identity of these angels. Some take them to be bishops or pastors of the churches. Others say that they truly are angelic beings, heavenly messengers of God. Still others have understood these angels as symbolic of the prevailing spirit of each church, that is, the church itself and its character.

In keeping with the whole character of Revelation, it is best to understand the angels of the churches as angelic beings, God's heavenly messengers. The word "angel" appears sixty-seven times in Revelation and, with the possible exception of the angels of the seven churches, it is quite clear that the referents of this word are *always heavenly messengers or figures*.

In 8:1–2 seven angels take over from the Lord Christ the task of mediating the message to John. These seven trumpet-angels are likely the seven angels of the seven churches. The fact that in Revelation heavenly angels are used by God to mediate his word to human beings is not surprising, for God used angels to mediate the Law to Moses on Mt. Sinai (Acts 7:38, 53; Gal 3:19; Heb 2:2), to announce the birth of Jesus (Mt 1:20; Lk 1:26–27; 2:8–9), and to proclaim the resurrection (Mt 28:2–7).

THE PREPARATORY FUNCTION OF THE SEVEN LETTERS

Each of the seven letters was written to a particular church and was relevant to that specific situation at the time of writing. However, like Paul's canonical letters, the seven letters to seven particular churches are also sacred Scripture addressed to all churches and to all Christians until the end of time. It is for this reason that at the end of each letter this statement—reminiscent of Jesus' own encouragement (e.g., Mt 13:9)—is made: "The one who has an ear, let him listen to what the Spirit says to the *churches*" (e.g., Rev 2:7).

The seven churches then symbolize the entire church of Jesus Christ under the motivating influence of the Holy Spirit (the "seven Spirits" in 1:4). In Revelation the number twelve and its multiples twenty-four and 144,000 represent the church of God as church; the number seven symbolizes the sevenfold presence of the Spirit and the church under the control of the Spirit.

The *seven sins and failings* mentioned in the letters seem to suggest a pattern or sequence. That is, each sin, when encountered in temptation and then in commission, leads to the following temptation or sin. When Christians leave their "first love" for Christ (2:4), there then follows the sin, or at least the temptation, of fear (2:10). Fear then gives way or leads into the sin of attempting to serve both God and mammon, and thus the danger of idolatry as exampled by Balaam and Balak (2:14). The sin or temptation of idolatry can lead into the error of the teaching of Jezebel (2:20), which denies the uniqueness of Christianity, and which in turn gives way to a deadness (3:1) of faith and heart. Once this has happened there is no longer the desire to take full advantage of opportunities to serve others in proclaiming the Gospel (3:8). The final sin which results from these is that of being "lukewarm" (3:16) in one's relationship with the Lord Christ. Once this has happened, one is fit only to be separated from the Lord by being cast of out of his holy presence.

Each sin or failing not only endangers one's faith, it also, unless repented of, can lead to the other sins; thus all the more is the Christian's faith and life put at terrible risk. Awareness of this is necessary for repentance, *a godly repentance which prepares the heart to receive the message of Revelation.*

As with the seven sins, the *seven identification marks* of the speaker can be viewed individually and then in total. The Lord Christ shows himself in the first letter as the one who holds the seven stars and who walks about in the midst of the seven lamps (2:1). By such an identification he declares that he is the Lord of the church and the one who through the angels is the mediator of the revelation of God (1:1). In the second letter he points to himself as the Savior of the church when he says that he is the First and the Last, the one who died and rose again (2:8). In the third letter he identifies himself as the judge by referring to the two-edged sword (2:12). In the fourth letter, to the church of Thyatira, the Lord Christ points to the fact that he is omniscient and always present with his power and majesty by reminding the church of his flaming eyes and brass-like feet (2:18). In the fifth letter, by reference to the seven Spirits and seven stars (3:1), the Lord reminds his church that he is the one who sends the Comforter, the Holy Spirit, and administers the care of the angels for the sake of his saints. In the sixth and seventh letters he reminds the church that he governs the opportunities for proclamation of the Gospel by reference to the key of David (3:7) and that he is the confirming witness of that Gospel message as the agent and source of God's new creation (3:14).

These seven descriptions detail for the reader the makeup of what it means to view Jesus Christ as the "Son of Man" (1:13), as the exalted Lord of the church. Thus the appearance of Jesus Christ as the Son of Man in Revelation 1 is interpreted in chapters 2 and 3. All this is for sake of the church, so that she will take warning and especially comfort in her Lord. Finally this detailed picture of the Son of Man reminds the church that the exalted Lord has a mission for his people on earth, and that he will supply her every need for that mission as she lives in repentance and faith.

While each letter focuses (usually toward the beginning) on the sins and failings of the church for the purpose of repentance, the goal of each is the strengthening of the church's faith in the victory of Christ; hence, each letter ends in a *promise* of eternal blessing for the one who conquers. The seven Gospel promises are given in expressions that refer to the *future,* so as to remind the hearer that the victory of Christ finds its full and final meaning before the very presence of God in eternal life. Certainly these eschatological promises encourage the church to recognize God's love for her and the honor that he bestows upon her in Christ. The Christian who conquers is one who endures the period of temptation and suffering and is faithful until the end of earthly life.

The church, however, is not yet in that eternal glory. She is still in the great suffering as she is sustained by faith and carries out the mission her Lord has given to her. The visionary and prophetic message of Revelation, which begins with chapter 4, will be her guide and instruction, her comfort and inspiration in that mission. By indicting sin, calling for repentance, and extending Gospel encouragement, the seven letters in chapters 2 and 3 prepare the heart of the church to receive this revelation.

REVELATION 2:1–7
TO THE ANGEL OF EPHESUS

TRANSLATION

2 ¹To the angel of the church in Ephesus write,
"These things says he who holds the seven stars in his
right hand, the one who walks about in the midst of
the seven golden lampstands: ²'I know your works
and toil and your endurance, and that you are not
able to bear evil people, and you have tested those
who call themselves apostles and are not, and you
found them to be liars. ³You also have endurance
and you bore up on account of my name and you
have not grown weary. ⁴However, I have something
against you, namely, that you have left your first
love. ⁵Remember then from whence you have fallen
and repent and produce the first works. And if you
don't, I am coming to you and I will remove your
lampstand from its place, if you don't repent. ⁶But
this you have, namely, that you hate the works of the
Nicolaitans which I also hate. ⁷The one who has an ear,
let him listen to what the Spirit says to the churches.
To the one who conquers I will grant to eat from
the tree of life, which is in the paradise of God.'"

COMMENTARY

WHO SPEAKS? (2:1)

The exalted Christ identifies himself as the *author* of this letter by referring
to himself as the one who holds the seven stars and walks about in the midst
of the golden lampstands. This identification directs our attention back to 1:12
and 1:16. In the commissioning vision (1:9–20) the Lord Christ holds the seven
stars and is in the midst of the golden lampstands. The stars are the angels of the
seven churches and the lampstands are the churches (1:20). In thus identifying
himself by a partial reference to his appearance as "the Son of Man" (1:13),
the Lord Christ reminds the church that he is both her *Lord and judge. As the*

church's judge, he calls the church to repentance (2:5), because of his love and concern.

WHAT HE KNOWS (2:2–4)

The Lord knows the *activity of the church.* In particular he recognizes how alert the church is toward false apostles, false teachers who by their deceptive teachings are enemies of the truth (see 1 Jn 4:1–6). He also recognizes the patience by which the church endures in the face of weariness brought about by constant toil and watchfulness (see Rev 1:9; 3:10). The patience of God's saints in the midst of turmoil and sufferings is a mark which identifies them as God's people on earth (13:10) and by which they display their faith and obedience to God's commandments (14:12).

What the Lord finds wrong in the church at Ephesus—and it is, of course, a danger for all Christians—is that God's people have left their "first love" (2:4). John is known as the disciple of love not only because of his nearness to Jesus Christ (Jn 19:26) but also because he testifies so abundantly to God's love in Christ toward the world. Jesus told his disciples to love one another as he loved them (Jn 13:34) and that there is no greater love than that someone should lay down his life for his friends (Jn 15:13). It is this love that moved God to give his own Son for the life of the world (Jn 3:16). This is the "first love" (Rev 2:4), the original love: the love of God in Christ. It is the genesis of all other love and of all of love's works.

From this love the church had fallen—a love that redeemed and saved her. Her members had forsaken this love of God that possessed them and bound them to each other; it was no longer of first importance in their lives. "You have left your first love" (2:4) is the chief sin, from which all the others mentioned in the following six letters evolve and result. How the church had left her first love is not mentioned, but the sins and failings mentioned in the six following letters indicate what she had done to manifest her loss of it.

CALL TO REPENT (2:5–6)

The church has fallen, and *if she does not repent,* the Lord threatens to remove her from her place in his presence (2:5). Remembrance of that first love and how she now has fallen from it is a prerequisite for repentance. God's Spirit, through this letter in this book of Revelation, gives that reminder and works contrition and faith. God's love and forgiveness in Christ are received anew. Works worthy of repentance will follow (cf. Mt. 3:8), that is, works which flow from this first love and which demonstrate it to others. Such were the "first works" (2:5) of the Ephesian Christians—and all Christians.

The church at Ephesus had not fallen so far as to embrace the licentious works of the Nicolaitans. To have done so would have compromised their faith with false worship and pagan activities of lust and evil (cf. Rom 1:18–31). The fact that those addressed in this letter hate the ways of the Nicolaitans and that

Jesus refers to them as "the church" (2:1) shows that they are *believers who are in the world*, not unbelievers who are of the world. As such, they are commended for their steadfast vigilance against evil and false people (2:2) but also warned and called to constant repentance, for the Christian in this world *lives in repentance.*

PROMISE (2:7)

The Lord implores his church to repent, and those who do so by heeding the warning word of the Spirit will receive the blessed assurance of eternal life. This is their victory, even their faith (cf. 1 Jn 5:4). The "tree of life" and "paradise" (Rev 2:7) give promise of eternal life in the new heaven and earth, the restored Garden of Eden.

TO THE ANGEL OF SMYRNA

TRANSLATION

2 ⁸And to the angel of the church in Smyrna write, "These things says the First and the Last, the one who was dead and came [back] to life: ⁹"I know your suffering and your poverty, but you are wealthy, and [I know] the blasphemy from those who say that they themselves are Jews and are not but rather [are] the synagogue of Satan. ¹⁰Stop fearing what you are about to suffer. See! The devil is about to throw some of you into prison so that you will be tested, and you will experience suffering ten days. Be faithful unto death, and I will give to you the crown of life. ¹¹The one who has an ear, let him listen to what the Spirit says to the churches. The one who conquers will certainly never be harmed by the second death.'"

COMMENTARY

WHO SPEAKS? (2:8)

The Lord Christ identifies himself as "the First and the Last" (2:8). This title is immediately interpreted by that which follows, "the one who was dead and came [back] to life." The Lord Christ is the First and the Last *because* he died and rose again. He thus is the first, the *cause* of the Christian's faith and life because of his death and resurrection, and he is the last, the *goal and object* of the believer's faith and life because he is the Lord and giver of eternal life with the Father (cf. also 22:13; Heb 12:2). This identification as the First and the Last would be a great comfort to the Christians who were daily faced by the fear of suffering and death.

WHAT HE KNOWS (2:9)

At this particular time the church at Smyrna was evidently experiencing such fear of persecution. In addition they were suffering material poverty, a common hardship among Christians of the first century. Though they were poor in the material wealth of the world, they were rich in the spiritual wealth given by God (see 3:17–18, where spiritual poverty is contrasted to material wealth). Not only were they poor, they were also persecuted by their Jewish neighbors, some of whom seem to have infiltrated their Christian community. These Jews claimed that they (and not the Christians) represented the true inherited faith of Moses and the prophets (see Gal 3:1–14). But the Lord names these oppressors for what they are: the synagogue of Satan—referring metaphorically to the fact that they, as a group, follow the lies of Satan.

COMFORT, EXHORTATION, AND PROMISES (2:10–11)

The suffering of the Christians at Smyrna, their poverty, and the opposition they suffered from Jewish neighbors were certainly ample causes for fear. The Christians were *already* full of fear; they are being enjoined to "stop fearing" (2:10). Therefore the Lord Christ speaks his word of comfort. He is aware that his people will suffer, even intensely. But they are not to be afraid, for the time of their suffering is set by God ("ten days," 2:10). To be afraid of the sufferings in persecution at the hands of people is fear misdirected, and as such it could open up the Christians to a weakening or even a loss of faith. Fear of anything or anyone besides God is a sin that not only endangers faith, but can, unless repented of, lead to idolatry (e.g., offering worship to Caesar).

Faith-threatening fear of suffering violence at the hands of people is a temptation for any Christian. God's people are open to this sin if they have left their "first love" (2:4). Fear then follows because the heart no longer looks to the love of God in Christ but to other things (see Mt 14:28–31). The Lord Christ, in his love and concern for his people, tells them not to be afraid for he has overcome the world (Jn 16:33). *The remedy for fear, then, is to repent and look with faith to Jesus Christ.* Through repentant, faithful focus on Christ there is reborn that first love (1 Jn 4:16–19; 5:1–5), which sustains endurance through persecution (cf. Heb 12:1–3).

To those who are "faithful" Christ promises the crown of life (Rev 2:10; cf. 4:4). In this context "faithful" refers to repentance and faith (see Rom 1:17 and Hab 2:4). Like the crowns given to victorious athletes (1 Cor 9:25), "the crown of life" (Rev 2:10) is a symbol of victory—victory over fear and death and the grave (1:17–18; 2:8) which results in the gift of eternal life (3:21; 7:13–17). Jesus Christ wears that crown, because by his death and resurrection he won the victory (14:14; 19:12). Crowns are worn by the twenty-four elders and the woman in chapter 12, who represent the church (4:4, 10; 12:1). On the Last Day the bestowal of "the crown of righteousness" inaugurates the Christian's hope of reigning with Christ forever after death (2 Tim 4:8). This crown is so precious to each Christian that he is to guard it so as not to lose it (Rev 3:11).

REVELATION 2:12–17

TO THE ANGEL
OF PERGAMUM

TRANSLATION

2   ¹²And to the angel of the church in Pergamum write,
"These things says the one who has the sharp two-
edged sword: ¹³'I know where you dwell—where the
throne of Satan is. Yet you hold to my name and you
have not denied my faith even in the days of Antipas
my witness, my faithful one, who was put to death in
your presence, where Satan dwells. ¹⁴Nevertheless, I
have a few things against you because you have there
some who are holding to the teaching of Balaam,
who taught Balak to cast an offense before the sons of
Israel [so as to cause them] to eat meat offered to idols
and to commit sexual immorality. ¹⁵In like manner,
you also have some who are holding to the teaching
of the Nicolaitans. ¹⁶Repent then! If not, I am coming
to you quickly and I will make war with them by the
sword of my mouth. ¹⁷The one who has an ear, let
him listen to what the Spirit says to the churches.
To the one who conquers I will give of the manna
which has been hidden, and I will give to him a white
stone, and upon that stone a new name written which
no one knows except the one who receives it.'"

COMMENTARY

WHO SPEAKS? (2:12)

The sender of this letter identifies himself as the Lord who has the sharp
two-edged sword, a reference to 1:16, where, in the commissioning of John, the
Son of Man has such a sword. The sword symbolizes the judgment of God. The
fact that the Son of Man wields the sword demonstrates that he, under the authority of the Father, will execute the judgment. When he comes in judgment at
the End, the Son of Man will bear this sword of judgment (19:15). That the Lord
of the church should identify himself also as the one who executes the judgment

of God suggests that the church is also under this judgment. But even more, it shows that he is the defender of the church as he judges the enemies of God who afflict his people.

WHAT HE KNOWS (2:13–15)

The "throne of Satan" indicates the source of the sufferings that the church of Pergamum was undergoing. The suffering may have been ridicule and hostility from a pagan society, or it may have been persecution resulting from these Christians' steadfastness in faith. Behind every form of opposition was Satan, the devil. The critical feature of this letter's introduction, then, is that the Lord Christ, the Lord of the church, knows of their dangerous situation and cares for them as their avenger who will judge their adversaries.

The church in Pergamum remained faithful even when tested and tried to the limit. The martyrdom of a notable member of their community, Antipas, must have shaken profoundly the hearts and faith of his fellow Christians; nevertheless, they held to their faith in Jesus Christ.

Yet lurking alongside their steadfast loyalty to Christ was a sin and failing that posed a threat to their victorious faith. Some in the fellowship held to the "teaching of Balaam" (2:14). The sin of Balaam, as can be deduced from the role he played between the Moabites (and Midianites) and Israel, was that of wanting both God and money (Mt 6:24). When the temptation came to him by way of Balak to curse Israel, he knew that he had to remain faithful to God and his word. But at the same time he desired the honor and riches that were promised to him if he heeded Balak's request. If only he could remain true to God while at the same time pleasing to Balak, he could have both God and earthly gain and wealth. *The sin and teaching of Balaam was the attempt to serve two masters, God and mammon (human honors and material wealth, Mt 6:24).* This sin ended in disaster: Balaam's own death, and his influence on many in Israel to add to their worship of God the worship of a false god. It resulted in leading many in Israel into sexual immorality and idolatry, and finally death (Num 25:1–2; 31:13–17, cf. 2 Pet 2:14–15).

In the pagan society in which the Pergamum Christians lived the temptation was to compromise their faith and witness to gain earthly honor (and perhaps also material wealth) and security, as well as the freedom to engage in illicit relationships. When they fell into this temptation and sin, they not only lost their faith but also encouraged other Christians to engage in syncretistic idolatry. What the Lord of the church had against them was twofold: their sin of compromising their faith for the sake of worldly gain and pleasure, and the sin of doing nothing to correct it (cf. 1 Cor 5:1–13).

To make matters worse, some within the church were holding to the antinomian heresy of the Nicolaitans, which encouraged Christians to misuse their Christian liberty for the purpose of licentious living. This latter sin worked along with and abetted the sin of Balaam (cf. Rom 1:32).

CALL TO REPENT (2:16)

God leads believers to repent and to view with horror the temptations to sin and the sin itself. Within that horror and fear of judgment, the Spirit of God brings forth sorrow and contrition that moves the penitent heart to bring the sin and its guilt to the throne of God's mercy (2 Cor 7:8–10). In faith the sorrowing heart sees Jesus Christ, who assumed our guilt and by the blood that was shed on the cross earned forgiveness, life, and salvation for sinful human beings (Rev 7:13–17; cf. Heb 4:14–16).

PROMISES (2:17)

Through faith worked by the Spirit of God, Christians hear the word of grace, the sentence of innocence (the white stone) and the promise of new and everlasting life (the heavenly manna). For those who hear the Spirit, there is the peace of victory over sin and death.

The promises are phrased in language that recalls Baptism (the "new name") and the Lord's Supper ("the manna which has been hidden"). In the Lord's Supper, Christians receive "a foretaste of the feast to come" (LSB 955; cf. Mt 26:29). That "feast to come" is the wedding supper of the Lamb (19:6–9). The Lord's Supper is *hidden* manna (2:17) because the future banquet is now hidden from view, and the presence of Christ in the Supper is also hidden, not visible, but nevertheless real and as certain as Christ's own promise: "This is my body. ... This is my blood" (Mt 26:26, 28). Hence, the church can hymn, "At the Lamb's High Feast We Sing" *even now,* affirming "eat we *manna* from above" (LSB 633:4).

REVELATION 2:18–29

TO THE ANGEL
OF THYATIRA

TRANSLATION

2   [18]And to the angel of the church in Thyatira write,
"These things says the Son of God, the one who has
his eyes like a flame of fire and his feet like burnished
brass: [19]'I know your works and your love and faith
and service and your endurance, and [I know] your
last works are more than the first ones. [20]However, I
have something against you, namely, that you tolerate
that woman Jezebel, who calls herself a prophetess
and teaches and deceives my very own slaves to
commit immorality and to eat meat offered to idols.
[21]And I gave her time so that she might repent,
but she does not wish to repent of her immorality.
[22]Behold I [am going to] cast her onto a sickbed,
and those who have committed adultery with her
into a terrible suffering, unless they repent of her
works. [23]And her children I will kill with death so
that all the churches will know that I am the one
who searches the innermost thoughts and the hearts,
and I will give to you each according to your works.
[24]But I say to you—the rest who are in Thyatira, as
many as do not hold to this teaching, who have not
known the depths of Satan (as they say)—I will not
put upon you another burden. [25]Nevertheless, what
you do have, hold firmly until whenever I come.
[26]And the one who conquers and who keeps my works
up to the end, I will give to him authority over the
nations, [27]and he will shepherd them with an iron
rod, as clay vessels are broken in pieces. [28]And as I
have received from my Father, so also will I give to
him the morning star. [29]The one who has an ear, let
him listen to what the Spirit says to the churches.'"

WHO SPEAKS? (2:18)

The Lord of the church now identifies himself as the Son of Man by referring to his fire-like eyes and brass-like feet, both of which are a part of his appearance when commissioning John (1:14–15). The flashing, fire-like eyes suggest the Lord's righteous anger over against the agents of darkness, the enemies of the truth, whether inside or outside the visible church. The brass-like feet demonstrate his firmness and determination to trample under foot these same enemies (cf. Dan 2:33, 40–41). For the first and only time in Revelation Jesus refers to himself as "the Son of God" (Rev 2:18). The Lord impresses upon his church, his people, that he, as true man and true God, is the only one who holds within his hands the destiny of the entire human race, the world itself and all history. He calls the church to listen carefully to his voice because he speaks for its eternal well-being.

WHAT HE KNOWS (2:19–20)

The Lord knows and acknowledges the works of his church, in particular its faithful service and patience. He knows also that the believers are increasing and growing in faith and Christian service. But all their faith, steadfastness, and service will be of no avail unless they realize the grave sin in their midst: the woman of sin within the congregation, Jezebel. Whether she was an actual woman who was the cause of the evil, or whether the name Jezebel served as a symbol of the sin itself which many fell into or were tempted by, it is quite clear by John's use of the OT figure what the sin and evil was.

Jezebel stands for and represents the sin of syncretism, a universalistic belief that all religions are of value and are able to be of benefit before God. In the pluralistic society of the Greco-Roman world, in which many religions were believed to be acceptable before God, this syncretism of religious ideas was a particular threat to the Christian community. To witness to and to live in the truth that Jesus Christ is the only truth about God and the only name by which human beings can be saved was to court economic and social ostracism, possibly even danger and death (cf. Acts 4:1–12; 5:27–32). The temptation was always present to tone down one's witness or even to deny Christ by silence or action in order to escape such treatment and persecution. Believers might all too easily compromise the Christian truth and faith, so that the unique and nonconforming dictates of their Christian faith and conscience might not stick out and gain attention.

CALL TO REPENT (2:21–23)

The Lord of the church in his patience urges those who are practicing this sin and are influencing others toward it to repent. He gives them time to do so. In order to help lead them to repent he lays affliction upon them. For those whom he loves, he chastens and disciplines, even painfully so at times, in order that they might avoid the coming fearful judgment (see Heb 12:1–13; cf. 2 Cor 12:6–10). It is clear that, though the Lord chastens, it is not his will that sinners die but that they repent and live in God's forgiving grace (Ezek 18:23, 32). Those who do not repent will suffer his judgment now and eternally. This judgment will now be seen by others as a warning and as a witness to the truth that the Lord Christ alone searches the hearts and thus is able to exercise God's judgment (Is 11:3–5).

EXHORTATION (2:24–25)

The "depths of Satan" (Rev 2:24) is another way of referring to the teaching and sin of Jezebel. The sins of syncretism and universalism deny the uniqueness of Christianity—the only true and saving knowledge of God. They are lies of Satan by which he attempts to subvert the truth of Jesus Christ. As for those Christians of Thyatira who, though severely tested by this sin, held firm to their Christian witness, the Lord will not further burden them—perhaps in the sense that he would not test them further (cf. 1 Cor 10:13). They have suffered enough. Instead, they are exhorted to hold on faithfully until their Lord returns (see Rev 2:10). Those who thus hold on and conquer do so by holding to the works of Jesus Christ, namely, his redeeming death and triumphal resurrection for their eternal well-being. These works of Christ they also exhibit to others in their Christian witness and life.

PROMISES (2:26–28)

The blessing of God's grace is pronounced upon such faithful slaves of Christ. They will share in his authority over the nations and in his demonstration of judgment. He will separate them from the ungodly as a shepherd separates the sheep from the goats with his staff (see Ps 2:6–12; Mt 25:31–46). At his resurrection and ascension, Jesus Christ receives the honor of being the bright star in the firmament of God's heavenly host, including both angels and saints. He promises to share this glory with those who conquer and remain faithful to him (see Rev 22:16–17).

REVELATION 3:1–6

TO THE ANGEL OF SARDIS

TRANSLATION

3   ¹And to the angel of the church in Sardis write,
"These things says the one who has the seven Spirits of
God and the seven stars: 'I know your works, that you
have a reputation that you are alive, and you are dead.
²Be watchful and strengthen the remaining things,
which were about to die, for I have not found your
works perfected before my God. ³Remember, then,
how you have received and heard, and keep [it] so
that you repent. If, then, you do not keep watch, I will
come as a thief, and you will certainly not recognize
in what moment I will come upon you. ⁴However,
you have a few names in Sardis that have not polluted
their garments, and they shall walk with me in white
[garments] because they are worthy. ⁵The one who
thus conquers will be clothed in white garments, and
I will certainly not remove his name from the book
of life, and I will confess his name before my Father
and before his angels. ⁶The one who has an ear, let
him listen to what the Spirit says to the churches.'"

COMMENTARY

WHO SPEAKS? (3:1A)

The Lord Christ here identifies himself as "the one who has the seven
Spirits of God and the seven stars" (3:1). In 1:4 the seven Spirits before the
throne of God represent the Holy Spirit. Here the Lord Christ claims the Spirit
of God; he is the one who sends the Spirit and who through the Spirit is present
with his church. The seven stars, which Jesus holds (1:16), are (represent) the
seven angels of the seven churches (1:20). By mentioning the seven stars here
Christ indicates that, as the exalted one, he is the Lord of the angels of the
churches. Thus the Lord reminds his church that through the Spirit and by
means of the angels he communicates his word here and throughout Revelation
to the church, God's people (see 8:1–6).

WHAT HE KNOWS (3:1B–2)

Of the seven letters, this one has one of the most severe condemnations. The Christian works and activities of the church are dead works (see Is 64:6). Though the Christians of Sardis purport to be alive, they are actually headed for death—spiritual death and, if there is no repentance, "the second death" (Rev 20:14; 21:8). The church, while still outwardly performing *rituals of godly pretence,* has lost faith and heart toward Christ and God, or at least is in danger of doing so.

That the church had not completely lost everything is indicated by the way the Lord encourages those who still had faith to be on their guard and to strengthen what was left of their faith and their numbers. Nevertheless, the danger to those still remaining is great, for they had come into a state in which they were about to die (3:2). Their works were not "perfected" (3:2), perhaps meaning that they had become complacent about the gift ("you have received," 3:3) of God's love, which manifests itself in works of love. Perhaps they had become weary of doing good and had not completed the course of action they had begun so well in faith (cf. Gal 6:9).

CALL TO REPENT (3:3)

Genuine repentance comes only from remembering what they had originally received and heard, the Word and message by which they had first come to faith (see Gal 3:1–4). Holding to that Word through the enabling power of the Spirit, they could then be brought to repentance (cf. Rom 10:17; 2 Cor 7:5–12).

PROMISES (3:4–5)

The "remaining" faithful ones (cf. Rev 3:2) who have not fallen prey to this deadness of faith and heart give evidence of their living faith by their outward way of life. Their works demonstrate not a dead faith but rather that they have washed themselves in the blood of the Lamb (7:13–14), and they thus walk about in the righteousness—the whiteness—of Christ. They are the worthy ones (3:4), made worthy in being recipients of God's favor.

The ones who are victorious, who remain faithful to the End (2:10), are clothed in white garments (3:5). The white garments refer to the blood and righteousness of Christ, which covers all who repent, are baptized, and believe. Those who have been baptized into Christ have been clothed with Christ (Gal 3:27) and washed clean with water and the Word (Eph 5:26), which saves by virtue of Christ's death and resurrection (1 Pet 3:18–22). What the redeemed have by faith on earth will be theirs in full at the End when they stand before the Lord. In Rev 7:13–17 the saints of God stand before his heavenly throne because they have washed their garments in the blood of the Lamb and thus have made them white (cf. 1 Jn 1:7; 2:1–2). Having washed their robes in the blood of the Lamb, they will have authority to partake of the tree of life and will be inhabitants of the new heaven and earth (Rev 22:14).

The saints in white garments also have their names written forever in "the book of life" (3:5). This recalls the "new name" (2:17; cf 3:12) and the baptismal allusion implicit in the theology of God's naming. This book of life is the register of God in which all who belong to him have their names inscribed. No one can take out of that register a name which God has entered; it designates that person an heir of eternal life. Those dressed in white will also be declared openly as Christ's followers and God's people before all the heavenly hosts (see Zech 3:1–7; Mt 25:31–40; Lk 12:8).

REVELATION 3:7–13

TO THE ANGEL OF PHILADELPHIA

TRANSLATION

3   [7]And to the angel of the church in Philadelphia write, "These things says the holy one, the true one, the one who has the key of David, the one who opens and no one can close and closes and no one opens: [8]"I know your works—behold, I have placed before you an opened door which no one is able to close—namely, that you have a little power and that you have kept my Word and you have not denied my name. [9]Behold, I [am going to] hand over those of the synagogue of Satan who call themselves to be Jews and are not, but rather they lie. Behold, I am going to force them so that they will come and they will fall down before your feet and shall acknowledge that I have loved you. [10]Because you have kept the Word of my endurance, I will also protect you from the hour of the trial that will most certainly come upon the whole inhabited earth in order to test those dwelling upon the earth. [11]I am coming quickly. Hold what you have so that no one may take your crown. [12]The one who conquers, I will place him as a pillar in the temple of my God, and he will never again go outside, and I will write upon him the name of my God and the name of the city of my God—the new Jerusalem, which is coming down out of heaven from my God—and my own new name. [13]The one who has an ear, let him listen to what the Spirit says to the churches.'"

COMMENTARY
WHO SPEAKS? (3:7)

As with the church of Smyrna, the Lord Christ has no explicit criticism of the church at Philadelphia, but there is a veiled indication of the Lord's disquiet. In the letter to the church in Smyrna, the Lord urged the Christians of Smyrna to "stop fearing" (2:10). That church was in danger of falling into the sin of misdirected fear. In the case of the church of Philadelphia, the Lord's anxious concern can be noted in the words "you have a little power" (3:8). Though they recognized the "opened door" (3:8) before them, the believers were not taking full advantage of the (mission) opportunity. *This letter to the church of Philadelphia has to do with the mission of the church.*

The exalted Lord identifies himself as "the holy one, the true one" (3:7). This directs the hearers' attention to the prologue (1:1–8), in which Jesus Christ is called "the witness, the faithful one" (1:5). Jesus Christ is *the* true witness of God to the human race (Jn 3:31–36; 8:13–18; Rev 1:2), which witness the church is now to carry to the world.

The Lord further identifies himself as the one who has "the key of David" (3:7), recalling the commissioning of John, in which Jesus says that he has "the keys of death and the grave" (1:18). The expression "key of David" in Is 22:22 is used with the same words as here in Rev 3:7, "what he opens no one can close, and what he closes no one opens." In Isaiah these words were spoken by the Lord to the chief steward of Hezekiah. The steward was directed to exercise complete control over the household of the king (Is 22:15–24). As possessor of "the key of David" only he could open locked doors, and no one else could lock doors he opened. Jesus uses the words of Isaiah to proclaim that *he alone* has the authority to control entrance into the household of God. He earned this authority by his death and resurrection. The keys of death and the grave symbolize his victory. His opened tomb shows that he has the key to open the grave for his followers to be raised. He has shut forever the door of eternal death ("the second death," Rev 2:11; 20:6, 14; 21:8) and the grave for those raised with him. The expression "key of David" symbolizes this authority.

WHAT HE KNOWS (3:8–9A)

The "opened door" (3:8) represents opportunities for bringing the message of Christ's victory to others. In 1 Cor 16:8–9 Paul plans to remain longer in Ephesus before going on to Corinth "because a great door has opened to me." The "great door ... opened" before Paul was a God-given opportunity to proclaim the Gospel. So great was this opportunity that Paul postponed a critical visit to Corinth (1 Cor 16:5–9). In 2 Cor 2:12 Paul uses a similar expression to refer to an opportunity to proclaim the Gospel of Christ. The apostle asks the Colossians to pray for him "that God may open to us a door for the Word, to speak the mystery of Christ" (Col 4:3).

The Lord Christ had opened such doors of opportunity for the Christians of Philadelphia. He then expected his people to enter and take advantage of these opportune seasons. The Lord Christ expects his people to carry out the mission of the church, the proclamation of the Gospel, at all times—whether convenient or not (2 Tim 4:2), but he especially expects his church to take full advantage of golden opportunities which he himself has taken special measures to provide

The Christians of Philadelphia had recognized the "opened door" and had used it to proclaim the Gospel, but not to full advantage. Though they had kept his Word and not denied their Lord's name, they were weak in their mission activities, to the extent that the Lord's desire for all to hear of God's grace was hindered. The eternal well-being of those who have not heard the Gospel depends upon their hearing and reception of it in faith (Rom 10:13–14). The exalted Christ wants all to hear the gracious message of life through his death and resurrection (Mt 28:18–20; Lk 24:46–49; Rev 10:11).

The rift and the conflict between the unbelieving Jewish people (as represented by the Jewish synagogue) and the Christians (Jews and Gentiles in Christ) was causing much suffering and possibly even persecution for the church. The Jewish people who claimed to be the Israel of God but who did not believe in Jesus of Nazareth as their Messiah had forfeited their membership in the covenant of Abraham (Gal 3:6–14). The true children of Abraham, the true Israel, were those Jews and Gentiles who accepted Jesus as the Messiah and who believed in him as the fulfillment of the covenant of Abraham. As the Christians of Philadelphia, both Jews and Gentiles, proclaimed that only in Christ was salvation (cf. Acts 4:12), opposition to that message was aroused, in particular among the Jewish people of the synagogue (cf. Acts 5:17–32). Despite that opposition, the Christians remained faithful in their witness of the message and to their Lord.

PROMISES (3:9B–11A)

Because of their faithfulness by the Spirit in the grace of God, the Lord Christ promised that their opponents would come to the Christians and "fall down before" them and acknowledge that God loved them (3:9). Either upon their conversion (Is 45:14; 49:23–26; 60:3–6, 14) or at the judgment (Phil 2:9–11), these Jewish people would acknowledge that God's love is only through Jesus Christ (Jn 3:35–36; 8:42; 14:21–24).

A second promise is given to the Christians of Philadelphia. Because they had kept Christ's Word during their trials and showed endurance as they waited on their Lord, the Lord of the church and of all history would defend them when the great trial and tribulation came upon the whole human race. This is an evident allusion to the terrible times preceding the second coming (the parousia) of Jesus Christ at the End (Mk 13:14-2-23; Mt 24:15–28). In Revelation this time of great testing and affliction is called Armageddon (16:12–16) and the battle of

Gog and Magog (20:7–10). No matter how much suffering and persecution the church may experience, the Lord will see his people through that hour of trial so that they do not lose faith (Mk 13:20; Jn 17:14–17; Rev 7:13–17).

The letter concludes with this promise: "I am coming quickly" (3:11; cf 1:3). Revelation also ends with the same word of promise from the Lord Christ: "Yes, I am coming quickly" (22:20). The fact that this promise of the imminent coming of Christ at his parousia is given in this letter to the Christians of Philadelphia—a letter that deals with the mission of the church and the end of this world—indicates the close relationship between the church's mission and the nearness of the End. The completion of that mission and the Lord's return are linked, that is, when God decides that the mission is completed, then the Lord will come (Mt 24:14; 28:16–20). Here in Rev 3:11 there is an element of *urgency* in the thought: "Be quick about it," that is, "Quickly complete the mission, for I am coming quickly."

EXHORTATION (3:11B)

Following upon this promise of his imminent return, the Lord Christ says, "Hold what you have so that no one may take your crown" (3:11). In the letter to the Christians of Smyrna, the Lord encouraged the church to remain faithful in the midst of their suffering *in view of the promise of the crown of life* (2:10). In the epilogue, in response to the promise of the Lord's quick return, John answers with this prayer: "Amen, come now, Lord Jesus" (22:20). Christians hold to their faith in the midst of suffering by looking to Christ, their coming Lord. Their hearts throb with the prayer, "Amen, come now, Lord Jesus." This prayer and hope will not go unanswered (Lk 2:29–32; Jn 14:1–3).

MORE PROMISES (3:12–13)

Finally, the Lord promises victory as portrayed here with these words: "I will place him as a pillar in the temple of my God" (Rev 3:12). Each saint is now assured that he or she is, by faith, a member of God's temple, his church; for the Lord's saints, the victory will be complete in the new Jerusalem. The new Jerusalem, which comes down from heaven (3:12) and is described in 21:1–27, is a place of perfect, everlasting life with God in the new heaven and earth. One's citizenship in the heavenly kingdom of God is confirmed by the name of God, the name of the new Jerusalem, and by Christ's new name being written upon the child of God. In Holy Baptism the name of God is conferred (Mt 28:19; 1 Cor 6:11; Rev 2:13). One is registered *by name* as a citizen of the new Jerusalem in the book of life (3:5). And one is assured of entrance into the new Jerusalem because his or her name is in the book of life (21:27). The Christian always bears the name of Christ. But when Christ comes, what the name of Jesus means—and what it means for the Christian to bear it—will be fully made known (19:11–16; cf. Phil 2:9–11).

REVELATION 3:14–22

TO THE ANGEL
OF LAODICEA

TRANSLATION

3 ¹⁴And to the angel of the church in Laodicea write,
"These things says the Amen, the witness, the faithful
and true one, the source of the creation of God: ¹⁵'I
know your works, namely, that you are neither cold
nor hot. Would that you were cold or hot! ¹⁶Because
you are thus lukewarm and neither hot nor cold, I
am going to spit you out of my mouth. ¹⁷For you are
saying, "I am wealthy and I have acquired riches and
I have need of nothing more," but you do not know
that you are the wretched one and pitiful and poor
and blind and naked. ¹⁸I advise you to purchase from
me gold which has been refined by fire so that you
may be wealthy, and white garments so that you may
clothe yourself and the shame of your nakedness
may not be seen, and eye salve to rub on your eyes
so that you may see. ¹⁹All whom I love I myself
reprove and discipline. Be zealous, then, and repent!
²⁰Behold, I stand at the door and knock. If anyone
should hear my voice and should open the door,
then I will enter to be with him, and I will dine with
him and he with me. ²¹The one who conquers, I will
grant to him to sit with me on my throne, even as I
myself have conquered and have sat down with my
Father on his throne. ²²The one who has an ear, let
him listen to what the Spirit says to the churches.'"

COMMENTARY

Of the seven letters this is the harshest. It is disturbing to hear the Lord
Christ speaking in such acrimonious terms. While one can understand why
Jesus would so speak to his enemies (Mt 23:13–36), it is distressing to think of
him speaking in this manner to his own followers. The context of this seventh

letter suggests that such harsh speech must be interpreted by the thought of Rev 3:19: those whom the Lord loves he reproves and disciplines.

WHO SPEAKS? (3:14)

The Lord Christ refers to himself as "the Amen, the witness, the faithful and true one" (3:14). This identification points back to the prologue, where Jesus Christ is called "the witness, the faithful one" (1:5). Jesus Christ is the one who witnesses to the truthfulness and validity of the message as he mediates it to John and to the churches (1:1–2). In the initial act of mediating the message to John, Jesus' witness to it is mentioned (1:2). When God speaks, he gives some kind of witness, a witness that in human terms could stand up in court. Jesus Christ is *the* witness because of and by means of his incarnation, his baptism, his ministry, his miracles, and especially by his death, resurrection, and ascension. And his witness is faithful and true (Jn 5:31; 8:14).

The self-designation "the Amen" affirms that Jesus Christ is "the faithful and true" witness of God's actions and words (Rev 3:14). When "amen" is spoken in affirmation, it usually comes *at the end* of what is being said and thus means, "this is most certainly true." Since Jesus Christ himself is "the Amen," this affirmation comes *first,* before any other words of self-identification. First Jesus says, "I am the Amen," and then he speaks. That is why in the gospels Jesus says "amen" *at the beginning* of his teaching, for it is *"the Amen"* who is speaking— with *authority.* When the church *responds* to what Jesus has spoken and ratified by his witness to it, she does so with "amen." Thus at the end of Revelation, John attaches "amen" to the Lord's earlier words, affirming the truthfulness of the Lord's promise, and then prays, "Come now, Lord Jesus" (22:20

The speaker of the letter further identifies himself as "the source" of God's creation (3:14). This is the only time in the entire NT that Jesus is called "the source, first (cause), beginning" of God's creation. In the gospel of John he is called "the Word" by which all things were created and who was there "*in* the beginning" (Jn 1:1–3), but he is not called "*the* beginning."

In Prov 8:22–23 in the Septuagint wisdom says, "The Lord created me the beginning of his ways for his works; before the age he established me in the beginning." Here "beginning" has the sense of time, that is, before the world was established, the first thing God created was wisdom. In Jn 1:1 too "beginning" refers to the time before the creation of the world, but Christ, the Logos ("the Word"), is eternal and uncreated. Here in Rev 3:14 "beginning" seems to have the sense of primacy, that is, that from which everything came about.

In Col 1:18 Paul calls the resurrected Christ the "first, source," but the context is not referring to God's creation but rather to the church. Jesus is "firstborn from the dead" and so he is the "first" and the "source" of all those who, lying in their graves, will be raised to life eternal. He is the Lord and power by which the dead will be called from their graves and raised bodily into the life of the new creation.

It is in that sense that "source" in Rev 3:14 is to be understood. Christ is the source, the power by which God's new creation comes into existence and will continue to exist. The "creation" here in 3:14 refers not chiefly to God's original creation, but rather to the *new* creation, the new heaven and earth (21:1–22:5). When the new heaven and earth will be created, Christ will be both the mediating agent and the power-source through whom and by whom it will come about. From the very beginning, Christ has always been the "Word" by whom God creates all things, but now by right of his redeeming work Christ has been given the honor by God of not only being the "Word" and "agent" of the new heaven and earth, but also the "first" and "source" of this new creation of God.

WHAT HE KNOWS (3:15–17)

Though the Lord Christ acknowledges her works, he speaks no commendation over the church in Laodicea, only judgment. He found her works neither hot nor cold. The sin is apathy. *The church was living primarily for earthly wealth and selfish desires. The works the Christians were producing from such an attitude demonstrated neither anger nor enthusiasm toward God.* Their lives and their plans and hopes were self-centered. Faith and love toward God in a life of service were of secondary importance, at best. This apathy toward God's Word of stinging Law and comforting Gospel is utterly distasteful to God. While Christ in patience forgives a Christian who sins even seventy-seven times and who lives in sorrow and repentance and always looks to God for mercy (Mt 18:21–22), the Lord does not tolerate a life of imagined self-sufficiency which needs no repentance and no forgiveness (cf. Lk 12:16–21). Such a state of lukewarmness is like being dead. To warn the church of such a final judgment, the Lord Christ speaks a terrifying and harsh word of Law, for he would wake the church from its spiritual torpor, which puts it in danger of eternal death.

CALL TO REPENT (3:18–20)

The Lord Christ urges his church not only to heed the warning but also to hear his gracious counsel and invitation. He speaks a stinging word of Law, of anger and judgment—the strongest in all of the seven letters—so as to prepare his church to hear his Gospel invitation. His call to purchase from him gold refined by fire (cf. Mal 3:2–3), which has eternal value, is reminiscent of God's gracious call to Israel in Is 55:1–3. As God there urged his people to come and purchase from him bread and wine which would really satisfy, at no cost to them, he was inviting them to come to the everlasting covenant promised to David. So the Lord Christ calls his church to come to him for spiritual wealth—spiritual sight and clothing—so that the shame of her sin could be covered with the garment of salvation.

Christ's word of severe judgment and then of gracious invitation is motivated by his love. For those whom he loves he disciplines (Rev 3:19), as a loving father disciplines a wayward child—not for the purpose of casting him out, but for the end result of repentance and forgiveness, for full restoration in his Father's love. The Lord *seeks* the lost; he comes to the very door of the heart and knocks for entrance. The picture of Jesus at the door is used in Matthew as a reference to the nearness of the End (Mt 24:33). It is used in James 5:9 for the Lord who stands at the door as a judge (cf. Lk 12:36). In Rev 3:20 the Lord is a friend who stands at the door and knocks, for he wishes to enter in order to dine with his people (cf. Jn 6:53–58). The one who hears and knows the voice will open the door to welcome his Savior and Lord (Jn 10:1–5; 14:23). Such a hearing of the voice of the Lord and such an answering of the knock are worked by the Holy Spirit, for only the Spirit can open the ear to hear and move the heart to respond (Rom 10:17; 1 Cor 12:3).

PROMISE (3:21)

This letter concludes with an eschatological confirmation of the victory of the Gospel. To the victor goes the crown and the right to sit on the Lord's throne. While he was on earth, Jesus promised his disciples that they would sit on thrones when he had assumed his rightful place (Mt 19:28). In Revelation 4 John will see a fulfillment of the Lord's promise as the twenty-four elders are sitting on thrones around the great throne of God (4:4; cf. 20:4). The throne is another metaphor, like that of a crown, for reigning with Jesus Christ and the Father forever in the new age (2:10; 3:11). The image of the throne of both Jesus and his Father appears also in 7:17 and 22:3.

And so this last of the seven letters reinforces the message of them all: the Lord Christ reigns as the Son of Man and will come again soon to judge and to save. Repent and trust in his promise!

THE PROPHETIC MESSAGE

4:1–5:14 **The Inaugural Vision of Heaven, Introducing the Message**

Excursus		*The Inaugural Vision of Heaven (4:1–5:14)*
4:1–11		The Throne of God and His Heavenly Court
5:1–14		The Coronation and Enthronement of the Lamb: The Seven-Sealed Scroll
Excursus		*The Lamb of God*

6:1–16:21 **The Prophecy**

Excursus		*Three Prophetic Visions of History, Each from Christ's Ascension to the End (6:1–16:21)*
6:1–8:5		First Sevenfold Vision of History from the Cross to the End (The Seven-Sealed Scroll Introduced by the Lamb)
6:1–17		The First Six Seals: Tribulations and the End
6:1–8		The First Four Seals: The Four Horsemen
6:9–11		The Fifth Seal: The Saints beneath the Altar
6:12–17		The Sixth Seal: The End and Its Terror
7:1–17		Interlude: The Church Militant and the Church Triumphant
Excursus		*Angelic Mediators in Jewish Tradition and the Book of Revelation*
8:1–5		The Seventh Seal Introduces the Second Sevenfold Vision

8:6–11:19	Second Sevenfold Vision of History from the Cross to the End (The Seven Trumpet-Angels): Disorders in Nature Accompanied by Sufferings of Evil Afflict Humanity
8:6–13	The First Four Trumpet-Angels: Upheavals in Nature
9:1–21	The Fifth and Sixth Trumpet-Angels: Demons from the Abyss and the Last Battle
10:1–11	First Scene of the Interlude: The Mighty Angel from Heaven Commissions John
Excursus	The Identity and Function of the Mighty Angel of Revelation 10
Excursus	The Mediators of Revelation: Guides to the Structure of the Book
11:1–14	Second Scene of the Interlude: The Temple Measured and the Two Witnesses
11:15–19	The Seventh Trumpet-Angel: The End and Its Joy
Excursus	The Missiology of Revelation
12:1–14:20	Interregnum: The Cosmic War between Christ and Satan, between God's Saints and the Forces of Evil
12:1–18	The Woman with Child and the Dragon
13:1–18	The Evil Forces of the Dragon: The Beast from the Sea and the Beast from the Earth
14:1–5	The Conquering Lamb and the Victory Song of the Saints
Excursus	144,000
14:6–13	The Defeat of the Dragon and His Beasts Announced
14:14–20	The Son of Man and the Harvest at the End

15:1–16:21	Third Sevenfold Vision of History from the Cross to the End
	(The Seven Censer-Angels): Plagues of God's Wrath as God's Judgment Is Poured Out on the Human Race
15:1–8	Preparation for the Last Plagues: Introduction of the Seven Censer-Angels
16:1–11	The First Five Censers of God's Wrath
16:12–16	The Sixth Censer of God's Wrath: Armageddon
16:17–21	The Seventh Censer of God's Wrath: The End

17:1–22:5 The Conclusion: The End and the New Heaven and New Earth

17:1–18:24	The Judgment and Overthrow of the Forces of the Dragon
17:1–18	The Judgment of the Harlot
18:1–24	The Fall of Babylon and the Rejoicing of the Saints
Excursus	Is the Harlot the Antichrist?
19:1–21	Victorious Celebration
19:1–10	A Song of Victory and the Marriage Feast of the Lamb
19:11–21	The Second Coming of Christ at the End
Excursus	The Use of the Definite Article with "God"
Excursus	The Great Te Deum of Praise in Revelation
20:1–10	The Judgment and Overthrow of the Dragon
Excursus	The Millennium
20:1–6	The Millennium: The New Testament Era, When the Dragon's Power Is Restricted

20:7–10	The Battle of Gog and Magog and the Final Doom of Satan
20:11–15	The Bodily Resurrection and the Last Judgment
21:1–22:5	The New Heaven and New Earth Portrayed as the Heavenly City Jerusalem
21:1–8	The New Heaven and New Earth
21:9–27	The New Jerusalem
22:1–5	The Garden Restored
Excursus	*The Restored Physical Creation*

EXCURSUS

THE INAUGURAL
VISION OF HEAVEN

(4:1–5:14)

Chapters 4 and 5 together present a vision of God's heavenly glory. God on his throne is surrounded by his court, the heavenly host of saints and angels. While the focus of the heavenly majesty and glory is on God the Father, the purpose of the vision is to demonstrate the enthronement and exaltation of Jesus Christ, the Lamb who was slain.

Indeed, there is no break between chapters 4 and 5. In chapter 4 John's attention is focused on the throne and the holy presence on it, that is, the heavenly glory of Yahweh, the almighty Creator. Around the throne are the hosts of heaven: the saints, represented by the twenty-four elders; the four winged creatures; and countless angels. While John's eyes are fixed on the throne and the heavenly court, he hears with his ears the opening refrain and first stanza of the Te Deum (4:8, 11) which voices the praises of God the Creator. God is worthy of such adulation from his creatures, for because of him they exist and were created. *And while John is still looking at this wondrous scene of God's heavenly glory and while his ears are being filled with the beautiful words of the Te Deum* (which continues in 5:9–10, 12–14), *he also witnesses the elevation and the enthronement of Jesus Christ, the Lamb of God.* One sees the fullness of God's glory only when one sees also the enthroned Lamb who was slain. One praises God's glory rightly only when one also acclaims the enthronement of the crucified and risen Son of God.

VISIONS OF GOD'S GLORY

The Bible contains four extended descriptive visions of God's enthroned heavenly glory: Ezek 1:4–28 (cf. 8:1–3; 9:3; 10:1–22); Is 6:1–8; Dan 7:9–10, 13–14; and Rev 4:1–5:14. At various other times, an individual sees God's glory in heaven, but no extended description is given (1 Ki 22:19–23; Acts 7:55–56). There are also many references to God's enthroned heavenly glory that lack a report or description of how it was *seen*.

When these four biblical descriptions of God's heavenly glory are compared, there are both similarities and differences among the OT visions and Revelation. In the OT scenes the saints of God do not appear, though angels do. In Revelation's vision not only do the saints appear, but they are *prominently* represented by the twenty-four elders. Another major difference is that the Son of God is not mentioned in the visions of Isaiah and Ezekiel. However, he does appear as the Son of Man in Daniel (7:13–14). In Revelation the Son of God appears as the Lamb of God, and he is worshiped equally with God the Father (5:6–14). (In Rev 2:18 the Son of Man identifies himself as the Son of God, the only time in Revelation that he is called "the Son of God.")

Revelation's throne scene is explicitly Christological, while those of the OT center on God the Father. This is not surprising, since in the OT the Christ, the Son of Man, had not as yet come into his messianic glory, though in Daniel's vision it is prophetically displayed. What is surprising is the absence of any mention of the saints in the OT visions. The angels are present (as also in Revelation's vision), but not the saints of God. Is this due to the fact that Christ had not yet accomplished in earthly history the redemption of God's people? While the OT saints certainly were present with God in his heavenly glory (see Zech 3:1–5; cf. Lk 9:30–31), they were there because Christ *would* die for them. But because Christ had not yet died for them (at the time of those OT visions; cf. Heb 11:39–40), God (evidently) did not yet put them on public display. At any rate, in Revelation God's saints are on public display as a part of his heavenly presence and glory.

Thus the vision of God's heavenly glory and the exalted enthronement of Jesus Christ, the Lamb who was slain, in Revelation 4 and 5 introduces and ushers in the prophetic message; the prophecy begins with chapter 6. The purpose of this inaugural vision of God's heavenly court is to show to the church the coronation and enthronement of Jesus Christ, crucified and risen, as her Lord. Since his ascension to the right hand of God, the victorious Lamb of God, in his exalted status as the Son of Man, rules everything on behalf of his church and for the sake of her mission on earth. *Not only does this vision of God's glory and the reign of the crucified and exalted Christ introduce the prophetic message of Revelation, it also dominates it and shows the direction and conclusion of it.*

REVELATION 4:1–11

THE THRONE OF GOD AND HIS HEAVENLY COURT

TRANSLATION

4   [1]After these things I looked, and behold, an opened
door in heaven, and the first voice which I heard,
like that of a trumpet speaking with me, was saying,
"Come up here and I will show to you what things
are necessary to come about after these things."
[2]Instantly I was in the Spirit, and behold, a throne
was standing in heaven, and on the throne was
One sitting, [3]and the One who was sitting was
like in appearance to a jasper stone and a sardius,
and a rainbow-like halo encircled the throne, in
appearance like an emerald. [4]And around the throne
were twenty-four thrones and upon the thrones
were twenty-four elders, sitting, clothed in white
garments, and on their heads were golden crowns.
[5]And out of the throne come forth lightning flashes
and noises and thunders, and seven lamps of fire
were burning before the throne, which are the
seven Spirits of God. [6]And before the throne was
something like a glassy sea, like crystal. And in the
midst of the throne and around the throne were four
winged creatures full of eyes in front and in back.
[7]And the first winged creature was like a lion, and
the second winged creature was like a calf, and the
third winged creature had his face as of a man, and
the fourth winged creature was like a flying eagle.
[8]And the four winged creatures, each one of them,
had six wings each; they are full of eyes around and
within, and they do not cease, day and night, saying,
"Holy, holy, holy, Yahweh, the [only] God,
   the Almighty, the One Who Was and
   Who Is and Who Is Coming."

⁹ And whenever the winged creatures give glory and
honor and thanksgiving to the One sitting on the
throne, who lives forever and ever, ¹⁰the twenty-four
elders fall before the One sitting on the throne, and
they worship him who lives forever and ever, and
they cast their crowns before the throne, saying,
¹¹"Worthy are you, Yahweh our God, to receive
   [all] the glory and the honor and the power,
because you created all things, and on account
   of your will they exist and were created."

COMMENTARY

A NEW VISION (4:1–2A)

The opening words of 4:1 ("after these things"), introduce a new section
and a new vision. The phrase "these things" refers to the first vision, in which
John was commissioned by the exalted Christ to write the revelation (1:9–20). It
also includes the first three chapters. After John had seen the exalted Christ and
had received his commission and the seven letters to the churches, John then
experienced the vision—the sight—of the opened door of heaven through which
he saw God's heavenly glory.

John not only saw through the door into heaven, he probably entered heaven
through it, for the trumpet-like voice summoned him to "Come up here" (4:1).
John was called to leave his place on earth to view the throne scene of God's
glory. The *trumpet-like* voice, which John recognizes as the "first voice which I
heard" (4:1), identifies the voice of the exalted Son of Man, for he spoke with such
a voice in the commissioning vision (1:10). *The exalted Christ is thus the mediator
of the vision of God's heavenly glory, and he will be such until 8:1, when angels will
take over the mediation.* The second "after these things" (at the conclusion of 4:1)
emphasizes that the purpose of the exalted Christ's mediation is not only to warn
and encourage his church by the seven letters, but to reveal to his saints on earth
"what things are necessary to come about quickly" (1:1; cf. 1:19).

John could not by his own strength obey the call of Christ to come up to
the door of heaven and stand at its entrance and/or to enter it. Immediately he
was "in the Spirit" (4:2). This seems to have a different sense than in 1:10, which
seems to refer to a holy experience in which all Christians participate by means
of God's Word and Sacraments. The phrase in 4:2 bears a sense of some kind of
a mystical sensation by which the person experiences something above and beyond the ordinary capability and understanding of human reality. Possibly John
experienced what Paul testifies to in 2 Cor 12:1–4. There the apostle declares
that he was "snatched up" into paradise and heard things that were not proper

for a human being to repeat. Paul could not tell whether he was in the body or out of it when he had those "revelations" (2 Cor 12:1–2). The prophet Ezekiel seems to have had a similar experience (Ezek 8:1–3; see also 11:1). Ezekiel states that the Spirit lifted him up so that he was between earth and heaven and was taken from Babylon to Jerusalem in order to see visions of God. However all this may have been, it certainly is different from the way in which all Christians are "in the Spirit" by virtue of their Baptism and the indwelling of the Spirit (Acts 2:38; Rom 8:9, 11; 1 Cor 12:3). Perhaps like Paul, John could not tell whether he was in the body or out of it. Nevertheless, by the Spirit and in the Spirit, he was lifted up so that he could receive the visions of God which he was to share with the church (cf. Rev 21:10).

THE THRONE AND THE ONE SITTING ON IT (4:2B–3A)

John first sees the throne of God and the One sitting on it. He is the God of Israel, enthroned; he is the object of worship and is addressed by the Greek version of God's OT name "Yahweh," "God Almighty" (4:8). In his description of God, John gives no facial or bodily characteristics. Rather, he says that the majestic person on the throne was in appearance like the precious stones of jasper and sardius. Though the identification of these precious stones with modern equivalents is somewhat uncertain, the impression which they connote and reflect is unmistakable: even as light flashes through and from them with beauty and brilliance, so do the majesty and glory of God flash forth from the appearance of the One seated on the throne. John does not mean to say that God in his glory looked like the essence of these stones. Rather, the appearance of God's glory reflects the brilliance of God's presence and person in the same way that precious stones reflect the rays of the sun. One cannot look directly at the sun, but one can, by way of the reflection of its rays through precious stones, catch a glimpse of the beauty of the sun's light. (Otherwise, unreflected, the sun would appear only in its brilliant, blinding brightness.)

Isaiah in his vision of Yahweh sitting on his heavenly throne (6:1) says that Yahweh's robes filled the temple. The throne in Ezekiel was like sapphire; in addition Ezekiel says that a brilliant light surrounded him, which looked like a rainbow (Ezek 1:28).

THE RAINBOW-LIKE HALO, IN APPEARANCE LIKE AN EMERALD (4:3B)

John also mentions that surrounding the throne was a rainbow-like halo (Rev 4:3b) that looked like an emerald, green in color. Despite the differences in appearance, it seems that the bright rainbow in Ezekiel and the rainbow-like halo in Revelation fulfill the same function, that of a token of God's heavenly glory and majesty. The only other place in the Bible besides Rev 10:1 where a rainbow is mentioned is in Gen 9:13–16, where it functions as the sign given to Noah that God would not again destroy the world with a flood. The rainbow was also a visible sign or proof that God would bless the earth so that it would never cease to sustain life with its bounty and fruits (Gen 8:20–22; 9:12–17).

Yet the rainbow was more than a sign of God's promise of the physical well-being of the earth and human life. It was also a sign of God's salvation by grace for humankind. In Is 54:8–9 the promise and covenant made to Noah reminded the prophet of God's *saving mercy*. Though God in his anger destroyed the human race with a flood, Isaiah is reminded of God's oath that he would never again destroy the world with water. Though God was angry at Israel (his wife) and had hid his face from her for a time, he would again have compassion on her. God's *covenant to Noah* became then for Isaiah an assurance that God's *saving mercy* would now cover Israel's sins and that God's mercy would never cease, because Yahweh was Israel's Redeemer (Is 54:8).

In Jewish theology the rainbow was a reflection of God's glory and was holy and sacred. Whenever the rainbow appeared, God's people should be moved to praise him as their Creator (Sirach 43:11–12). Since the rainbow was a reflection and a reminder of God's creative glory, one should not attempt to look upon it, just as one would also not attempt to look at the glory and face of God. Rather, one should fall down upon one's face as did Ezekiel when the glory of God, together with its rainbow, appeared (Ezek 1:28). If one did attempt to look at the rainbow, one could be blinded. In rabbinic theology, the rainbow was thought to have been created on the eve of the Sabbath at twilight. The rainbow, then, also reminded God's people of the everlasting rest and peace to which the Sabbath pointed.

Because the rainbow-like halo surrounds the throne of God's heavenly glory, it certainly is a part of that glory as it reflects the majesty of God's position as the Supreme Being. He is the Creator of all that exists (Rev 4:11), and as such is to be worshiped by all creation. But with this majesty of God as reflected by the rainbow, John is reminded by the same rainbow of God's mercy toward his creation. *It is thus God's majestic mercy that the rainbow-like halo signifies.* God is the almighty Creator, but his almighty creative power is controlled and motivated by his love and mercy toward his creation.

The three precious stones—jasper, sardius, and emerald—were also part of the breastplate of Israel's high priest (Ex 28:15–21). Wearing these stones, the high priest represented Israel before God as he offered sacrifice for atonement (Ex 28:29; 1 Chr 6:49). Thus like the rainbow, the references to these stones suggest God's mercy toward his people.

THE TWENTY-FOUR ELDERS (4:4)

The word "elder" elsewhere in the NT designates a human being on earth. What is unique about the use of the word in Revelation is that it refers to *personages in heaven.*

The elders *dressed in white garments* are similar to the appearances of angels on earth, who sometimes are pictured as arrayed in white. However, the fact that they are *sitting on thrones* and *wearing crowns* indicates that these elders are *not* angels, but rather elevated saints of God. Nowhere in biblical or extracanonical literature do angels ever sit on thrones or wear crowns. Usually it is the Father, Jesus, or God's saints who are pictured sitting on thrones and/or wearing crowns. In Rev 19:12 Jesus Christ, as the exalted Son of Man, coming at the End in judgment, wears a many-faceted crown. Similarly in 14:14, at the harvest in the End, the exalted Son of Man wears a golden crown. The crown that the Lord Christ wears signifies *victory,* and because of that victory the merited glory of godly *royalty.* Likewise God's saints, when elevated, will wear crowns which signify the victory that the Lord Christ won for them and shares with them. Each Christian is promised the crown of life (2:10). In 12:1 the woman with Child wears a crown of twelve stars signifying that though she (that is, the church) suffers, she will be victorious because of the victory of the Christ Child.

Both Christ and the saints of God sit on thrones. While the heavenly throne in Revelation usually refers to God the Father's throne, there is one instance where the throne of God the Father is also spoken of as the throne of God the Son, "the Lamb" (22:3). In the new heaven and earth God the Father and the exalted Christ will share the same throne. Similarly in Mt 25:31, when the Lord Christ comes at the End, he will sit on his throne of glory. Also God's saints will sit on thrones because of the enthronement of Christ. When the Son of Man will take his seat on his throne of glory, those who follow him will also sit on thrones (cf. Mt 19:28; Lk 22:30).

Not only do angels wear white, also God's elevated saints are pictured frequently in Revelation wearing white robes or garments. In the great scene of God's saints in heaven in Rev 7:9–17, they wear robes that have been made white by the blood of the Lamb (7:14). The wearing of white garments by God's people, both on earth and in glory, is a common theme throughout Revelation. These robes of Christ's "blood and righteousness" are the Christians' "glorious dress" (LSB 563:1), reminiscent of the wedding garment in the parable in Mt 22:11–12 (cf. 1 Jn 1:7). The exalted Christ also wears or is enveloped in white. In the transfiguration Jesus appeared in white (Mt 17:2; Mk 9:3; Lk 9:29). In Revelation the Christ in glory has a head of white hair (1:14). He comes in judgment on a white cloud (14:14) and on a white horse (19:11), and in judgment he will sit on a white throne (20:11).

If, then, the elders are elevated saints of God, why the number twenty-four? John would *not* have understood the significance of the presence of *twenty-four* elders *only* in relationship to the twelve tribes of Israel. Rather, he would have understood them to be representatives of the believing people of God from *both* OT Israel and NT saints. From this perspective, the number twenty-four is best explained as *the elders (patriarchs) of the twelve tribes of Israel, who represent before God's heavenly throne saints from the Israel of old, and the twelve apostles, who represent saints from the Israel of the NT period.* In the OT the number twelve was often used to represent Israel before God and Moses. Examples include the twelve spies, one from each tribe (Num 13:1–16; Deut 1:23); the twelve stones in the high priest's breastplate (Ex 28:21; 39:14); the twelve cakes or loaves (Lev 24:5); and the twelve leaders, one from each tribe (Num 1:1–16; Josh 4:1–3). These instances of the number twelve are based on the actual twelve sons of Jacob, the fathers of the twelve tribes of Israel (Gen 35:22–26).

This use of the number twelve to represent Israel of the OT is carried over into the NT. Jesus tells the twelve apostles that in the new age they will sit on twelve thrones as judges of the twelve tribes of Israel (Mt 19:28). "The new Jerusalem, which is coming down out of heaven" (Rev 3:12), has twelve gates with the twelve names of the sons of Israel written on them, and there are twelve foundation stones upon which the names of the twelve apostles are written (21:12–14). There the twelve representatives of the tribes of Israel and the twelve apostles of Christ circumscribe the holy city as its gatekeepers and as its foundation. *These twenty-four elders thus pictorially represent the heavenly Jerusalem.*

The twenty-four elders before God's heavenly throne in Revelation 4 are, therefore, the twelve elders of OT Israel and the twelve apostles of Christ. *Together* they represent before God's heavenly glory *the totality of God's people.* They sit on thrones because they reign with Christ (Rev 3:21; 20:6; 22:3–5). They wear crowns because in the victory of Christ they are victorious (1:5–6; 3:5, 21; 12:11). They are dressed in white robes because the blood of Christ has cleansed them and made them righteous and holy (7:14). They are in the presence of God in his heavenly glory because that is where they, by grace, belong. They now reign with Christ as heirs of his eternal glory. As the exalted Christ's rightful place is with God the Father (22:3), so his bride (the church), as represented by the twenty-four elders, has her rightful place in God's holy presence.

PHENOMENA AROUND THE THRONE (4:5A)

The *"lightning flashes and noises and thunders"* (4:5a) that come out of God's throne are reminiscent of the thunder and lightning that accompanied God when he met Moses and the children of Israel at Mt. Sinai (Ex 19:16). These demonstrations of natural forces are symbolic of and a part of God's majestic and creative power. Although he does not explicitly mention these natural forces, Isaiah became fearful when he was in the presence of God's heavenly glory and the temple was shaken and filled with smoke (Is 6:4–5). Ezekiel saw lightning flashes in his vision of God's heavenly glory (Ezek 1:13). Elsewhere in the OT God reveals his awesome creative power and majesty through the natural forces of his creation (Pss 18:12–15; 77:16–19). In Revelation these theophany-like indicators of God's creative power and majesty appear at various places in the prophecy as a reminder of God's awesome and fearful presence (8:5; 11:19; 16:18).

THE HOLY SPIRIT (4:5B)

The presence of the Holy Spirit is signified in visible form by the *"seven lamps of fire"* (4:5b) which are burning before the throne of God. The seven lamps are identified with "the seven Spirits" first mentioned in the trinitarian stamp of approval of 1:4–5. In the tabernacle of Moses, the lampstand with its seven lamps (Ex 25:31–40; Num 8:1–4) stood before the place where God was present (Num 7:89–8:2). In the vision of God's heavenly presence here in Revelation 4, the lamps are present to remind John of the Spirit of Yahweh. In Zech 4:1–10 the lampstand with its seven lamps reminds the prophet that it is by the Spirit of Yahweh that God is active for his people, and the seven eyes illustrate the truth of God's omnipresence by his Spirit. In Revelation the Spirit of God is symbolized by both the seven lamps (4:5) and the seven eyes (5:6).

THE SEA, LIKE CRYSTAL (4:6A)

Before God's throne there was "something like a glassy sea, like crystal" (4:6). This suggests a great distance between John and the throne of God. In Ex 24:9–10, when Moses and the elders of Israel went up Mt. Sinai and appeared before God, they saw under his feet something that looked like a firmament or pavement made of sapphire and clear as the sky. According to Jewish thought the waters above the firmament joined the waters on earth to cause the flood of Noah (1 Enoch 54:7–10; cf. Gen 7:11–12). Thus the waters could be interpreted to be a reminder of God's judgment over his creation.

The "glassy sea" in Rev 4:6 is, then, a reminder of the separation between God and his creation. In particular *it reminded John that while he and God's people were still on earth, they were separated from that eternal glory which in faith they longed to inherit* (see Rom 8:23–25; 2 Cor 5:1–10; 1 Pet 1:3–9). Since sin is the cause of this separation, the sea could be said to symbolize separation from God because of his judgment over against sin. In the OT the sea monster Leviathan inhabited the sea and caused it to churn into a boiling rage (Job 41:31–32; cf. Ps 104:26), and nothing on earth was his equal; humanity was helpless before him (Job 41:8–10, 33–34). Rahab appears to be another name for this sea monster who inhabits the boiling rage of the sea (Ps 89:9–10). Only God himself can conquer and control this sea monster (Pss 74:13–14; 89:10; Is 51:9–10). In Is 27:1 Leviathan, the sea monster, is called the "serpent" which on a particular day, "that day" of judgment and deliverance, Yahweh will slay.

The connection between this sea monster and the serpent leads one to identify it as the devil. In Rev 12:1–9 the dragon is identified with the ancient serpent, the one called "devil" and "Satan." The sea in its boiling rage—as it is inhabited by this sea monster—is a symbol of the fury of human sin as it is stirred up by Satan. Neither the sea nor the monster who stirs it up can be controlled by sinful humanity. Only God can slay Leviathan. Only God can control and quiet the sea (Pss 65:7; 89:9; 107:29; Mt 8:26). So also only God can control and conquer the enemy and finally quiet the fury of human sin and its resulting ruin and destruction.

But the glassy sea in Rev 4:6 was like crystal, that is, transparent and quiet, quite the opposite from the usual raging sea of chaos and evil in the OT. The sea that is before God's heavenly throne has been tamed, conquered, and stilled. *Its crystal-like stillness reminded John that what had separated him from the glory of God's presence, the turmoil of his sin and God's judgment, is now stilled and quiet.* Though the sea reminds John of his separation from God, he is no longer afraid, for the sea is quiet; he knows that Christ has conquered Satan and taken away the raging torment of his (John's) guilt and the fearsome wrath of God's judgment (cf. Mt 8:26–27; 14:25–29). Now all is peaceful between himself and God, despite the fact that the sea reminds him he is not yet in that glory while still on earth.

Here on earth the sea is still in its boiling rage, as it is stirred up by the dragon. John himself is suffering, as are God's people. In Rev 13:1 the dragon conjures up *from the sea* a beast that wars against the woman, the church. So fearful is this warfare between God's people and the forces of evil that the battlefield is likened to *"a glassy sea mixed with fire"* (15:2). But in the End, when the dragon and his evil forces have been defeated and cast into "the lake of fire" (20:10), in the new heaven and earth, in the presence of God, the sea is not only quiet and at peace, it is forever gone (21:1). No longer will there be this reminder that God's people were once separated from him.

THE FOUR WINGED CREATURES (4:6B–8A)

"In the midst of the throne and around the throne," John sees "four winged creatures" (4:6). Though strange looking and awesome, these heavenly creatures are closer to God than any of the other angels and saints (elders), for they are "in the midst of the throne and around [it]." The designated location "in the midst" most likely means "in the immediate vicinity." They thus form an immediate and inner circle around the throne of God.

John does not identify these winged creatures as angels, nor does he call them cherubim or seraphim. He refers to them simply as "winged creatures." But it is quite apparent they are similar to or identical with the winged creatures that both Isaiah (6:1–3) and Ezekiel (1:5–26; 10:3–22) saw in their visions of God's heavenly glory. Isaiah calls them "seraphim" (Is 6:2) and Ezekiel "cherubim" (Ezek 10:3–5, 11, 15). In Isaiah they are above or before God and his throne (Is 6:2). In Ezekiel they seem to bear the throne of God (Ezek 1:22–26; 10:3–5, 18–19). According to Ezekiel, the cherubim move in whatever direction the Spirit wills to go (Ezek 1:15–21; 10:9–22). Evidently whenever and wherever

God moves, the cherubim move; hence the wheels within wheels in the vision enable the throne to move straight in any direction (Ezek 1:15–21). While in Ezekiel's vision the winged creatures move together with God and his throne, in the visions of both Isaiah and John, they seem to be positioned in one place, stationary with God's throne and presence.

In comparing the three visions of Isaiah, Ezekiel, and John, one notes similarities and dissimilarities in the appearances of the winged creatures. John mentions that each winged creature had one particular appearance or *face,* that of a lion, an ox, a man, or an eagle. Isaiah does not mention facial appearances. Ezekiel says that *each creature* had four faces, the face of a man, on the right side the face of a lion, on the left side the face of an ox, and then also each had the face of an eagle (Ezek 1:10). In the second appearance of the winged creatures to Ezekiel, in Ezek 10:14, each creature again had the four faces, but with one difference. The face of a cherub has taken the place of that of the ox. Perhaps John saw only one face for each winged creature because they were stationary, while Ezekiel saw each with four faces because they were moving—hence also the wheels that each creature had (Ezek 1:19–24; 10:15–17), which John does not mention.

In the three visions each creature has *wings.* In Isaiah (6:2) and Revelation the winged creatures have six wings each, but in Ezekiel each has four wings (Ezek 1:11; 10:21). Isaiah says that with two wings they covered their faces, with two they covered their feet, and with two they flew (Is 6:2). Ezekiel says that with two wings they touched the wings of another creature, and with two they covered their bodies (Ezek 1:11). John does not mention the function of the wings.

In John's vision the winged creatures are *full of eyes,* both "in front and in back" (Rev 4:6b) and "around and within" their wings (4:8a). Isaiah does not mention eyes. Ezekiel in his first vision perceives that the wheels have eyes (Ezek 1:18), and in his second vision, he sees that the bodies and the wings of the creatures are full of eyes (Ezek 10:12).

Both Isaiah and John hear the winged creatures *singing a hymn of praise,* a Te Deum. Ezekiel hears no hymn, but he does hear a loud rumbling-like sound or voice, which says, "Blessed is the glory of Yahweh from his place" (Ezek 3:12–13). Ezekiel hears this blessing in connection with the sound of the winged creatures.

Who or what are these winged creatures? In Ex 25:17–22 Moses was commanded to fashion two cherubim out of hammered gold. One was placed at each end of the lid of the ark; they faced each other with their wings outstretched over the lid. God promised to meet with Moses between the cherubim over the ark and speak with him (Ex 25:22; Num 7:89). Cherubim were also woven into curtains for the tabernacle and later the temple (Ex 26:1, 31; 2 Chr 3:14). For the temple, Solomon had two cherubim made of olive wood and overlaid with gold, ten cubits in height. They were placed in the temple's Holy of Holies, and their wings overshadowed the ark, which was moved there when the temple was finished (1 Ki 6:23–28; 8:6–7; 2 Chr 3:10–13; 5:7–8). Solomon's temple also had cherubim carved on the walls of both the Holy Place and the Holy of Holies, and also on the doors (1 Ki 6:29–35). Cherubim adorned the stands for the moveable bronze basins used in the courtyard of the temple (1 Ki 7:27–29, 36). Cherubim were carved all around the eschatological temple Ezekiel saw in a vision (Ezek 41:17–20, 25).

The cherubim in the Holy of Holies over the ark served as God's throne, the place of his majestic presence. In addition, the cherubim David planned for Solomon to build for the temple, whose wings were "for spreading and covering the ark of the covenant of Yahweh," are said to be God's chariot (1 Chr 28:18). Therefore Yahweh is said to ride upon the cherubim (Ps 18:10; cf. Ezek 9:3).

The other cherubim mentioned in the OT are those which God placed to the east of the Garden of Eden to guard the way to the tree of life (Gen 3:24). With these cherubim was the flaming sword, flashing back and forth.

The picture, then, that the OT presents is that wherever God's heavenly throne and majesty are revealed or described in detail, the cherubim always attend him. They either are the throne of his majestic presence, as in the Holy of Holies, or they attend his presence to serve and enhance that glorious presence and to sing his praises.

In some passages of Jewish literature, winged creatures play an important role as they accompany God's majestic presence (see 1 Enoch 14:14–25; 61:10–11; 71:7–8; 2 Enoch 21:1; 3 Enoch 21:1–4). *They are viewed as among the highest orders of angels.* It is not clear whether John related his vision of the four winged creatures to this Jewish tradition, but he probably was aware of it. More to the point, he certainly would relate and compare what he saw in the vision to that which Isaiah and Ezekiel saw.

The four winged creatures that John saw are, then, *a particular order of angels.* In his vision of God's heavenly glory and throne, they are closer to God than any other creature, angelic or saintly. As such their glorious task is to lead the heavenly host in the praise and adoration of God. They could be thought of as the choir masters of the heavenly choir, whose joy and thanksgiving it is to sing the praises of their Lord and Creator. They initiate the worship (Rev 4:9), and the saints and angels in heaven follow their lead (4:10–11; 5:11–12).

The *number* of the winged creatures is symbolic. Four suggests the totality of God's animate creation, "the four corners of the earth" (Rev 7:1; 20:8). *The winged creatures are, properly, representatives of God's total creation in worship before his heavenly throne* (see 5:13–14). The fact that they are full of eyes suggests that God in his ceaseless vigilance oversees his creation as it is represented by the four winged creatures. The four would represent the entire creation of God as it was before the fall and/or as it will be when restored (see Rom 8:18–25; Rev 21:1).

THE GREAT HYMN OF PRAISE BEGINS (4:8B–11)

Whatever else they may do as they attend and serve God in his heavenly glory, the four winged creatures are the choir masters of the heavenly host. John sees and hears them praising God day and night. He hears the same Trisagion ("holy, holy, holy") that Isaiah heard (Is 6:3). While Isaiah's verse next speaks of God's glory filling the whole earth, that of John speaks of God's almighty power as the Eternal One, though in Rev 4:11 (cf. Is 6:3) God's creative power is acknowledged in praise of God's glory.

The One who is worshiped, the One who sits on the throne, is identified as "Yahweh, the only God" and as "the Almighty, the One Who Was and Who Is and Who Is Coming" (Rev 4:8). These same designations and descriptive titles are used in 1:4 and 1:8 to refer to the first person of the triune God, the Father. Here in 4:8, "the Almighty, the One Who Was …" could be interpreted as in apposition to "Yahweh, the only God," thus meaning, "Yahweh, the only God, that is, the Almighty, the One Who Was …" However one takes it, this compound title for the first person of the Trinity emphasizes God's eternal holiness as it is expressed in his creative power. Thus, because he is the holy Creator, God is to be recognized and worshiped as the Almighty, the All-Powerful One.

The Trisagion can be understood as the opening *refrain* of this great Te Deum. Throughout Revelation this heavenly Te Deum continues to be sung, with stanzas being added at various points. Some of the stanzas are sung by angels (4:8; 5:12; 16:5–7); some by the twenty-four elders (4:11; 5:9–10; 11:17–18); some by all creation (5:13); some by all the saints in heaven (7:10); some by the whole heavenly host (7:12); some by the church on earth in warfare (15:3–4); and some by the church triumphant, the bride of Christ (19:1–8). It could be suggested that no greater Te Deum has ever been sung. But perhaps it is more correct to say simply that *this is the hymn by which all the heavenly host praises God.* The church on earth, even in suffering, also sings this hymn—triumphantly so in faith. Especially the bride of Christ, in heavenly triumph, sings and will continue to sing this great hymn of praise.

If "holy, holy, holy" (4:8) is the refrain which begins this heavenly Te Deum and is also the refrain sung at intervals throughout the hymn, then 4:11 can be seen as the first stanza of this great hymn. As the winged creatures continually (or at intervals) sing this refrain, the twenty-four elders, representing the entire people of God, sing a stanza which praises God as their Creator. The song of the winged creatures moves and directs the elders to fall down before God on his throne and worship him. As an act of worship the twenty-four elders cast before God's throne their golden crowns, indicating that they share in Christ's victory only because of God's mercy and grace. Then the twenty-four elders sing their hymn of praise, by which they worship God as their Creator. In this stanza of praise they worship God not only as their Creator, but also as the Creator of everything. And they can sing this hymn of praise because in Christ's victory they have been restored before God's holy presence. All glory and honor and power is attributed and given to God because he has created them and has now restored them through Christ.

The church fathers were correct when, in the ancient creeds of faith, they put as the First Article that which confesses God the Father and his work of creation. This was followed immediately by the Second Article, concerning Christ's redemptive work. Creation came first and then, after its fall, the redemption wrought by Christ. The first could not remain without the second. So also John *first* sees and hears and reports the praise of God the Creator and *then*, as he continues to relate this inaugural vision of God's heavenly glory (in chapter 5), he describes the enthronement of the Redeemer, Jesus Christ.

REVELATION 5:1–14

THE CORONATION AND ENTHRONEMENT OF THE LAMB: THE SEVEN-SEALED SCROLL

TRANSLATION

5   ¹And I saw in the right hand of the One sitting on the throne a scroll which had something written on the inside and on the back, sealed with seven seals. ²And I saw a mighty angel proclaiming in a loud voice, "Who is worthy to open the scroll and break its seals?" ³And no one in heaven or on the earth or under the earth was able to open the scroll nor to look into it. ⁴And I began to weep greatly, because no one was found worthy to open the scroll nor to look into it. ⁵And one of the elders says to me, "Stop weeping. Behold, the Lion who is from the tribe of Judah, the Root of David, has won the victory so as to open the scroll and its seven seals." ⁶ And I saw in the midst of the throne and of the four winged creatures and in the midst of the elders a Lamb standing as one who had been slain, having seven horns and seven eyes, which are the seven Spirits of God sent out into all the earth. ⁷And he came and took [it] from the right hand of the One sitting on the throne. ⁸And when he took the scroll, the four winged creatures and the twenty-four elders fell before the Lamb, each having a harp and golden censers full of incense, which are the prayers of the saints. ⁹And they begin to sing a new song, saying,

"Worthy are you to take the scroll
        and to open its seals,
because you were slain and you ransomed for God
        with your blood [a people] from every tribe and

tongue and people and nation,

[10]and you made them for our God a kingdom
and priests, and they rule on the earth."

[11]And I saw, and I heard the voice of many angels
around the throne and around the winged
creatures and the elders, and their number was
ten thousands times ten thousands and thousands
times thousands, [12]saying with a loud voice,
"Worthy is the Lamb who was slain to receive
[all] the power and wealth and wisdom and
strength and honor and glory and blessing."

[13]And all creation which is in the heaven and on
the earth and under the earth and on the sea and
all things which are in them I heard saying,
"To him who sits on the throne and to the Lamb
be [all] the blessing and the honor and the
glory and the dominion forever and ever."

[14]And the four winged creatures were continually saying
"amen." And the elders fell and worshiped.

COMMENTARY

THE VICTORIOUS LAMB AND THE OPENING OF THE SCROLL (5:1–7)

Jesus Christ is introduced in the vision of God's heavenly glory as the victorious Lamb. He is presented to the heavenly host as the one who can receive the scroll from God and look into it. His receiving the scroll from God is also a demonstration and a vindication that his death and resurrection were a victory for God and his people (5:9).

The Scroll (5:1)

John sees the scroll in the *right* hand of God. God's *right* hand works salvation for his people (e.g., Ex 15:6, 12). Whatever the contents of the scroll, it will have as its purpose the ultimate good and glory of God's people. That the scroll is written *on both the inside and the back* makes it all the more notable and suggests the completeness of its contents. The scroll that was given to Ezekiel in his vision of God's heavenly glory was also written on both sides, suggesting that God's words were complete and extensive (Ezek 2:9–10).

The scroll in John's vision is sealed with *seven seals*. Seals offer security and keep the contents safe from any unlawful usage. In Is 29:11 a scroll with words describing a vision is sealed to secure it against any unauthorized reading. In

Mt 27:66 the tomb of Jesus was sealed in order to secure it. It was a practice in Roman civil law for a last will and testament to be sealed with seven seals.

The scroll with its seven seals in the right hand of God contains a prophetic message that for the moment is closed to everyone. Yet, because Revelation begins with the idea that a revelation was about to be given concerning events that must soon happen (1:1–3), it is possible that the contents of the scroll focused on the future—a future which was unknown, but which also was important and necessary for God's people on earth to know. For the moment as John gazed at the sealed scroll, its message was hidden. It would remain closed and its contents unknown until the worthy person came to claim it.

"Who Is Worthy?" (5:2–5a)

A mighty angel sends out the call for such a worthy figure to come forward and lay lawful claim to the receiving and the opening of the scroll. There was no such figure in all of God's creation, not even among the angels. No one was worthy, for no one had earned the right to stand before the presence of God and lay legal claim to the scroll. John sensed the great need that someone be found to receive the scroll, for he began to weep. Possibly he inferred that the future destiny of God's people was at stake—and as events unfold in Revelation that will be proven to be the case.

Throughout Revelation angels help John as he receives and views the prophetic visions. They assist the prophet in interpreting scenes or lead him through a vision by pointing out details, focusing his attention on them (e.g. 17:1–3, 6–7). But in two instances an elder attends John (5:5; 7:13–14). *In the two visions that have most to do with the redemption and salvation of God's people and with the resulting triumphal reign of Christ, an elder attends John, not an angel.* Who better than an elevated saint, who himself has gone through the suffering but now is at peace before God's holy presence, to tell John to stop weeping by urging him to look at the Lamb of God? The imagery is reminiscent of the honor of proclaiming the Gospel that God gives to his church, his people on earth—an honor that not even the angels have in this same measure (see 1 Pet 1:12), though they had the honor of being the first heralds of Christ's birth (Lk 2:8–14) and resurrection (Mt 28:2–6).

The Victorious Messiah (5:5b)

The elder introduces John to the victorious Lamb by the titles that describe Jesus by way of his human nature. "The Lion who is from the tribe of Judah" and "the Root of David" (5:5) refer to Christ's human origin and descent. From the tribe of Judah the Messiah would come, and the lion was the symbol of his messianic royal reign and power (Gen 49:8–10). He would be a direct descendant of David, and as such would be the everlasting King upon whom all the nations would place their hope for salvation (Is 42:4; 49:1, 6).

In Jewish apocalyptic thought, the Messiah is represented by and symbolized as a lion. For example, in 4 Ezra 11:36–46 the Messiah as a roaring lion will judge the ungodly in the last days but in mercy will deliver God's people.

Likewise in Jewish literature, a descendant of David would judge and save all people who would call on the Lord. For example in the Testament of Judah (24:1–6) this deliverer is called the "Shoot of God Most High," and this Shoot would come from the root. This Shoot is also called the "Star from Jacob" and the "Sun of righteousness" (cf. Num 24:17; Mal 4:1–3; see also the Testament of Levi 18:1–5). In Psalms of Solomon (17:21–26), the son of David will rule over Israel and in wisdom and righteousness will judge the sinners, but he will gather God's people and will lead them in righteousness.

Thus these two titles from the OT, "the Lion who is from the tribe of Judah" and "Root of David" (Rev 5:5), influenced both Judaism and early Christianity in their respective messianic thoughts and hopes. The Jewish Christian apostles, however, had the advantage over Judaism, for they recognized Jesus of Nazareth as this Lion of Judah and Root of David. Before the birth of Jesus, Jewish people could only recognize the Christ prophetically; after the coming of Jesus of Nazareth many of them failed to see him as such. But Paul and John and others did. Paul recognized Jesus Christ as the seed of David because of his resurrection (2 Tim 2:8; see also Rom 1:2–4). Peter in his sermon at Pentecost also recognized that Jesus was the seed of David because of his resurrection (Acts 2:29–32). Now John, in the vision of Christ's enthronement, is introduced to the victorious Lamb by way of these two great messianic titles from the OT.

The Lamb Who Has Been Slain (5:6)

This messianic Lion of Judah and Root of David has conquered, and because of his victory he has earned the right to take the scroll and open it (5:5). *He is Jesus, the Lamb who was slain (5:6). The victory is won by Christ the Lamb, in his death on the cross and his resurrection. It is a victory that is shared with his faithful followers, the people of God* (e.g., 12:11). It is a victory which determines the Christian's life on earth (2:26), and it is the victory that guarantees life forever with God (21:7). Here in the vision of Christ's enthronement John's eyes are completely focused on the victorious Lamb, who is about to be received by God and about to have conferred on him the royal authority to receive the scroll.

The Lamb stands "in the midst of the throne and of the four winged creatures and in the midst of the elders" (5:6). As in 4:6, where the same expression is used, "in the midst" refers to the closeness of the Lamb to God and the heavenly host. Here it probably takes on more significance than merely being close or "in the immediate vicinity." The victorious Lamb, the exalted Christ, is now near to God and the heavenly host as the center of attention and as the recipient of honor and worship (see 5:9–12). The exalted Christ, because of his victory as the Lamb, will now rule the heavenly host, next to God the Father and by God's authority. In particular it is from the midst of the throne that the Lamb will care for the saints in heaven and lead them to the fountains of living waters (7:17).

As the Lamb stands "in the midst" (5:6), he does so as one who has been slain—a witness to his death on the cross. But it is also a witness to his resurrection, for though once slain, he now *stands* and lives forever (Rev 1:18; Heb 9:23–28).

As the victorious Lamb lives, he exercises total power on earth (cf. Mt 28:19), as symbolized by the "seven horns," and by means of the "seven Spirits" he is omniscient, all seeing and all knowing (Rev 5:6). In the OT the "horn" is a symbol or metaphor of power on earth in human affairs. For example, in Deut 33:13–17, in reference to Joseph, the horn symbolizes his majesty and power by which he subdues the nations—most likely a reminder of his role in Egypt but now used as a metaphor for the role that his two sons, Ephraim and Manasseh, play (cf. 1 Ki 22:11; Ps 112:9; Zech 1:18–19). Memorable are the ten horns of the fourth beast in the vision in Dan 7:7. The number ten there suggests supreme power exercised by human beings *in human affairs,* while seven, the number of the Lamb's horns here, points to his exercise of supreme power *over all life, human and spiritual.* The number seven suggests also that the exalted Lamb exercises this supreme authority and power through the "seven Spirits of God" (Rev 3:1; 4:5; 5:6; cf. 1:4), the Holy Spirit, for God the Father now gives his Spirit to act on behalf of the victorious Christ (cf. Zech 4:1–6). The exalted Lord Christ now exercises this supreme authority and power on behalf of God's people, in particular as he uses this power to defend them on earth, as will be revealed in the prophetic message of chapters 6–16. The "seven horns" (5:6) are a comforting reminder to John that the Lord Christ will defend him and his faithful hearers no matter what they experience and suffer, for he is the "horn of [their] salvation" (Ps 18:2–3; cf. 1 Sam 2:1; Lk 1:69).

Closely connected with the horns are the "seven eyes" (Rev 5:6), by which the exalted Lamb now knows and sees all things. In Zech 4:10 the seven eyes of Yahweh rove over the whole earth, that is, the Lord (by means of the seven eyes) sees and knows everything. In Zechariah's vision the seven eyes are symbolized by the lampstand with its seven lamps (4:1–3), and together they represent and symbolize Yahweh's presence by his Spirit (4:4–6). *Now this authority to oversee everything by the Holy Spirit has been given by God to the Lamb because of his victory.* The seven horns and eyes thus demonstrate the close relationship between the triumphant Christ and the Holy Spirit, for in Christ's exalted status he and the Spirit are inseparable, especially as Christ works with his church on earth through his Word and with the Spirit (Rev 2:1, 7, 11, etc.; cf. Jn 14:17; 20:22; Rev 4:5).

THE SIGNIFICANCE OF RECEIVING AND OPENING THE SCROLL (5:7)

Jesus Christ as the Lamb comes to God on his throne and takes from him the seven-sealed scroll. This presentation before God recalls the presentation of the Son of Man before the Ancient of Days in Dan 7:13–14. The Son of Man approached the Ancient of Days and was presented to him. He then was given authority and glory and power over all peoples and nations, and his dominion would be an everlasting reign. Here in Revelation John sees the Lamb approach the heavenly throne and receive from God the seven-sealed scroll. What are the contents of the scroll, and what does the action of receiving and opening the scroll signify?

John wept when no one was found worthy to open the scroll, because he sensed that the scroll was about the destiny of God's people. It becomes evident, as the Lamb opens each seal, that *the content of the scroll is the message that is prophetically made known to John,* the message of Revelation 6:1–22:5. The message of the scroll has to do with events on earth from the time of Christ's victory and ascension to the end of all earthly things. The prophetic message of Revelation is about the tribulation and suffering that the human race, including the church, will experience, from the ascension of Christ up to the end of this world. *But the most important part of the message concerns Christ's present and future reign in glory and the current faith and mission of the church in the midst of all the agony and death throes of the human race and its history.* As each seal of the scroll is opened in turn, the panorama of earthly events, together with Christ's reign with his people, will be poignantly displayed. *The ultimate purpose of Christ receiving the scroll and then revealing its contents to John and the church is to strengthen the church's faith and to encourage the church, in the midst of all the sufferings, to remain faithful to Christ and so to attain the promise of everlasting glory. That faithfulness involves carrying out the mission Christ has given to her, certain of the final outcome at Christ's return.* Thus the destiny of the whole human race and all history is involved as well, for that destiny is and will be determined by the reception or rejection of the church's witness to the Lord Christ. *The entire destiny of the church, of the human race, and of all history is thus revealed as the scroll is opened.* This is all under the lordship of Jesus Christ, for the glory of God and for the benefit of his people.

Thus the action of the Lamb receiving the scroll from God is of great importance and is laden with meaning for John and the church. Someone had to be in charge of opening the scroll if the human race's destiny was not only to be revealed but also controlled and was to have any hope for the future. The point is emphatically made to John in 5:3 that *no one anywhere* could receive the scroll and dominate its contents. No evil force, no creature, angelic or otherwise, no human, and certainly not human history and ambitions, could claim authority to receive the scroll. Only the chosen one of God, the Lamb, could do so. This means first of all that the entire destiny of the human race and its history is under the lordship and control of Jesus Christ. Humanity is *not* under the guidance of some mindless evolutionary force and is not subject to the ambitions and works of people, but rather it is under the will and power of God as now exercised by Jesus Christ. The governance of humanity and humanity's history and ultimate conclusion are under the control of God—his judgment and his love.

In receiving the scroll the Lord Christ received from God the authority (1) to reveal to John and the church the prophetic message of the scroll; (2) as Lord to control and dominate everything in it; and (3) to judge humanity and the events revealed. He earned and merited the right to be the Lord and judge of all human events and history by the shedding of his blood and by his victorious resurrection. As the Savior of the world, who died for all, Christ alone determines and will continue to determine the outcome of human history. He also is the one who dominates all evil, and he will control it for the benefit of the church and her mission. Finally at the End, he will judge the evil and deliver his suffering bride. *The Lord Christ thus rules everything on behalf of his heavenly Father and for the benefit of his church, so that she will be protected in faith and hope and will be enabled to carry out her mission unto the End.*

Finally, the event of the Lamb receiving the scroll is the *coronation* of Jesus Christ as the King of kings and Lord of lords (cf. 19:16). It is his exaltation to the right hand of God in order now to rule everything on behalf of his heavenly Father. It is the enthronement of God's holy Son, who not long before hung on a cross. It is the beginning of the everlasting reign of God's righteousness through his exalted Son, a reign that will be consummated at the resurrection and in the new heaven and earth (20:11–21:7).

THE WORSHIP OF THE LAMB (5:8–14)

When the Lamb had thus taken the scroll and had been enthroned at the right of God (cf. 7:9; 22:1–3), the heavenly host (as represented by the four winged creatures and the twenty-four elders) fell before the Lamb. The elders made preparation to worship him with harps and golden censer-like bowls full of incense. The censers of incense symbolize the prayers of the saints as they rise to the throne of God (Ps 141:2). Here in Rev 5:8 the elders offer to God the prayers of the saints as they prepare to sing their hymn attended by the harps. Possibly the four winged creatures also have harps and censers of the prayers, for an angel does offer before God's throne the incense and prayers of the saints (Rev 8:3). However this might be, the prayers of God's people are a fragrant part of the worship as the heavenly host begin their hymn of praise to the Lamb.

"A NEW SONG" (5:9)

With the singing of the hymn of praise to the Lamb we enter into the greatest scene of universal adoration in all of the biblical writings. Through the worship of the Lord Christ the heavenly Father receives his highest glory from his saints (cf. Jn 5:23; 8:54).

The hymn or ode of praise is called a *"new song"* (Rev 5:9). In 14:3 the church militant, as represented by the 144,000, sing something akin to the "new song" as they follow the Lamb, indicating that the worship and praise of God's people on earth is parallel to that of the saints in heaven before God and reaches toward it. In 15:3 the church on earth, as she is in deadly conflict with the beast, sings "the song of Moses ... and the hymn of the Lamb." In contrast to the "new song," the song of Moses and the Lamb is a hymn of victorious hope in the midst of conflict; it voices the assurance of victory here on earth despite the suffering caused by the beast. This song also expresses the rightness of God's actions in showing his anger and judgment on earth toward the beast and his evil forces. The new song, on the other hand, voices the peace of the ultimate victory in God's presence in heaven.

Here in 5:9 the hymn of adoration addressed to the Lamb is "new" because it has never been sung before. Unlike the song of Moses and the Lamb, it contains no direct OT quotes. The stanzas of the new song (5:9–10, 12–13) echo the stanza in 4:11 and thus join the new song to the great Te Deum begun in 4:8 and continued in 4:11. Added in 5:9–10 and 5:12 are stanzas that celebrate the victory and enthronement of the Lamb. While such a hymn might have been sung before, it would have only been in anticipation. Now it is sung because the promise has been fulfilled, for the Christ has come and has won the victory for God and his people. The hymn itself expresses why the Lamb is worthy to receive "[all] the power and wealth and wisdom and strength and honor and glory and blessing" (5:12): he ransomed for God with his blood a people from all quarters of the human race (5:9).

"A KINGDOM AND PRIESTS" (5:10)

These people purchased by Christ are now the "kingdom" of God and serve as his "priests" on earth (5:10). The royal priesthood of all believers is a royal-priestly reign of God's kingdom here on earth in which his people are involved. The fact that his people fulfill their royal reign as priests suggests that the purpose of God's kingdom on earth is an intercessory one. Through the proclamation of the redemptive victory of the Lamb, God's royal priests on earth hold up before his heavenly throne the atonement, as they point people through it to the mercy of God (see 1 Pet 2:5–9). Already Rev 1:6, part of the trinitarian stamp of approval, makes this important identification of God's people as "a kingdom, priests." Rev 20:6 again mentions this royal priesthood as a description of the role of the church in the "millennial" reign of Christ on earth. The fact that this note of God's people as his royal priests (5:10) is a part of the hymn which glorifies the Lamb demonstrates that they have this role because of Christ and that God honors his people as such. *The royal priesthood of God's saints is an image of the royal priesthood of Christ, a priesthood for the salvation of all people by his own blood and through the proclamation of the Gospel* (cf. Heb 4:14–5:10; 9:11–28; 10:19–25). This priestly reign of God's people on earth is not some future happening, but it is active *now* through the proclamation of God's Word (see Rev 10:11). *The royal priestly reign of Christ, the kingdom of God, is not some future event but is present now, though its present and future glory and its manifestation to the human race are not yet visible, for the reign of Christ is seen now only through faith.*

THE HEAVENLY HOST AND ALL CREATION JOIN IN PRAISE (5:11–14)

Though the hymn of praise is begun by the four winged creatures and by the twenty-four elders, all the heavenly host of angels joins in this acclamation of the Lamb (5:11–12). The whole heavenly host, saints in representative fashion and all the angels, worships and adores the Lamb now enthroned at the right of the Father. All the glory and honor and worship that was given to God the Creator (4:11) is now given in equal manner to the victorious and elevated Christ (5:12).

When comparing the two stanzas of praise, the first to God the Creator (4:11) and the second to the Lamb (5:12), one finds that the same ascriptive words of praise are used in both: "glory", "honor," and "power." But to the Christ further words of praise are ascribed: "wealth," "wisdom," "strength," and "blessing." These additional words of worship and praise are given to the Son of God because he merited and earned them in his earthly life of humiliation, suffering and death, and by his glorious resurrection. Because he is the Savior of the human race, God's saints laud him, for Jesus Christ is the wealth, the wisdom, the strength, and the blessing of God. In his creative activity God is the glory and honor and power of his people, but this creative activity of his glory and honor and power can be seen now in full measure only through Jesus Christ as his followers recognize and see in him the wealth and wisdom and strength and blessing of God. It is also through Christ's wealth and wisdom and strength and blessing that God's people receive from God the gift of salvation and the gifts of his creative activity, now because of and through the proclamation of the Gospel. Then in worship of God through the Christ the saints give it all back to God and his Christ in acknowledgement that everything comes from God and belongs to him.

And so all creation renders equal praise to both God on his throne and to the Lamb with the ascriptive words of "[all] the blessing and the honor and the glory and the dominion" (5:13). Finally then, all the ascriptive words of worship and praise are given equally to God and to the Lamb, all except "wisdom" and "wealth," which remain alone with the Lord Christ.

Jesus Christ is both "the Word" (Jn 1:1) and "the Wisdom" (of God (1 Cor 1:21). While the *creative power* of God can be discerned in the things he has made (the natural revelation of God, Rom 1:18–23) so that people should honor and glorify God, God's *Word* is *incarnate* and his *Wisdom* is *embodied* and recognized only (by faith) in Jesus Christ. This is especially seen to be true when wisdom is connected with wealth. Wealth in this context refers to spiritual, not material, wealth. It sums up everything that Christ has done to redeem and save the human race. *It is only in Christ that the human race receives and acknowledges the "wealth" of God's saving grace, and it is only in the Lord Christ that the "wisdom" of God is received and acknowledged, especially that wisdom which leads the human heart in repentance to a saving faith.* Thus "wisdom" and "wealth" are credited alone to Jesus Christ, for these cannot be seen or received by way of the "natural knowledge" of God but only through the knowledge of and faith in Jesus Christ.

The four winged creatures conclude the stanzas of this great Te Deum, the "new song" (5:9) of praise to the Lamb and to God for the salvation of God's people (5:9–10, 12–13), by pronouncing "amen" (5:14). The Greek tense suggests that, as the heavenly hosts were singing the new stanza of the Te Deum, the four winged creatures were continually saying or singing "amen." Especially at the end does their "amen" ring out in affirmation, "This is most certainly true." As the four creatures initiated the great Te Deum with "holy, holy, holy" in 4:8, so now they conclude this stanza with the affirming "amen." The heavenly hosts, both saints and angels, under the direction of the choir masters (the four winged creatures), thus voice this mighty hymn to God, their Creator and to the victorious Lamb. But it is in particular the *saints of God,* as represented by the twenty-four elders, who, at the crescendo of the four winged creatures' "amen," conclude the worship of God as their Savior in Christ by falling down before him (5:14).

THE ENTHRONEMENT AND THE CELEBRATION

This glorious vision of God's heavenly majesty and the coronation and enthronement of Jesus Christ are among the most beautiful chapters in the entire Bible. Revelation 4 and 5 picture the end result of God's creation and in particular God's redemption and restoration of the human race through his Son, Jesus Christ. This is where the whole story of God's revelation to humanity ends: before his heavenly throne, under the reign of Jesus Christ. The whole purpose of God's activity toward all peoples and his creation is that it all would end in the worship and praise of God as the Creator and Savior through his Son. The actual conclusion to this heavenly vision is when the new heaven and earth have come about at the resurrection in the End (20:11–22:5).

When did the enthronement of Jesus Christ, pictured in Revelation 4–5, take place? Several factors suggest that it took place at the ascension of the Lord Christ. It is certain that it took place after the suffering and death and resurrection of Jesus, for the victorious Lamb appears in the scene as one who has been slain but now is alive (5:6). The Scriptures reveal that Jesus Christ would come into his heavenly glory after his resurrection. In his intercessory prayer for his disciples (John 17), Jesus prays that finally they might be with him to see his glory—a reference to his glory at the right hand of God in his heavenly majesty (Jn 17:24). In the accounts of the transfiguration, the glory of the Christ which was displayed was the glory that he would come into after his death and resurrection (see especially Lk 9:31–32). Just before Stephen was led away to his martyrdom, he looked into heaven by the Spirit and saw Jesus Christ in glory at the right hand of God (Acts 7:55–56). According to Peter, the exaltation of Jesus at the right hand of God was after the resurrection and before the sending of the Holy Spirit at Pentecost, that is, at his ascension (Acts 2:32–35; cf. Jn 7:39; Acts 3:12–13).

Revelation 4 and 5 are a dramatization of the exaltation of Jesus Christ at the right hand of God, as it appeared from heaven's view. The description of Acts 1:6–11 is from the perspective of those on earth. We thus have two complementary visual descriptions of Christ's ascension. As the disciples saw the Lord taken up from them to disappear into the heavens, at the same time Jesus was received by his heavenly Father, as pictured in Revelation 4 and 5. At his ascension he was enthroned and crowned as Lord so as to rule everything on behalf of his Father. The action of God giving the scroll to the Lamb represents this coronation and enthronement. What John sees in Revelation 4 and 5 is a reenactment of that which, in earthly time, had taken place some years before, at the Mount of Olives (Lk 24:50–51). However, the celebration that began and was initiated at the Lord's enthronement was still going on when John saw the dramatization of it. It is still going on and will continue into eternity. Christ's exaltation as Lord continues, as does also the celebration with the singing of the "new song" in the Te Deum, for that "new song" is ever new and the One it celebrates is ever present with his church.

There has never been a celebration like that which began when the Son returned to his heavenly Father. For some two thousand years it has been taking place, and it will continue forever. Heaven broke into joyful song and celebration when the Son came back victorious. He was received by the Father and was given the authority, then and up to the End, to rule everything on behalf of God (see 1 Cor 15:20–28). But one can imagine how, not long before this, all heaven was in mourning when the Son was crowned with thorns and placed on a cross—witness the darkness that came over the face of the earth (Mk 15:33). In reality Jesus' coronation, by which he created a kingdom for God and by which he himself became a king, was at his suffering and death (see Jn 12:27–33; Rev 5:9–10). But while his kingship was earned in his suffering and death, it would be a kingdom and a reign in glory. The crown of thorns gave way to a crown of many diadems (Rev 19:11–14; cf. Mt 26:63–64). The glory of the cross is now fully seen in the glory of the exaltation of Christ at the right hand of God in his heavenly majesty. Heaven is no longer in mourning; celebration has taken its place forever.

THE ENTHRONEMENT AND THE PROPHETIC MESSAGE

Finally, this vision of God's heavenly glory and the enthronement of Jesus Christ and of the celebration begun and now ongoing not only introduces the prophetic message of Revelation, it also dominates and controls it and shows how it is all going to end. Jesus Christ is the Lord of the message. After his coronation (Revelation 4–5), he himself (6:1–7:17) introduces the message to John. (The message from 8:1 to 22:5 is *from* Jesus *through* angels.) Jesus controls it for the purpose of strengthening the saints, of aiding his church to carry out her mission on earth, and of judging the powers and persons of wickedness and evil. *Everything seen and heard in the prophetic message is to be interpreted in view of this inaugural vision of Christ's coronation, for then and only then will the individual components of the message yield their proper interpretations.*

EXCURSUS
THE LAMB OF GOD

The Lamb of God is a beautiful concept that is derived from the OT. Perhaps there is no other description or title of Jesus Christ that so touches the heart of the Christian. Related to it is the idea that Jesus Christ is also the Good Shepherd. Because Jesus was the Lamb of God who was sacrificed for the sins of the people, he became as a result their Shepherd. It is not by accident that the twenty-third psalm is possibly the single most quoted chapter of the Bible, for it prophetically draws together what Christ means to his followers. John in his gospel relates to us how John the Baptist pointed out Jesus as the Lamb of God, who takes away the sins of the world (Jn 1:29). John's gospel also describes how Jesus is the Good Shepherd (John 10). Jesus became the Good Shepherd by laying down his life for the sheep (Jn 10:11). In Revelation Jesus is referred to as both the Lamb of God and as the Shepherd of God's people (7:17).

Both motifs, the Lamb of God and the Good Shepherd, are deeply embedded in the OT. According to the author of Hebrews, the lambs (also bulls and rams) prescribed for sacrifice in the OT were examples or patterns (Heb 9:23) of the sacrifice of Christ's death (Heb 9:6–10:18). Peter says that Christ, as a blameless and spotless Lamb, redeemed God's people by his blood (1 Pet 1:18–20). That brings to mind the kinds of lambs that were required for sacrifice in the OT (Lev 3:1–2, 7–8; 4:32–34; Num 6:12). Isaiah prophetically describes how the Suffering Servant carried the guilt of the sheep who had gone astray and was thus led like a lamb to the slaughter (Is 53:5–7; cf. also Jer 11:19). Ezekiel speaks of Yahweh becoming the Shepherd of his scattered sheep (Ezek 34:11–16), and how he will do this by placing over his flock one Shepherd, his Servant, a new David, who would tend and lead the sheep. Thus Yahweh will save his flock (Ezek 34:22–24; cf. Is 40:10–11; Micah 5:2–4). Throughout the OT God was thus looked upon as the Shepherd of his people.

In particular, the Passover lamb played an important role in the liturgical and devotional life of the people of the OT. The sacrifice of the lamb and the eating of it initiated the Passover festival. The lamb had to be a year-old male and without defect (Ex 12:5; Num 28:19). Before the first Passover meal was eaten the blood of the lamb had to be smeared on the doorframes of the house. The Passover sacrifice and meal were celebrated in commemoration of the deliverance from slavery in Egypt. On the night of the first Passover, as the Passover lamb was eaten, the Lord destroyed the firstborn sons of Egypt, but he passed over the houses of the Israelites because of the blood of the lambs smeared on the doorframes of their homes.

The slaying of the firstborn sons of the Egyptians and the redemption of the firstborn sons of the Israelites (Ex 13:1–16) could have been a picture of God's promised sacrifice of his own Son for the redemption of the world (see also Gen 22:1–18). Such an explicit connection is made in the NT. Paul in 1 Cor 5:7 says that Christ is the sacrificed Passover Lamb. In the accounts of the Passover meal before Christ's death, there is an apparent connection between Christ's body and blood and his coming death, and the Passover lamb whose blood was shed (Mt 26:28; Mk 14:24; Lk 22:20). Apart from Paul, however, no other NT author explicitly calls Christ the Passover Lamb, but the fact that Paul does so—and does so without explanation—seems to imply that such a connection was widely known. Certainly it was known to the early church fathers, for they often saw in the Passover lamb a type of the sacrifice of Christ.

Of NT authors, John makes the most use of the concept of Jesus Christ as the Lamb of God. The OT picture of the lamb and its shed blood introduces Jesus to the public at his baptism (Jn 1:29, 36). John emphasizes the blood and water from Jesus' side at his death (Jn 19:34). In 1 Jn 1:7–9, the blood of Jesus cleanses the sins of those who confess. Together with the water and the Spirit, the blood testifies that Jesus is God's Son (1 Jn 5:5–9). In Revelation it is the picture of the Lamb who was slain that is used to introduce the Lord Christ at his presentation to God on his heavenly throne (5:6, 9, 12–13), and it is by the blood of the Lamb that the saints of God also stand before his heavenly Father (7:13–17).

While the Christology of Revelation deals primarily with the exaltation of Jesus Christ and his glorious reign, the foundation for this exalted Christology is the theology of the Lamb of God, who suffered and died and rose again. By this suffering, death, and victory he merited the eternal glory of his Father, the glory he now shares with his people. Throughout Revelation the exalted Christ is the focus of the prophetic message. But also throughout the message of Revelation there is a constant reminder that Jesus Christ is the exalted Son of Man and Lord of lords and King of kings *because he was and is the Lamb of God, who was sacrificed for the sins of God's people.*

6:1–16:21

THE PROPHECY

EXCURSUS
THREE PROPHETIC VISIONS OF HISTORY, EACH FROM CHRIST'S ASCENSION TO THE END

(6:1–16:21)

With chapter 6 the prophecy of Revelation begins. *It consists of three visions of events taking place on earth* (6:1–8:5; 8:6–11:19; 15:1–16:21). Each vision covers the same time period, from the ascension of Jesus up to the end of this present world upon Christ's return. In addition to these three visions of earthly events there is a vision of the cosmic war between God and Satan which is interspersed between the second and third visions (12:1–14:20). After these three visions, there is also a lengthy conclusion which contains visions of the End, the judgment, the resurrection, and the new heaven and earth (17:1–22:5).

Each of the three visions of earthly events has *seven scenes,* making a total of twenty-one scenes. (See below for a discussion of why there are *three* visions of *seven* scenes each.) The first five scenes of each of the three visions cover the same time period: from Christ's ascension up to the last great battle (Armageddon, 16:16) just before the End. The sixth scenes in the second and third visions cover this last great battle. In the first vision, the sixth scene (the sixth seal) pictures the end of this world, while in the second and third visions it is the seventh scene (the seventh trumpet and the seventh censer, respectively) that pictures the End. While the three visions cover the same time period and while each depicts events on earth, the three are not repetitious, for each vision displays its own particular events.

The events displayed in the three visions are not given for the purpose of predicting particular events in human history. Rather, they are presented so as to portray conditions, circumstances, situations, environments, and contexts in which people find themselves during the time period covered. While particular events in human history are to be, and must be, interpreted in view of and by these conditions, circumstances, and so on, no particular historical event or person at any given time exhausts the condition as prophetically revealed, for the conditions revealed in this prophetic message are prevalent throughout all of human history. *The end result of the prophetic message, then, is not to give a predictable view of history, but rather to give a predictable view of the human condition in suffering and defeat because of human evil and rebellion against God, and a predictable knowledge of God's terrible judgment. The purpose is to move all people to repentance and faith before the End, which in turn serves the ultimate purpose of displaying Christ's majestic sovereignty for the salvation and hope of those who listen, repent, and believe.*

Many of the events displayed for the purpose of depicting these conditions, contexts, and so on are dramatized by means of symbols. The circumstantial events are presented by these symbols not only to educate, but also as visual aids to grip the heart and the emotions, as well as the mind, so that the conditions they represent will not so easily be forgotten. On the one hand, the symbols strike fear in the human heart. On the other hand, for those who repent and trust in the slain Lamb, they fill the heart with peace and joy and hope. To accomplish both ends—fear and comfort—different symbols are used.

This question may be asked: Why are there *three* visions of events on earth, all covering the same time period? Could not all the events, twenty-one in total, be revealed in one sweeping vision instead of in three? It could be suggested that the twenty-one scenes contain too much information for John to digest all at once. Perhaps for that reason, after John had received the first sevenfold vision, he was given time to digest and to record it before the next set of seven scenes was given to him in the second vision. Then after he assimilated that, finally the third and last set of seven scenes was visually displayed before him. That may be true. But there are two other possible answers, the first arising from a consideration of the literary design and structure of Revelation, and the second from the theological thrust of its message.

The literary structure of Revelation is controlled by *the number seven.* The prophetic message is to be given to seven churches, and the message itself is visually presented in three visions of seven segments each. This sevenfold pattern is modeled after the seven days of creation. It is for that reason that the number seven in biblical literature usually is reserved for God, for his holy and complete presence and for his holy and perfect creative activity, especially when related to the seventh day. If the contents of the twenty-one scenes were given in a single visual presentation, this sevenfold literary structure would be lost. It was important for John and his audience to receive and understand the message of Revelation by way of this sevenfold pattern, so that they would realize that the message is from God's own holy and perfect presence, and that it is his holy and complete revelation.

A sevenfold structure, present in the three visions in 6:1–16:21, is a common motif in the Jewish tradition known to John. The number *seven,* the holy number of God, was the chief number in recording the chronology of historical time periods, especially in view of eschatology. This was because all history was seen to be under the providence of God. The use of the number seven in this manner may also have arisen because the solar year of 364 days was divisible by seven, resulting in a year of fifty-two weeks. Seven became the number for interpreting the meaning of history, because God created the world in seven days.

The ultimate purpose and thrust of the message itself suggests a second possible reason why the twenty-one scenes were given in three visions. While it may be true that it would have been too much for John to assimilate the entire message in one visual presentation, it is also true—and more to the point—that in this scheme John and his hearers have *three opportunities to understand and apply the same message,* one portion at a time. For the message to accomplish its purpose, *time* is needed for the mind to receive each of the three visions in turn. After the first vision of seven scenes has been observed and digested, *then* comes the second, and after that the third. Each of the three visions is complete in and of itself, as structurally indicated by the number of seven scenes in each, and each is to accomplish basically the same purpose.

The purpose of each vision is to work repentance and give the encouragement of faith and hope. The hearer is meant to receive each vision in such a way that, as he fearfully heeds its sevenfold message, he is moved to repentance and faithful hope in the reigning Christ. If one takes lightly the *first* warning of the first sevenfold vision, he will be hit harder by the *second* warning of the second vision, and thus be given another opportunity to repent. Finally there is the dire *third* warning, in which the reader is impacted even harder. Thus the *three sevenfold* visions are *three* warnings by which God endeavors to bring home to his people on earth the seriousness of what he desires his church to hear and heed. God's people are to believe in the reigning Christ and to hope in his promise to come soon. *Indeed, the ultimate purpose of Revelation is to inspire the church to pray with John* (in response to the Lord's promise in 22:20, "Yes, I am coming quickly"): *"Amen, come now, Lord Jesus"* (22:20).

There are biblical precedents for this structure of *three* warnings and for *sevenfold* warnings. For example, in Leviticus 26, God instructed his people that if they would follow his decrees, he would bless their earthly life (Lev 26:1–13). But if they did not listen and did not carry out his instructions, God first warned that he would strike them with earthly plagues (Lev 26:14–22). If they did not heed *that* warning, then God warned them a second time that he would strike them with the sword of their enemies (Lev 26:23–26). And if they *still* would not listen and repent, then he warned a third time that he would punish them for their sins by destroying their children and bringing them into exile among the pagan nations (Lev 26:27–39). These three warnings aimed to move the people to live in constant repentance, so that they might also live under the grace of God according to his faithful covenant with them (Lev 26:40–45). Four times in Leviticus 26 God says that he would afflict and punish his people *"seven times over"* if they did not repent (Lev 26:18, 21, 24, 28).

So also now in Revelation, in *three* successive visions, God urges his people—and the world—to heed the message, the *"seven* times over" message of warning and hope. This is all for the purpose that they may enjoy the "Sabbath rest" (Heb 4:9) of God's covenant with them in Christ.

6:1–8:5

FIRST SEVENFOLD
VISION OF HISTORY FROM
THE CROSS TO THE END
(THE SEVEN-SEALED SCROLL
INTRODUCED BY THE LAMB)

REVELATION 6:1–17

THE FIRST SIX SEALS: TRIBULATIONS AND THE END

TRANSLATION

6 ¹And I looked when the Lamb opened one of the seven seals, and I heard one of the four winged creatures saying, as a voice of thunder, "Come." ²And I looked, and behold a white horse, and the one sitting on it had a bow, and a crown was given to him, and he went forth conquering so that indeed he might conquer. ³And when he opened the second seal, I heard the second winged creature saying, "Come." ⁴And another horse went forth, a red one, and to him who sat on it was granted to take peace from the earth and that they should slay one another, and a great sword was given to him. ⁵And when he opened the third seal, I heard the third winged creature saying, "Come." And I looked, and behold a black horse, and the one sitting on it had a weighing scale in his hand. ⁶And I heard something like a voice in the midst of the four winged creatures saying, "A measuring quart of wheat for a denarius, and three measuring quarts of barley for a denarius, and the olive and the wine do not spoil." ⁷And when he opened the fourth seal, I heard the voice of the fourth winged creature saying, "Come." ⁸And I looked, and behold a ghostly green horse, and the one sitting upon it—his name was Death, and the grave was following along with him, and there was given to them authority over the fourth of the earth, to kill by sword and by famine and by death and by means of the wild animals of the earth. ⁹And when he opened the fifth seal, I saw underneath

the incense altar the souls of those who had been
slain because of the Word of God and because of
the testimony which they held. [10]And they cried
out with a great voice, saying, "How long, O
Master, the only holy and true One, are you not
going to judge and to avenge our blood from those
dwelling upon the earth?" [11]And a white robe was
given to each of them, and it was said to them that
they should rest yet a little time, until their fellow
slaves and their brothers, who are going to be
killed even as they were, should also be fulfilled.
[12]And I looked when he opened the sixth seal, and
there came about a great earthquake, and the sun
became black as hairy sackcloth and the whole moon
became like blood, [13]and the stars of heaven fell to the
earth as a fig tree casts its unripe figs when shaken
by a great wind, [14]and the heaven was split open as
a scroll rolled up and every mountain and island
were moved from their places. [15]And the kings of the
earth and the exalted persons and the high ranking
officials and the wealthy and the powerful and every
slave and freeman hid themselves in the caves and
in the rocks of the mountains, [16]and they say to the
mountains and to the rocks, "Fall upon us and hide
us from the face of the One sitting on the throne and
from the wrath of the Lamb, [17]because the great day
of their wrath has come, and who is able to stand?"

COMMENTARY

FIRST FOUR SEALS: THE FOUR HORSEMEN (6:1–8)

The opening of the first four seals of the scroll by the Lamb of God introduces four horsemen who go forth to spread terror and sufferings of one kind or another. Throughout the Middle Ages, and earlier, the four horsemen were used in pictorial art and in literature to symbolize the ravages of war and pestilence, famine and death. The symbolism of the horsemen indicates that the tribulations are of the sort that humans frequently experience in this fallen world; they are common and natural, not of the supernatural. In apocalyptic literature, whenever an author wanted to portray events or personages common to human experience and senses, he would make use of symbols taken from human, earthly life. But when he wanted to portray supernatural events or personages which were beyond human experience and intelligence, he would create symbols which do not exist in empirical human knowledge. God employs these natural phenomena to express his judgment against human sin.

The Lamb opens "one of the seven seals" (6:1). Though the exalted Lord Christ opens the seals, it is the four winged creatures who, in turn, invite John to look at the four horsemen. This is in contrast to what happens when the Lamb opens the fifth and sixth seals, for then no mediating angelic figure plays a role. This may be due to the fact that the four horsemen introduce and represent tribulations and sufferings which are under the sovereign God's permissive will, which is carried out at times through his heavenly angels (e.g., 2 Ki 19:35–37). But when, in the opening of the fifth and sixth seals, there is revealed the souls of the saints before God in heaven and then the End itself, no mediating heavenly angelic figure is used to announce it, *for these two last seals and what they introduce are for the hope and comfort of God's people.*

THE FIRST HORSEMAN

The first horse is white. Its rider has a battle bow and wears a crown. He comes forth for the purpose of conquering. He exists solely to conquer and be victorious in his effort. *The bow is the symbol of intention to conquer by military might and prowess..* The crown that the rider of the white horse wears proclaims that in his conquering role he will be victorious. The white color of the horse indicates that the horseman claims that his conquering ability and his victories are by the authority and majesty of God.

The interpretation that best fits the description of this first horseman and his role is that of a spiritual evil that causes military, tyrannical dominance. *The rider of the white horse symbolizes and represents every form of tyranny which is won and acquired by power and force, usually warfare or forms of it, and which then by a dictatorial rule exploits, enslaves, dominates, and terrorizes.* It can take the classical form of military might and conquest. However, it also refers to *any* human entity—institutional or individual, lawful or unlawful—which misuses its authority to exert tyranny over its subjects. It can be a governmental, educational, or economic system; a spouse, parent, or any person or agency in authority in any sphere of life. Such tyranny often justifies its dominance by a claim of divine or quasi-divine authority, hence the horse's color of white. It will use force—of arms, of mind, of wealth, or of any other resource—to establish its authority and the exercise of it; hence the bow. And it will be victorious. *The picture presented by this rider on the white horse is one of a tyranny that will dominate and be the rule, not the exception, throughout the time period from the ascension of Christ up to the end of history.* It gives a terrifying depiction of how human beings treat each other: *people's inhumanity to other people through fear and exploitation.* Human freedoms will be the exception. Human tyrannical slavery in all its fearful forms will be the rule.

The Second Horseman

The following three horsemen come in succession in the wake of the conqueror on the white horse. *The result of tyranny is bloodshed, which in turn is followed and accompanied by scarcity of goods and famine, so that the end result is death and the grave.* While each follows in the wake of the other as they are introduced to John, once they have all been introduced, they accompany each other as they ravage the earth. While there are some difficulties in identifying the first horseman, there is no problem in identifying the following three. When the second seal is opened by the Lamb, at the voice of invitation of the second winged creature, John sees a second horseman ravaging humankind. The horse is red, perhaps blood red, and the one sitting on it has permission to take peace from the earth by human beings slaughtering one another. The "great sword" (6:4) that was given to him symbolizes this role of destroyer of peace. The fact that the "great sword" is *given* to him indicates that he is acting by the permissive will of the exalted Lord Christ, the Lamb who with the opening of the second seal ushered in this rider.

Clearly the rider of the red horse symbolizes warfare, but in addition he represents any sort of unlawful killing and murder. Throughout the time period covered by the prophetic message of Revelation, from the victory of the Lord Christ up to his second coming, peace and tranquility will be the exception. The general rule will be wars and rumors of war, violence, murders, insurrections, and the like (see Mk 13:7–9). It is for this reason that Paul urged his fellow Christians to pray for peace and for an orderly and quiet life (1 Tim 2:1–2), for he knew that only God could grant such.

The Third Horseman

The opening of the third seal introduces the next horseman. His steed is black, the color of death, which in the ancient world often resulted from famine (cf. Jer 14:1–2; Lam 5:10). He has in his hand a "weighing scale" (Rev 6:5), that is, a pair of scales attached and suspended from a beam or yoke (hence the scale is designated by the Greek word for "yoke,"). Here in 6:5–6 the scale is used to measure out foodstuffs by volume, which is then given a monetary value.

As John views the rider with the scales, he hears a voice which comes from "the midst of the four winged creatures" (6:6). The voice is not identified.

Of the thirteen times in Revelation that John hears such an unidentified voice (6:6; 9:13; 10:4, 8; 11:12, 15; 12:10; 14:13; 16:1, 17; 18:4; 19:5; 21:3), it seems that most (if not all) of the times the voice is that of an angel in a deferential relationship to God (e.g., 16:1). However that may be, in each instance the voice is certainly speaking for God *under his authority* and glory.

Here in 6:6 the voice comes from the midst of the winged creatures. *Probably* it is a voice of *an angel speaking on behalf of God,* for what the voice says concerns God's providential care of the earth's bounty in the midst of scarcity, which care the angelic voice sounds.

The picture given in 6:6 is one of imbalance and scarcity of foodstuffs in the market. The "measuring quart" most likely is the Greek measure of almost a quart. It took a worker's daily wage, "a denarius" (Rev 6:6), to purchase just one "measuring quart of wheat" or "three measuring quarts of barley." Both the wheat and barley were costly, but at least a worker and his family could subsist—though barely. The announcement that the two grains were set at a certain price suggests that price-control measures were being taken to counter the runaway inflation that comes when vital goods are scarce. For example, in AD 92 a decree was made during the reign of Domitian when there was a severe scarcity of grains but a plentiful grape harvest. The decree instructed that half of the vineyards were to be destroyed to stabilize the price of the fruit of the vine. A surplus would result in a low selling price, and then farmers and merchants may not make enough profit to enable them to afford the expensive grain necessary for their sustenance. So unpopular was this decree that it was later rescinded. The voice that John hears also commands that the olive oil and wine were not to be harmed, probably meaning that they were to be kept from being spoiled or soured.

Whatever the details may be, the overall picture presented in 6:5–6 is a condition of *both scarcity and plenty,* that is, *an economic imbalance in the supply of food and the daily necessities of life.* Despite human attempts to adjust this imbalance economically, the end result, from place to place, will be hunger and even at times starvation. In such situations famine begins to stalk large portions of the human population. The horseman on the black horse, then, suggests that *throughout the entire period from the Lord's ascension until the End, there will always be present, at various times and places, hunger and famine.*

THE FOURTH HORSEMAN AND THE FOUR TOGETHER

At the end of the day or at the end of an era of such hardship, the only victor visible to the human eye is death, attended by the grave. So when the fourth seal is opened, John sees the "ghostly green horse, and the one sitting upon it," whose "name was Death" (6:8). This grim reaper fells his harvest, and as he is followed by his attendant, the grave receives the gleanings of this horseman and of the three preceding. The rider on the ghostly green horse symbolically demonstrates that death is the result of the tyranny, the bloodshed, and the famine of the first three horsemen, and that death together with the grave reigns on this earth. Throughout the whole time period covered by this first sevenfold vision, at any given moment a fourth of the earth's population may be dying because of the sword, famine, diseases, and the wild animals of the earth.

John sees first one horseman and then the other three, following one after the other. But when all four are finally present, he sees them all together—side by side—ravaging the human race throughout the whole period of history. Certainly also in recent centuries the human race has witnessed the horrors depicted by the four horsemen, in deadly scene after deadly scene. Millions upon millions have perished through wars and famine and bloodshed and diseases. How long is this to go on? *Until the end of time!* History continues to unfold, in particular in all the sufferings of God's own people here on earth, of which John is reminded when the fifth seal is opened (6:9–11).

FIFTH SEAL: THE SAINTS BENEATH THE ALTAR (6:9–11)

At the opening of the fifth seal John sees underneath the incense altar the souls of God's people who had been martyred because of their witness to the Word of God. He hears them crying out loud to God, asking him how long it would be until he avenges their blood from those who had put them to death (cf. Heb 12:24). They did not avenge their own blood, nor did their Christian brothers avenge them, but now these in glory are asking God to do so. Christians are not to exact vengeance (see Lev 19:18; Rom 12:19). But *God's own* vindication of his people is a common note in the OT (see Gen 4:10; Ps 79:10; 94:1–6).

While Christians pronounce the judgment of God upon the wicked who are unrepentant, they do not execute that judgment. That is for God alone. But it is proper for Christians to pray for justice in God's own time and manner, for such requests arise from their concern for the reputation of God. It is for the honor of the exalted Christ and for the confirmation of the truthfulness of his Word, to which they gave witness and for which they gave their lives, that the Christians in glory thus pray for God to avenge their blood.

The souls of the saints of God are *underneath the incense altar* that is before God's heavenly throne. Because the incense altar is a symbolic reminder of the prayers of all God's people, on earth and in heaven, it is underneath and before the altar that John sees the souls of God's heavenly saints praying (cf. Rev 5:8; 8:3–4). In the OT the priest would pray and offer up incense on the altar in the temple for the people of God as they stood outside and also prayed (Ex 30:7–8; 40:26–28; cf. Lk 1:8–10). So now the souls of God's saints, as his priests (Rev

1:6; 5:10; 20:6) in God's heavenly temple, pray while God's people on earth, who are also priests (1:6), are still in their suffering and are praying for deliverance (15:2–4).

In answer to their prayer there is given to each a "white robe" (6:11). The white robe symbolizes the salvation of Christ which now covers them, so that they are righteous before God's holy presence (3:18). They were clothed with Christ in Baptism (Gal 3:27; cf. Is 61:10; Eph 4:24; Col 3:10, 14). They are reminded that, because they have been cleansed by the blood of the Lamb (7:14), they thus stand pure and holy and righteous before God. Here in 6:11 the white robes are also a vindication of the martyred Christians' trust in and faithfulness to God, and of God's faithfulness to them—faithfulness that includes God's judgment of those who had slain his people.

Also in answer to their prayer they are told "that they should rest yet a little time, until their fellow slaves and their brothers," who are going to be martyred even as they were, "should also be fulfilled" (6:11). They "should rest," be at peace, until all their fellow Christians on earth have been martyred and have joined their glorious company before God in heaven. The rest that they experience and enjoy can be identified with the rest that the Lord Christ gives to all who "labor and are heavy laden" and who come to him (Mt 11:28). It is the rest that was promised in the OT, the eternal Sabbath rest which the Messiah himself would bring about (Heb 4:9–11, 14–16). It is the rest that God's people on earth experience in faith, and the completion of which they long to receive before God in heaven and at the resurrection (Rev 14:13). The moment the souls of the saints were ushered before God's heavenly throne, they received and possessed this heavenly rest (cf. Lk 23:43). But now they are reminded that, just assuredly as they have this rest now, they should in that rest confidently place their prayer that in God's justice and in his time he will avenge their blood.

They are to rest, to be at peace and patiently wait, until all their fellow Christians on earth have joined them. Whether one understands, "should be fulfilled," numerically, that is, until the full number of their fellow believers is filled up and completed or as referring to the completion of the mission of their fellow Christians, that is, until the mission of their fellow Christians on earth is fulfilled and completed by their martyrdom, it refers to the time when God would avenge their blood in the great judgment at the end of this world's existence and history. Perhaps it is best to receive both interpretations. When the mission that the Lord Christ has given to his followers on earth is complete, then the full number of the elect chosen by God will have entered his kingdom, and then at that time God will avenge their blood (see Mt 22:1–10; Rom 8:28–30; Rev 19:1–9). The emphasis is on completion, for then the vengeful judgment will take place. God will avenge his people; he will vindicate their trust and faith in the Gospel of Christ's salvation; he will openly display his church in his glory; and he will judge and destroy her enemies once and for all. All this is for his glory and that of the exalted Christ, which redounds for the benefit of his holy people. This divine vindication will appear at the End, not before (see Dan 7:21–22). While God's people will participate in his judgment (see 1 Cor 6:2–3), they do not execute such judgment now on earth nor in the judgment at the End. The execution of judgment has been given by God only to his Son, Jesus Christ (Jn 5:22–23, 27; Acts 10:40–42; 17:31). This is the peace and comfort in which God's saints can rest: God will avenge their blood when all is finished (cf. Rev 21:5–6).

The *martyred* saints in heaven—and those to be martyred who are still here on earth—portray a picture of the suffering church all during the time period that the four horsemen are ravaging the earth, from the time of the ascension of Christ to the End. *All* Christians are martyrs in the sense that they *all* give witness by their faith, their mouths, and their lives to the victorious Lamb, who died and rose again. Because all Christians give that testimony, they all suffer because of it. It is a glorious witness and song they give, and a part of that song is to pray for each other, all to the glory of the One on the throne and to the exalted Lamb (15:2–4; 19:6–8). *It is her glory to complete her mission in martyrdom and thus glorify the cross and resurrection of Christ and his exaltation at the right hand of the heavenly Father.*

SIXTH SEAL: THE END OF THIS WORLD AND ITS TERROR (6:12–17)

With the opening of the sixth seal John receives a visionary scene in which is depicted the end of all things, together with the preceding and accompanying cosmic disturbances. The prophecy of Hag 2:6–7 might have entered John's mind as he viewed the great shaking of the cosmos, for the prophet declared that once more God would shake the heavens and earth as well as all nations. According to the author of Hebrews this once-more shaking of the earth and heaven would make evident that which would be destroyed and would also demonstrate that that "which could not be shaken" would remain, namely, the kingdom of God (Heb 12:26–28). John sees the heavenly bodies—the sun, moon, and stars—shaken and disturbed. The imagery of Joel 2:30–31 comes to mind, where the prophet says that the sun will be turned into darkness and the moon into blood. In Joel 3:15 the sun and moon will be darkened and the stars will no longer show their light (cf. Is 34:1–4). Joel speaks of this cosmic shaking taking place just before the coming of the great and terrible (terrifying) day of the Lord (Joel 2:31). In John's prophetic scene in Rev 6:12–17, this cosmic shaking and these disturbances happen just before and at the great day of the wrath of the One sitting on the throne and of the Lamb (6:16–17). In the gospel of Mark Jesus says that all these cosmic disturbances will precede and attend his coming at the end of this world (Mk 13:24–27; cf. Mt 24:29–31; Lk 21:25–28).

The suddenness of this cosmic, earthquake-like shaking is graphically portrayed by the heavens being split open and rolled up, as if a scroll were split and each half rapidly rolled up around its spindle. The apostle Peter speaks of how the heavens will be destroyed by fire and the elements will be dissolved, melted, in a tremendous heat. All this will happen so that a new heaven and earth can take their place (2 Pet 3:12–13; cf. Is 65:17).

When this cosmic, earthquake-like shaking hits the earth as the mountains and islands begin to move and disappear, the peoples of the earth will be struck with a terror and a hopelessness that staggers the imagination and surpasses any horror yet experienced by humanity. Calling upon the rocks and hills will be to no avail, for they cannot hide the people who thus cry out in fear from the anger and judgment of God and of his Christ (see Is 2:10–22; Hos 10:8; Lk 23:29–31). All peoples of the earth—king and subject, free and slave, rich and poor—all who did not heed the call to repentance and the invitation of the Gospel of the victorious Lamb will attempt to flee in terror. But there is no place to hide from the presence of the almighty God (cf. Gen 3:8–10).

It is "from the face of the One sitting on the throne and *from the wrath of the Lamb*" (Rev 6:16) that they would attempt to flee. While mercy and forgiveness might be expected from "the Lamb," here there is only "wrath"—anger and judgment. The fact that God has given the execution of his judgment to Jesus Christ is usually expressed with reference to Christ as "the Son of Man" (e.g., Jn 5:27; cf. Mt 26:64) and not as "the Lamb." However, it is because Jesus was the Lamb of God that he not only earned the right to save God's people from God's judgment against their sin, he also earned the right to judge those who do not repent of their sins. While it is as the Son of Man that he will execute the judgment of God, *he will do this precisely because he was the Lamb who died in that judgment on the cross.* In Rev 14:1–20 Christ is portrayed both as "the Lamb" (14:1) and as "the Son of Man" (14:14), thus emphasizing his dual role of both savior and judge. But even more to the point for understanding "the wrath of the Lamb" here in 6:16 is Revelation 19:11–16, where only Christ's role of judge is described and where he is pictured only as the Son of Man. There too John is reminded that Jesus is this judge because of his suffering and atoning death, signified by the "garment that had been dipped in blood" which he wears (19:13). Therefore he alone "treads the winepress of the wine of the fury of the wrath of God" (19:15). He alone has the right and the authority to carry out the judgment of God.

All this cosmic shaking happens because *"the great day"* (6:17) of God's wrath, and that of the Lamb, has come. In the OT, similar designations, such as "the (great) day of Yahweh," appear as references to the time when the Lord God will execute his judgment on the human race. While this "day of the Lord" is "a day of wrath" to the world (Zeph 1:15), it is to the people of God a day of vindication and deliverance. Nonetheless, it is still called a "day of wrath," for its purpose is the judgment of God. In 2 Pet 3:10 "the day of the Lord" will come suddenly as a thief, and it is the day in which the present heaven and earth will be destroyed (cf. 1 Thess 5:2). In Rom 2:5 Paul calls it the "day of wrath," and in Jude 6 it is called "the great day."

The first sevenfold vision is one of horror, tribulation, suffering, and fear, from the time of the Lord's resurrection and ascension up to the End. The whole vision is nothing but woe and lament, even for God's own people. One can imagine that as John mystically experienced the horrors and sufferings depicted and saw at their conclusion only death and the grave and then finally the terrifying judgment of God, he might have been tempted to fall into a hopeless despair

John of course knew, from his own experience and that of his congregation, that suffering and finally death would be their lot. The Lord Christ while still on earth had told him as much. To see it so graphically and fearfully portrayed before his eyes, however, must have stirred John's heart to the very depths and core of his being. But he must have kept in mind what he had seen previously—the glory of God in heaven and the coronation of the exalted Jesus Christ (Revelation 4–5), with the twenty-four elders (representing the church) enthroned around him (4:4). The Lord says, in effect, "Yes, John, there is suffering now. But remember, what you have just seen and will experience—all that tribulation and horror—is not and will not be *your* end. Your end is to share in my exalted glory (cf. Rom 8:18). You are my prophet who, in the midst of your sufferings, speaks of my glory as the victorious Lamb. And no matter what you suffer for my name's sake, I will defend you and keep you until I take you to myself."

As the prophetic message of Revelation continues, the Lord Christ will now lift up John to see something beautiful and full of hope and comfort (Revelation 7, an interlude). *He and the reader* will be lifted up and encouraged before being given the second sevenfold vision of terrifying events on earth (Rev 8:6–9:21; 11:15–19).

REVELATION 7:1–17

INTERLUDE: THE CHURCH MILITANT AND THE CHURCH TRIUMPHANT

TRANSLATION

7 ¹After this I saw four angels standing on the four corners of the earth, holding back the four winds of the earth so that a wind would not blow upon the earth nor upon the sea nor upon any tree. ²And I saw another angel going up from the rising of the sun, having the seal of the living God, and he cried out with a loud voice to the four angels to whom it had been given to harm the earth and the sea, ³saying, "Do not harm the earth neither the sea nor the trees, until we have sealed the slaves of our God upon their foreheads." ⁴And I heard the number of those who had been sealed, one hundred forty-four thousand, who had been sealed out of every tribe of the sons of Israel:

⁵From the tribe of Judah twelve thousand who had been sealed;
From the tribe of Reuben twelve thousand;
From the tribe of Gad twelve thousand;
⁶From the tribe of Asher twelve thousand;
From the tribe of Naphtali twelve thousand;
From the tribe of Manasseh twelve thousand;
⁷From the tribe of Simeon twelve thousand;
From the tribe of Levi twelve thousand;
From the tribe of Issachar twelve thousand;
⁸From the tribe of Zebulun twelve thousand;
From the tribe of Joseph twelve thousand;
From the tribe of Benjamin twelve thousand who had been sealed.

[9]After these things I looked, and behold a great
crowd which no one was able to count, out of every
nation and tribes and peoples and tongues, standing
before the throne and before the Lamb, clothed about
with white robes and palm branches in their hands,
[10]and they were shouting with a loud voice, saying,
"[All] the salvation is with our God, who sits
    on the throne, and with the Lamb."
[11]And all the angels had taken their stand around
the throne and the elders and the four winged
creatures, and they fell before the throne on
their faces and they worshiped God, [12]saying,
"Amen: [All] the blessing and the glory and
    the wisdom and the thanksgiving and the
    honor and the power and the strength be
    to our God forever and ever. Amen."
[13]And one from the elders replied, saying to me,
"These who are clothed about with white robes,
who are they and whence have they come?"
[14]And I say to him, "My lord, you—you know."
And he said to me,
"These are those who are coming out of the great
    tribulation, and they washed their robes and
    made them white in the blood of the Lamb.
[15]On account of this they are in the presence
    of the throne of God, and they worship
    him day and night in his temple,
and the One sitting on the throne will
    spread his tent over them.
[16]They will never again hunger nor ever again thirst,
    neither shall the sun smite them nor any heat,
[17]for the Lamb, who is in the midst of the
    throne, will shepherd them, and he will lead
    them to fountains of the waters of life,
and God will wipe every tear from their eyes."

COMMENTARY

INTERLUDE: A VISION OF COMFORT

Between the sixth and seventh seals (6:12–17 and 8:1–5, respectively) there is an *interlude* in which John sees two scenes. In the first scene he sees the 144,000 sealed (7:1–8), and in the second scene he sees the glorious picture of the saints before God's throne in heaven (7:9–17). The 144,000 represent God's people on earth in perfect order and thus ready to march. This is interpreted to be the church militant, poised and ready to carry out the marching orders—the mission—that her Lord has given to her. In the second scene John sees the great multitude of people before God's heavenly throne. Their number is so great that it cannot be counted. This is the most beautiful picture in the entire Bible of the saints of God in heaven: the church triumphant.

What John sees in this interlude *comforts* him. After the horrifying scenes introduced by the first six seals, scenes that could have melted John's heart like wax in awe and terror, he is now lifted up by what he sees next. The two scenes, of the church militant and the church triumphant, would at any time and place appear beautiful, instilling peace and hope in the Christian heart. But here in this setting, in sharp contrast to the horrors of suffering and despair and darkness and death depicted by the first six seals, these scenes appear even more beautiful to John.

In the scene of the 144,000, he sees God's people on earth as they are ready to carry out their mission and thus enter the valley of the shadow of death (see 14:1–5; 15:2–4). But before the onslaught he sees them sealed. John is comforted and encouraged by this sealing, for it means that no matter how much he and God's people on earth suffer as they fulfill the mission of their Lord, God will protect them in their faith. And when, in the second scene, he sees the church triumphant—all those who are coming out of the great tribulation and suffering—he is full of joy and enthusiasm. The church militant will suffer and die in the Lord's mission, but she will not lose faith, for her God will defend her in that faith (see 2 Cor 1:10; 2 Tim 1:12; 4:18). In the end the church militant will become the church triumphant. Not only is the church sealed and kept in her faith no matter what she suffers, she will soon be elevated and glorified just as the Lord Christ was. Thus John—and through him God's people—are comforted and full of hope, for God will protect them on earth and soon take them to the glorious company of the saints in heaven. He and his readers are now all the more encouraged and emboldened to be about the mission of Christ on earth, so long as God gives breath and life.

THE FOUR ANGELS HOLDING BACK THE FOUR WINDS (7:1)

After the opening of the sixth seal, which introduced to John the scene of the collapse of the heavenly bodies and the great day of the wrath of God and of the Lamb (6:12–17), John sees "four angels standing on the four corners of the earth, holding back the four winds" (7:1). When Scripture uses the description "the four corners of the earth," it does not imply that the earth is a flat square (Is 11:12; Rev 20:8). Rather, this is a metaphorical expression which refers geographically to the entire earth *without implying any shape or form of the earth*. So here in Rev 7:1 it means that the four angels stand astride over the whole earth.

As the angels stand on the "four corners of the earth," they hold "back the four winds of the earth" (7:1). In Jewish thought the angels under God's providence controlled and thus were the keepers or custodians of the elements and forces of nature. For example, in the Book of Jubilees (2:2), the angels of the elements and forces of nature are listed: "the angels of the spirit of fire, and the angels of the spirit of the winds, and the angels of the spirit of the clouds and darkness and snow and hail and frost, and the angels of resoundings and thunder and lightning, and the angels of the spirits of cold and heat and winter and springtime and harvest and summer" (cf. 1 Enoch 66:1–2; 2 Enoch 19:4). In Rev 16:5 an angel of the waters is mentioned. Of the biblical writings, only Revelation refers to these angels of the natural elements and forces.

The four winds are to be identified or associated with the four horsemen of Revelation 6 and thus are another symbol of destruction and suffering. This connection is made because of Zech 6:1–8, where the four chariots and their horses are interpreted for the prophet by an angel as the four winds of heaven sent out by God over the earth. A similar identification is made in Dan 7:2–3, where the "four winds of heaven" stir up the sea and the four beasts come out of it. Thus the "four winds" symbolize the tribulations and sufferings which take place all over the earth under the permissive will of God; they express his anger and judgment over against the sinful human race. Also the destructive power of the winds is metaphorically used to refer to acts of God's anger visited on the earth. For example, in Jer 49:36–39 God tells the prophet that he will bring upon Elam the "four winds from the four corners (or extremities) of heaven." By these four winds God would drive out the people of Elam so that they would no longer be a nation. God's acts of judgment, symbolized there by the four winds, would be by the sword of Elam's foes (Jer 49:37). It would be quite natural, then, for John to recognize a relationship between the horsemen and the "destructive capacity" of the winds.

A FIFTH ANGEL AND HIS WORK OF SEALING THE SAINTS (7:2–3)

The "four angels" hold back the "four winds" so that they "would not blow upon the earth" (7:1), that is, afflict it, until "the slaves of our God" (7:3) had been sealed. The winds of eschatological wrath are restrained so that the work of sealing God's people may be accomplished. A fifth angel now comes from "the rising of the sun" (7:2), from the east.

Ezek 43:1–4 may explain this angel's coming from the east. In a vision of the future, the prophet Ezekiel sees the glory of the Lord coming from the east (Ezek 43:2), and as a result all the land of Israel would be made radiant by God's glory. The prophet remembered that in a former vision he had seen the glory of the Lord leaving by the east gate (Ezek 10:18–19) before the destruction of the temple and the city of Jerusalem (Ezek 10:1–22; 33:21). Now in the vision related in 43:1–4 Ezekiel sees that Jerusalem will be restored, which restoration is signified by the glory of Yahweh entering the city by the east gate (Ezek 43:4)—the same glory which had lit up the whole land (Ezek 43:2).

The east, the place of the rising of sun, does not, then, refer merely to the direction of the east. Rather, it is a symbol of the working of God's permissive will to judge the peoples of the earth, similar to the symbolical use of the "four winds of heaven" (Dan 7:2). That permissive will also unleashes the wicked actions of humans so as to punish the people of the earth. But also the same symbol serves as a blessed reminder of the motion of God's grace in the one who would bring back the glory of Yahweh to God's people and thus enlighten the whole human race, the one who is the Messiah, the "Sun of righteousness" (Mal 4:2). Here in Rev 7:2, the fact that the angel comes from "the rising of the sun" indicates that though God's people would suffer because of the four horsemen and the four winds, the motion of God's grace through the sealing of his people would protect them.

This fifth angel, who comes "from the rising of the sun," has "the seal of the living God" (7:2). This seal could be the equivalent of a signet ring of God. Pharaoh gave his signet ring to Joseph so that he could act with Pharaoh's authority (Gen 41:41–42; cf. Esth 3:10; Dan 6:6–9). Signet rings were used by Oriental kings of the ancient world to authenticate documents and protect people in their service by marking them as their property. Here "the slaves of our God" (Rev 7:3) are thus to be sealed so that they are marked—identified and signed with God's own signature—as God's personal property and under his authority, care, and protection. The seal (signet ring) of God represents God's special way or manner of identifying his people and marking them as his own for their protection and eternal well-being. God does know those who belong to him (Jn 10:14; 1 Cor 8:3), but beyond or in addition to this knowledge of God, John sees here those who belong to God being sealed. Is this sealing some kind of public acknowledgement like that in which God marked out Jesus of Nazareth as his Son in his baptism (Mt 3:16–17; Jn 1:32–34)?

Perhaps Paul gives the best clue as to what the seal of God is. In 2 Tim 2:19 he says, "The firm foundation of God stands, having this *seal*: the Lord knows those who are his." Paul maintains that the "foundation of God" is certain because it has this "seal": the Lord knows those who belong to him. The Christian can be absolutely certain and sure of his salvation and faith because it rests on the truth of God's Word and God's seal within that Word: "the Lord knows those who are his." Thus it is through his Word that God seals his people, assures them by his Spirit that they belong to him and that he will protect them in their faith. Paul says that Christians are "sealed" by the Holy Spirit, given to the Christian as God's "pledge" or "guarantee" of the inheritance that God has promised (Eph 1:13–14; see also 2 Cor 1:22). The Holy Spirit, the "pledge" of God's promise, seals the Christian in his heart. The seal of God, then, assures the believer that he belongs to God and is known by God. The Holy Spirit does this through the Word of God's promise, which has been brought to fulfillment by Jesus Christ.

Thus the Spirit's presence and activity in the heart through God's spoken and written Word, creating and sustaining the Christian's faith in Christ, is this precious sealing work of God. Does the sealing also take place by the Spirit through the Sacraments? The baptism of Christ, when the Father declared audibly and visibly (by the Spirit descending as a dove) that Jesus is his beloved Son, and biblical thought about "signs," "marks," and "seal(ing)" support the answer yes.

In Ezek 9:1–6 the people of God who grieved and lamented over the idolatry in Jerusalem and in the temple had a "mark," an *x* or a cross placed on their foreheads so that they would escape the terrible judgment and slaughter that would come upon the city. Whether it was a visible sign, or whether the marking was merely a symbolical way of saying that God identified the faithful Israelites even if he alone could see who they were, God did in fact recognize and protect his people. In the gospel of John the miracles of Jesus are called "signs" because they visibly demonstrated God's gracious presence. Of particular importance in both testaments is the labeling of circumcision as a "sign" because it was an identifying mark of God's people that could be seen (Gen 17:11; Rom 4:11). Paul connects that "sign" with God's "seal" when he says that Abraham "received the sign of circumcision as a seal of the righteousness that is through faith, which he had while still uncircumcised" (Rom 4:11). Paul also sees the sign of circumcision as a precursor to Baptism, which he calls "a circumcision not done with hands" because in Christian Baptism it is God, not people, who puts off the sinful flesh of the person baptized, raises him up to new resurrection life with Christ, and freely forgives all his transgressions (Col 2:11–13).

God's Spirit, then, does use signs, visible marks or actions, in the sealing of God's people. Even as Jesus' ministry was accompanied by "signs" (Acts 2:22), so also the ministry of the apostles was accompanied by "sign(s)"—perceptible activities of the Spirit—which confirmed that their ministry of preaching the Gospel (Acts 2:14–35), baptizing (Acts 2:38, 41), and the breaking of the bread (Acts 2:42) was of God. The Sacraments of Baptism and the Lord's Supper are visible signs, that is, tangible elements (water, bread and wine) accompanied by words of God promising the forgiveness of sins (Mt 26:28; Acts 2:38). *Through these signs, Baptism and the Lord's Supper, the Spirit works according to those words and promises of God, and the Spirit thereby seals God's people and confirms that they are indeed his people. Thus the Spirit of God, in his gracious activity through God's Word and the Sacraments of Baptism and the Lord's Supper, seals God's people so that they know they belong to God and that he will protect them in their faith in the midst of all the tribulations they endure.*

One other place in Revelation mentions this sealing on the foreheads of God's people on earth. In Rev 9:1–6, in the second vision of events on earth, in the fifth scene (the fifth trumpet-angel) of the vision, John sees scorpion-like demons from the abyss (hell) afflicting the human race. But the command was given to these demons that they should afflict only those who did not have the seal of God on their foreheads. *Whatever these demon-like afflictions were to be, God's own people were defended and kept safe from them, because they bore the seal of God on their foreheads.*

In addition there are two references in Revelation which speak of God's people bearing his *name* upon their foreheads. In 14:1, 3, the only other times the 144,000 are mentioned, God's people are standing on Mt. Zion with the name of the Lamb and of his Father on their foreheads. Here the name of God seems to have the same purpose as the seal of God, namely, the identification and protection of his people. The other reference is in 22:4, where also the name of God and the Lamb is on the foreheads of his people. But in this case God's slaves are in his presence in the new heaven and new earth. The archenemy of God also marks his minions with the name and number of the beast to indicate that they belong to the evil one (13:16–17; 20:4). The people thus marked are thereby enabled to carry on their earthly pursuits of money and honor and power. A different Greek word is used for the mark of the evil one than that used for God's "seal." This means that those under the influence of the evil one do not bear a "seal" that affords them salutary protection under him, but rather they bear his "image" or "representation" so they may be used by him for his own evil purposes. Throughout the time period covered by the prophetic message of Revelation, from Christ's ascension to his return, the slaves of God and the slaves of Satan each have a mark that identifies them as belonging to their respective masters. And there are no "neutral" or independent people who serve no one; every person is a slave, either of God or of Satan.

The sealing of God's people in 7:2–8 does not refer to their initial sealing, though this is in the background, that is, it does not refer to their conversion, for the slaves of God are already his people when John sees them as the 144,000. Rather, the sealing here in Revelation 7 refers to the *ongoing* work of the Spirit through God's Word and Sacraments by which the Christian is kept in faith and protected in godly hope through all the tribulations and sufferings and persecutions illustrated by the four horsemen. No matter how dire the dangers become for the Christian, God will not permit his people to be lost. He will keep them in their faith and hope regardless of what is thrown at them, even death itself (see Phil 3:12–14; 2 Tim 4:6–8). This sealing of God is most relevant and comforting at those times in the "good fight of faith" (1 Tim 6:12) when all seems to be only darkness and despair and defeat. God's Spirit, working through the Gospel in his own special way, assures the believing heart of God's eternal presence and grace: "You are mine, and nothing can pluck you out of my hand"—the hand of the Good Shepherd, the victorious Lamb (see Jn 10:11, 14–15, 27–30).

The four winds and the four horsemen are held back—restrained—until God's slaves are sealed. When they have been sealed, the four horsemen will be unleashed to cause their havoc and destruction. Throughout the time period covered by the prophetic message of Revelation, from the time of Christ's resurrection victory on earth to his second coming, the four horsemen are held back while God seals his people. In each Christian's life, in each Christian community and church, God *restrains* the horrors represented by the horsemen until each Christian and each church are mature and ready by his Spirit to meet the onslaughts of the world as they carry out Christ's mission on earth (cf. Eph 4:11–16; 1 Pet 1:3–7).

Rev 7:1–8 thus suggests a pastoral application for each church and each Christian. At any given time throughout human history and in relation to each church and each Christian, the horsemen may be either restrained or let loose. They are restrained so that Christians may grow in grace and knowledge for the faith and steadfastness needed in the activity of God's kingdom on earth in the midst of their suffering (cf. 2 Cor 4:7–15). The horsemen may be let loose on Christians who have been matured and made ready to take their place in the mission of Christ's church despite the persecution and sufferings inflicted by the opposition. Once Christians are sent out into the world, they will be hit by all the forces of the opposition and all the evils perpetrated by humanity (the four horsemen). They would be overwhelmed unless sealed by God, that is, unless identified and protected and matured by the work of the Spirit through God's Word and Sacraments. The horsemen are held back until each Christian has been fortified by the Spirit for sacrificial Christian service.

THE 144,000 FROM THE TWELVE TRIBES: THE WHOLE CHURCH ON EARTH (7:4)

The number of the slaves of God who are sealed is 144,000—God's people from all the twelve tribes of the sons of Israel. In all of Scripture this number appears only here in Rev 7:4 and in 14:1, 3. The number 144,000 is symbolical and refers to *the whole body of Christians, Jews and Gentiles, on earth throughout the time period covered by Revelation* (from Christ's ascension to his return at this world's end) and at any given time in that period. Since John sees them in the context of a vision of events *on earth* (7:1–3), they are the church militant on earth.

The fact that John calls those who have been sealed "of every tribe of the sons of Israel" (7:4) would, on the surface, suggest that they are Jewish Christians. The 144,000 are described in OT terms, as the twelve tribes of Israel. But it is not uncommon for NT authors to refer to the church of Jesus Christ, *both Jews and Gentiles,* in OT language. For example, Jesus promised the disciples that they would "sit on twelve thrones, judging the twelve tribes of Israel" (Mt 19:28; Lk 22:28–30). Paul says that the believers in Jesus, both Jews and Gentiles, are the true Israel of God and the true sons of Abraham (Romans 4:1–12; 9:6–8; 11:11–27; Gal. 3:26–29; 4:21–31; Phil. 3:3). Historically, by the time of the NT, not all of the twelve tribes of the sons of Jacob were identifiable, especially the ten northern tribes which were scattered and disappeared in Assyria (though some remnants survived). Nevertheless, both the ethnic Jews and the Jewish and Gentile Christians still used the designation "the twelve tribes of Israel." To most adherents of Judaism, the restoration of the twelve tribes was an apocalyptic hope; to the Christians (Jews and Gentiles in Christ), that restoration was already a theological reality in Jesus Christ and his followers. It was, then, quite appropriate for John to use OT language in describing the Christians of his day, both Jews and Gentiles, for in Christ they were now the true Israel of God. In the context of the entire book of Revelation, the use of this designation would have to be interpreted in light of other descriptions of God's people, such as the twenty-four elders (4:4), the seven churches (2:1–3:22), the great multitude of saints in heaven (7:9), the woman and her seed (12:13–18), the 144,000 standing with the Lamb on Mt. Zion (14:1), and the bride of the Lamb (19:5–10).

The 144,000

While John's use of "every tribe of the sons of Israel" (7:4) can be understood as a description of all the followers of Jesus Christ, what does his use of the number 144,000 mean? Interpreting 7:4 in its narrower and broader biblical context leads to the understanding that this number must be symbolical and not literally numerical. According to the scene of the saints in heaven, their number is so great that the crowd could not be counted (7:9). In the second mention of the 144,000 in Revelation, it would be impossible to take the number literally, for there the 144,000 are depicted as male virgins (14:1–5). *The number is a multiple of twelve: twelve times twelve thousand. It suggests a total completeness. It gives a numerical picture of God's people on earth in perfect marching order, in perfect step. It suggests that God's Israel, the church of Jesus Christ, as it advances to battle in the mission given it, is a perfect and complete army, fully equipped and ready to do God's work.*

There is biblical precedent for this picture of the tribes, counted and marshaled, in perfect order as they follow Yahweh. In Num 2:1–34 the Lord instructed Moses to arrange the twelve tribes around the tabernacle so that Israel at rest, encamped in the wilderness, presented a perfect numerical pattern: three tribes to the east of the tabernacle, three to the south, three to the west, and three to the north. Each tribe had its assigned position. When Israel journeyed, it was also according to this pattern. In particular, when the tribes went to war, it was from this formation. *Israel was thus already in the wilderness organized as a military camp for the conquest of the promised land.* In the war against the Midianites, one thousand men were chosen from each of the tribes, twelve thousand in all for the battle (Num 31:1–6). A census of all the males twenty years and older from all the tribes was taken to determine the number and size of the army that could be called upon (Num 1:1–46; cf. Num 26:1–64), but often only a representative number went out to battle, with equal numbers from each tribe. David also organized his army in twelve equal divisions, 24,000 men in each division (1 Chr 27:1–15). (It could be conjectured that the equal numbers were so that no tribe could take credit for the victory, only God; cf. Ex 14:14; 2 Chr 32:8.) The community at Qumran idealized the army of eschatological Israel. For example, the Temple Scroll describes the composition of the king's guard. It was "to be made up of 12,000 'chosen men,' 1,000 from each tribe."

John is within this tradition when he describes the sealed people of God as 12,000 from each tribe, totaling 144,000. The number is symbolic of perfection, similar to the perfectly square dimensions of the new heavenly Jerusalem, whose four walls each measure 144 cubits (Rev 21:17). The new Jerusalem has twelve foundations and twelve gates with twelve angels, one at each gate, and the twelve gates are inscribed with the names of the twelve tribes of Israel, while the twelve foundations are inscribed with the names of the twelve apostles (21:12–14). *The 144,000 thus present a picture of the church militant throughout the entire period of the prophecy of Revelation and at any given moment in this time period.* The church of Jesus Christ is always in perfect marching order as she stands ready to carry out the mission given to her by the Lord. To the human eye the church looks anything but perfectly ordered as she is torn asunder by schisms, tribulations, and persecutions. But in God's eyes she is in perfect pattern and position for the purpose of Christ's mission (cf. Eph 5:27). This is so because she has been sealed (Rev 7:1–8). She will not lose faith. She will not deny her Lord. Unto death she will remain faithful to the Lamb of God.

THE TWELVE TRIBES (7:5–8)

The list of the twelve tribes in 7:5–8 is unlike any in the OT, for it is not according to birth order or birth mother nor according to the allotment of the land. For example, Judah is mentioned first, but he was actually the fourth born. Joseph and Benjamin are correctly listed eleventh and twelfth according to the order of birth. Manasseh, who was a son of Joseph and a grandson of Israel and who is listed as one of the twelve tribes in the allotment of the land, is mentioned (7:6). But Manasseh's brother, Ephraim, is completely missing even though he (like his brother) was allotted a portion of the land! Another son of Israel by birth and also one of the twelve tribes allotted a portion of land was Dan. But he too is completely missing from John's list of the tribes. *In this list in Revelation, Levi and Joseph, who were sons of Jacob but who were not allotted a portion of the land, have taken the place of Ephraim and Dan, who were allotted portions (though one of them, Ephraim, was a grandson of Jacob).*

John gives no explanation for these differences between his list and those in the OT. However, certain conclusions can be surmised. Judah is probably mentioned first because the Messiah came from this tribe. Dan is missing probably because it was in this tribe that graven images were erected, so that Dan became associated with idolatry (Judg 18:1–31; cf. Gen 49:17). Later in the history of Israel Dan was one of the two places where King Jeroboam set up a golden calf for the people to worship, in opposition to the true place of worship, the temple in Jerusalem 1 Ki 12:25–30). In Jewish intertestamental writings Dan was thus associated with apostasy and idolatry. Testament of Dan 5:6 says that the prince of Dan was Satan. The church fathers Irenaeus and Hippolytus state that Dan was left out of the list in Revelation 7 because the Antichrist will come from Dan. Ephraim was connected with this apostasy and idolatry because it was in league with Dan (Judg 17:1–13; cf. Judg 18:1–7, 18). Possibly for this reason Ephraim also was left out of the list. *It is clear that a redefined list of the twelve tribes of Israel is used in Rev 7:5–8: a list that has been cleansed of any association of apostasy and idolatry; a list that emphasizes faithfulness to God, hence the inclusion of Joseph and Levi; and in particular a list that focuses on the Messiah because of the placement of Judah.*

Thus in Rev 7:4–8 the twelve tribes of the sons of Israel serve to symbolize the church of Jesus Christ. The use of the number 144,000, twelve thousand from each tribe, points to the church militant, ready for mission, in her marching order. The specific names in the redefined list show she is cleansed from idolatry and apostasy. Moreover, she is sealed, protected in her faith, as she stands as a witness in the time of tribulation.

THE COUNTLESS HOST (7:9)

The second scene in this great interlude is in sharp contrast to the first. "After these things" in 7:9 (cf. 4:1) indicates a fresh and new sight to be viewed, a sight that probably none on earth had ever been permitted and privileged to behold. The church militant on earth appeared as the 144,000. Though symbolic, this number suggests a much smaller crowd of people than the great host in heaven that is too numerous to count (7:9). In addition, the church militant on earth (as witnessed by the orderly arrangement of the twelve tribes) was prepared to march out in mission. In contrast, the great multitude of people before the heavenly throne of God is at rest and peace, celebrating the results of the mission of the church on earth. As the 144,000 stand poised to be launched out into a world of turmoil and suffering, they are quite aware of the peril they face, though they are confident of God's sealing protection. But the church triumphant, at rest and peace and awaiting the final act of God's judgment and the resurrection at the End, will never again experience tribulation and persecution on earth. For them the latter part of Paul's words has come true, "I reckon that the sufferings of this present time cannot be compared to the glory that shall be revealed to us" (Rom 8:18).

The crowd of people before the throne of God is *countless*. This may have reminded John of the promise made to Abraham, Isaac, and Jacob that their descendants would be beyond counting—as numerous as the sand of the seashore and as the stars in the heavens. This crowd standing before God's throne is from every ethnic group of people on earth. Certainly this demonstrates that the true Israel of God, represented on earth by the 144,000 and in heaven by this countless crowd before God's throne, is all those who have the same faith as Abraham, both Jews and Gentiles. That faith alone justifies, the faith in the faithfulness of Jesus Christ (Rom 3:21–31; 9:7–8, 30–31).

The great crowd is *arrayed in white robes*. This is the third time that John sees heavenly figures dressed in white robes. The first time was the twenty-four elders sitting on thrones around God's heavenly throne (4:4). The second was the souls of the martyrs beneath the incense altar in heaven (6:11). In addition two earlier references (3:4–5 and 3:18) mention people *on earth* wearing white or white robes; they are those who remained faithful to their Lord. Here in 7:9 (as in 4:4 and 6:11), those who are so dressed are before God *in heaven*. As in the instances of the elders and the martyrs, the white robes here in 7:9 symbolize the purity and righteousness of Christ, which purity and righteousness have been given to his people because of his blood (7:14).

The heavenly crowd is also *carrying palm branches* in their hands. Biblical and Jewish sources associate palm branches with victory and celebration. In the ancient Near East the palm tree often appears in artistic form as the tree of life on cylinder seals. In the OT palm branches are associated with the Feast of Booths or Tabernacles (Lev 23:40; Neh 8:13–17). In Jewish celebrations, as when Simon Maccabeus delivered Jerusalem from the pagan enemy, palm branches were used in the victory celebration. In 2 Macc 10:5–8 palm branches were carried at the celebration of the purification of the temple; the people were thus reminded of the Feast of Tabernacles (10:6).

John would have been aware of this tradition. As he reflected on the sight of the palm branches, he may have thought of the crowd that went out to meet Jesus as the King rode *triumphantly* into Jerusalem (Jn 12:12–13, the only other reference to palm branches in the entire NT). Whatever their thoughts or the motivation of their actions, including their waving of the palm branches, they were consciously taking part in a celebration. With the palm branches they were participating in a godly reception of the promised King, the Son of David, who would cleanse the temple.

Now John sees again palm branches in the hands of celebrants. This time the crowd is much larger, and a host of people from every nation is in heaven before God. The palm branches in their hands allude to the triumph of Christ.

THE HYMN OF PRAISE (7:10–12)

John hears the multitude shouting *a hymn of praise* in which God's people attribute their salvation to God and to the Lamb (7:10). No greater praise can be given to God than that his creatures attribute their salvation to him and to his Christ (cf. 5:9–14). This hymn of praise for salvation is a new stanza to the great Te Deum begun in 4:8. In the glorious vision of God's throne in heaven and of the enthronement of the Lamb in Revelation 4–5, the heavenly host added new stanzas of praise to the Te Deum, a stanza giving glory to God for creating all things (4:11); two stanzas lauding the Lamb for the salvation purchased by his blood (5:9–10 and 5:12); and another stanza extolling both God and the Lamb (5:13). Similarly now in 7:10 a great heavenly crowd adds yet another stanza in praise of God and the Lamb for their salvation. As John hears the large crowd thus crying out their stanza of praise, he most likely thought of the twenty-four elders and the four winged creatures and their stanza of praise to the Lamb, in which they exclaimed how the Lamb had purchased for God a people "from every tribe and tongue and people and nation" (5:9). The similar language (though in a slightly different order) that is used to describe the multitudes of 7:9–10 suggests that they are the people mentioned in 5:9. As in the vision of God's heavenly throne and the coronation of the Lamb (Revelation 4–5), so also here in Revelation 7 all the angels around the twenty-four elders and the four winged creatures hymn a stanza of praise (5:11–12; 7:11–12). Similar to the stanza in 5:13, sung by "all creation," "[all] the blessing and the glory and the wisdom and the thanksgiving and the honor and the power and the strength" are ascribed to God (7:12). Here the stanza of praise is given only to God the Father. Why is the Lamb not also the object of the praise, as he is together with God in 5:13? Perhaps the reason is that here we can imagine him presenting this great crowd (7:9), washed in his shed blood (7:14), to his heavenly Father. As their Shepherd he now leads them to the "fountains of the waters of life" before God in heaven (7:17). However this is interpreted, the heavenly Father is singled out as the object of the heavenly host's praise, for he as their Creator is the source of the salvation of his people through the blood of the Lamb. He sent the Shepherd to the earth to gather his people (Jn 10:14–18, 27–30). Now the Shepherd, as the victorious Lamb (Rev 5:9–10), presents the flock to his heavenly Father. At the end of the stanza of praise by the angels to God, as at its beginning, "amen") is spoken (7:12). In 5:14 the four winged creatures spoke it. Here in 7:12 "amen" is spoken by the host of angels.

It is worth emphasizing here that it is *the angels* who sing to their God and Creator this hymn of praise (7:12). In 5:12 the host of angels around the throne of God and around the four winged creatures and around the twenty-four elders also sang the praises of the Lamb because of his victory for God and his people (see also 5:9–10). Now here the angels around the throne and around the winged creatures and elders again sing a hymn of praise, but this time to God the Father (7:11–12). This great Te Deum, begun in 4:8 by the four winged creatures, has stanzas throughout Revelation. Some are sung by angels, some by the saints of God, and some by the whole heavenly host. One can imagine this heavenly choir of God singing the Te Deum antiphonally, stanza by stanza. The angels praise God and the Lamb for the salvation of human beings; they praise God for rescuing a fallen humanity through his Son, who is also their Lord. The angels praise God for his every action, but in particular they praise him for *the redemption of his people in Christ as the most important action since his creation of all life.*

THE IDENTIFICATION OF THE COUNTLESS HOST (7:13–14)

One of the twenty-four elders asks John, "These who are clothed about with white robes, who are they?" (7:13). Of course the elder himself knows, for he, together with the other twenty-three, represents all the saints before God's heavenly throne (4:4). One would have expected John to have asked the question. He was perhaps so awe-struck by the appearance of the great crowd in heaven that he had said to himself, "Who are these?" Sensing John's private wonder the elder then asked the question for him in 7:13. John responded, "My lord, you—you know" (7:14). The elder not only asked John who this great crowd was, but also, "whence have they come?" (7:13). When John saw in Revelation 4–5 the vision of God's heavenly glory and the enthronement of the Lamb, he beheld the elders and the winged creatures as well as the thousands of angels, but he did not see a multitude of people. So in chapter 7 he evidently was wondering not only who they were but also from where they came. The elder included this in his question to John, as if John had asked, "From where did these people come, for I did not see them before?"

An elder, and not an angel, attends John in this vision of the saints in heaven. This is the second and final time that an elder stands with John as he looks at a vision or a scene within a vision and helps interpret it for him. The

first time that an elder thus attended John in a vision was in 5:5, when he served
John by pointing out to him the victorious Lamb. Both in 5:5 and now here in
7:13 the scene or vision has to do very pointedly with the victory of the Lamb *for
the purpose of God's people.* So in both instances God gives to one of the elders,
representatives of God's people, the honor of attending John as he views the
scenes. All the other times throughout Revelation it is an angel, or angels, who
accompanies John to help him interpret and understand the visions and their
scenes.

THE GREAT TRIBULATION

In answer to the question of the identity of the crowd and its origin, the
elder states, "These are those who are coming out of the great tribulation, and
they washed their robes and made them white in the blood of the Lamb" (7:14).
John had already observed the tribulations and the horror caused by the four
horsemen (6:1–8), and he had seen the souls of the martyred saints in heaven
praying to God for vengeance, which vengeance would come only after their
brothers and sisters had endured the horror of the same persecutions and sufferings (6:9–11). Are the things described in Revelation 6 "the great tribulation"
that the elder speaks about here in 7:14?

Elsewhere Revelation pictures tribulation as a continuing reality for all
Christians. In 1:9, at the beginning of John's description of how the exalted
Christ commissioned him to write Revelation (1:9–20), John states that he was
sharing "in the suffering/tribulation" that other Christians were experiencing
at that time (1:9). Certainly his exile to the island of Patmos was a part of that
tribulation. John had likely suffered other forms of persecutions and tribulations
in his long life of witness to Christ. He was not unfamiliar with hardship; his
own brother James had suffered martyrdom (Acts 12:1–2). In one of the letters
to the seven churches, the Lord Christ acknowledged that his people on earth
were and would continue to experience "suffering/tribulation," part of which
was the suffering of persecution and imprisonment (Rev 2:9–10). But these
tribulations were not described as "the *great* tribulation" (as in 7:14). Christians
of all ages are always suffering tribulations of one kind or another, including
persecutions. In encouraging the Christians in Lystra, Iconium, and Antioch,
Paul once stated that "through *many tribulations* it is necessary for us to enter
the kingdom of God" (Acts 14:22; cf. Jn 15:20; 2 Tim 3:12).

*The fact that the tribulation here in Rev 7:14 is called "great" seems to indi-
cate that it is the worst of the common tribulations that all Christians in general
experience throughout history. The "great" tribulation is the time toward the end*
of the "thousand years" (the millennium, which is the NT church age) when
Satan will be let loose for a short time (20:7).

In Mt 24:15–31 (cf. Mk 13:14–27; Lk 21:20–28) Jesus describes the terrifying days before the end of this present world, and before his second coming,
in which he says that there would be a "great tribulation" as had never been

experienced before since the beginning of the world's existence (Mt 24:21). This "great tribulation" would be so horrible that even God's own elect would not be saved unless those horrific days were cut short for their sake (Mt 24:22). And the Lord Christ said (Mt 24:15) these last days of this "great tribulation" would be introduced by the "abomination of desolation" prophesied by Daniel. Jesus' discourse concerning the sufferings of the last days before his second coming is concluded with these words (Mt 24:29–30):

> And immediately after the tribulation of those days, the sun will be
> darkened and the moon will no longer give its light and the stars will
> fall from heaven and the powers of the heavens will be shaken, and
> then the sign of the Son of Man will appear in heaven, and then all the
> tribes of the earth will wail and they will see the Son of Man coming
> on the clouds of heaven with great power and glory.

The evil days *immediately before Christ's second coming,* together with their sufferings and persecutions, are called the "great tribulation" (Mt 24:21) and "the tribulation of those days" (Mt 24:29).

Is the "great tribulation" of Mt 24:15–31 the same as that of which the elder speaks in Rev 7:14? It certainly seems so, for the Lord's words in Matthew locate the "great tribulation" in a sequence of historical events leading up to the return of Christ at the End (cf. "when," Mt 24:15; "immediately," Mt 24:29). However, the elder's words in Rev 7:14 (especially the present participle "coming" in the phrase "those who *are coming* out of the great tribulation") also suggest that the picture here is of a condition out of which all the saints are being delivered, not only through the "great tribulation" just before the End, but also through tribulations throughout the whole time period covered by the prophetic message of Revelation.

Thus this vision of the church triumphant has a message of comfort for all Christians, including those who go through death long before the "great tribulation" at the End. Since every Christian experiences testings of faith and witness, every such trial points to the future "great tribulation" at the End and becomes at that moment in time existentially a great tribulation for that believer. For example, when Jesus describes the last days before his second coming as the "great tribulation," he speaks also of the destruction of the temple and the evil days of suffering preceding it (Mt 24:1–14). Jesus uses the word "tribulation" in referring to those days of sufferings and persecutions which the residents of Jerusalem and Judea would endure. The foretelling of the destruction of the temple and of Jerusalem, and the preceding days of tribulation, while serving as an admonition *then,* serve in turn also as a *prophetic type* of the end of this world and of the days of the "great tribulation," which will come right before the End. Immediately following Jesus' warning about the destruction of Jerusalem and the temple is his discourse about the last days of the "great tribulation" and his second coming at the End (Mt 24:15–31). It is evident that, *for the people of*

Judea and Jerusalem, their sufferings preceding the fall of the city in AD 70 were their "great tribulation" before the end of their lives in the holy city.

The picture of eternal glory of Rev 7:14 is for the comfort of all Christians of all times as they experience whatever tribulations sorely test their faith and patience. Some tribulations and sufferings will be so piercing and poignant that the very faith and foundation of the believer's hope will be severely tried, almost to the point of despair and defeat. For that Christian at that moment, his sufferings and trials are his great tribulation. And every Christian will experience tribulation.

THE COMPLETE CHURCH IN ITS ESCHATOLOGICAL STATE

The people in the great crowd which John sees before the throne of God in heaven have already experienced "the great tribulation" (7:14) and have come out of it. The present participle in the phrase "those who are coming out" (7:14) suggests that Christians are continually emerging from this tribulation, adding to the crowd in heaven. *John is looking at the whole people of God entering and becoming the church triumphant. The crowd that John sees represents the whole church as if it were already triumphant, as if it were already compete, as it will be at the resurrection at the End.* In contrast, the souls of those who had been martyred, which John saw in heaven at the foot of the incense altar, were not yet complete in number (6:9–11). Also only their "souls" (6:9) were mentioned, which implied that the resurrection of the body had not yet taken place, while in 7:9–17 no such differentiation between body and soul is made concerning the great crowd before God's heavenly throne. This suggests that the great crowd of the church triumphant is complete in number, but uncountable. *John is looking at the church in its eschatological state,* which state the souls of all Christians enter the moment of their death and which is consummated at the resurrection of the body at the End.

The crowd of saints comes out of the great tribulation victorious because they had "washed their robes and made them white in the blood of the Lamb" (7:14; cf. 15:2, 4). Because of the redeeming death of Jesus Christ and because he now as the victorious Lamb presents them to the heavenly Father, the crowd of people stands pure and holy in the presence of God (cf. Rom 3:21–26; Heb 4:14–16). With sins forgiven by the blood of Christ (1 Jn 1:7–9; 2:1–2), and covered now with the righteousness of the Lamb (Rom 3:22; 10:4), they share in the victory of the Lamb before the heavenly Father. The *active* Greek verbs "washed" and "made ... white" (7:14) with the people as the subject suggest that the saints did the washing. They were the recipients of God's grace, with the result that as they held to Christ in repentance and faith, they "washed" their garments and "made them white" in his blood by means of Word and Sacrament. Yet there is no contradiction between passages that speak of Christians washing their robes

(7:14; 22:14) and those that refer to Christians being washed. Since salvation is by grace alone, it is impossible for a person to wash himself or his clothes so as to (actively) achieve the forgiveness of sins (e.g., Jer 2:22; Job 9:30–31). God alone can turn scarlet sins to "white" (Is 1:18). God must wash the sinner clean from sin (e.g., Ps 51:2, 7; Is 4:4), as confirmed by the baptismal language about God's "washing" of his church (Eph 5:26; Titus 3:5). Therefore when God calls for people to wash themselves clean from sin (Is 1:16) or "be baptized and wash away your sins" (Acts 22:16), and when Christians are described as having washed their robes (Rev 7:14; 22:14), it is always with the theological understanding that God is the one who instills the desire, prompts the action (Phil 2:13), and accomplishes the result: forgiven sins and eternal glory.

LIFE ETERNAL IN COMMUNION WITH GOD (7:15–17)

The crowd of saints shares in the heavenly celebration of the victorious Lamb (cf. Rev 5:8–10). As they stand before the throne of God, "they worship him day and night" (7:15). As the four winged creatures "do not cease, day and night," singing the "holy, holy, holy" of the great Te Deum (4:8), so now the saints of God continually participate in the heavenly worship. Here their worship is noted but not described in any detail. Rather, their relationship to God and the Lamb is emphasized.

The one who sits upon the throne "will spread his tent over them" (7:15). The verb here translated "spread his tent" points to an earthly dwelling in which people share the intimacy of family living. In biblical literature it carries an incarnational idea of God living in an earthly form or abode that can be experienced through the senses. In Jn 1:14, when the Logos became flesh, he "tabernacled" or "tented" among God's people. The verb emphasizes a familial, intimate dwelling together in an earthly sense. It could be that, in using this word, God is condescending to our human understanding of existence and manner of speaking. But more likely, the word is used to direct attention to the fact that God's people, considered in their eschatological existence, raised from the dead, will live intimately *in the flesh* with God in the new heaven and new earth (21:3), and in a familial, intimate way, he will dwell with them in a manner that can be experienced also with the human senses (see 1 Jn 1:1–3). The future tense of the verb "will spread" emphasizes the "not yet" aspect of this promise. *Now* this is understood and experienced only through the mind and eyes of faith, but *then, after the resurrection,* it will be a sensory reality (see Job 19:25–27; 2 Cor 5:1–5; cf. 2 Pet 1:13–15). Here in Rev 7:15 John is assured that God will dwell with his saints who have come out of the great tribulation. God dwells with them forever in a manner that is in keeping with what Jn 1:14 reveals: the Word became flesh and came to dwell among us in the person of Jesus Christ.

Because God will tent among his saints in heaven, "they will never again hunger nor ever again thirst" (Rev 7:16). This description and those which follow are to be received in an eschatological, incarnational sense. The state of existence that is being described, though true now for all the saints before God's heavenly presence as "souls" (6:9), will reach its final and full meaning *at the resurrection of the body in the new heaven and new earth.* For example, in describing life with God in the new heaven and earth, John says that every tear will be wiped from the eyes of God's people (21:4), and all who are thirsty will drink from the fountain of living water (21:6). While Revelation 21 does not explicitly speak of never again being hungry nor thirsty, it does say that in the new heaven and earth there shall never again be any pain or sorrow or death (21:4). Again, while all this is understood as true *now for the souls* of God's people with him in his heavenly presence, it finds its final and complete meaning *after the resurrection of the body* in the eternal life with God in the new heaven and earth.

Though 7:16 describes the blessed state of existence as the *absence* of physical traumas, it touches the very core of natural human life and needs. Hunger, thirst, and burning, scorching heat are especially applicable to living in a desert-like wilderness as the children of Israel did (Ex 16:1–3; 17:1; cf. Rev 12:6). They are, nevertheless, woes common to all life in this fallen world. These words of Rev 7:16 call to mind the promise that God gave through Isaiah (49:8–10). God said to his people that in the day of his salvation he would help them and restore them to their land. When that happened they would not hunger nor thirst, nor would the heat of the desert or the sun smite them (Is 49:10). What John heard in Rev 7:16 may have reminded him of the manna in the wilderness and the miraculous way God provided water (Ex 16:4–5; 17:3–7). It also may have evoked his memory of Jesus feeding the five thousand (Jn 6:1–15). John must have remembered the words of Jesus to the woman at Jacob's well that whoever drinks the water he gives will never thirst again (Jn 4:7–15). Jesus also said that because he is the bread of life, whoever comes to him will never hunger again, and whoever believes in him will never thirst again (Jn 6:35).

As John reflected on what he had heard in Rev 7:16 and related it to such words and deeds of the Lord, he must have been comforted with this thought: God always keeps his promises. *John now sees and hears the final end of God's promise concerning his people.* Now in their existence as "souls" (6:9) in heaven before God and the Lamb, and in his vision of the future final fulfillment after the resurrection of the body in the new heaven and earth, John sees God's people at rest, never again to be pained by the harshness of life as they formerly experienced it in their earthly existence. In their new life with God—now before his heavenly throne and then in the new heaven and earth—the Lamb "will shepherd them, and he will lead them to fountains of the waters of life" (7:17; cf. 21:6).

Before his death and resurrection Jesus had identified himself as the Good Shepherd (Jn 10:11–14). In the OT Yahweh had promised his people that like a shepherd he would look after them in order to rescue them and care for them. In order to carry out this word, God then promised to provide his people with a shepherd who would tend them. This promised shepherd would be his servant, a new David (e.g., Ezek 34:23). According to Jesus' own words, he himself is this servant, this David. It was also well known at the time of Jesus' earthly ministry that the Messiah would be born at Bethlehem from the seed of David. The relationship between God and his people, as pictured by his being their shepherd, was revealed so beautifully in the twenty-third psalm. In this psalm, as the psalmist declares that Yahweh is his shepherd, he says that his Lord will lead him to "quiet waters" and thus restore his soul (Ps 23:2–3). Now in Rev 7:17 John sees and hears the final outcome of these promises in the OT and of the Lord Christ himself. The shepherd of Yahweh has now been provided. By his death and resurrection, the servant David has rescued God's people (5:5–6). As their Good Shepherd he tends the flock, caring for them and leading them through "the great tribulation" (7:14) to the quiet waters of eternal life—already now on earth, then in heaven with God, and finally forever in the new heaven and new earth.

"Fountains of the waters of life" (7:17) is an expression for the source of life. God himself is that source of life (Ps 36:9; cf. Rev 21:5–6). Jesus Christ leads the flock to God for the gift of life. As God the Father has life in himself, he has also given to his Son to have life in himself (Jn 1:4; 5:26). In order to give the gift of life to God's people, the shepherd laid down his life for the sheep (Jn 10:11). In his resurrection he received his life back (Jn 10:17–18) so as to lead his followers to God, the ultimate source of life.

A final truth describes the rest and the peace of the crowd of saints before God's throne in heaven: "God will wipe every tear from their eyes" (Rev 7:17). Tears and laments are part of the experience and character of the faithful people of God while on this earth. Tears are shed over one's sins and the sins of others (Is 22:4; Pss 6:6; 39:12; Lk 7:37–38), over the ruin and sufferings experienced by others (Jer 9:1, 18; 13:17), over one's own afflictions (Job 16:16; 30:31), when confronted with God's anger (Ps 80:5), when alone and in sorrow (Ps 102:9), at death (2 Sam 18:33–19:4; Jer 31:15; cf. Mt 2:16–18; Lk 8:52; Lk 23:26–31; Jn 11:33) and at other times of sadness (Acts 20:18–19, 37–38; 2 Cor 2:4; 2 Tim 1:4. Jesus warned his disciples and followers that they would weep and mourn while the world would rejoice (Jn 16:20).

In this life the shedding of tears is as much—at times even more—the experience of Christians as are joy and laughter. While it is of the nature of the people of God to weep and lament, it is the gift of God's grace to turn the weeping and sorrow into joy (Ps 126:5; Jn 16:20), for he has promised a day when "the Lord Yahweh will wipe away tears from all faces" (Is 25:8). *John now sees (in*

Rev 7:17) *the complete and final fulfillment of this promise of God. The final word describing the peace and joy of the saints before God in heaven says it all: "and God will wipe every tear from their eyes."*

CONCLUSION: AN INTERLUDE OF COMFORT AND ENCOURAGEMENT

While the inaugural vision of God's heavenly glory and the coronation and enthronement of Jesus Christ (Revelation 4–5) controls and dominates the prophetic message of Revelation, the vision of the church militant sealed by God and of the church triumphant shepherded by the Lamb encourages and nurtures a comfort and hope that permeates the same prophetic message. *The purpose of Revelation 7, the interlude between the sixth and seventh seals, is to encourage John and his hearers—despite the fears and horrors already introduced by the first six seals and also in view of all the tribulations yet to be revealed.* While John and the seven churches have experienced the sufferings and persecutions revealed in Revelation 6—and will continue to experience them until the end of this world, when Christ returns—they are not to forget that what they had seen in the inaugural vision (Revelation 4–5) controls everything for the sake of God's glory and that of the Lamb, and for the benefit of God's people on earth. Now for their own encouragement and comfort and hope, they are also not to forget what they had just seen and heard in this interlude. God will protect his people as they carry out the mission of their Lord here on earth. He will not forsake them. He will not permit them to lose their faith and hope. He promises soon to conduct them to the glorious citizenship of the church triumphant. That is to be their end—not the suffering here on earth, but instead the glory of God and of the Lamb. How much John and his hearers will need such knowledge and encouragement in their faith, for even more dreadful portents are yet to be revealed after the seventh seal is opened!

EXCURSUS
Angelic Mediators in Jewish Tradition and the Book of Revelation

ANGELS AS MEDIATORS OF THE VISIONS

Beginning in 8:6 angels take over from the Lamb the mediating role of the remainder of the message of Revelation. But the fact that the seventh seal introduces this portion of the message indicates that Jesus Christ is still the overall mediator. He directly mediates to John the first part of Revelation's message (2:1–8:5), and through the angels indirectly mediates the remainder of the prophetic message (8:6–22:5).

In the prologue (1:1–8) John is told that the "revelatory-unveiling of Jesus Christ" was from God, who had given it to Jesus Christ, and that Jesus Christ, in turn, would give it to John through an angel (1:1). This suggests that (for whatever reason) the Lord Christ would use an angel and/or angels in mediating the message of Revelation to John. So John probably was not surprised when angels began (as of 8:6) to mediate the message in place of and for Jesus Christ.

But as to why this happens, and why beginning here at 8:6 and not elsewhere, John neither receives nor gives an answer. The Lord Christ certainly *could have* mediated the entire message, or he *could have* used angels as his mediating agents throughout the entire message, but he does neither. The triumphant Lord begins mediating the first part of the prophetic message of Revelation (2:1–8:5), and then, after the first vision, angels take over and in the stead of Christ mediate the remainder of the message. The Lord Christ disappears from view; he will not again confront John until the epilogue (22:6–21). Through the first vision of events and up to 8:6, angels within the vision and its individual scenes helped to interpret for John the scenes (with two exceptions, where elders did so). But these angels never were the mediators of the visions. Now, from 8:6 onward, angels not only continue to attend John within the visions and their various scenes, they also for the first time mediate the visions and their scenes. Why might this be?

THE REASON FOR ANGELIC MEDIATORS

We know from elsewhere in the Bible that no human being in this present age of sin and unrighteousness can actually see God in his majestic holiness and live to tell of it. God must condescend in some way or in some form so that

he can meet people and communicate with them. Even heroic men of God like
Moses, while still on earth, could not with their human eyes behold God in all
his holy righteousness and glory (see Ex 33:18–20). God used various natural
forms through which he approached and spoke to human beings, things such
as the burning bush (Ex 3:2), a cloud (Ex 19:9; cf. Mt 17:5), a pillar of cloud (Ex
13:21; Ps 78:14), and a pillar of fire (Ex 13:21; cf. Ex 14:19–20). In certain instances God appeared to individuals *in the form of an angel* or *by a heavenly figure in
human form*. To Abraham (Gen 18:1–2), to Jacob (Gen 32:24–30), to Moses (Ex
3:1–4), to Joshua (Josh 5:13–15), to Gideon (Judg 6:11–16), to Samson's parents
(Judg 13:3–11), and to others (e.g., Gen 21:14–19) God thus appeared and communicated. The NT also reports that God gave the Torah to Moses on Mt. Sinai
through angels (Acts 7:38, 53; Gal 3:19; Heb 2:2).

Jewish tradition held that God used mediating angels to appear to and
confer with human beings because that was the only way the spoken words of
God could be received. For example, in the Book of Jubilees (1:26–2:1) the angel
of God's presence spoke to Moses the Word of God, including the creation story,
which Moses was to write into a history that could have been the Pentateuch.
Such angelology thus developed in Judaism because of the belief in the remote-
ness and transcendence of God, a part of which was due to his terrifying and
overpowering majesty, which no human could approach.

Was this the reason that Jesus Christ used angels to mediate the major
part of the prophetic message of Revelation—that in his exalted status as the
glorified Lord, no human could stand before him? This appears to be the case.
In Rev 1:17, when the exalted Son of Man appeared to John to commission him
to write Revelation, John could not stand before the majesty of the glorified
Christ but rather fell before him as dead (cf. Mt 17:5–7). No human being in the
fallen state of this earth could any more stand before the glorified Christ than
he or she could stand before the holy majesty of God and see his face and live
(cf. Acts 9:3–6; 22:6–11). Only by the grace and strength of the gracious God
can any mortal, sinful human being stand before God. In like manner only
when touched by the right hand of Christ could John stand before the heavenly
majesty and holy power and presence of the Lord Christ (Rev 1:17). As God in
the OT had his angel (or angels) through whom he appeared and communicated
with his people, so now Christ in his exalted status has his angel (or angels) by
which he also approaches and speaks to his prophet John.

THE REASON WHY JESUS HIMSELF MEDIATES THE FIRST PART

If this is so, why then does the exalted Christ begin mediating the first
part of the message of Revelation directly to John before turning the role of
mediator over to angels? No explicit answer can be derived from Revelation, nor
does Scripture elsewhere reveal the mind of Christ in this action of mediation.

However, one may conjecture that the exalted Christ first wanted to establish beyond doubt *that this revelation came from God and himself.* Once this was established, then he could turn the mediation of the message over to angels. The unique and esoteric character of the message of Revelation, different from the other writings of the Scriptures, would make it difficult enough to receive. If, in addition, there were any doubt as to its origin, it would perhaps not have been received at all by the earliest church, even if it had come from angels out of heaven, for they alone could not vouch for its godly veracity. *But since the exalted Lord Christ himself by direct appearance and command told John to receive and write the revelation (1:1–3, 12–16, 19; cf. 22:6–7, 16), there is no doubt or question as to its origin and godly purpose.* Moreover, John immediately recognized the One who appeared to him and told him to write, for he had seen him before like this in his glorified state—at least in a preview of it—at the transfiguration (cf. Mt 17:2; Rev 1:16). *Once the Lord Christ had established the origin and the authority of Revelation by mediating the first part of it, he could safely turn over the mediation of the remainder of the revelatory message to angels, knowing that John would surely continue to receive it as from Christ himself.* John would assuredly know that, though angels were now to mediate the following message of Revelation, the seventh seal's control of the rest of the message would indicate that the mediator is still Jesus Christ, his Lord, even though angels now take Christ's place.

Another possible reason that the Lord Christ began the mediation and then gave it over to angels is that he wanted John to know without doubt that, because Jesus was now in his glorified state as the Lord of lords (19:16), John could no longer stand before his holy presence and see his face—just as Moses on Mt. Sinai could not look on God's face. To do so would mean death. Even while still on earth Jesus began to make this point. After his resurrection he told Mary Magdalene not to continue to hold on to him because, although he had not yet gone to his heavenly Father, he was soon to do so (Jn 20:17). Their relationship, when he would be in his state of glory and she still in her earthly life of decay, would sensately be quite different. After Christ had come into his exalted glory and met John in that glory on Patmos, this new relationship was clearly defined, for John fell down before the mighty Lord as one dead (Rev 1:17). Now he could no more approach the Lord Christ and look on his face than he could attempt to look on God's holy face. Unless Christ had given him a special grace, he would have remained dead. But the exalted Son of Man did give him that grace by touching him with his right hand (1:17–18). John could now, for the moment, stand before the majestic and all-powerful Lord.

The point, then, that the Lord Jesus wanted to make was this: John could not *continue* to stand face to face before the holy, majestic presence of Jesus because of his earthly state of decay and Christ's exalted state as holy God. *The Lord Christ, for the moment, permitted and empowered John to stand before him until John knew for certain that the message of Revelation was of God.* But after that moment the Lord Christ withdrew his visible presence and gave the remainder of the message through angels. "Flesh and blood" of sinful humankind "are not able to inherit the kingdom of God," are not able to live in the presence of the holy God and his exalted Son, the Christ (see 1 Cor 15:50). John would have to wait for that gift when he had, in the resurrection, put on an immortal body in an incorruptible state (1 Cor 15:53–55).

Therefore, just as God in the OT had angel(s) by whom and through whom he spoke to Moses (and others), so now Jesus Christ in his state of heavenly glory also has his angel(s), through whom he speaks to John (see Rev 1:1; 22:6, 16). These angels through whom Christ will now continue the revelatory message are introduced to John in 8:1–5.

REVELATION 8:1–5

THE SEVENTH SEAL INTRODUCES THE SECOND SEVENFOLD VISION

TRANSLATION

8 ¹And when he opened the seventh seal, a silence
came about in heaven for about half an hour. ²And
I saw the seven angels who stand in the presence of
God, and seven trumpets were given to them. ³And
another angel came and stood at the incense altar,
holding a golden censer, and much incense was given
to him so that he might place it, in connection with
the prayers of all the saints, on the golden incense
altar, which is in front of the throne. ⁴And the smoke
of the incense together with the prayers of the saints
ascended from the hand of the angel in the presence
of God. ⁵And the angel took the censer and filled it
from out of the fire of the incense altar and emptied
it on the earth, and there came about thunders and
noises and lightning flashes and an earthquake.

COMMENTARY

THE SILENCE FOR ABOUT HALF AN HOUR (8:1)

When the Lord Christ opened the seventh seal, there was "a silence … in
heaven for about half an hour" (8:1). This half-hour period of silence seems to indicate an intermission between the first act of this revelatory drama (Revelation
6–7) and the second (chapters 8–11). But for what purpose? Oecumenius (sixth
century) says that the opening of the seventh seal refers to "the second coming
of the Lord and the giving in return of the good things". He says that the half-
hour silence is a reminder of the silence that will be at the advent of the King of
creation when at the consummation of the kingdom of God every angelic power
will be astonished at the superlative glory of the One who has come. By referring
to creation in the context of the *seventh* seal, Oecumenius may be suggesting
that this silence, which will come about in the new creation at the Lord's second

coming, corresponds to the seventh day of rest after the first creation (Gen 2:2). Thus one may infer that the silence portends the eternal rest of the heavenly Sabbath (cf. Heb 4:1–11).

Perhaps Rev 8:1 does not refer directly to the eternal heavenly rest to be initiated at the end of the present world, but it is, nevertheless, similar to the silence which preceded God's original creation according to an intertestamental Jewish tradition. According to this tradition there was a silence before God spoke and thus created light (Gen 1:3). 4 Ezra 6:39 says that darkness *and silence* covered everything before God commanded light to appear. According to 2 Baruch 3:7, at the original creation there was *silence*. Also according to this tradition, a silence would occur before God's new creation. 4 Ezra 7:30–36 states that there will be a "primeval silence," like that of the first creation, which will precede the resurrection and the judgment at the End (cf. 2 Baruch 3:5–9). Whether John himself, in his reflective thoughts on this silence in Rev 8:1, connected it to the silence of God's first creation, and perhaps also to the eternal Sabbath rest, can only be conjectured.

If one searches Jewish tradition for an interpretive direction, perhaps more to the point is the silence of God which preceded the revelation of his judgment on Pharaoh and the Egyptians. In the Wisdom of Solomon (18:14–19), a silence and peaceful rest preceded the angel of death's descent from heaven to strike the doomed land. Like the plagues that struck Egypt in God's wrath and judgment (Exodus 7–11), so the first four trumpet-angels reveal natural plagues that will strike the earth (Rev 8:6–12), plagues that are somewhat similar to some of those sent upon Egypt. The natural woes revealed by the trumpet-angels also have a similar purpose, that of serving God's people (cf. Ex 7:1–5; Rev 8:6–13; 16:1–9).

In the OT a silence is enjoined or commanded from time to time. In Hab 2:20 the whole earth is to keep silent before the Lord because he is in his holy temple (cf. Zech 2:13). In Zeph 1:7 God's people are urged to keep their peace in his presence, because the day of Yahweh is near. When Pharaoh and his army approached the Israelites before the Red Sea and the people were terrified, Moses told them not to be afraid but to stand firm and they would see the great salvation of the Lord. Moses told them to stop voicing their unbelief and to "be silent," for God would act for them (Ex 14:10–14). In Ps 46:10 God speaks, "Be still and know that I am God." Human strength and action cannot save; God himself will put an end to war, and so the Lord is about to be exalted among the nations and exalted in the earth. The silence enjoined upon God's people of the OT was an act of faith and worship before the awful majesty of God's action of judgment toward their enemies, which actions would also save his people. The judgment and salvation brought about in and by the great day of Yahweh moves God's saints to a fearful and awe-inspired silence before the mighty God as he acts for his people. John would be mindful of this OT theme of silence as he experienced and later meditated on the "silence" of the "half an hour" (Rev 8:1). It was a silence of awe and mystery as the exalted Son of God made ready to unfold the remainder of the message of Revelation (involving the acts of the judgment of God upon the earth), which would be revealed by the seven angels. All these acts are for the glory of the exalted Lord Christ and for the assistance of his church on earth.

The silence lasts "for about half an hour" (8:1). It is a relatively short but nevertheless significant break in an otherwise rapidly moving chain of events. It is not known whether it was a common practice to reckon time in the interval of a half hour. The NT often refers to a (full) "hour," and perhaps an hour-long interval could have been just as beneficial. But John says "about half an hour." John often uses the word "hour" as a designation of an interval of time. In 1 Jn 2:18 the word is used in an eschatological sense to refer to the time before the End. The "hour" in 1 Jn 2:18 could possibly refer to the whole time period from the time of Christ's first advent up to his second coming, but with an emphasis on the time just before the End. If one were to see in the "half an hour" of Rev 8:1 an eschatological nuance, it would suggest that while in the end time of the "hour" mentioned in 1 Jn 2:18 the End itself would not come until the seven angels had sounded their trumpets. Throughout the time period covered by Revelation, the Christian is to stand before God in faith, in fear and awed silence, as he witnesses the judgments of God. This awe-inspiring silence (Rev 8:1) is to be a part of the Christian's daily worship of the Lord Christ. The "half an hour," then, reminds the Christian to take time out for intervals of silent meditation in view of God's acts of judgment on earth—acts which, though fearful now to behold, will in the end serve the Christian's eternal hope.

THE SEVEN ANGELS (8:2A)

John sees seven angels before the presence of God. Because of the article ("the") these seven angels are a definite group. John evidently assumes that they are known and recognized by his hearers and readers. But which group of seven are they? A Jewish tradition holds that there are seven archangels. This tradition goes back at least to the second century BC In Tobit 12:12–15 Raphael identifies himself as one of the "seven holy angels" who enter into the presence of God and offer up the prayers of God's people. In 1 Enoch 20:1–7 the names of six of these seven "holy angels" are given together with their respective duties. Only two archangels are known from the Bible: Michael and Gabriel. Though the designation "archangel" does not appear in the OT, terms such as "the great prince" (Dan 12:1, rendered in Greek as "the great angel") probably were instrumental in the creating of the term "archangel." Apparently "archangel" appears for the first time in literary form in the NT. In Jude 9 Michael is called an "archangel," and in 1 Thess 4:16 Paul speaks of the "voice of an archangel" which will announce the second coming of the Lord. In Jewish literature terms for "archangel" began to be used about the same time (one appears in 4 Ezra

4:36, written around AD 100). As a group of seven, these angels seemed to have been at first called "holy angels" (1 Enoch 20:1–7), but because they stood before the holy presence of God in heaven, they were also known as the "angels of the presence" (Jubilees 1:27, 29; 2:1; 15:27; 31:14).

This Jewish tradition thus speaks of seven archangels, but no reference to seven such archangels exists in either the OT or the NT. In fact, no group of seven angels is ever mentioned in Scripture, except in Revelation. Most commentators offer the seven archangels of Jewish tradition as the only known group of seven angels to which the article in Rev 8:2 could refer. However, there is another possible interpretation of the seven angels of 8:2.

In Revelation groups consisting of seven angels are mentioned ten times. In addition, the seven angels of the seven churches mentioned in 1:20 are referred to, one by one, as the recipients of the letters sent to the seven churches. Six of the seven trumpet-angels of 8:2 are also listed separately, one by one, as they sound their trumpets.

These references to groups of seven angels can be divided into categories. First, there are references to the seven angels of the seven churches (chapters 2 and 3), who are symbolized by the seven stars in the right hand of the exalted Son of Man (1:20). A second category of references is to the seven trumpet-angels (8:2), who introduce the seven scenes of the second vision of earthly events (8:6–11:19). The third category of references is to the seven censer-angels (15:6–8), who introduce the seven scenes in the third vision of events on earth (16:1–21). Each of these three categories has a group of seven angels to whom a different task is assigned: the angels of the seven churches, the angels with the trumpets, and the angels holding the seven censers. *Does this mean that there are three different groups of angels, making twenty-one in all? Or do the same seven angels fulfill all the functions in the three categories of references?* The use of the article (8:2) may help to determine the answer, as well as to suggest a possible identification of the angels.

The article first appears in the mention of the seven trumpet-angels (8:2, 6). The use of the article here serves as a "pointer" to these angels as a definite, known group. *It is the interpretation of this commentary that John used the article "the" to point to a group of seven angels mentioned earlier in Revelation.* That means that *the seven trumpet-angels are to be identified with the seven angels of the churches.*

When John introduces the seven censer-angels in 15:1, he does not use the article. This may suggest that these censer-angels are not the same as the trumpet-angels and the seven angels of the churches, but rather a second group of seven angels. However, the absence of the article in 15:1 does not of itself rule out the possibility that the seven censer-angels are also the seven trumpet-angels, as well as the angels of the seven churches. When a substantive, in this case the seven censer-angels, is well known because of previous appearances, the article is not needed to make a substantive definite. Thus the absence of the article when the seven censer-angels are introduced (15:1) may actually identify these seven angels with the previously known seven angels, who are the angels of the churches and of the trumpets.

While there is no description of the dress of the trumpet-angels, the seven censer-angels have a unique dress (15:6). Another difference between these two groups of angels is that the seven censer-angels receive their assigned mission from God through one of the four winged creatures (15:7), while the trumpet-angels begin their tasks (8:6) after the introduction of the angel of the incense altar (8:3–5). These differences could suggest that these are two different groups of angels. However, the differences could just as well demonstrate that the same group of angels has a different role later.

It is the interpretation of this commentary that there is only one group of seven angels fulfilling three different roles: in chapters 2–3 they are the messengers to the seven churches; in 8:6–9:21 and 11:15–19 they are the mediating angels of the seven trumpets; and in chapters 15–16 they are the mediating angels of the seven censers.

The identification of the trumpet-angels with the angels of the seven churches agrees with the purpose and subject matter of the second earthly vision and its seven scenes, which are introduced by the trumpet-angels. While the first vision of earthly events, introduced by the seven seals, had as its purpose the assurance that the church will be defended and kept in her faith no matter what she suffers, the purpose of the second earthly vision is the assurance that God will protect the church in such a way and manner that she will be enabled to carry out her mission—again, no matter what she suffers. As the trumpet-angels introduce each scene in the second vision, the plagues that are unleashed have as their purpose to strike in particular the *unbelieving* portion of the human race (9:4), all in the service of aiding the church in her mission (9:20; cf. 11:3–6). Who better to introduce these scenes than the angels of the seven churches? In the whole context of the prophetic message of Revelation, and in particular within the second earthly vision in relationship to the rest of the message, *it thus seems better to interpret the trumpet-angels as the angels of the seven churches rather than the seven archangels of Jewish tradition.*

THE SOUNDING OF THE TRUMPETS (8:2B)

Trumpets were given to the seven angels. With the sounding of his trumpet each angel in turn introduces events to take place on earth. Trumpets in the ancient world were used not so much in musical entertainment but as instruments to give signals for the initiation of events like battles in a war or to accompany announcements of important events (Num 10:1–10; Josh 6:4–9, 13, 16, 20; 1 Ki 1:34, 39; 2 Ki 9:13). In particular trumpets are referred to in the announcement of eschatological events. The great day of Yahweh is likened to the day of the trumpet (Zeph 1:14–16), that is, a trumpet will be a part of that which will announce its coming and arrival. In Is 27:13 the blowing of a trumpet heralds the promised deliverance of Israel. In Zech 9:14 the sound of a trumpet attends the appearance of the Lord in judgment against the enemies of Israel and at the same time announces the deliverance of his people. In 4 Ezra 6:23 a loud blast of a trumpet will announce the coming of the Lord in judgment, which judgment will be accompanied by plagues of various kinds (4 Ezra 6:18–22). When people hear the trumpet blast, they will be filled with terror (4 Ezra 6:23). The Apocalypse of Abraham 31:1–3 says that God will sound a trumpet to announce the coming of his "chosen one" who will summon his people and judge the wicked with the fires of hell. Thus in both the OT and in Jewish tradition, trumpets are associated with the eschatological coming of the Lord God in judgment, which judgment results in the vindication and deliverance of his faithful people.

The NT continues this tradition of the OT and of Judaism. At the second coming of the Lord Christ, angels will be sent out with a great trumpet to gather God's elect (Mt 24:29–31). A trumpet sound will accompany the resurrection at the End (1 Cor 15:52; 1 Thess 4:16). In Revelation the voice of the exalted Lord Christ is likened to the sound of a trumpet (1:10; 4:1). The remainder of the references to trumpets in Revelation are all in connection with the trumpet-angels—with one exception. Rev 18:22 states that, because of God's judgment, never again will the sound of trumpeters be heard in Babylon.

The trumpets given to the seven angels here in 8:2 are to be used to announce various plagues, both natural and demonic, which will strike the human race—in particular those who do not belong to God. The purpose of these acts of God's judgment is to move people to repentance (9:20–21). Such acts of judgment, the plagues, aid the church in her ministry of announcing the judgment of God (Law) against human sin and rebellion, and this in the end serves the proclamation of the Gospel to those who are brought to repentance by the Law (10:11; 11:3–12). The trumpets, and the plagues of God's judgment which they herald, thus point to the judgment and deliverance in the great day of the Lord at the end of this world (10:7; 17:1; 21:9).

Why do the angels use trumpets and not loud voices (as an angel does in 5:2; cf. 14:6–7, 9; 18:1–2; 19:17)? Because the exalted Son of Man speaks with a trumpet-like voice (1:10; 4:1), the trumpets given to the angels demonstrate that the angels act within and under the mediation of the Lord Christ even though he now no longer stands before John as the visual mediator of the message (cf. 8:13).

"ANOTHER ANGEL": PRAYERS GO UP AND FIRE GOES DOWN (8:3–5)

Before the seven trumpet-angels can begin to mediate the second earthly vision, an angel enters who carries out an action which prepares the way for them to begin their task. It is "another" angel (not one of the seven) who enters the heavenly scene of God's throne (cf. 8:2). He takes his position by standing before (over?) the altar. Here the altar is clearly the incense altar and not a sacrificial or burnt offering altar.

The angel has a golden incense censer, filled with a large quantity of incense. The incense has the purpose of attending the prayers of the saints. As the smoke and sweet odor rises from the smoldering incense on the altar, so the prayers of God's people rise to his heavenly throne. The angel here is analogous to the priests who daily ministered in the holy place of the temple in Jerusalem, offering up incense while the people before the temple prayed (Lk 1:9–10; cf. Ex 30:7–8). As God—in anthropomorphic language—loves the fragrant smell of offerings and of incense (Gen 8:21; Lev 2:1–2), so he loves the prayers of his saints. For this reason the psalmist prays that God will accept his prayer as incense (Ps 141:2). Paul says that the gifts of Christian love are a fragrant offering and sacrifice acceptable to God (Phil 4:18). So also are the prayers of God's people.

As the smoke and the fragrant odor of the incense, together with the prayers, ascend to God, the angel takes the incense censer and fills it with fire from the altar. The tense of the verb ("took") both heightens the drama of the scene and suggests the continuity of the results of the action of the angel. This means that the angel takes fire from the altar and continues to pour it out on the earth, while the seven angels, one after the other, blow their trumpets. The other angel's censer is not completely emptied until the seventh angel has sounded his trumpet. Then, with the seventh trumpet-angel, the wrath of God is completed, and, as the reader may envision it, also the other angel's censer of fire is emptied (see Rev 10:7; cf. 15:1).

When the angel empties his censer and thus casts fire upon the earth, it is an action of judgment. A similar action is recorded in Ezek 10:1–8. In a vision Ezekiel sees a man dressed in linen who is commanded by God to go among the cherubim of God's heavenly throne and fill his hands with coals of fire. He is then to scatter the burning coals over the city of Jerusalem (Ezek 10:2, 6–7). The scattering of the burning coals indicated the judgment of God and the resulting punishment and suffering (Ezek 11:1–2). In the OT fire often represents or manifests the unapproachable holiness of God, so that only the cleansed and purified may approach him (Ex 19:10–19; cf. Heb 12:18–21). In particular the fire here in Rev 8:5 images God's fierce and consuming anger, which can sorely punish and even destroy all before it on the face of the earth. When David was delivered from the hand of Saul, he sang a hymn of praise in which he declared how God's anger blazed like a consuming fire with burning coals, before which the earth trembled and quaked (2 Sam 22:8–9; cf. Pss 50:3; 97:3). So here in Rev 8:5, as the fire hits the earth, it will tremble and shake under God's judgment, resulting in all manner of suffering for the human race (8:6–13).

As the angel poured out the fire on earth "there came about thunders and noises and lightning flashes and an earthquake" (8:5), that is, a great trembling and shaking of the earth occurred. In Revelation descriptions similar to the one here in 8:5 are used only in reference to God's majesty and awesome presence (see also 4:5; 11:19; 16:18). These descriptions are related to and reminiscent of God's awesome and fearful presence on Mt. Sinai. In Ex 19:16–18 when God came down to meet his people, the holy mountain was covered with a thick cloud and there were lightning flashes and thunder. The smoke was like the smoke of a furnace (cf. Rev 9:2) as God descended on Sinai in a fire, and the whole mountain was violently shaken. Though involving natural phenomena known in this world, this display and demonstration of God's holy presence was so awesome and fearful that the people of Israel were terrified (Ex 20:18; Deut 9:18–21; Heb 12:18–21). In Rev 4:5 these phenomena, which draw attention to the awesome and terrifying presence of the holy God, were present when John saw the majesty of the One sitting on the heavenly throne. Here in 8:5, in connection with the angel pouring out fire on the earth, this extraordinary display of natural phenomena attending God's majestic presence attests to the holiness of God, whose *anger* is being poured out on the fallen earth. As Mt. Sinai shook violently because of God's presence, so the whole earth will be violently shaken (cf. Heb 12:25–29) by the plagues that will strike the earth with the blowing of the trumpets by the angels (Rev 8:6–13). The fact that these "thunders and noises and lightning flashes and an earthquake" (8:5), signals of God's holy presence, accompany the casting of this fire upon the earth attests that the judgments introduced by the seven trumpet-angels and caused by the pouring out of the fire (8:5) not only come about because God *permits* them, but even because he *sends* them. The plagues that strike the earth serve his purpose and ultimate glory and are for the benefit of his people, as were the ten plagues that shook ancient Egypt.

SECOND SEVENFOLD VISION OF HISTORY FROM THE CROSS TO THE END
(THE SEVEN TRUMPET-ANGELS): DISORDERS IN NATURE ACCOMPANIED BY SUFFERINGS OF EVIL AFFLICT HUMANITY

REVELATION 8:6–13

The First Four Trumpet-Angels: Upheavals in Nature

TRANSLATION

8 ⁶And the seven angels who have the seven trumpets prepared themselves so that they might blow the trumpets. ⁷And the first blew his trumpet, and there came about hail and fire, [both] having been mixed in blood, and it was cast to the earth, and a third of the earth was burned up and a third of the trees were burned up and all green grass was burned up. ⁸And the second angel blew his trumpet, and something like a gigantic mountain burning with fire was cast into the sea, and a third of the sea became blood, ⁹and a third of the creatures which are in the sea—which had life—died, and a third of the ships were destroyed. ¹⁰And the third angel blew his trumpet, and there fell from heaven a great star, burning like a flaming torch, and it fell upon a third of the rivers and upon the springs of waters, ¹¹and the name of the star was called Wormwood, and a third of the waters were poisoned and many of mankind died from the waters because they had been made bitter. ¹²And the fourth angel blew his trumpet, and a third of the sun was struck and a third of the moon and a third of the stars, so that a third of them should be darkened and the day should not be daylight [for] a third part of it, and the night likewise. ¹³And I looked and I heard one eagle flying in mid-heaven, calling in a great voice, "Woe, woe, woe to those dwelling upon the earth because of the remaining voices of the trumpet of the three angels who are about to blow their trumpets."

COMMENTARY

After the priestly action of the angel before the incense altar and after he emptied the incense censer of its fire onto the earth (8:3–5), the seven angels with their trumpets were ready to begin introducing the seven scenes of the second vision of events on earth. The prayers of the saints had been offered as sweet incense, and now God will answer the pleadings of his people as each angel blows his trumpet (cf. 6:9–11). The plagues introduced and ushered in by the first four trumpet-angels are reminiscent of some of the features of the judgments and plagues that struck Egypt (Exodus 7–10).

THE FIRST TRUMPET-ANGEL (8:7)

At the sound of the first trumpet "hail and fire, [both] having been mixed in blood" (Rev 8:7) were poured out on the earth. In Ex 9:13–33 a plague of hail struck the land of Egypt. As the hail rained on Egypt, it was accompanied by thunder and flashes of lightning (Ex 9:23–24). So destructive was the hail storm that it crushed everything in the fields, plants and trees, as well as hurting animals and human beings (Ex 9:25). However, no blood is mentioned. Perhaps here in Rev 8:7 the "blood" describes the awesome color of the storm . In the Sibylline Oracles (5:375–85) the imagery of fire and blood falling on people like rain from heaven symbolizes the destruction of warfare on the land and people. Whether one interprets the hail and fire mixed with blood as a natural phenomenon of the elements or as a symbol of the horrors of warfare on the land, the devastation to the earth, with its foliage of plants and trees and grasses, is catastrophic. One third of the earth's vegetation is burned and ruined. While warfare is terribly destructive to the earth's vegetation, so as to leave it desolate and unproductive for years, here in 8:7 the emphasis is more likely on the destruction caused by the natural elements of nature. However all this is understood, all through the time period covered by Revelation the earth's surface will be unable to yield produce according to its Edenic original capacity. As a result humanity will suffer from such a devastation of the earth's plant life.

"A third" (8:7) suggests partial, not total destruction. The expression "a third" appears in the OT with a similar meaning. For example, in Ezek 5:8–12 God tells the prophet that because of his judgment of Jerusalem a third of its population will be destroyed by famine, a third will be killed by the sword, and a third will be scattered to the winds and pursued by the sword (Ezek 5:12; cf. Zech 13:7–9). This prophecy of judgment is introduced by Ezekiel performing the symbolical action of dividing the hair shorn from his head into three parts: a third to be burned, a third to be struck by a sword, and a third to be scattered to the wind (Ezek 5:1–2). The expression "a third" thus appears throughout the second earthly vision in connection with each of the first four trumpet-angels. Each of the plagues, as it strikes the earth and its environment, destroys "a third" of what the plague hits. While the first four plagues (plagues of seemingly natural forces) strike the earth directly, humanity is also affected as a result (see 8:11). But in the fifth and sixth plagues (which are not disturbances of nature but demonic in character), a third of the human race is directly affected (9:15, 18). All through the prophetic time period of Revelation (between Christ's ascension and return) the plagues of this second sevenfold vision will destroy a part of natural life as well as a large portion of the human race.

THE SECOND TRUMPET-ANGEL (8:8–9)

The second trumpet-angel introduces a scene in which John sees "a gigantic mountain burning with fire" that "was cast into the sea" (8:8). Perhaps it can be imagined as a huge ball of fire being thrown into the bodies of water. Because of this plague a third of the seas become blood, and, as a result, a third of the seas' creatures perish and a third of the ships are destroyed—that is, a third of man's commercial activity as well as human life is affected. This is somewhat reminiscent of the first plague that struck ancient Egypt: the plague of blood (Ex 7:14–24).

As John later meditated on what he had seen here in Rev 8:8–9, he may have thought of volcanic activity among the Aegean island, perhaps even of the volcanic eruption of Mt. Vesuvius, which devastated the Bay of Naples in AD 79. Perhaps he recalled the imagery in Jer 51:24–25: in God's judgment Babylon, once "the burning mountain ... that destroys the whole earth" would be destroyed like a burned-out mountain. 1 Enoch 18:13–15 depicts seven stars (symbolizing seven evil angels) like burning mountains that had apparently fallen from heaven to the place of imprisonment, that is, hell. The fiery mountain that John sees probably symbolizes natural events that strike the earth's seas, that is, volcanic eruptions (rather than evil angels). Such hurling masses could readily be described as burning mountains falling into bodies of water. From such eruptions, and to whatever other natural forces the human imagination can relate such imagery, the earth's bodies of water will be so affected that much of the marine life will be destroyed. Consequently, humanity itself will be made to suffer as people traverse the seas. When a third of the seas become blood, it symbolizes this maritime death and destruction.

THE THIRD TRUMPET-ANGEL (8:10–11)

With the blowing of the third trumpet John sees a burning star, perhaps a meteor. It strikes the rivers and springs, that is, the bodies of fresh water. As a result, the fresh waters of the earth are embittered and made unfit to drink, perhaps even poisoned, so that people die from drinking their water. "From heaven" (8:10) suggests not only the star's place of natural origin, but also metaphorically the origin of the judgment which the star represents. The judgment is from God, just as was the case with the plagues of Egypt (Ex 9:1–3; 11:1). All through the time period of Revelation (from Christ's ascension to his return) a portion of the fresh waters of the earth will be so polluted as to make them unfit for human consumption.

The falling star is given the name "Wormwood." In the OT a Hebrew word often translated "wormwood" is a kind of bitter poison. As a divine punishment, it represents sorrow and bitterness in the human heart (e.g., Lam 3:19; cf. Prov 5:3–4). In Jer 9:15 the prophet is told that the Lord God has given the people wormwood to eat and poisoned water to drink because they had sinned against him. Thus embittered and poisoned waters represent God's judgment and punishment. However, God in his mercy can restore such bitter and poisonous waters to their original purity and sweetness so that they again become suitable for human use, as he did in the case of Moses and the Israelites in the desert (Ex 15:24–25). The "third of the waters" (Rev 8:11) can also mean, then, that, according to God's will that permits but also limits the extent of the plague, not all the fresh waters will be embittered. But the emphasis here in 8:11 is that a portion of the waters at any given time will be so polluted as to be unfit for human consumption.

THE FOURTH TRUMPET-ANGEL (8:12)

At the sound of the fourth trumpet a third part of the heavenly bodies is struck—so much so that the sun, moon, and stars are not able to give their full light and brightness to the earth (cf. Job 9:7). This causes a third part of the day and night to be darkened. In the ninth plague that struck ancient Egypt, a darkness came over the whole land, a total darkness for three days (Ex 10:21–23). Here in Rev 8:12 the darkness is not total nor is there a time limit, for this partial darkness lasts throughout the period of Revelation's prophecy (from Christ's ascension to his return). It is difficult to relate this partial darkness to human experience. Partial or total eclipses of the sun or moon are, of course, common. However, eclipses of the sun and moon do not seem to correspond completely to this inability of the heavenly bodies to produce their full light for the benefit of life on earth. Could it be that, throughout the time period that Revelation covers, clouds and smog and pollution of the atmosphere will so cover the earth that it will be increasingly difficult for the light of the heavenly bodies to penetrate?

Throughout the Bible darkness is often used as a metaphor for human sin and wickedness and for God's judgment, in contradistinction to light, which symbolizes God and the purity and holiness he would graciously give to mankind (see Jn 1:5, 9; 1 Jn 2:8–11). In Is 13:9–10, when the day of the Lord comes, the sun and moon and stars will be darkened and not shine forth. However, even if what John saw in Rev 8:12 could be understood as a symbol of this *spiritual* darkness (as demonstrated by the darkening of the heavenly bodies in the day of the Lord), that does not seem to relate to what John here describes. Here the heavenly bodies are not totally destroyed or made incapable of producing their light—as they will be in the End (see 6:12–14; cf. Joel 2:31).

Perhaps even more important, the plague that hits the heavenly lights is not so much a *symbol* of the darkness of God's judgment as it is a *sign* of his judgment. The *actual* heavenly bodies are being struck, and, because they are no longer able to give their full light on earth, life in general and mankind in particular will suffer accordingly.

Whatever this plague of the heavenly bodies implies and entails, it is a part of the total picture of what the first four trumpet-angels introduce. All through the time period covered by the message of Revelation, nature and its components are being physically struck, and, as a result, humanity is made to suffer. This is to display God's anger and judgment against the human race, *for the purpose of moving human beings to repentance* before it is too late to repent (see 9:20–21). In particular, the partial darkening of the heavenly bodies points to that End; this partial darkening is a sign of God's judgment which urges all people to *repent* while there is still time, for the *total* darkness of God's final judgment will soon envelope the earth, and then repentance will no longer be possible (see Rev 10:5–7, 11; Jn 9:4).

THE EAGLE IN MID-HEAVEN (8:13)

There is a transition from the natural disasters of the first four trumpets to *demonic* woes that will be shown to John in the scenes of the remaining three trumpet-angels. To emphasize this transition from natural calamities to those that are demonic, and then to the End itself, an eagle flying in the highest point of heaven cries out in a loud voice for all to hear, "Woe, woe, woe to those dwelling upon the earth because of the remaining" three trumpet-angels and what they will cause (8:13). So terrible and horrifying (in comparison to the scenes of the first four trumpet-angels) will be the scenes which the last three angels will introduce that they are called woes.

This eagle is the only earthly creature in Revelation which God uses to speak a word. In all other instances where God speaks through an intermediary, an angel speaks. Since angels are always used elsewhere, it would be natural to expect an angel here in 8:13 to fly "in mid-heaven" and to speak for God a word of warning to the human race. In 14:6–7 such an angel does fly "in mid-heaven" (as in 8:13) and cries out in "a loud voice" (as in 8:13). He also cries out a similar warning to the inhabitants on earth to repent, actually, "to fear God and give to him glory, because the moment of his judgment has come" (14:7). However, the angel in 14:6–7 proclaims not only judgment but also urges the people on earth to worship God the Creator, and he has the eternal Gospel, which is to be proclaimed to all people. Thus the roles of the eagle in 8:13 and of the angel in 14:6–7 are not identical, for the one proclaims only woes while the other proclaims both judgment and grace. Still, one might well have expected an angel here in 8:13.

In Mt 24:28 Jesus refers to an "eagle" or "vulture" in connection with the finality of God's judgment. This would be somewhat similar to the bird here in

John's vision, though the eagle in Mt 24:28 does not speak. That the inspired writer would see and hear an eagle as a spokesman for God would not be out of keeping with what he saw elsewhere in Revelation. In the heavenly throne scene of God's glory three of the four winged creatures are pictured as similar to earthly creatures: like a lion, like a calf, and "like a flying eagle" (4:7), and they do speak for God (6:1, 3, 5, 7). Perhaps here in 8:13 the Lord God used an eagle to speak the woes in connection with the last three trumpet-angels because the eagle serves as a transition from the natural plagues to those of demonic character. The natural plagues in the scenes introduced by the first four trumpet-angels are bad enough, but the cry of the eagle signals that the remaining three plagues are going to be far worse.

The eagle cries out "woe, woe, woe" (8:13), one woe for each of the three following scenes in this earthly vision. The three woes of the flying eagle point to the horrors of the demonic plagues of the fifth and sixth trumpet-angels (9:1–21) and to the horror and fear of the unbeliever in the judgment at the End (11:15, 18). The threefold woe suggests that the situation is very, very grave.

The eagle cries out the three woes in reference to "the remaining voices of the trumpet of the three angels who are about to blow their trumpets" (8:13). "The trumpet" of "the three angels who are about to blow their trumpets" is singular. The plural might have been expected. The singular here could refer to *the one* trumpet, the trumpet-like voice of the exalted Lord Christ (1:10; 4:1). "The *trumpet*" (8:13) that the last three angels will blow is on behalf of Jesus Christ, for it is in his stead that they sound their individual trumpets as they mediate the woes.

REVELATION 9:1–21

THE FIFTH AND SIXTH TRUMPET-ANGELS: DEMONS FROM THE ABYSS AND THE LAST BATTLE

TRANSLATION

9 ¹And the fifth angel blew his trumpet, and I saw a star which had fallen out of heaven to the earth, and the key of the shaft of the abyss was given to him. ²And he opened the shaft of the abyss, and smoke came up out of the shaft like smoke of a large furnace, and the sun and the atmosphere were darkened by the smoke from the shaft. ³And out from the smoke came forth locusts onto the earth, and authority was given to them like the authority which the scorpions of the earth have. ⁴And it was said to them [to the locusts] that they should not injure the grass of the earth nor any green [herbage] nor any tree, only those men who do not have the seal of God upon their foreheads. ⁵And it was given to them [to the locusts] that they should not kill them, but rather that they should be tormented for five months, and their [the locusts'] tormenting was like the tormenting of a scorpion when it stings a man. ⁶And in those days the men [without the seal] will seek death but they will never find it, and they will long to die but death will flee from them. ⁷And the appearances of the locusts were like horses prepared for battle, and on their heads were something like crowns in appearance like gold, and their faces were as faces of men. ⁸And they had hair like hair of women, and their teeth were like lions' [teeth]. ⁹And they had breastplates like breastplates of iron, and the noise of their wings was like the noise of the chariots of many horses galloping into battle. 10And they have tails in appearance like those of

scorpions and stings, and in their tails is their power
to injure men for five months. [11]They have over them
a king, the angel of the abyss. His name in Hebrew is
Abaddon, and in Greek he has the name Apollyon.
[12]The first woe has come and gone. Behold, two
more woes are to come after these things.
[13]And the sixth angel blew his trumpet, and I
heard one voice from the four horns of the golden
incense altar which is before God [14]saying to the
sixth angel, the one who has the trumpet, "Release
the four angels who have been bound at the great
river Euphrates." [15]And the four angels, who had
been prepared for this hour and day and month and
year, were let loose in order that they might kill a
third of the human race. [16]And the number of the
soldiers of the cavalry was twenty thousands times
ten thousands. I heard their number. [17]And this is the
way I saw the horses in the vision and those sitting
on them. They had fiery red and bluish and sulfur-
yellow breastplates, and the heads of the horses were
like heads of lions, and out of their mouths come
forth fire and smoke and brimstone. [18]From these
three plagues a third of the human race was killed—
from the fire and the smoke and the brimstone
which was coming out of their mouths. [19]For the
authority of the horses is in their mouths and in
their tails, for their tails are like serpents, having
heads, and by means of them they cause injury.
[20]And the remainder of mankind, who were not killed
in these plagues, did not even repent of the works of
their hands, so that they might no longer worship
the demons and the gold and silver and brass and
stone and wooden idols, which are able neither to
see nor to hear nor to walk about. 21And they did
not repent of their murders nor of their witchcrafts
nor of their sexual immorality nor of their thefts.

COMMENTARY

The revelations of the fifth and sixth trumpet-angels are called woes (8:13; the third "woe" applies to the seventh trumpet-angel's revelation in 11:15–19). This sets them off from the plagues revealed by the first four trumpet-angels and indicates their greater seriousness. Moreover, the descriptions of the locusts and of the fearful calamities that will be visited on the earth's human inhabitants are given more attention, more detail. In addition, unlike the four horsemen in Revelation 6 and the natural forces and heavenly bodies in Revelation 8, the images and symbols that confront John in the scenes of the fifth and six trumpet-angels are other-worldly. The locust-like creatures introduced by the fifth trumpet-angel and the cavalry-like creatures with both human and animal features following the sounding of the sixth trumpet are not visible except to the human imagination. This means that whatever the fifth and sixth scenes involve, what they portray and symbolize is not within natural human understanding and experience but is of the supernatural and thus understood only within the spiritual realm.

THE FIFTH TRUMPET-ANGEL (9:1–12)
THE STAR WITH THE KEY TO THE ABYSS

At the trumpet sound of the fifth angel, John sees a star that had fallen out of the skies, and it is given the key of the abyss. This star is not the same as the star in 8:10–11 (named "Wormwood") which fell into the waters and embittered and poisoned them; this star represents a personality. The star, as a stand-in for the one who has the key of the abyss and who is a ruler, has a *personal* name (in Hebrew Abaddon and in Greek Apollyon) and is identified as the "angel of the abyss" (9:11). The identity of this star is unmistakable, for it is the same personality that is embodied by the dragon in 12:3 and who is identified as the devil and Satan (12:9).

Jewish tradition sometimes depicts the fallen angels as fallen stars. For example, in 1 Enoch 21:1–6 seven fallen, burning stars represent angels who had "transgressed the commandments of the Lord" and thus now are bound. Such imagery may have been derived from Is 14:12, which speaks of a star that had fallen from heaven; this refers to the fall of the king of Babylon, and then, by way of analogy, the casting of Satan out of heaven (Is 14:11–15; cf. Rev 12:7–9). 1 Enoch 86:1–6 describes a star which had fallen to the earth and had caused terror among its inhabitants; in 1 Enoch 88:1 this fallen star is bound and thrown into the abyss. This tradition of a fallen star is similar to the picture in Lk 10:18, where Jesus said that he saw Satan falling from heaven like lightning (cf. Rev 12:3–4, 7–9; 20:1–3).

Satan, the devil, is here introduced into the prophetic message of Revelation. He will play a prominent role throughout the remainder of the message. Here in Revelation 9 he appears as a star and is identified as the angel of hell and the king of the demons who come out of the abyss. In Revelation 12, he will appear as the dragon, the archenemy of God and Christ and the church on earth. His minions and cohorts are represented by the two beasts of Revelation 13 and by Babylon, which consists of the first beast and the harlot (Revelation 17–18). He is the perpetrator of Armageddon in Revelation 16 and of Gog and Magog in Revelation 20. Finally, at the second coming of the Lord Christ, he will be cast forever into hell (Revelation 19–20).

The fallen star, the angel of the abyss, unlocks the depths of hell and from its hellish interior comes forth a smoke as from a large furnace of fire. The smoke is so widespread that the entire earth and its atmosphere are enveloped. It is so dense that the sun is unable fully to penetrate it and so appears darkened. The smoke and its darkness graphically portray the spiritual darkness that is perpetrated by the angel of the abyss, a darkness that covers the entire earth and its human population (cf. Gen 19:27–28; 2 Cor 6:14; Eph 2:2).

The Locust-Like Creatures from the Abyss and Their Purpose

Out of the rising smoke from the pit of hell (cf. 1 Enoch 21:7) come locust-like creatures who have the authority and power of scorpions on the earth. Their purpose is to afflict the human race, not the grass or trees or plant life. The trees and plant life and other natural entities important for sustaining life were afflicted by the plagues introduced by the earlier four trumpet-angels. Now out of the human race those who do not bear "the seal of God" (Rev 9:4) are singled out for affliction (see 7:1–8). Locusts have long been a natural phenomenon plaguing vegetation and as a result causing loss to human commerce and food production. Swarms of such locusts can wipe out entire crops and thus the live-lihood of people. In Ex 10:1–20 a plague of locusts descended on ancient Egypt and destroyed the vegetation of all the land. Joel 1:1–2:11 paints a terrifying, graphic picture of an invasion of locusts. All plant life before the horde of these creatures is wiped out (Joel 1:2–4). In Joel the locusts and the destruction they wreak portend the coming fury of God's judgment (Joel 1:13–15; 2:1–2, 11). Just as no human can stop and reverse the swarm of locusts and their devastation, so no one can abide and endure the dark and dreadful day of the Lord (Joel 2:11). Jesus in his earthly ministry also spoke of scorpions as representatives of the power of the enemy and his forces (Lk 10:17–20; cf. Lk 11:12).

As the locusts in Joel, so also the locust-like creatures here in Rev 9:3–4 embody something of the evil spiritual realm. In Joel they are a frightening phenomenon of nature to portray the terror of God's coming judgment. Here in Revelation 9 they portray the hordes of demons from hell which fall upon the human race. In John's vision the locusts have the ability to injure people as scorpions do. While locusts do not directly injure human beings, these locusts in John's vision, because they are like scorpions, do injure mankind. And while scorpions do not swarm and thus by their numbers darken the sky, these scorpions do so because they are like locusts.

These demons from the abyss afflict only those of the human race who do not belong to God. In the same way that the children of Israel were protected from the plagues that hit the Egyptians (Ex 8:20–23; 9:1–7, 25–26; 10:21–23), so now in this scene John hears the word that these locust-like scorpions are not to touch God's own people. This does not mean that God's people will not suffer at all from the onslaught of Satan and his hordes of demons. But that suffering will be pictured and emphasized later in Revelation in the warfare of the dragon against the church (12:13–18; 13:1–18). Here in Revelation 9 Satan is set loose to afflict only those who are not followers of the Lamb. God permits this to happen in order to move people to repentance (9:21). Consequently, Satan and his demons cannot kill but only injure. The warfare of the dragon against the church on earth is different.

Who gives to these locust-like, scorpion-like demons authority at this time to injure those not sealed with God's name? Behind the passive voice "was given" (9:3) stands the agency of God. As in the case of Job (1:6–12; 2:1–6), it is God who permits these demons to strike, in this case those who lack God's name. The demons and their king can go so far and no farther, for it is God's will that no sinner should die but that all should come to the knowledge of the truth (Ezek 18:23; 1 Tim 2:4; 2 Pet 3:9).

For a period of "five months" (Rev 9:5) unbelieving mankind is to be tormented. This time period may be modeled after the life cycle of locusts and thus suggests that the sufferings caused by the demons are not constant. At any given time throughout the period covered by Revelation's message (from Christ's ascension to his return), those not marked with the seal of God will suffer the anguish of these demonic torments, whether of a mental or physical kind. These sufferings will not always be present in a particular unbeliever's life, and when they are, they will not necessarily last an entire lifetime. The pain and suffering is likened to the sharp pain resulting from the sting of a scorpion. While not deadly, the pain and suffering inflicted by these demons, of whatever nature, will bring excruciating anguish—so severe that people will desire death. But no matter how much these unbelievers will long for death, thinking that death would bring release from the torment inflicted upon them, death will not come. This hindrance which blocks death from coming to them must be viewed as part of God's will. God does not permit this torment in order that this demonic affliction should *kill,* but rather that it (painfully) bring people to an awareness of their lost condition.

Job 3:20–26 is a graphic expression of the anguished cry of the soul which longs for death—death which never comes. The despairing soul searches for death as for a hidden treasure and a time of rejoicing (Job 3:21–22). But instead, as death and the grave continually recede, all the soul has is fear, restlessness, and despair (Job 3:26). In the case of Job, who was a man of God, his longing for death was not primarily for relief from the torments of Satan, but the desire to be reconciled to and present forever with his Savior God. The release would come in God's good time (Job 19:23–27; cf. Phil 1:21–23). Here in Rev 9:6 it is the ungodly person who is being so tormented. His belief that death would bring relief is a delusion, for without the sealing of God, physical death will bring "the second death" (20:6, 14; 21:8). Death flees from him so that he may have time to repent as he bears his torments and sufferings (cf. 9:20–21).

The locust-like, scorpion-like creatures resemble cavalry horses prepared to rush forward against a battle line. Upon their heads are crowns that *appear* to be of gold, giving the appearance of victory. However, the fact that their crowns only *seem* to be of gold indicates that the creatures are merely being *employed* by God for his own good purposes. Their overall appearance is grotesque and terrifying. The description of them is reminiscent of that of the locusts of Joel 2, overwhelming the land before the day of Yahweh. Thus the demon-like creatures of John's vision here in Revelation 9 will overwhelm the human race, in particular the ungodly.

These demons have faces like humans and hair like that of women. They will act with human intelligence in cunning deception as well as with human beauty in cruel attraction. Their teeth are like those of lions. In Joel 1:6, when the invading locusts are likened to an invading nation, they are pictured with teeth of a lion and fangs of a lioness. The demon-like creatures here in Revelation 9 will be ferocious and savage in their attack, though they will not physically tear asunder their victims. However, the fierceness of their attack in the mental and spiritual dimensions, which could affect one's physical health as well, will be as if the victim were being torn apart, but not fatally so.

Their armor is that of a foot soldier. Thus in their attack these evil creatures from the abyss would be protected from counterattack. The noise of their attack, as sounded by the loud buzzing of their wings, was in human ears like the noise of chariots and horses rushing into battle. Whether taken as a physical noise of numerous chariot wheels and horses' hoofs, which could be deafening the closer they approached, or whether this noise is taken as a metaphor, the fear alone caused by even the rumor of their approach will instill terror in the intended victims.

Like scorpions, these locusts dressed in battle armor have tails in which are embedded stings by which they torture their prey. While the sting of the venomous tail of a scorpion is usually not lethal to humans, it can be torturously painful. Again, their ability to torment mankind is for the period of "five months" (Rev 9:10). As in 9:5, this period of time suggests an on-again, off-again ordeal to which these demons subject their victims. Like a cat playing with a terrified and helpless mouse, so the human victims of these hordes from hell are playthings of their craft and cunning.

The locust-like, scorpion-like creatures have over them a recognized leader, a king who directs and rules their actions. He is identified as "the angel of the abyss" (9:11). This angel of the abyss is pictured in 12:3–9 as the dragon who attempts to destroy the Child of the woman but fails. In 12:7–9 he is the leader of the rebellious angels and is identified as "the ancient serpent, who is called the devil and Satan" (cf. 20:1–3). He bears the name "Destroyer" here in 9:11. This is the only instance in the Bible where "Destroyer" is a personal name of the devil. His more common name is Satan, which means "the Adversary." Both names, "Satan" and "Destroyer," define the devil's character and purpose. He attempts *to destroy* all that is holy and godly. His most grievous attempt was the destruction of the Christ Child (Rev 12:3–4; cf. Mt 2:16–18; 4:1–11). But now his destructive powers are used against the church, God's people on earth, the body of Christ (Rev 12:13–18). The devil also attempts *to accuse* God's people in such a manner that they would believe that their sins are not forgiven (see Rev 12:9–12).

Here in 9:1–11, however, the victims of the angel of the abyss and his demonic hordes in their attempt to destroy and accuse are not God's saints, but rather the ungodly portion of the human race. The attempt of the devil and his minions to destroy and falsely accuse the Christians will be visually portrayed from 12:13 onward. But here the devil and his servants are set loose so as to attack human beings not sealed with the seal of God. The emphasis here in Revelation 9 is on his *destructive* character rather than his slanderous accusations. His ultimate purpose is the destruction of the human race, that people not believe the Gospel and so not enjoy the fruits of Christ's victory. But he and his demonic, locust-like monsters are restrained from achieving the complete destruction of these human beings. God permits them only to injure and torment, but not to kill (9:3–5). The Lord Christ is still in control.

"The first woe has come and gone" (9:12). Of the final three woes introduced by the last three trumpet-angels, the first dire warning has sounded; two more are to come. But the time is short (1:3).

THE SIXTH TRUMPET-ANGEL: THE LAST BATTLE (9:13–21)

At the sound of the trumpet of the sixth angel, John hears "one voice" coming "from the four horns of the golden incense altar which is before God" in heaven (9:13). The voice could be that of the angel of the altar who has a censer of incense which represented the prayers of God's saints (8:3–5), or it could be the voice of the souls of God's saints who are beneath the incense altar, that is, the collective voice of their prayers to God (6:9–11). Most likely it is both; these two sources are in harmony, so united they comprise "*one* voice" (9:13). The prayers of the saints implore God to judge the people on earth who had caused their suffering (6:10), and the smoke from the censer of the angel at the altar, together with the prayers of the saints, rises to God as he is about to show his anger and judgment on the inhabitants of the earth by way of the trumpet-angels (8:4–5). The voice speaks under the authority of God and for the sake of his people.

The voice instructs the sixth trumpet-angel, who has already sounded his horn, to "release the four angels who have been bound at the great river Euphrates" (9:14). The first five trumpet-angels blew their horns and thus introduced the respective scenes of the second earthly vision, but they had no part in the action that each scene depicted. Here in the sixth scene the trumpet-angel not only introduces the scene by the blast of his horn, he also is part of the action that is displayed. If the seven trumpet-angels are the angels of the seven churches, then the angel of the sixth church is also this sixth trumpet-angel.

The sixth church is the church in Philadelphia. In the letter to the angel of that congregation (3:7–13), the exalted Son of Man says that in the hour of the "trial" which will come upon the whole earth, and which thus will "test" its inhabitants, those who have kept his Word will be kept safe (3:10). Then the Lord says that he *is* coming quickly (3:11). The contents of that sixth letter fit and relate to what is now to be revealed to John by way of the sixth trumpet-angel. In the sixth scene John will see intense testing of the inhabitants of the whole earth as the four angels are let loose, the "trial" (3:10) that will take place just before the End at Christ's return. Rev 9:13–21 does not speak specifically of God's people, but when this "trial" envelopes the earth, they too will experience it (see 20:7–10), and (according to 3:10–11) they will be kept safe no matter how much they suffer. The sixth trumpet-angel is the angel who, under God's authority, *controls* the forces that are to be let loose so that they cause much affliction (as described in this sixth scene) but do not overturn God's ultimate plan of salvation.

The Four Angels from the Great River Euphrates

At the instruction of the angel of the incense altar, the sixth trumpet-angel releases the four angels who up to this moment have been bound, held inactive, at the River Euphrates. This river in Mesopotamia, together with the Tigris River, ran through the territories of Assyria and Babylonia, Israel's ancient enemies. God had promised to Abraham the land from the Nile in Egypt to the Euphrates. From the northeast, across the Euphrates, the enemies of Israel often came to afflict her, and if possible, to destroy her (Is 8:1–10; 2 Ki 25:1–26). Thus the enemies of Israel are frequently described as coming from the north (Is 43:5–6; Jer 1:13; 4:5–6; 25:8–11).

Because the Euphrates and the north were the place and direction from which the *historical* enemies came to bring fear and destruction to Israel, this area came to be used also as a symbol for the place from which the *eschatological* enemies of God's people would come. So Ezekiel prophesied that Gog of the land of Magog would come from "the far north" and with his hordes advance against Israel and cover the entire land like a dark cloud (Ezek 38:15–20). All this would happen by God's permission, according to his will in judgment. When that judgment had accomplished its purpose, God would then turn on Gog and destroy him as he rescued his people (Ezek 38:21–23; 39:1–8). So here in Rev 9:14 the River Euphrates is used as a symbol of the place from which will come the eschatological hordes of evil that will be unleashed upon the human race.

Who are "the four angels" (9:14) who are held back—restrained—at the great river Euphrates? They have been prepared for their particular task (9:15). They stand ready to be unleashed at a certain predetermined time. Whatever they represent and whatever they will do, these four angels are not operative all through the time period covered by the message of Revelation (from Christ's ascension to his return). Rather, they will be set in motion and will work in a set time defined as an "hour and day and month and year" (9:15; see further comments below).

The definite article ("the") suggests that these four angels are a definite, particular group of four. Their association with the evil forces that will assault the human race could lead one to conjecture that they were demonic, fallen angels. But that is not likely, for the word "angel" throughout Revelation always refers to the holy angels of God, unless identified otherwise. Rather, these four angels are a definite group of holy angels acting under God's will. The only other place in Revelation where four angels are mentioned is in 7:1–3. In 7:1 four angels hold back the four winds (representing the four horsemen of 6:1–8) until God's people on earth are sealed. Here in 9:14 the four angels have a similar task, that of holding back the forces of evil until the appointed time of their release, when the evil forces would afflict the human race. The definite article here in 9:14–15 could indicate that they are the same angels who held back the four winds in 7:1–3. Perhaps here the identification is that of roles rather than of persons, that is, the four angels of 9:14–15 have a similar role to play—that of restraining evil forces—but are not necessarily the same angels as those in 7:1–3.

The four angels in 7:1–3 and also here in 9:14–15 are angels of judgment and punishment. Within Judaism the idea of angels meting out punishment on behalf of God is not uncommon. For example, in 1 Enoch 53:3–5 angels dispense plagues and punishment on the earth (cf. 1 Enoch 62:11). In 1 Enoch 56:1 such angels are called "the angels of punishment," and in 1 Enoch 63:1 they are referred to as "the angels of his [God's] punishment" (cf. also 2 Enoch 10:1–3; Testament of Levi 3:3). This tradition of angels of punishment is most likely derived from Gen 19:1–29, which describes how angels, on behalf of God, punished and destroyed Sodom and Gomorrah (cf. also 2 Ki 19:35–36; 2 Chr 32:20–21; Is 37:35–37). The four angels here in Rev 9:14–15, who are held back and then released, act under the authority of God, as indicated by the fact that the angel of the incense altar is the one who gives the command that they be released. The fact that the sixth trumpet-angel is the one who, at that command, actually releases them demonstrates that their release is for the aid of the church and her mission (see 8:1–5; 10:8–11).

The four angels are prepared and will act during a definite time period—not the whole period from Christ's ascension to his second coming, but rather a period of time within that greater length of time. The time period of an "hour and day and month and year" in 9:15 appears only here in Revelation and, in fact, in the entire Bible. In Greek a single definite article (rendered in this commentary's translation as "this") introduces the entire phrase, suggesting a specific period of time

Whatever this expression may mean, it certainly points to a definite time within the whole period covered by the prophetic message of Revelation (from Christ's ascension to his parousia). The fact that it is mentioned in the sixth trumpet-angel's revelation could indicate that this time period may be just before the end of earthly time, which will be described in what the seventh trumpet-angel will reveal (11:15–19). The time period could thus suggest that the sufferings perpetrated by the evil forces let loose on the human race will occupy every moment of every day, every day of every month, and every month of each year in the evil times just before the Lord's return.

The evil forces let loose from under the angels' control, by permission of the will of God, will destroy a third of the human race. Up to now, the elements and forces of nature on earth and the elements and natural bodies above the earth have been struck (as revealed by the first four trumpet-angels, 8:6–13) and as a result have caused mankind to suffer. Also the human race was tormented by the demonic spirits from the abyss (as revealed by the fifth trumpet-angel, 9:1–11). However, no one of the human race was killed by such natural and demonic assaults (cf. 9:5). But now a large portion—one-third—of the human race is killed. When in the fifth scene John saw the locust-like demons tormenting mankind, people sought death but it eluded them (9:6). Now death seeks them out and grasps them as a result of the evil forces released on the earth. While only a third die, the number of people killed will be staggering. The remaining two-thirds, while escaping death, will live under its terror (cf. Heb 2:15).

As in the fifth scene (9:1–12), the forces of evil that wreak such havoc upon the human race in this sixth scene are demonic in character, as attested by their number and grotesque appearance (9:16–19). They number in the millions, an unimaginable, countless force of cavalry that invades the earth. Such a vast number is reminiscent of the tens of thousands upon thousands of holy angels and chariots which attended God when he left Sinai for his sanctuary, as declared in Ps 68:17 (MT 68:18; cf. Deut 33:2; Dan 7:10). Such a number would be staggering, but John attests that he actually heard their number (Rev 9:16). The horses in their visionary appearance had heads like lions, demonstrating that they would terrorize and conquer all before them. In 9:8 the locust-like demons had teeth like those of lions, by which they would torment but not kill. Here these demonic creatures have heads of lions by which they not only torment but also kill. From their mouths they breathe out fire and smoke and brimstone, by which they plague and kill a third of the human population. Those who sat on these fire breathing monsters had breastplates which matched the fiery smoke and brimstone of the lion-like mouths of the beasts they rode. This cavalry force is invincible as it invades and kills. Those who are not killed by the plague of fire are killed by the plague of smoke and by the plague of brimstone. Did this bring to John's mind the rain of fire and brimstone that destroyed Sodom and Gomorrah (Gen 19:24–28)? Most likely John would have remembered the destruction of Pompeii in AD 79 by the eruption of Mt. Vesuvius as a possible illustration of the devastation these demonic-like monsters would unleash on the entire human race.

The authority and power of these cavalry-like demons to attack the human race is not confined to their mouths, for by their tails they also strike people. Their tails have heads and are like serpents. By the three plagues of their mouths they kill; by their serpent-like tails they injure and torment people (compare 9:19 to 9:10). This suggests that the two-thirds of humanity that is not killed is nevertheless tormented and made to suffer. None will escape their fury.

Tragically, even though they see their fellow human beings fearfully killed and even though they themselves suffer, those who temporarily evade death do not repent of their works (9:20). They do not let themselves be turned away from worshiping "the works of their hands" (9:20). "The works of their hands" (9:20) is an expression denoting the full range of human activities in life, particularly occupations and livelihoods. It can also, as here in 9:20, refer to idols which people have fashioned and set up before themselves. The idols of gold and silver and other materials are the lifeless objects of their worship (cf. Is 44:9–20; 1 Sam 5:1–5), worship inspired by demons. As a result of their idolatry they are really worshiping demons, whether knowingly or unknowingly. Pagan idolatrous worship throughout the Bible is attributed to demons, and such worship is also offered to demons (Ps 106:36–38; 1 Cor 10:19–20). Such idolatrous, demonic worship comes from a mind that is unfit and ruined because it ignored and re-jected the knowledge of God the Creator (Rom 1:18–25). The intended purpose of idolatrous worship is always the betterment of one's own fortunes in life. Therefore it seeks to glorify creatures, in particular human beings, instead of God, their Creator and Redeemer. Of this worship the people did not repent.

Therefore any alternative to Christ and to faith in him alone is idolatry (1 Jn 5:21). The idols fashioned by people can never respond to their worship, heed their prayers, or sustain and save their life, for these idols have no heart, no love, no ears—no preserving or redemptive ability (Ps 115:4–7; cf. Ps 135:15–18; 1 Ki 18:27–29; see also Deut 4:32–35; Deut 32:16–17; Ps 96:5; Jer 10:5; 1 Cor 8:4; 1 Cor 10:19).

Of such idolatrous worship the people do not repent. Under the influence of the demons they worship, and hardened because of their lack of repentance, they commit murder and robbery of all kinds and indulge in witchcraft and all manner of sexual immorality. Idolatry leads to increasingly shameful acts, escalating guilt, and encouragement to sin all the more as they applaud each other in their degeneracy (Rom 1:24–32). The Greek word in Rev 9:21 for "witchcraft, magic" at the time of John's writing of Revelation included any form of witchcraft and spiritism, occult or magical arts, which included drugs, spells, rituals, ostensibly "good" magic, and discernment of the future. In Gal 5:20 in the list of sins of the flesh, witchcraft is mentioned after idolatry, and in Rev 21:8 people who are engaged in witchcraft and idolatry do not enter the new heaven and new earth (cf. 22:15).

This sixth scene (9:13–21) in the second earthly vision (8:6–11:19), of the demonic hordes unleashed from the control of the four angels, is related to the scene which the sixth censer-angel introduces (16:12–16) in the third earthly vision (15:1–16:21). Both are for a particular time period, and both are the sixth of seven scenes. The sixth scene of the third earthly vision depicts the battle of Armageddon just before the end of this world at Christ's return. This last battle is also connected with the River Euphrates (16:12). Here in 9:13–21 John receives the first glimpse of that last battle, the last great affliction. In it he sees the forces of evil poised and ready to be unleashed. As they are released they afflict the human race with death and suffering. In 16:12–16 John sees again a view of this last battle. It is not just a duplication of what he saw in 9:13–21, for in the second view of it he sees this same demonic host, pouring out from the Euphrates over all the earth, actually gathered for and engaged in battle at a place called Armageddon. This second view complements the first. Finally, a third time he will see this last battle just before the End when, in a vision, Gog and Magog appear (20:7–10). This third view of the battle depicts its conclusion and the final defeat of the evil forces involved in it.

REVELATION 10:1–11

FIRST SCENE OF THE INTERLUDE: THE MIGHTY ANGEL FROM HEAVEN COMMISSIONS JOHN

TRANSLATION

10 [1]And I saw another mighty angel coming down out of heaven, who was clothed about with a cloud, and the rainbow-like halo was upon his head, and his face was like the sun, and his legs like pillars of fire, [2]and he has in his hand a small scroll, which has been opened. And he placed his foot, the right one, on the sea, and the left one on the land. [3]And he cried out in a loud voice as when a lion roars. And when he cried out, the seven thunders spoke their own voices. [4]And when the seven thunders spoke, I was about to write, but I heard a voice from heaven saying, "Seal what the seven thunders have spoken, for you must not write those things." [5]And the angel, whom I saw standing on the sea and on the land, raised his hand, the right one, toward heaven, [6]and he swore by the One who lives forever and ever, he who created the heaven and the things in it and the earth and the things in it and the sea and the things in it, [he swore to affirm] that no longer will there be time, [7]but rather [that] in the days of the sound of the seventh angel, when he is about to blow his trumpet, then will have been completed the mystery of God, as he graciously promised to his own slaves, the prophets. [8]And the voice which I heard from heaven again was speaking with me and saying, "Go, take the scroll which has been opened in the hand of the angel who is standing on the sea and on the land." [9]And

I went up to the angel, saying to him to give to me
the small scroll. And he says to me, "Take and eat
it, and it will embitter your stomach, but in your
mouth it will be sweet as honey." [10]And I took the
small scroll from the hand of the angel and I ate it,
and it was in my mouth as sweet honey, but when I
ate it, my stomach was embittered. [11]And they say
to me, "It is necessary that you again prophesy over
many peoples and nations and tongues and kings."

COMMENTARY

As in the first vision of events on earth (6:1–8:5), so also now in the second
earthly vision (8:6–11:19) there is an interlude between the sixth and seventh
scenes. In the first earthly vision the interlude (7:1–17) came between the sixth
and seventh seals, and it had to do with the protection and the comfort of the
church in the midst of her sufferings on earth. In the second earthly vision, the
interlude (10:1–11:14), placed between the sixth and seventh trumpet-angels,
pictures the church in mission and God's protection of her in that mission.

The interlude consists of two scenes. In the first a mighty angel from heaven
commissions John to proclaim the prophetic message to all the world (10:1–11).
In the second scene John sees two witnesses, who symbolize the church in
mission, proclaiming the message as they fulfill the mission of their Lord
(11:3–14). That second scene, which graphically pictures the church in mission,
is introduced by a glimpse of John measuring the temple of God (11:1–2). The
measuring of the temple, with its worshipers within, assures John that the two
witnesses—the church—will be protected by God so as to enable them to carry
out their mission.

ANOTHER MIGHTY ANGEL
FROM HEAVEN (10:1)

The first thing that John sees in this first scene of the interlude (10:1–11)
is an "angel coming down out of heaven" (10:1). The angel is introduced as
"another" angel. This means that this angel is not one of the seven angels of the
churches who have the trumpets, the angels who mediate the second earthly
vision and its scenes. While the seven trumpet-angels are mediators of the
prophetic message on behalf of the Lord Christ, this angel from heaven has an
entirely different role, that of commissioning (or recommissioning) John on
behalf of the exalted Christ.

"Mighty"

The angel is furthermore introduced as a "mighty" angel (10:1). Only three
angels in Revelation are designated as "mighty": (1) the angel who cried out

asking whether there was anyone worthy to receive the scroll and open its seals and by this action introduced the victorious Lamb in the heavenly vision of God's throne (5:2); (2) the angel here in Revelation 10; and (3) the angel who demonstrates the judgment of Babylon (18:21, who probably is the same angel mentioned in 18:1, where he in a "mighty" voice announces the fall of Babylon, 18:2–3). "Another" (10:1) suggests that this mighty angel in Revelation 10 is probably not the same as the mighty angel in 5:2.

This distinctive adjective "mighty" often connotes godly strength or might from God, or it describes the might of God himself. Though the Greek translation of the OT does use this word to describe both people and things on earth (e.g., Gen 41:31; Num 13:31), it never uses it for an angel or any heavenly figure other than God

In the NT "mighty" appears twenty-nine times, nine in Revelation. Among its uses are references to Jesus Christ as "mightier" than John the Baptist (Mt 3:11; Mk 1:7; Lk 3:16) and to the "mighty man" who metaphorically represents Satan (Mt 12:29; Mk 3:27; Lk 11:21), though Jesus is represented by the comparative form "a mightier man" (Lk 11:22). But it is never used of an angel. Of the nine times that "mighty" appears in Revelation, one is in connection with God (18:8); two are in connection with human beings (6:15; 19:18); one is in connection with Babylon (18:10); one with a voice of a crowd of people which is likened to "mighty, crashing" thunders (19:6); three with angels (5:2; 10:1; 18:21); and one with a "mighty" voice of an angel (18:2). Revelation is the only book in the entire Greek Bible which uses "mighty" to describe or identify an angel.

John probably was aware of all of this. Nevertheless, he, alone of all biblical translators and authors, does use such a word for an angel here in Revelation 10.

Because the angel here in 10:1 is called "mighty," some have conjectured that this is a cryptic way of identifying this angel as Gabriel. Gabriel in Hebrew does mean "mighty one of God." Both the angels Gabriel and Michael appear in Daniel, and some have suggested that as Michael has a role in Revelation (12:7), so also Gabriel appears in a role as the "mighty" angel from heaven here in 10:1. However, John does not recognize this angel as Gabriel. When John does recognize the angel Michael, he will identify him in 12:7. Since Gabriel is well known not only from the book of Daniel but also from the role he played in the birth of Jesus (Lk 1:19, 26), most likely John would have recognized him as Gabriel, and even if not, the angel would have identified himself as such. But since John does not recognize him and since the angel does not identify himself as Gabriel, most likely this "mighty" angel is not that particular archangel.

The fact that this angel is called "mighty" does not mean that this angel has divine power inherent in his own nature and character. Rather, identifying the angel as "mighty" suggests a *divine-like power* by which and under which he carries out his role on behalf of God. Thus, the description of the angel of Rev

10:1 as "mighty" could indicate that he is close to God's heavenly glory and acts in his power and under his powerful authority.

"Coming Down Out of Heaven"

The angel is "coming down out of heaven" (10:1). Heaven is the dwelling place of God (11:19). "Out of heaven" declares that this angel is from God's holy presence and is sent out by God. In 3:12 and 21:2 "out of heaven" and "from God" appear in apposition, suggesting that to come from heaven means to come from God. Two other times John sees an angel descending from heaven. In 18:1–2 an angel announces in a "mighty voice" the judgment of Babylon, the archenemy of God's people on earth. This angel appears to be the same as the "mighty angel" in 18:21, who throws a millstone into the sea, symbolic of Babylon's destruction. In 20:1–2 John also sees an angel coming down out of heaven to bind Satan. In all three cases the angel acts under God's authority and in his stead. "Clothed About with a Cloud"

The angel is "clothed about with a cloud" (10:1). In the OT a cloud is often associated with God, in particular with his presence among his people. In the form of a pillar the cloud indicated God's presence by which he led and protected Israel in the wilderness (Ex 13:21; 14:19–20; Num 9:17–21). It was through a cloud that God spoke to Moses on Mt. Sinai and at the entrance of the tabernacle (Ex 24:15–18; Deut 31:15–16). The cloud was also a demonstration of God's glory (Ex 16:10), in particular when the cloud covered the tabernacle (Ex 40:34–35). In Ezek 10:3–4 a cloud similarly conveyed the presence of God's glory in and out of the temple. The cloud is also referred to as a conveyance or heavenly vehicle of God (Ps 104:3; Is 19:1; Ezek 1:4).

On occasion a cloud is associated with a heavenly figure who is designated by a term or terms other than "God" or "Yahweh," but in these cases the figure nevertheless seems to be God or a person of the triune Godhead. In Dan 7:13 in the heavenly court the Son of Man approaches the Ancient of Days accompanied by clouds. In Ex 14:19–20 "the angel of God" is connected with the pillar of cloud by which God protected Israel from the Egyptians, and "the angel of God" (Ex 14:19) is apparently the same as "Yahweh" (Ex 13:21; 14:24). Thus the cloud is associated with both Yahweh himself and the angel of God.

This significance of the cloud is carried over into the NT. God speaks to Jesus from a cloud on the mount of transfiguration (Mt 17:5; Mk 9:7; Lk 9:35). Like the Son of Man in Dan 7:13, Jesus, the Son of Man, will come on clouds when he returns to earth in judgment at the End (Mt 24:30; Mk 13:26; Lk 21:27). A cloud also received Jesus as he ascended into heaven (Acts 1:9; cf. 1 Thess 4:17; Rev 11:12).

In Revelation "cloud" appears seven times, either in the plural or singular, and in every instance for a supernatural purpose. Rev 1:7 says that Jesus Christ will come "with the clouds" and everyone will see him, even those who pierced him. In 11:12 the two witnesses, who represent the church in mission, after their resurrection are taken into heaven "on the cloud," similar to the Lord's ascension when a cloud enveloped and removed him from the sight of his disciples. In 14:14–16, at the coming of the Lord Christ, a "white cloud" appears, and the Son of Man is sitting on the cloud and on or from it he executes the "harvest" at the End.

Here in 10:1, because the angel is "clothed about with a cloud," it seems clear that the cloud was not a *conveyance* by which the angel descended from heaven (as it will be at the second coming of Jesus; cf. also Mt 24:30). Nor does the angel *speak* to John from the cloud, as God did to Jesus and the three apostles (Mt 17:5). Rather, the mighty angel is *clothed, wrapped around,* with a cloud as if it were his garment. The form of the Greek verb indicates that *before* the angel descended from heaven, he was "clothed about" with a cloud *by someone other than himself* (cf. Zech 3:3–4). Thus the angel came to John not on his own authority but by that of God.

Elsewhere in the entire Bible, only God is ever spoken of as having been covered or clothed with a cloud. In Lam 3:42–44 God covers himself with a cloud in order to conceal himself from his people because of his anger over their sins. Nevertheless, a cloud could also be *a majestic covering which exhibits the glory of God.* In Ezek 1:4 the cloud with flashing lightning reflects the heavenly glory of God (cf. Ezek 1:28). Like the pillar of cloud in the wilderness, which was at night a pillar of fire and light (Ex 13:21–22), so also the majestic covering of the cloud, by which God clothed himself, could be a covering of light. The cloud in Ezekiel, with its flashes of lightning (Ezek 1:4, 13), was also connected with a rainbow (Ezek 1:28), and thus all the more was God's heavenly glory visually exhibited.

Other than God, the angel of Rev 10:1 is the only figure in the Bible who is clothed with a cloud. (He also has a rainbow; see below.) In the case of God the cloud can conceal his glory (Lam 3:44) or it can exhibit and display it (Ezek 1:4, 28). In the case of the angel of Rev 10:1 the cloud can be both for concealment and display. The angel's own person and identity is *concealed* in order to show and emphasize that he is acting not on his own authority, but rather on that of God. The cloud also represents the glory and majesty under which he acts on behalf of God in order to *demonstrate* that his mission is a godly and glorious one. The cloud is thus a token or heraldic emblazonment which points to the fact that the angel is a herald and messenger acting directly within God's glory and under his authority. The angel wears the mantle of God as he commissions John to proclaim the message to all peoples (10:11).

"THE RAINBOW-LIKE HALO"

A second identifying mark of the angel is "the rainbow-like halo" (10:1). A rainbow-like halo in 4:3 encircled the heavenly throne of God (cf. Ezek 1:28). There the rainbow appears as a reminder of God's promise to the human race and his creation (Gen 8:22; 9:13–17) and also of his gracious covenant of salvation toward humankind (Is 54:8–9). The fact that the definite article ("*the rainbow*") introduces the angel's rainbow suggests that it is to be identified with or related to that of God's throne. *The angel's rainbow has the same significance as the rainbow that surrounds God's throne. God has placed on the angel the visible token and sign of his covenant of grace with the human race.* The angel's rainbow is a reflection of the rainbow encircling the throne of God, and it thus reminds John of God's merciful covenant by which he has bound himself to the human race and his creation.

The particular Greek word for "rainbow" that John uses here ("iris") might have led some of his hearers to think of Iris, a messenger of the gods in Greek mythology. In particular this messenger was known as the goddess of the rainbow and was the attendant and messenger of Juno, the wife and queen of Jupiter. When Iris acted as a messenger, she wore a garment of many colors—the colors of the rainbow. When a rainbow appeared in the skies, those familiar with Greek mythology might think of this goddess messenger and wonder whether the gods were sending some kind of message to human beings on earth. Whether John was conscious of this when he used this word is a matter of conjecture, but he is the only translator or author in the Greek Bible (OT and NT) to use this word for "rainbow." If John used this word with knowledge of its pagan mythological background, he did so to indicate that *the angel of Rev 10 is a messenger of the one true God, who has bound himself with his creation in a covenant.*

This angel is on a heraldic mission in which he demonstrates and reflects both God's glory and mercy—God's glory as the Creator and God's mercy in his covenant with the human race. The angel's mission is one by which this divine glory and saving mercy will be proclaimed and adorned.

"Face … Like the Sun"

A third identifying indicator is the face of the angel: "his face was like the sun" (10:1). While the cloud and rainbow-like halo demonstrate a relationship with God the Father, the sunlit face suggests a relationship with Jesus Christ, for in 1:16 the "appearance" of Christ as the Son of Man shines like the sun. In the OT this description of a "face … like the sun" is not encountered. But the skin of Moses' face shone (Ex 34:29–35), and the Shulammite is described as "looking down like the dawn, beautiful like the moon, bright like the sun" (Song 6:10). Also the Aaronic benediction pronounces the blessing "Yahweh make his face shine upon you" (Num 6:25), a thought echoed in the psalms. In the above instances, however, God's sun-like glory is reflected and/or directed toward individuals. But the sun is used as a symbol for glory only for God (e.g., Is 60:1–3, 20; Ps 84:11) and for the messianic figure mentioned in Mal 4:1–2.

It is in the NT in particular that this explicit description of a face like the sun is used. In Matthew's account of the transfiguration Jesus' face "shone like the sun" (Mt 17:2). This indicates that Jesus has God's radiant glory, to which he will return after his death and resurrection (Mt 17:9; cf. Jn 17:1–5; 2 Pet 1:16–18). In Rev 1:16, when the exalted Christ appeared to John to commission him to write the revelation, his face and appearance were like the sun, thus demonstrating that he is now in glory (cf. Jn 1:4; 8:12; Heb 1:3).

The only other figure in the NT whose face is like the sun is this angel of Revelation 10. While other angels are associated with light and glory (Rev 18:1; cf. Lk 9:26; Acts 12:7) and with the sun (Rev 19:17), only the angel here in Revelation 10 has a "face … like the sun." There are, however, three stated differences between the exalted Christ's appearance, which shone like the sun (1:16), and that of the angel. First, 1:16 says that Jesus' "appearance" was like the sun. Here in 10:1 only the "face" of the angel was like the sun. This is a marked and important difference. In Mt 17:2, in his transfigured glory, only Jesus' face was like the sun, as is the angel's face here in Rev 10:1. However, because Jesus' outer garments were "white like the light," Christ's *whole appearance* was like the "light" of the sun (Mt 17:2). Furthermore, when the exalted Lord Christ appears to John in Rev 1:16, it is clearly stated that not only his face but also his whole appearance was like the sun. Because only the angel's face is like the sun and not his whole appearance, *with no hint that his outer garment was like the light but rather with the statement instead that it was a cloud,* the angel is not the light as Christ is. Rather, he reflects that sunlit glory, that light of the exalted Christ.

This interpretation is supported further by the second stated difference. Rev 1:16 states that Christ's appearance "was like the sun when it shines *in its full power,*" in its most brilliant light. In contrast, the angel's face is only "*like* the sun" (10:1), indicating the sun in its lesser or dimmed light. This suggests an element of comparison, namely, that the appearance and the face of Jesus were brighter than that of the angel. While both the exalted Christ and the angel radiate the glory of God, they do not do so in equal measure. The exalted Lord Christ radiates God's glory in full strength, because he actually shares in that glory. The angel also radiates that same glory, but in a lesser degree of brilliance, for he is not a sharer of that glory as Christ is.

The third difference is that because of the brilliant appearance of Christ "like the sun when it shines in its full power" (1:16), John fell down at Jesus' feet "as dead" (1:17). He could not possibly stand before the Lord Christ in all of his exalted glory. When Christ appeared on the mount of transfiguration—a preview of this exalted glory into which he would enter after his resurrection at his ascension—the disciples fell on their faces at the voice of the Father from heaven (Mt 17:6). It was a voluntary falling down, an act of worship. But when Christ appeared to John to commission him to write Revelation, the apostle did not fall down voluntarily in worship. He was knocked down and became "as dead," so overwhelmed was he by the brilliant glory of the exalted Christ (cf. Jn 18:6). In Revelation 10, however, even though the angel's face was like the sun,

John did not fall down before him, either involuntarily or voluntarily, in awe or in an act of worship.

"Legs Like Pillars of Fire"

The final thing John notes about the angel's appearance is that "his legs" were "like pillars of fire" (10:1). No other figure in biblical literature is so described. However, the angel's legs are reminiscent of the feet of Jesus Christ in 1:15 and of the legs of the angelic figure (the Son of Man) in Dan 10:4–6. In Jewish literature such legs or feet are not unknown. For example, in the Apocalypse of Zephaniah (6:13), a great angel is described with feet of bronze which had been melted in fire. In the OT, in the Song of Songs (5:15) the male lover is described with legs that were like pillars of marble (cf. Dan 2:31–35). But none of these figures has feet or legs like the angel of Revelation 10. The only pillar of fire mentioned in the Bible is that of Exodus 13–14, the pillar of cloud and of fire by which Yahweh and his angel led and protected Israel in the wilderness. Whatever interpretation can be derived from the brass-like feet of Jesus in Rev 1:15 (such as representing victory and dominance over enemies like death and the grave) or from the symbolism of the pillar of fire in the OT (such as guidance and protection), the legs of this angel suggest a stability and fearful power which cannot be resisted. Perhaps the angel's legs, like pillars of fire, combine both the symbolism of Jesus' brass-like feet and of the pillar of fire. Because Jesus is the conqueror of death and the grave, symbolized by his brass-like feet, this angel now (as a result of that victory) is on a mission for God and Christ, a mission that will prevail and be victorious. Just as it was by means of the pillar of cloud and fire that God protected his people at the exodus (Ex 14:19–20), so now this angel's legs, being like pillars of fire, remind John that, as the mission of the angel is carried out, God will protect and guide his people in that mission.

AN OPENED SMALL SCROLL (10:2A)

The angel has "in his hand a small scroll, which has been opened" (Rev 10:2). Though the "scroll" is identified in the Greek as both a "small scroll" (10:2, 9, 10) and a "scroll" (10:8), it is probably smaller in size than the seven-sealed scroll of 5:1, 4, 8. Also the fact that the seven-sealed scroll of the victorious Lamb controls the entire prophetic message of Revelation, of which the angel of Revelation 10 and his scroll are a part, supports this interpretation.

More important than the size, however, are the contents of the scroll and its symbolical role. The exact contents of the scroll are not stated, but surely it is related in some way to the seven-sealed scroll in Revelation 5.

The symbolical usage of this "small scroll" helps to determine its possible subject matter, for John is to eat it and then proclaim its contents to all peoples (10:11). We may conclude that the small scroll contains part or all the seven-sealed scroll of Revelation 5. The seven-sealed scroll contained the prophetic message of events to take place from the ascension of Christ up to his second coming; that same message (symbolized now by the scroll of the angel) is given to John to receive (to eat) and then to proclaim to all people. First John was instructed to proclaim the revelation of Jesus Christ to the seven churches, that is, *to all of God's people on earth* (1:4, 11). The revelation is encapsulated in the seven-sealed scroll (Revelation 5). Now in Revelation 10 John is also to proclaim this same prophetic message, symbolized now by the angel's scroll, *to the entire population of the earth* (10:11). The scroll of the seven seals at first was unopened; its message was secret until the victorious Lamb received it from God (5:1–5). The scroll of this angel is already opened (10:2, 8), signifying that its message is known to John, for it is the same message as that of the seven-sealed scroll. Its contents need not be identified here, for the purpose of the angel's small scroll is not to give a further explanation of nor to repeat the same message of the seven-sealed scroll, but rather to act as *a symbol of the seven-sealed scroll's message.* John's eating of the scroll symbolizes the action of John to take the one prophetic message, to make it first a part of himself, and then to proclaim it to the world. If the angel's scroll were smaller in size, perhaps it would be because the prophetic message given to the church (the seven-sealed scroll) would contain more; for example, the seven-sealed scroll included the suffering the church would endure and how God would protect and comfort his people (7:1–17). The message (of the angel's small scroll) that is now to be proclaimed to the world by John and the church, while *in essence* the same as the message that reveals and alerts the Christians as to what is to happen (4:1, the seven-sealed scroll), would *not necessarily* be given *in the same amount of detail.* The proclaimer needs to know the full message of Law and Gospel even if he is to speak to others only a condensed summary of it.

STANDING ASTRIDE SEA AND LAND (10:2B)

The angel "placed his foot, the right one, on the sea, and the left one on the land" (10:2) while still holding the scroll in his hand. In the OT, "sea" and "land" are elements in a formula that expresses the totality of all things created: the heavens and earth and sea. While the formula is often used in contexts that have in view God as the Creator of all things, including the heavens, here in 10:2 "land" and "sea" focus just on the totality of the earth (Ps 146:5–10; 1 Cor 15:25–28; Eph 1:20–22). By straddling the entire earth the angel demonstrates that he—and the mission on which God sent him—will dominate the earth, its history, its people, its present and future—everything. In particular, the angel and his mission dominate the two beasts that come out of the sea and land as pictured in Revelation 13. These two beasts under the direction of the dragon (12:17–13:3) are the great enemies of God's people and their mission on earth. But for the sake of that mission the angel places his feet on the sea and land, that is, on the two beasts (cf. Gen 3:15; Rom 16:20).

The fact that the angel stands astride the entire orb of the earth indicates his gigantic size. His size is not actually mentioned. It is left to the imagination of the reader. But the stature of the angel must have been colossal. The idea of a very large angel may be based on angels such as the one David saw standing over Jerusalem with a drawn sword (1 Chr 21:16; cf. 2 Sam 24:16–17). That angel stood "between heaven and earth" (1 Chr 21:16). This seems to suggest an angel larger than ones encountered elsewhere by human beings (cf. Num 22:21–31; Josh 5:13–15). Most likely John was familiar with this OT example.

The size of the angel here in Revelation 10 draws attention to the *important mission* for which he has been sent by God. The angel dominates everything on earth. As he stands astride the earth, no power, human or demonic, can push him aside or overthrow him. That is to say, the mission which the angel represents will rule everything on earth, so much so that not even the "gates of hell" (Mt 16:18) can oppose and overcome it. The whole dress and demeanor of the angel also enhances his stature. He comes to John in the majesty and authority of God himself as he stands in place of Christ to commission John and the church on earth. No one and no power can resist this angel and the mission he represents, the mission of John and the people of God which Revelation portrays as about to commence.

A VOICE LIKE THAT OF A ROARING LION (10:3A)

The roar of a lion indicates that the angel speaks with the majestic authority of God through his word. No other figure in Revelation speaks with the voice of a lion, as does the angel here, and he does so only once. In the OT God is likened to a lion. In Job 10:16 God's majestic power is compared to the lion's prowess as a hunter (see also Hos 5:14; Amos 3:12). In Amos 3:8 the Word of God impels the prophet to speak it just as surely as the roar of the lion incites fear (see also (Is 31:4; Jer 25:30–38). While the lion is used on occasion in reference to mighty men of renown (e.g., Prov 19:12; 20:2; cf. Gen 49:9; Ezek 19:1–6), in the OT it is never so used in reference to angels. In all of biblical literature, only the voice of God (Hos 11:10) and that of the angel of Revelation 10 are likened to the voice of a lion.

The lion-like voice of the angel points to the strength, volume, and depth of his voice. There is no other voice that is equal to his, for it is with the voice of God that the angel speaks. The lion's voice—like the cloud and rainbow, the angel's radiant countenance, his legs of fire, and especially his gigantic size—demands attention for the sake of the mission which he will command John and the church to undertake (10:11). In the same way that the roar of a lion instills fear and awe (cf. Amos 3:8) and the lion possesses a roar which no human can outshout, *so the mission of John and the church as they speak the message of God will overcome all opposition.* It is a mission that will instill fear because the message is one of judgment—judgment that serves the purpose of repentance if the message is heeded (Jer 25:30–38; cf. Rev 9:20–21; 16:10–11). Thus the importance of the lion-like voice of the angel is not in its content—John does not report what the voice says. Rather, its importance lies in directing John's attention to the voice which speaks the commands from heaven, "Go, take the scroll," and "it is necessary that you again prophesy" to all peoples (10:8, 11).

THE SEVEN THUNDERS SPEAK (10:3B–4)

When the angel cries out with his lion-like roar, John hears "the seven thunders" speaking "their own voices" (10:3). Nowhere else in either the OT or NT are seven thunders mentioned. However, the presence of the definite article ("the") indicates that these thunders are a specific or familiar entity. It may be that background for these seven thunders is twofold: the divine associations of the number seven (as in 1:4 and 5:6) and the fact that in the OT God's voice was likened to thunder (Ps 29:3; Is 30:30; Joel 3:16; Amos 1:2). Whatever the exact source of these seven thunders, it is apparent that they accompany the lion-like voice of the angel *to enhance his stature as a spokesman for God.* The angel, in commissioning John and the church to proclaim the message, acts under the majestic and authoritative command of God, as if the thunder-like voice of God himself were speaking. As John received the message by way of the angel and the scroll, the speaking of the "seven thunders" could suggest that he was to proclaim the message of God to all peoples and tongues.

Upon hearing the voices of "the seven thunders" (Rev 10:3), John "was about to write" (10:4), either what they were saying or something about the impression they had made on him. Whether the voices were intelligible to John is not stated. The fact that it says he "was about to write" could suggest that he probably did understand what they were saying. If John did understand the voices of the thunders, they were not revealing any further material that God desired to be included in the prophetic message of Revelation. Rather, they likely were uttering holy things of God's heavenly glory that were too sacred and beautiful for anyone to hear while still on earth. Perhaps John did not understand what the thunders were saying, but rather was about to write down the glorious impression and the holy thoughts about God's heavenly majesty that the thunders inspired and motivated him to think. Whatever the contents of the voices of the thunders, whether intelligible or not, John's desire to write what they were saying or inspiring him to think is understandable, for he had been instructed by the Christ to write what he saw and heard (1:1–3, 19). In 10:4 we have the only suggestion anywhere in Revelation that John had pen in hand to write down immediately everything he saw and heard.

But a "voice from heaven" tells John, "Seal what the seven thunders have spoken, for you must not write those things" (10:4). This must be the voice of God or of one directly authorized by God, for God/Christ alone could command John not to write something which he was hearing, because it was by God's command that he should write in the first place. Only God could counter an original command which he alone had given.

With this voice from heaven and its command not to write and reveal what the thunders were saying, the purpose of these thundering voices becomes clear. It is definitely *not* to give to John a further revelation of events on earth or in heaven. *Rather, their purpose is to enhance and thus make stand out in bold relief all the more the lion-like voice of the angel for the ultimate goal of highlighting the importance of the angel's mission.* The voices thus act as God's stamp of approval on the angel's voice and mission. As God once spoke with his majestic, thundering voice at Mt. Sinai, so he once again speaks to John in the presence of this angel in Revelation 10.

THE ANGEL'S OATH (10:5–7)

The angel astride the earth raises "his hand, the right one, toward heaven" (10:5) and takes an oath, swearing by the living God, who is the Creator of the earth and all life. The overall intent of the oath is to dramatize the certainty and truthfulness of the contents of the scroll in the angel's hand, that is, the message that John is to proclaim to all peoples. In the OT God is sometimes portrayed as swearing—taking an oath—often raising his (right) hand to heaven (Ex 6:8; Is 62:8; Ezek 20:15, 23). Deut 32:40, in the Song of Moses, says that God swears by lifting up his hand to heaven, and he swears by himself because he lives forever. Since God cannot invoke anyone greater than himself, he swears by himself (Gen 22:15–16; cf. Heb 6:13, 18).

When John saw and heard the angel lifting his right hand to heaven and taking an oath by God, he may have been reminded of a similar oath in Dan 12:7, where an angelic, heavenly figure raised both hands to heaven and took an oath by the One who lives forever. That angelic figure dressed in fine linen took an oath to assure Daniel that there would be a completion of the things prophesied to him.

Similarly here in Rev 10:5–7 the angel takes an oath in order to assure John and all Christians that there will be a fulfillment, a completion of those things revealed by the seven trumpet-angels, as well as of the whole prophetic message of Revelation. In particular, when the events dramatized by the seventh trumpet-angel come to pass, all things will have been fulfilled and completed; when the seventh trumpet-angel blows his trumpet, then the mystery of God will have been brought to its end, finished.

Here in 10:7 the "mystery" itself is not explained to John in so many words. But by the way it is used in reference to the seventh and last scene in the second vision of events on earth, its interpretation becomes evident. Just as Paul uses the word to refer to the entire plan of God's saving grace in Christ and the Gospel message which proclaims it (Rom 16:25–27; 1 Cor 2:1–2; Eph 1:3–10; Col 2:2–3; 4:2–3; 1 Tim 3:16), so here in Rev 10:7 the "mystery" is the prophetic message of Revelation, which shows and announces to John the culmination of that Gospel message as it reveals the goal and end result of that saving grace of God in Christ.

As it is expressed in Revelation, the "mystery" is the coming about of the kingdom of the cosmos of Yahweh and of his Messiah at the end of the present world (11:15). By means of the seventh trumpet-angel John will see the completion of this mystery of God, when, in his kingdom and that of his Christ, God will rule forever (11:15–19). The "mystery" is qualified and interpreted by the following words, "graciously promised to his own slaves, the prophets" (10:7). The prophets of the OT knew of this mystery of God. For example, 1 Pet 1:10–12 says that the prophets of old carefully examined and searched what had been prophetically spoken concerning the Christ, both his suffering and his coming into glory, and they searched for when this would all happen (cf. Is 53; 60:1–6; 63:1–6). It is called a mystery because the plan of God's salvation and the announcement of it were hidden in former times and kept secret from those of the human race who were the enemies of Christ (Col 1:26; Acts 2:23; 1 Cor 2:6–9).

JOHN AND THE SMALL SCROLL (10:8–10)

John again hears the voice which spoke to him in 10:4. This time it speaks not a prohibition but a command. The heavenly voice tells him to take the scroll from the angel, to eat it whole, and to proclaim the prophetic message of God in Christ among all peoples on earth. The image of a scroll was at times used to symbolize a message that was to be received and then announced to others (e.g., Is 29:11; Zech 5:1–4). Tablets and scrolls were used symbolically to assure and confirm the truthfulness and certainty of a message, and that the message could not be destroyed no matter the opposition (cf. Ezek 3:1–9). The action of eating the scroll and digesting its contents is reminiscent of a similar action by the prophet Ezekiel. In the inaugural vision of God's heavenly glory (Ezekiel 1–3), in which the prophet is commissioned to speak a prophetic message (Ezek 2:3–4), Ezekiel is given a scroll to eat, after which he is to speak God's words (Ezek 2:9–3:4). When Ezekiel ate the scroll, it was sweet as honey in his mouth (Ezek 3:3), but a bitterness in the stomach is not mentioned. However, a short time later Ezekiel did experience a bitterness in his spirit when he embarked on his mission to proclaim the message of God (Ezek 3:14–15).

The symbolical action of eating the scroll in both the cases of Ezekiel and of John suggests that before they proclaim the prophetic word to others, they must first "inwardly digest" it themselves (see the prayer for "Grace to receive the word," LSB 308). The message of God that they were to announce must first be heard, internalized, and applied to themselves. As John heard the message for himself and meditated on it for his own edification, it would be both sweet and bitter. The message would be full of sorrow for him and his hearers because of the woes and the judgments of God, for the Law and just pronouncements of God's anger are never pleasant to hear (Is 6:5; Jonah 1:1–3). The message also brings joy—to the proclaimer himself, as he rejoices in its Gospel comfort, and then the same joy to his hearers. The forgiveness of sins, deliverance from the suffering and persecution of this evil age, and participation in the reign of

Christ on earth and in the new heaven and new earth are part of the scroll's message too (cf. Rev 7:14–17; 20:1–6; 21:1–22:5).

JOHN IS TOLD HE MUST PROCLAIM THE MESSAGE OF GOD (10:11)

The whole purpose of the appearance of the gigantic angel and his scroll rings out loud and clear. John must ("it is necessary," 10:11) proclaim the message of God among all peoples of the earth. No one is to be excluded from hearing the message of God and his Christ. The visionary appearance of the angel is a powerful reminder to John and the churches that they must be engaged in the mission that Christ gave to his church on earth (see Mt 28:16–20). In particular, the angel of Revelation 10 stands in the place of the exalted Christ as John is commissioned, by way of the scroll and the command from heaven, to proclaim the prophetic message. The exalted Lord Christ himself, as the Son of Man, was the first to commission John to receive and then to proclaim the prophetic message (1:9–20). In that first commissioning John was instructed to give the message to the seven churches, God's own people (1:11). In this second commissioning (or recommissioning) in chapter 10, done through the angel in the stead of Christ, John (and, by implication, the church) is instructed to proclaim the message to the whole human race. First the church is to receive it for her own warning and comfort and hope (1:11; 6:1–7:17). Then the church is to proclaim the message to the world (11:1–13; cf. 8:1–9:21; 15:1–16:21).

The way in which the colossal angel takes his stand, then, symbolizes the mission of the church, that is, in particular the power of God in that mission. Just as the gigantic angel astride the earth dominates everything, so now the church in mission will dominate all human life and events and history. As the exalted Lord Christ rules absolutely everything on behalf of God's people in order to protect them in their faith (7:1–8) and in order to prosper the church in her godly mission on earth (11:1–13), so the angel demonstrates that nothing can stop the church in her mission. As little as any human being or force or any demonic opposition can overthrow this mighty angel, so it is impossible for the church on earth to be destroyed. As the angel stands invincible, so the church will be triumphant in her mission. No matter what she suffers, even death, the church will carry out and complete the mission given to her by God.

The symbolism is furthered by the dress and insignia of the angel. He bears the emblems of God's majesty and glory and those of the exalted Christ, and he is accompanied by the thundering voice of God as he himself roars like a lion. All the divine authority that these descriptive emblems of the angel symbolize is conveyed to the church, so that it can be said of the church that in her mission she is emblazoned with the majesty of God and of the exalted Christ. As she carries out her godly mission, the church is accompanied by the awesome, thundering voice of almighty God. The angel clearly demonstrates how much

God esteems his faithful people on earth as they carry out their most important mission to the world.

However, the angel himself is not the authority that commissions and gives the word of command to John to proclaim the message. It is the voice from heaven which gives the command (10:4, 8, 11). While "the voice" is singular (10:4, 8), the command to John is expressed in a plural verb form, "they say" (10:11). If this verb had as its subject the "voice" from heaven (10:4, 8) or possibly the voice of the angel (10:9), one would have expected the singular form. The plural verb form suggests several possibilities. It could be a reference to the heavenly voice in 10:4, 8, with the plural suggesting the Trinity (see 1:4–5). It could well be the equivalent of the passive ("it was said") without any reference as to its source. However, the fact that this form is plural most likely rules out the interpretation that understands this to have been said by the voice of the (one) angel, for he has just spoken to John in 10:9 about how the eating of the scroll would affect him. If the angel were the speaker again in 10:11, it would be most natural for the singular form to be used as it was in 10:9. The most likely interpretation is that the plural form refers to God together with the entire heavenly court of his angels around him. As God (or an angel speaking for him) gives the command to John, the whole angelic court joins in by speaking an affirming word, perhaps "amen" (cf. 5:14). However this may be, *the angel himself is not the commanding authority; that is reserved for God himself.* Rather, the angel is a representation of this commanding authority of God and as such serves as a symbolic affirmation of the importance of the church's mission on earth. The angel is thus a visible sign of God's stamp of approval on that mission.

EXCURSUS

THE IDENTITY AND FUNCTION OF THE MIGHTY ANGEL OF REVELATION 10

Because of the wonder and awe that the angel of Revelation 10 evokes and because of his uniqueness in biblical literature, speculation as to his identity abounds. However or with whomever this angel is identified, it is quite clear that he is acting on behalf of God and of Christ. As he acts on behalf of the triune God, he stands in his place in order to commission or recommission John to proclaim the message. Just as surely as the exalted Christ commissioned John to give the prophetic message to the churches (Rev 1:9–20; 4:1), so surely does the Lord Christ (by way of the angel) now commission John to proclaim the message to all peoples of the world. The second commissioning is just as valid as the first. John recognized that the commission to proclaim the message to the nations came from God and his Christ. Whether this was from Christ *in the guise of an angel* or from the Lord Christ *through an angel* chosen for the role, *it was still the Lord Christ who commissioned John.*

The probability is that the angel is not Jesus Christ himself but rather an angel appointed by God to act on behalf of the Lord Christ. For one thing John gives no indication that he recognized the angel as Christ. If he had, he probably would have fallen down (cf. 1:17), and he certainly would have bowed down to worship him (cf. 4:10), as he attempted to do—and was stopped from doing—before two glorious angels (19:10; 22:8–9). In the OT when the angel of the Lord appeared to a human being on earth, the individual often voluntarily bowed in worship (Num 22:21–31; Judg 13:3–22) or was commanded to do so (Ex 3:1–6). Even when individuals did not immediately bow down, after the event they recognized that they had seen God (e.g., Gen 16:7–14). But perhaps of even more import, when the angel of the Lord spoke, he did not speak as one sent under another's authority, but always in the first person in his own right and authority (Gen 22:11–18; cf. Mt 9:1–6). If John had recognized the angel of Revelation 10 as the Lord Christ, then John, as a Christian in the Jewish tradition of worship and awe toward the angel of Yahweh, would have bowed down before him—*but he didn't.* This suggests that John did not so recognize him.

Another telling point is that the angel swears by God (10:5–6). This the angel of the Lord never did in the OT, nor for that matter did Jesus Christ. In the case of the angel of the Lord, just the opposite happened, for he swore by himself as God does (Judg 2:1). *This the angel of Revelation 10 does not do, indicating that he is not the Lord Christ himself.*

What the description of the angel of Revelation 10 does suggest is that he is the angel of Jesus Christ and of Christ's Father, the angel through whom the prophetic message is given to John. Rev 1:1 reports that the revelatory message of God was given by Jesus Christ to John through his (Christ's) angel. Rev 22:6, at the conclusion of the book, says that God the Father sent his angel to show these things to John, and 22:16 states that Jesus Christ sent his angel to witness these things to the churches. *The angel of Revelation 10 is a pictorial representation of the angel through whom God the Father and God the Son mediated the message to John. In particular he represents the idea and the fact that God (the Father and the Son) used an angel (or angels) to convey the prophecy to John.* Whether it was always the same angel or different angels at various times acting in this role of a mediating angel, *the angel of Revelation 10, as he stands before John, is a mediating angel who represents the mediating role of all angels.* In particular here in Revelation 10, the mediating angel of God and of Christ now reminds John of this by commissioning him to proclaim the message, the message that this angel (and other angels) have been and are mediating to John on behalf of God and Jesus Christ.

Jesus Christ used an angel (or angels) to speak to John because the apostle could not, on this side of heaven, stand before Christ in all of his exalted glory. Just as God could not speak the Torah directly to Moses but did so through angels (e.g., Acts 7:38), so also Christ, because of his holy glory and presence, cannot speak directly to John but rather has to do so through angels. In Revelation 10 we have a picture of such a mediating angel, who is the angel of God and of Christ.

EXCURSUS

THE MEDIATORS OF REVELATION: GUIDES TO THE STRUCTURE OF THE BOOK

The prophetic message of Revelation can be divided into two parts: that part which is mediated to John by Jesus Christ himself (2:1–8:5) and that which is mediated by angels (8:6–22:5). Jesus Christ as the exalted Son of Man dominates and controls the mediation of the first part, that part which directly affects the seven churches. The angels, in particular the seven angels of the seven churches, control the second part, that which John and the church are to proclaim to the world. However, though the angels are the mediators of the second part of the message, the Lord Christ still dominates the message, for the angels are mediating it in his stead and on his behalf. Jesus Christ is still the one mediator of the message. To emphasize that he is the overall mediator (though now through angels), the mighty angel of Revelation 10 appears to John. This mighty angel represents all the angels who are used to mediate the second part, that is, he models the mediating role that they play. He is, so to speak, the chief angel who is in charge of this mediating role, and he is such because he stands in the place of the Lord Christ. So then, while he represents the mediating role of the angels, he stands in the place of Christ as their overlord, for through him Jesus Christ still exercises his lordship as the mediator of God's message to John and the churches.

The prime revelator of the message of Revelation is Jesus Christ. The secondary revelator is the mighty angel of Revelation 10. Similarly, as the exalted Christ is the first to commission John to receive and then send to the churches the message (1:1–2, 9–20), so now the mighty angel (in the place of Christ) commissions John to proclaim the message to the world (10:9–11). While it can be said that John thus receives two commissions, there is in reality only one, that of and from Jesus Christ (1:9–20). The commissioning of John by the angel is a *reminder* of the commission first given to him by Jesus Christ. John is mindfully *recommissioned* by the angel so that he will know that, though the revelatory message now comes through angels, it is still from the Lord Christ and that he must proclaim it to the world. The message is not only for the churches (1:4, 11; chapters 2–3; 22:16) but also for all nations, and that same message is to be proclaimed by the churches to the world (10:11).

The line of communication of the message of Revelation, as stated in 1:1 and 10:11, is thus: God the Father (the source), Jesus Christ, Christ's angel (the angel of Revelation 10), John, the churches, and finally all peoples and nations. This order of communication is demonstrated by the following.

OUTLINE OF THE MEDIATING STRUCTURE OF REVELATION

Prologue (1:1–8)

Jesus Christ Himself Commissions John (1:9–20)

Jesus Christ Mediates

Letters of Preparation to the Seven Churches (2:1–3:22)

Heavenly Vision of the Throne of God (4:1–11) and of the Exaltation of the Lamb, the Seven-Sealed Scroll (5:1–14)

First Sevenfold Vision: The Seven Seals of the Scroll (6:1–8:5)

Angels Mediate: The Mighty Angel (10:1–11) Stands in the Place of Christ and Represents All Angelic Mediators

Second Sevenfold Vision: The Seven Trumpet-Angels (8:6–11:19)

The Cosmic War (12:1–14:20)

Third Sevenfold Vision: The Seven Censer-Angels (15:1–16:21)

The Parousia (17:1–22:5)

Epilogue (22:6–21)

NOTES

The heart of the prophetic message of Revelation is the three cycles, each with a sevenfold vision (A, B, and C of the outline). Each of these cycles reveals events that take place over the same time period, the NT era from the ascension of Christ to his second coming. Thus the second cycle, though with different events and emphases, recapitulates what is revealed in the first, and the third recapitulates what is revealed in both the first and second cycles.

The seventh seal (8:1–5) of the first cycle (which concludes A of the outline) introduces the second cycle (B of the outline), which is followed by the third cycle (C of the outline). Because the first cycle is mediated directly by the Jesus Christ and the second and third cycles are mediated through angels (epitomized by the mighty angel of chapter 10) who stand in the place of Christ, the Lamb is still the overall mediator who controls the entire revelation.

The three visions of (1) the throne of God and the exaltation of the Lamb, (2) the woman and her Child, and (3) the parousia (I, II, and III of the outline) overshadow or overarch the three cycles of sevenfold visions (A, B, and C of the outline). *Thus the three cycles of sevenfold visions are to be interpreted in view of these three overarching visions.*

The seven letters to the churches (chapters 2 and 3) are preparatory in nature. Their function is to call the hearers to repentance in order to prepare them to receive the message which begins with chapter 4. The letters are mediated by Jesus Christ to the seven angels of the churches, the seven angels of God's presence (see the commentary on 8:2). Throughout the rest of the book of Revelation (8:6–22:5), whenever anything is to be received as relevant for the church and directed to it, it is mediated by angels on behalf of Christ, which mediation is epitomized by the mighty angel of Revelation 10.

REVELATION 11:1–14
Second Scene of the Interlude: The Temple Measured and the Two Witnesses

TRANSLATION

11 ¹And a cane like a measuring rod was given to me, and someone said, "Rise and measure the temple of God and the incense altar and those who are worshiping in it. ²But the court which is outside of the temple leave out and do not measure it, because it has been given over to the pagan nations, and they will trample underfoot the holy city for forty-two months."

³"And I will appoint my two witnesses so that they will prophesy one thousand two hundred sixty days clothed about with sackcloth. ⁴These are the two olive trees and the two lampstands which stand before the Lord of the earth. ⁵And if anyone wishes to harm them, fire will come forth from their mouth and devour their enemies; and so if anyone should wish to harm them, thus it is necessary that he be put to death. ⁶These [witnesses] have the authority to close heaven so that rain will not shower during the days of their prophetic proclamation, and they have authority over the waters to turn them into blood and to strike the earth with any plague as often as they should desire.

⁷"But whenever they have completed their witness, the beast which is coming up out of the abyss will make war with them and will conquer them and will kill them. ⁸And their body will be on the plaza of the great city, which is spiritually called Sodom and Egypt, where also their Lord was crucified.

⁹And individuals from the peoples and tribes and

tongues and nations look at their body for three
and a half days, and they do not permit their bodies
to be placed in a tomb. [10]And those dwelling upon
the earth rejoice over them and celebrate, and they
will send gifts to one another, because these two
prophets tormented those dwelling upon the earth.
[11]"But after the three and a half days, the spirit
of life from God entered into them, and they
stood on their feet, and great fear fell upon those
watching them. [12]And they heard a great voice
from heaven saying to them, 'Come up here.' And
they went up into heaven on the cloud while their
enemies watched them. [13]And in that moment a
great earthquake came about, and a tenth of the
city fell, and seven thousand men of renown were
killed in the quake, and the rest of them became
fearful and they gave glory to the God of heaven."
[14]The second woe has come and gone.
Behold, the third woe is coming quickly.

COMMENTARY

THE MEASURING OF THE TEMPLE AND THE TRAMPLING OF THE OUTER COURT (11:1–2)

Beginning with chapter 10 John's role is more than merely that of a viewer:
he now becomes a witness and an active participant. In 10:8–11 he takes the
opened scroll from the angel and is told to eat it and to proclaim its message.
In chapter 11 John's active participation continues, as he is told to "measure the
temple of God" (11:1). John's active role should not be surprising because chapters 10 and 11 have most to do with the church's mission on earth, witnessing
about Jesus Christ to the world. John has long been a part of that ministry and
will be until his death.

John is given a "measuring rod" in the form of a "cane," by which he is to
"measure the temple of God" (11:1). The prophet Ezekiel had a similar experience (Ezek 40:1–5). In a vision he saw a heavenly figure with a measuring rod
(Ezek 40:3) in his hand. The measuring of the temple (Ezekiel 40–42) was a
promise that the temple would be rebuilt and the glory of Yahweh would return
to the temple and Yahweh would live among his people forever (Ezek 43:1–7;
48:35). God's promise for the future was so certain that even now it could be

physically measured as a concrete reality. Also the prophet Zechariah had a vision in which he saw a heavenly figure with a "measuring line" (Zech 2:1–5). In that case Jerusalem was to be measured, symbolizing the promise that God would protect the city and that he also would be its glory. Thus the instruction to John to use a measuring rod puts him in line with this prophetic tradition. His measuring of the temple of God and its dwellers indicates that God's people, his holy dwelling, will be protected as they carry out the mission given to them—the proclamation of the Gospel.

The incense altar (Rev 11:1) is included in the prophetic and protective measuring. The incense altar represents the prayers of God's saints ascending to his holy presence (see 5:8; 6:9–11; 8:3–4). The worship life of God's people in prayer and praise is a part of their mission on earth, and it will also be protected and maintained.

The outer court of the temple is *not* to be measured, for "it has been given over to the pagan nations" who will "trample [it] underfoot" (11:2). In the temple of Solomon there were two courts (1 Ki 6:36). The "inner court" (1 Ki 6:36) was called "the court of the priests" (2 Chr 4:9). The other was a large court with no designated purpose mentioned (2 Chr 4:9). In Ezek 10:5 an "outer court" is mentioned. Also in the later vision in which Ezekiel saw the heavenly temple there is an "outer court," but again no designated purpose is mentioned (40:17–19). In the rebuilt temple complex of Herod there was both an inner and an outer court around the temple proper. The inner court was divided into three sections: one for the priests, one for Israelite men, and a third for women. The outer court was for the Gentiles. Separating the inner court(s) and the outer court was a partition or barrier on which was inscribed a warning of death to any Gentile who entered the inner court (cf. Eph 2:11–18). This outer court came to be known as a place or house of prayer for the Gentiles (see Mk 11:17; cf. Is 56:6–7). Here in John's vision in Rev 11:1–2 the outer court (the court of the Gentiles) is *not* to be measured. It will *not* be protected by God from desecration, for the pagan nations will turn against it as a place of prayer and attempt to destroy both it and the temple of God. That is to say, the church of Jesus Christ, the people of God, will be under severe attack. Though the church will be protected by God so that she can carry out her mission, she will suffer persecution and even death as a result of the pagan nations' opposition.

The outer court and the "holy city" (11:2) will be trampled. The "holy city" is later identified as the "new Jerusalem" coming down from heaven (21:2, 10); it is the locus of the holiness of life with God in the new heaven and earth (cf. Gal 4:26; Rev 3:12). But in 20:8–9, where it is called "the beloved city," the holy city of God is under siege by the hosts of evil (Gog and Magog) that have been trampling it underfoot here on earth. *The holy city, both now and in the new heaven and earth, represents God dwelling in the midst of his people. It thus is the holy symbol of the church of Jesus Christ, the place where God dwells incarnationally among and in his saints, both here on earth now and triumphantly in God's presence in the new age to come.* Here on earth the holy city, the church of God, is being trampled underfoot, that is, persecuted. While the temple of God and its outer court symbolize the place of God's real presence in the continuing worship life of the church, the holy city itself represents the church as it dwells here on earth. The church is sustained in her faith and godly life by God's presence as the focus, source, and center of her worship, as indicated by the temple and its outer court. While the holy city, the church, is being persecuted, she is sustained and protected in her faith and also (as is emphasized here in Revelation 11) in her mission so that she can carry it out and complete it. But she will suffer because of her mission, as portrayed by the outer court being trampled. Her worship life will be sorely tested but not destroyed, for the incense altar is measured, is protected by God. The outer appearance of the church (the holy city) may well be destroyed. At times even the visible appearance of her worship (the outer court) may be trampled. But her inner soul of worship and faith (the altar and temple) will be nourished and kept by God through Word and Sacrament, so even in dying she will still witness and thus complete her godly mission.

FORTY-TWO MONTHS OR
1,260 DAYS (11:2–3)

The length of time that the outer court will be trampled underfoot is given as "forty-two months" (11:2). This same time period is also represented as "one thousand two hundred sixty days" (11:3), the length of time that the two witnesses will prophesy. Though expressed in two different ways, it is the same time, for while the outer court is being trampled the two witnesses will be prophesying. This same time period is mentioned three more times in Revelation. In 12:6 the woman, after delivering her Child, is protected for 1,260 days while she is being pursued by the dragon. In 12:14 this same woman is again mentioned as cared for and protected by God during the same time period, but now the time period is given as "a time and times and half a time"— best understood as meaning three and a half years. (Three and a half years of lunar months—30 days per month—equals forty-two months and also equals 1,260 days.) In 13:5 again this same time period, in this case given as forty-two months, is referred to as the length of time that the beast from the sea will afflict the woman and her seed. Though it is designated by three different reckonings of time, days (1,260), months (forty-two), and years (three and a half), it is the same time period in all cases. (There is also the period of three and a half *days* in 11:9, 11; see below.)

Why the same time period is given in three different ways, is not stated and cannot be determined from the contexts in Revelation. However, these different reckonings are derived from and patterned after the chronology in Daniel. In Dan 7:25 the time period during which the fourth beast will dominate the saints of God is given as three and a half "times," which could refer to years. This is the equivalent of the time period of forty-two months during which the beast from the sea in Rev 13:5 will persecute the woman and her seed (13:1–10). Dan 12:7 mentions the time period of three and a half "seasons," which again could be years. It is the period of time during which the saints of God will endure all the "astonishing things" (Dan 12:6) prophesied to Daniel. In Dan 12:11 again the same time period is referred to, but this time as days—"1,290 days." The 1,290-day period of time in Daniel is the time during which the saints of God will have to endure the "abomination of desolation" (Dan 12:11). In Daniel, as in Revelation, the three and a half "times," "seasons," or years and the 1,290 (1,260 in Revelation) days designate the same time period. However, as in Revelation, Daniel also does not give an explanation as to why the same time period should be designated by different reckonings of time. (Daniel does not use the designation of forty-two months, as does Revelation, to refer to the time period.)

In both Daniel and Revelation this time period is that period of time when God's people on earth will be trodden underfoot by the pagan nations. Daniel sees this time of suffering and persecution prophetically in the future, while John sees it as the time in which he is living, a time that will also continue until the end of the present world at Christ's return. Jesus' teaching on the endtimes (Mark 13:1–26; cf. Mt 24:1–31; Lk 21:5–28) indicates that this time period begins with his own suffering, death, and resurrection and extends to his second coming. In other words, it is the entire church age, from Christ's first advent to his second advent, when this world will end, the final judgment will take place, and then the new heaven and new earth will be the eternal home of God's saints. The entire church age is a time of tribulation, though toward the end of it, persecution shall increase to the point where it becomes a great tribulation. In Lk 21:24 this entire period of persecution is called the "times of the nations/Gentiles." The terrifying days before the fall of Jerusalem are a type of the suffering which will be endured by God's people *throughout the church age*—suffering which reaches a terrible depth just before the End. Here in Rev 11:1–3 this period of time between Christ's passion and ascension, and his second coming is that time when the outer court will be trampled underfoot. During this time of the Gentiles, expressed as forty-two months, the church will suffer affliction and persecution (11:2). But during this same time of the Gentiles, expressed now as 1,260 days, the two witnesses will also carry out their prophetic ministry (11:3). Though the church in prophetic ministry (as represented by these two witnesses and "the holy city," 11:2) will suffer through the trampling, *because the temple is measured* the church will be protected and enabled by God to carry out her mission and complete it.

Why this time period is designated by three different reckonings—forty-two months (11:2; 13:5), 1,260 days (11:3; 12:6), and three and a half years (12:14)—is not explained. Taking into consideration also the three and a half "times," "seasons," or years of Daniel (7:25; 12:7) and the 1,290 days of Daniel (12:11), it is possible that the well-known period of draught and famine during the prophetic ministry of Elijah (1 Ki 17:1; 18:1, 42–45; cf. Lk 4:25; James 5:17) established the type from which the expression of three and a half years might have been derived. Another period of three and a half years that became especially well known to Jewish people was the reign of terror in Judea instigated by Antiochus Epiphanes. Another period of similar length could be the Jewish war of AD 67–70, which ended with the destruction of Jerusalem and the temple. While these memorable periods of suffering in John's religious background and tradition would come to mind as possible types for the symbolical use of three and a half years in 12:14 and thus point out the horror and suffering of the whole time period covered by the prophetic message of Revelation, there seem to be no corresponding types for the forty-two months and the 1,260 days. Certainly the three-and-a-half-year period suggests a time of dire suffering for the church as she carries out her mission. But just as God took care of Elijah during the time of persecution under Ahab and Jezebel and during the three-and-a-half-year famine, so also God would protect and provide for his people to enable them to complete their godly mission.

Finally, the number three and a half suggests only a *portion* of the total time period of God's ordinance and providence. To express such a total and complete time of God's grace numerically, the number seven would have been used. The age of the Messiah, the age of the new covenant, would be numerically symbolized by the number three and a half (Rev 12:14; cf. 11:2, 3, 9, 11). By inference, then, there must be a prior period of three and a half to total seven. Another age that could be symbolized by three and a half is that of the prophets, the age of the old covenant. Both ages added together under God's ordinance of time would have been symbolized by the number seven, if a number were to be used to symbolize and thus designate the complete time of the earth's existence under God's covenants of mercy.

THE TWO WITNESSES (11:3–13)

THE TWO WITNESSES PROPHESY (11:3–6)

The "two witnesses" of God are "clothed about with sackcloth" (11:3). Sackcloth in biblical literature is a coarse, hairy garment worn as a sign of grief (Gen 37:34) or of sorrow and repentance over sin (1 Chr 21:16; Jonah 3:5–8; Mt 11:21). That the two witnesses are dressed in sackcloth demonstrates that they will conduct their prophetic ministry in a penitential attitude of humble and sacrificial service. The prophets of old were thus dressed at times, as they carried out their own ministry as Yahweh's spokesmen (2 Ki 1:8; Is 20:2; Zech 13:4); the last of them was John the Baptist (Mk 1:6).

The two witnesses are further described as "the two olive trees and the two lampstands which stand before the Lord of the earth" (Rev 11:4). This descriptive imagery is similar to that of Zech 4:2–14. In a vision the prophet Zechariah saw a golden lampstand with seven lamps (Zech 4:2). On either side of the lampstand were two olive trees (Zech 4:3). The lampstand with its seven lamps of light represented the seven eyes of Yahweh by which he penetrates the whole earth with his omniscience (Zech 4:10)—which sevenfold omniscience is exercised by his Spirit (Zech 4:6). When Zechariah asked what the two olive trees were or represented, he was told that they were two individuals who were anointed to serve Yahweh, the Lord of all the earth (Zech 4:11–14). In the context of Zech 4:2–14, it appears that the lampstand is Israel, the people of God, under the sevenfold guidance of Yahweh's omniscience as exercised by the Holy Spirit, and that the two olive trees represent the anointed priesthood (at that time in the person of Joshua) and the anointed royal house of David (in the person of Zerubbabel, Zech 2:1–6:15). The two olive trees supply the oil for the lamps of the lampstand; that is, the priesthood and the royal house of David are God's anointed representatives by which the Holy Spirit cares for Israel, for it is not by might but by the Spirit of Yahweh that God's people are delivered and kept safe (Zech 4:6).

Rev 11:1–4, then, employs some of that imagery from Zechariah 4, but in a new context, and so transformed. The lampstand under the sevenfold light of the Spirit (Zech 4:2) now represents not OT Israel, but rather (as *two* lampstands) "the temple" and "the holy city" (Rev 11:1–2), that is, the NT church, God's saints on earth. The two olive trees now represent not Joshua and Zerubbabel, but the two witnesses anointed by God to proclaim the prophetic Word throughout the era of the new covenant.

It is noteworthy that the one lampstand in Zechariah has become two lampstands in Revelation 11. John has already been told that the seven churches, which represent the entire church on earth, are the seven lampstands (Rev 1:20). Putting together Zechariah 4 and Revelation 1 and 11, one can say that the people of God, first of all, are viewed and represented in Zechariah 4 by *one* lampstand that is supplied with oil from two olive trees (Zech 4:2–14). Second, the church can also be represented by *seven* lampstands because she is under the sevenfold omniscience of God's Holy Spirit (Rev 1:20). Third, she can be symbolized by *two* lampstands as seen through and by way of the prophetic ministry, the royal priesthood (combining the priesthood and the line of kings), of the two witnesses (Rev 11:1–4).

Thus prima facie the church is looked upon as the single lampstand with its seven lights (as suggested by Zechariah) or as seven lampstands (as seen in Rev 1:20). But here in Rev 11:1–4 the church is represented by the two witnesses who in turn are symbolized by the *two* lampstands and the two olive trees, for the church is the royal priesthood of God here on earth as she carries out her prophetic ministry (as depicted by the two witnesses; see 1:6; 5:10; 20:6). *Thus the two witnesses are symbolized by the two lampstands because they represent the church in her royal, priestly, prophetic witness to the Gospel message of Christ to the world. They are also symbolized by the two olive trees because God, through his anointed prophets and ministers, edifies and nourishes the church as she (through them and as represented by them) witnesses to the world.*

These two witnesses belong to the speaker—God the Father or Jesus Christ—for they are identified as such by the possessive pronoun "my" in 11:3. The definite article ("the" indicates that John evidently understood them to be two well-known figures. If it were necessary to identify them as specific biblical persons, the most likely candidates would be Moses and Elijah, because they appeared with Jesus on the mount of transfiguration (Mt 17:3; Mk 9:4; Lk 9:30). The fact that according to Luke (9:31) they spoke about Jesus' coming "exodus," which was soon to happen in Jerusalem, also lends credence to this identification. The description of their godly powers in Rev 11:5–6, which speaks of fire from their mouths (cf. 2 Ki 1:10–14) and the closing of heaven so that it would not rain (cf. 1 Ki 17:1) and the ability to turn water into blood (cf. Ex 7:14–21), encourages this same identification as well. However, Moses and Elijah only serve as models for the two witnesses, who in turn are symbols of the entire church in her mission of witnessing to Christ. Though it seems that Moses and Elijah *best fit the description of the two witnesses* and likely came to the mind of John, the two witnesses are not *actually* Moses and Elijah, nor any other OT prophets. In the same way that John the Baptist was in spirit that Elijah who was foretold, so now these two prophetic witnesses are in the spirit of Moses and Elijah as they symbolize the church, for the church carries out that prophetic ministry in that same spirit of Moses and Elijah, which spirit is now symbolized by the two witnesses.

The church is symbolized by *two* witnesses most likely because of Deut 19:15, which prescribes that for a testimony to be received it must be established by two or three witnesses. In his earthly ministry Jesus followed this Mosaic tradition when he urged his audience to receive his testimony because of two witnesses to it (Jn 8:16–18), and he practiced this when he sent out the twelve disciples and the seventy-two in teams of two (Mk 6:7; Lk 10:1; cf. Acts 15:39–40). This practice of having testimony concerning Jesus established by two witnesses is illustrated by the testimony of the two witnesses on the mount of transfiguration, Moses and Elijah. So now the church is to proclaim prophetically the testimony of Jesus to the world as it is also thus confirmed to be the truth.

The end of Rev 11:4 states that the two witnesses "stand before the Lord of the earth." They are in his presence, his glory and holiness, as they minister for him in their prophetic witness to Christ. The fact that they stand in God's presence also suggests that they (that is, the church) are under God's protection. During the time of their witness (cf. "the days of their prophetic proclamation,"

11:6) no one can "harm them" (11:5). Their ministry cannot be stopped or
destroyed, for "not even the gates of hell can overcome it" (Mt 16:18).

The imagery of fire from their mouth which destroys their enemies (Rev
11:5) is reminiscent of God's protection of Elijah when King Ahaziah in Samaria
sent messengers to take the prophet into custody (2 Ki 1:1–15). Fire twice came
from heaven and destroyed the messengers so that the king could not place
his murderous hands on Elijah (2 Ki 1:10, 12). Fire also came from heaven on
Mt. Carmel to devour the sacrifice of Elijah as a demonstrative proof that the
true God is Yahweh and not the Baal of the false prophets (1 Ki 18:38–39). The
language here in Rev 11:5 is more likely to be metaphorical of God's manner of
protecting his witnesses. Similarly, "the authority to close heaven so that rain
will not shower" (Rev 11:6) is like that of Elijah when he announced to Ahab
that there would be no rain for several years (1 Ki 17:1). God himself is the one
who controls and dictates how even the forces of nature will aid the prophetic
ministry of the church.

The witnesses also "have authority over the waters to turn them into blood
and to strike the earth with any plague" (Rev 11:6). Under God's will and judgment against Egypt, Moses exercised such authority (Ex 7:19–20). Again, God
himself, in aid of his people, controls and directs all earthly powers, natural and
human. As the prophet declares, it is God who sends plagues on the earth to aid
the prophet's ministry (Amos 4:10).

Because of this descriptive imagery of God's protective power in Rev
11:5–6, it is quite natural to see Elijah and Moses as the prototypes of the two
witnesses. However this may be, the two witnesses certainly are a representation
of the church's prophetic witness to Jesus Christ. As the church carries out this
prophetic ministry, no one and no power—human or demonic—can stop her
mission. This is because God himself, in his sovereign and gracious rule through
the exalted Christ, will provide for and protect his church in her godly mission.
John must (10:11) and she must carry out and complete this mission for the sake
of the human race (10:8–11).

THE TWO WITNESSES ARE KILLED (11:7–10)

Nevertheless, the church will suffer as a result of completing her mission.
When the two witnesses "have completed their witness," the beast from the
abyss "will make war with them and will conquer them and will kill them"
(11:7). While the church is active in God's mission, the fury of the enemy and
its opposition never slackens, and finally, when the church has completed the
mission, this fury of the enemy will be unleashed to destroy the witness of the
church.

This enemy is symbolized by "the beast which is coming up out of the
abyss" (11:7). Already in 9:1–11 John had seen the demonic forces from the abyss
afflicting the human race. The leader of this demonic force was "the angel of
the abyss" whose name is "Abaddon" and "Apollyon" (9:11), which both mean

"Destroyer." Here in 11:7 "the beast," identified by the definite article ("the"), is clearly the angel of the abyss (9:11), also identified as the dragon and Satan (12:9). In particular, because the devil is called "the beast" here in 11:7, this designation refers to the dragon who operates against the church through the two beasts of Revelation 13 and who is thus a symbol of all the enemy forces (human in particular) who are under demonic influence and control (see 11:9–10).

Even though it causes much suffering (12:13–18), the fury of the enemy cannot stop the church as she witnesses. But when her mission of witnessing is completed, then she will be put to death and her prophetic voice will, for the moment, be stilled. In God's own stewardship of time, not that of the two witnesses, when their prophetic ministry is completed, God will permit the beast to overcome them and kill them. Their death will be illustrative of the death of their Lord Christ (cf. 2 Cor 4:10–11). Their bodies will be unburied for a time and on display, thus bringing to mind the depravity of the place where they died (Rev 11:8).

Wherever the church is trodden underfoot, that place and its inhabitants are as evil before God as Sodom and Egypt. In its most evil days of apostasy, Judah was likened to Sodom and Gomorrah, so much so that God for a time would no longer receive their worship and prayers (Is 1:8–15; cf. Ezek 16:46, 55). The place where the bodies of the two witnesses lay unburied is also likened to Egypt, which was the place of slavery for the Israelites. "Sodom" and "Egypt" are to be understood "spiritually" (Rev 11:8) and connected to Jerusalem, where the Lord was crucified. Every place where the witnesses carry the message of redemption becomes, for the time of their prophetic ministry, a holy place, like the holy city of Jerusalem. But when the inhabitants of that place reject their witness, the place of their ministry becomes like apostate Jerusalem, like Sodom and Egypt, for to reject the witness of the church is to come into a depraved and idolatrous state (like Sodom), resulting in a spiritual slavery (like bondage in Egypt).

Many of the inhabitants of the city, now in a depraved exile from all that is holy, do not permit the bodies to be buried. The denial of proper burial was an insult by which scorn and ridicule could be placed upon those left exposed to the public eye. Ps 79:1–4 presents a terrifying description of how the pagan nations defiled God's temple and shamed his people, so much so that the mockers of God did not even permit the bodies of those of his people whom they killed to be buried (Ps 79:3). To prevent such shame in Israel, the Mosaic Law stipulates that dead bodies were not to be left unburied (Deut 21:22–23; cf. 1 Sam 31:8–13; Jn 19:31). But the bodies of these two witnesses in Revelation 11 were not to receive burial. This is to be interpreted symbolically. Though there have been instances of bodies literally left unburied for public ridicule, this description metaphorically suggests the ongoing shame and ridicule that the unbelieving world heaps on the testimony of the church, especially in her demise, and particularly on her martyrs.

The bodies of the witnesses are left unburied for "three and a half days" (11:9, 11). This number of days can be compared to the number of years of their prophetic ministry: 1,260 days (11:3), if converted to years (twelve lunar months of thirty days each month), would result in three and a half years. That is, in microcosm, for three and a half days, their death and the stillness of their prophetic voice is a reminder of the whole NT era, which is symbolized by the three and a half years during which they prophesied. However, their death and the silencing of their prophetic and living voice of witness does not eliminate their influence. Though silenced, even their unburied bodies are a testimony, a testimony that haunts those who rejected their witness, for these people cannot quite stamp the witnesses' testimony out of their memory. In the end that testimony will judge them (see Jn 12:48). For the place and for the people of that place who heard their witness and then put to silence the voice of the church, that silence will endure. The next time that they will hear that witness will be in the judgment at the End—for their eternal ruin. The silence of the church for three and a half days in any given place at any time throughout the entire period from Christ's exaltation to his second coming is also a warning that the people who live there and their children may not again have an opportunity to hear the Gospel voice of God.

The people not only shame the bodies by leaving them unburied; they also "rejoice over them and celebrate and ... send gifts to one another" (11:10). They no longer are "tormented" (11:10) by the witnesses; they no longer have to listen to that prophetic voice that reminded them of God's holy laws and their sins and that there is only one way to salvation, the cross of Christ.

The Two Witnesses Come Back to Life (11:11–12)

But the joyful celebration over the demise of the church is short-lived, for after the three and a half days the two witnesses come back to life. The resurrection of the Christians at the End is the final and great coming back to life from death. Here the bringing to life by the Spirit of God refers more to the church being raised up again to witness after a time of persecution. From the time of Christ's ascension to his second coming (the 1,260 days or forty-two months or three and a half years), the church—at one place or another—is continually being trodden underfoot and then raised again. Here and there the voice of the witness of the church is stilled, but after a period of time (the three and a half days) the church comes back to life to continue her witness. Just when the enemy thinks the church's witness to Christ is silenced, God raises up the church again, giving to her new life by which she begins again to shout out the Gospel of Christ.

As the two witnesses stand again on their feet, "a great voice from heaven" calls them to "come up" to God's presence. "And they went up into heaven on

the cloud" (11:12). Their prophetic ministry on earth was finished according to
God's plan; their apparent end on earth was a humiliating death, without burial.
But their real end is to ascend into God's heavenly glory. Thus their ministry
of witness comes to the same conclusion as their Lord's had: death, then resurrection and ascended glory (cf. 2 Cor 4:7–15). As the Lord Christ ascended into
heaven and was received by a cloud, the two witnesses ascend to heaven "on
the cloud" (Rev 11:12). The definite article ("the"/) before "cloud" most likely
relates the cloud to the cloud of Jesus' ascension (Acts 1:9), possibly also to the
clouds upon which he will come again at the end of this world (Mt 24:30; 26:64).
However this may be, the fact that the cloud is mentioned indicates how much
God glorifies his two witnesses. The unbelieving world shames them, but God
envelopes them in his glory, the glory of the ascended Christ.

"A Great Earthquake" (11:13)

The church is raised in such a way that "great fear fell upon those watching"
(Rev 11:11). As they continue to watch God's people ascend into heaven (11:12),
these enemies of the church are struck by a further fear when they experience
"a great earthquake" (11:13). The earthquake causes "a tenth of the city" to be
destroyed and seven thousand prominent people to perish (11:13). Earthquakes
often accompany and attest God's mighty acts (Ezek 38:19–20; Hag 2:6–9; Zech
14:1–5). Matthew's account of Jesus' death (Mt 27:51) reports that the earth was
shaken as in an earthquake and the rocks were split in two, and at his resurrection a great earthquake happened (Mt 28:2). In the epistle to the Hebrews it says
that before the End, God will once again shake the earth and the heavens (Heb
12:26).

The earthquake of this verse occurs as a demonstration of the majestic and
awesome glory that attends the church as God raises her up. However, the earthquake in particular is a pointer to the majestic and fearful judgment of God that
strikes the unbelieving world because of the way the pagan nations treated his
people. For this judgment the saints in heaven have been praying (6:9–11). God
shaking the earth refers not only to literal geophysical tremors, but also (and
perhaps more often) metaphorically to political, economic, and sociological
shakings by which God shows his displeasure and anger over the way the world
treats his church and her witness. Examples of this are evident when political
systems have silenced the witness of the church in their effort to destroy God's
people. Imperial Rome was shaken by God so that it eventually lay in ruins
while God raised and preserved his church. At the close of the twentieth
century, political and economic powers lay in ruins after trying to destroy God's
church. Yes, "the Word of our God stands forever" (Is 40:8; 1 Pet 1:25).

The earthquake kills "seven thousand men of renown" (Rev 11:13), either
famous or notorious persons. "Seven thousand" is a symbolic number, indicating the control of the sevenfold Spirit and the will of God (see 1:4; 3:1; 4:5; 5:6).
Whatever the actual number of those who perish in any given instance, it is

according to God's mind and judgment and not according to some arbitrary fate or accidental chance, for such a capricious understanding of historical events would be idolatrous in character (see Deut 32:39–43; Ezek 31:15–17; Amos 4:6–13). "Seven thousand" is in proximity to the "tenth of the city" (Rev 11:13) which was toppled by the same earthquake. In God's shaking, great damage was done to the city, and, as a result, many people perished. This catastrophe even causes some of the former hardened unbelievers to "[give] glory to the God of heaven" (11:13). Does this mean that some repent and come to believe the church's witness to Christ? Possibly so, for the expression "give glory to God" can indicate such repentance (see Lk 5:25; Acts 13:48).

ANNOUNCEMENT ABOUT THE SECOND AND THIRD WOES (11:14)

The second "woe" (8:13) had been revealed by the sixth trumpet-angel in 9:13–21, the scene of the last battle before this world's end. "The second woe has come and gone. Behold, the third woe is coming quickly." These words in 11:14 are a bridge between 9:13–21 and 11:15–19, and thus they introduce the scene of the seventh trumpet-angel, that is, the third woe. The three woes are, then, the last three scenes of the second vision of events on earth: the demonic forces attacking the human race (9:1–12); the last battle (9:13–21); and the end of the present world itself (11:15–19). Between the sixth scene (second woe, 9:13–21) and the seventh scene (third woe, 11:15–19) there is situated an interlude (10:1–11:14) consisting of two scenes (10:1–11 and 11:1–14).

CONCLUSION

The interlude of 7:1–17 pictured the church militant and the church triumphant for the purpose of encouraging the Christians on earth with the promise that God would keep them in faith no matter what they suffered. The interlude of 10:1–11:14 portrays the missionary witnessing role of the church: Christians are encouraged to know that despite the persecution of the world, God will protect them in their mission and will provide for them so that they may complete their prophetic ministry.

The two witnesses symbolize the entire church during the whole of the NT era. They also represent the entire church during a particular time period within the greater period between Christ's ascension and his second coming—whether during the time of John, during the time of the twentieth century, or any other time. What is symbolized by the two witnesses can also be applied to a particular church or congregation, or even to the life span of an individual Christian. For the church as a whole, as well as for each particular part of it and for each Christian, there is a specific time span during which she may complete her ministry, a time span given by God himself. When that time span is fulfilled and her ministry is completed, God may permit the enemy to trod underfoot the church or individual Christians and thus silence their witnessing voice on earth. But after such a demise God may again lift up his church, reviving or resurrecting her so that she can again witness to the world (cf. the Reformation). As for individual Christians, after their allotted time on earth for witnessing has come to an end, they too will experience a lifting up and then participate in the heavenly worship portrayed in, for example, 4:4, 10–11; 7:9–17.

Thus the picture given by the scene of the two witnesses is that the Christian church—composed of individual Christians—is always living in witness, dying for that witness, and being raised again for further witness. This happens all through the time period covered by the prophetic message of Revelation, the time from Christ's ascension to this world's end. When the church and/or a segment of it is crushed by the enemy, many, if not most, of the individual Christians of that particular church may die, in which case their own being filled with the spirit of life and standing up again (11:11) will be when they ascend to God's glory in heaven (11:12). When that particular church is revived so that she can again witness, her witnessing ministry will be carried on by new Christians who have taken the place of those who have gone to heaven. However, some of the individual Christians who have suffered through the crushing of the church may survive, and instead of ascending to heaven, they may be a part of that church's revived and new mission.

The final and terrifying assault on the church and her witness to Christ will be Armageddon (16:12–16) and the battle of Gog and Magog (20:7–10). The final and great instance when the church will be caused to stand on her feet (11:11) and called to "come up here" (11:12) will be the resurrection at the End, when the Lord Christ will come to claim his bride for eternal life in the new heaven and new earth (19:1–21; 20:11–15; 21:1–22:5). Each revival of the church here on earth in order to witness again, and each raising of a Christian to God's heavenly glory throughout the time period of the NT era, is a type and foreshadowing of the great and final revival—the resurrection at the End.

REVELATION 11:15–19
THE SEVENTH TRUMPET-ANGEL: THE END AND ITS JOY

TRANSLATION

11 [15]And the seventh angel blew his trumpet, and
there came about great voices in heaven, saying,
"The kingdom of the cosmos has become
   our Lord's and his Christ's,
and he will reign forever and ever."
[16]And the twenty-four elders who are before
God sitting on their thrones fell upon their
faces and worshiped God, [17]saying,
"We give thanks to you, O Yahweh, the [only] God,
   the Almighty, the One Who Is and Who Was,
because you have taken your great power
   and you have begun your reign.
[18]And the pagan nations were made angry,
   and your anger has come,
   and the time of the dead to be judged [has come]
and [the time] to give the reward to your slaves,
   the prophets, and to the saints and to those
   who fear your name, the small and the great,
and [the time] to destroy those who
   were destroying the earth."
[19]And the temple of God, which is in heaven, was
opened, and the ark of his covenant was seen in his
temple, and there came about lightning flashes and
noises and thunders and an earthquake and large hail.

COMMENTARY

THE VICTORY SONG OF
THE GREAT VOICES (11:15)

With the sound of the seventh trumpet-angel the seventh and last scene of the second vision of events on earth appears. "Great voices in heaven" pronounce or sing out the glorious news that "the kingdom of the cosmos has become our Lord's and his Christ's" (11:15). Whether the song is another stanza in the great Te Deum begun in 4:8 and continued in 4:11; 5:9–14; and 7:10–12 or whether it is an independent shout of praise, it is a voice and verse of celebration. The hymn celebrates the victory of God and his Anointed One.

This shout of joy and praise is in sharp contrast to the opening of the seventh seal and the ensuing silence (8:1)—the seal which concluded the first vision of events on earth (the seven seals) and introduced the second vision (the seven trumpets). The silence then suggested the fear and awe and the anticipation that the mighty God was about to act in and through the events to be displayed in the second vision, the scenes of which were then introduced by the seven trumpet-angels. Now the mighty acts of God's judgment have been completed, and God's people in their faith are now vindicated at the moment when God openly takes his reign at the end of all things. The "great voices in heaven" now recognize this final triumph of God through his Christ—which is also the triumph of his people.

The voices are not identified. In 7:9–10 the saints in heaven (the church triumphant) shout out with a "loud voice" their praise of God and the Lamb. In 19:1 "an immense crowd in heaven" proclaims in a "loud voice" its joy that God has judged the great enemy of his people, the harlot. In 19:6 John will hear the "voice of an immense crowd" praising God because he, at the End, has taken his reign; it is a shout of celebration that is similar to that of 11:15. Though the voices in Revelation 19 are not identified, they seem to be that of the heavenly host of saints, as in 7:9–10. The reason for the praise in the scene here in 11:15 is the kingdom and reign of God and his Christ. That reason is similar to the one in 5:9–10, where the heavenly hosts, both saints and angels, praise the triumphant Lamb at his exaltation, for he has made the saints "a kingdom and priests, and they rule on the earth" (5:10). This similarity suggests that in 11:15 (cf. also 11:17) the cause for the celebration includes God's reign over and through his saints and so the saints are likely to be prominent among those expressing the acclamation. Another similarity is the proximity of the twenty-four worshiping elders in both 5:8 and 11:16, and these elders represent the entire church—the saints of both testaments.

"THE KINGDOM OF THE COSMOS HAS BECOME OUR LORD'S AND HIS CHRIST'S"

The heavenly host sings in celebration because "the kingdom of the cosmos has become [their] Lord's and his Christ's." Saints and angels celebrate the fact that the entire creation of God, because of Christ's redemptive and reconciling victory, has now become God's again (see Rom 8:18–25; 2 Pet 3:11–13; Rev 21:1, 5). As was promised in Ps 2:4–9 and in Zech 14:9, the Lord Yahweh through his Anointed One will become King of the earth, and on that day when it happens, the whole earth will acknowledge that there is but one God, whose name is Yahweh, and only one anointed King through whom he saves and through whom he is known (cf. Acts 4:10–12). However one interprets "cosmos," at the End it belongs to God and to the one who won it back for him, the Christ.

The "cosmos" can refer to the entire created universe or to any part of it, in particular the earth and the human race. Here in 11:15 the cosmos is that part of God's creation that was/is contested by the forces of evil, that part the devil claimed as his own. It thus refers to that part of God's creation which rebelled against him, the human race, but also to that creation itself which was placed under the judgment of God because of human sin (Gen 3:17–19; Rom 8:18–23). *At the End in the final display of the victory of Christ, God will openly claim all of his creation as his own, in particular that part of creation that was once under the prince of darkness. God will publicly display his reign over all his creation as he lays claim to that realm of his creation that has been restored through Christ's redemption.* Thus God in his Christ will gloriously demonstrate that he is once again the Lord of all creation and alone its sovereign Lord.

THE SONG OF CELEBRATION (11:16–18)

This is cause for celebration: God's everlasting reign through Christ over his cosmos and especially over his redeemed people. The "twenty-four elders" (11:16) continue the hymn of celebration by adding their stanza of thanksgiving to the Te Deum. In the vision of the elevation and coronation of the Lamb in 5:6–8 the twenty-four elders, together with the four winged creatures, praised the Lamb because by his blood he purchased a people for God and thus made them his kingdom. Now at the End the elders again sing in thanksgiving to God, but this time by a hymn of praise in which they laud him because he has assumed his great power and has begun his reign. As in 5:6–8 the elders represent the entire people of God, the church universal both before and after the incarnation of Christ. This rejoicing at the End, when God takes his reign, John will see once again (19:6–8), but then it will be expressed by all the saints as the bride of the Lamb.

When God takes his reign at the End, it means a time of judgment for the pagan nations, a time for destroying those who were destroying the earth. It is therefore designated the third woe (see 8:13; 9:12; 11:14). While the Christians celebrate in worship of God, the unbelieving nations are suffering their woe, their eternal judgment (cf. 2 Thess 1:6–7).

The fact that the pagan nations "were destroying the earth" (Rev 11:18) is a descriptive way of saying that they were participating with the devil and all evil forces in their attempt to usurp the power of God and take over his reign. In the OT the destroying or defiling of the earth and especially the sacred land of Israel was often stated to be the result of the sinful depravity of the people, a spiritual corruption which even physically cursed the land (see Amos 4:7–9). In Lev 18:24–28 the Israelites are warned by God not to defile themselves and the land by the sins of the people around them (Lev 18:1–23), for the pagan nations had committed such horrifying actions of depravity that the land was moved to vomit out its inhabitants (Lev 18:28; cf. Ezra 9:11). Here in Revelation 11 the pagan nations were destroying the earth because they were *unclean*, and they made the land *unclean*. But now they are judged.

As God takes back his reign from the usurpers, the pagan nations seethe with anger. But their fury at God as he vindicates his righteousness and that of his people in Christ is quickly turned into a terrified fear. God's wrath overwhelms them as he now claims his kingdom (see 6:15–17). The time had come "for the dead to be judged" (11:18). Judgment will take place at the resurrection so that both those still living at Christ's return and the raised dead (1 Thess 4:15–17) will stand before God's judgment seat (Rom 14:10; 2 Cor 5:10; cf. Mt 25:31–46; Rev 20:11–13).

THE APPEARING OF THE TEMPLE AND THE ARK (11:19)

After the judgment all is ready for the heavenly temple of God to appear and be opened in plain view to be seen by all. God's saints, in the perfect righteousness into which their mortal bodies have been raised (see 1 Cor 15:52–55), will now see God's presence and glory face to face (cf. 1 Jn 3:2; Rev 22:3–4).

The ark of the covenant (Rev 11:19) in God's heavenly temple also appears in clear view for all to see. In the OT the ark of the covenant (1 Ki 8:1) was the symbol of God's covenantal presence with his people. The ark which first stood in the tabernacle later resided in the Holy of Holies in Solomon's temple (1 Ki 8:6). When Nebuchadnezzar destroyed Jerusalem and the temple, probably the ark was also destroyed (2 Ki 25:9). Jeremiah (Jer 3:16) prophesied that the ark would no longer be missed nor even come to mind and that another one would not be made. This suggests that the ark itself would never be found again. This would explain why the ark is absent from the list of temple furnishings brought back from exile to the second temple (Ezra 1:7–11; 5:14–16; 7:19). The mention of the ark of the covenant here in Rev 11:19 is an indication that the promise of God's saving mercy, as represented by the ark, has come to its glorious conclusion before his heavenly presence.

The "lightning flashes and noises and thunders and an earthquake and large hail" (Rev 11:19) are (as at Mt. Sinai) a majestic affirmation of God which speaks a loud "amen!" Such manifestations of nature attend God's holy presence (see Ex 19:16; Rev 8:5; 16:18). At such manifestations all fall face down in fear and awe.

EXCURSUS

THE MISSIOLOGY
OF REVELATION

The Revelation of St. John may well be the most evangelistic book of the entire Bible. Certainly it is unique in the way it proclaims the Gospel and empowers the church for her mission.

There is a twofold purpose of Revelation. As the prophetic message of the book unfolds its view of events on earth from Christ's first advent up to the present world's end at his return, it presents to us (1) a Christology of the exalted reign of Christ and (2) a theology of the church and her mission.

These two purposes are related. Christ reigns so as to enable the church to carry out and complete her mission. Among all the tribulations and sufferings on earth, the Lord Christ unveils his exalted glory for the comfort of the church and for the empowerment of her mission. From the time of Christ's victory and ascension up to the End, all history is controlled by the Lord Christ for the sake of his church and her mission of witness. When that mission is completed, the curtain will fall on this world's existence and the Lord will come to claim his bride.

How important is the mission of the church in her role of witnessing to Jesus Christ as the Savior of the world? Two visions in particular give an answer: the mighty angel of Revelation 10 and the woman with Child in Revelation 12. The mighty angel astride the entire earth (10:1–2) exhibits the importance of the church and her mission, for all people everywhere and throughout history must hear the message of God that the church proclaims. John, on behalf of the church, is told that he must prophesy to "many peoples and nations and tongues and kings" (10:11), for the eternal destiny of each member of the human race depends upon hearing and believing the message of Christ crucified and risen.

The woman with Child in Revelation 12 who is hunted by the dragon portrays the suffering of the church during her mission, but she also reveals the glory and honor with which God, for the sake of the Child, adorns his church. The church is pictured like the Virgin Mary, as the one who births Christ, the Savior, into this world (12:5). No other entity in human history is so honored. The church and her mission are the most important aspects of human experience and world history, for she bears the cross of Christ and the love of God, the cross and love that extend to the spatial and temporal ends of the earth.

The entire book of Revelation can be interpreted in view of the mission of the church, for that mission is carried out and completed under the exalted glory and reign of her Lord Christ.

I. Introduction (1:1–3:22): The time is short and the church is not yet ready.

    A. The prologue (1:1–8) conveys the *urgency* for the church to complete her mission. The events will transpire soon (1:1) and Christ will return in glory (1:7). Now that Christ has freed his church from her sins (1:5), the church has a priestly role (1:6) of witnessing to the Word of God (as did John, 1:2) and proclaiming Christ's imminent return (1:7–8).

    B. The Lord in his grace places his right hand on John and *commissions him for the mission* (1:9–20). The apostle represents the church since he is a "brother and partner in the suffering and kingdom" (1:9). He is unprepared for the mission task as he stands before the overpowering glory of the exalted Christ and falls down "as dead" (1:17), utterly incapable of serving as his witness to the world. But Jesus, by the power of his resurrection, commissions John to write the revelation (1:18–19).

    C. The seven letters to the seven churches (2:1–3:22) instill repentance and faith and thereby prepare the people of God for the mission of witnessing to Christ. The seven letters to the churches point out seven deadly sins with which the churches are being tempted and thus hindered in their witness.

        1. The sin of abandoning their first love (2:4).

        2. The sin of the fear of suffering for Christ's sake (2:10).

        3. The sin of serving mammon and engaging in false worship (unionism, syncretism) while trying to serve God, which leads to idolatry and sexual immorality (2:14).

        4. The sin of crediting salvation to those outside of Christ, to adherents of non-Christian religions in a pluralistic society, which sin also leads to immorality and idolatry (2:20).

        5. The sin of pretense, outwardly conforming to the Christian faith but inwardly dead, slumbering, or worshiping something else (3:1–2).

        6. The sin of neglecting opportunities to witness, the door opened by the Lord (3:8).

        7. The sin of apathy, of being lukewarm (3:15–16).

The Lord Christ calls the church to repent of these seven deadly sins. He chastises and trains those whom he loves (3:19; cf. Heb 12:4–11). The church is lifted up in the grace and mercy of Christ to be motivated and empowered for the mission given to her. Each of the seven letters closes with a Gospel promise for "the one who conquers" (Rev

2:7, 11, 17, 26–28; 3:5, 12, 21). Martyrdom is the most powerful witness to Christ.

II. The prophetic message (4:1–22:5): By the grace of God, the church lives and carries out her mission. For the sake of the church and her mission the exalted Son of Man controls all history and all events.

   A. The inaugural vision (4:1–5:14) of the enthronement of the Lamb and the exalted reign of the Lord Christ at the right of the heavenly Father is central for all that follows in Revelation. The focus and object of the church's faith and worship is the exalted Christ. With this vision she lives in hope and is empowered for her mission of witness. The Te Deum of the angels and saints is the hymn of the church in mission (4:8, 11).

   B. The mission is fraught with danger, suffering, and death as exhibited by the three visions of events on earth (6:1–16:21). These visions are introduced by the seven seals of the scroll (6:1–8:5), the seven trumpet-angels (8:6–11:19), and the seven censer-angels (15:1–16:21).

     1. The church is not immune from the tribulations and sufferings that afflict the human race because of its sin and rebellion against God (6:1–8:5). These include tyranny and oppression (6:1–2); war and bloodshed (6:3–4); economic depression and famine (6:5–6); and death and the grave (6:7–8). Through it all the church suffers as she witnesses, even unto death, for her witness by word is sealed in martyrdom (6:9–11). She is comforted in her mission by the scenes of the church militant on earth (7:1–8) and the church triumphant in heaven (7:9–17).

     2. The church in mission should be prepared to face further dangers to mankind (8:6–11:19).

       a. There are disorders and calamities on earth and in the heavens in the form of natural disasters and plagues (8:6–13).

       b. There are also supernatural torments from hell spawned by the demons led by their king, the angel of the abyss (9:1–11). She will face the last battle (9:13–21).

       c. She is reminded of the purpose and the necessity of her prophetic ministry by the mighty angel in Revelation 10.

       d. The two witnesses, who are martyred then raised, dramatize that her prophetic witness will prevail, even unto death and glory (11:1–14).

       e. The seventh trumpet will bring the end of the present world, and the church in mission will join the heavenly worship with great joy (11:15–19).

3. The church in mission is engaged in the cosmic battle between God and Satan (12:1–14:20).

a. Though her spiritual warfare on earth against the dragon and the beasts is intense, God keeps his church in his watchful care and honors her as his bride for the sake of the victory of the holy Child, the Christ (12:1–18). The dragon is unable to destroy the church's holy Child because the dragon was utterly defeated by the Christ (12:1–5; cf. Mt 2:13–23; 4:1–11; Jn 12:27–33). Satan is thrown out of heaven so that he can no longer accuse the saints before God's heavenly throne (Rev 12:7–9). The dragon takes out his hatred of God and His Christ on the woman and her seed on earth, the church, in order to destroy her and her witness to the holy Child (12:13–18). In her earthly pilgrimage the church wanders in the wilderness, but she is cared for and protected by God because the church is to be Christ's bride (cf. 19:6–8).

b. To assist the dragon in his war against the church he conjures up two beasts: a political beast from the sea (13:1–10) and a religious beast from the earth (13:11–18).

c. The church militant is comforted by the vision of the church on earth after she has completed her mission and the Lamb returns for her (14:1–5).

d. The dragon and his beasts will be defeated (14:6–13).

e. The fruit of the church's mission will be gathered at the harvest at the present world's end (14:14–20).

4. The church continues her mission in the third sevenfold vision of events on earth from Christ's first advent to his return (15:1–16:21).

a. As the church proclaims the Gospel of Jesus Christ, she follows her Lord singing the Te Deum, even as she suffers and goes into death (15:1–4). In nature and in the history of human affairs there are no accidents of fate. Everything is under God's sovereign authority and power (15:5–8).

b. The acts of God's judgment are an aid for the mission of the church (16:1–11). The plagues of God's wrath are poured out on the earth in order to lead the human race to repentance. The church in her prophetic witness to Christ must affirm these acts of God's judgment as she proclaims the Word of God (16:5–7).

c. The church is given a second vision of the final battle just before the End (16:12–16).

d. The church sees that even in the final plague of God's judgment as this world comes to its end, humanity as a whole is not led to repentance, but stubbornly blasphemes God (16:17–21).

C. God will bring the church's mission to its triumphant consummation in eternity (17:1–22:5).

1. Even though the world and its powers and wealth are aligned with the harlot (the anti-church) against the church in mission, Babylon (the harlot riding the beast) will be defeated and fall (17:1–18:24).

2. After the church completes her mission according to God's schedule, Christ will claim her as his bride and celebrate the wedding feast (19:1–21).

3. Satan is bound during the NT era so that the church can carry out and complete her mission (20:1–6). At the End he is let loose only to be defeated at the last battle (20:7–10).

4. The result of the church's mission will be revealed on Judgment Day: all those whose names are written in the Lamb's book of life (20:11–15).

5. Her mission completed, the church, the bride, will live forever with her Lord in the new heaven and new earth (21:1–22:5).

III. The epilogue (22:6–21), like the prologue (1:1–8), stresses the urgency of the church's mission because the events will happen quickly (22:6) and Christ is returning soon (22:20). Like a codicil, the epilogue attests the truthfulness of God's words (22:6), which are not to be altered in any way (22:18–19) as they are proclaimed in the mission of the church. The Lord of the church declares that he is coming quickly (22:20). Hence, the church answers with John, "Amen, come now, Lord Jesus!" (22:20). That is the constant prayer of the church in mission as she waits for the fulfillment of her Lord's promise.

12:1–14:20

Interregnum: The Cosmic War between Christ and Satan, between God's Saints and the Forces of Evil

REVELATION 12:1–18

THE WOMAN WITH CHILD AND THE DRAGON

TRANSLATION

12 [1]And a great sign appeared in heaven: a woman clothed about with the sun, and the moon underneath her feet, and upon her head a crown of twelve stars, [2]and she was carrying [a Child] in her womb, and she cries out loud as in birth pains and as she strains in anguish to give birth. [3]And there appeared another sign in heaven: behold, a great red dragon who had seven heads and ten horns and upon his heads seven diadems, [4]and his tail sweeps down the third of the stars of heaven and he threw them down to the earth. And the dragon stood before the woman who was about to give birth in order that, when she should give birth, he might devour her Child. [5]And she gave birth to a Son, a male Child, who is going to shepherd all the nations with an iron rod. And her Child was snatched up to God and to his throne. [6]And the woman fled into the wilderness, where she has there a place prepared by God, so that there they might care for her one thousand two hundred sixty days. [7]And there came about war in heaven, for Michael and his angels had to make war with the dragon. And the dragon went to war and also his angels, [8]but he did not prevail nor was a place found for them any longer in heaven. [9]And the great dragon was thrown out, the ancient serpent, who is called the devil and Satan, the one who deceives the entire inhabited [world]; he was thrown down to the earth, and his angels with him were thrown out. [10]And I heard a great voice in heaven saying,

"Now has come about the salvation and the
    power and the kingdom of our God,

and the authority of his Christ,
> because the accuser of our brothers has been
>> thrown out, the one who was accusing them
>> in the presence of our God day and night.
[11]And they conquered him because of the blood of
>> the Lamb, and by the word of their witness,
> and they did not hold their life dear
>> even in the face of death.
[12]On account of this break out in celebration,
>> O heavens, and those who dwell in them!
> But woe to the earth and to the sea, because
>> the devil has come down to you,
> having great fury, knowing that he
>> has but a short time!"

[13]And when the dragon saw that he was thrown down to the earth, he tore after the woman who had given birth to the male Child. [14]And the two wings of the great eagle were given to the woman so that she might fly into the wilderness to her place where she is cared for there a time and times and half a time from the face of the serpent. [15]And the serpent spewed out of his mouth after the woman water like a river so that he might cause her to be swept away in its flood. [16]And the earth heard the cry of the woman, and the earth opened its mouth and swallowed the river which the dragon spewed out of his mouth. [17]And the dragon became furious at the woman and went away to make war with the rest of her seed—those who are keeping the commandments of God and who hold the witness of Jesus. [18]And he stood on the edge of the sea.

COMMENTARY

INTRODUCTION TO REVELATION 12–14, AN INTERREGNUM

Chapters 12–14 serve as an interregnum, that is, *a pause* between the second (8:6–11:19) and the third (15:1–16:21) sevenfold visions of events taking place on earth. During this pause opposing forces vie to rule. This break between the second and third earthly visions is more than an interlude, such as those that appeared between the sixth and seventh seals (7:1–17) and the sixth and seventh trumpet-angels (10:1–11:14) in the first two sevenfold visions. In this break between the second and third visions there is a lengthy pause or cessation by which the normal flow of the visionary prophecy in Revelation concerning events on earth is interrupted. The portrayal of events on earth is *suspended* in order to permit John to see a cosmic vision expounding events that *overarch* what he has been seeing happening on earth. What John views in Revelation 12–14 *dominates and controls* the events that he sees taking place on earth. *These chapters visually explain to John why the events on earth are occurring.*

The events depicted in this interregnum are cosmic in character because the actions depicted occur both above and on the earth. What is portrayed before the eyes of John is nothing less than the cosmic war between God and the prince of darkness, a war that takes place in the heavens and then drops down to earth. This warfare between God and Lucifer (the fallen angel, see Is 14:12; cf. Is 27:1; Lk 10:17–18) is the *source and cause* of the warfare between God's people on earth and the forces of evil. Revelation 12–14 is thus an exposition and an explanation of all that John sees happening on the earth from the time of Christ's exaltation up to the end of this present world at Christ's return.

Chapter 12 presents the awesome scene of the woman with Child, the dragon who attempts to destroy the Child, and (after the Child is taken to heaven) the war in heaven which results in the expulsion of Satan from God's heavenly presence. The chapter concludes with the dragon venting his fury on the woman and her offspring. The vision continues in chapter 13 with the scene of two terrifying beasts that the dragon conjures up for use in his warfare against the woman and her seed. The cosmic vision of this interregnum concludes in chapter 14 with scenes of victory and rejoicing over the judgment and overthrow of the evil forces of the dragon.

A GREAT SIGN IN HEAVEN: A WOMAN (12:1–2)

"A great sign" (12:1) appeared in heaven. A "sign" in the biblical sense is a visual presentation that exhibits something of the divine. It could be a visible token which serves as a confirmation of a gracious promise of God, or a visible guarantee of God's presence (see Gen 9:12–17; Ex 3:12; 7:3). In his gospel John called miracles of Jesus "signs" because they were visible evidences of the saving presence of God in Jesus Christ. Strikingly, here in 12:1 the word refers to "a woman clothed about with the sun" and with "the moon underneath her feet." She is referred to as a "great sign," implying that what she is and represents is of great importance. The sign of the woman appears "in heaven," indicating that her presence is before God in heaven (see 4:4; 7:9–17). She is from God, that is, she is related to his saving presence. Yet the woman and what she represents is also on earth (12:13).

The woman was *clothed in* the brilliance of Christ as exhibited by the sun. Her face and appearance *themselves* do not shine like the sun, for that is reserved for the exalted Son of Man (Rev 1:16; cf. Mt 17:2) and for the angel that stands in the place of Christ and represents him when commissioning John and the church (Rev 10:1, 11). But God has put around her the brilliant, sunlit glory of his Christ, signifying that in Christ and because of him she stands in God's holy presence. "Clothed about with the sun" also suggests how much God in Christ honors the woman.

The moon is "underneath her feet." While "clothed about with the sun" indicates glory, "the moon underneath her feet" suggests dominion. In the OT the sun and moon are mentioned on occasion in reference to the glory and beauty of a human being (Song 6:10). Here in Rev 12:1 the sun is also used as a symbol of glory and honor, but the moon, because of its position under the feet, is used more as a symbol of dominion and authority which the woman exercises as she carries out her mission given by God (see 10:11; 11:1–13).

The woman wears "a crown of twelve stars" on her head. The crown or wreath was a reward given because of victory in a contest or struggle of some kind. Her crown is made up of or contains twelve stars. In 1:20 seven stars in the right hand of the exalted Son of Man represent the seven angels of the churches. Here the twelve stars of the woman's crown represent twelve of the twenty-four elders enthroned around the great throne of God in heaven in 4:4. Prior to her Child's birth, her twelve stars signify the twelve elders representing the twelve tribes of Israel, who in turn represent the people of God in the OT. After her Child is born and is taken to heaven, the crown of twelve stars would then represent the other twelve elders, who stand for the twelve apostles and the NT church. The twelve stars of the crown signify that the woman represents the entire people of God, both Israel and the church of Christ. "Salvation is of the Jews" (Jn 4:22) and so Jesus is born of Mary, *but* he was born to be the Savior of all people, Jew and Gentile alike. The woman wears the victor's wreath as an indication that the people of God are victorious because of her child, the Christ Child.

With the exception of Jesus Christ, no human figure in the entire Bible is so clothed and glorified as this woman. This should not be surprising when it is noted that she bears a Child "who is going to shepherd all the nations with an iron rod" (Rev 12:5), that is, the Messiah. Mary is called "favored of God," because the grace of God was with her (Lk 1:28–30). In addition Mary would be called blessed among women because she would bear the Christ Child (Lk 1:31–33, 42). Here in Rev 12:1–2 this honor is typified by the sun and the crown with which the woman is adorned, and the dominion she inherits through her Son is typified by her feet on the moon.

Mary, the mother of the Christ Child, is the model for the woman here in 12:1–2, for the woman, as does Mary, symbolizes and represents the church. The woman thus represents the faithful people of God who longed for the Messiah to come, and who by their faith can be said metaphorically to be the mother of the Child and thus to have given birth to him. After the birth and the ascension of the Child, the woman becomes and represents the church of the apostles.

In Revelation three women appear and illustrate important roles. The woman of 12:1 illustrates the church in her beauty and position before God. The harlot of 17:1–18:24 in her deceptive beauty represents the anti-church and as such is the archrival and enemy of the woman of 12:1. The bride of the Lamb in 19:7–8 is to be identified with the woman of 12:1 as she meets her husband, the Lord Christ, at the End.

ANOTHER SIGN IN HEAVEN:
A DRAGON (12:3–4A)

"Another sign" appeared in heaven: "a great red dragon" (12:3). As in the case of the woman with Child, the fact that this other appearance is designated as a "sign" points out that what it pictures is important—yet not as important as the *"great* sign" (12:1) of the woman. The sign of the dragon also appears in heaven, thus indicating that what it depicts is *above* the earth, though it will greatly influence what happens *on* the earth too. The dragon has "seven heads and ten horns and upon his heads seven diadems" (12:3). The "seven heads" are similar to the *seven* horns and the *seven* eyes of the Lamb in 5:6. The number seven is God's number, in particular symbolizing the sevenfold presence of Yahweh through his Holy Spirit (1:4; 3:1; cf. 1:20). The fact that the Lamb in Revelation 5 has seven horns and seven eyes signifies that the exalted Christ is all-powerful (the horns; cf. Lk 1:69; Deut 33:17; Dan 7:8, 24–25) and all-knowing (the eyes, 2 Chr 16:9; Prov 15:3) and that he exercises this power and authority by the Spirit. The dragon's seven heads reflect his deceptive claim that *he*, and *not* the Christ, is the spirit who has all knowledge to supervise all earthly matters. Each head is crowned with a diadem reflecting his deceptive claim that he possesses all royalty and lordship. The ten horns point to the boastful claim that the dragon has supreme earthly power. The number ten means that while other earthly powers exist, the dragon has dominating power and authority to exercise it. Any other earthly power, symbolized by a single horn, can exist and exercise that power only under the consent and sanction of the dragon and by his guidance. By such an appearance the dragon boasts that he has all wisdom and all power over all the peoples and kingdoms on the earth (cf. Mt 4:8–9). Of course this is all a lie (Jn 8:44)—but a lie that will spell doom for those who believe it. The color of the dragon is red, the color of murder and bloodshed (see Rev 6:4) of both a spiritual and a physical nature.

The dragon sweeps down with his tail "the third of the stars of heaven" and he throws them "down to the earth" (12:4). Stars represent the angels (1:20). In 9:1 a star falling from heaven represents the angel of the abyss, the devil (9:11; cf. Lk 10:18). Elsewhere in the Scriptures angels are represented by stars (Judg 5:20; Job 38:7) and fallen angels, especially the devil, by fallen stars (Is 14:12). Here in Rev 12:4 the casting of the stars out of heaven to the earth dramatically portrays the dragon pulling other angels with him in his rebellion against God (cf. 2 Pet 2:4; Jude 6). A third of the stars were involved with the dragon in this rebellion. Whether one takes "the third" as a literal number or as a symbolical number, it suggests not a majority, but a sizable minority of the angelic host. This is the only reference in the Bible which suggests the number of angels that the dragon took with him in his opposition to God.

THE DRAGON AND THE CHILD (12:4B-6)

The dragon awaits the birth of the Child so that at his birth he might destroy him. The dragon's opposition is not at first against the woman, but against the Child, for the Child is the focus in the dragon's warfare against God. Only after the Child has escaped his clutches and is safe in heaven does he vent his rage on the woman (12:13).

Ancient mythologies have a number of stories of a woman with child who is pursued by a monster or dragon. These myths provide evidence that ancient peoples had heard the truth of a woman whose Child would deliver the human race from the forces of evil and darkness, embodied in the ancient serpent or dragon. These myths originated from the original promise God gave to Adam and the woman when he said that the Seed of the woman would crush the serpent's head (Gen 3:14-15). By the time that these ancient myths were recorded in the extrabiblical literatures in which they are preserved, they had already been distorted and given shape by pagan ideas and influences. Nevertheless, in their core they witness to the one true, original story of a Child from a woman who would rescue the human race. John, the author of Revelation, would know of some of these stories, and in this retelling of the ancient story of the woman with Child and the dragon, he sets the record straight. There was an original, true promise of a woman and her Child, the Child who would save the human race from the clutches of the dragon. That Child is the Christ Child.

The woman gives "birth to a Son, a male Child" (Rev 12:5). The "male Child" is clearly identified as the One who would "shepherd all the nations with an iron rod." In Psalm 2 the "Anointed One" ("his [Yahweh's] Messiah"; "his Christ"; Ps 2:2), who is the "King" installed by God on Mt. Zion (Ps 2:6) and who is declared to be his "Son" (Ps 2:7), will rule over all other kings and over all the peoples of the earth (Ps 2:1-2, 8, 10). He will reign with an "iron rod," breaking them to pieces like pottery (Ps 2:9). The "iron rod" looks beyond Christ's present hidden reign in grace to his future reign in revealed power and glory, when all opposition to him will be shattered. He will begin that reign after the end of this world at his return, as indicated by the future sense of "who is *going to* shepherd" (Rev 12:5). In light of that *future* reign in wrath over his foes, all peoples and all kings are invited *now* to fear and love him and thereby through faith enter his present kingdom of grace and escape God's future wrath (Ps 2:11–12). But that invitation is not extended to the dragon; he can only look forward to the termination of his evil rule and to his own destruction, hence his fury against the Child.

In Lk 1:31–32 the angel Gabriel said that the male Child to be born to Mary would rule the house of Jacob on the throne of David forever. Here in Rev 12:5 through the quote of Ps 2:9 the male Child is unmistakably identified as the Messiah of God, the Christ, the Anointed One, and also as the Child of Mary, the promised Savior, whose name is Jesus (see Lk 1:31; cf. Mt 1:21). In his earthly ministry Jesus of Nazareth declared that he was the shepherd promised by God who would lay down his life for the sheep (Jn 10:11–15; cf. Ezek 34:15–24). His staff or rod symbolizes the care of his people (see Jn 10:27–28; cf. Zech 11:7–10) but also represents his authority in judgment by which, like a shepherd, he will separate the sheep from the goats, God's people from unbelievers, and thus in judgment vanquish the enemies of God (Mt 25:32–33; cf. Ps 2:9; Ezek 34:17–22). According to Rev 2:26–27 this shepherding authority of the Christ Child will be shared by God's people: in the letter to the church of Thyatira, every Christian who is victorious and keeps doing Christ's work to the End "will shepherd them [the nations] with an iron rod." God's people will share in Christ's authority over the nations and in his demonstration of judgment.

The Child is "snatched up to God and to his throne" (12:5). Here the incarnation and the entire ministry, passion, death, resurrection, and ascension of Christ are compressed into the words "snatched up to God." John's purpose is to emphasize the *final outcome* of Christ's incarnation and passion and resurrection, that is, the dragon's failure to destroy the Child and the victory of the Christ over the enemies of God's people. The fact that Christ was taken "to God and to his throne" (12:5), his ascension, demonstrates and vindicates his victory over the dragon and the forces of death and evil. *He* is exalted and enthroned, not the dragon. Christ's session at the Father's right hand is the ultimate confirmation of his victory, and here it is reenacted and dramatized for John in order to confirm his faith in the victory of the Lamb over the dragon, won years before at the cross and empty tomb.

The dragon tried his utmost to destroy the Child when the woman gave birth. The action of King Herod in killing the infants of Bethlehem in his effort to destroy the infant Christ is certainly a part of the dragon's design against the Child. But the Child was snatched from Herod's wicked hands and taken to Egypt (Mt 2:13–18), a type of the final snatching to God at Christ's ascension. Also Jesus' temptation in the wilderness is to be viewed in connection with the dragon's continued effort to intimidate and to destroy the Christ (Mt 4:1–11).

Throughout Jesus' earthly ministry the devil attempted to thwart his mission (see Heb 4:15). But despite the agony and the suffering that the Lord Christ endured, the dragon did not and could not destroy the Child.

After the ascension of the Christ to God, "the woman fled into the wilderness" (Rev 12:6). The woman at first, after the model of Mary, typified Israel, the people of God of old. Now she becomes the new and larger Israel, the Christian church, the people of God, both Jews and Gentiles (cf. Eph 2:11–22). The church would not immediately share in the exalted glory of the ascended Christ, for the woman flees "into the wilderness." As was prophesied of Mary, so now the church would be pierced with a sword (Lk 2:35). The "wilderness" brings to mind the wanderings of Israel in the Desert of Sinai after the deliverance and exodus from Egypt (Ex 19:1–2; Num 14:20–35; Deut 8:2). So now the new Israel, the church of Christ, enters her wilderness experience after having seen and been the recipient of the great salvation worked by the Lamb of God. As the Israelites of old were cared for by God in the barren desert with manna and food and water and safety (Ex 16:4–5, 13; 17:3–7; 23:20), so now the church would be nourished and defended by God in her harsh and dangerous environment. Here in Rev 12:6 the 1,260 days symbolize the length of time that the church will be in exile here on earth and that God will care for her. It is the same period of time, also designated as 1,260 days, that the two witnesses carry out their prophetic ministry (11:3). Since it amounts to three and a half years, it is also the same length of time as the "forty-two months" when the church, represented by the holy city and its temple, is trampled underfoot (11:1–2). These time periods designate the same period of history, which spans the church age: from the ascension of Christ to the end of the present world at Christ's return.

WAR IN HEAVEN (12:7–9)

What is now announced and portrayed to John staggers the human imagination. That there should be war before God's presence in heaven would seem to be unthinkable, utterly out of place. The angels sang at the birth of Jesus, "Glory in highest places to God and *on earth peace*" (Lk 2:14). The pilgrims who welcomed Jesus on Palm Sunday as he rode triumphantly into Jerusalem sang a similar hymn of blessing: "*In heaven peace* and glory in highest places" (Lk 19:38). According to Luke, then, the Christ was born to bring peace to earth and through his death and resurrection was about to bring peace in heaven. But what does that "peace" mean? While human warfare on earth includes physical struggles and bloodshed, to the Christian on earth the most horrible battle is a spiritual one fought against forces *in the heavenly realms*: "our fight is not against flesh and blood, but against the rulers and authorities and cosmic powers of this darkness, against the spiritual forces of evil *in the heavenly realms*" (Eph 6:12). While Christ's birth, death, and resurrection established peace between God in heaven and humanity on earth, that peace is now being contested by evil spiritual powers in heavenly realms who seek to sever the peace between

God and people achieved by Christ. *The warfare in heaven must be interpreted as a spiritual struggle in which the dragon attempts to displace the Christ Child, the victorious Lamb who was slain, in order to establish himself again in the presence of God as the prince of the angels and as the one who has dominion over humanity on earth, and specifically as the one who has the authority to stand before God and accuse people for their sins.*

At the center of this warfare in heaven is Satan's ability to stand in God's holy presence and accuse the saints of God (Rev 12:10). It is a war, so to speak, of words—the words with which Satan accused God's saints of their sins (e.g., Job 1–2; Zech 3:1–5). With these words Satan claimed that he, not the Christ, truthfully represented the saints before God's heavenly throne. This warfare, though of words, is deadly serious, for if Satan's accusations were validated in the heavenly court, then God's justice would require him to deny even his own people because of their sin. But for that to happen God would have to deny the claim of his own Son to be the rightful representative and advocate for God's people. Christ's victory has earned for him the right to represent fallen humanity; he is the one "who loves us and set us free from our sins by his blood" (Rev 1:5). Therefore the accusations of Satan are thrown out of court, and Satan himself is thrown out of heaven (12:8–10). Because of the rightful claim of Christ to represent God's people with Christ's own sinlessness and righteousness, the very presence of Satan in heaven was now an offense to God and all the heavenly host.

The war in heaven was concluded by "Michael and his angels" against "the dragon" and "his angels," that is, it reached its climax when Michael cast the dragon out of heaven (12:7–9). This war, this casting of Satan out of heaven, took place as a result of Christ's victory and at his ascension and session at the right of God (see 5:1–14). There was no room for *two* opposing advocates, each claiming to be the rightful representative of sinful humanity. No longer could God tolerate Satan's presence, since his accusations were rendered false by the victorious Lamb, who now returned to heaven. At the command of God, Michael and all the faithful angels drove out the dragon and his angels. The dragon and his hordes were not to take part in the celebration that ensued among the heavenly hosts—the celebration of Christ's coronation at his ascension. Once the Messiah of God, the Savior and Champion of his people, had defeated the prince of darkness and had taken his seat at the right of God, the dragon was expelled by Michael. Now dethroned from his seat in the council of angels (see Job 1:6; Zech 3:1), the dragon could never again appear before God.

The idea that God would hold court in the heavenly council can be seen in biblical references. In Dan 7:10, for example, the assembly of angels around the throne of God is called "the court." Related to this idea of God holding court is the fact that angels are often pictured surrounding the heavenly throne of God (Is 6:1–8; Ezek 1:22–28; Dan 7:9–10; Lk 2:13; Rev 4:6; 5:11).

In 12:7 Michael, while not called an "archangel," is the captain of the host of angels engaged in the war with the dragon and his hosts. The verbal construction "had to make war" suggests that the war was at God's command and that they "*had* to make war" because of the exaltation of the Christ Child before God in heaven. As a result of Christ's victory on the cross and his public vindication over the dragon at his ascension and exaltation, there was no longer any room in heaven for the accuser. The dragon *had* to be thrown out of heaven, for Christ's vicarious atonement and justification of the saints made Satan's accusations false—lies—and an offense against God's gracious justice in Christ. Once Christ was elevated and enthroned, the slanderer was held in contempt of God's court and "was thrown out" (12:9), never again to appear before God's heavenly presence.

The dragon did not want to leave his lofty place before God. But although he struggled to maintain his position, it was to no avail. At his expulsion the dragon is clearly identified to John: he is "the ancient serpent, who is called the devil and Satan" (12:9; cf. Gen 3:1–5; Mt 4:10; Lk 4:3). The word "Satan" means "adversary" or "enemy," sometimes also "accuser" (cf. 12:10). Likewise "devil" means "slanderer" or "false accuser" (Jn 8:44), and true to his name he "deceives the entire inhabited [world]" (Rev 12:9). He and his host of evil angels are now confined to the earth and its sphere.

When did this war, this expulsion of the dragon and his evil host, take place? According to 12:5, it happened when the "Child was snatched up to God and to his throne," that is, at the ascension of Christ. Apparently before Christ's victory and ascension, the devil could at will stand before God and bring accusations against God's saints. There are two well-known instances of this in the OT. In both Job (1:6–11; 2:1–5) and Zechariah (3:1–7), Satan stands before God's heavenly presence to accuse two of his saints: Job and Joshua the high priest. But at Christ's enthronement at the right of God, Satan was forever banished from God's presence and his place in the heavenly court was taken from him.

This war in heaven in Rev 12:7 is not the original rebellion of the devil against God, which took place before the fall of Adam and the woman (Gen 3:1). *The war and expulsion described in Revelation 12 happened as a result of Christ's victory and elevation.* Not only is Satan judged, because of Christ's triumphant return to his heavenly Father's throne, Satan is now expelled and banished forever from God's presence. Finally, at the End when Christ returns, Satan and all his fellow evil spirits will be cast forever into hell, the lake of fire (Rev 20:10; cf. 2 Pet 2:4; Jude 6). The conclusion that the expulsion of Satan from heaven here in Revelation 12 is the result of Jesus' ministry of redemption agrees with Jesus' statement at the return of the seventy-two, when he said, "I was watching Satan falling like lightning from heaven" (Lk 10:18). Jesus also said, "*Now* the ruler of this world will be thrown out outside, and I, when I am lifted up from the world, will draw all people to myself" (Jn 12:31–32).

THE SONG OF VICTORY (12:10–12A)

"A great voice in heaven" now calls forth a declaration of victory and celebration, for "the accuser" of God's saints "has been thrown out" (Rev 12:10). The saints here are called "our brothers." Because of that designation, the "great voice" apparently is not that of an angel or one of the four winged creatures (e.g., 4:6–8; 6:1; 7:2). Most likely it is spoken by the twenty-four elders, since the elders represent OT Israel and the NT church (see 4:4, 10; 5:5; and the commentary on 4:4). If so, then the elders, together with all the saints in heaven and on earth, had to suffer the accusations of the devil as he stood before God, but now they suffer no longer.

Therefore, the "great voice" declares, "Now has come about the salvation and the power and the kingdom of our God, and the authority of his Christ" (12:10). The victory was won on the cross (5:6; cf. Jn 12:31–32), and the completeness of that victory is demonstrated by the resurrection of the Christ for all to see and witness (Rev 1:17–18; cf. Acts 2:29–36). Now at the ascension and elevation of the Christ of God, that victory is fully displayed and consummated in the heavens when the dragon is expelled and can never again stand before God's heavenly glory. The devil can never again bring accusations against the saints before the heavenly throne (see Rom 8:31–39).

The phrase "the kingdom of our God, and the authority of his Christ" (Rev 12:10) is similar to "the kingdom of the cosmos has become our Lord's and his Christ's (11:15). In 11:15 the total and cosmic comprehensiveness of "the kingdom" is emphasized. Here in 12:10 the sovereignty and power of that kingdom in its completeness is emphasized. "The authority" of Jesus Christ is displayed now in all its power and grandeur at the expulsion of Satan. The Lord Jesus partially exercised and displayed some of this authority during in his earthly ministry, though not all recognized it (e.g., Mk 1:27; 2:10; 3:22–27). Now this "authority" of Christ is seen in all its consummating power, before which no enemy can stand and by which Christ completely exonerates his followers and the faith they have in him (cf. Phil 2:7–11).

The saints of God, the followers of Christ, were not destroyed or condemned by God based on the accusations of the devil. Though tormented by his accusations because of their guilt over sins they had indeed committed, they never gave in to despair. Their faith was that their sins were washed away in the blood of the Lamb (see Rev 7:13–14). Now it becomes evident for all to see that the guilt of sin no longer clings to believers in Christ. God's people had trusted that they were innocent despite the accusations of "the old evil foe" (LSB 656:1). They knew that truth because of the Word of promise to them (cf. Jn 17:15–17). "The blood of the Lamb" was the actual cause of their acquittal, and "the word of their witness" (Rev 12:11) was the result that testified to their victory in Christ. They gave "witness" to that truth of God's forgiveness because of the blood of the Lamb. They held to that witness even in the face of threats, suffering, and death (see 2:10, 13; 3:10–12). Their faith was their victory because they held firmly to the victorious Christ (1 Jn 5:4–5). For that victory in faith they were not afraid to die. Thus they were a living demonstration of Jesus' words: "The one who loves his life loses it, but the one who hates his life in this world will keep it for eternal life" (Jn 12:25; cf. Mt 10:39; Mk 8:35).

The "great voice" (Rev 12:10) then calls upon the very "heavens" themselves and all "those who dwell in them" to "break out in celebration" (12:12)! At various times the heavens were invoked to hear and to testify to God's words and promises (e.g., Deut 32:1; Ps 19:1; Is 1:2). Now they praise God for the fulfillment of those words and promises. The angels are invited to rejoice with the elders and all the people of God. Though the angels are not the recipients of the saving victory of Christ, they, nevertheless, celebrate with the followers of the Lamb (cf. Rev 5:11–14). They also celebrate because their Lord, the Christ of God, has returned triumphantly to claim his rightful seat at God's right in the council of angels.

THE DRAGON AND THE WOMAN ON EARTH (12:12b–18)

The "great voice" (12:10) also cries out, "Woe to the earth and to the sea, because the devil has come down to you" (12:12)! He has been thrown out of heaven and is now confined to the earth and sea, and he will attack its inhabitants in his evil designs of destruction. No longer able to vent his hatred or plot evil against the Christ of God, and no longer able to express his hatred and cunning craft in lies before God concerning God's saints, he takes out his fury on the human race and life on earth. The dragon also knows "that he has but a short time" (12:12) to attempt the destruction of God's creation. The End is soon to come, and then the dragon will be forever separated from all of God's creation. This "short time" is the time from Christ's ascension to the end of this world.

The dragon vents his anger and evil designs especially against the woman, the church, the bride of the exalted Christ. While the devil, as "the angel of the abyss" (9:11), assails the entire human race (as depicted in 9:1–11), it is the woman who is the focus of his intense warfare. In particular he hates the woman because she gave birth to the Child, and now he vents his hatred of the Child upon the woman, the church, because she puts her trust and life into the care of Christ and refuses to worship and serve the dragon. But the woman is cared for by God and is protected so that she will not be destroyed. The metaphorical imagery of this godly care, "the two wings of the great eagle" (12:14), is reminiscent of the care by which God succored the people of Israel in their wilderness pilgrimage: in Ex 19:4 the Lord God reminds the people of Israel, "I carried you on eagles' wings, and I brought you to myself" (see also Is 40:31; cf. Deut 32:10–11; Ps 91:4). The woman, the church of Christ, like Israel of old, is now on a desert pilgrimage here on earth as the devil hunts her down, causing her all manner of fear and suffering and depredation. God's loving care, however, will sustain her through it to the promised land.

The length of time of her fear and anxiety in the wilderness is given as "a time and times and half a time" (Rev 12:14). This time period of the woman's suffering probably represents three and a half years and is equivalent to the "forty-two months" in 11:2, when the holy city of God will be trampled underfoot by the pagan nations; to the 1,260 days in 11:3 during which the two witnesses of God will carry out their prophetic ministry; and to the 1,260 days in 12:6, during which the woman is sustained in the place prepared for her in the desert. The time period symbolized by these three equivalent expressions is the time between the ascension of Christ and the end of this world at his return. A model and type for it is the wilderness sojourn of the children of Israel. The fact that the dragon is referred to as "the serpent" (12:14–15) indicates that in the dragon's warfare against the woman, the most dangerous onslaught against her will be the temptation to leave the truth of Christ in the quest to become her own god in wisdom and saving care—the same temptation by which the serpent successfully lured Eve and Adam (Gen 3:1–6). This suggests that the most severe suffering caused by the dragon will be of a spiritual nature, in particular the temptation and pressure to commit the sin of apostasy (see Eph 6:12; Rev 2:12–14).

Though God cares for the woman by hindering and restraining the serpent, nevertheless the serpent causes her much anxiety and pain. "The serpent spewed out of his mouth" a raging flood of "water like a river" in order to drown the woman (12:15). In great terror the woman cries out, and God hears her cry and responds by causing the earth to swallow the river. The people of God have always been confronted by the dragon and the fear of being overwhelmed by the torrents and raging floods of evil (see, e.g., Pss 18:4–5; 32:4–7). But God always hears the cries of his endangered and fearful people. In Ps 124:2–5 the psalmist declares that if God had not been by his side when the torrents and the floods of evil had engulfed him, he would have perished. And in Is 43:1–2 the prophet hears the promise of God that when he would travel through waters and rushing rivers, they will not sweep him away, for the Lord God, his Redeemer, would be with him (cf. Ps 18:6). One may also recall how God stopped the flow of the Jordan River so that his people could cross on dry land (Joshua 3), as well as the crossing of the Red Sea (Exodus 14–15) and the universal flood (Genesis 6–9), during which God protected Noah and his family, typifying Holy Baptism (1 Pet 3:20–21).

The earth swallows the water. This brings to mind how the earth opened its mouth in God's service to swallow up Korah and those with him in his rebellion against Moses (Num 16:1–3, 28–34), a miracle by which the people of Israel would know that Korah was really opposing God. In this manner God delivered the faithful Israelites from the sin of apostasy. The use of such imagery here in Rev 12:16 suggests that, if necessary, God will rescue and defend his people from the onslaughts of the evil one even through miraculous events (cf. 11:5–6). Rebels may oppose God and usurp the authority of those properly called to shepherd God's flock, and such schisms may lead some of the flock astray, but the church will be preserved by grace and ultimately the schismatics will be put to shame.

Since even the earth takes part in God's work of protection, the dragon becomes even more furious that he cannot destroy the woman. So now he focuses his attention on "the rest of her seed," her children (12:17). The dragon could not destroy the Christ Child. He could not destroy the woman, the church. So he attempts to destroy her seed, at least some of them. So the devil "went away to make war" with her children, "those who are keeping the commandments of God and who hold the witness of Jesus" (12:17). This description of her children, who are the individual members of the church, indicates that despite the dragon's attempt to destroy the church and the dire threats of annihilation, many tenaciously hold to their faith. Still, individual Christians become the targets of the dragon's desperate designs by which some, at least, *could* be destroyed.

The next stage in the dragon's warfare against the children of the woman is to stand at the edge of the sea, the place of chaos and evil. He will first conjure up the beast from the sea (13:1) and then the beast from the earth (13:11). With these two beasts and what they represent, the dragon will carry on his evil war against the members of Christ's church. The two beasts under the control and inspiration of the dragon will be the cause of all the tribulations and sufferings that the church and her children will endure throughout the remainder of the message of Revelation.

REVELATION 13:1–18

THE EVIL FORCES OF THE DRAGON: THE BEAST FROM THE SEA AND THE BEAST FROM THE EARTH

TRANSLATION

13 ¹And I saw a beast coming up out of the sea having ten horns and seven heads, and upon its horns ten diadems, and upon its heads the name[s] of blasphemy. ²And the beast which I saw was like a leopard, and its feet were like [those] of a bear, and its mouth was like the mouth of a lion. And the dragon gave to it his own power and his throne and great authority. ³And one of its heads was as if it had been fatally wounded unto death, but its wound of death had been healed. And the whole earth was full of amazement at the beast. ⁴And they worshiped the dragon because he gave his authority to the beast; they also worshiped the beast, saying, "Who is like the beast and who is able to go to war with it?" ⁵And there was given to it a mouth speaking great things and blasphemies, and authority to be active for forty-two months was given to it. ⁶And it opened its mouth for [the purpose of] blasphemies against God, to blaspheme his name and his sanctuary [and] those dwelling in heaven. ⁷And [the authority] to make war with the saints and to conquer them was given to it, and also authority was given to it over every tribe and people and tongue and nation. ⁸And all those dwelling upon the earth will worship it—[every person] whose name has not been written in the book of life of the Lamb who was slain from the foundation of the world.

[9]If anyone has ears, let him listen!

[10]If anyone is for captivity, into captivity he goes;
if anyone is by sword to be killed,
he by sword is to be killed.

Here is the patience and the faith of the saints! [11]And I saw another beast coming up out of the earth, and it had two horns resembling a lamb's, but it was speaking like the dragon. [12]And it exercises all the authority of the first beast in its presence, and it makes the earth and those dwelling in it so that they will worship the first beast, whose mortal wound was healed. [13]And it produces great signs, so that it could even make fire to come down out of heaven onto the earth before men. [14]And it deceives those dwelling upon the earth by the signs which were given to it to perform before the [first] beast, saying to those dwelling upon the earth to make an image to the beast which has the mortal wound of the sword but came back to life. [15]And there was given to it [the ability] to put a spirit/breath into the image of the beast, so that the image of the beast could also speak and so that it could make it so that those who would not worship the image of the beast would be killed. [16]And it forces all—the small and the great, and the wealthy and the poor, and the free and the slaves—so that there would be given to them a mark upon their right hand or upon their forehead, [17]and that no one could be able to purchase or sell except the one who had the mark—the name of the beast or the number of its name. [18]Here is wisdom! He who has the intelligence, let him figure out the number of the beast, for it is a human number, and the number of it is six hundred sixty-six.

COMMENTARY

THE BEAST FROM THE SEA (13:1–10)

THE APPEARANCE OF THE BEAST FROM THE SEA

The first "beast" or evil creature that the dragon conjures up in his warfare against the woman and her seed comes up "out of the sea" (13:1). In 11:7 "the beast" which comes "out of the abyss" makes war with the two witnesses (representing the Christian church) and kills them. The use of "beast" here in 13:1, the same term as in 11:7, suggests that these two beasts are related, though they are not the same. The beast "coming up out of the abyss" in 11:7 is to be is identified with "the angel of the abyss" in 9:11, who in turn is to be identified with the "dragon" of Revelation 12: all three are Satan. Here in 13:1 the beast is not the dragon (the angel of the abyss), but it is under the control of the dragon (Satan himself).

The "sea" in 13:1 is, then, similar to "the abyss" (hell) in 9:11 and 11:7. Just as Satan is the "beast" from "the abyss," that is, hell (11:7), similarly the "beast" here in 13:1, which is under Satan's control, is from "the sea," which indicates a sinister origin. In 12:18 (ET 13:1) the dragon (Satan) stands on the shore of the "sea" in anticipation as he awaits the beast to come forth at his bidding. If one faces out toward the Aegean Sea from Patmos, the island off the coast of Asia Minor where John wrote Revelation (1:9), one is looking in the general direction of Rome, which was for John and for the Christians of his time the epitome of evil worldly power, just as Babylon was for ancient Israel.

In the OT the "sea," especially in its boiling rage, is frequently portrayed as the place of the fearful chaos and destruction caused by mankind's sin and rebellion against God. As such it is the dwelling place of the sea monsters Leviathan and Rahab, which terrorize the human race (Job 41; Ps 89:9–10; Is 51:9–19). In Is 57:20–21 the wicked are likened to "the tossing of the sea" which has no rest or peace and whose waves are always casting up sludge and filth. Only God himself can control the fury of this sea—as exhibited in Jesus' stilling of the tempest (see Ps 74:13–14; Mt 8:26).

The first beast has "ten horns and seven heads" (Rev 13:1), exactly like the dragon (12:3). This identifies the beast, and what it represents, as the instrument and agent of the dragon. The beast, like the dragon, also has "diadems" (13:1). However, the diadems—the sign of royal authority and dominion—are not upon the monster's heads, as was the case with the dragon, but on its horns. The dragon, and not either of the two beasts he conjures up, has diadems on his heads, because *the dragon* is the supreme mastermind of evil who will motivate and inspire the beasts.

The horns of the beast symbolize earthly power which it exercises in and over human affairs through individual authorities. The fact that the beast, like the dragon, has *ten* horns means that it will be the dominant earthly power before whom no other worldly authority can stand. The diadems on the horns of the beast suggest that once its heads are inspired by the dragon, the individual authorities whom the horns represent will act on their own power in so far as God will allow them. While the horns of the beast wear diadems, its heads wear name(s) or title(s) of "blasphemy," for these rulers seek to blaspheme God and his saints. Blasphemy is the defaming and abusive speech by which God and all that belongs to him are ridiculed and mocked (see Mt 12:31).

In appearance the beast looks "like a leopard," but has "feet ... like [those] of a bear" and "its mouth was like the mouth of a lion" (Rev 13:2). This beast appears to be a composite of the four beasts Daniel saw in Dan 7:2-7. In Daniel's vision, the beasts came out of the sea (Dan 7:2) in succession, and each took the place of the one before it. After the first three had come and gone, the fourth beast continued on alone to "devour all the earth" (Dan 7:23). This fourth beast had "ten horns" and then another horn which supplanted three of the ten; all of the horns represent kings through whom the beast exercised his destructive power (Dan 7:7, 24-25). The additional horn would also war against the saints and (temporarily) defeat them, for they are given into his hand for a length of time: "a time and times and half a time," probably indicating a figurative three and a half years (Dan 7:21, 25; cf. 11:36-45; 12:7, 11-12). This horn also spoke "great/arrogant/boastful things" against God, perhaps referring to blasphemies (Dan 7:8, 20, 25; cf. 11:36).

Thus the description of the beast from the sea in Rev 13:1-2 suggests that it resembles the fourth beast from the sea in Dan 7:7. John sees only one beast because by his time in history the first three had come and gone. After the fourth beast which Daniel prophetically saw had taken the place of the first three, it would remain active throughout the whole time period designated by "a time, times, and half a time" (Dan 7:25)—three and a half figurative years. This is the same time period that the beast in Rev 13:1-2 would be active, but in 13:5 that period is designated as forty-two months, an equivalent expression. While the fourth beast in Daniel 7 had not yet come into existence during the lifetime of Daniel, it had by John's time, for in Revelation 12 the casting out of the dragon from heaven and the initiating of his warfare against the woman on earth took place at the ascension of Christ into heaven (12:5, 7-9, 13). The time period during which the beast would be active, designated and symbolized by 1,260 days (11:3; 12:6), forty-two months (11:2; 13:5), and three and a half years ("a time and times and half a time," 12:14), would be the whole period of church history, from Christ's ascension up to the end of this present world at Christ's return.

John sees only one beast from the sea. While it resembles the fourth beast of Daniel 7, it also carries forward into its own royal authority and power the prerogatives and trappings of the first three beasts in Daniel 7. The beast John sees has characteristics of (1) the leopard, (2) the bear, and (3) the lion (Rev 13:2). Those same three animals are mentioned by Daniel, but in the opposite order:

the first beast was like a lion, the second was like a bear, and the third was like a leopard (Dan 7:4–6). This reversed order suggests that *through the one beast from the sea which John sees, John looks backward in time toward the first three beasts in Daniel 7, which are now incorporated in this one beast.* Like the fourth beast in Dan 7:7, the beast which John sees also has "ten horns" (Rev 13:1), clearly associating it with the ten-horned dragon of 12:3 and also the ten-horned fourth beast seen by Daniel. That fourth beast seen by Daniel in the sixth century BC has now come into its reign and power, bearing all the trappings of the first three, which at John's time (the first century AD) are no longer in existence. However, unlike the fourth beast of Daniel 7, the beast from the sea which John sees has "seven heads" (Rev 13:1), which provide further evidence that it is to be identified as a minion of the seven-headed dragon (12:3). A connection to the Roman Empire is supported by the links (discussed immediately above) between this beast and the fourth beast in Daniel 7, for it is during the era of the fourth beast in Daniel 7 that the "one like a Son of Man" comes, receives power and glory from the Ancient of Days, and establishes his kingdom, which will last forever (Dan 7:13–14, 18, 22, 27). The "Son of Man," of course, is Christ Jesus who established the kingdom of God, which indeed will last forever. Christ's life, ministry, death, resurrection, ascension, and exaltation in glory took place during the era when the Roman Empire was the dominant world power.

IDENTIFICATION AND INTERPRETATION OF THE BEAST FROM THE SEA

Many commentators today identify the beast of Rev 13:1–2 with the Roman Empire. However, this interpretation must be broadened: *the beast represents and symbolizes every human authority and everything of the human nature that the dragon can corrupt and control and use in his warfare against the woman (the church) and her seed (individual Christians):* political, governmental, social, economic, philosophical, and educational systems, as well as individuals. No one entity or person at a given time in history will exhaust what the beast signifies. In John's day and long after, the beast of 13:1–2 did indeed represent Rome. While a personage like Hitler or Stalin might for a time and in a particular region epitomize what the beast represents, that personage also would not exhaust such representation. Other human forces and people too would be at work under, beside, or apart from such typical fulfillments of what the beast symbolizes. Furthermore, what the beast signifies will be *worldwide at all times,* and not present only where an epitomized human individual or human organization exists at the moment.

THE POWER AND AUTHORITY OF THE BEAST FROM THE SEA

To this first beast "the dragon gave … his [the dragon's] power and his throne and great authority" (13:2). This beast is a vassal of Satan himself, for it owes its position to him and it rules by his authority and sanction.

"And one of its heads was as if it had been fatally wounded unto death, but its wound of death had been healed" (13:3). The Roman emperor Caligula (ruled AD 37–41) had once become seriously ill then unexpectedly revived and recovered (Suetonius, *Lives of the Twelve Caesars*, Gaius Caligula, 14). Perhaps for John this would have served as an example of one of the beast's heads dying but then being healed. Caligula also attempted to set up a statue of himself in the temple in Jerusalem (Josephus, *Antiquities*, 18.8. 2–9). This attempt could well have been for John an example of a name of "blasphemy," as on each of the beast's heads (13:1).

Closer to the time when John received the revelation, the emperor Nero (AD 54–68) could also have served as an example of one of the beast's heads being mortally wounded. His reign was filled with wickedness; for example, he initiated a fearful persecution of Christians in Rome. Eventually, after being condemned to death by the Roman Senate, he committed suicide in order to escape the fate of dying shamefully as a public enemy. Though he was given a public funeral, the rumor was spread that he had not died but had escaped to Parthia. It was further rumored that he was attempting to raise an army and would return to Rome to regain his throne. In the years after his death several imposters claimed to be Nero. Near the end of the first century AD the rumor of his return eventually died, but it was replaced by the curious belief that he would rise from the grave and thus reclaim his imperial throne (Tacitus, *Annals*, 15:44; *Histories* 2:8; Suetonius, *Lives of the Twelve Caesars*, Nero, 16, 57).

While Caligula and Nero can serve as examples of the mortally wounded head of the beast, and thus also as models or types of future tyrants, the overall picture in 13:1–10 is that at any given time, there will be many human powers that represent the beast. There always will be authorities which are overthrown and replaced by others. The longing for a former ruler or power (or at least one like him) to return, as if risen from the dead, may remain in the hearts of many people.

The powerful and fearsome tyranny exhibited by the beast engages the attention of much of the human race, so much so that people in awe marvel at the beast (13:3). They "worshiped the dragon," the mastermind behind the beast, as "they also worshiped the beast" (13:4). Worship of the Roman emperors had been encouraged ever since the reign of Augustus, but it was not until the latter part of the first century AD that such worship was widespread. Wherever people actually engage in formal worship of the state and its leaders, or when they place their hope and trust in human institutions and affairs and resort to them in place of God, they are worshiping the dragon. So strong is the beast's stranglehold on people that they are helpless in opposing it, even if they would desire to do so, for no one can "go to war with it" (13:4). No one "is like the beast" (13:4); no one can stand up to it. Christians also are not spectators but also suffer because of the dragon's warfare against the woman of Revelation 12, who represents the church, but they never worship the beast. Though the church suffers oppression and even martyrdom as she obeys God rather than man (Acts 5:29), she turns the other cheek (Mt 5:39; cf. Rom 13:1–10) because she is not called to wage an earthly war, but a spiritual war (Eph 6:10–22).

While the whole human race (Rev 13:3) is afflicted by this henchman of the dragon, it is particularly the saints of God on earth who are the focus of the beast's warfare and tyranny. It is for that reason that the beast is given a mouth by which it speaks "great things" (13:5)—arrogance, hybris—and blasphemes God's name, his holy habitation, and all who are dwelling there (13:6; cf. Ps 23:6). In its warfare, it sets out to conquer, to destroy God's holy people by subverting their faith and outlawing their witness to the Lamb who was slain. As the beast exercises authority "over every tribe and people and tongue and nation" (13:7), the woman and her seed will be isolated and tormented to no end, for throughout the whole time period from Christ's ascension up to the End at his return (the era symbolized by the forty-two months, 13:5), she will have no relief from the beast's oppression. But the church will not perish, for the names of God's people are indelibly "written in the book of life of the Lamb who was slain from the foundation of the world," and thus can never be removed from the heart and gracious care of God (13:8; see also 3:5; 17:8).

COMFORT FOR THE SAINTS

The "book of life" is a metaphor which symbolizes that the names of God's saints are written in his mind and on his heart. God knows each of his people by name (see Jn 10:3, 27), and no one can pluck any of them out of his hand nor that of the Lamb (Jn 10:28–30). God's saints belong to him because of the Lamb and his victory (Rev 5:5, 9; 7:3, 14). Thus "the book of life" is called "the book of life *of the Lamb*" here in 13:8 (and in 21:27). When John will see the new heaven and new earth, he will be told that only "those who have been written in the book of life of the Lamb" will enter the heavenly city (21:27; cf. Lk 10:20).

"If anyone has ears, let him listen" (13:9) is an admonition by the Spirit of God for *anyone and everyone* to heed what is to follow. This was also Jesus' admonition to all who heard him (e.g., Mt 11:15; 13:9, 43). The admonition at the end of Revelation 13 (13:18) suggests that every Christian must seek and receive wisdom from God in order to understand the chapter (and indeed, all of Revelation and all of Scripture). Similar calls to the churches are given at the end of each of the seven letters in Revelation 2–3: "the one who has an ear, let him listen to what the Spirit says to the churches" (2:7, 11, 17, 29; 3:6, 13, 22). The purpose there is for the Word of God to call forth repentance and faith (e.g., 2:16–17). In 13:9, the admonition is more for the purpose of instilling patience and faith (13:10b).

While in God's estimate the time is short, for the Christian undergoing persecution and suffering the time can seem endless. Especially then will Christians be tempted to take things into their own hands. But the Spirit of God warns the Christian not to do so. Rather, accept what God allows, even if it is cruel and unjust, and do not resist it. No human being can stand against the beast or control it, since "on earth is not his equal" (LSB 656:1). In God's governance the woman is destined to suffer the warfare of the beast. To whatever degree "captivity" and being "killed" (Rev 13:10) come upon the Christian and whatever form imprisonment and martyrdom take, the Christian is to suffer them patiently in faith for the sake of the Gospel and the Lord Christ (see 1 Pet 2:18–25; 3:14; 4:14). "Here is the patience and the faith of the saints" (Rev 13:10) because it is in such suffering and trials that the faith of the saints shines forth to the world, and the saints realize what God is accomplishing in permitting the beast to conquer them. As stated in 11:7–13, their persecution will be used by God for the sake of the church's Gospel mission and in view of her ultimate glory (cf. 15:2–4). In such "patience" and "faith" the church entrusts her own care to God, knowing that in God's own time he will also mete out justice upon her foes.

THE BEAST FROM THE EARTH (13:11–18)

The second beast or monster that the dragon enlists in his warfare against the woman and her seed comes "up out of the earth" (13:11) and thus is different from the beast from the sea (13:1). While the beast from the sea represents external oppression that forces its dominating tyrannical rule upon people and thus enslaves them, the beast from the earth and what it represents works from within and among people, springing up from humanity's own native soil, as it were. The beast from the earth does not force itself upon people but rather insinuates itself into their confidence and then leads them astray.

This beast has "two horns resembling a lamb's, but it was speaking like the dragon" (13:11). A lamb suggests meekness and innocence. However, this is deceptive for its voice is like "the dragon," that is, it speaks for the dragon of Revelation 12, who is the devil. Oecumenius (sixth century) in his Greek commentary cites 2 Thess 2:9 and interprets the beast to be "the Antichrist, whose coming is by the working of the devil." The beast appears as if it were the Christ, the Lamb of God, but since it speaks for the dragon, it is in reality a false christ (cf. 2 Cor 11:13–14). *While the beast from the sea represents every tyranny by human power and enterprise (political, social, economic, educational, and so forth), the beast from the earth represents religious tyranny. In brief, the first beast can be called the "political beast," while the second is the "religious beast."*

This religious beast is the "false prophet" mentioned in Rev 16:13; 19:20; and 20:10 and is to be identified also with the "harlot" of Revelation 17–18. While Revelation retains the symbol of the beast from the sea (the political beast) throughout, the symbol of the beast from the earth (the religious beast) appears only here. Later in Revelation "the false prophet" (16:13; 19:20; 20:10) replaces it and then the "false prophet" in turn is finally replaced by and becomes "the harlot" (in Revelation 17–18. This suggests that while the religious beast at first represents all false religions and spiritual movements, including gross idolatry and pseudo-Christianity (13:14–15), as time goes on it develops and evolves into its more deadly form, that of the apostate Christianity of the pseudo-church, the Antichrist (see 1 Jn 4:1–3).

ACTIVITIES OF THE BEAST FROM THE EARTH

The beast from the sea is the dragon's prime agent in his warfare with the woman. The beast from the earth is a spiritual power which aids the first beast in its effort to destroy the church. This second, religious beast acts with and under the authority of the political beast in order to enhance and legitimize the stranglehold that the political beast has on the human race. He does this by inspiring the human population of the earth to "worship the first beast, whose mortal wound was healed" (Rev 13:12). The political powers come and go, as signified by the first beast's head that died and returned to life, giving the impression that at times the political beast is weak or dead. But the second beast continually sanctions the first beast's hold on the human race by moving all to stand in fear and awe before it. The fact that one of the first beast's heads has revived from its mortal wound even adds to its mystique, which is also encouraged by the second beast's spiritual servitude to the beast from the sea. This service that the religious powers render to the state for its enhancement and legitimation in its tyrannical hold on the people was obvious under the Roman Empire. The state of Rome used religion to sanctify the fear and obedience of its subjects toward their government. The twentieth century has seen this same attempt in Germany under Hitler, who invoked the ancient Aryan culture and its pagan religion and attempted to use the church to support his regime. But this kind of endeavor is everywhere present (at least potentially), the endeavor of the political and social structures of each generation to garner support by calling upon religious powers and loyalties.

The beast from the earth is capable of producing "great signs" (13:13) in its support of the political beast. The word "signs" suggests miraculous activities: pseudo-miracles. Genuine miraculous works accompanied and attended the true church in her mission (Jn 14:12). But false prophets also produced pseudo-miracles in order to demonstrate and to attempt to validate their spiritual authority (2 Thess 2:9). These miraculous activities are trials for the saints on earth, by which even they could be deceived unless protected by God (see Mk 13:21–23). To "make fire to come down out of heaven onto the earth" (Rev 13:13) was a true miracle of God which attested the prophetic ministry of Elijah (1 Ki 18:36–40; see also 2 Ki 1:10–14; cf. Rev 11:5). In like manner this beast calls fire "down out of heaven" in the attempt to prove that it is the true spiritual power and authority.

Much of the earth's population is deceived "by the signs" which the beast produces (13:14). Those who are deceived are moved "to make an image to the beast" which had been mortally wounded and had come "back to life" (13:14). The making of the image sanctifies the political beast and encourages a cultic worship of what it represents. Few can resist such cultic worship of the state and of other human powers and agencies because they are sanctioned by the religious powers and influences of the moment.

The religious beast is granted the ability "to put a spirit/breath into the image" of the political beast so that it can "speak." Whoever did not heed the speech of the image and thus "worship" it would suffer the penalty of death (13:15).

Magical trickery, spiritism, and witchcraft were widespread and also influential at John's time. They could well be used in the dragon's attempt through the beasts to deceive even Christians (see 1 Jn 4:1–3). But all of this in a wider sense is a type that symbolizes the manner in which the world's religious systems align themselves with the secular powers in the effort to destroy the church and her witness to Christ. As the church resists this pressure by refusing to deny her Lord, and as she steadfastly continues her witness, she will pay the price.

The Mark of the Beast from the Earth

The earth's populations are so under the control of the religious beast that they are forced to be marked so as to be identified as those who belong to the beast. The "mark" (Rev 13:16) could be any kind of stamp, brand, tattoo, image, or representation by which a person in his or her manner of dress and/or conduct declares his or her spiritual loyalty. Slaves were branded or marked by their masters, and worshipers of a particular god were often branded with a mark or tattoo to indicate their devotion to it.

John was probably aware of these practices, and they could have served for him as examples or types of the "mark" of the beast, although, as with the seal of God, John did not expect the mark to be visible to the eye. The dragon and his two beasts know and recognize those who belong to them, even as God knows those who are his saints. The saints of God are sealed on their foreheads (7:3; 9:4), and that seal is spiritual and invisible; Holy Baptism does not leave a physical mark on the Christian (though it may be recalled by a physical gesture such as making the sign of the cross). The adherents of the beast may also be sealed on the forehead (13:16), for the forehead is the seat of knowledge. To wear a "seal" on the forehead means that the person's mind and intelligence belong to the one who is represented by the seal.

The seal may also protect the one who wears it. In the case of the people of God, the seal exhibits that they are protected by God from being destroyed by the warfare of the dragon and his beasts (see 7:1–3; 9:4). OT precedent is found in the Passover signing and in Ezek 9:3–6. In the case of the followers of the beast, the seal indicates that they will be protected by the beast during the warfare conducted by the dragon against the church. They can continue to live without the fear and harm which befall the Christians. As an alternative to the seal on their foreheads, the followers of the beast can have the seal on their "right hand" (Rev 13:16). Such a seal would signify that the activities of the person are done with the sanction of the beast and at his direction. Only those with the beast's mark can legally make a livelihood in commerce and transact earthly affairs. The saints of God on earth do not have such a seal, indicating that God will not necessarily protect their earthly affairs and their pursuits of livelihood, even when they abide by the state's laws. Rather, they will be hindered and even persecuted as they live in this world.

THE NUMBER OF THE BEAST

The mark or brand of the beast is identified with "the name of the beast or the number of its name" (13:17), that is, the name is represented by its number. Ancient Hebrew and Greek used letters of the alphabet to represent numerals. Among the Jewish people in particular there arose the practice of representing the name of a person by the numerical value of the letters of his or her name. Thus each name could bear a particular numerical value. This practice was known as *gematria*.

Rev 13:18 is perhaps the most perplexing verse in the whole of Revelation. However, for John the author this was evidently not so, for he says that just as anyone who has ears should hear (13:9), whoever "has the intelligence" should "figure out the number of the beast, for it is a human number" (13:18). Not everyone would have this intelligence and ability, but evidently some do or did. Those who were versed in gematria could "figure out the number of the beast" if that were the method John had in mind. In Eph 1:17 Paul, in his prayer for the believers in Ephesus, asks that God would grant them the "Spirit of wisdom and of revelation in their knowledge of him [Jesus Christ]." The wisdom and intelligence that John speaks of is the knowledge and revelation of Christ, which a person can understand only by the aid of the Spirit. Whether or not it involves a particular cryptographic hermeneutic like gematria, he evidently expects those who have such knowledge and spiritual wisdom to exercise it.

The number of the beast "is a human number" (Rev 13:18), for the number "six hundred sixty-six" is expressed in human language and words. Furthermore, since man was created on the sixth day (Gen 1:26–31), the number six could represent humanity and anything of the human nature, just as the number seven represents God. Thus 666 would represent and point to one particular individual. The person most commonly accepted is that of Nero. If "Nero Caesar" is transliterated into Hebrew letters, equivalent to NRON QSR, then the total would be 666 (N [50] + R [200] + O [6] + N [50] + Q [100] + S [60] + R [200] = 666). If this is the solution, only a part of John's recipients could have solved this cryptogram.

If Nero is the particular person to whom the number 666 cryptically refers, he is the type or model of what the beast really represents, and he is not the final fulfillment, for he had been dead around twenty years when John wrote

Revelation. Nero could serve as one example of what the beasts represent: *all* anti-Christian forces. As a *type* the deeper significance of the number is that which it *typifies*—the *unholy trinity* of the dragon (Revelation 12), the beast from the sea (13:1–10), and religious beast from the earth (13:11–18). In the context of chapter 13, the number is the number of the beast from the earth, the second beast. Nevertheless, the number applies also to the dragon and to the first beast, the beast from the sea. The number applies to all three members of the unholy trinity, especially to whichever one is most active and most prominent at any given time and in any given situation.

If the number 777 were to be used, it would refer to the holy Trinity, God the Father, Son, and Holy Spirit; hence, 666 would be an evil trinity that mimics the Holy Trinity but always falls short. *"The wisdom" referred to at the beginning of 13:18 is then the wisdom that comes from God and enables the Christian to know and understand what this unholy trinity is and represents at any given time here on earth. This wisdom enables the Christian to discern how the evil forces of the dragon, both secular and religious, are always and everywhere active, at war to destroy the church and her witness to Christ.* Such wisdom comes only from God, but it is a wisdom that he graciously and richly confers on all his people in Christ.

REVELATION 14:1–5

THE CONQUERING LAMB AND THE VICTORY SONG OF THE SAINTS

TRANSLATION

14 [1]And I looked, and behold there was the Lamb standing on Mount Zion and with him were the one hundred forty-four thousand who had his name and the name of his Father written on their foreheads. [2]And I heard a voice from heaven like the sound of many waters and like the sound of a great thunder, and the voice which I heard was something like that of harpers harping on their harps. [3]And they were singing as if it were a new song before the throne and before the four winged creatures and the elders. And no one was able to learn the song except the one hundred forty-four thousand, who had been purchased from the earth. [4]These are those who were not made unclean with women, for they are [male] virgins; these are the ones who are following the Lamb wherever he goes. These were purchased from among men as a firstfruit for God and for the Lamb. [5]And in their mouth a lie was not found; they are unblemished ones.

COMMENTARY

THE LAMB AND THE SAINTS ON MOUNT ZION (14:1)

John sees "the Lamb standing on Mount Zion" (14:1). This is John's second vision of the Lamb in Revelation. In the throne scene of God's heavenly glory in 5:6, John saw the Lamb for the first time. There he viewed the exaltation and coronation of the Lamb, portrayed by the Lamb receiving the seven-sealed scroll.

Now John sees the Lamb on Mt. Zion leading the 144,000. How fitting it is that after the horrifying warfare of the dragon and his two beasts depicted in Revelation 12–13 John now sees the host of God's saints in the church militant accompanied by a song of victory. Though they were conquered in the earthly warfare by the beasts (13:7, 15), they are still victorious. This victory is now demonstrated by them following the Lamb on Mt. Zion and about to join the church triumphant, which sings "a new song" (14:3) before the throne of God in heaven.

Only here in Revelation does John speak of Mt. Zion, and it is quite appropriate that it is the holy place where the Lamb stands together with the 144,000. The Lamb who was slain stands where the temple with its sacrificial altar once stood. Now the Lamb has come to deliver God's people from the horrifying warfare waged by the unholy trinity of the dragon and the two beasts (Revelation 12–13). This scene of the Lamb and the 144,000 on Mt. Zion signals the beginning of the end of this present world, which is pictured in 14:14–20 as a harvest.

Rev 14:1–5 is the second and final time that the 144,000 are mentioned. In Rev 7:1–8 they represented the church militant, the Christians on earth, who were sealed by God in preparation for the conflict before them. In 14:1 they accompany the Lamb, who, as the Son of Man, is about to execute the judgment of God in the harvest of the earth at the End (14:14–20). They have completed their mission, and though they were in deadly conflict with the two beasts of the dragon (Revelation 13), they now stand victorious because of the Lamb's own victory on their behalf (see 5:6–10; 7:9–17). They are, for the moment, still the church militant on earth (on Mt. Zion), but now their warfare is over and they are about to join the church triumphant in heaven. The seal of God that the 144,000 bore when in warfare (7:1–3) is now identified as "his [the Lamb's] name and the name of his Father" (14:1). The repetition of the identical number (144,000) here in 14:1 suggests that God has preserved his church through the intervening warfare. Now the 144,000 stand beside the Lamb as he delivers them and as he, as the "Son of Man" (14:14), is about to judge their enemies. As the church militant (as pictured in 7:1–8) they had been waiting in hope to join that heavenly multitude of God's saints who have washed their robes in the blood of the Lamb (7:9–17). The prayers of those saints beneath the incense altar before God's heavenly throne are now about to be answered (6:9–11); they prayed for the deliverance of the church militant in tribulation and that the saints on earth would join the church triumphant.

THE SAINTS AND THEIR NEW SONG (14:2–5)

The 144,000 standing on Mt. Zion with the Lamb hear a loud "voice" (14:2) breaking out in the singing of "a new song" (14:3). Because the "new song" is being voiced in heaven before God's "throne and before the four winged creatures and the elders" (14:3), it is the voice of the church triumphant, the heavenly multitude of the saints of God standing before him clothed in white garments (7:9–17). As the church triumphant sings this "new song," the 144,000, who represent the church still on earth standing with the Lamb of God on Mt. Zion, hear the song and learn it (14:3). Momentarily they too will be in heaven, singing that song with the glorified saints, as they are even now learning to sing it on earth, in the heart and in the hope born of faith. Only those who "had been purchased from the earth" (14:3) by the blood of the Lamb (cf. 1 Cor 6:20; 7:23; 1 Pet 1:19) are able to learn and sing the hymn.

There is a profound message here about the church's worship. Even now, here on earth, the church learns the hymns sung by our glorified brothers and sisters in Christ. The church on earth joins the church in heaven to form *one* holy church, united in faith expressed through hymns sung in unison. In worship the church on earth raises her voice to participate in the heavenly worship. This truth is articulated in the Preface: "With angels and archangels and with all the company of heaven we laud and magnify your glorious name, evermore praising you and saying-..." (e.g., LSB 208).

It is "a new song" (Rev 14:3) that is sung. It is part of the ongoing chorus that extends throughout Revelation (see the excursus "The Great Te Deum of Praise in Revelation"). The words and content are not given here, but they must be similar to if not identical with those of the "new song" in 5:9. *Thus the song is "new" to the 144,000 (the Christians on earth who will soon be glorified), since it is the song of the new creation in Christ, but it is the same "new song" that has been sung by the saints and angels in heaven ever since the victory and ascension of the Lamb.* While being sung by the saints in heaven, it is also ever "new" to them as well since it celebrates Christ's work of redemption and renewal. This "new song" is mentioned only twice in Revelation (5:9 and 14:3), but it is certainly being voiced continually as a part of the heavenly worship and praise of the victorious Lamb.

The words of the new song are given in 5:9–14. It contains three stanzas. The first voices the truth that the Lamb is worthy to receive the scroll because he "ransomed for God with [his] blood" a people from all the nations and thus made them "a kingdom and priests" to God (5:9–10). In the second stanza the Lamb is praised and lauded as worthy of receiving all honor and glory because he was slain (5:12). And in the third stanza both God and the Lamb are given honor and glory (5:13). This is the new song that the 144,000 learn as they await their deliverance; they will shout it when they are brought to the heavenly throne. One is reminded of the "new song" in Ps 96:1–2, which is a song celebrating the salvation of Yahweh (cf. Pss 40:3; 98:1; 144:9–11). In Ps 33:2–3 this "new song" is accompanied with the playing of the harp.

The new song is introduced, and most likely also accompanied, by music that sounds like "harps" (14:2). The sound of the harps was of such a volume that it was like the roaring of rushing waters and like loud thunder crashes. In 5:9–14 the twenty-four elders each have a harp as they sing the new song, together with the four winged creatures and all the angelic host. In 14:1–3 all the saints in heaven, and the 144,000 on earth in anticipation, sing the new song. The angelic hosts also join in as they did in 5:9–14, and in 14:1–3 perhaps it is the twenty-four elders who are playing their harps to accompany the singing.

The 144,000 are identified as "[male] virgins" (the Greek word is masculine) who "were not made unclean with women" (14:4). Scripture often portrays the church on earth as a pure virgin or bride (Rev 19:7; 21:2, 9; 22:17). The church is the bride of Christ, and since she is washed and cleansed by him (Eph 5:25–27), she is a virgin and holy to her Lord. In the OT God's people, Israel, are described as a virgin bride (e.g., Jer 31:4). One also finds the custom of not having sexual relations in preparation for encountering the holy (Ex 19:15; 1 Sam 21:5; cf. 2 Sam 11:9–13). The NT nowhere commands such abstinence but does refer to voluntary and temporary abstinence for the sake of prayer (1 Cor 7:5). Spiritually speaking, Paul says that those who had been converted through his ministry had been pledged to Christ as a virgin bride is betrothed to her husband (2 Cor 11:2; cf. Eph 5:25–27). Therefore, when the 144,000 are described as "virgins" in Rev 14:4, this signifies that through faith in the redemption of Christ, the church on earth is pure, holy, and without blemish in God's sight (see Rom 3:21–26; 5:1–11; 7:7–25).

But why are these virgins in Rev 14:4 male? Often throughout the Scriptures the female gender is used for God's people on earth, pictured either collectively as his bride or as an individual woman representing his church on earth. Yet the Scriptures can also portray the people of God or the church on earth as an individual or group with the male gender. For example, Israel, Jacob, and Judah are names that can designate God's OT people, whom he also calls "my son" (Hos 11:1). In some of Jesus' parables, a male figure or figures can represent the church (and also individual Christians), such as the prodigal son (Lk 15:11–32) or the workers in the vineyard (Mt 20:1–16). Because the 144,000 both in Rev 7:1–8 and here in 14:1–5 is used to depict the church militant as God's army in warfare, the male gender is appropriate, for in the ancient world armies were almost always composed of men.

The 144,000, as if in marching order, follow "the Lamb wherever he goes" (14:4). Throughout the time period from Christ's ascension to the End, the church on earth follows after her Lord in faith, in the mission Christ has given to her, and finally in hope to eternal glory.

Not only were the 144,000 "purchased from the earth" (Rev 14:3), but also they "were purchased from among men as a firstfruit for God and for the Lamb" (14:4). In the OT the firstfruits were the firstfruits of the harvest, which were offered to God in thanksgiving. To call the saints on earth "the firstfruit" suggests that they are an offering to God for the sake of the mission of Christ. As Paul puts it in Rom 12:1, Christians are exhorted to offer, through the mercies of God, their "bodies as a living, holy sacrifice acceptable to God." This offering is an act of "worship" which honors God and Christ. It is an act of offering which places at God's disposal in Christ one's whole being and existence and production—all of one's talents and members and faculties of body and mind—as slaves of Christ and his righteousness, all for God's honor (see Rom 6:15–23).

A final description and identification of the 144,000 is given in these words: "and in their mouth a lie was not found; they are unblemished ones." In the OT speaking the truth and not lying were important characteristics of God's prophets and people, by which the truthfulness of Yahweh, the only true and faithful God, was demonstrated (Ps 15:1–2; Prov 16:13; Zeph 3:13). In the NT it is the devil who lies and is the sponsor of all lies, and all who are liars are children of this father of lies (see Jn 8:44; cf. 1 Jn 2:21, 27; 3:8). In contrast, those who are of God's truth in Christ do not lie but speak the truth.

As ones who speak the truth, the 144,000 are blameless or "unblemished ones" (Rev 14:5). They are not tainted or polluted by lies and liars (cf. Rom 16:17–20) but rather are dressed in the righteousness and truth of God. Their "unblemished" status as witnesses to the truth stands in sharp contrast to the "perverse" and "depraved" people of this sinful world (Phil 2:15). They stand with God in a blameless state of purity and holiness because they have been presented to him by Christ, the "unblemished Lamb" (1 Pet 1:19; cf. Ex 12:5) who was sacrificed for us.

EXCURSUS

144,000

In Revelation the number 144,000 is used as a numerical symbol for the church militant on earth (7:4; 14:1, 3). According to 7:4–8 the number results from 12,000 multiplied by twelve, that is, 12,000 from each of the twelve tribes of Israel.

Elsewhere in Revelation, it is possible to uncover sources for the use of 12,000 times twelve for a total of 144,000. Twelve is the basic number used in Revelation to symbolize in representative fashion the church or people of God. In 4:4 the twenty-four elders before God in heaven represent the OT church and the NT people of God—the fathers of the twelve tribes plus the twelve apostles. In Revelation 12 the woman pictorially symbolizes at first God's people in the OT (12:1–6) and then (after the birth and ascension of the Child) the church of the NT (12:13–18). To symbolize God's people in that way, she wears a crown of twelve stars (12:1). In 21:9–17 the holy city Jerusalem, that is, the bride of Christ, has twelve gates in its wall and twelve foundations upon which the wall rests. The names of the twelve tribes of Israel are written on the gates (21:12), and the names of the twelve apostles are written on the foundations (21:14). The first basic number from which 144,000 is derived is thus the number twelve.

When the number twelve is squared (twelve times twelve) the result is 144. The holy city Jerusalem described in 21:9–17 lies foursquare, that is, its length and width are each 12,000 stadia, so that the area of the city is 144,000,000 square stadia. Moreover, the wall of the city measures 144 cubits (21:17). Thus the second number in helping to determine the source for 144,000 is the number 144, the number that results when twelve is squared (twelve times twelve, for example, the twelve gates and the twelve foundation stones, 21:12–14).

The third number that plays a part in formulating 144,000 is the number 1,000. While there is a biblical tradition behind the use of this number, it is more its appearance within Revelation itself that determines how it is used in connection with 144,000. It appears only once in Revelation, but this one appearance is critical. In 20:1–6, the period of 1,000 years appears as the time during which Satan is bound and cast into the abyss. In the OT the number 1,000 indicated perfection or completeness in terms of natural life and periods of time here on earth. One thousand times 144 equals 144,000. Thus the number 144,000 results first from twelve being squared, then that result, which is 144, being multiplied by 1,000.

The resulting number of 144,000 thus symbolizes the church militant—God's dwelling place here on earth, the church militant whose foundation is the twelve apostles (Eph 2:20), the heirs of the twelve patriarchs of Israel. The time allotted to the church to complete her mission is symbolized by the 1,000 years, the NT era.

The number 12,000, the number for each of the twelve tribes in Rev 7:4–8, can also be related to the expanse of the holy city Jerusalem which, in the new heaven and new earth, is stated to be 12,000 stadia in width, length, and height (21:16). This number when multiplied by the twelve gates of the wall of the holy city (or by the twelve names of the twelve tribes, which are written on the twelve gates; or by the twelve foundations, which bear the names of the twelve apostles) results in 144,000.

Thus 144,000 is a number that is derived from numbers that are used in Revelation, numbers that have a spiritual and theological significance in their usage.

REVELATION 14:6–13

The Defeat of the Dragon and His Beasts Announced

TRANSLATION

14 [6]And I saw another angel flying in mid-heaven, having the eternal Gospel to proclaim to those residing on the earth and to every nation and tribe and tongue and people, [7]saying in a loud voice, "Fear God and give to him glory, because the moment of his judgment has come, and worship him who made the heaven and the earth and sea and springs of waters." [8]And another angel, a second one, followed, saying, "Babylon the great has fallen, fallen—she who has made all the nations to drink from the wine of the fury of her sexual immorality." [9]And another angel, a third one, followed them, saying in a loud voice, "If anyone worships the beast and its image and receives the mark upon his forehead or upon his hand, [10]he himself will drink from the wine of the fury of God which has been poured out full strength [that is, undiluted] into the cup of his wrath, and he will be tormented in fire and brimstone in the presence of the holy angels and in the presence of the Lamb. [11]And the smoke of their torment arises forever and ever, and they have no rest day and night—those who worship the beast and its image, and if anyone receives the mark of its name. [12]Here is the patience of the saints, those who keep the commandments of God and the faith of Jesus." [13]And I heard of a voice from heaven saying, "Write: Blessed are the dead who are dying in the Lord from now on."

"Yes," says the Spirit, "so that they will receive rest from their labors, for their works accompany them."

COMMENTARY

Three angels in succession (14:6, 8, 9) now announce the judgment of God on the two beasts conjured up by the dragon. Each angel is introduced as "another angel." This indicates that they are not from among the seven trumpet-angels. They are among the many angels who appear throughout Revelation who are not part of the seven (e.g., the angels in 5:2; 7:1, 2; 10:1; 18:1; 19:17).

THE "ETERNAL GOSPEL" (14:6–7)

The first angel, "flying in mid-heaven" has "the eternal Gospel to proclaim" to all the inhabitants of the earth (14:6). At first glance this phrase seems to be incongruous in this context, for the terms "Gospel" and "to proclaim [the Gospel]" usually involve "Good News" that brings joy, specifically the forgiveness of sins through faith in the work of Christ (e.g., Rom 1:16–17). But here they include somber news of judgment, for the angel's loud cry calls for all to "fear God … because the moment of his judgment has come" (Rev 14:7). However, several factors indicate that this "eternal Gospel" includes more than the announcement of judgment (Law). The surrounding context is explicitly Christological, with 14:1–5 depicting the victorious Lamb and the victory song of the saints. In particular John most likely had in mind the "judgment" at the Lord Christ's second coming at the End, which would also be the time of the final deliverance of God's people from the dragon, his two beasts, and their hosts (19:1–16). This aspect of the "eternal Gospel" is pointedly suggested in 14:13 when a *blessing* is pronounced upon those who have died and are dying "in the Lord." In addition, even when the "eternal Gospel" is proclaimed to all the nations for the initial purpose of moving people to "fear God" (14:7) because of their sins and his coming judgment, such proclamation has as its *goal* the repentance and salvation of all through the announcement of Christ's forgiveness. Thus the "eternal Gospel" is the eternal message of God—of both judgment and grace—based on the person and saving work of Jesus Christ.

The stated purpose of proclaiming the "eternal Gospel" is to move people to "fear God" and "give to him glory" and "worship him," all in view of his coming judgment (14:7). Here is a clear definition of the purpose of proclaiming the eternal message of God. The "fear of Yahweh is the beginning of wisdom" (Ps 111:10; cf. Job 28:28). Such fear comes from learning about God through hearing his Word (Deut 4:10). Fear of God is an essential part of contrition over sin and repentance (Acts 2:37) and is also a part of one's faithfulness to God (Acts 9:31; Rev 11:18). Glory is given to God in and through Jesus Christ (Jn 17:5, 22–24; cf. 13:31–32). In particular, God is glorified when people come to him in Jesus' name (Jn 14:13–14; 15:7–8) and when they thank him for what has been done to them by Jesus (Acts 4:21–22; 11:17–18). Moreover, it is God's purpose that he himself thus be glorified through Jesus Christ (1 Pet 4:11), for his Son in exaltation is God's glory (Acts 7:55). To worship God as the Creator is the end result of fearful repentance and giving glory to God through the redemption wrought by Christ. The heavenly hosts worship God as their Creator (Rev 4:8–11). The saints now join in this worship of God because of the victory of the Lamb on their behalf (5:9–14), for the end purpose of God's redemption is the restoration of his creatures so that they recognize and worship him as their God and Creator.

THE FALL OF BABYLON (14:8)

The second angel announces the judgment of Babylon, "she who has made all the nations drink ... of her sexual immorality" (14:8). This is the first time that Babylon is mentioned in Revelation. (It will be mentioned again in 16:19; 17:5; 18:2, 10, 21.) Its appearance is somewhat sudden and unexplained. Evidently John assumes that his audience will recognize to what or to whom he is referring. In Revelation Babylon is always a name for the evil enemies of Christ's church on earth; it is the name of the harlot as she sits on the beast (17:3–17). In Revelation 17–18 Babylon is the symbol of the two beasts of Revelation 13 *but now presented as the harlot and a single beast, both of whom carry out the plan masterminded by Satan.*

Babylon symbolizes the *sociopolitical* dimension of the two beasts that are under the control of the dragon. That is why in Revelation 17 the first beast—the political and societal one—is still present as the beast upon which sits the harlot. (She is the new form of the religious enemy.) Therefore Babylon is a symbol of these two enemies in their most deadly form: *when the harlot sits on the beast, that is, when the false religious entities, and in particular apostate Christianity, attempt to use or work with the existing political and social powers to destroy the church of Christ.* For John, Rome epitomized and was that historical enemy of the church. Under the name of "Babylon," Rome would also serve as a typological model for all future enemies of God's people, enemies both within and outside the church—enemies who, like Rome, may be called "Babylon."

FIRE AND BRIMSTONE (14:9–11)

The third angel announces the judgment of God on anyone who "worships the beast and its image" and who demonstrates allegiance to them by bearing "the mark upon his forehead or upon his hand" (14:9). In 13:14–17 the beast from the earth (the second, religious beast) symbolizes all false spirituality, and in particular pseudo-Christianity (see 13:11). That beast motivates the human race to make an image for the beast from the sea (13:1, the first, political beast) and thus to worship and serve the political beast. In addition, the religious beast marks or brands all those who belong to it so that only those who obey its religious mandate to worship the political beast can engage in the economic and social activities regulated by the ruling powers. Now here in 14:9–11 all the followers and adherents of the political beast and its image (the people who are motivated by the religious beast to be such adherents) are to be judged. This judgment will finally and completely be executed at the End when Christ returns, after which these adherents "will be tormented in fire and brimstone" (14:10).

Eternal suffering is a result of God's anger, meted out as undiluted wine (14:10), that is, anger that is not tempered with any mercy. At the conclusion of this world's history, God will show no mercy in his judgment against those who are adherents of the beasts. Wine in its full strength is undiluted with water. Wine was an intoxicant and is often used as a metaphor for the judgment of God. For example, in Rev 16:19 Babylon is given to drink "the cup of the wine of the fury of his [God's] wrath" (cf. also Ps 75:7–8; Is 24:1–23, in particular 24:20; Jer 25:15–16).

This torment of "fire and brimstone" (14:10) will last forever; there will be no relief "day and night" (14:11; cf. Lk 16:22–24). Similarly, the beast and the false prophet and the devil will be forever tormented in the lake of fire and brimstone (Rev 19:20; 20:10). This judgment will be witnessed by "holy angels" as it is carried out "in the presence of the Lamb" (14:10). Because of his redemptive victory on behalf of God's saints, the exalted Christ will oversee this judgment of God, and he will do so in the presence of the heavenly host of angels (as partially described in 14:14–20; see also Mk 13:24–27; Rev 19:11–16; cf. Jn 5:22–27).

THE PATIENT ENDURANCE
OF THE SAINTS (14:12)

The saints of God still in the warfare (and its suffering) hear the announcement of this promised judgment upon their enemies. A godly characteristic of the saints is their patient endurance in their deference to God's judgment and his timetable of executing it. In Rev 13:9–10, they wait for God to avenge their blood (cf. 6:9–11) and to strike down those who have blasphemed the Gospel and God's holy name (11:7–13; 13:6; 16:9–21). They do not take into their own hands the execution of this judgment, though they participate in its announcement (Heb 10:30–31; Rev 10:11; cf. Lk 9:51–55). Elsewhere in Revelation this patient endurance in faith is related to and/or equated with *wisdom*, a wisdom that only God can give (Rev 13:18; 17:9). Through such wisdom God gives the Christian the ability to interpret events *in view of and in relation to God's end-time judgment* (James 1:2–5). This wisdom, by which Christians wait in faithful patience, enables them to know that, even though now they are being defeated on the human plane by the beasts (Rev 13:7), they are and will be victorious as they follow the Lamb (15:2–4; cf. 1 Jn 5:4–5). Thus their patience is a victorious and certain hope in the promise of God (cf. Rom 5:3–5).

The saints are described as "those who keep the commandments of God and the faith of Jesus" (Rev 14:12). In Jn 10:17–18 Jesus states that it was the commandment of the Father that he should lay down his life and take it up again. Christ's whole life and ministry were thus under the will of his heavenly Father expressed in this commandment. Jesus knew that for him to carry out the will of God would result in "eternal life" for those who followed him (Jn 12:50). The *faithfulness of Jesus* is the cause of the believer's salvation, and "the faith of Jesus" in Rev 14:12 (cf. Rom 3:22, 26) refers first of all to *his* faithfulness, then also to the believers' faith in Jesus. By faith the saints cling tenaciously to Christ amid temptations and persecutions which pressure them to worship the beast. Moreover, they persist in Christian love, for the new "commandment" that Jesus speaks of in Jn 13:34 is that the Christians should love one another as he has loved them (cf. Jn 14:15; 1 Jn 4:21). 1 Jn 2:7–11 states that the commandment which is both ancient and new is to love one another because "the darkness is passing away and the true light is already shining" (1 Jn 2:8).

A BLESSING (14:13)

At the conclusion of the three announcements of God's judgment by the three angels (14:6–12), John hears "a voice from heaven" which speaks a beatitude or blessing on all "who are dying in the Lord" (14:13). Though the source of the voice is unidentified, it emanates from heaven on behalf of God, for it speaks *his* blessing on *his* people. It also receives the divine Spirit's affirmation (14:13b). While faithfulness to God and Christ results in suffering and martyrdom for the Christians, they have the blessed hope and certainty of an eternal rest and victorious peace. This is the second of the seven beatitudes announced in Revelation. The first (1:3) is spoken to those who read and hear "the words of this prophecy" of Revelation "and who keep the things written in it." The sixth (22:7) is similarly addressed. The other five beatitudes are spoken in view of eternity. Here in 14:13, in contrast to the *eternal* torment for unbelievers (14:9–12), this beatitude is a spoken comfort to those who are dying and who are going to die in the Lord. They are blessed *because* they are dying in the Lord, dying in their hope in him and in his saving care. Death cannot rob them of life and peace, for they are in the hands of the Good Shepherd (Jn 10:27–28). This great consolation for the dying is also a solace and balm for the grieving Christians they leave behind (temporarily!) in this world.

Those who are blessed because of their death in the Lord Christ now "receive rest from their labors" (14:13). In their life on earth they heard the gracious invitation spoken by Jesus (Mt 11:28), "Come unto me all who are laboring and who are heavily burdened, and I will give you *rest*." Burdensome toil and the burden of the grief caused by sin were results of the judgment of God on the sin of Adam (Gen 3:17–19). Even though the Christians all their earthly life suffer this anguish, aggravated by the dragon and the two beasts, they know in faith's hope (1 Pet 5:7), having heeded the invitation of Jesus, that they will finally be delivered. Now as they are dying in their Lord, they come at last into that eternal rest and peace which the Spirit of God alone can give (1 Pet 4:14). The followers of Christ have this eternal rest, in stark contrast to those who worshiped the beast, who never have any rest from their eternal torment (Rev 14:11).

Those who are entering this eternal rest are accompanied by their works (14:13). Those in eternal torment who persecuted them *are never* separated from their sins and guilt (cf. Mt 25:41–46). In contrast, the saints *are* separated from their guilt and shame but *are not* separated from their godly works, for *those* works follow them. While the Christians lived on earth, their works—by which they adorned the Gospel—honored Christ and glorified God the Father (Titus 2:10; cf. Mt 5:16). Therefore, such works will be cited by God at the final judgment (Mt 25:31–40).

REVELATION 14:14–20

THE SON OF MAN AND THE HARVEST AT THE END

TRANSLATION

14 ¹⁴And I looked, and behold—a white cloud, and on the cloud there was someone sitting like the Son of Man, who had upon his head a golden crown and in his hand a sharp sickle. ¹⁵And another angel came out from the temple, crying out in a loud voice to the One sitting on the cloud, "Send out your sickle and reap, for the moment has come to harvest, because the harvest of the earth is ready [fully ripened]." ¹⁶And the One sitting on the cloud cast his sickle onto the earth and the earth was harvested.

¹⁷And another angel came out of the temple which is in heaven, who also had a sharp sickle. ¹⁸And another angel [came out] from the incense altar who had authority over the fire, and he spoke out in a loud voice to the one who held the sharp sickle, saying, "Send forth your sharp sickle and gather the grape clusters of the vineyard of the earth, for its grapes became ripe." ¹⁹And the angel cast his sickle onto the earth, and he gathered the vineyard of the earth and cast [the grapes] into the winepress, the great one, of the fury of God. ²⁰And the winepress was trampled underfoot outside the city, and blood came out of the winepress up to the bridles of the horses as far away as a thousand six hundred furlongs.

COMMENTARY

THE APPEARING OF THE SON OF MAN (14:14)

The scene of the harvest at the End is introduced by the awesome sight of the Son of Man on a cloud. This scene of the parousia is the conclusion to the interregnum (12:1–14:20) depicting the startling and breathtaking war between God and the dragon, and between the beasts and the church. It culminates in the great harvest, which is the judgment of God. The phrase "like the Son of Man" (14:14) identifies the same person who first appeared in 1:13, when John was commissioned to write Revelation. As in 1:13, the phrase also recalls the glorious appearance of the Lord Christ at the transfiguration (Mt 17:2; cf. Rev 1:16).

In Dan 7:13, the Son of Man came "with clouds of heaven." Similarly in Rev 14:14, he comes into the scene "on the cloud." In Mt 24:30 Jesus himself said that at the End everyone would see him as "the Son of Man coming on the clouds of heaven," and he would come "with power and great glory." Jesus testified to this same truth also when standing before the high priest at his trial (Mt 26:64). The clouds are an identifying mark of his entrance into his heavenly glory at his ascension (Acts 1:9–10), and now at the End, the "white cloud" (Rev 14:14) is also such a mark at his return to the earth. In the OT the cloud was a visible sign of God's majestic presence with his people, in particular when he spoke his word (Ex 19:9; 24:15–18; 34:5–7). It was through a cloud that God spoke on the mount of transfiguration (Mt 17:5). In Rev 10:1 the "mighty angel" is clothed with a cloud when he comes to John to speak the word of God which instructed John to proclaim the Gospel to all peoples (10:8–11). In the prologue of Revelation (1:1–8) is the promise that Jesus Christ will come "with the clouds" (1:7).

Here in Rev 14:14 the cloud is "white." In Ps 97:2 a cloud and deep darkness surround God in his majesty. If the *whiteness* of the cloud here is to be emphasized, it could signify the righteousness of God in judgment (Rev 20:11), and in particular the righteousness of Christ. The white cloud would then suggest that, in the majesty of God, the Lord Christ will execute the judgment *in his righteousness*. In Rev 19:11, in Revelation's second vision of the parousia, the Son of Man "in righteousness judges and wages war," and so he is pictured riding a "white horse."

Upon his head is "a golden crown" (14:14) that denotes him as the victor. In the second vision of the parousia in Revelation (19:11–16), he will wear "many diadems" (19:12), for there he is pictured coming as the "Kings of kings and Lord of lords" (19:16).

The "sharp sickle" (14:14) in his hand depicts the victorious Christ coming at the end of time to reap and gather the harvest. The purpose of wielding the sickle at the harvest is to cut the grain so that it can then be gathered and placed in the granary. As the grain is cut, weeds and tares among the grain are also cut, but then the grain is separated, and the weeds are put to the fire (see Mt 13:24–30). The imagery in 14:14–16 is of a harvest of *grain,* which takes place after the green and growing plants have matured. The statement that the harvest had fully ripened (literally "had dried out," 14:15) may mean that the rainy growing season was over and the hot, dry summer had come. The picture in 14:17–20 also includes a "sharp sickle" (14:17), but there the sickle is employed to cut the ripe grape clusters from the vine.

REAP THE HARVEST (14:15–16)

"The moment" for the beginning of the harvest is signaled by the voice of "another angel." The angel "in a loud voice" instructs "the One sitting on the cloud" to begin the task of harvesting (14:15). While at first glance it may seem strange that an angel should give a command to the exalted Lord Christ, the command to begin the harvest comes from the Father, and the angel is merely relaying the command to the Lord Christ. The harvest and the judgment are executed by the exalted Christ because he won that right by his death and resurrection (see, e.g., Jn 5:19–23; 12:31–33), but they are done under the authority of God the Father, who determines the exact hour or moment that it will be carried out (see Mk 13:32; cf. Acts 1:7).

"And the One sitting on the cloud cast his sickle onto the earth" (Rev 14:16) to execute the judgment of God, metaphorically pictured here as a harvest. Jesus may have attendants (see Mk 13:24–27), but only the Lord Christ as the exalted Son of Man is worthy to preside over the judgment. He alone suffered the judgment of God pronounced on the sin of the entire human race. Having suffered that judgment on behalf of all mankind, he alone has the right to be the judge, by the authority of his Father.

In both the OT and the NT the picture of the harvest is used as a symbol of the judgment of God at the End. In Joel (3:13) the gathering of the nations before God for judgment is described as a harvest and as the trampling of grapes in the winepress. In the parable of the wheat and the tares (Mt 13:24–30, 36–43) both results of God's judgment are pictured: condemnation and fire for the wicked but compassion and deliverance for the saints (cf. Mt 9:35–38; Mk 4:26–29). The church is always to keep in mind that her mission on earth is intimately related to this harvest at the End. As Jesus himself sent out the seventy-two, he urged them to pray for workers in the harvest (Mt 9:37–38; Lk 10:2). So the church is always to pray as Christians are sent out to be servants working for Christ that his harvest may be more plentiful (Jn 4:34–38). The entire period from Christ's first advent to his return in glory at the End is the season of the harvest. At no time may the church on earth consider her work to be done or imagine that all opportunities have been exhausted. Until that final call for Christ to send forth his sickle, there is much work that the church must do—and do soon (cf. Rev 10:6–7, 11)!

GATHER IN THE VINTAGE (14:17–20)

The picture of the grain harvest illustrating the ingathering of the human race for the judgment of God now changes and becomes a picture of the gathering of the vintage of the earth. While the grain harvest (14:14–16) symbolizes the ingathering of both the people of God and the wicked, the vintage of the earth (14:17–20) emphasizes the gathering and judgment of the *unbelievers*, that is, those who worshiped the beast and its image (14:9–11). An angel had announced that every worshiper of the beast "will drink from the wine of the fury of God which has been poured out full strength into the cup of his wrath" (14:9–10). With this figure of speech John stresses the severity of the judgment. The trampling of the grapes extracts their blood, which provides the wine that is poured out into the cup of God's wrath. Thus there is a slight shift in the imagery: in 14:9–10 the idolaters (unbelievers) will *drink* the cup of wrath, but in 14:17–20 the unbelievers are the trampled grapes whose blood *fills* the cup of wrath.

John sees an angel executing this negative side of the judgment of God, for "another angel came out of the temple" of God in heaven with "a sharp sickle" (14:17). While Christ is the Lord over the entire ingathering for the judgment and in particular is present to mete out compassion and mercy to God's own saints, and while angels attend him in the gathering of the saints (cf. Mk 13:24–27), he will delegate to an angel the task of separating the unbelievers from his followers and thus prepare the unbelievers for the terrifying judgment and punishment of God (cf. Mt 13:30).

The angel with the sickle came out of the heavenly temple. Still another angel in "a loud voice" tells the angel with the sickle to commence the reaping and gathering of "the grape clusters of the vineyard of the earth" (14:18). This second angel, who gives the command to the angel with the sickle, is identified as the angel "from the incense altar," who has "authority over the fire" (14:18), that is, the fire of the incense altar, the fire that causes the incense to smolder and its sweet smell to rise. This may be the same angel who, in Rev 8:3–5, stood before the incense altar with a censer of smoldering incense, which represented the prayers of the saints. That angel took the censer and filled it with fire from the incense altar and then poured it out on the earth. That action of the angel before the incense altar introduced the seven trumpet-angels of the second sevenfold vision of events on earth (8:6–11:19). If this identification is correct, then that angel of the incense altar, who signaled the seven trumpet-angels to begin the revelation of the second earthly vision, now gives another signal for the angel of the sickle to commence the gathering of the vintage of the earth.

The prayers of God's martyrs in heaven are now answered in the final act of God's judgment and punishment of their enemies. Throughout the time period covered by the prophecy of Revelation, from Christ's ascension to his second coming, the martyred saints are continually praying that God avenge their blood by judging the inhabitants of the earth (6:9–11). These prayers are symbolized by the incense that rises from the incense altar before God's heavenly throne (6:9–11; cf. 5:8). In the prophetic picture of the second vision of events on earth (8:6–11:19) those prayers are partially answered, so to speak, when John sees the seven trumpet-angels introducing natural and demonic plagues which afflict the human race, in particular those people who were not sealed by God as his own (9:4–6). The commencement of those plagues was signaled by the angel of the incense altar (8:3–5). Now at the End John sees the completion of God's answer to the prayers of his saints in the gathering of the vintage of the earth for the judgment of his anger. The commencement of this judgment was signaled by the same angel—the angel of the incense altar (8:3–5)—here described as the angel who has authority over the fire upon the incense altar (14:18).

The harvest of the vintage is completed and the judgment carried out when "the winepress was trampled underfoot" (14:20). This judgment and punishment of the worshipers of the beast and its image (14:10) takes place "outside the city" (14:20). Most likely the "city" is Jerusalem and thus to be identified symbolically with the "holy city" in 11:2. While the "holy city" (that is, God's church on earth) was trampled underfoot by the pagan nations ("trample," in 11:2 as in 14:20), now the pagan nations in turn are "trampled underfoot" in the winepress of God's fury and judgment (14:20). John would have remembered that it was outside the city (see Heb 13:12) where the judgment of God trampled underfoot (so to speak) his Son, when he suffered the judgment and punishment for the sins of the world. Jesus was trodden in this winepress as he endured God's anger alone and suffered in the stead of the human race. Isaiah saw, in a vision of the day of God's vengeance and redemption, one single person (Is 63:3) whose garments were red from treading alone the winepress of God's anger (63:1–6). In the vision it was in Edom and the Edomite city of Bozrah, enemies of Israel and thus outside the holy city, that the Messiah alone would tread in the winepress (Is 63:1). Edom had rejoiced in the plunder and destruction of Jerusalem (Obad 8–14). Now the tables are turned, as Christ tramples underfoot the pagan nations in God's anger and judgment and makes Edom and the rest drink the cup of his wrath (Obad 15–16).

This judgment of the nations would also take place "outside the city" (Rev 14:20). In Joel 3:2, 12 (cf. Zech 14:1–5), the judgment would be executed in the Valley of Jehoshaphat, linked by tradition with the Kidron valley between Jerusalem and the Mount of Olives.

So extensive and terrifying is the judgment of God that "blood came out of the winepress up to the bridles of the horses as far away as a thousand six hundred furlongs" (Rev. 14–20), that is, around 184 English miles. The OT sometimes refers to grape juice or wine as the "blood of grapes" (Gen 49:11; Deut 32:14), but "blood" in Rev 14:20 refers to human blood. Such a flow of blood is beyond human experience and comprehension.

Various interpretations of the distance of 1,600 furlongs have been given. That it is the product of the square of four times the square of ten suggests it is a reference to completeness and thus symbolizes the whole earth, especially if 1,600 is taken as the square of forty. More importantly, the number, together with the depth of blood reaching the bridles of the horses, points symbolically to the completeness and totality of God's judgment and the horror of its punishment. As prophesied by Isaiah (63:6), the blood of the pagan nations would be "poured out onto the ground" after God had trampled them underfoot in his wrath and judgment. 1 Enoch 100:1–13, which graphically portrays the final judgment of all sinners, says that a "horse shall walk through the blood of sinners up to his chest; and the chariot shall sink down up to its top" (1 Enoch 100:3). Thus the picture of the blood "up to the bridles of the horses" here in Rev 14:20 symbolizes the totality of God's judgment from which no human person can escape, for it will sweep all into a terrible and fearful bloodbath.

15:1–16:21

THIRD SEVENFOLD VISION OF HISTORY FROM THE CROSS TO THE END

(THE SEVEN CENSER-ANGELS): PLAGUES OF GOD'S WRATH AS GOD'S JUDGMENT IS POURED OUT

REVELATION 15:1–8

PREPARATION FOR THE LAST PLAGUES: INTRODUCTION OF THE SEVEN CENSER-ANGELS

TRANSLATION

15 ¹And I saw another sign in heaven, a great and marvelous one: seven angels who have seven plagues, the last ones, because in them the fury of God is brought to an end. ²And I saw something like a glassy sea mixed with fire, and [I saw] those [who, though being conquered] by the beast and by its image and by the number of its name, were nevertheless conquerors standing on the glassy sea holding harps of God. ³And they were singing the song of Moses the slave of God and the hymn of the Lamb, saying,

"Great and marvelous are your works,
   O Yahweh, the [only] God, the Almighty;
righteous and true are your ways,
   O King of the nations.
⁴Who will not fear, O Yahweh,
   and will glorify your name?
For [you] alone are holy,
   for all the nations will come
   and will worship in your presence,
because your righteous judgments
   have been made visible."

⁵And after these things I looked, and the sanctuary of the tabernacle of the testimony in heaven was opened. ⁶And the seven angels who have the seven plagues came out of the sanctuary clothed in pure and shining linen and girded around the chests with golden cinctures. ⁷And one of the four winged

creatures gave to the seven angels seven golden censers filled with the fury of God, who lives forever and ever. ⁸And the sanctuary was filled with smoke from the glory of God and from his power, and no one was able to enter into the sanctuary until the seven plagues of the seven angels were finished.

COMMENTARY

THE THIRD SEVENFOLD VISION OF EVENTS ON EARTH

Chapters 15 and 16 of Revelation display the third and last vision of events on earth. As in the first two earthly visions (6:1–8:5 and 8:6–11:19), there are seven scenes. In this third vision, each of the scenes is introduced by an angel with a censer. The first five scenes (16:1–11) depict events that take place concurrently: each covers the same time period, from Christ's ascension up to Armageddon. The sixth scene (16:12–16) describes the last battle, here called Armageddon, which takes place just prior to the end of this present world at Christ's return. The seventh scene (16:17–21) envisions the End at the second coming of Christ.

A SIGN IN HEAVEN (15:1A)

For the third and final time John calls a visionary scene a "sign in heaven" (15:1). The two other scenes which he designates as a sign in heaven are the woman with Child in 12:1 and the dragon in 12:3. In contrast to the "great sign" of the woman with Child (12:1) and "another sign," the sign of the dragon (12:3), this scene in 15:1 is called "another sign in heaven, a great and marvelous one." While the "seven angels who have seven plagues, the last ones" (15:1), initially are the "sign," they introduce the seven plague scenes of the third and last earthly vision, and so the whole vision can be understood as this "great and marvelous" sign. The plagues come from God himself as signs of his anger (15:1, 7).

THE SEVEN CENSER-ANGELS AND THEIR TASK (15:1B)

Who are these "seven angels who have seven plagues," these censer-angels? While an argument can be made for identifying the trumpet-angels (8:1–6) with the angels of the seven churches (Revelation 2–3), it is more difficult to identify these seven censer-angels. While the seven trumpet-angels are introduced with the definite article ("the") in 8:2, there is no definite article modifying the censer-angels when they are introduced in 15:1. (The definite article does appear in 15:6, but this may be only to further identify the seven angels of 15:6 with those in 15:1.)

However, this absence of the article here in 15:1 does not necessarily rule out an identification of the censer-angels as the trumpet-angels. If a term or subject matter is of itself definite or well known because of its familiarity, the article is not necessary to make it definite. This may be the case here. Twice before, groups of seven angels have appeared. When the second group appears—the seven trumpet-angels (8:1–6)—the article is used to suggest that it is the same as the first group: *the* seven angels of the seven churches (1:20; 2:1–3:22). Now when the group of seven angels appears for the third time, no article is needed because these seven angels are by now well known. Even without the aid of the definite article, the reader can identify them as *the same seven angels* who appeared twice earlier. The fact that John does not use the word "another, other" when introducing the seven censer-angels could support the interpretation that these seven angels of 15:1 are the same as the seven trumpet-angels and the angels of the seven churches, for John often uses "another, other" when he wants the reader to know that another, different angel is now appearing.

Moreover, the purpose of the third earthly vision (15:1–16:21) is similar to that of the second (8:6–11:19), namely, to show God's wrath and judgment against the enemies of his church. Who would be better to announce these judgments, in both the second and the third earthly visions, than the angels of the churches?

The specific task of these seven censer-angels is the revelation of the "seven plagues, the last ones," by which God will have vented and completed his "fury" (15:1). They are on a godly mission. On behalf of God and for the sake of the churches, they herald the last great effort of God to move the human race to repentance before it is too late. The revelation of and the sending out of the plagues of God's fury are called a "great and marvelous" sign (15:1), for it is by these last plagues that God will display his righteous judgments and thus show forth the glory of his name.

A VISION OF THE BATTLEFIELD (15:2)

After John sees the seven angels standing prepared and ready to pour out their censers of God's wrath, he sees the battlefield on which the warfare between the church and the beasts of Satan is taking place. He sees the battlefield as "a glassy sea mixed with fire" (15:2). Surely John was reminded of the "glassy sea, like crystal" before the heavenly throne of God (4:6). However, in 4:6 the heavenly sea, though reminiscent of the past turmoil of the warfare on earth, was quiet and peaceful. Thus it was a reminder to John that the saints in heaven, though they had been in the warfare, were now at rest and peace before God's heavenly presence (see 6:9–11; 7:9–17). Now in 15:2 the "glassy sea mixed with fire" is a reminder of the horrifying warfare with its suffering that the people of God on earth are experiencing. But in this terrifying conflict, though they are conquered by the beast and its image (13:5–7), through death and martyrdom they come out of the struggle victorious, just as their Lord did on their behalf (19:15; cf. Is 63:1–6). Throughout the whole time period of suffering, from

Christ's ascension up to the End at his return, the church exhibits this victorious faith by confidently singing the hymn of salvation, even as she goes into death.

The beast and its image had already been introduced to John in Revelation 13, where the first beast, the beast from the sea, represents all earthly powers of the human nature (society, politics) that the dragon gets under his control and uses in his warfare against the woman, who represents the church (13:1–10; cf. 12:13–18). The image or idol of this first, political/social beast is made by people who are coerced by the second beast (13:14)—the beast from the earth, the beast that symbolizes everything of a false *religious* nature. This second, religious/spiritual beast serves the political beast by compelling the human race to fashion the idol of the first beast and to worship and serve the first, political beast (13:11–18). This unholy trinity of the dragon (chapter 12) and his two henchmen, the political beast and the religious beast (chapter 13) war against the church, even though one or another may be most firmly in control at any given moment. Here in 15:2 the political beast and its image are at the front in the dragon's warfare against the church.

Though defeated by the beasts (11:7; 13:7), the church is nevertheless victorious. It is a victory that is not apparent on earth, except by faith. It is a victory that will be fully realized as each Christian is taken through suffering to God's heavenly throne. It will be fully exhibited at the End for all to see at the judgment and resurrection (see 19:1–10; 20:11–15; cf. 7:9–17). Though experiencing suffering and defeat on earth, even as Christ did, the church is totally confident of victory because of Christ's victory, so she voices in song her faith in the victory—even as she goes into death.

THE VICTORY SONG (15:3–4)

Her song is first called "the song of Moses" (15:3). This song of "the slave of God" (15:3) was sung after the great deliverance of the Israelites at the Red Sea (Ex 14:19–31). The song itself (Ex 15:1–21) expresses thanksgiving to God who alone brought about the salvation of his people through the waters (Ex 15:1–10). It also expresses the confidence that God will deliver his people from all future enemies (Ex 15:11–16). Finally it voices a confident hope that the Lord in the end would bring them safely to his eternal abode (Ex 15:17–18). The song in Ex 15:1–21 emphasizes God's great redemptive action by which he delivered his people from the tyranny and suffering in Egypt. That saving act pointed forward to the deliverance wrought in Jesus Christ.

The song is also called "the hymn of the Lamb," a hymn of God's redemptive care. In contrast with the "new song" in 14:3, which celebrates the final deliverance at the end of this world, this song of Moses and of the Lamb celebrates the deliverance from the enemy in any particular suffering at any time throughout the pilgrimage of the church on earth. It joins the OT church ("the song of Moses") to the NT church ("the hymn of the Lamb") in one grand unity. The Lord is *always* delivering his church in times of turmoil and death so that she can have another day in which to witness. Throughout the time period of the church's witness she is *always* being defeated, but she also is *always* being delivered in order to carry on her mission. *This continual saving action and care of her Lord is daily celebrated by the song of Moses and of the Lamb.* In the final deliverance at the end of each Christian's life and in the final deliverance of the entire people of God at the End, the "new song" of 14:3 is sung. But throughout an individual Christian's *earthly* life and the life of the entire church *on earth,* the song of Moses and of the Lamb is sung daily in celebration and in thanksgiving to God for his continued redemptive care *in the midst of all the church's suffering in the warfare of the beasts* (15:2).

The words of the song glorify God as the Lord and Judge of all nations in view of the fact that only he is holy (15:4). The song pointedly celebrates that the Lord God shows forth his just and righteous judgments. The words of the hymn and its thoughts are taken from the OT. "Great and marvelous are your works, O Yahweh" are words reminiscent of Ps 111:2–3, in which the psalmist extols the works of Yahweh, which move the heart. In particular the psalmist praises the righteousness of God as a work that endures forever (Ps 111:3; cf. Ex 34:10; Ps 139:13–15). The name of God used in 15:3, "Yahweh, the [only] God, the Almighty," recalls the Greek translation of passages such as Amos 4:13.

Among the reasons given here why the Lord's name is to be feared and glorified is that his ways, his actions, are "righteous and true" (Rev 15:3). This wording recalls Moses' song of praise in Deut 32:4 as well as Ps 145:17. The conclusion of the hymn in Rev 15:4 states that God's "righteous judgments have been made visible." God's "righteousness judgments" are his holy actions which are motivated by and are in keeping with his own inherent righteousness, which was revealed in Christ. The righteous actions or judgments of God are also the holy standard by which he expects all humankind to live as it is expressed in his Torah—not just the Pentateuch, nor just the portion of the OT that is doctrinal Law, but God's teaching, his revelation (both Law and Gospel). Mankind cannot fulfill these just requirements, but God in Christ has fulfilled them himself for all people. Through "the Spirit of life in Christ Jesus" (see Rom 8:2), mediated through the Gospel, God has set his people free because he has fulfilled the righteous requirement of the Law in Christ.

Here in Rev 15:4 the phrase "righteous judgments" refers specifically to those actions by which God shows his anger and displeasure at the sins of all people who refuse his gracious invitation to his mercy in Christ, that is, the followers of the beasts (cf. 15:2 and chapter 13) and the enemies of his saints on earth. These "righteous judgments" of God will be displayed and poured out on the earth in the form of the plagues from the seven censer-angels as described in 16:1–21. The purpose of making visible his righteous judgments (15:4) is to move the unbelieving world to repentance before it is too late (16:9, 11). At the End, when he returns, the Lord Christ will carry out the judgment of God according to this righteous standard in his own righteousness (19:11).

In this song of Moses and of the Lamb, the saints on earth laud these "righteous judgments" of God. These righteous actions of God not only vindicate their faith and hope in Christ, but also support and confirm their witness to the judgments of God from which only Christ can deliver people. These judgments of God in the form of the plagues poured out by the censer-angels are the setting and arena in which the church's witness to the victory of Christ's death and resurrection are made all the more poignant and telling. As the saints go through suffering and persecution into death, they gloriously sing the song as an expression and witness of their prayer that God will use his "righteous judgments," and even their own deaths (cf. 11:7–13), to move people to fear and glorify his name (15:4) and thus to come and worship him in repentance and faith before the cross and empty tomb of his Christ.

THE TABERNACLE AND THE CENSERS (15:5–8)

After John had seen the church's battlefield, "the glassy sea mixed with fire" (15:2), and the saints victoriously singing, the apostle's sight is lifted heavenward. He sees "the sanctuary of the tabernacle of the testimony," not here on earth but in heaven (15:5). This "sanctuary of the tabernacle of the testimony" appears to be a reference not to Solomon's temple but to the tabernacle, the tent of witness. This was God's dwelling place, the visible home of God's presence with his people in their wanderings in the wilderness after the exodus from Egypt (Ex 25:8–9; 40:34–38). This tabernacle was sometimes called "the tent of the testimony" (Num 17:22–23; 18:2; 2 Chr 24:6), because the ark of the covenant containing the "testimony" of the Law was placed within the sanctuary, the Holy of Holies, of the tabernacle (Ex 40:20–21). The tabernacle was also called "the tent of meeting/assembly," because God would meet with Moses personally and with his people at the entrance to the tent of meeting and because the people of Israel would assemble there when Moses spoke God's testimony to them.

As the tabernacle of Moses was the focal point of Israel's life with God, so now the heavenly tabernacle reminds John that, because of God's covenant and testimony of mercy and righteousness, God's holy presence is the center and core of the life of his saints in his heavenly glory. The earthly tabernacle was a type of "a greater and more perfect tabernacle, not made of human hands"—the heavenly one, which the exalted Christ entered as high priest into the very presence of God with his own blood as the ransom price for the sins of God's people (Heb 9:11–12). That is to say, *as the earthly tabernacle embodied God's presence through his covenant with his people in the wilderness, so now the heavenly tabernacle reminds John that God, through the covenant of his Christ, is with his saints on earth with his "righteous actions" (Rev 15:4) for the protection of his church and for the judgment of her enemies.*

From the opened heavenly tabernacle and from God's holy presence come the seven angels with the seven plagues of God's righteous judgments. They are "clothed in pure and shining linen" and "girded around the chests with golden cinctures" (15:6). The "shining linen" indicates that the angelic servants of God appear in the brilliance and purity of his holiness (cf. Mk 9:3). The "golden cinctures" or belts indicate royalty. In Rev 1:13 the Son of Man is girded with a "golden sash" or cincture around his chest. Thus the seven angels are clothed in the holiness and righteousness of God and his Christ, with the sign of royalty indicating that they are acting on behalf of God and in particular on behalf of Christ their Lord and King.

Acting as a servant of God, one of the four winged creatures gives to the seven angels the "seven golden censers filled with the fury of God" (15:7; cf. Is 6:6; Ezek 2:9). The censers contain the anger and judgments *of God,* and what fearful actions they represent are by God's authority and come from him alone. The seven angels are merely the dispensers. Only one other group of individuals in Revelation holds censers: the twenty-four elders in Rev 5:8, but there the censers are full of incense, which is identified as the prayers of God's saints. The prayers of the saints in heaven in 6:9–10 petition God to judge those on earth who persecuted them unto death. As representatives of the entire people of God (the OT and NT church) before his heavenly throne, the twenty-four elders hold the prayers of the saints, which prayers were answered in 8:1–11:19 and now again are to be answered in 16:1–21.

After the seven angels received their censers, "the sanctuary was filled with smoke from the glory of God and from his power" (15:8). In the OT smoke was associated with the awe-inspiring presence of God. For example, when God descended on Mt. Sinai, smoke covered the mountain like smoke from a furnace, for Yahweh had descended on it in fire. As a result the whole mountain shook violently, and then God spoke to Moses (Ex 19:18–20; cf. 40:34). When Yahweh of hosts appeared to Isaiah in a vision, seated on his heavenly throne and being worshiped by the seraphim, the temple shook violently as smoke filled it. So terror-stricken was the prophet that he cried out in fear, "Woe is me, for I am destroyed" (Is 6:1–5). Here in Rev 15:8 the heavenly sanctuary filled with smoke indicates the awesome and terrifying presence of God in his power as the seven angels stand ready to pour out his anger and fury upon the earth.

"No one was able to enter into the sanctuary until the seven plagues of the seven angels were finished" (15:8). Perhaps John was reminded of the tabernacle of Moses, when the cloud of God's glory filled it and Moses could not enter it as long as God's glory rested upon it (Ex 40:34–35; cf. 1 Ki 8:10–11). So terrifying would be God's holy judgments in the form of the plagues which John was about to witness that no one could penetrate these inscrutable righteous actions of God until they were completed at the End itself (see Rev 10:5–7; cf. 16:17–21; 19:1–8), when the Lord would come.

REVELATION 16:1–11

THE FIRST FIVE CENSERS OF GOD'S WRATH

TRANSLATION

16 ¹And I heard a great voice from the sanctuary saying to the seven angels, "Go forth and pour out the seven censers of the fury of God onto the earth." ²And the first went forth and poured out his censer onto the earth, and there came about a grievous and painful sore upon the men who had the mark of the beast and who worshiped its image. ³And the second poured out his censer on the sea, and there came about blood as from a corpse, and every life of a living thing died which was in the sea. ⁴And the third poured out his censer on the rivers and the fountains of the waters, and they became blood. ⁵And I heard the angel of the waters saying,

"Righteous are you, the One Who Is and
　　Who Was, the Holy One, because you
　　are dispensing such judgments;
⁶for the blood of saints and prophets they shed, and
　　so [now] blood you have given to them to drink.
Deserving are they!"
⁷And I heard from the incense altar saying,
"Yes, O Yahweh, the [only] God, the Almighty,
　　true and righteous are your judgments."
⁸And the fourth poured out his censer upon the sun, and [license] was given to it to burn men with fire. ⁹And men were burned with an intense heat, and they blasphemed the name of God, who has such authority over these plagues, and they did not repent to give him glory. ¹⁰And the fifth poured out his censer upon the throne of the beast, and its kingdom became darkened, and they were biting their tongues from the pain. ¹¹And they blasphemed

the God of heaven from their pains and from their
sores, and they did not repent of their works.

COMMENTARY

A GREAT VOICE FROM THE TEMPLE (16:1)

The speaker of the voice in 16:1 is unidentified. Since the voice comes from
the temple, it is probably the voice of God himself, for no one else can enter the
temple until the plagues are completed (15:8). The "great voice" commands the
seven angels to begin their task of pouring out their censers, which are full of
God's wrath.

The seven plagues that the angels are to pour out on the earth have similarities to some of the ten plagues of Egypt (Ex 7:14–11:9) and to the calamities
upon the earth that the trumpet-angels introduced (Rev 8:6–9:21; 11:15–19). In
all three cases the plagues and calamities come from God with the purpose of
moving hardened hearts to repentance.

The severity of God's judgments will increase as the end of this world at
Christ's return draws nearer. In fact, *this is the overall emphasis in this third
vision of earthly events. While some of the events presented in this third vision
repeat those in the second, in the third vision they are all intensified in order to
portray God's final warning of the seriousness of his judgment at the End.* For
example, in 8:8–9, one third of the sea is contaminated and one third of ocean
life perishes, but in the corresponding plague in 16:3, *all* seawater becomes
blood and *all* sea creatures perish. Thus the plagues of God's wrath in the third
vision urge the human race to repent before it is too late since *no one* will escape
the final judgment.

In 8:1–5, when the trumpet-angels were preparing to introduce the calamities about to strike the earth, smoke from the incense altar and the prayers
of the saints were involved in the preparation. Here, in the preparation of the
censer-angels, the majesty of God and his heavenly temple are involved. The
trumpet-angels acted on behalf of God at the prayerful behest of his saints. The
censer-angels act on behalf of God at his direct command and on his own initia-
tive, and not primarily in response to prayer.

THE FIRST THREE PLAGUES (16:2–4)

The plague of the first censer-angel strikes all those who, in opposition
to God and his saints, worship the beast and its image (13:14) and who bear
its mark or brand of recognition. The plague is described as a "grievous and
painful sore" (16:2). This is reminiscent of the plague of boils or blisters that
struck Egypt (Ex 9:8–12). While the plague of boils in ancient Egypt was for
a short period of time, this plague will strike the human race all through the
time period from Christ's ascension up to the End. It is not that all people at
any given time will be plagued by them, nor that an individual will suffer from

them throughout all of life, but they will be a constant menace and many will suffer from them. In general, the plagues will grow worse as the time of Christ's return draws near, even as the ten plagues on the Egyptians grew worse before the exodus.

The plague of the second censer-angel strikes the seas and the bodies of water so that they become "blood as from a corpse" (Rev 16:3). The flow of blood (not yet coagulated) is such that only a person who has just died could produce it. While the human race itself is not directly struck, this "blood as from a corpse" is a horrifying plague that strikes the seas. Whatever form this plague takes at any given time, it will affect all life in the seas. The first plague upon ancient Egypt turned the waters of the Nile into blood (Ex 7:19–21). As a result the fish died, and water turned into blood was everywhere. The stench of the Nile was so bad that the people could not drink the waters. In Rev 8:8–9 when the second trumpet-angel sounded his horn the seas were struck so that a third of them became blood and caused a third of the fish and of the creatures in the seas to die. As in 8:8–9, the specific earthly forms of this plague here in 16:3 can be left to the imagination. Whatever is involved, it certainly suggests that increasingly the seas will be made unfit for people or beasts, and that some of the basic requirements for sustaining human life will be severely hindered. For example, the cycle by which ocean water evaporates and then provides rain to water the earth could fail. All life in the seas will die in this plague (in contrast to just one third of the sea's living things in 8:8–9), indicating that as the time of judgment at the End draws nearer, more and more of the seas of the earth will be so plagued.

When the third censer-angel empties his censer, the rivers and bodies of fresh water are struck by a plague so that they also become blood (16:4). In 8:10–11, when the third trumpet-angel blew his horn, the fresh water supplies of the rivers and the springs were hit so that they became bitter and poisonous and thus unfit to drink. As a result many people died from drinking such polluted water. But only one third of the rivers and springs were embittered. Here in 16:4 *all* the fresh water supplies are plagued. It is difficult to imagine how all the rivers and springs would be so polluted, for that would seem to imply that no drinking water would be safe for human consumption. Life would thus become impossible. Probably what is suggested is that at any given time during the period from Christ's ascension up to the End, the waters will be so affected that increasingly they will become so dangerous that no life can survive there. As in the case of the seas (16:3), the closer the end of this world draws near, the more the supplies of fresh water will become so unhealthy that many people will die. Whole regions of the earth may become uninhabitable.

A RESPONSE (16:5–7)

Between the plagues of the third and fourth censer-angels John hears "the angel of the waters" (16:5) proclaiming a response to these acts of God's fury. In

7:1 angels of the four winds appeared, and 14:18 spoke of an angel with authority over the fire on the incense altar in heaven. Within Judaism angels under God's authority were understood to be in charge of the elements of creation. Whether or not "the angel of the waters" (16:5) was in charge of these waters in the sense of Jewish tradition, he evidently has some responsibility for oversight and care of the waters.

As the waters are plagued, this angel cries out in response to these acts of God's judgment. It is a cry of worship in which the angel acknowledges the justness of God in dispensing and pouring out on the earth his anger. The angel's words of worship can be understood as an "antiphon" to the canticle of worship of God in 15:3–4, "the song of Moses ... and the hymn of the Lamb." In that song the saints of God were victoriously singing even as they were suffering earthly defeat and death, because at the same time they were emerging victorious over the beast (15:2). The saints acknowledged that God was righteous and just in declaring his punishing judgments on their enemies—the acts of judgment about to be introduced by the seven censer-angels. Now, as these acts or plagues of God's fury are poured out, the angel of the waters cries out a similar word acknowledging the righteousness of God's judgments.

The angel confesses that God, "the One Who Is and Who Was, the Holy One," is "righteous" (in so judging the human race. This holy name of God, "the One Who Is and Who Was," is an explanatory form of the name of Yahweh. This is the fifth time that a form of this holy name has appeared in Revelation (1:4, 8; 4:8; 11:17; 16:5). Three times it is given in a fuller form: "the One Who Is and Who Was and Who Is Coming" (1:4, 8) or "the One Who Was and Who Is and Who Is Coming" (4:8). In 11:17 and here in 16:5 it is given as "the One Who Is and Who Was." The "Who Is Coming" part of the holy name is probably absent in 11:17 because Yahweh, the Lord God, is no longer the Coming One, since in 11:15–19 the seventh trumpet-angel introduces the seventh and last scene of the second earthly vision, which is the scene of the end of this world. Here in 16:5 "Who Is Coming" is also absent. Though John will see a scene of the End in 16:17–21, the element in the holy name that looks toward the future is absent probably because the angel of the waters recognizes that these plagues of the seven censer-angels are the *last* plagues, which give God's third and *final* set of warnings—warnings that illustrate and inaugurate the final judgment at the End.

Yahweh, "the Holy One," is just and "righteous" in judging the earth by these plagues (16:5). In the canticle of 15:3–4 it is because God, who is the Holy One, is also true in all his ways and works as the Redeemer that he has the right to so judge the human race. Here in the antiphon of 16:5–6 "the Holy One" is just in his acts of anger because he is judging the enemies who had shed the blood of his "saints and prophets" (16:6). The judgment takes the form of exacting vengeance by shedding the blood of those enemies. In the same way and measure that they persecuted the "saints and prophets," so also in that same way and measure the persecutors will be judged and punished (cf. Mt 7:2). This is their righteous punishment as judged in the scales of God's justice.

A voice from the incense altar speaks the amen to the antiphon of the angel. In Rev 9:13 John heard a voice from one of the corners of the incense altar which instructed the sixth trumpet-angel to release the four angels who had, up to that moment, held back the evil forces about to be unleashed at the River Euphrates (9:14–19). In 14:18 the angel who had the fire of the altar came from the incense altar and told the angel with the sharp sickle to begin the harvest (14:17–18). Whether or not the voice here in 16:7 is the voice of the angel of the incense altar, the voice speaks for the saints and their prayers, since the incense represents the prayers in which the saints petition God to judge their enemies on their behalf (6:9–11; cf. 8:3–5).

The amen is a resounding yes to Yahweh, the Lord God Almighty. It confirms his acts of anger because God is true and righteous in his judgments as they are revealed (15:3–4). These acts of judgment will be even more visibly displayed in the following four plagues.

THE FOURTH AND FIFTH PLAGUES (16:8–11)

In the second vision of events on earth (8:6–11:19) in the scene introduced by the fourth trumpet-angel, a third of the sun, moon, and stars was darkened, and thus a third of the day and night did not have light (8:12). Here in the fourth scene of the third sevenfold vision of events on earth, when the angel pours out his censer upon the sun, it burns people with an extreme heat, just the opposite from the plague in 8:12. In both cases part of the created order is disrupted so that humankind is endangered.

One can only imagine how this might take place, in the natural phenomena in the heavens above the earth. In various periods mankind has suffered from excessive heat from the sun. In this scene of the fourth censer-angel, it appears that this excessive heat from the sun will not kill humanity but only increase to the point that at various times many people will cry out in their suffering without any apparent relief.

When humanity suffers in this way under God's judgment, people blaspheme the name of God and do not repent of their sins by giving him glory (16:9). Regardless of whether they attribute this judgment to the true God, in their idolatrous state of unbelief they vent their anger and express their hatred toward God. This idolatry would include ascribing their suffering to fate or random chance or a false god or religion. Whether or not they recognize the hand of God in this judgment against their sins and unbelief, they do not have the wisdom to understand that God is doing it for their own eternal well-being. Instead they blaspheme God and his name—that name by which alone mankind can be saved (Acts 4:12; cf. Phil 2:10–11).

These are general statements about *humanity as a whole;* they do not preclude the possibility that *some* may repent and believe in the true God. These general statements also are primarily about unbelievers—those with the mark of the beast (16:2). Christians too might suffer along with the rest of humanity but would be penitent. However, most people will mock God (cf. Rom 2:24) and refuse to acknowledge their sin and shame and turn in repentance to God for mercy. Revelation mentions repeatedly this hardness of heart in refusing to repent (9:20, 21; 16:9, 11).

When the fifth angel pours out his censer, the kingdom of the beast becomes "darkened" (16:10). Since the worshipers of the beast and its image (see 13:12–15) refuse to repent, even though struck by these various plagues, God now strikes the object of their worship and allegiance. Even though it is not stated here how or in what form this judgment of the beast and its kingdom takes place, in Revelation 18 John gives a graphic picture of this judgment when he describes the fall of Babylon and the destruction of the harlot. However, in Revelation 18 the picture is more about the *final* judgment and destruction of this enemy of God's people, when Christ returns in glory. Here in 16:10 John sees the beast and its kingdom being struck by God, however and in whatever ways he does it, *throughout the whole time period between Christ's first and second advents.* This takes place in order to warn *the people* to cease their worship of the beast and to come instead to the only true God and Savior of the human race (cf. 18:4–5).

As the adherents of the beast see the judgments of God strike the beast's throne, they also suffer, in turn, because they are members of the beast's kingdom. Their suffering is such that they bite their tongues (16:10). But the worshipers of the beast and its image do not listen nor take heed. Instead, they only grow more vehement in their anger and hatred toward God. The more they suffer from the consequence of their sins and their worship of the beast, the more they blaspheme "the God of heaven" (16:11). Even though they see the kingdom of the beast crumbling around them, and even though they at least should have recognized the futility of their allegiance, they still refuse to repent (cf. 18:9–10).

REVELATION 16:12–16

THE SIXTH CENSER OF GOD'S WRATH: ARMAGEDDON

TRANSLATION

16 [12]And the sixth poured out his censer onto the great river Euphrates, and its water dried up so that the way of the kings who are [coming] from the rising of the sun might be made ready. [13]And I saw [coming] out from the mouth of the dragon and out from the mouth of the beast and out from the mouth of the false prophet three unclean spirits like frogs; [14]for they are spirits of demons producing signs, [spirits] which go forth upon the kings of the whole inhabited earth to gather them together for that war of the great day of God, the Almighty. [15]"Behold, I am coming as a thief. Blessed is the one who stays awake and guards his garments, so that he might not walk about naked and so that they might not see his shame." [16]And he assembled them at the place which is called in Hebrew Armageddon.

COMMENTARY

THE SIXTH SCENE (16:12)

The sixth censer-angel introduces a scene that is parallel to the scene introduced by the sixth trumpet-angel: the last battle between the forces of evil and the church. The devil's war against the church continues throughout the entire NT era (as portrayed in 12:13–17), but it culminates in one last and greatest battle before the End at Christ's return. In 9:13–21 John received his first visionary view of this last battle. There, when the sixth angel sounded his trumpet, he saw a terrifying host gathered and poised at the River Euphrates. This host was about to be unleashed on the human race, and when let loose, it would kill a third of the human population. That vision revealed that this evil force was positioned to be let loose at a definite and certain time, "this hour and day and month and year" (9:15), just before the End (see 10:5–7; 11:15–19). This evil host is described in such nightmarish terms that it is clearly of demonic origin. Here in 16:12–16 John receives a second view of the last battle. It is designated as "that war of the great day of God, the Almighty" (16:14), and the place of battle is designated as "Armageddon" (16:16). A third and final time John will see a scene of this last battle when, in connection with the final defeat of the devil, he sees the forces of Gog and Magog destroyed (20:7–10).

When the sixth angel pours out his censer, it is upon "the great river Euphrates" (16:12). It is the same Euphrates River as in 9:14, where John previously saw an evil host gathered and about to be unleashed. The fact that God here (16:12), through the sixth censer-angel, strikes the Euphrates suggests that he will use the occasion of this last battle to judge and destroy the enemies of his saints on earth (cf. 20:8–9). This will be their final and utter defeat on earth, followed by their eternal punishment in hell (20:10).

The great river is dried up in order to prepare the way for the evil host from the east to invade and surround the people of God (cf. 20:9). This drying up of the Euphrates is somewhat reminiscent of the dividing and drying up of the Red Sea, which furnished the escape route for Moses and the Israelites and also prepared the way for Pharaoh and his army to be destroyed (Ex 14:21–31). It is also reminiscent of the miniature reenactment of the exodus miracle when God split the waters of the Jordan River so that Israel could cross into the Promised Land (Josh 3:9–17). Moreover, Rev 16:12 fulfills the prophecy of Is 11:15. Envisioning the future day of deliverance in terms of the past, God promised a greater exodus when he would dry up "the tongue of the sea of Egypt and wave his hand over the river" so that his people could cross over in sandals, just as he did "for Israel on the day he [Israel] came up from the land of Egypt" (Is 11:15–16). As recognized by most translations and commentaries, "the river" (Is 11:15) is a reference to the Euphrates. God will do all this for his people as a result of the righteous "Branch" coming from the "stump of Jesse" (Is 11:1–14; cf. Is 51:9–10; Zech 10:10–11).

On this prepared highway the kings would come from the east. The enemies of ancient Israel often came from the east, from Mesopotamia, the region between the Tigris and the Euphrates. At the time of John's own ministry the Parthians in the east were a constant threat and danger to the eastern frontier of the Roman Empire. A rumor at the time said that Nero had not died but had escaped to Parthia, from where he would lead a Parthian army to retake his imperial throne.

In Rev 16:12 John uses the phrase "from the rising of the sun" symbolically. Geographically the east, in particular the region of the Euphrates, was the direction from which Babylon, the great enemy, which in Revelation represents all the enemies of God's people, came to destroy Judah and take her into the captivity of the Babylonian exile. John now recalls this historic circumstance and uses the east ("the rising of the sun") and the Euphrates (16:12) as symbols. He suggests to the minds of his hearers that another and greater enemy will hurl itself at the church of Christ in one last battle in the attempt to destroy her. The origin of this evil host will not be a *geographic* location but rather a *spiritual* locus.

THE UNHOLY TRINITY (16:13)

The power and influence behind the kings and their hosts are identified as "the dragon ... the beast and ... the false prophet" (16:13). This is the same unholy trinity which is found in Revelation 12–13. "The dragon" (16:13) is the "great red dragon" (12:3) of Revelation 12, who is Satan himself. He attempts to destroy the male Child (Christ Jesus) of the woman, who represents the Christian church (12:3–4). After the Child is taken to heaven (12:5), the dragon pursues the woman in order to destroy her and the rest of her offspring—the Christians (12:13–17). "The beast" (16:13) is the "beast ... of the sea" (13:1) described in 13:1–10. The third partner of this unholy trinity is identified here in 16:13 as "the false prophet."

This is the first time in Revelation that this "false prophet" is mentioned. In 13:11–18 the third partner of the unholy trinity was the "beast ... of the earth" (13:11), who bore the number 666. It appears that the evil spiritual entity previously called the "beast ... of the earth" is here called "the false prophet." This identification becomes a certainty when one compares 13:13–14 to 19:20. Rev 19:20 says that it was the false prophet who made the signs by which he deceived those who received the mark of the beast and who worshiped the image of the beast (that is, the image of the beast from the sea). In 13:13–14 it was the "beast ... of the earth" (13:11) who deceived the inhabitants of the earth by producing the signs and who motivated the peoples of the earth to "make an image to the beast" (the beast from the sea). Revelation will mention "the false prophet" one more time: in 20:10 the beast (that is, the beast from the sea, 13:1–10) and the false prophet are with the dragon after he is cast into the lake of fire. Furthermore, this third spiritual entity, called the beast from the earth and the false prophet, will also be called the harlot in Revelation 17 and 19. Therefore, while the dragon and the first beast (the beast from the sea, 13:1–10) remain the same throughout Revelation, the second beast (the beast from the earth, 13:11–18) appears in three different guises: as the second "beast" (13:11–18), as "the false prophet" (16:13; 19:20; 20:10), and as the "harlot" (17:1, 5, 15–16; 19:2).

In the economy of this unholy trinity, the dragon is the mastermind. He works through the beast from the sea and the false prophet (the beast from the earth) in order to deceive the peoples of the earth in his warfare against the woman—the church (12:13–13:1). In this warfare the beast from the sea represents all political, social, and economic powers that are harnessed by the devil. For that reason this commentary labeled it "the political beast." The beast from the earth, now called the false prophet, represents all false religions and also the corrupted and apostate elements within the Christian church—those that may be called "Christian" but which really are not. For that reason this commentary referred to the second beast as "the religious beast." This false spirituality of the beast is emphasized all the more when (as here in 16:13) it is referred to as "the false prophet."

This unholy trinity empowers the human hosts that John now sees unleashed at the River Euphrates. Three "unclean spirits like frogs" were leaping out of the mouths of the three partners of this unholy trinity (16:13). The "three unclean spirits" motivate the kings under the influence and control of the unholy trinity. That these unclean spirits are likened to frogs may be due to the fact that in Lev 11:9–11 (cf. 11:41) all creatures living in water who do not have fins and scales were to be considered unclean and unfit for human consumption. Surely John was also reminded of the plague of frogs in ancient Egypt (Ex 8:1–15). Like the frogs that covered everything in Egypt (Ex 8:3–4), so this host under demonic influence will cover the entire earth.

THE UNCLEAN SPIRITS GATHER KINGS FOR BATTLE (16:14)

By means of miraculous "signs" the unclean spirits, which in 16:14 are called "spirits of demons," "go forth upon the kings of the whole inhabited earth to gather them together" for the great battle, "that war of the great day of God, the Almighty" (16:14). In his earthly ministry Jesus warned that in the last days before the End (Mt 24:6, 13–14), "false messiahs and false prophets" would produce "signs" by which they would deceive many (Mt 24:23–28). Here in Rev 16:14 the kings and their hosts are so deceived by the "signs" produced by the demons that they gather together for war in order to destroy God's saints on earth. Rev 20:7–9 portrays this same sequence of events but ascribes the deception to Satan himself and pictures the attackers as all the nations of the earth under the leadership of Gog and Magog. Rev 20:9 also makes explicit that *the war is against God's saints and against his beloved city.* The war will take place on "the great day of God, the Almighty" (16:14). The people of God were told in the OT that such a war would take place (e.g., Ezekiel 38–39). The prophet Joel stated, "Great is the day of Yahweh, and utterly terrifying," so much so that no one will be able to "endure it" (Joel 2:11; cf. Zeph 1:14). It is a day when the Lord God "will gather all the nations for judgment in the Valley of Jehoshaphat" (Joel 3:2). All the previous days of judgment—such as Assyria's conquest of Israel, the fall of Jerusalem to Babylon, and the destruction of Jerusalem by the Romans in AD 70—and all the persecutions and calamities suffered by Christians and churches throughout history up until the present time pale in comparison to that terrifying day. At the same time, those calamities and the present warfare of the church militant portend that coming day. They also remind the church that even when she seems defeated, she is not, for the Lord himself ultimately will crush her enemies and by grace she shall emerge victorious (cf. Rev 15:2–4).

A WORD FROM THE LORD CHRIST (16:15)

In the midst of the visionary imagery of the last battle before the End at Christ's return, John hears a voice speaking in the first person, "Behold, I am coming as a thief" (16:15). This is the voice of the Lord Christ, for elsewhere in Revelation *only he* declares in the first person, "I am coming." In the letter to the angel of the church in Philadelphia, the Lord Christ urges the saints to hold on to his Word (3:8, 10) so that they would not lose their crown, reminding them, "I am coming quickly" (3:11). In the letter to the church at Sardis, the exalted Lord says, "I will come as a thief" (3:3). His coming will be so unexpected that no one will be able to predict the moment of his arrival. In Mt 24:36–44 Jesus describes the coming of the Son of Man at the End, saying that it will be like the coming of a thief (Mt 24:43). In 1 Thess 5:2 Paul says that "the day of the Lord will come like a thief coming in the night."

While the suddenness and unexpectedness of the coming of the Lord Christ at the End is a warning which all Christians need to heed at all times (Rev 3:3), *it is also a promise of encouragement and hope* (3:11). This is the reason why the prophetic message of Revelation to John concludes with this promise, "Yes, I am coming quickly," to which John answers, "Amen, come now, Lord Jesus" (22:20). In 16:15 this word of promise is attached to a beatitude, which is the third of seven beatitudes in Revelation. The beatitude here is an encouragement for the Christian to keep watch and guard his garments, that is, the clothing washed in the blood of Christ (7:9, 13–14), the garment of righteousness (Job 29:14; Is 61:10; Zech 3:4) worn by all who believe and have been baptized into Christ, since in Holy Baptism a person is clothed with Christ. It is a word of promise that encourages the people of God on earth to remain faithful in the midst of the fearful days of this last battle before the End. The fear of suffering in the battle could be a temptation to surrender to the enemy and thus forfeit Christ's garment and stand "naked" in one's "shame" (Rev 16:15). For this reason the Lord urges his church in Laodicea to remain clothed in white garments so that the shame of her nakedness would not appear (3:18). But especially this is a word of promise which engenders hope, for the Lord is coming quickly (1:3; 22:6–7). The battle will soon be over and the victory will extend throughout eternity!

ARMAGEDDON (16:16)

The enemy hosts are assembled "at the place which is called in Hebrew Armageddon" (16:16). While Armageddon (from the Hebrew for "mountain of Megiddo") is a geographical place name, John lifts it out of any particular historical context and uses it as a symbol for this last battle before the End. The natural environment surrounding Megiddo offered springs and supplies of fresh water, as well as forage and spatial expanse, so that armies could sustain themselves and be deployed easily. Thus it was one of the few suitable places in ancient Israel where vast armies could assemble for battle. It had been the place of the battles of the Israelites under Barak and Deborah with the hosts of Sisera (Judg 4:14–24) and the warfare between the Israelites and the Egyptians in which King Josiah was killed (2 Ki 23:29–30). It was also at Megiddo that Ahaziah king of Judah died after having been mortally wounded in a battle with Jehu (2 Ki 9:27) and where Joram king of Israel was killed (2 Ki 9:23–29). As mountains have often witnessed great events (Is 44:23; Ezek 6:3–13; cf. 35:12; 36:1–7), so here in Rev 16:16 the mountain of Megiddo will witness this final battle on the great day of the Lord.

Thus Armageddon is used here not as the designation of a particular geographic place, but as a terrifying metaphor of a war that will cover the expanse of the entire earth, since the whole human race will be caught up in it (see 20:9). The enemy's intent in this last battle before the End will be the destruction of the people of God, the church of Jesus Christ (20:9; cf. Ezek 38:7–16). But the enemy shall not prevail (Rev 16:19; 20:9–10), and the kingdom shall belong to the Lord forever and ever (Obad 21; 1 Chr 29:11).

REVELATION 16:17–21

THE SEVENTH CENSER OF GOD'S WRATH: THE END

TRANSLATION

16 ¹⁷And the seventh poured out his censer upon the air, and a great voice came forth out of the sanctuary from the throne, saying, "It is completed." ¹⁸And there came about lightning flashes and noises and thunders, and a great earthquake came about of such a kind that has not occurred from the time when man came into being on the earth—so large-scale was this earthquake. ¹⁹And the great city was broken up into three parts, and the cities of the pagan nations fell. And Babylon the great was remembered in the presence of God, to give to her the cup of the wine of the fury of his wrath. ²⁰And every island passed out of sight, and mountains vanished from view. ²¹And great hail like hundredweight stones comes down from heaven upon the men, and the men blasphemed God on account of the plague of hail, because the plague of it was great—exceedingly so.

COMMENTARY

THE SEVENTH CENSER (16:17)

When the seventh censer-angel pours out his plague, John again hears "a great voice" (16:17). In 16:1 a "great voice" came forth from the temple. This time the voice is from "the throne" within the temple. As in 16:1, the speaker of the voice is not directly stated, but it most likely is the voice of God himself, for throughout the chapter it is God who is the source of the plagues. The only place in Revelation where God the Father is explicitly identified as the speaker in the first person is in 21:5–6. In 21:6 God says, "It has come into being," a form of the same Greek verb translated here as "it is completed." Therefore it appears that the speaker here in 16:17 is also God. The voice shouts out that the final act follows: this is the End.

"It is completed" (16:17). Now comes the End itself. This is the fourth time that John receives a view of the End. In the first vision of earthly events

(6:1–8:5), when the Lamb opened the sixth seal, John saw the End in terms of the fear and the terror it evokes (6:12–17). In the second vision of events on earth (8:6–11:19), when the seventh angel blew his trumpet, John again saw the End, but in terms of the joy that it brings to God's people (11:15–19). John saw the End for a third time in the interregnum (12:1–14:20), which concludes with a depiction of the great harvest at the End (14:14–20). Now for a fourth time John is given a prophetic picture of the End in the seventh scene of this third vision of events on earth, the scene introduced by the seventh censer-angel.

As the angel pours out the seventh plague "upon the air" (16:17), the plague is accompanied by this great voice of God, thus indicating that this is the final plague, the very End itself. "The air" that is struck is the entire atmosphere that surrounds the earth, including the air that people breathe. This last plague encompasses and impacts the entire earth and all the human race, much more than did the first six. Not only are the earth and the sea and the fresh water supplies and the sun struck, but now the necessary element of human existence is blighted, the air which surrounds people and which they breathe, without which they would quickly die. John is not shown or told *how* the air is struck or how the plague prevents people's ability to breathe. But what he is shown in 16:18–21 is a cataclysmic and violent disturbance that shatters the entire earth's surface. This would suggest that in these verses we have an explanation of the result of the "air" being plagued.

The voice from the heavenly throne shouts out that everything necessary has been accomplished so that the End can now come. The phrase "it is completed" not only refers to that which has been displayed and brought to a completion (that is, the first six plagues), it also points to the final act, the last plague. The first six plagues of God's wrath have shown to mankind his displeasure and anger over their allegiance to the dragon and his partners, the beast and the false prophet. Through those plagues God has given the reason why humankind should repent, and he has also given people the time to do so. But the seventh plague proclaims emphatically that the time is up, for the End is here and it is time for the final judgment. The cry from the cross "It is finished" signaled the end of Jesus' suffering and as a result also signaled the completion of everything necessary for the new beginning of a new life at the resurrection. So here this cry in 16:17 signals the end of the time for repentance and an end of God's merciful patience. It also signals that the judgment at the End has begun and indeed has come. One more time (21:6) John will hear the voice of God cry out the same verb, when he is shown the new heaven and earth (21:1–8). This would suggest that while the penultimate "it is completed" is the final judgment at the End, the ultimate completion of that cry is the creation of the new heaven and new earth and the beginning of resurrection life in the eternal state.

THEOPHANY AND JUDGMENT (16:18–21)

When the voice cries out, it is accompanied by phenomena similar to what occurred when God descended and spoke on Mt. Sinai: lightning flashes, thunder, and a violent shaking (Ex 19:16–20; cf. Judg 5:5; 2 Sam 22:8; Ps 18:7). In Rev 4:5, in the scene of God's heavenly glory, "lightning flashes and noises and thunders" came out from the heavenly throne of God, accompanying and manifesting his awesome and fearful presence. When the angel of the incense altar poured out his censer of fire onto the earth (introducing the seven trumpet-angels), "thunders and noises and lightning flashes and an earthquake" attended his action (8:5). At the conclusion of the scene of the End introduced by the seventh trumpet-angel, "lightning flashes and noises and thunders and an earthquake" were present (11:19). When these phenomena occur in Revelation in the scene of the *heavenly* sphere of God's presence (4:5), the "earthquake" is not present. But in the scenes where God's actions of judgment *strike the earth and the human race* (8:5; 11:19), the "earthquake" is a result. So here in 16:18, at the final judgment at the End, the "earthquake" also occurs together with the other natural phenomena. This suggests that when the awesome and fearful presence of God (indicated by the "lightning flashes and noises and thunders") descends *to earth* for the purpose of *judgment*, then the "earthquake" demonstrates that God is now present in his fearful majesty for the purpose of executing the judgment of the human race. But the earthquake that attends the majesty of God's presence at the End is much greater than the ones referred to in the OT and in 8:5 and 11:13—greater than any that has ever been. It is so much greater because this is the final quake to shock the human race, thus portending the enormity of God's *final* reckoning in the judgment at the End.

These natural phenomena, signifying God's majestic presence for the purpose of judgment, now strike the earth as cataclysmic occurrences, and as a result "the cities of the pagan nations fell" (16:19). "Babylon the great" is singled out in particular. At the End all the cities and everything they represent (civilizations, culture, commerce, wealth, and the social life and ambitions of the human race) come to an end in God's judgment. Especially the "great city" (16:19), here identified as "Babylon the great," is "remembered in the presence of God" so that she will drink "the cup of the wine of the fury of his wrath." Especially to John Rome represented satanic powers opposed to Jesus Christ and his church. But Rome, here signified by "Babylon the great" (16:19), became a type or example for all future time of every human institution—in particular political, economic, and social orders, and pagan spiritual philosophies—which, under the dragon's influence, attempts to destroy God's saints on earth. Because of Nebuchadnezzar's destruction of Jerusalem and the resulting Babylonian captivity, the ancient city of Babylon became a type of all future enemies of God's people (in both the OT and NT eras). In the same way, because of the Roman conquest of Judea in 63 BC, the destruction of the Jerusalem temple by the Romans in AD 70, and the Roman persecution of the early church, Rome became an umbrella-like type for all future enemies of the Christ and his church. Thus for John, Rome was the modern Babylon.

The fact that "the great city was broken up into three parts" (16:19) suggests the totality of its destruction in God's judgment. In Rev 11:13 only "a tenth of the city fell" because of an "earthquake." Here the entire city was demolished. So sudden and total was the destruction of the city that there was no longer time for change of heart and repentance.

Also the topography of the earth's surface was altered by the great earthquake: "every island passed out of sight, and mountains vanished from view" (16:20). Apparently these topographic features were leveled and abolished so as to be no longer discernable to the human eye. Christ's first advent is portrayed as transforming creation in a similar way: "Every valley shall be filled in; every mountain and hill shall be made low" (Lk 3:5, quoting Is 40:4). But Christ's second advent, which brings this world to its end, alters the creation radically, violently, and completely. In the scene of the End in the first sevenfold vision, the sixth scene (6:12–17), "every mountain and island were moved from their places" (6:14). In the scene of the judgment at the End in 20:11–15, before the fearful and majestic presence of God, "the earth and the heaven fled." Certainly this indicates that the earth and its immediate environment will be greatly altered. This climatic change of the old earth and sky opens up the way for the creation of the new heavens and the new earth (Rev 21:1–22:5).

Finally, the enormity of the destruction caused by God's judgment is emphasized by the unimaginable depiction of fantastic hailstones so large that they each weigh a hundred pounds. While the earth's surface and its cities are being shaken and demolished, so that human beings flee in terror for safety but find none, the earth and its inhabitants are further afflicted by hailstones so large that it is difficult to think any human being or animal or plant could survive. (Yet some people apparently do, for they blaspheme God in 16:21.) Whether such hail is only a metaphor for God's punishing judgment or whether such physical hail attends his coming presence in judgment—or both—the result is the same. The hail emphasizes the climax of God's divine wrath in his anger over the sins and rebellion of humankind. In the OT God sometimes punished the enemies of his people on earth with hail. In imagery that is close to what John sees here in the plague of the seventh censer-angel, Ezekiel saw how God promised to destroy Gog and his evil host just before the End (Ezek 38:18–23). When Gog will be judged and destroyed, God in his wrath will send an earthquake so that all life on the face of the earth will tremble, mountains will be thrown down, and torrents of rain, accompanied by hailstones and burning sulfur, will pour down upon this great enemy of God's people (Ezek 38:22; cf. Rev 20:8–9).

Despite all the evidence furnished by God's plagues, signifying the punishing actions of his judgment, the enemies of his saints do not repent, for people "blasphemed God" (16:21) on account of his judgment at the End. Their adherence and allegiance to the dragon and his henchmen is unshaken. They even do this in the face of eternal suffering in hell (cf. 19:20–21; 20:10).

17:1–22:5

The Conclusion: The End and the New Heaven and New Earth

17:1–18:24

The Judgment and Overthrow of the Forces of the Dragon

REVELATION 17:1–18

THE JUDGMENT
OF THE HARLOT

TRANSLATION

17 ¹And one of the seven angels who have the seven
censers came, and he spoke with me, saying,
"Come, I will show to you the judgment of the
great harlot who sits upon many waters, ²with
whom the kings of the earth committed adultery,
and those dwelling on the earth were made
drunk from the wine of her immorality."
³And he carried me away in the Spirit into a desert.
And [there] I saw a woman sitting on a scarlet
beast full of the names of blasphemy, having seven
heads and ten horns. ⁴And the woman was clothed
in purple and scarlet and was gilded with gold and
precious stone and pearls, holding in her hand
a golden cup full of abominable things, indeed,
the unclean things of her immorality. ⁵And on
her forehead a name had been written, a mystery:
"Babylon the great, the mother of harlots and of
the abominable things of the earth." ⁶And I saw the
woman in a drunken stupor from the blood of the
saints and from the blood of the witnesses of Jesus.
And I marvelled with great awe when I saw her.
⁷And the angel said to me, "Why were you amazed?
I will explain to you the mystery of the woman
and of the beast which bears her, which has the
seven heads and the ten horns. ⁸The beast which
you see was, and is not, and is about to come up
out of the abyss, and it goes away into destruction.
And those dwelling upon the earth whose name
has not been written in the book of life from the
foundation of the world will be awe-struck when
they see the beast—that was, and is not, and shall

be present. ⁹Here is the mind which has wisdom!
"The seven heads are seven hills, upon which the
woman is sitting. And they are seven kings. ¹⁰Five
have fallen, one is [present], the other has not yet
come, and when he comes it is necessary that he
remain a little while. ¹¹And the beast which was, and
is not—also he himself is the eighth and is from the
seven and goes away into destruction. ¹²And the ten
horns which you see are ten kings who did not yet
receive a kingdom but receive authority with the beast
as kings for one hour. ¹³These act with one mind so
that they give their power and authority to the beast.
¹⁴These will wage war with the Lamb, but the Lamb
will conquer them because he is the Lord of lords
and the King of kings, and those [who conquer] with
him are the called and chosen and faithful ones."
¹⁵And he says to me, "The waters which you see where
the harlot sits, they are peoples and crowds and
nations and tongues. ¹⁶And the ten horns which you
see and the beast, these will hate the harlot, and they
will make her desolated and naked, and they will
eat her flesh, and in fire they will burn her up. ¹⁷For
God has given into their hearts to do his will and
to act with one mind and to give their kingdom to
the beast until the words of God will be completed.
¹⁸And the woman whom you see is the great city
which has dominion over the kings of the earth."

COMMENTARY

THE FINAL VISION OF THE END (17:1–22:5)

At the end of the third vision of events on earth (15:1–16:21), after the
seventh censer-angel introduced the last scene, which depicted the End
(16:17–21), John receives a vision in which he again sees the end of the present
world (17:1–22:5). But this vision of the End does not give another dimension
and emphasis, as do the first four scenes of the End. Rather, it is a lengthy vision
which summarizes and concludes all that John has seen earlier in the previous
four scenes concerning the End. This fifth, lengthy vision of the End draws to a
conclusion the entire prophetic message of Revelation. It does this by means of

several scenes, each of which depicts a certain aspect of what will take place at the End. Each of these scenes in turn also brings to a conclusion certain other things that John has seen before, not only in the four earlier scenes of the End, but also what he has seen in other parts of the prophetic message.

The first thing that John sees in this concluding vision of the end of the present world is the judgment and destruction of the two henchmen of the dragon: the beast and the harlot, which together are called Babylon (17:1–18:24). Then in chapter 19 John receives a beautiful visionary depiction of a celebration, which includes a song of victory (19:1–4), the marriage feast of the Lamb (19:5–10), and the second coming of the Lord Christ (19:11–21). At the return of the Lord Christ and its attendant celebration, there appears a prophetic picture of the judgment and overthrow of the dragon himself—Satan, the mastermind of the beast and the harlot (20:1–10). This judgment of the dragon is presented to John by way of two scenes, that of the millennium, which represents the entire church era, the time between Christ's first and second advents (20:1–6), and that of Gog and Magog (20:7–10). At the end of chapter 20 John receives a glimpse of the resurrection of the dead and the final judgment of the human race (20:11–15). Last of all, when lifted up by the Spirit, John is led by one of the censer-angels through a glorious picture of the new heaven and new earth, the heavenly city Jerusalem (21:1–22:5). This picture of the new heaven and earth concludes the prophetic message of Revelation.

THE VISION OF THE HARLOT (17:1–6)

The Great Harlot Sitting on Many Waters Controls the Nations (17:1–2)

The seven angels, who had the censers full of the plagues of God, emptied their censers and so introduced the seven scenes of the third and last vision of earthly events (15:1–16:21). One of those angels now invites John to follow him and view "the judgment of the great harlot" (17:1). It is quite fitting that one of these seven angels should show this judgment to John, for, if we are correct in our interpretative identification of them, they are the same angels as the angels of the seven churches, the angels to whom the seven letters are addressed in Revelation 2–3. Throughout the period of time from Christ's ascension up to his return at the End, the harlot, riding the beast (17:7), is the great enemy of God's saints on earth. As the angels of the churches were the mediators of the prophetic message of Revelation to the churches, which mediation they carried out and completed by way of the seven trumpets (8:1–11:19) and the seven censers (15:1–16:21), it is more than fitting that one of them now should show to John the judgment and overthrow of that enemy which had caused the church so much suffering. One of these same angels will also show to John the heavenly Jerusalem, the church finally at rest forever with God in the new heaven and earth (21:9; cf. 22:1, 8–9).

For the first time the enemy of the church is called "the great harlot" (17:1). In 17:7 she is pictured riding on the beast "which has the seven heads and the ten horns." The beast which bears the woman is clearly the beast from the sea in 13:1, which also has "ten horns and seven heads." In 13:11–18 at the dragon's bidding another beast arises which also plagues the church: the beast from the earth which has "two horns resembling a lamb's [it imitates Christ], but it was speaking like the dragon [it speaks for Satan]" (13:11). As the prophetic message of Revelation unfolds, this beast from the earth is later identified as "the false prophet" (16:13; 19:20; 20:10) and "the great harlot" (17:1, 5, 15–16; 19:2).

The first beast, which has the seven heads and ten horns, represents every-thing of the human sphere (society, government, economics) that the dragon uses in his warfare against the church. That so-called "political beast" does not evolve but remains the same. In contrast, the lamb-like beast, which speaks for the dragon represents every *spiritual* and *religious* entity that the dragon deceit-fully uses against the true church of Christ. This so-called "religious beast" evolves and develops until it finally and especially represents false Christianity and the apostate church. Therefore what this second beast represents *changes* from *all* false religions and spirituality in general into the false prophet and the harlot, that is, pseudo-*Christianity* and the false *church*, the most deadly form of the religious beast.

In Revelation 17, the use of "harlot" to designate the apostate pseudo-church is reminiscent of the practice of ancient fertility religions using cultic prostitution and many other forms of sexual immorality as part of their worship and also of God's complaint that his people Israel had become a harlot because of their idolatry in the worship of false gods (e.g., Hos 4:10–15; (Is 1:21–23; Jer 2:20). John will combine Babylon and the harlot as symbolic representatives of the pseudo-church using political power to destroy the true church of Jesus Christ, exampled in John's own day by Rome and her empire (see 17:5, 9; 18:2–4, 19–20). It is therefore quite understandable that a harlot now becomes a visual representation of the *false* people of God, that is, those who outwardly appear or claim to be part of the Christian church but are inwardly and spiritually apostate.

By means of "the harlot" the pseudo-church is presented as an attractive woman (cf. 17:6). She offsets and counters the woman of Revelation 12, who rep-resents the true people of God, also called the bride of the Lamb in 19:7. While the woman who bore the Child (Christ, 12:1–2, 5) is hunted down by the dragon and as a result suffers all manner of persecution and tribulations in the world (12:13–18), in contrast the harlot is honored and courted by the world (17:2, 4; 18:3),for she flatters and encourages the lifestyles of the ungodly. Now she enjoys the acclaim of the world (cf. 18:3, 9–15), but on that final day she will experience destruction and eternal ruin under the judgment of God (cf. 18:1–2, 5–6). On the other hand, the woman of Revelation 12 (Christ's church) is despised and rejected and persecuted by the people of the world under the motivation of the harlot and the beast (cf. 12:13; 13:7, 15–18), for she denounces the world and its lifestyles of unbelief and ungodliness as she witnesses to the only true God and Savior of the world (11:3–10). But in the End she will be claimed and acclaimed by God as the bride of his Son, Jesus Christ (19:6–8; cf. 11:11–12).

The harlot "sits upon many waters" (17:1). Jeremiah's prophecy against Babylon (Jer 51:1–64) makes reference to Babylon as the city which "resides upon many waters" (Jer 51:13, the phrase quoted in Rev 17:1). Ancient Babylon was situated on the Euphrates River and was known as the city of many waters because of the system of canals which carried and distributed the waters of the Euphrates throughout the city and to the surrounding area. According to 17:15 the "waters" symbolize "the peoples and crowds and nations and tongues" over which she holds sway. Now here in Revelation 17 and 18 Babylon upon the "many waters" (17:1) is to be judged by God.

The harlot has dominion over the nations. She is described as a harlot, "the mother of harlots" (17:5). The kings of the earth commit adultery with her, and the people under her influence become "drunk from the wine of her immorality" (17:2). The references to adultery and immorality refer to all manner of ungodly and licentious living, which is illustrative of the peoples' idolatrous adherence to the harlot, such as those who followed the idolatrous worship of Rome. But Rome, which was the harlot and Babylon of John's own age, is also the type of all future spiritual powers (especially apostate Christianity) and political powers which would war against the church and her witness to Christ.

The people become "drunk from the wine of her immorality" (17:2; cf. 18:3). In Jer 51:7–8 Babylon is pictured holding such a cup from which the whole earth drank and became intoxicated and as a result was in a stupor of mindlessness. "The kings of the earth" (Rev 17:2) are under her influence. It is often true that as the rulers go, so go the people under their governance.

JOHN IS TAKEN TO THE DESERT AND SHOWN THE HARLOT (17:3A)

While John is invited by an angel to come and see "the judgment of the great harlot" (17:1), it is by "the Spirit" that he is "carried ... into a desert" (17:3). This is the third time that John is caught up "in the Spirit." In 1:10 John "on the Lord's day" was "in the Spirit" when the exalted Son of Man appeared in order to commission him to receive and then to send the prophetic message of Revelation to the churches (1:9–11). In 4:2 John was carried "in the Spirit" into heaven to view the throne and presence of God. Here in 17:3 it is by the Spirit that John in a vision is carried away "into a desert" in order to view and prophetically witness "a woman sitting on a scarlet beast."

One further time John will be carried by the Spirit: when he is shown the heavenly city Jerusalem (21:10). Here in 17:3 (as in 4:2 and 21:10) "in the Spirit" suggests that John was empowered by the Spirit of God in some kind of mystical experience so that he not only saw the woman in a desert but was actually "carried" to the place to experience the scene he was shown. This was a mystical revelatory experience in the Spirit by which he was lifted up, whether in the body or out of the body (cf. 2 Cor 12:1–4), and brought into the desert to view the woman. Possibly John's experience was like that of Ezekiel, who was in Babylon when, he says, "the Spirit lifted me up between the earth and heaven and brought me to Jerusalem in visions of God" (Ezek 8:3; see also Ezek 11:24).

While the harlot in 17:1 is pictured as sitting "upon many waters," symbolizing the nations of the earth (17:15), here in 17:3 she is sitting on a beast in "a desert." In 12:6, 14 the woman, after the birth of her Child, "fled into the wilderness/desert." There the desert is patterned after the wilderness experience of the Israelites in the exodus and symbolizes the current wilderness-like experience of the woman, that is, the church. For the church (and for individual Christians), life in this world is a pilgrimage through a desert in which only God can care for and sustain her (12:6, 13–14). While the dragon pursues the woman in the desert (12:13–18), here in 17:3 the harlot on the beast is stationed in the desert. Does this harlot also station herself in the desert *so that she can pretend that she is the true church and thus by her immoral deceptiveness wean people away from the church of Christ?*

The imagery of the "desert" could also imply that this will be the end of the harlot, that is, she will end her life in the desolation and ruin of the desert. For the woman of Revelation 12 (the church of Christ) the desert only typifies her earthly life, but not her end. Her journey's end will be in the glory of God as the bride of Christ (19:6–8). But for the harlot, her end will be desolation in the desert, as Isaiah similarly prophesied about ancient Babylon when, in "an oracle about the desert," he spoke of her ruin (Is 21:1–10; cf. Is 13:21; Jer 50:12; 51:43). So now the harlot and the beast face the judgment of God in total desolation in which they will be destroyed and will never again be able to rise up and hurt God's people.

The beast upon which the woman is sitting is "scarlet" in color and has "seven heads and ten horns" (Rev 17:3). The seven heads and ten horns clearly identify this beast as the beast from the sea in 13:1, which had ten horns and seven heads and which the dragon conjured up as one of his henchmen in his warfare against the woman (12:17–18; 13:1, 7). The dragon himself (Satan, 12:9) originally had the "seven heads and ten horns" (12:3). But he delegated his wisdom and power to the beast that he brought up from the sea, the place of chaos and evil, and so now the beast bears the seven heads, symbolic of wisdom, and the ten horns, symbolic of power (13:1; 17:3). By the "*seven* heads" the dragon claimed *all spiritual* wisdom, and by the "*ten* horns" he arrogated to himself *supreme dominion* and power over *human* affairs. Now Satan's deceptive claims are the boast of the beast.

THE HARLOT SITS ON A SCARLET BEAST (17:3B)

The beast's color is mentioned for the first time in 17:3: "scarlet." Most likely the beast has this color because it is one of the colors of the harlot (17:4), and she has conferred it on the beast to indicate that she dominates it and that it acts on her behalf and for the purpose of magnifying her splendor. As mentioned in the commentary on 17:1, this is the political beast.

The fact that here the woman *rides* the beast suggests that, at the moment, *the beast serves the purposes of the harlot.* At other times, the relationship is reversed, and the harlot serves the beast. This happens when the harlot is in the guise of the beast with the number 666 (13:11–18) or the false prophet (16:13; 19:20; 20:10), and she serves the beast with the seven heads and ten horns (13:13–14; 19:20; cf. 17:3, 7). At still other times these two minions of the dragon (who together with him make up the unholy trinity) seem to work as equals in tandem (16:13–14). And finally, at times they squabble and fight among themselves, as if the dragon is not always able to keep them in line. This becomes evident when, near the End (and possibly at other times as well), the beast turns upon the harlot to destroy her (17:16), most likely as a part of God's judgment on her.

THE BEAST IS "FULL OF THE NAMES OF BLASPHEMY" (17:3C)

The beast is also described as "full of the names of blasphemy" (17:3; cf. 13:1). The blasphemous character of Rome had its epitome in the deification of the emperors, for they arrogated to themselves titles such as "Lord," "Savior," "divine," and "Lord of the world," in addition to encouraging emperor worship. Throughout the entire period covered by the prophetic message of Revelation, from Christ's ascension to the End at his return, this political beast (represented by Rome in John's era) will carry on and sponsor such a program of idolatry so as to deceive the peoples of the earth in the dragon's warfare against the church of Christ.

THE HARLOT IS SUMPTUOUSLY DRESSED (17:4A)

The woman who sits astride the beast is dressed sumptuously; she is "clothed in purple and scarlet and ... gilded with gold and precious stone and pearls" (17:4; cf. 18:12, 16). In ancient Rome "purple and scarlet" demonstrated luxury and splendor. In the OT "purple" was used for royalty (e.g., Judg 8:26; Dan 5:7; cf. Mk 15:17), and "scarlet" could signify royal splendor (Nah 2:3) or luxury (2 Sam 1:24; Jer 4:30). The harlot's pearls, costly jewels, and gold would exhibit the extravagant and profligate lifestyle by which the woman demonstrated the wealth of dominion over kings and nations—a lifestyle into which she drew them.

THE HARLOT HOLDS A CUP OF ABOMINABLE THINGS (17:4B)

In her hand the "golden cup full of abominable things, indeed, the unclean things of her immorality" (Rev 17:4) symbolizes all the immoral, evil, and corruptive attitudes, practices, and influences that she proffers to the peoples and their rulers (cf. Jer 51:17). She is quite successful in enticing the rulers and their peoples to drink of her cup, by which they themselves become inebriated in wealth, and in luxurious and sensual and immoral lives (cf. Rev 18:3, 9, 11, 15). All who are under her spiritual influence, a false substitute for Christianity, justify such immorality as godly and righteous.

THE MYSTERY OF THE HARLOT'S NAME (17:5)

Climactically, the woman is identified as "Babylon the great" and described as "the mother of harlots and of the abominable things of the earth." The name of Babylon identifies the harlot as the enemy of God's people, just as ancient Babylon was the historical enemy of Israel of old. As ancient Babylon destroyed the temple and the holy city of Jerusalem and carried off its people into exile, so now the woman on the beast makes war against the saints of God in Christ in order to destroy them and carry them into the bondage of her immoralities.

The name "Babylon the great" is called a "mystery" (17:5). Literally the word means "secret" and can refer to a "secret rite," "secret teaching or knowledge," or a "mystery" in the sense of something that can be known only by a special revelation or initiatory wisdom. Here the word is used in the sense of a symbolic representation and implies that the identification of the harlot as "Babylon the great, the mother of harlots" is a "mystery" because no one can know or understand that that is who she is unless given special knowledge or revelation (until Christ's return and the End, when everything will be revealed publicly). Perhaps also her designation as Babylon is called a "mystery" because to the world at large her true identity as the *false* church and great *enemy* of God's saints on earth will not be fully disclosed until the End, when it will be revealed by her judgment by God (cf. 2 Thess 2:1–8). Until that time, most people believe her lie that she is the true church and the true bride of Christ, and not the harlot.

The Harlot Is in a Drunken Stupor (17:6)

John next relates how he saw the woman in a drunken stupor "from the blood of the saints and from the blood of the witnesses of Jesus" (17:6). Bloodbaths occur from time to time throughout the history of the human race. But here the woman is not in an occasional drunken bout; rather, this is a description of a condition in her lifestyle that is constantly occurring. *Her steady diet is the blood of God's people.* The "saints" and "witnesses of Jesus" most likely are not two different classes of God's people, but rather a twofold description of all those who follow Christ on earth, for all Christians are saints and also witnesses of Jesus Christ (cf. 1:1–2, 5–6, 9). The "blood" that the woman drinks is a metaphor for the sacrificial witness in which all the followers of Christ participate. This witness incurs opposition from and persecution by the world (cf. 1:9). In her opposition to and persecution of the saints the woman indulges in this drunken orgy. What is most painful and trying to the saints is that she who claims to be true godliness and the genuine church of God (though she is not) should drink the "blood of the witnesses of Jesus"—just as the unbelieving world does, but for her own reasons.

As the harlot sits on the beast, dressed in her finery and drunk from the blood of God's saints, John is moved to marvel greatly (17:6). Though John is shortly to be shown the judgment and ruin of the woman (17:16; 18:2, 9, 19), of which judgment he had already been told (17:1–3), he sees for the moment the woman in all of her beauty and adornment and influential power. This must have been momentarily incomprehensible to John; hence, he is awestruck by her presence and appearance.

THE ANGEL'S EXPLANATION (17:7–14)

The mystery of the woman bearing the name "Babylon the great" (17:5) is explained to John by "the angel" (17:7), one of the seven censer-angels (17:1) attending John in this vision of the description and judgment of the harlot (17:1–18:24). For John and his first readers the model after which the woman and the beast were patterned most likely was Rome, and during John's time they also represented Rome and her empire (see 17:9, 18). But the *religious* power (the harlot, an incarnation of the *religious* beast in 13:11–18) and the *political* power (the beast, which is the *political* beast in 13:1–10) represented by Rome and her empire are merely types of *all enemies* of God's saints and his witnesses, from John's day to the end of this world at Christ's return. This mystery is now to be explained to John.

THE BEAST (17:7–8)

The angel asks John, "Why were you amazed?" (17:7). The angel treats his amazement as a legitimate question. The angel begins explaining the mystery of the woman by first referring to the beast. The heavenly messenger identifies the beast, by way of "the seven heads and the ten horns" (17:7), as the beast from the sea already seen by John in 13:1–10. As John now looks at the beast, the angel further describes it as the beast that "was, and is not, and is about to come up out of the abyss, and it goes away into destruction" (13:8). The first time that John saw this beast, one of its heads was mortally wounded, but then the head was healed (13:3; cf. 13:12, 14).

The ability of the beast, either partially with one of its heads or in its whole being, to be resuscitated or even resurrected time and time again moved the inhabitants of the earth to marvel and be awestruck. *The beast and what it represents come and go in one form or another throughout the entire period from Christ's ascension up to the End at Christ's return.* The beast disappears in one particular makeup or disguise—possibly because it has outlived its usefulness to the dragon and/or perhaps because God has brought it down—and then rises up in another form and entity to plague the church of Christ. Human institutions of every kind, and "-isms" of all sorts, come and go. As symbolized by the beast they last for a while as terrifying threats to the saints of God, but then they disappear, only to be replaced by other entities under the control of the dragon.

The source of everything that is represented by the beast is the abyss. The beast is ultimately from the abyss because Satan, who summoned the beast, himself is from the abyss. In Rev 11:7 Satan is pictured as "the beast" that comes up from the abyss (cf. also 13:7). The abyss is the abode and place of origin of all demons (9:1–6) and of their leader, "the angel of the abyss" (9:11).

After the end of the present world, when Christ returns, the dragon and his two partners, the beast and the false prophet, will be thrown into "the lake of fire" from which they will never again arise to torment the followers of Christ (Rev 19:20; 20:10). Thus the abyss is both the place of origin and the final prison of the beast. While now it wars against God's people, its destiny under God's judgment is its own eternal destruction in hell. Although it seeks to destroy the saints, and it enjoys a measure of success in this world, ultimately it will be destroyed and its demonic, hellish intent to destroy the church will fail. Nevertheless, during its warfare in this world, the people of the earth whose names are not "written in the book of life" stand in awe before the beast (17:8) because it, and what it symbolizes, has the ability to resuscitate itself time and again. But this awe and amazement of people will be short-lived, and unless repented of, it will be to their eternal ruin (see 13:8; 14:9–10; cf. 18:4).

THE BEAST'S SEVEN HEADS (17:9A)

He who has "the mind which has wisdom" can know the mystery of the "seven heads" of the beast, for they are "seven hills, upon which the woman is sitting" (17:9). Already in 13:18 John heard that the one who has "wisdom" and the "intelligence" to use it can "figure out" the number of the beast from the earth, the number 666. Here the same wisdom is necessary to figure out what the seven heads of the beast, that is, the seven hills where the woman is sitting, symbolically represent. John and all readers of Revelation during the first and second centuries certainly would know that the "seven hills" pointed to the city of Rome, for Rome was known as the city of seven hills, as many of her authors and poets proudly declare.

It would seem that no special wisdom was needed to understand that the "seven hills" indicate Rome. But it might take special wisdom to make the connection between ancient Babylon and Rome, and in particular to understand that the seven heads and hills also point to seven kings, and to understand which kings. More likely what 17:9 means is that *it takes special wisdom to understand what all this means for the saints of God (past and present) in their earthly pilgrimage.* This indeed requires wisdom that only God can grant (James 1:5–6; Prov 2:1–6; cf. Job 12:13).

THE SEVEN KINGS PLUS ONE (17:9B–11)

The "seven kings" (17:9) are described as if some had come and gone, and others are still to come. In 17:10 the angel says, "Five have fallen, one is [present], the other has not yet come, and when he comes it is necessary that he remain a little while." Throughout the centuries since the writing of Revelation, commentators have attempted to identify these seven kings. For the most part Roman emperors have been matched with the seven kings, but not always the same emperors.

Difficulties abound in attempting to identify the "seven kings." These difficulties only increase when in 17:11 the beast itself is described as an "eighth" king who also "was, and is not ... and goes away into destruction." Similar to the seven kings, the beast as an eighth king comes and goes and comes again and then finally goes to destruction. Already in 13:3 one of the beast's heads (that is, one of the seven kings) was mortally wounded. But the head was resuscitated, thus giving to some Christians credence to the legend of Nero's return, and as a result Nero came to be identified as the eighth king, or the type of whomever that future king might be. If one were to match a name with this eighth king, Nero would be a likely candidate, for according to the legend he was to return and regain his power to reign as emperor. He thus would be the "head" of the beast which "had been fatally wounded unto death, but its wound of death had been healed," as described in 13:3. To many pagan authors, and to some Christian ones, Domitian resembled Nero so much that Nero was almost personified in Domitian. Attempting to match a list of seven kings with the seven kings in 17:9–10 does not yield a satisfactory result. One must seek elsewhere for a solution to the mystery of the seven kings and the beast itself as the eighth. The most that be can said for attempts to identify the seven kings by name is that, even if one could satisfactorily make such matching identifications, they would only serve as models or types of all such earthly rulers and the powers they exercise. All oppressive earthly rulers that come and go throughout the entire period of time covered by the prophetic message of Revelation (Christ's ascension to his return) are symbolized by these seven kings as well as by the beast itself. *The number seven is symbolic and represents all earthly powers and rulers who claim spiritual authority by which they justify and sanction their despotic dominion over their subjects, in particular as it is used in opposition to the church of Christ.* In the case of Rome as the model and type of such rulers, the seven kings represent its imperial power under and together with the pretense of the spiritual and divine-like authority she claimed, as it was displayed, for example, by emperor worship. The emperors come and go, but each in turn continues to carry out the imperial and despotic rule of Rome. The fact that the beast itself is designated as the eighth king is perhaps best understood as a summary statement. That is to say, as the emperors come and go, and even at times when one is weak and ineffective because of madness (such as Caligula), imperial Rome continues, for she herself is the power no matter who the emperor is. Thus imperial Rome herself could be designated the eighth king serving as a symbol of the "eternal" power of Rome which all emperors exercised. That the beast itself, under the designation of the eighth king, could be pictured as coming and going suggests that imperial Rome itself comes and goes, weakened and then strengthened again, until she together with all her emperors finally goes into eternal ruin and destruction.

For John, the beast represented Rome, but it must be remembered that for him the beast as Rome also served as a symbol and a type or model of all future ruling powers which, like Rome, would persecute the church. *The beast then, together with its seven heads, becomes and is for all time until the End a terrifying symbol that represents all earthly powers and dominions and rulers that exercise tyrannical authority under the pretense of divine sanction of some kind or other.* The outward form of this despotic governance will come and go, one form disappearing and being replaced then by another. It can even be severely wounded and weakened so much that at times it seems to have disappeared (to the relief of Christians). Then it arises again in similar or different guises to terrorize once again its subjects. So it goes until in God's judgment it is destroyed, at the End when Christ returns.

THE TEN HORNS WILL WAGE WAR
AGAINST THE LAMB (17:12–14)

The picture of the political beast is not yet complete, for there are "the ten horns" which represent "ten kings who did not yet receive a kingdom" (17:12). While the seven kings symbolize ruling powers acting with wisdom as sanctioned under the pretense of divine authority, metaphorically depicted by the number *seven* (*divine* authority) and by the *heads (wisdom),* the ten horns would indicate ruling powers in all their naked might and total oppression, sanctioned not by the claim to divine authority but by the action of conquering power itself under its own authority. Because they do not claim spiritual and divine sanction for their ruling power and authority, these "ten kings" most likely are not Roman emperors. They could be lesser kings or rulers dependent on Roman sponsorship for their governing positions—for example, the Herodian kings of Palestine or the rulers of Egypt.

The ten kings "receive authority with the beast" for a short time (17:12). The beast, the Roman Empire, while recognizing the kings' right to rule within the claims of the empire, allows them to do so only as clients. These ten kings "did not yet receive a kingdom" (17:12), for they do not possess their own authority and power to rule. However, the implication is that at any time in the future these ten kings may become independent of Rome and thus acquire their own kingship. Similar to the ten horns of the fourth beast in Daniel (7:7, 24), which is a prophetic prototype of the beast here in Revelation 17, they seem to be kings who are connected with the Roman Empire and then come out of it or come after it.

There could be many possible ways in which one might imagine the ten kings of the beast's horns in relation to the seven kings of its heads on a historical plane at the time of the writing of Revelation. *Clearly they symbolically represent all earthly ruling powers, during the entire time period from Christ's ascension to his return at the present world's end, which do not claim any particular divine sanction or authority (as do the seven kings).* The ten rule instead under the authority that is gained or sanctioned by naked power. Only their *power* to rule legitimates their right and authority to rule. On occasion they may make cause with the seven kings who legitimatize their right to rule under the pretense of divine sanction. But the ten kings maintain their rule by their tyrannical and fear-evoking power and it alone. *The beast then, with its seven heads and ten horns, symbolizes all earthly powers of whatever sort and makeup which are under the influence of the dragon (Satan) in his warfare with the followers of Christ* (see 12:13–18; 13:1, 11). This is the beast upon which the harlot sits (17:3), and as she does so she is called "Babylon the great" (17:5).

These ten kings (as the seven, in their own way) "act with one mind," and "they give their power and authority to the beast" (17:13). They agree in supporting the goal of the beast, which is to dominate and to destroy the church, the bride of Christ. In actuality, though, they "wage war with the Lamb" (17:14), for the conflict has always been between the dragon (Satan) and God. This war reached its climax at the cross on Calvary, for it was there that Jesus Christ, on behalf of God's people, won the victory as the Lamb of God (Jn 1:29; 1 Pet 1:18–21; Rev 5:5–10). When he was lifted up on the cross, "the prince of this cosmos" was cast out (Jn 12:31–32). Cast out of heaven at the glorious ascension of the victorious Lamb, the devil is never able again to accuse God's saints before God's heavenly throne (Rev 12:5–12; cf. Phil 2:5–11). The casting of the dragon out of heaven is described in terms of warfare: "Michael and his angels had to make war with the dragon. And the dragon went to war and also his angels" (Rev 12:7). As a result, "the great dragon … the ancient serpent, who is called the devil and Satan," was thrown out of God's heavenly presence, never again to appear before him (12:9). The war between God and the dragon was over. But when the dragon realized that he could not continue his warfare against God in heaven and that he had failed to destroy the Christ Child (the male Child of the woman, 12:3–5), and also knowing that he could no longer stand before God and mock God's saints (cf. Job 1:6–12; 2:1–7; Zech 3:1–4), he then took out his anger on the woman on earth and her seed. He set about to make war with the church of Christ on earth (Rev 12:13–18).

Since the ascension of Christ, the warfare between the dragon and God is now confined to that which takes place between Satan and God's saints *on earth*. In this warfare with the woman and her seed, the dragon enlists two allies: the two beasts described in Revelation 13. Much of what John sees in Revelation concerns this warfare on earth. Though the warfare is between this unholy trinity—the dragon and the two beasts—and the church, its ultimate purpose is to shame and belittle God and his Christ. The dragon can no longer defy God before his face, so now he attempts to do so, even though banished from God's heavenly presence, by shaming and destroying God's saints on earth and their witness to the Christ. But though the target of the battle is the church, actually the war is against the Lamb, for he is the champion and the defender of God's people on earth. In fighting against the church, the evil forces of the dragon (to their own astonishment) discover that they are really fighting against the Lord Christ himself. In this contest the Lamb faces them not like a lamb that was led to slaughter in humility and weakness (Is 53:7; Acts 8:32–33) but as the mighty God who is "the Lord of lords and the King of kings" (Rev 17:14). His "called and chosen and faithful ones" (17:14), his followers, face the enemy always with the conquering Lamb before them, for it is through his victory of the cross and resurrection that the church is defended. By the right of that victory the Lamb always stands between his witnesses and the evil forces of the dragon in order to keep his saints safe and finally to deliver them (cf. 14:1–5; 15:2–4).

The Lamb here in 17:14 is identified as "the Lord of lords and the King of kings," which is the designation the Son of Man will use when he comes in judgment at the End (19:11–16). Because of this identification, the victory of the Lamb over the beast and its kings (17:14) could be viewed as taking place at the End (cf. 16:12–16; 20:7–10). Certainly the final conflict in which the evil forces will forever be destroyed lies in the future, when Christ returns and the final judgment takes place. But also now and throughout the time of the church's mission on earth, the Lamb will prevail over the beast so as to enable his church to carry out and complete her mission. Throughout the history of the church, the enemies who on the human plane conquered the saints (13:7) at a given time were in turn overthrown and now lie in the dust heaps of history. It is a constant warfare in which enemies are always arising and falling, only to be replaced by others. *But throughout it all the Lamb defends his church and conquers her enemies.* Finally, at the Lord's return, the beast will be totally defeated, never again to rise in any form to threaten God's people.

THE ULTIMATE DEMISE
OF THE HARLOT (17:15–18)

After having seen the harlot on the beast in all of her amazing beauty, and after having received an explanation of the mystery about the woman (who she is and what she represents, together with her beast), the angel then tells John how the woman will be ruined and destroyed under God's judgment. The angel first tells John that the waters upon which the woman is sitting are "peoples and crowds and nations and tongues" (17:15). She dominates, or at least desires to dominate, the entire human population. This way of designating the human race by means of such a grouping is used elsewhere in Revelation for the people of God, who have been brought out of the human race to be his saints (5:9; 7:9). It is also used to describe the pagan population of the world (10:11; 11:9; 13:7;

14:6). Here in 17:15 it describes the peoples of all nationalities in the Roman Empire at the time of John's writing. As imperial Rome dominated all the peoples in the various classes and races, so the harlot now sits in dominion over the nations and peoples of the earth. Included in this grouping (it seems) are God's own people, for when Babylon's judgment comes, God calls his people out of her midst (18:4).

When the angel first announced in 17:1 that he would show to John the judgment of the harlot, she was pictured as sitting on these "many waters." That these waters are mentioned again in 17:15 seems to emphasize that she who was dominating the peoples of the earth is now to be judged. In 17:2–14 John does not yet see her judgment but instead is given an awesome and fearful description of her immoral reign and that of the beast with her. But now in 17:15 the angel brings John back to what he had said in 17:1 about her judgment—only this time it will be described. The description begins by referring again to the position of her dominance over the peoples of the earth, for the one who deceived the nations of the earth is now to be brought to her ruin and destruction.

Rev 17:15–18 serves as a brief and partial description of her judgment. This serves to introduce a lengthy and detailed account (in chapter 18) of her overthrow and the eternal ruin for which she is destined in hell. These final verses of chapter 17 tell how the beast with the ten horns turns on the woman, under God's sovereign motivating power, to begin her downfall. *The political and ruling powers of the earth which had been cohorts with the harlot in her immoral and demonic-like spiritual reign over the earth now become agents of God which initiate her final ruin.* God has in store for the harlot, "Babylon the great, the mother of harlots" (17:5), a carefully laid out plan to tear her apart as he brings her to total destruction in his anger and judgment. These verses (17:15–18) reveal the beginning of this plan.

It is a telltale sign of her coming final judgment when the beast and the ten horns begin to "hate the harlot" and turn on her (17:16). It is interesting that the beast turns to hate the woman with its *ten horns* and not its seven heads. Historically, Rome was finally brought down not so much by her own emperors but rather by kings and ruling powers of her client states and from neighboring states with whom she flirted but whom she could never completely bring under her sway. The disintegration of the harlot's false spiritual and Christlike power begins not so much because of the political and ruling powers which legitimatized their authority under the pretense of divine sanction (the seven heads, or seven kings, 17:9), but rather because of those ruling powers which seize and sanction their authority to rule by brute and naked force (the ten horns, or ten kings, 17:12).

When they turn against the woman in hatred, "they will make her desolated and naked, and they will eat her flesh, and in fire they will burn her up" (17:16). This certainly is a grisly description of how they will treat the harlot. It is reminiscent of the judgment of God that Ezekiel prophetically pronounced against the two adulterous sisters representing Israel and Judah (Ezek 23:1–34). In God's judgment their former lovers would turn on them and, as described in graphic terms, would rip them apart. They would strip them naked (Ezek 23:10, 29) in their hatred (Ezek 23:29). They would cut off their noses and ears and burn them in fire (Ezek 23:25). The two adulterous sisters would drink of the cup to its utter dregs and then in drunkenness tear at their own breasts (Ezek 23:32–34). In a similar description, the harlot here in Rev 17:16 is prophetically pictured as being ripped apart by her former lovers, her associates in her immoralities by which she polluted the peoples of the earth.

The beast and the ten horns act in this way toward the harlot because "God has given into their hearts" to carry out his will "until the words of God will be completed" (17:17). This is another instance of what has often happened in the past: that the powers of evil were used by God to serve his own purposes. For example, after ancient Babylon had served God's purpose in the captivity and exile of Judah, Babylon in turn under God's judgment was punished and brought to ruin by other pagan nations. So here in the judgment of the harlot, her former associates in evil turn against her and destroy her. In the end all such powers of wickedness will serve God's ultimate purpose: the salvation of his people and their deliverance from all enemies. This will happen according to "the words of God" (17:17) which were spoken by his prophets.

As the beast and its ten horns turn on the harlot, John is told again that she is "the great city which has dominion over the kings of the earth" (17:18). As ancient Babylon was at one time mistress of the world, and as imperial Rome was such at the time of John's receiving the message of Revelation, both are types or manifestations of the harlot sitting on the beast, the significance of whose meaning goes far beyond that of ancient Babylon and Rome, the city of the seven hills. There will always be such "mistresses" (whether cities or governing powers and nations) which will, even unknowingly, be under the control of the dragon (Satan) for the purpose of making war against the woman and her seed, the church (12:17). But all such mistresses will be brought to total destruction in God's judgment, a judgment that God will execute on behalf of his saints (19:1–2).

REVELATION 18:1–24

THE FALL OF BABYLON AND THE REJOICING OF THE SAINTS

TRANSLATION

18 ¹After these things I saw another angel coming down out of heaven who had great authority, and the earth was bathed in light by his glory. ²And he cried out in a mighty voice, saying, "She has fallen; Babylon the great has fallen and has become a dwelling place of demons and a prison of every unclean spirit and a prison of every unclean bird and a prison of every unclean and hated beast, ³because from the wine of the rage of her immorality all the nations have drunk, and the kings of the earth committed sexual immorality with her, and the merchants of the earth became wealthy by the power of her luxurious sensuality." ⁴And I heard another voice from heaven saying, "Come out from her, O my people, so that you do not participate in her sins and so that you do not receive from her plagues, ⁵for her sins have been piled up as high as heaven, and God has remembered her crimes. ⁶Give back to her as she gave out, and render twice the double things according to her works; in the cup which she mixed, mix double for her; ⁷as much as she glorified herself and lived in sensual luxury, give to her in like measure torture and grief, because in her heart she says, 'I sit as queen and I am not a widow and I will never see sorrow.' ⁸On account of this, in one day her plagues will come, death and mourning and famine, and in fire she will be utterly consumed because mighty Yahweh, the [only] God, is the one who judges her.

⁹And the kings of the earth who committed sexual immorality with her and lived luxuriously [with her] will weep and wail over her when they see the smoke of her fiery burning, ¹⁰as they stand at a distance because of the fear of her torment, saying,
" 'Woe, woe, the great city,
    Babylon the mighty city,
for in one moment your judgment has come.'
¹¹"And the merchants of the earth weep and shed tears over her because their merchandise no one any longer buys— ¹²merchandise of gold and silver and precious stone and pearls, and of cloth of fine linen and of purple and of silk and of scarlet, and every scented wood and every ivory vessel and every vessel of most precious wood and of brass and of iron and of marble, ¹³and cinnamon and spice, and incenses and perfumed ointment and frankincense, and wine and olive oil and refined wheat flour and grain, and cattle and sheep, and [merchandise] of horses and chariots and slaves, and the souls of men.
¹⁴"And the fruit of your passion for
    life has departed from you,
and all costly and splendid things have been
    destructively taken from you, and no
    longer will they ever find them.
¹⁵"The merchants of these things, who became wealthy by her, will stand at a distance because of the fear of her torment, weeping and shedding tears, ¹⁶saying,
" 'Woe, woe, the great city, she who was clothed in
    fine linen and purple and scarlet, and who was
    gilded in gold and precious stone and pearl,
¹⁷for in one moment such wealth was incinerated.'
"And every sea pilot and everyone who sails for a place and mariners and as many as work the sea, at a distance they stood, ¹⁸and they kept on crying out as they watched the smoke of her conflagration, saying, 'What is like this great city?' ¹⁹And they threw dust

on their heads, and they kept on crying out as they
were weeping and shedding tears while saying,
" 'Woe, woe, the great city,
by means of which all those who own ships on the
    sea were made wealthy by her abundant wealth,
because in one moment she has been
    brought to total ruin.'
[20]"Rejoice in celebration over her, O heaven
    and you saints and apostles and prophets,
because God has executed your judgment on her."
[21]And one particular mighty angel lifted
up a stone like a large millstone and
he threw it into the sea, saying,
"In the same way with violence shall Babylon,
    the great city, be thrown down and
    will surely never again be found.
[22]And the sound of harp players and of musicians
    and of flute players and of trumpeters
    will never again be heard in you,
and any craftsman of any skill will
    never again be found in you,
and the noise of a mill will never
    again be heard in you,
[23]and the illumination of a lamp never
    again will give light in you,
and the voice of a bridegroom and of a bride
    will never again be heard in you,
because your merchants were the power
    brokers of the earth, because in your
    sorcery all the nations were deceived,
[24]and [because] in her the blood of prophets and
    of saints was discovered and [the blood] of
    all those who were slain upon the earth."

COMMENTARY

THE FINAL JUDGMENT OF THE HARLOT (18:1–8)

After John had seen the awesome picture of the harlot and the beast (which together comprise Babylon, 17:1–14), and then the beginning of her downfall (when the beast turned on her as part of God's sovereign judgment, 17:15–18), he then sees her total destruction (described in chapter 18). The first words of chapter 18, "after these things," are a common formula throughout Revelation for connecting two sections. It is used not only to introduce the next section (or the next item within a section), but also to move the subject at hand to its final conclusion or goal. *In this case it serves as a pointer to John that tells him to expect a conclusion to what he had just seen, that is, the final judgment of the harlot.*

In this concluding scene of the harlot's final judgment, John first sees "another angel coming down out of heaven" (18:1). This is not the angel who has been attending John through this entire last portion of Revelation (the End, 17:1–22:5); that attending angel (17:1, 7, 15; 19:9–10; 21:9, 15; 22:1, 8–9) is one of the seven censer-angels (17:1; 21:9; the seven censer-angels were introduced in 15:7). Rather, this other angel acts out a role in the visionary scene itself, announcing the judgment of Babylon. He has "great authority," and his presence lights up the entire earth "by his glory" (18:1).

Only one other angel in Revelation has such a commanding presence: the "mighty angel" of Revelation 10, who dominated the earth and commanded John to proclaim the message to everyone (10:1–2, 11). That angel's face was "like the sun" (10:1) and he "cried out in a loud voice" (10:3). The angel here in Revelation 18 also "cried out in a mighty voice" (18:2), and while he is not depicted with a face like the sun, the brilliance of his glory does light up the earth (18:1). The angel of Revelation 10 was dressed in the majestic insignia of God the Father's glory (the cloud and the rainbow-like halo) and the glory of Christ (the sun, 10:1). He also came directly out of heaven, that is, from the presence of God (10:1). He thus stands in for God (particularly the Father and the Son) as his angel in reminding John of the mission that God has given to his church on earth (10:8–11). The angel here in Revelation 18 also comes directly from the presence of God, and, while not described as one dressed in the insignia of God's glory, he does bear and reflect that glory, for the glory of the angel which lights up the earth is not his own, but that of God. Because he came directly and so recently from the holy presence of God, the angel still bears his brilliant glory as Moses did when he came down from Mt. Sinai (Ex 34:29–35).

Because of these similarities the angel here in Revelation 18 may well be the same as that angel in Revelation 10. This identification is supported by the roles they play, for each has to do with *the mission of the church* as that mission is related to the very presence and glory of God. The seven angels of the seven churches stand in for the churches as the recipients of the message of Revelation (Revelation 2–3); they are also, for the sake of the church, the dispensers of God's acts of judgment on the earth against those who oppose the mission of the church (the seven trumpet-angels in 8:6–11:19 and the seven censer-angels in 15:1–16:21). But the two majestic angels of Revelation 10 and 18, on the other hand, stand in for God and his Christ. They do so as *heralds of God, announcing the mission of the church and the final judgment of the enemies of the church.* While they could be two different angels, the fact that they each appear alone, executing a single action on behalf of God as his majestic angel, seems to suggest that they are one and the same.

"The earth was bathed in light by his [the angel's] glory" (Rev 18:1). In Ezek 43:1–5 it is the glory of God that will light up the earth as his glory returns to the temple in Jerusalem. Similarly here in Revelation 18, as the Lord God prepares the way for the coming of the Son of Man at the End to claim his kingdom, God illuminates the earth with his glory as he announces through the angel the judgment of the harlot.

The angel "cried out in a mighty voice" (18:2). This is not just a "loud" voice, but a "mighty" voice. Other angels call out in a "loud" voice (e.g., 5:2; 7:2; 10:3; 14:6–7), but this angel calls out in a "mighty" voice like that of God. The word "mighty" in biblical literature—with the exception of Revelation—is never used of angels but only of God. (On the earthly plane it is used of people.) The angel in 18:2 heralds the fall of Babylon. Similar was the prophetic announcement of the fall of ancient Babylon by the prophet Isaiah (21:6–9). In that prophetic announcement the same words appear as here in Rev 18:2: "She has fallen; Babylon has fallen" (Is 21:9). Isaiah's prophecy of Babylon's fall (cf. Is 47:1–15; Jer 50:1–51:64) did not come to pass until long after the prophet's death. So now John hears the announcement that Babylon, which is composed of the harlot and the beast, will fall, never to rise again as a threat and terror to God's people. In John's era, Rome represented "Babylon," and the Roman Empire finally crumbled away under pressure from various barbarian hordes in the fifth century AD Therefore, John would not live to see his prophecy fulfilled even in the form of Rome's fall, but it would surely come to pass. As the angel's announcement comforted John and his initial hearers with regard to Rome, so also does it comfort Christians throughout the era from Christ's ascension up to his return at the end of the present world. Though a "Babylon" will always exist to afflict Christians in this life, they know the certainty of her overthrow.

Babylon's judgment is so destructive that instead of being a house of wealth and pleasure (Rev 17:4; 18:11–18), she becomes a house of destitution full "of demons and … of every unclean spirit and … of every unclean bird … and hated beast" (18:2). A dwelling place that has become devoid of human life because of famine and other disasters is finally occupied only by scavengers as they feed on the corpses (cf. 19:17–21). So total and final will be the destruction of Babylon that only scavengers such as the "unclean bird" and the "unclean and hated beast" are left. Demons and unclean spirits could here be more than merely the memories that haunt the empty shell of Babylon. They could be the actual demons of hell itself which—under the guidance of the dragon, the chief of demons—have been all along the companions of the harlot as they inspired her to carry out her anti-Christian activities. Now at her demise, having used her for their own devilish purposes, all that is left of the once proud city are the demons hovering over her corpse.

The reason for Babylon's overthrow and judgment is because "from the wine of the rage of her immorality all the nations have drunk, and the kings of the earth committed sexual immorality with her, and the merchants of the earth became wealthy by the power of her luxurious sensuality" (18:3). This describes how all the pagan nations and political and economic rulers and powers shared in her deceptive piety. Sanctioned by her perverted form of Christianity, they received from her license to indulge in and live by filthy lucre and sensual power and immorality (cf. 1 Tim 3:3, 8; Titus 1:7, 11; 1 Pet 5:2).

Two groups of people in particular are affected by the spiritual and imperial dominance of Babylon: the political rulers and the mercantile class. They are emphasized because nations flourish or diminish by them and through their influence. As these two classes were empowered and made wealthy under the license of the harlot and the beast, so their nations also lived by the sufferance of the harlot as dispensed by their rulers and merchants.

As John views the judgment and overthrow of Babylon, he hears "another voice from heaven" calling God's people to come out from Babylon so that they would not "participate in her sins" and suffer "from her plagues" (18:4). This voice is not that of the angel of 18:1–2. As happens often in Revelation, the source of the "voice" is not identified. However, the fact that the possessive pronoun "my" is used to identify "the people" that are being called suggests that the speaker is God, for nowhere else in Revelation does an angel use the possessive pronoun in the first person. Moreover, an angel, when speaking for God or representing him, *never* uses first person language. However, as the voice continues to cry out in 18:5, it certainly seems not to be the voice of God the Father, for God is spoken of as distinct from the voice. Could the voice then be that of God the Son, Jesus Christ (cf. 2:13; 11:3)? The voice urges God's people to "come out from" the midst of Babylon lest they perish with her in her sins (18:4). Similarly, both Isaiah and Jeremiah called upon God's people to come out from ancient Babylon so that they would escape her destruction (Is 48:20; Jer 50:8; 51:6, 45). Jesus, just before his own death on the cross, warned his followers that when they saw "the abomination of desolation standing where it ought not be," they should flee and not look back or go back to rescue anything (Mk 13:14–16; cf. Mt 24:15–18; Lk 21:20–21). Similarly, Paul warns Christians not to be in fellowship with unbelievers in their pagan idolatry and manner of living, and then he cites Is 52:11 in urging his readers "to come out from their midst" (2 Cor 6:14–17; cf. Eph 5:6–11). At all times God's people are to come out of any association or fellowship which denies the truth of Jesus Christ. The pending judgments of God are near. In view of the present world's end, when the harlot will be made desolate, God's people are to flee without delay from the terrifying destruction that is to be her end.

The judgment of the harlot must come "for her sins have been piled up as high as heaven, and God has remembered her crimes" (18:5). So great were the sins of Sodom and Gomorrah that they reached God in heaven (Gen 18:21–22). Jeremiah cried out that ancient Babylon could not be rescued from destruction because her judgment had reached as high as the sky, as high as the clouds (Jer 51:9). In like manner the sins of the harlot—the apostate church, Babylon, the mother of harlots—were so great and horrifying that God would no longer put up with her. She had to be destroyed and would forever suffer God's judgment in the pit of hell (see Rev 19:20).

It is a terrible thing to fall into the hands of God's vengeance and wrath (see Heb 10:29–31). So John is told that Babylon will be paid back double according to her works, for she will drink of the cup of her evil deeds twice over (Rev 18:6). The cup of poisonous dregs which she mixed for others will be the potion that she herself will now drink. The word is given, "Give back to her as she gave out," and "render twice the double things" (18:6).

To whom is the word addressed? Whoever it is will be of God's own choosing. As stated in Rev 17:15–18, among these dispensers of God's justice will be the beast and all that it represents of human structures—in particular, political powers of human governments and societies—as it turns in hatred on the harlot to destroy her. Also involved among these retributive agencies could be the forces of natural elements such as earthquakes and other upheavals and disorders (see 8:6–13; 16:1–11; cf. 18:8). The divine punishments administered by the trumpet-angels and censer-angels, which are aimed especially at unbelievers and the forces of evil (9:4; 16:10), suggest that angels could participate too. However and by whomever she is paid back, Babylon will drink from the "cup which she mixed" (Rev 18:6), for it is now the cup of God's wrath from which she will drink as she is paid back in God's judgment (cf. Ezek 23:32–34).

The harlot's punishment and misery will be in proportion to her self-aggrandizement, for "as much as she glorified herself and lived in sensual luxury," she in turn is to receive "torture and grief" (Rev 18:7). She boasted that she was a "queen" (18:7), whom all peoples would love and applaud as they participated in her deadly games of wealth and power and immorality. But all the while she was a wicked witch who spun her devilish wiles over the human race, wiles that were presented in sensual and luxurious beauty to make her spiritual dominion attractive and acceptable. Thus all false spirituality—and in particular *apostate*

Christianity—presents itself and acts accordingly. As a harlot in her youthful beauty promotes an arrogance that knows no bounds and still does so even later when her beauty fades, so the *apostate church* which parades herself in the beauty of Christ boasts that she will never be "a widow," will never be deserted, and "will never see sorrow" (18:7; cf. Is 47:7–8; Ezek 23:11–21). Imperial Rome boasted that she would be ageless and eternal. Though she thus boasted that she would never be a widow and that no one would ever ravage her, yet she would be destroyed by God and brought down to hell.

But suddenly, "in one day her plagues will come," plagues such as "death and mourning and famine" (Rev 18:8). In the case of historic Babylon, Isaiah prophesied that "in one moment, in a single day" she would become a widow (Is 47:9), for disaster would suddenly come upon her (Is 47:11). So too in Revelation, Babylon, the harlot and mother of harlots, in one day will be plagued, and "in fire she will be utterly consumed" (Rev 18:8). As Jeremiah (51:1–64) prophesied that the destruction of ancient Babylon would be accompanied by fire (Jer 51:25, 30, 32, 58), so too apostate Christianity and the false church will be destroyed by fire (cf. Ezek 23:25–31). This reference to fire is affirmed in Rev 19:11–16: when the Son of Man returns at the End, "the beast" and "the false prophet" will be thrown into "the lake of fire" (19:20).

The time interval of "one day" (18:8) emphasizes the suddenness and completeness of the harlot's destruction. The "one day" also could refer to the day of Yahweh, also called "that day" (e.g., Is 27:1–2) and by other designations. This is the day in which Yahweh will hold judgment. This interpretation is somewhat supported by the fact that "mighty Yahweh, the [only] God" (Rev 18:8) will be her judge. While under God's sovereign will others may initiate and participate in her judgment, at the very End it will be the Lord God who will execute the judgment. However the "one day" in 18:8 is understood, God himself will be the harlot's judge and executioner (cf. Jer 50:34).

THE LAMENT OVER FALLEN BABYLON (18:9–19)

Rev 18:9–19 describes the lament and mourning—the dirge—over the judgment and destruction of Babylon. Particular attention is given to the mourning of the political rulers (18:9–10), that of the merchants (18:11–17a), and that of the seafarers and mariners (18:17b–19). This dirge is similar to that which is voiced in Ezek 27:1–36, the lament over Tyre that is made by kings (27:35; cf. 26:15–18), mariners (27:29), and merchants (27:36). These three groups each wail and mourn over Babylon not only because of her end but also because their own luxurious and sensual livelihood would disappear when she lay in ruins. They had depended on the harlot for their power and wealth and commerce and trade, but in the ashes of Babylon lies also the devastation of their own lives and positions. Her end will be their end.

Standing at a distance on account of the fear of the harlot's torment, the kings of the earth weep and wail over her when they see the smoke of her fiery burning (Rev 18:9–10). Those political powers that "committed sexual immorality with her and lived luxuriously" with her (18:9) witness her terrifying and awesome destruction, and that evokes fear in their own hearts. These kings are most likely not those (symbolized by the horns and the beast in 17:8–17) who turned on the city to destroy her, but rather are those who lived and ruled under her license and prospered and felt secure under her spiritual patronage. Now, as they stand on the sidelines far enough away so as not to be sucked into her torment and fiery ordeal, they perceive that their security and well-being and future may also go up in the smoke of the harlot's torture. *If "in one moment" (18:10) the judgment of the harlot has come, in what "moment" will their own downfall come?*

The *kings* mournfully cry a dirge which is that of a husband over a paramour or mistress. It is a cry of sorrow over the loss of a lover; but it is also a cry of fear, for the husband now realizes that his mistress was struck down because of her sins and their illicit affair, so that the judgment that hit the kings' lover would sooner or later come to them (cf. Rev 8:13; Mt 11:21–24). The cry "woe, woe" (18:10) echoes Ezek 16:23, where the prophet refers to Jerusalem as a paramour who offered her beauty in shameful promiscuity to her illicit lovers, which adulterous acts were her idolatry (Ezek 16:24–26). So also the harlot Babylon in Revelation 18 now hears a lament of woes. To apostate Jerusalem, God promised that he would establish an eternal covenant. God himself would make the atonement for her sins, and those who repented would receive forgiveness (Ezek 16:59–63). That atonement was made by Christ on the cross at his first advent. But Babylon here is being judged at the end of the present world, when Christ returns, and the time for repentance has expired. Therefore there is no such possibility for forgiveness for Babylon, the mother of harlots.

The *merchants* join in this woeful dirge (Rev 18:11–17a). Their lament seems to be even more full of hopeless sorrow, for they weep and shed tears over the harlot, because no one any longer buys their merchandise (18:11). She through whom and by whose license they had become wealthy is now gone. Their own wealth disappears because their merchandise and goods are now worthless (cf. James 5:1–3; cf. Lk 6:25). Thus the lament of the merchants is like that of the political rulers, a lament that voices sorrow over the demise of the harlot, but in addition the merchants lament their own hopeless economic state of affairs.

Rev 18:12–13 lists the merchandise that no one any longer buys. Similarly, the dirge over Tyre in Ezekiel 27 contains an inventory of merchandise that could not save the city from ruin (Ezek 27:3–24, 36). The goods listed in Rev 18:12–13 are of several categories: monetary items, produce, and living creatures. The list of the goods, while not the same for all merchants at all times in human history, nevertheless is typical of all trade goods of whatever sort which sustain mercantile wealth throughout the world.

Noteworthy in the list are the last two items in 18:13, "slaves, and the souls of men." The first item is "bodies," a word that occasionally denoted "slaves," especially when used as an item of trade and merchandise. Slavery was widely prevalent in the Roman Empire. It was not based on race, for slaves often came from the same ethnic groups (including Greeks and Romans) as their owners. Besides military conquest, another major source of slaves was piracy. In the Greco-Roman world, slavery itself was accepted, but even so trading in slaves generally was regarded with contempt and disgust because of the deceit, fraud, and appallingly inhumane practices that were routine in that industry. Paul lists slave traders (1 Tim 1:10) in a list of heinous sinners who oppose God's Law and are contrary to the sound doctrine of the Gospel (1 Tim 1:8–11). Rev 18:13 portrays slavery as an institution that is part of this corrupt world order sponsored by "Babylon" (18:10), which consists of the beast and the great harlot. The harlot is the antichurch, the opposite of all that the church should be and is by God's grace. Slavery, and the other activities and institutions fostered by Babylon's prostitution, will pass away forever when this sinful world ends.

The last item in 18:13, "the souls of men" (cf. Ezek 27:13), is not so easily understood. Here "slaves" are already denoted by the word "bodies." There might not be any purpose for adding another word or designation that has a similar meaning. However, if "souls of men" is taken in apposition to "bodies," then both together would mean, "slaves, that is, souls of men." This understanding of the two phrases would emphasize the evil of the slave trade in that it expresses the thought that slaves, body and soul, belonged to the master as property. Human slaves were thus considered no different than any other merchandise commodity of value.

The "souls of men" (18:13), that is, of people, however, could bear another meaning. In 1 Chr 5:21, "souls of people" refers not to slaves but to *captives* taken in warfare. Such captives were commonly sold as slaves, as were those kidnapped by pirates, with the Roman government closing its eye to such slave trafficking. If the phrases here in Rev 18:13 are understood in this light, then they would be understood as "slaves, and captives." However these phrases at the end of 18:13 are interpreted, they reveal the horror of what it meant to be caught up in the evil web of merchants who were slave traders under the sufferance of the harlot.

While the merchants lament the loss of their own wealth because their goods are no longer valuable, they also give expression to the fact that the harlot's "fruit of [her] passion" has departed, together with "all [her] costly and splendid things," which were a part of her passion and love for life (18:14). The "fruit" symbolically refers to the harlot's treasure, which she has stored up and saved and which is now ready to be tapped in leisure time or retirement for easy, comfortable, and luxurious living. This is all gone now, for the harlot as well as for the merchants, for they will never realize the dreams that their stored treasure created and sponsored (cf. Lk 12:16–21). When the outward "costly and splendid things" have been destroyed, their passion for life, their joy of living fades away and is replaced by dark despair in the face of the coming eternal abyss (cf. Rev 19:20).

The merchants' lament concludes with the same double woe (18:16) that was expressed in the dirge of the kings (18:10). While the woes of the kings were uttered with regard to the instant destruction of the great city, Babylon ("in one moment," 18:10), that of the merchants is uttered as an expression of fearful awe in view of the devastation and ruin of the wealth of "the great city" (18:16). Even wealth of such a magnitude as possessed by Babylon, wealth of gold and precious stones and costly clothing, could not save the doomed city. Gold and finery that once clothed the harlot and hid from view her shameful nakedness was now stripped away. All that was left was a stinking and rotting corpse. In terror and fear the merchants stand at a distance (18:15), as did the kings (18:10), as they watch her demise in her fiery torment. The first part of 18:17 belongs to the conclusion of the merchants' dirge and is the final thought introduced by the two woes that begin 18:16. The shock of the destruction and ruin of their paramour, the harlot of Babylon, was not only evoked by the totality of her downfall, but also by its suddenness, "for in one moment such wealth was incin- erated" (18:17). The dirge of the kings ended on the same terrifying note (18:10). There the suddenness of the harlot's "judgment" was noted. Here in 18:17 the suddenness of the destruction of her wealth is marked out.

The *seafarers* also take up and continue the dirge over fallen Babylon (18:17b–19; cf. Ezek 27:25–32)). John knew the certainty that Babylon the harlot would be destroyed in God's wrath and anger. So now there rings in John's ears the woeful dirge and wailing of the mariners over the fallen harlot, their paramour.

Not only the mariners and pilots who actually work and sail the ships wail and lament, but also "everyone who sails for a place" joins the lament (18:17). This description is difficult to interpret. Most likely it is a reference to "pas- sengers." These all stand on the shore "at a distance" (18:17) as they watch the smoking ruins of the great city.

In Rev 18:19 the seamen also shout out the double woe in their mournful lament, woes that express the shock and fearful awe that "the great city" (Rev 18:19) should be so devastated. Their woes also express the hopeless fear that because "the great city" is gone, their own wealth, which they earned with their ships by carrying and receiving Babylon's goods, would now disappear also and be lost forever. Their dirge concludes with the cry "in one moment she has been brought to total ruin" (18:19). Thus each of the three segments of this wailful dirge—that of the kings (18:9–10), the merchants (18:11–17a), and the mariners

(18:17b–19)—ends with the unbelieving cry "in one moment," marking the *suddenness* of her judgment and destruction. In the ending of the lament of the kings, "in one moment" emphasizes the suddenness of the harlot's judgment (18:10). In the case of the merchants, "in one moment" points out the ruin of such "wealth" that the harlot possessed (18:17a). In the case of the mariners, "in one moment" stresses the suddenness with which Babylon becomes totally ruined (18:19).

THE CALL TO CELEBRATE (18:20)

The prophetic announcement of the judgment of Babylon, which consists of the harlot and the beast (17:3, 7), concludes with a call to heaven and to the saints and prophets and apostles to break out in celebration (18:20). When this command and invitation is given, an angel casts a millstone into the sea to dramatize the finality and totality of Babylon's destruction in the judgment of God. As the angel throws the millstone he proclaims that Babylon will never again arise and never again will there be any sign of life in her (18:21–24).

"Rejoice in celebration" (18:20) not only means "be happy, rejoice," but "be joyful by having a celebration." This call prepares for the wedding feast in 19:6–9. In contrast to the mournful dirge of the kings and merchants and mariners (18:9–19), heaven and its people break out in celebration. Throughout their earthly lives, the "saints" (18:20) of God had been bedeviled and harassed by the harlot and the beast, even unto death (see 13:7, 14–15; 15:2), but now they rejoice and celebrate over their fallen enemy. The "apostles and prophets" (18:20), the witnessing foundation of the saints (see Eph 2:20; cf. Rev 21:12–14), were mocked and ridiculed (cf. 11:7–10). Now they are vindicated in their testimony to Christ, which vindication they celebrate as they are lifted up before the heavenly throne of God (cf. 7:11–12; 11:11–12). Perhaps John was reminded of the concluding verse of Moses' song in Deut 32:1–43: "Rejoice, O heavens, with his people, because he [God] will avenge the blood of his slaves" (Deut 32:43). As God passes judgment on Babylon here in Rev 18:20, his people shout out in praise and celebration, for their Lord has given to the harlot the judgment she executed on his people.

THE MIGHTY ANGEL (18:21–24)

In dramatic fashion a certain angel illustrates the total and final destruction of Babylon by this act: he "lifted up a stone like a large millstone and he threw it into the sea" (18:21). This is not just *an* angel, but *one* particular angel, a noted angel, for the angel is designated as "one particular mighty angel." (The fact that he is called "mighty" could be a way of identifying him as the "mighty" angel of 5:2, the angel who helped to introduce the victorious Lamb in the vision of God's heavenly glory, or as the "mighty" angel of 10:1, who commissioned John (and through John the churches) to proclaim the message of God and his Christ to all peoples (10:11). The use of this word "mighty" in designating these angels (or one single angel) suggests that they are particular, noteworthy angels of God's presence, angels who stand before God, prepared and waiting to be sent on a mission. When they are sent and present themselves, they appear as angels who command attention.

In Revelation there are five angels who appear with such a commanding presence, because they are called "mighty" (5:2; 10:1; 18:21), and/or because of their majestic visible appearance (10:1; 18:1; 19:17). All five play important individual roles (5:2; 10:1; 18:1, 21; 19:17). In addition two of them are pointedly marked out as "one particular angel" (18:21; 19:17). Three of the five stand out especially because of their appearance. The angel of 10:1 has a rainbow-like halo on his head, he is clothed with a cloud, and his face is like the sun. The angel of 18:1 has such a glory that the earth is illuminated by it. And the angel of 19:17 stands "in the sun." These three are dressed in these majestic emblems of God the Father and Christ to indicate that they are special angels who represent God as they carry out their missions. The other two (5:2; 18:21), while not described in such terms of God's majesty, also have special missions as they represent God, and so they are called "mighty."

The five stand out especially *because of the roles they play.* The "mighty" angel of 5:2 in the very presence of God introduces the victorious Lamb to the heavenly hosts. The "mighty" angel of 10:1, dressed in the cloud and rainbow and whose face is like the sun, commands John, representing the church on earth, to proclaim the message of Christ to all people (10:11). The angel in 18:1, whose glory illuminates the whole earth, announces the judgment of God on the harlot Babylon. The "mighty" angel here in 18:21 dramatizes the fall of Babylon by heaving a large stone, like a millstone, into the sea. And the angel in 19:17 stands in the sun and commands the birds of prey to come to the banquet of God at the End and feed on the fallen enemies of God's people.

The important roles of these angels involve *the church's mission on earth:* commissioning the church to proclaim the message (10:1–11); announcing the final judgment of the great enemy of the church's mission (18:1–3); illustrating that judgment by throwing the millstone-like stone (18:21); and announcing the banquet of God at the present world's end(19:17–18). While the angel in 5:2 does not immediately affect the church's mission, he does invite the Lamb to open the scroll with seven seals, and that opening of the seals by Christ does directly involve the church's mission. This similarity in the purpose of these angels—each involving the church's mission—could indicate that these special angels are one and the same angel. Whether that is true or not, they have remarkable roles that they carry out, roles on behalf of God and for the sake of his church, and specifically for the sake of her mission.

This angel took "a stone like a large millstone and he threw it into the sea" (18:21). The millstone sinks into oblivion, never again to rise to the surface. So the ancient and ongoing enemy of the church—she who had tormented God's saints all through the time period from Christ's ascension up to his return at the End, the harlot Babylon—now sinks forever into the bottomless pit. She is now gone forever and will "never again be found" (18:21). This is reminiscent of the way in which the army of Egypt, the first enemy of Israel, sank in the depths of the sea like a stone and like lead during the exodus (Ex 15:4–5, 10). The angel's casting of the large stone into the sea, to symbolize the complete disappearance of the harlot Babylon, is also similar to Jeremiah's casting of a scroll into the Euphrates River to symbolize that ancient Babylon would sink and never again rise to plague God's people (Jer 51:60–64).

As in a ghost town, not a sound will be heard—not a movement of a worker, not the light of a lamp, not the joyful voices of a married couple. The list in 18:22–23 of activities and sounds that will pass away is similar to descriptions of God's judgment given through certain of his prophets (Is 24:8 [cf. Jer 7:34]; Jer 25:10; Ezek 26:13). The cessation of all life and its activities is especially witnessed to by the fact that "the voice of a bridegroom and of a bride will never again be heard" (Rev 18:23).

The latter part of 18:23, together with 18:24, gives in summary fashion the reasons for the judgment and devastation of the harlot Babylon. Her ruin came about because her "merchants were the power brokers of the earth" (18:23). Commercial gain and money were the gods that drove and controlled the human race under the license and sufferance of the harlot. In particular, *apostate Christianity* (the most pernicious form of the harlot) encouraged and sanctioned sensual and luxurious self-indulgence gained by power grabs and the love of wealth. Another sin for which the harlot will be condemned is her pseudo-Christianity in the form of her "sorcery" by which "all the nations were deceived" (18:23). "Sorcery" here is understood in its broadest sense as a reference to the harlot's false spirituality, wonder-working signs, and apparent miracles (see 13:13–14; cf. Mt 24:24; 2 Thess 2:9) by which she deceived and led astray people to believe that they had security through their trust in her. Sorcery can also include the use of drugs and occult practices. As people trusted Rome as "the eternal city," so nations trusted the harlot Babylon for their spiritual well-being. The final sin for which the harlot will be damned is her persecution and execution of "prophets" and "saints" of God, as well as "all those who were slain upon the earth" (Rev 18:24). Their blood cried out for vengeance (Rev 6:9–10; cf. Gen 4:10; 2 Macc 8:1–4; Heb 12:24), and now God will exact that vengeance in her judgment (cf. Rev 19:1–2).

EXCURSUS

Is the Harlot the Antichrist?

Is the harlot Babylon the Antichrist? While the term "Antichrist" does not appear in Revelation, it does appear in two of the Johannine letters (1 Jn 2:18, 22; 4:3; 2 Jn 7)—but nowhere else in the NT. In 1 Jn 2:18 Christians are reminded that it is the "last hour" (or, "last moment") and that the Antichrist is coming. In 1 Jn 2:22 the Antichrist is described as "the liar" who denies that Jesus is "the Messiah/Christ" and thus also denies God the Father. According to 1 Jn 2:18 there were also many "antichrists" already present when the epistle was written but there was one Antichrist who was coming very soon. Similarly in 2 Jn 7 we are told that there are many "deceivers" who have come into the world and who deny that Jesus Christ has come in the flesh, but in particular there is one deceiver, "*the* deceiver," who is the Antichrist.

In Mt 24:24 (also Mk 13:22) Jesus said that one sign of the last times before his second coming would be the arising of "false christs" and "false prophets" who would deceive, if possible, even God's elect people. In Revelation "the false prophet" (16:13; 19:20; 20:10) is a member of the unholy trinity, together with the beast and the dragon (the devil). The Lord Christ does not speak of one single false Christ. Possibly the many antichrists of 1 Jn 2:18 are the same as, or are related to, the false christs mentioned in Mt 24:24.

If one were to identify someone or something in Revelation as the Antichrist, it would be the dragon, Satan (12:3–4, 9), for the dragon claims all spiritual power (as symbolized by the seven heads) and all earthly power (as symbolized by the ten horns). Thus the dragon stands opposite to the Christ and opposes him (12:3–4), as well as the church (12:13–18). He is the great enemy of Christ and of his church on earth, and he is the one who deceives the whole earth (12:9). *Strictly speaking, in the human plane on earth, that which offsets and stands opposite to the church of Jesus Christ, and thus opposes her, is the harlot of Babylon.* There are two women in Revelation. One represents and symbolizes the true church of Christ: the woman with Child in Revelation 12 (who is the bride of Christ in 19:6–9). The other woman symbolizes the false church: the harlot, who, together with the beast she rides (17:3, 7), comprises Babylon in Revelation 17–18. So in Revelation that which stands opposite *Christ* is the dragon in chapter 12, the Antichrist, and that which stands opposite *the church of Christ* is the harlot in chapters 17–18, the antichurch. However, since in 13:1–18 the dragon gives to the beast from the sea and to the beast from the earth his authority and power to act on his behalf (13:2), the harlot in Revelation 17–18—who is the beast from the earth, the beast that bears the number 666

(13:18), and who rides the beast from the sea (17:3, 7)—becomes and is (in the stead of the dragon) that entity which has come to be known as the Antichrist.

Though John himself in Revelation does not use the term "Antichrist" in reference to the harlot, some of the early church fathers implied that there was a connection. Irenaeus, in his great literary work *Against Heresies,* is among the earliest to do so. In speaking about the Antichrist he applies the "man of lawlessness" described in 2 Thess 2:1–12 as a prophetic description of the Antichrist. He also equates the "abomination of desolation" spoken of in Daniel (11:31; 12:11) with the Antichrist. Irenaeus relates the beast with the seven heads and ten horns in Rev 13:1–10 and Babylon in Revelation 17–18 to the same topic: the tyranny and deception fostered by the Antichrist. Since Babylon in Revelation 17–18 consists of the harlot and the beast, this may imply that Irenaeus thought of the harlot as the Antichrist. A similar example is Victorinus (third century), who in his Latin commentary on Revelation, when commenting on 14:6, 8, interprets Babylon to be the Antichrist.

Specific historical identifications of the Antichrist were also made. Nero seems to have been the first to be identified as the Antichrist. (Nero was also connected with the number 666.) Nero was held to be the Antichrist not in his first lifetime, but when (according to legend) he would return after his death. The papacy has also been identified with the Antichrist. Other identifications have been suggested, such as the Muslims and Turks, and in more recent times political leaders like Stalin and Hitler. But those latter identifications did not endure. While false religions, such as Islam, and persecutors of the church, such as Hitler and Stalin, can be counted among the many antichrists, *the Antichrist itself, as illustrated by the harlot, is Christian in outward appearance.*

The clearest identification of the harlot Babylon is that *she represents apostate Christianity and the false church.* She looks genuinely Christian to the extent that she might at times deceive even God's own elect people (see Rev 17:6–7; cf. Mk 13:14–23). Since the harlot of Revelation 17–18 seems to be the same anti-Christian entity as the "abomination of desolation" in Dan 11:31; 12:11 and as the "man of lawlessness" in 2 Thess 2:1–12, then whoever and whatever she is at any given time, she dwells right in the bosom of visible Christianity, right in the sanctuary of that which represents God's presence on earth. In the same way the "man of lawlessness" (2 Thess 2:4) calls himself God and takes his seat right in the temple of God, and the "abomination of desolation" also is placed in the temple of God (Dan 12:11; Mk 13:14; cf. 1 Macc 1:54).

The description of the harlot in Rev 17:3, 7 as riding the beast (the political beast of 13:1–10) suggests that she is present especially when the apostate church employs political and economic powers in order to force participation in her false worship (cf. 13:15–17). She will continue her deceptive work throughout the time period of the Christian era until the present world's end, when she will be destroyed by God at the second coming of Christ (2 Thess 2:7–8; Rev

19:11–21). In particular, she will be a terrifying threat to the true church of Christ in the last days just before the End (Mk 13:20–23). This "Antichrist," under the control of Satan, is able to perform all kinds of counterfeit miracles and works of wonder to deceive people (2 Thess 2:9–10; Rev 13:11–14). For that reason, John warns, "Children, guard yourselves against the idols" (1 Jn 5:21).

19:1–21

VICTORIOUS CELEBRATION

REVELATION 19:1–10

A SONG OF VICTORY AND THE MARRIAGE FEAST OF THE LAMB

TRANSLATION

19 ¹After these things I heard something like a loud
voice of an immense crowd in heaven saying,
"Hallelujah!
[All] the salvation and the glory and the power
     are of our God, ²because his verdicts
     of judgment are true and just,
for he passed sentence on the great harlot who
     corrupted the earth in her immorality,
and he avenged the blood of his slaves from her hand."
³And a second time they said,
"Hallelujah!
And her smoke ascends forever and ever."
⁴And the twenty-four elders and the four
winged creatures fell down, and they worshiped
the [only] God, the One who sits on the
throne, saying, "Amen, hallelujah!"
⁵And a voice came out from the throne saying,
"Praise [him who alone is] our God,
     all you his slaves,
and those who fear him,
     the small and the great."
⁶And I heard something like a voice of an immense
crowd and like the sound of many waters and
like the noise of crashing thunders saying,
"Hallelujah!
For Yahweh, our God, the Almighty,
     has taken his reign.
⁷Let us rejoice and let us celebrate and thus
     we will give the glory to him,

because the marriage of the Lamb has come
and his bride has prepared herself.
[8]And there was given to her that she should
be clothed in pure, bright linen,
for the linen is the righteous deeds of the saints."
[9]And he says to me, "Write, 'Blessed are those who
have been invited to the feast of the marriage of the
Lamb.' " And he says to me, "These are the true words
of God." [10]And I fell before his feet to worship him.
But he says to me, "See that you do not [do that]! I
am a fellow slave with you and with your brothers,
who have the witness of Jesus. Worship only God! For
the witness of Jesus is the Spirit of the prophecy."

COMMENTARY

THE FIRST STANZA OF THE HALLELUJAH CHORUS (19:1–4)

After the judgment and destruction of the harlot and the beast (which together comprise Babylon) had been announced and demonstrated in chapters 17–18 ("after these things," 19:1), John hears "something like a loud voice of an immense crowd in heaven" (19:1) fulfilling the call for rejoicing in 18:20. Perhaps the "loud voice" (19:1) comes across to John as "*something like* a loud voice" because of a heaven-like quality. Whatever the explanation, John now hears the "Hallelujah Chorus" of the great Te Deum, the continuing song of praise to God, the beginning of which he had heard in 4:8 and stanzas of which he heard every so often throughout the prophetic message of Revelation. With this tremendous Hallelujah Chorus the great Te Deum comes to a climaxing crescendo.

Who is the "immense crowd" (19:1) that shouts out this Hallelujah Chorus? In 19:4 the twenty-four elders represent the church of both testaments, while the four winged creatures are angels. Because this Hallelujah Chorus continues through 19:8, it seems that the whole heavenly host of *both* angels *and* God's saints make up this choir. Perhaps the various stanzas of the chorus are sung antiphonally by the saints and the angels, with the twenty-four elders and the four winged creatures as the choir masters of the saints and angels, perhaps respectively (see 19:4; cf. 4:9–10; 5:8, 14).

Whatever the exact makeup of the choir, its Hallelujah Chorus celebrates the readiness of the bride for marriage to the Lamb and celebrates the invitation to the wedding feast itself. The bride of the Lamb—the communion of the saints of God, the church—is prepared first of all in that God has judged and "passed sentence on the great harlot" (19:2). She who had "corrupted the earth in her immorality" and shed "the blood of [God's] slaves" (19:2) is now gone forever, never again to threaten and hurt God's people. God himself wrought deliverance from this archenemy of his saints on earth, through the victory of the Lamb demonstrated at his resurrection (see 1:17–18; 5:2–10). This deliverance from Babylon was part of God's entire redemptive program (cf. Mk 13:19–20).

Therefore the heavenly choir in this Hallelujah Chorus attributes all "the salvation and the glory and the power" to God (19:1). Because the Christ suffered in the stead of God's people and received God's judgment against their sins, God is now "righteous" (16:5) and his "verdicts of judgment are true and just" (19:2; similarly 16:7) in handing down to the harlot the sentence of eternal death. She "who corrupted the earth in her immorality" (19:2), that is, she who motivated the peoples of the earth to worship the goddess of sensual self-indulgence as if that were the true form of Christianity, receives the sentence of the eternal fires of hell (see 19:20).

In Rev 19:3 a second "hallelujah" is raised to God in praise as the heavenly choir sees the evidence of the harlot's destruction as "her smoke ascends." Her confinement in hell and her torment will be permanent, without hope of ever ending. This second "hallelujah" is not merely a repetition of the first, but something like a climatic encore in view of the fact that the harlot's judgment is final. Therefore, her rising smoke demonstrates the finality of her judgment and moves the heavenly host to shout out a second "hallelujah" in response (cf. Is 34:8–10). And so here in Rev 19:1–3 the first stanza of the Hallelujah Chorus ends as it began, with a mighty shout of "hallelujah."

In response, "the twenty-four elders and the four winged creatures," the choirmasters of the heavenly singers, affirm the choir's Hallelujah Chorus by falling prostrate in worship and praise before God, and in this worshipful posture they, perhaps antiphonally, shout out their own "hallelujah" (19:4). In Revelation 4–5, during the worship of God on his throne and of the victorious Lamb in the heavenly vision of God's glory, the twenty-four elders prostrated themselves (4:9–10; 5:8, 14; also 11:16) while the four winged creatures (as the chief choirmasters) led the whole heavenly host in the opening stanzas of this great Te Deum. Here in 19:1–4, as the Hallelujah Chorus concludes this glorious hymn of praise, once again the twenty-four elders fall down before the throne of God, but this is the first time the chief choirmasters, the four winged creatures, also prostrate themselves before God. Perhaps the winged creatures did so to indicate that this is the end of the hymn and nothing more is to be added.

ALL GOD'S PEOPLE ARE INVITED TO JOIN IN THE WORSHIP (19:5)

A "voice came out from the throne," inviting all of God's people, both "the small and the great," to worship and praise him (19:5). Because the voice invites the slaves of God ("his slaves") to worship him, most likely it is an angel who is speaking, perhaps one of the angels of God's presence who stand before him and wait on him (e.g., see Lk 1:19).

God's people are identified as "his slaves, and those who fear him, the small and the great." The identification echoes 11:18. There the prophets of God are called "slaves" and the saints of God are "those who fear [his] name, the small and the great." The designation "the small and the great" includes all people of whatever social, economic, or educational rank or status (cf. 19:18; 20:12).

THE MARRIAGE FEAST OF THE LAMB
(19:6–10)

This call to worship is the prelude to the announcement of the marriage feast of the Lamb and an invitation to the same (Rev 19:6–10). John hears "something like a voice of an immense crowd" (19:6). Most likely this is the same crowd that is mentioned in 19:1–3 and consists of the heavenly hosts of God's saints and angels. In 19:1–3 the heavenly hosts celebrated God's judgment of the harlot. Here (19:6–8) the same heavenly hosts rejoice at the pending marriage feast of the Lamb.

As the church triumphant sings, it is in a voice "like the sound of many waters" (Rev 19:6). The church militant, pictured as the 144,000 standing on Mt. Zion with the Lamb (14:1–5), previously heard coming from heaven the "new song" (14:3; cf. 5:9) that was likened to the "sound of many waters" (14:2). While still on earth, they too learned to sing the "new song" of the church triumphant in heaven (14:3). In 14:1, the church militant stood in readiness for the judgment of Babylon at the present world's end and in joyful readiness to be received before God in heaven and thus to join the church triumphant. Hence, the whole church anticipated the second coming of Christ (14:14–20) as she sang the "new song." Here again in 19:6–8 the entire people of God, and this time joined by the angelic hosts, shout out in a loud voice "like the sound of many waters" in joyful anticipation of the marriage of the Lamb and also of Christ's immediate second coming to receive his bride (19:11–16).

The loud voice was also "like the noise of crashing thunders" (19:6). The adjective "crashing, mighty" connotes divinity in 5:2; 10:1; 18:2, 21, where in each case an angel acts or speaks for God himself. In 18:8 the adjective describes the Lord God himself. Apparently John actually heard the thundering voice of Yahweh when the "mighty angel" (Rev 10:1) cried out with a voice "as when a lion roars," since it was accompanied by the voices of "the seven thunders" (10:3–4). That could perhaps also be the "noise of crashing/mighty thunders" John hears here in 19:6. Certainly all this indicates that the shout of the heavenly hosts of both saints and angels was overwhelming, since it is likened to the sound of rushing waters and the deafening noise of crashing thunders. There could be no greater shout than that which announced the marriage of the Lamb with his bride and its ensuing banquet, for it was like the shouting, mighty voice of God himself, as if he were the one announcing the marriage of his Son (cf. Mt 22:2–3). But God gave this honor to his church triumphant, accompanied antiphonally by the angelic hosts.

Whereas the first stanza of the Hallelujah Chorus (19:1–3) celebrated the judgment of the harlot in the salvation and glory of God, the second stanza (19:6–8) celebrates the inauguration of the royal reign of Yahweh, God Almighty, which inauguration actually comes about by means of the marriage of the Lamb and its feast. (It is by the marriage of his Son that God will exhibit his everlasting reign for all to see; cf. 1 Cor 15:24–28; Phil 2:9–11.) Thus the two stanzas of the Hallelujah Chorus proclaim in words of praise the final deliverance of God's people and the unveiling of the kingship of the Lord God in the ceremony of the wedding of his Son, all to the praise and glory of him who is the Creator and King of all life.

The first thing mentioned in the second stanza of the Hallelujah Chorus sung by the heavenly choir of saints and angels is that Yahweh, God Almighty, "has taken his reign" (19:6). The form of the verb suggests a completed and single action by which the Lord God *enters into his reign as King*, an action or event by which *he takes his kingdom and exhibits that he alone is King*. Of course, God never lost his kingdom, for he is the eternal King (1 Tim 1:17), and he has always ruled everything through *power* and judgment. But his *gracious* reign over the human race was interrupted by humanity's sin of rebellion, beginning with Adam and Eve (Gen 3:1–24). God would win back mankind and again exercise his reign of grace and love, and thus (so to speak) take back his kingdom. This he did through the incarnation, death, and resurrection of his Son.

The OT anticipates this coming of the kingdom in Christ. It says Yahweh reigns especially when he acts in history to save and deliver his people (e.g., Ex 15:18). At his first advent Jesus announced the arrival of the kingdom of God (e.g., Mt 3:2; 4:17) and was crowned as King on the cross (Mt 27:29, 37). His accession to the throne of David (Is 9:6–7 [MT 9:5–6]) was signaled by his victorious resurrection (Rom 1:3–4).

The book of Revelation begins on this very note: *through the victory of his Son, Jesus Christ, God regained his gracious reign over his people.* Rev 1:5–6 testifies that by his blood Jesus Christ set God's people free from their sins and thus "made us to be a kingdom, priests to his God and Father." This theme is repeated in 5:9–10 at the exaltation and coronation of the Lamb, when the heavenly hosts praise the Lord Christ because he ransomed with his "blood [a people] from every tribe and tongue and people and nation, and ... made them for our God a kingdom and priests." During earthly life this reign of God over his people, while present through the eyes and the knowledge of faith (see e.g., Lk 17:20–21), is not openly seen by God's people (see e.g., 1 Cor 2:9–10; Heb 2:7–9), nor is it acknowledged by the unbelieving people of the world (see e.g., 1 Cor 2:6–8). *But at this world's end, when the Lord Christ at his second coming displays his exalted lordship over the entire human race for all to see and acknowledge* (Mt 24:29–31; 26:64; cf. Phil 2:6–11), *God will claim his rule over all people in full view of every human eye. In particular, he will openly enter his eternal reign over his saints* (see e.g., 1 Cor 15:20–28). Here in Rev 19:6 John hears that the Lord God has come into that gracious reign over his own people. As Yahweh, the God of his people, enters his reign, he is identified as "the Almighty" (19:6). In the Greek translation of the OT this title for God is used primarily to translate the Hebrew word "Sabaoth," meaning "hosts, armies"). The title or epithet "Yahweh of hosts" expresses the idea that Yahweh is the God over all powers, human and angelic and spiritual. Now at the End and by way of the wedding of the Lamb and his bride, the church, the Lord God will openly display this sovereign lordship over the entire universe as Yahweh, the Lord of hosts, "the Almighty" (Rev 19:6).

This gives cause for the rest of the second and final stanza of the Hallelujah Chorus, in which all the heavenly hosts burst out as they "rejoice" and "celebrate" (19:7–8). The immediate cause for the rejoicing and celebration is the "marriage of the Lamb" (19:7). Because this marriage of the Lamb with his bride is the occasion by which Yahweh, the Almighty God, openly enters his reign and receives his kingdom, the real and actual purpose of the rejoicing and celebrating is to "give the glory to him" (19:7). The marriage of the Lamb causes and motivates the celebration, but its purpose and end result is to glorify Yahweh, God Almighty.

The concept of the divine marriage is deeply rooted in the OT. The OT usually pictures Israel as Yahweh's *wife* and implies that the original marriage *already took place* at the exodus (e.g., Hos 2:14–16, 2:19–20; 3:1–3; Is 54:5–8; 62:5; Ezek 16:8). This imagery of the divine marriage between God and his people is carried over into the NT. However, the NT pictures the relationship as an *engagement,* with the wedding still in the *future* (unlike the OT, which portrays Israel as the wife already married to Yahweh.) Now the Son of God, Jesus Christ, is the bridegroom of the bride, the church. In the parable of the marriage feast (Mt 22:2–14), the kingdom of the heavens is likened to a king who plans a marriage for his son. (Though the bride is not mentioned, she is presupposed.) In Mt 9:15 (Mk 2:19; Lk 5:34) Jesus refers to himself as "the bridegroom" (cf. Jn 3:28–29). Paul in 2 Cor 11:2 speaks of the believers in Corinth as a "chaste virgin" whom he pledged to one husband, who is Jesus Christ. Paul also uses the imagery of the divine marriage in Eph 5:22–33 when he likens the relationship between husband and wife to that of Christ and the church (cf. Rom 7:1–6).

Among the Israelites and later among the Jewish people at the time of Christ, marriage had two major events: the betrothal and the wedding itself accompanied by a feast. Betrothal was taken very seriously; it was tantamount to marriage, but the betrothed couple did not come together and live as husband and wife until the wedding and its feast. The wedding ceremony and the marriage feast usually took place at the house of the bridegroom (see, e.g., Gen 29:21–22) and could last for a week or more (Judg 14:12; Tobit 8:19–20). Often the groom would pay a betrothal price to the bride's father (Gen 34:12; Ex 22:16; 1 Sam 18:24–27; 2 Sam 3:14; cf. Ruth 4:10).

God chose the seed of Abraham to be his people, his bride, Israel. She proved to be unfaithful and adulterous, but amazingly God promised to pardon her and to betroth himself to her again forever at a price he himself would pay: "I will betroth you to myself in righteousness and in justice and in mercy and in compassion; and I will betroth you to myself in faithfulness" (Hos 2:19–20). How poignantly this was carried out in the life and crucifixion and death and resurrection of Jesus Christ! This was the betrothal price that God paid in order to purchase his people as his bride. Paul reminds his readers (e.g., 1 Cor 6:20; 2 Cor 11:2) that they were purchased at a price and therefore belong to Christ as his betrothed (cf. 1 Pet 1:18–19; Rev 1:5–6; 5:9–10). It was in the "righteousness" of Christ that God made his chosen people to be his betrothed wife.

Thus the bridegroom has *purchased* his betrothed and made her to be his *promised* wife. That promise will be fulfilled when Christ returns for his bride at the End. Now John hears that "the marriage of the Lamb has come and his bride has prepared herself" and is now ready for her husband, the Lord Christ, to claim her and receive her (Rev 19:7). The Lord Christ himself, when he chose her to be his wife, made her worthy of such an honor by paying the betrothal price.

Purchased by means of the betrothal price which Jesus Christ himself paid to make her his bride, now as his betrothed she prepares herself for the wedding. "There was given to her that she should be clothed in pure, bright linen" (Rev 19:8). This garment is not the same as the robes of the saints in heaven in 7:9–17, for those robes were made white by the blood of the Lamb (7:14). The robe of each of the saints in the church triumphant, before God's heavenly throne, is the robe of *Christ's blood and righteousness* by which they are covered and thus stand forgiven and righteous before him (7:13–17). The wedding garment here in 19:8 is defined as "the righteous deeds of the saints" (19:8).Ever since she was betrothed to her husband and covered by his garment of righteousness, she has adorned herself with works and actions that demonstrated that she belonged to Christ and to no other. "The righteous deeds of the saints" (Rev 19:8) are those acts wrought in them by the Holy Spirit. *These good works of Christian piety and sanctification are as much a gift of God's grace in Christ as is the saving status of righteousness merited by his sacrificial work.* It is by these "righteous deeds" that God's people on earth glorify him (Mt 5:16) and by which they adorn the preaching and teaching of the Gospel of Christ's saving victory (Titus 2:10). It is these works of Christ's love that God will use in the judgment at the End as evidence to demonstrate that they are his faithful people (Mt 25:31–40).

In reality it is Jesus Christ, her husband-to-be, who fashions the wedding garment, the "righteous deeds" with which she is clothed. Hence, at the wedding and its feast she is clothed in the garment of deeds wrought by herself but given to her as a gift from her husband-to-be. Now the bride stands ready to be received by her husband. The Lord Christ had purchased her as his bride by paying the betrothal price, and he has thus clothed his betrothed in the robe of his righteousness. All through the time of her betrothal, the time of her exile here on earth, she prepared her wedding garment ("prepared herself," Rev 19:7) through "righteous deeds" (19:8). Clothed in this wedding garment, granted to her from her husband, she was ready for the wedding and its feast to begin (cf. Mt 22:11–14; Rev 21:2).

Perhaps while the Hallelujah Chorus was still ringing in his ears, John hears someone saying to him, "Write, 'Blessed are those who have been invited to the feast of the marriage of the Lamb' " (19:9). Most likely the speaker is the same angel (one of the seven censer-angels from Revelation 15–16, who also are the seven angels of the seven churches in Revelation 2–3) who has been John's guide since the vision of the End began in 17:1.

The angel says, "Blessed" (19:9). Seven times in Revelation this word appears, each time to introduce a beatitude. These may be called "the seven beatitudes" of Revelation; in the Sermon on the Mount (Matthew 5–7) there are nine beatitudes (5:3–12). The first beatitude in Revelation (1:3) pronounces a blessing upon the one who hears and keeps the prophetic message of Revelation. In 14:13 a blessing is spoken over those who die in the Lord and who have received rest from their earthly toil, and "their works accompany them." In the third beatitude (16:15) the blessing is spoken to the one who watches and is ready for the Lord's second coming at the End; such a Christian guards his "garments" so that the shame of his nakedness will not be visible.

The fourth beatitude, here in 19:9, appears in a logical thought sequence after the second and third beatitudes. The works that follow those who die in the Lord (14:13) are now pictured as the wedding garment of "pure, bright linen" (19:8) worn by the bride of the Lamb. The "garments" that cover the individual Christian's shame in 16:15 are the same as the robe of righteousness from Christ (7:14) by which his people were betrothed to him and which in 19:8 is now adorned with the wedding garment given to the bride. And so the fourth beatitude here 19:9 is pronounced over all those who have been invited to the wedding of the Lord Christ and his bride. The bride has kept her garment of righteousness, which covers her nakedness and keeps her pure and virgin (16:15), and her wedding garment is ready to wear, for her works have followed her (14:13). She is now ready and her husband receives her. How "blessed" are those invited to the wedding!

So then the fourth beatitude is now spoken to the invited guests. But who are these guests who attend the wedding and its feast? The manner in which the metaphorical figure of the bride is used for the church might suggest that the guests are different from the bride. But in reality they are one and the same.

The bride in the collective sense consists of the guests who have been invited and who have been brought in, as pictured in the parable of the marriage feast in Matthew (22:1–14; cf. Lk 14:15–21). In the parable, some of those invited did not accept the invitation. In Rev 19:9 the blessing is addressed to and realized only in those who are actually brought in and who then sit as guests at the feast. They are now the guests of honor at the marriage feast of the Lamb, for they are the bride of the Lord Christ. So while all who heard the gracious invitation of God were blessed in that they were recipients of the invitation, only the guests now ushered into the banquet hear the blessing and receive the contents of it: to sit in the presence of God as the bride of his Christ (cf. 3:21).

This invitation to "the *feast* of the marriage of the Lamb" recalls how banquet language is used elsewhere to describe God's salvation. There is Isaiah's prophetic pronouncement about "a banquet of rich foods, a banquet of aged wines" (Is 25:6–8) and Jesus' words concerning those who would "recline with Abraham and Isaac and Jacob in the kingdom of the heavens" (Mt 8:11; cf. Lk 13:28–30). The parable of the marriage feast (Mt 22:1–14) and the words that Jesus spoke at the Last Supper, "I will not drink again of this fruit of the vine until that day when I will drink it anew with you in the kingdom of my Father" (Mt 26:29) would also come to mind.

Here in Rev 19:9 the heavenly banquet furnished by God takes place at the End. It is the marriage feast of Christ and his bride, the saints of God. The angel's pronouncement, "These are the true words of God" (19:9),certainly is an appropriate assessment of all Scripture. However, this particular affirmation of divine authority is aimed specifically at this beatitude, as well as the whole section of the prophetic message beginning with 17:1 through 19:9, for it seems to be the same angel who guides John throughout the message concerning the present world's end (17:1–22:5) who now speaks these words of affirmation. Two further times a similar affirmation of God's divine authority will be spoken concerning a part of the message of Revelation: in 21:5 in connection with the revelation of the new heaven and new earth and in 22:6 at the beginning of the epilogue. Here in 19:9 the definite article ("the") before "words" makes it all the more emphatic that these words are "*the* words" of God, and that they are true and trustworthy.

At the conclusion of the Hallelujah Chorus and at the words of the affirmation that God's words are true, John "fell before his [the angel's] feet to worship him" (19:10). Apparently John fell before the angel to worship him because he was so overwhelmed by what he had just seen and heard (from 17:1 to 19:10) by God's revelation and word that he fell before the angel in awe and reverence.

With a sharp rebuke, "See that you do not [do that]!" (19:10), the angel immediately rejects any and all such forms of worship. Even though he is a godly and heavenly messenger, given such an overwhelming revelation and word from God, he is still just a "fellow slave" of God like John himself and all John's "brothers" and fellow saints, "who have the witness of Jesus" (19:10). Angels are never to be worshiped, for as stated elsewhere, they are created beings and so are far lower in status than the Lord Christ, who is the Son of God and is himself God (e.g., Heb 1:4–13). Whenever angels are sent to earth by God, they carry out his mission as servants who are ministers to God's saints, the heirs of Christ's salvation (Heb 1:14). So the angel identifies himself as "a fellow slave" of God just as John is, and just as are all God's saints on earth (Rev 19:10). Thus the angel and John stand before and under God as slaves equally. Though they have different roles of service, God alone is the author of whatever service they are called upon to do (cf. 1 Cor 3:5–9).

The directive of the angel to "worship only God" is placed between the mention of those "who have the witness of Jesus" and the statement that "the witness of Jesus is the Spirit of the prophecy" (Rev 19:10). The double mention of "witness" in this context suggests that the saints on earth, God's slaves, worship God by being witnesses of Jesus to the world. This brings to mind what Jesus said to the disciples in Lk 24:44–48: the message of the Torah of Moses and the Prophets and the Writings of the OT was fulfilled in his death and resurrection, and in his name the forgiveness of sins is to be proclaimed to all nations, for the disciples were *"witnesses of these things." "The witness of Jesus is the Spirit of the prophecy"* (Rev 19:10), *that is, the witness that the Spirit gave in the prophetic writings of the OT is the same witness that the apostles and John and the saints of God now hold concerning Christ (cf. 1 Pet 1:10–12), and it is the witness which they proclaim to the world. By this witness they worship God.* To worship an angel would signify that their witness was not to Christ and his saving victory, but to an angel, and this they are never to do.

Does "the witness *of* Jesus" mean "the witness *about* Jesus" or "the witness *from* Jesus," the witness which Jesus himself gives? Often this way of speaking does not sharply distinguish between these two possibilities so as to be one and not the other, but rather includes some elements of both possibilities. *It is the witness which Jesus gave concerning himself in his ministry on earth* (e.g., Mk 2:10–11) *and which he now continues to give by the Spirit* (Jn 15:26) *through the witness of God's people on earth* (e.g., Jn 15:27; Acts 1:8). It is also the witness which tells about Jesus' victory for the human race, that is, the Gospel message about his birth and ministry and life and death and resurrection (see, e.g., Rom 3:21–26; Gal 2:15–21; cf. Acts 2:32–38). Here in Rev 19:10 this "witness" is that message about Jesus' saving work, which is witnessed to by Christ himself and which he gave to the church to hold and proclaim to others, namely, that Christ is the Savior of the world.

"The Spirit of the prophecy" identifies "the witness of Jesus" as the same witness that the Spirit gave to and through the prophetic message of the OT. This is the witness concerning the death and resurrection of the promised

Messiah, which witness is now conveyed through the "true words" (19:9) of the Gospel message of Jesus Christ.

REVELATION 19:11–21

THE SECOND COMING OF CHRIST AT THE END

TRANSLATION

19 [11]And I saw heaven opened, and behold a white horse, and the one sitting upon it [called] faithful and true, and in righteousness he judges and wages war. [12]And his eyes were like a flame of fire, and upon his head were many diadems. He has a name written which no one knows except he himself. [13]And he was clothed with a garment that had been dipped in blood, and his name was called the Word of God. [14]And the hosts which are in heaven were following him on white horses, dressed in pure, white linen. [15]And out of his mouth came a sharp sword so that by means of it he might strike the pagan nations, and he will shepherd them with an iron rod; and he himself treads the winepress of the wine of the fury of the wrath of God, the Almighty. [16]And he has on his garment and on his thigh a name that has been written: King of kings and Lord of lords. [17]And I saw one particular angel standing in the sun, and he cried out in a loud voice, saying to all the birds which fly in mid-heaven, "Come, gather together for the great banquet of God, [18]so that you may eat the flesh of kings and the flesh of rulers of thousands and the flesh of mighty ones and the flesh of horses and of those sitting upon them, and the flesh of all free people as well as of slaves, and of small and great ones." [19]And I saw the beast and the kings of the earth and their hosts gathered together to make the war with the one sitting on the horse and with his host. [20]And the beast was seized, and with it the false prophet who had before it produced the signs by means of which he deceived those who

had received the mark of the beast and those who
worshiped its image. While [still] alive these two
were thrown into the lake of fire which [continually]
burns with brimstone. [21]And the remainder were
put to death by the sword of him who sits upon the
horse, [the sword] which came out of his mouth,
and all the birds were satiated with their flesh.

COMMENTARY

THE APPEARING OF THE WORD OF GOD (19:11–16)

In these verses Jesus Christ, the Son of Man, is described as the "King of kings" (19:16) and the Lord of the hosts of heaven coming at the present world's end. Though the rider on the horse is not designated as the Son of Man, "his eyes … like a flame of fire" (19:12) together with the "sharp sword" (19:15) that issues from his mouth point out that he is the Son of Man (see 1:13–14, 16; 14:14; cf. 2:18). This is the second time in Revelation that the second coming of the Lord Christ is portrayed. In the vision of the harvest of the earth at the End in 14:14–20, the first view of his second coming, the Son of Man was pictured as the Lord of the harvest. Here in 19:11–16 he is described as the mighty warrior, the Lord of hosts, who comes at the End to execute the judgment of God and to carry out the sentence of that judgment (19:17–21).

The vision begins with "heaven opened" (19:11). In 4:1 John saw "an opened door in heaven" so that he could enter into the very presence of God. That began the visionary revelations through which the prophetic message of Revelation was given to him. Here in 19:11 heaven is opened and John sees the Lord Christ coming to inaugurate the events that occur at the End. The epiphany which began at the incarnation is about to be concluded in the display of the glory of God in this appearance of his Son as the victorious and conquering champion of his people, for Christ's return is the conclusion of that mission which began with his life on earth. During his first advent Jesus completed his mission of offering the sacrificial atonement for the world's sin. He also set in motion the church's worldwide mission of Gospel proclamation. Now the time allotted for the church's mission is concluded. Christ's return at the End is the fulfillment of the promise that the two angels (the two "men" dressed in white) made to the disciples on the mount of the ascension when they said that the Lord would come again to them in the same manner in which they saw him ascending into heaven (Acts 1:10–11).

The Lord Christ is described as "the one sitting upon" a white horse, and he is designated as the one who is "faithful and true" (Rev 19:11). The return of Christ is generally associated with the clouds (14:14; Mt 26:64; cf. Mt 24:30; Dan

7:13; Acts 1:9–11). But here in Rev 19:11 he comes upon a "white horse." While clouds will accompany his coming as the emblem of God's heavenly glory, his coming on a "white horse" points out that he comes as a *warrior*, a warrior who has been victorious in battle and now comes in triumph to claim his spoils, his rightful rewards (Is 40:10; 53:12; 62:11).

He is called "faithful and true" (Rev 19:11). In the prologue of Revelation Jesus Christ is presented as "the witness, the faithful one" (1:5). In 3:14, at the beginning of the seventh letter, he is called "the witness, the faithful and true one." (The Lord Christ is the true and faithful witness from God and for God—the witness to all that is true about God and the human race. As he comes at the present world's end to execute the judgment of God, he comes as the only true and faithful one to witness to the truth of the only God. Thus he alone has the right to judge humanity on behalf of God and to determine the ultimate destiny of every last man, woman, and child, because of his incarnation, death, and resurrection (1:17–18).

The Lord Christ comes in righteousness to judge and make war (19:11). In 19:15 the symbol of his judgment and warfare is "a sharp sword." In the OT it is *Yahweh himself* who is presented as the mighty, all-conquering warrior who comes with his sharp "sword" (e.g., Josh 5:13; Is 27:1; 31:8; 66:16) and with his hosts to make war (Is 13:4) against his enemies and those of his people. But even in the OT the role of Yahweh as a warrior (Ex 15:3; Deut 10:17; Is 42:13) was pictorially and prophetically delegated and assigned to the Messiah, and as in Rev 19:15, he would conquer by means of the Word in his mouth (Is 11:1–5; 49:2; cf. Josh 5:13–15). This idea that the Messiah would carry out Yahweh's role as warrior is continued in the NT. In 2 Thess 2:8 the Lord Jesus at his second coming "will kill by the spirit of his mouth" the "man of lawlessness" (cf. Mt 10:34). Now here in Rev 19:11 John sees in dramatic fashion the Lord Christ coming as the warrior of Yahweh to judge and destroy the enemies of God and of his saints—now the beast and the false prophet—by casting them into hell (19:19–21).

"His eyes were like a flame of fire" (19:12) directly identifies the one sitting on the white horse as "the Son of Man" (1:13) who appeared to John in 1:9–20 and commissioned him to write Revelation (1:19). Such eyes indicate a penetrating look of holy purification before which no human can stand unless covered and cleansed by the forgiveness and righteousness of God (Ex 19:10–19; Mal 3:1–4; 4:1–3). Nothing is unknown or hidden from such searching, searing eyes (Heb 4:12–13).

"Upon his head were many diadems" (Rev 19:12). The diadem signifies kingly royalty and authoritative sovereignty, and he who wears it exercises absolute and lordly power. In the first vision of the second coming of Christ at the harvest at the End (14:14), "the Son of Man" wore a crown which represented his victory. By right of his victory (see 5:5–10), he was rewarded with the authority to be the Lord of the harvest. Here in the second vision of his return at the End, the Son of Man now wears "many diadems" (19:12) because he comes as the absolute Ruler and Lord to execute God's judgment as his mighty warrior. He comes now as the regal Lord who already became the Victor at his resurrection.

In 12:3 the dragon (Satan, the devil) wore seven diadems and by them falsely claimed that he was the spiritual ruler of the universe. Despite that pretense, Jesus, during his temptations in the wilderness, refused to ascribe to Satan such royal sovereignty (Mt 4:8–9), for that sovereignty would be conferred upon God's Son by his Father (cf. Pss 2:6–8; 110:1–2). In Rev 13:1 the beast from the sea, the first henchman of the dragon, wore ten diadems, by means of which it arrogantly boasted that it was the supreme ruler on earth in human affairs. Now the Lord Christ as the mighty warrior wears "many diadems" (19:12), far more than the seven of the dragon and the ten of the first beast. The "many diadems" could be understood as *all* the diadems, which now are on the head of the Son of Man, for at his coming to judge no one will dare to wear a diadem of any sort.

The rider on the white horse has "a name written which no one knows except he himself" (19:12). This calls to mind the incident related in Gen 32:22–32, when Jacob wrestled with the mysterious divine presence in the form of a man. When Jacob asked his name, he answered, "Why do you ask my name?" No name was given. Nevertheless, the "man" blessed him, and Jacob realized that he had seen "God face to face." Could the name of 19:12 be the sacred tetragrammaton ("Yahweh"), a name so awesome and holy that Jewish custom refrained from pronouncing it? (In place of it the Hebrew term for "my Lord" usually was pronounced.) In the NT the Lord Christ is associated with and identified as the visible presence of Yahweh, the ineffable God.

However, "Yahweh" is probably not the unknown name here written, for the name of Yahweh was known and could have been read and identified. The name in Rev 19:12 was written and evidently was visible to John, but it could not be deciphered. In 2:17 the one "who conquers," that is, the faithful Christian, will be given "a new name written which no one knows except the one who receives it." In 3:12 the Lord Christ says that he "will write upon" the one who conquers "the name of my God and the name of the city of my God—the new Jerusalem, which is coming down out of heaven from my God—and my own new name." Is the unknown name here in 19:12 the "new name" of the Lord Christ which will be revealed only when he has returned and established the everlasting reign of God in the new heaven and new earth? Is it that "new name" which he will also share with God's faithful saints and thus only he and they will know? Whatever the exact meaning, it seems to imply a name which is now hidden from those on earth but expresses the mystery of Christ's own person and exalted status as the Son of Man. It is a mystery that only the Son of God fully understands but which his true believers, after the parousia and their resurrection and entrance into the new heaven and new earth, will also have and know (cf. 1 Cor 13:12).

When the exalted Son of Man appeared to John in Revelation 1, he was dressed in a long flowing robe like that of the high priest (1:13). Here at his second coming he is a warrior clothed "with a garment that had been dipped in blood" (19:13). In Is 63:1–6 the prophet sees the Messiah, the one who says, "I am speaking in righteousness and am great enough to save" (Is 63:1), coming from Edom. Edom represents the enemies of God's people, and the vision portrays the battle through which the Messiah delivered the people from their enemies, including their sins. As evidence that he destroyed the godless nations, he wears garments that are stained in red because of the blood that spattered on them as he trampled the enemies in his anger (Is 63:2–3). His garments looked like those of a person "treading [grapes] in a winepress" (Is 63:2). In this prophecy by Isaiah the trampling of the enemy was for both judgment and redemption (Is 63:4). Therefore the blood spattered on his garments included the blood of redemption, which the Messiah alone could provide (Is 63:3a; cf. Is 53:4–5, 8, 12)—that is, the Messiah's own blood, shed in the battle he fought to save his people. The blood also was that of his enemies, shed because of his judgment against them—and this is the main emphasis in Is 63:1–6.

Upon reflection there likely came to the mind of John this reference in Isaiah, for now he sees in this vision of the Son of Man in Rev 19:13 what was prophetically received by the prophet. The emphasis here in 19:13, as also in Is 63:1–6, is that the blood on his garment is the blood of the enemies crushed in the judgment of God which he as the Son of Man executes. While he comes as the Redeemer to his own people (Is 62:12; 63:4), to unbelievers he comes as the judge and warrior of God. He comes to tread the winepress in the anger and judgment of God (Rev 19:15). But John surely would have thought also of the "blood of the Lamb" (1:5, 9; 7:14; 12:11). The prophetic passage of Is 63:1–6 would also lead to such an interpretation. By the shedding of his own blood to defeat the enemy, and thus bring salvation to God's people, Christ earned the right now to judge those enemies by the shedding of their blood. The warrior on the white horse who is called "faithful and true" (19:11) bears a name, "the Word of God" (19:13). With the possible exception of Heb 4:12, the expressed thought of a personal "Word" is confined to Johannine literature. In the gospel of John the title is used as a personal name by which Jesus Christ is introduced as "the Word" who was "made flesh"—incarnate (Jn 1:1–14). In 1 Jn 1:1 the title "the Word of life" is used in reference to Jesus Christ. In Jn 1:3, 10 the Word is presented as the person through whom all creation came about, and thus he is the agent of God's creation. The Word is identified as the "only-begotten God who is in the bosom of the Father" (Jn 1:18). The Word is described as the person who brings light and life (Jn 1:4; 1 Jn 1:1–5). He is identified as the only-begotten (Son) of God (Jn 1:14, 18), Jesus Christ (Jn 1:17).

Here in Rev 19:13 the Son of Man is called "the Word of God." Is the exalted Son of Man as the warrior-judge named "the Word of God" because he speaks for God and is the agent who carries out and executes the judgment on behalf of God? In the OT the designation "the word of the Lord" frequently appears for the prophetic messages that came from God to the prophets. The fact that John calls Jesus Christ "the Word of God" certainly implies that he is *the* prophetic spokesman for God. He is the complete and perfect and final revelation of God to humankind in his person and work and in his teachings (see Heb 1:1–4). Now, as the exalted Son of Man, "the Word of God" will speak and execute the judgment of God.

When he comes as the warrior-judge bearing the name of "the Word of God," this name suggests that his role as the spokesman of God is not only for the judgment of God's enemies. The name also hints that as "the Word of God" he will, by means of the judgment and after it, carry out an active role in a new creation, for in Johannine literature the "Word" (Logos) is always presented as the powerful Word of God that creates and brings to life. While the emphasis here in Rev 19:11–16 is on the warrior-like role of a fearful judge, the fact that he is named "the Word of God" indicates that, after his second coming at the End, the Christ is going to do something more than judge—something positive by the grace of God, something creative and new.

"The hosts which are in heaven" (19:14) attend the Lord Christ as he comes. They are "dressed in pure, white linen" (19:14). "Hosts" in Greek (also twice in 19:19 and once in 9:16) designates "soldiers, armies of armed troops." The closest OT equivalent is the Hebrew word for "hosts, armies." In the OT this plural form often appears as a part of a title for God, "Yahweh of hosts," and it refers to the ranks of God's people (e.g., Ex 12:41; 1 Sam 17:45; 2 Sam 7:26–27) and also to the heavenly bodies, the stars or the angels or both, for stars often represent angels (e.g., Job 38:7). Here in Rev 19:14 the "heavenly hosts" are the angelic hosts who follow and attend and serve the Lord Christ (cf. Zech 14:5; Mt 26:53).

The heavenly angelic hosts are "dressed in pure, white linen" (19:14). The bride of Christ is dressed in "pure, bright linen," which garment is "the righteous deeds of the saints" (19:8). Here the clothing of the angels suggests the purity and holiness of God's righteous judgment to be executed now by the exalted Son of Man as he is attended by the angels in this holy task. While the "pure, white linen" (19:14) might suggest that the heavenly hosts are the saints of God (cf. Rev 7:14), here the hosts are *angels* for they, and not the saints, elsewhere are associated with Christ as he comes at the End for the purpose of judgment (e.g., Mt 24:29–31). The 144,000, representing the church *militant on earth,* do follow the Lamb as an army (though not wearing white)—but they do so for a different purpose. Here the divine warrior coming from heaven to earth is followed by the heavenly hosts of angels sitting "on white horses" (19:14; as does Christ himself, 19:11) for the purpose of judgment. The saints of God, either on earth as the 144,000 or those in the church triumphant, do not follow the Lord Christ *for the purpose of executing God's judgment.*

The "sharp sword" which comes out of the mouth of the Son of Man (19:15) is reminiscent of his appearance in 1:16, but there the purpose of the sword was to chastise the impenitent, for in 2:12–17 (the letter to Pergamum) the sword out of Christ's mouth (2:12) was for such a stated purpose (2:16). Here in 19:15 Christ's purpose is to wield his sword against those who are *outside* the church, for the Son of Man comes to "strike the pagan nations" (19:15). His sword represents the deadly power of the word of judgment that issues from his mouth, as in Is 11:4, where the Branch (Is 11:1) will "strike the earth with the rod of his mouth" and thus will kill the wicked. He earned the right to wield the sword of justice and judgment because he himself was struck by the word of God's justice and judgment against the world's sin in order to deliver the people from such a sword (see e.g., Zech 13:7–9).

In addition to the sword, the Son of Man will also use "an iron rod" to "shepherd" the pagan nations (Rev 19:15). Is the "iron rod" the same as the sword? In Is 11:4 it is a rod or staff from the Branch's mouth, but in Is 49:2 the mouth of the servant of the Lord is likened to a sharp sword. This could suggest that the sword which strikes the pagan nations is similar to the "iron rod" by which he thus shepherds or rules the nations in judgment. The fact that the Son of Man is described as one who shepherds the nations implies that as he comes to destroy the pagan nations, he first *separates* them from his own followers with the "iron rod" and then strikes them down with the sword. As prophesied in Ps 2:6–9 the Son of God would shepherd the nations with "an iron rod" and would "break them in pieces like pottery." Thus in several figurative thoughts the Son of Man coming at the End in judgment comes as the victorious *Warrior* wielding the sword of justice, as the *King* with his ruler's scepter, as the *Shepherd* employing his staff as a rod to separate his sheep from the pagan nations before executing that justice, and perhaps the added figure, implied by way of the quote from Ps 2:9, that like a *potter* he will shatter those earthen vessels that displeased him (Jer 18:1–10; Rom 9:19–24).

Another figurative thought at the conclusion of Rev 19:15 pictures the warrior-like Shepherd carrying out his role of judge and destroyer: "he himself treads the winepress of the wine of the fury of the wrath of God, the Almighty." As 19:13 described, his garment is "dipped in blood," *the blood that he himself shed because he bore transgressions and God's judgment in the stead of sinful humanity.* Now as he comes in judgment at the End, his blood-red garment illustrates the truth that he will tread down the pagan nations in the winepress of God's anger as grapes are trodden underfoot (cf. Joel 3:12–14). It is a terrible thing to fall into the hands of a vengeful God (Heb 10:30–31). Divine judgment and hatred of sin is as much a part of the message of Revelation as is divine affection for mankind. Without question God will destroy forever in hell (Rev

19:21; cf. 20:15) the sinner who rejects the only true God, the Almighty, by deny-
ing his Son as the Savior of the world (1 Jn 2:22–23).

The scene of the second coming of the Lord Christ (Rev 19:11–16) is
concluded with the statement that the Son of Man "has on his garment and on
his thigh a name that has been written: King of kings and Lord of lords" (19:16).
The "garment" is probably the same garment that is covered with blood (19:13).
Though covered in blood, his "garment" also bears a written name which is
above every other name. The name was also written on "his thigh" (19:16).
Whether the name is written once, on that part of the garment which covers the
thigh, or twice, on the garment and also underneath on his thigh itself, John
pointedly records that it was on "his thigh."

In Gen 32:25 (MT 32:26) Jacob's "thigh" was touched by God when Jacob
wrestled with him. The Israelites abstained from eating the muscle of the thigh
(ET Gen 32:32) out of respect, because it was a sign of what had happened
between God and Jacob when his name was changed to Israel. The name "Israel"
was a reminder that, while Jacob fought with God (in the form of an ordinary
man; cf. Is 53:1–3) and conquered him (Gen 32:28) and was thus blessed by God
(Gen 32:29), God touched Israel's thigh so that he limped (Gen 32:31). God did
this to remind Jacob that, while he fought and overcame God, he did so because
of God's condescending love and mercy to him.

Does this suggest that the name was written on the "thigh" of the Lord
Christ in order to indicate that the real "conqueror of God"—the one who successfully endured the judgment and anger of God the Father—is Jesus Christ?
Or could it recall the humility of God in Christ, who became a mortal man
in weakness and allowed himself to be "defeated" by his human adversaries,
for the purpose of providing the atonement for their sin—and the sin of the
whole world? In either case, Jesus Christ is the ultimate "Israel" who, in God's
condescension, love, and grace, suffered and thereby conquered the anger and
judgment of God so that God would always favor humankind. The name on
the thigh would then be the mark which identifies Jesus Christ, having once
conquered sin and death by his own death and resurrection, as the true Israel, of
which Jacob of old was a prefigurative type. Matthew (2:15), when narrating how
God called the Christ Child out of Egypt, interprets that call as the fulfillment
of God's call for Israel to come out of Egypt (Hos 11:1). In this way Matthew
identifies Jesus Christ as the true Israel of God's people. Similarly here in Rev
19:16 God may be making the same identification by revealing to John that Jesus
Christ has his conquering name written on his "thigh."

For a third time in 19:11–21, the Son of Man in his role of warrior-judge
is given a name. First "he has a name written which no one knows except he
himself" (19:12). Next his name is called "the Word of God" (19:13). Now he is
said to bear the name "King of kings and Lord of lords" (19:16).

This title has a rich background in Scripture. In Deut 10:17 Moses declared that Yahweh, the God of Israel, is "the God of gods and the Lord of lords," and therefore is "the only God, the great and the warrior and the fearful." In Psalm 136, as the psalmist urges the hearer to "give thanks to Yahweh because he is good, because his mercy is forever" (Ps 136:1), he then says that the hearer should "give thanks to the God of gods" and "the Lord of lords" (Ps 136:2–3). In Dan 2:47 Nebuchadnezzar, after his dream had been interpreted by Daniel, praised the God of Daniel as "the God of gods and the Lord of kings," because he alone reveals mysteries. In 1 Tim 6:14–15 Paul refers to Jesus Christ as "the King of those who are reigning and Lord of those who are lording." Paul uses this appellation in reference to Christ when he will, at his "appearing" or "epiphany," exhibit himself as "the blessed and only Sovereign."

Now here in Rev 19:16 John sees this holy and awesome title of Yahweh applied to Jesus Christ as he comes at the End to call to account the entire human race and its history. It is a name which shouts out that the Lord Christ is the universal Ruler of the entire creation, the only King and Emperor of the human race, and the Lord before whom all people of whatever race and nation and tongue will kneel and acknowledge as the only Lord and as true God (Phil 2:6–11). By right of his victory and under the authority of his Father he will determine the end result and destiny of the peoples of the world. He will judge and bring all history to its conclusion, and he will bring to an end the present physical world. Even now as his followers, the saints of God on earth, struggle in the battle against the harlot and the beast, they know and honor the Lamb as "the Lord of lords and the King of kings" (Rev 17:14). On earth they may suffer defeat (11:7; 13:7), but ultimately they will triumph because their Lord has triumphed and will triumph (12:11; 17:14).

THE CONCLUSION OF THE WARFARE
(19:17–21)

At the coming of the Son of Man as the commander of the heavenly hosts (19:14, 19), John sees the conclusion of the warfare between the Lord Christ and the hosts of the beast and the false prophet. The beast and false prophet are cast into hell, and their hosts are destroyed (19:20–21). Just as before the destruction of Jericho "the commander of Yahweh's army" (Josh 5:14) met Joshua to encourage him to know that the hosts of Jericho would be destroyed, so now John is comforted by the Son of Man in the knowledge that the hosts of the enemies of God's people would be overcome and victory would belong to the Christ and his church.

The scene of this conclusion is introduced by "one particular angel standing in the sun" (Rev 19:17). The fact that the angel is identified as "one particular angel" suggests that he is the same angel which John saw in 18:1 and again in 18:21. In chapter 18 the angel who announced the judgment of Babylon (which consists of the harlot and the beast, 18:1–2) and who demonstrated the destruction of that great enemy of the church by throwing a millstone into the sea (18:21) is called "one particular mighty angel" (18:21). In 18:1 that same angel had "great authority," and "the earth was bathed in light by his glory."

Here in 19:17 the "one particular angel" apparently is that same angel from 18:1, 21 who now appears again. The fact that he stands "in the sun" (19:17) reinforces the identification of this angel with the one of 18:1. His standing "in the sun" indicates that it is *in the majesty of the Lord Christ* that he announces the final and total destruction of the hosts of the beast and the false prophet. In 18:1–2 the angel announces the coming judgment of the beast and the harlot (who together comprise Babylon) and, as he does so, he lights up the whole earth with his glory—that is, with *the glory of Christ,* which he reflects. The same angel, now "in the sun," stands *in the majesty of Christ, from which he shouts out the final and complete victory.* It is fitting that the same angel who announced the judgment of Babylon (18:1–2) and who illustrated the finality of that judgment by throwing the millstone into the sea (18:21) should now be the angel who heralds the final destruction of the hosts of the beast and the false prophet.

The angel "cried out in a loud voice, saying to all the birds which fly in mid-heaven, 'Come, gather together for the great banquet of God' " (19:17). From his position in the sun the angel can easily command these birds. Certainly the birds will obey, for the angel cries out to them in the majesty of their Creator and Lord. The "mid-heaven" or "zenith" was the same place where John saw an "eagle" or "bird of prey" which cried out three woes upon those dwelling on the earth (8:13), and from where John also saw an angel calling out to the people on earth to fear God and to give him glory because "the moment" of his judgment had come (14:6–7). Now here in 19:17, from the same part of heaven—its highest point in its arch above the earth and the point at which the sun is directly overhead and also is at its brightest—the angel invites the birds of prey to "gather together."

They are to gather as invited guests, as it were, at "the great banquet of God" (19:17). This particular banquet, at which the birds are to feed upon the corpses, appears to be the counterpart of the marriage feast of the bride and the Lamb (19:7, 9). While the marriage feast for the bride—the Christian church—is taking place, "the great banquet of God" is also being prepared and eaten. The banquet at which the birds feed on the corpses is in terrifying contrast to the marriage feast of joy and celebration. It is called the banquet "of God" because God has planned this banquet and brought it about by his judgment. He has set it up and has provided its provisions: the corpses of the fallen hosts of the enemies of Christ and his church. As gruesome and revolting as this scene of God's banquet must have been to John, on reflection there must have come to his mind the similar banquet prepared by God in Ezek 39:17–20. The prophet Ezekiel saw the hosts of Gog and Magog making war upon God's people and overwhelming them (Ezek 38:1–23). But God would intervene and destroy the hosts of Gog and Magog (Ezek 39:1–29) and as a result would prepare a banquet at which every bird (Ezek 39:17) and all the wild animals would feed on the corpses of their fallen hosts. This banquet of the fallen hosts of Gog and Magog is also *God's* banquet because he says it will be at "my table" that the birds and wild animals will feed on the corpses (Ezek 39:20). Though the scenes in Ezekiel and Rev 19:17 are repelling, the point of such a graphic banquet is to impress upon the reader the horrible fate that awaits those who war against God, and the comforting promise to the viewer that these fallen hosts will never again arise to haunt and hurt God's people. Rev 19:18 identifies the fallen hosts. They are made up of all ranks and kinds of people, the mighty and the lowly, the slave and the free. They include all who were adherents and worshipers of the beast and its image and who received the mark of the beast (13:11–18), all who fornicated with the harlot (17:1–18:3), and all who believed the preaching of the false prophet, who deceived many (16:13; 19:20; 20:10). Their bodies lie unburied on the field of conflict to be prey for predators who gorge themselves upon them. To remain unburied and preyed upon was especially repugnant in the ancient world. That was the usual fate of victims who were impaled or crucified (cf. 2 Sam 21:10). Horses are also mentioned as part of the banquet's fare. In the banquet pictured in Ezekiel horses are mentioned because the men and soldiers of Gog and Magog rode upon them (Ezek 39:20). When the riders fall as casualties, the horses that bore them also fall. In modern parlance one can imagine that whatever the adherents of the harlot used in their spiritual and physical warfare against the saints of God, those vehicles and incarnations of evil will be destroyed with them.

In Rev 19:19–21 a description of the actual battle is given, in particular its end. The human hosts under their "kings" are arrayed in order "to make the war with the one sitting on the horse and with his host" (19:19). This is a battle presented in spiritual dimensions, for the human hosts of the harlot and the beast are now fighting against the warrior-judge, who is the King of kings and Lord of lords, and against all the angelic hosts of heaven. The hosts of the harlot and beast had already fought against the saints of God on earth and had conquered them (13:7, 15; cf. also 11:7). However, that victory was ephemeral, for the saints (though bloodied and dying) came out victorious because of the Lamb. In their arrogant audacity, having laid low the church of Christ, the harlot (who is also the false prophet) and the beast and their human hosts now take on the Lord Christ himself and his angelic hosts. It is an impossible undertaking on their part (17:14), for they are instantly thrown down and laid waste, fit now only to be gorged upon by the birds of the air. As Ezekiel prophesied, just when the hosts of Gog and Magog had all but destroyed the people of God, God himself intervened with fire from heaven and annihilated their forces (Ezek 38:22–23; 39:3–6; cf. Rev 20:7–9). Thus there is present in these verses a reference to the battle of Armageddon (16:12–16), in particular its end, emphasizing the total destruction of the human hosts of the harlot and the beast. These are not two different battles, but two different visions of the same battle immediately preceding the present world's end at the return of Christ. John will see the conclusion of this last battle before the End one more time: in 20:7–10, where the forces of the false prophet and the beast are typified by this imagery of Gog and Magog.

Here in 19:19–21 the end of this great battle emphasizes the overthrow and destruction of these human hosts together with the beast and the false prophet. In 20:7–10 the emphasis at the end of this last battle will be the casting of Satan, the mastermind behind the beast and the false prophet, *into hell*. While only the beast and the false prophet in particular are mentioned in 19:20 as being "thrown into the lake of fire," which is hell or "the *second* death" (20:6, 14: 21:8), all the human hosts of their adherents who worshiped the beast and received its mark are also destined for hell (20:11–15; contrast 20:4), and so is Satan himself (20:10). For now, the human hosts are only "put to death by the sword of" the Lord Christ (19:21). As slain corpses they are preyed upon by the birds of the heavens as they await their impending judgment at and after the resurrection.

CONCLUDING THOUGHT:
THREE WOMEN

Three women appear prominently in the book of Revelation: (1) the woman clothed with the sun with the moon under her feet and with a crown of twelve stars, who gave birth to the "male Child" (12:1–6, 13–17); (2) the harlot clothed in purple and scarlet and arrayed in gold and precious stones, who sits on the beast with seven heads and ten horns, and who bears the name "Babylon" (17:1–19:3); and (3) the bride of the Lamb, who is clothed in the wedding garment of pure, shining linen (19:7–8; 22:17; cf. 21:2, 9).

The woman of Revelation 12 represents the people of God, who in the OT are often called the wife of Yahweh and in the NT are called the bride of Christ. She first represents the OT community of God's faithful, and then, after the birth of the "male Child" (12:5), she represents the church of Jesus Christ. The crown of twelve stars would represent the twelve tribes of Israel, then after the birth of the "male Child" they would represent the twelve apostles. Especially in her role of giving birth to the Christ Child, the woman of Revelation 12 is embodied in the Virgin Mary. In a way Mary represents the OT people of God (cf. Lk 1:54–55; Rom 9:5). She is also the mother of our Lord (Lk 1:43) and the first to believe that Jesus is the Son of God, and so she can represent the NT church.

The woman of Revelation 12 is arrayed in the splendor and majesty of God and of his Christ, thus signifying how much God in the Christ loves and honors her. Though arrayed in the honor and love of God, her life is one of hardship in her exile-like existence in the wilderness of her life on earth. She is hunted down and pursued by the dragon and, though he is not able to destroy her, he causes her untold pain and suffering. The prophecy of Simeon that a sword would pass through the soul of Mary (Lk 2:35) was true of the entire existence of the woman of Revelation 12, that is, the church of Jesus Christ.

The harlot of Revelation 17–18 represents the *antichurch,* and she and the beast she rides (17:3, 7) are the two henchmen which the dragon uses in his warfare against the church, who is represented by the woman of Revelation 12. The harlot fares sumptuously and is clothed in the costliest of garments and precious stones. She is wealthy and is held in honor by the world which worships at her feet. She wields by way of the beast (which is the political and economic beast of 13:1–10) enormous political and economic power. She is the spiritual force that encourages and motivates the peoples of the world in their own lusts and desires for position and power and wealth. She is the queen of her world. All this power of position and influence and spirituality she uses against the church, her rival "stepsister," in order to destroy her. She wants to believe that she is the most beautiful and encourages the people of the world to receive her as the true bride of Christ. *For this reason the harlot is also called "the false prophet"* (16:13; 19:20; 20:10). But in her heart she knows she is not that bride, for someone else holds that position before God, her "stepsister" whom she hates and taunts. Though her poor "stepsister," is dressed, to the human eye, in rags and is the laughing stock of the world, the harlot is terribly jealous of her, for she knows that one day the despised woman in rags—and not she herself—will be the bride of Christ. In contrast, her own end will be to be stripped naked (17:16; cf. 16:15) and shamed before God and then cast into hell. The bride of Christ of Revelation 19, who on earth was the woman of Revelation 12, now is no longer in exile—tormented, bereaved (12:17), and driven to endless suffering by the dragon through the beast and the harlot (or false prophet). During her earthly life she was spiritually clothed in the righteousness of Christ and washed in his blood, but to the human eye she was destitute, dressed in rags, spurned by the world, and mocked by the harlot. Now at the End she is publicly honored by God for all to see as the bride of his Son. Now she is arrayed in her wedding garment, as she is presented to her husband (cf. Zech 3:1–5). The day for which she, the church, so ardently longed has arrived. The bride comes to her Lord with rejoicing and with the hymn of the Hallelujah Chorus, for now the time of weeping and fasting has passed, and she joins the angelic choir in singing the Te Deum to her God and Savior. From now through all eternity she will bask in his majestic presence and behold his unveiled face.

EXCURSUS

THE USE OF THE DEFINITE ARTICLE WITH "GOD"

In Revelation the use of the definite article "the" with "God" demands more attention than it has usually been given. The grammatical use of the definite article in Greek is quite different from its usage in English—though there is the common factor that in both languages it makes the word it is modifying definite.

What is striking about the appearance (or absence) of the definite article with "God" in Revelation is that, with but three exceptions, "God" is always attended by the definite article. In Revelation the Greek word for "God" appears ninety-six times, always with the definite article except in 7:2; 21:3, 7. ("God" occurs three times in 21:3, the first two times with the article and the third time without it.) This overwhelming consistency is surprising, for substantives that are definite on their own merit (such as proper names and "God") do not need the definite article. Why then does John so often use the definite article with "God," when in common grammatical usage it would not be needed?

While the definite article with "God" certainly *does* reinforce that it is definite and thus identifies which "God" is the "God" in the context, its appearance with the word does *more*, for it emphasizes the fact that *the "God" under discussion is the "only true God," apart from whom there is no other*. It is for this reason that the article with "God" can be translated as "the *only* God."

This use of the definite article for pointing out the *absolute uniqueness of God* is also seen in Revelation with "Christ," "the Word," and "the Lamb." For example, in 12:10, the article appears with "Christ," even though the word without the article would be sufficient to indicate to Christian readers that Jesus Christ is meant, since the pronoun indicates that the "Christ" is "*his* Christ," that is, *God's* "Christ" (cf. Ps 2:2). But the attending definite article points out that *this Christ is the only Messiah and Savior of the human race, apart from whom there is no other* (cf. Acts 4:12; Rev 20:6). Similarly, the definite article is used with "Word" and with "Lamb" to indicate that there is only one Word of God and only one Lamb who was sacrificed for the salvation of the world.

EXCURSUS
THE GREAT TE DEUM OF PRAISE IN REVELATION

The great Te Deum of Revelation is a hymn of praise to God for his creation of all life and for his salvation of his people through the victory of the Lamb. Its stanzas are sung at various times and places throughout the book. It begins with the singing of "holy, holy, holy" (4:8) in the vision of God's heavenly glory and of the ascension, coronation, and enthronement of the Lamb (4:1–5:14). It concludes with the Hallelujah Chorus in the vision of the bride of Christ at the End (19:1–10). This Te Deum presents a liturgical context which attends the prophetic message of Revelation as a response, a response from both the saints of God and the angelic hosts. It is an act of worship by which the heavenly choirs of saints and angels, joined also by the suffering church on earth, laud and magnify God and his Christ. The lasting impression is given that this is the greatest activity and work of God's saints and angels: the voicing and the singing of his praises.

The themes expressed in the Te Deum and by the other related voices include God's holiness (4:8), his creation (4:11), his salvation and redemption through the Lamb (5:9–10, 12; 7:10, 14–17; 12:10–12; 19:6–8), and his judgment upon his enemies, who are also the enemies of his church (11:17–18; 15:3–4; 16:5–7; 19:1–3). Doxologies abound throughout. All of these themes are appropriate for the church militant to sing too, though it is significant that the verses extolling God's judgment are, for the most part, sung by the saints and angels *in heaven* and by the church *on the Last Day*. The picture presented in Revelation is that of *one grand service of worship* whose participants include the saints on earth, still suffering in warfare, as well as the saints and angels in glory. This worship also has a *timeless* quality, as though all who participate are engaged in the *eternal* service of God, regardless of whether they are, for the moment, still on earth or whether they are in heaven. Striking too is the *unity* of this *corporate* worship; all participating voices blend in perfect harmony.

This great hymn can be understood to have an opening refrain, after which three parts follow: the hymn of the heavenly choirs; the hymn of the church; and the hymn of the bride. In addition, in several other places another voice serves as a cantor to explain or affirm the Te Deum.

THE OPENING REFRAIN

The Te Deum begins with the heavenly choirs. It is introduced by "holy, holy, holy" sung by the four winged creatures (4:8).

> *Holy, holy, holy, Yahweh, the [only] God, the Almighty,*
>> *the One Who Was and Who Is and Who Is Coming.*

Because it is stated (4:8) that the four winged creatures never cease singing this Trisagion (*Ter Sanctus*), it may be a refrain that is sung antiphonally before and after each of the following stanzas, or perhaps it is even continuously sung as an accompaniment to the stanzas, throughout the singing of the entire Te Deum.

THE HYMN OF THE HEAVENLY CHOIRS

If the Trisagion is the opening refrain, then the hymn proper begins with the first stanza sung by the twenty-four elders sitting around God's heavenly throne (4:11). It is a stanza that praises God as the Creator.

> *Worthy are you, Yahweh our God,*
>> *to receive [all] the glory and the honor and the power,*
> *because you created all things,*
>> *and on account of your will they exist and were created.*

At the enthronement of the Lamb, after he had received the scroll with seven seals, the twenty-four elders (and most likely also the four winged creatures) sing the following stanza in which they laud and praise the Lamb as the Savior of God's people (5:9–10). It is called "a new song" (5:9) because this stanza (5:9–10) and those that follow (5:12, 13) were sung for the first time at Christ's ascension and thus were added to the first stanza (4:11).

> *Worthy are you to take the scroll and to open its seals,*
>> *because you were slain and you ransomed for God*
>>> *with your blood [a people] from every tribe and*
>>> *tongue and people and nation, and you made*
>>> *them for our God a kingdom and priests,*
>> *and they rule on the earth.*

Then the hosts of angels add a stanza to the new song, in which they also praise the Lamb for his redemptive work (5:12).

> *Worthy is the Lamb who was slain to receive*
>> *[all] the power and wealth and wisdom and*
>> *strength and honor and glory and blessing.*

And finally all creation joins the heavenly choirs in praise of God and the Lamb (5:13).

> *To him who sits on the throne and to the Lamb*
>> *be [all] the blessing and the honor and the*
>> *glory and the dominion forever and ever.*

The four winged creatures then say "Amen" (5:14). They continuously sing or say the amen, suggesting that, just as the Trisagion is the opening refrain that introduces the stanzas, the amen concludes each of them.

THE HYMN OF THE CHURCH

The Te Deum continues as the prophetic message of Revelation unfolds before John. As the Lamb opens the seven seals of the scroll and reveals to John the first vision of events on earth (6:1–8:5), from the midst of all the sufferings John sees the church triumphant clothed in white before God's heavenly throne, and he hears them singing a stanza (7:10).

> *[All] the salvation is with our God, who sits*
> > *on the throne, and with the Lamb.*

The angels in heaven then add their own stanza to that of the church triumphant (7:12).

> *Amen: [All] the blessing and the glory and the wisdom and*
> > *the thanksgiving and the honor and the power and*
> > *the strength be to our God forever and ever. Amen.*

These two stanzas by the church triumphant and the angels, while sung in heaven, *are for the comfort and inspiration of John and the church on earth in the midst of their sufferings.* It can be said that as they look heavenward, they also sing these stanzas in faith and longing.

In the second vision of events on earth (8:6–11:19), when the seventh angel blows his trumpet and thus introduces the second scene of the End, the twenty-four elders on behalf of the entire people of God add a stanza which celebrates the judgment of God (11:17–18).

> *We give thanks to you, O Yahweh, the [only] God, the*
> > *Almighty, the One Who Is and Who Was,*
> *because you have taken your great power*
> > *and you have begun your reign.*
> *And the pagan nations were made angry, and your anger has*
> > *come, and the time of the dead to be judged [has come]*
> *and [the time] to give the reward to your slaves, the*
> > *prophets, and to the saints and to those who*
> > *fear your name, the small and the great,*
> *and [the time] to destroy those who were destroying the earth.*

The final stanza of the church is sung at the beginning of the third vision of events on earth (15:1–16:21) as a part of the introduction to that vision. It is sung by the church militant as she is in warfare with the beast. Though suffering defeat, she is nonetheless victorious. It is called "the song of Moses" and "the hymn of the Lamb," and it celebrates the righteousness of God in his judgments

on his enemies and the enemies of his church on behalf of his suffering people
(15:3–4).

> *Great and marvelous are your works,*
>> *O Yahweh, the [only] God, the Almighty;*
> *righteous and true are your ways,*
>> *O King of the nations.*
> *Who will not fear, O Yahweh,*
>> *and will glorify your name?*
> *For [you] alone are holy,*
>> *for all the nations will come*
>> *and will worship in your presence,*
> *because your righteous judgments have been made visible.*

THE HYMN OF THE BRIDE

The last part of the Te Deum is the hymn of the Lamb's bride as she is
received by her Lord at the End (19:1–10). It is sung by a great crowd in heaven,
and it celebrates the judgment of the harlot and then the wedding feast of the
bride and the Lamb. It is the Hallelujah Chorus by which the Te Deum reaches
its climax and conclusion (19:1–4, 6–8). The first part of the Hallelujah Chorus is
in 19:1–3.

> *Hallelujah!*
> *[All] the salvation and the glory and*
>> *the power are of our God,*
>> *because his verdicts of judgment are true and just,*
> *for he passed sentence on the great harlot*
>> *who corrupted the earth in her immorality,*
> *and he avenged the blood of his slaves from her hand....*
> *Hallelujah!*
> *And her smoke ascends forever and ever.*

At this place in the Hallelujah Chorus (19:4), the twenty-four elders and the
four winged creatures worship God by adding the third hallelujah.

> *Amen, hallelujah!*

The Hallelujah Chorus then continues and concludes with a stanza honor-
ing the bride of the Lamb (19:6–8).

> *Hallelujah!*
> *For Yahweh, our God, the Almighty, has taken his reign.*
> *Let us rejoice and let us celebrate and thus*
>> *we will give the glory to him,*
> *because the marriage of the Lamb has come*
>> *and his bride has prepared herself.*

And there was given to her that she should be
clothed in pure, bright linen, for the linen
is the righteous deeds of the saints.

Comments of Other Voices

There are several places throughout the Te Deum where another voice—that of an elder or an angel or a voice speaking for God—attends the stanzas of the Te Deum. These voices relate to the Te Deum perhaps like a cantor who sings solos interspersed with the choirs in order to explain what is happening as the stanzas progress. In the liturgical context these other voices serve a similar function to the way in which a narrator assists in the movement of a narrative account.

In 7:14–17 one of the twenty-four elders identifies for John the great crowd in heaven who is dressed in white and who is singing a stanza of the Te Deum.

These are those who are coming out of the great tribulation,
and they have washed their robes
and made them white in the blood of the Lamb.
On account of this they are in the presence of the throne of
God, and they worship him day and night in his temple,
and the One sitting on the throne will
spread his tent over them.
They will never again hunger nor ever again thirst,
neither shall the sun smite them nor any heat,
for the Lamb, who is in the midst of the throne,
will shepherd them, and he will lead them
to fountains of the waters of life,
and God will wipe every tear from their eyes.

In 11:15, when the seventh angel sounded his trumpet, "great voices in heaven" introduced the stanza sung by the twenty-four elders in which they celebrated the judgment of God.

The kingdom of the cosmos has become
our Lord's and his Christ's,
and he will reign forever and ever.

In 12:10–12 a great voice in heaven explains why the church is so joyous as she sings her hymn as part of the Te Deum.

Now has come about the salvation and the power
and the kingdom of our God,
and the authority of his Christ,
because the accuser of our brothers has been
thrown out, the one who was accusing them

> *in the presence of our God day and night.*
> *And they conquered him because of the blood of the*
> *Lamb, and by the word of their witness,*
> *and they did not hold their life dear even in the face of death.*
> *On account of this break out in celebration, O*
> *heavens, and those who dwell in them!*
> *But woe to the earth and to the sea, because*
> *the devil has come down to you,*
> *having great fury, knowing that he has but a short time!*

In 16:5–7 "the angel of the waters" affirms the last stanza of the hymn of the church (15:3–4), in which the church had celebrated the righteousness of God in his judgments.

> *Righteous are you, the One Who Is and Who Was, the Holy*
> *One, because you are dispensing such judgments;*
> *for the blood of saints and prophets they shed, and so*
> *[now] blood you have given to them to drink.*
> *Deserving are they!*

Then in seconding affirmation another voice, from the incense altar in heaven, says,

> *Yes, O Yahweh, the [only] God, the Almighty,*
> *true and righteous are your judgments.*

THE JUDGMENT AND OVERTHROW OF THE DRAGON

EXCURSUS
The Millennium

Except perhaps for the number 666 (13:18), no other portion of Revelation has caused more confusion and consternation than the first six verses of chapter 20, which describe what has come to be known as the millennium. One could receive the impression from the amount of interest caused by these verses that they are the most important and influential in the entire book. In fact, the manner in which commentators view the millennium determines to a large degree how the whole of Revelation is interpreted. Since these verses which describe a thousand-year period are a part of John's vision of the End at Christ's return (17:1–22:5), they should be interpreted first of all in relationship to the other events described in this section of Revelation. The description of the millennium (20:1–6) is placed between two scenes: the scene of the overthrow of the beast and the false prophet at the second coming of Christ (19:11–21) and the scene of the last great battle when Gog and Magog are defeated and Satan is thrown into hell (20:7–10), where the false prophet and the beast had already been cast (19:20). This suggests that whatever the millennium is and to whatever time it refers, its placement between these two scenes determines how it is to be interpreted and, more importantly, how it is to be viewed in relation to the rest of Revelation. This commentary's exposition of 20:1–10 will show that the millennium began with the binding of Satan at Christ's first advent (his incarnation, ministry, death, resurrection, and ascension) and will conclude when Christ returns in glory to bring this present world to its end.

There are today three prevalent interpretations of this thousand-year period, usually labeled "premillennialism," "amillennialism," and "postmillennialism." Those who advocate the premillenarian interpretation believe that Jesus Christ will return to earth before *(pre-)* he establishes his kingdom *on earth*. His believers will then rule with him in this earthly kingdom for a literal thousand years, and such a millenarian kingdom is still in the future. Amillennialists believe that the millennium began with Christ's death, resurrection, and ascension and lasts up to Christ's return at the end of this present world, when the final judgment will take place, followed by the creation of the new heaven and new earth. In this interpretation the millennium is equivalent to the NT era and thus is *not (a-)* a literal thousand years. Postmillennialists believe that the Christian church will influence the entire world gradually and increasingly, making it more and more righteous and thus fit for the Lord Christ to return. This will eventuate in a period of peace and righteousness among the peoples on earth that will last for a thousand years, *after* which *(post-)* the Lord will come to earth. There are many variations of all three of these interpretations.

JEWISH MILLENNIAL VIEWS

Even before John wrote Revelation there was a tradition within Judaism concerning a millennium. According to this tradition the history of the world consists of seven periods of a thousand years each, patterned after the seven days of creation. There would also be an eighth day, an eighth thousand-year period which would come after the seven millennia of the present world, and this eighth would continue without end (2 Enoch 32:2–33:2). The seventh day, the seventh thousand-year period, would be a millennial day of rest (2 Enoch 32:2–33:1), in which the Messiah would reign, after which would be the resurrection and judgment (4 Ezra 7:28–33); the messianic reign would endure until the present evil world has come to an end (2 Baruch 40:1–4). When the Messiah would come, he would bring a time of rejoicing, peace, and plenty. At the coming of the Messiah, the evil one would be subdued so that he no longer would be able to afflict God's people (2 Baruch 40:1–3; cf. Jubilees 23:24–31). Satan would be bound in a pit of darkness by the angel Raphael so that all the people would not perish (1 Enoch 10:4–8; cf. 14:5; 88:1). In 1 Enoch 10 the devil is called by the name of Azazel, which in the OT was the name of the "scapegoat" that was sent out and exiled into the desert on the Day of Atonement (Lev 16:7–10).

The tradition of a millennium in Judaism does not seem to fit a single, agreed upon pattern. Rather, one finds fragments of various schemas. Nevertheless, Jewish tradition does envision a millennium which would be the age of the Messiah and in which God's people would be protected from the onslaught of the evil one.

A HISTORY OF CHRISTIAN VIEWS

The Christian church too has expressed a variety of millennial views, though these are more similar to each other than the Jewish conceptions, and most of the Christian views draw on a particular interpretation of Rev 20:1–6.

Throughout the history of the church, interpretations of the millennium have varied. Often particular views have come and gone and then reappeared. In the early church a premillennial interpretation was seemingly prevalent, partly due to the influence of the church father Papias, who may have known and listened to the apostle John. According to the church historian Eusebius (ca. 260–ca. 340), Papias (ca. 60–ca. 130) thought that after the resurrection of the dead there would be a millennium, at which time there would be an earthly kingdom of Christ. According to Eusebius it was due to Papias that so many adopted this view.

The first Christian author whose statements specifically about the book of Revelation have survived is Justin Martyr (ca. 100–ca. 165). In *Dialogue with Trypho*, 80–81, Justin expressed the belief that after the resurrection of the dead Christians, the millennium would then commence. Other church fathers who may have held this view or a similar view were Irenaeus (ca. 130–ca. 200),

Tertullian (ca. 160–ca. 225), Hippolytus (ca. 170–ca. 235), and Victorinus (third century). .

In the third century the church began to turn away from a premillennial interpretation and increasingly espoused what today would be called amillennialism. Tyconius (died ca. 400), a Donatist theologian and layman of considerable influence, wrote a commentary on Revelation which sadly is lost to us today. However, from excerpts of his other writings some of his thoughts on Revelation can be reconstructed. Tyconius thought the millennium represented the period of time from Christ's first advent up to his return. He believed that the first resurrection is the spiritual raising to life of Christians which occurs in Baptism (cf. Rom 6:1–4; Col 2:11–13), and the second is the physical resurrection of all people at the present world's end. Because Tyconius was a Donatist, later theologians were hesitant to endorse his views even if they agreed with his interpretation.

One such theologian was Augustine (354–430). In *The City of God* he argued that the millennium was not a literal one thousand years. Latin commentators and biblical scholars followed Augustine's interpretation and helped to spread his views on the millennium. These include the great biblical scholar and translator Jerome (ca. 342–420) and also Primasius (sixth century) in his Latin commentary on Revelation. While Jerome was at first a premillennialist, under the influence of Augustine he adopted the amillennial interpretation. Some of the later Greek commentators on Revelation, such as Oecumenius (sixth century), Andreas (sixth century), and Arethas (tenth century), also followed the interpretations of Tyconius and Augustine on the millennium.

Tyconius' and Augustine's interpretation of the millennium dominated, for the most part, the Western church's theology up to the late twelfth century, especially in Europe. But in the twelfth century the church began to review its interpretation. For example, Joachim of Fiore (1135–1202) revised Augustine's interpretation of the millennium—so much so that he was the cause of premillennialistic views being entertained again. *However, it was not until the Reformation in the sixteenth century that premillennialism began to become popular and take its place alongside of the amillennialism of Augustine.* Luther (who had been an Augustinian monk) and Lutheranism opposed the reintroduction of premillennialism. However, it was sponsored by such fanatical leaders as Müntzer and Bockelson. Calvin himself also rejected premillennialism, but later Calvinists like Johann Heinrich Alsted (1588–1638) accepted and advocated it. Throughout much of Protestantism up to and through the twentieth century this new chiliasm (premillennialism) has been influential.

Along with the rebirth of premillennialism there has also arisen the postmillennial view. In the eighteenth century in both England and America this interpretation had strong advocates such as Philip Doddridge (1702–51) and Jonathan Edwards (1703–58).

A BIBLICAL PERSPECTIVE

The position which has been expressed throughout this commentary and will be evident in the exposition of Rev 20:1–6 is shaped by several overarching considerations. Of first importance is the centrality of God's grace in Christ. Above all, every interpretation of Scripture must be in harmony with the central teaching of all Scripture, which is God's plan of redemption by grace alone and through faith in Christ alone. That focus precludes, for example, dispensational premillennialism, which allows for a two-covenant plan of salvation (one for Jews, another for Gentiles) or even a multiplicity of ways to salvation. Whenever Scripture speaks of redemption and the restraint and final destruction of evil, God accomplishes that in and through Christ, and through Christ alone. All of God's promises are and will be fulfilled in Christ (2 Cor 1:20). Moreover, God has already accomplished that salvation through the incarnation, ministry, suffering, death, and resurrection of Christ. While we still await the future consummation of God's promises when Christ returns, no additional or future actions by God nor by human beings are necessary to effect our redemption because Christ's work is finished and is completely sufficient.

A related consideration is the nature of the kingdom of God established by Christ and the full effect of Adam's sin (cf. Rom 5:12–21). Fallen human beings are inherently corrupt and depraved (cf. Rom 1:18–32; 2:9–24), and the present world likewise is characterized by futility and corruption. Therefore all hopes for a visible kingdom of God similar to kingdoms of this world, to be established among fallen human beings on this present earth, are misguided. That includes such hopes expressed by both premillennialists and postmillennialists. In particular, the two world wars in the twentieth century and the general worldwide decline of the human condition have largely eradicated the optimistic postmillennial view that things will get better and better. Jesus himself said that his kingdom is not of this world (Jn 18:36). The kingdom of God is not, and will never be, a worldly entity. God's kingdom comes invisibly and mysteriously, as the Holy Spirit attends the Gospel message and works in human hearts faith in Christ. To be sure, God is at work transforming Christians by his grace (cf. Romans 12), but the Christian's life in this world is always a struggle (Romans 7). In the plan of God the church will suffer worldly defeat (Rev 11:7; 13:7), and victory comes only through death and resurrection in Christ (2:10–11; 3:21; 12:11).

A final overarching consideration that may be mentioned is the hermeneutic of interpreting Scripture with Scripture. While many Christian groups, including Lutherans and fundamentalists holding various millennial positions, adhere to this hermeneutical principle, the decisive issue is *which* scriptural passages are to be used to interpret which other passages. The view of this commentary is that the eschatological outlook provided by the gospels and the epistles is clear, and that eschatological framework is the guiding principle for the interpretation of the apocalyptic visions in Revelation, rather than the other way around.

REVELATION 20:1–6

The Millennium: The New Testament Era, When the Dragon's Power Is Restricted

TRANSLATION

20 [1]And I saw an angel coming down out of heaven, who had the key of the abyss and a heavy chain in his hand. [2]And he took hold of the dragon, the ancient serpent, who is the devil and Satan, and he bound him for a thousand years, [3]and he threw him into the abyss and closed and sealed [it] over him so that he could no longer deceive the nations until the thousand years should be completed. After these [thousand years] it is necessary that he be released for a short time. [4]And I saw thrones, and they sat upon them, and judgment was given to them, and [I saw] the souls of the ones who had been beheaded on account of the witness of Jesus and on account of the Word of God, and who did not worship the beast nor its image, and who had not received its mark upon the forehead and upon their hand. And they came to life and reigned with Christ for the thousand years. [5]The rest of the dead did not come to life until the thousand years had come to an end. This is the resurrection, the first one. [6]Blessed and holy is the one who has a share in the first resurrection! Over these the second death does not have authority, but rather they are and will be priests of God and of the Christ, and they rule and will continue to rule with him for [the] thousand years.

COMMENTARY

SATAN THROWN INTO THE ABYSS (20:1-3)

John sees "an angel coming down out of heaven" (20:1). Apparently John did not recognize this angel as one of the angels that had appeared earlier in a vision or scene, for no adjectival identifying word is used to introduce him.

Frequently John uses the words "after these things" before "I saw." The fact that here in 20:1 John does *not* say "after these things I saw an angel ..." indicates that there is no "order of time" in relating the vision of the angel binding Satan to the visions that preceded it. We are not necessarily to understand that what John sees in 20:1-10 *follows in time* what he has just seen in Revelation 19, the marriage feast of the bride and the Lamb (19:1-10) and the second coming of Christ at the End (19:11-21). If John intended for the reader to understand that the "thousand years" (20:2-3) was to take place *after* the second coming of Christ, he most likely would have indicated that by using a phrase such as "after these things" to introduce 20:1-10. For example, in 19:1 he uses "after these things" to introduce the scene of the celebration that takes place *after* the judgment and overthrow of the harlot and the beast described in Revelation 17-18. As to the *time* when the "thousand years" do take place, see the commentary below on 20:2-7.

The angel has "the key of the abyss and a heavy chain in his hand" (20:1). In 9:1 "the key of the shaft of the abyss" was given to the star which had fallen out of heaven. That star is to be identified as "the angel of the abyss" in 9:11, that is, Satan, the "king" of the demons. He opened the shaft of the abyss (9:2) from which then came the demons who afflict the human race (9:3-6). Now here in 20:1 John sees an angel *from heaven,* that is, *from the presence of God,* who has "the key of the abyss"—not just of the shaft of the abyss, but of the abyss itself. This time "the angel of the abyss" (9:11), the dragon (20:2), will himself be put into the abyss. He is named "Satan" (20:2). Satan was given a key by which to open the shaft and unleash the demons on humanity (9:1-2). Now with another key, the key to the abyss itself, the abyss will be closed and secured after Satan has been cast into it. Satan cannot open what is shut with the angel's key from heaven (cf. Is 22:22; Mt 16:19; Rev 3:7). Jesus Christ is the one who holds "the keys of death and the grave" (Rev 1:18) and "the key of David," which is the key that locks and unlocks, and no one else can undo what is done with that key (Is 22:22; Rev 3:7).

To ensure that Satan cannot escape from the abyss, he is bound by "a heavy chain" (Rev 20:1). The chain must be so heavy that it would not be possible for the dragon to break it, as the Gerasene demoniac had broken ordinary chains (Mk 5:3-4). Here in Rev 20:1 the chain is not a physical, earthly fetter, but a metaphor for God's power, exercised by the angel, by which the dragon is bound.

THE BINDING OF SATAN

The angel "took hold of the dragon ... Satan, and he bound him for a thousand years" (20:2). Is it possible to determine when this binding of Satan took place? In the synoptic gospels there is a reference to Satan being bound. Jesus was casting out demons, and he was accused of doing so by the power of "Beelzebub, the ruler of the demons" (Mt 12:24; Mk 3:22; Lk 11:15). In Jesus' response, he equates Beelzebub with Satan (Mt 12:26; Mk 3:23, 26; Lk 11:18). Jesus countered the accusation by saying that if he were casting out demons by the authority of Satan, then Satan is divided against himself and as a result will meet his end, like a kingdom divided against itself (Mt 12:22–27; Mk 3:20–26; Lk 11:14–19). Then Jesus explained why he was casting out demons. In a parabolic saying Jesus spoke about someone entering into the house of "a strong man" Mt 12:29; Mk 3:27; Lk 11:21) to rob him of his goods. But before robbing the strong man, he must first "bind" (a form of the same verb used in Rev 20:2) the strong man (Mt 12:29; Mk 3:27). *The "strong man" is the devil, and the one who had come to rob him by first binding him is Jesus Christ.*

By this parabolic saying Jesus answered his critics by asserting that *in his ministry of exorcising demons he was setting people free from the demonization and slavery of Satan and displaying the power and authority by which he was binding Satan. This reference to the binding of Satan in the synoptic gospels is the only other place in the NT which speaks of such a binding of the devil.* The gospel of John does not refer to the binding of Satan but describes Satan as being "judged" and "cast out" when Jesus would be lifted up on the cross (Jn 12:31–33; cf. 16:11). *According to the four gospels, then, the devil was bound, conquered, judged, and cast out as a result of Jesus' saving ministry, culminating in his death on the cross and his resurrection. Therefore, the binding of Satan, the dragon, took place at Jesus' victory, accomplished by his ministry, death, resurrection, and ascension* (cf. also Rev 12:5, 7–10)—*at the beginning of the "thousand years"* (Rev 20:2).

Other references that may be of help in determining when the binding of Satan took place, *and so also when the "thousand years" or millennium started,* are 2 Pet 2:4 and Jude 6. In 2 Pet 2:4 the apostle says that the angels who sinned were put into "chains of darkness" by God. While the word there for "chain" is not the same as the one used in Rev 20:1, it bears a similar meaning, a chain or rope by which someone is bound in order to be carried off to prison or kept there. Their place of confinement in 2 Pet 2:4 is "hell." Having been bound with "chains of darkness" in hell, they are "being kept [there] for the purpose of judgment." This reference in 2 Pet 2:4 could well be describing the same event depicted in Rev 20:1–3. Jude 6 says of the angels who left their "dwelling," that is, their heavenly life with God, the Lord has and is keeping them by means of eternal chains under darkness for judgment of the great day. This reference in Jude says essentially the same thing that 2 Pet 2:4 does: the fallen angels are bound by chains and are kept in the darkness of hell until and for the purpose of judgment at the End. It seems that the event of the fallen angels being bound by chains and cast into the dark abyss is the same event that John sees in Rev 20:1–3, except that only the dragon, the leader of the fallen angels, is mentioned in 20:1–3. The biblical statements about binding in 2 Pet 2:4 and Jude 6 do not tell *when* Satan and the demons were bound. But they do affirm that the demons are bound in the abyss up to and for the purpose of the final judgment. If Rev 20:1–3 refers to this same action (and it probably does), it adds a time element during which the demons are bound—"a thousand years" (20:2)—and it also adds a description of what is taking place on earth during that same period in the following verses, 20:4–6.

The angel threw the dragon "into the abyss and closed and sealed [it] over him" (20:3). In Revelation 9, the demons under their king (9:11), the angel of the abyss, pour forth out of "the shaft of the abyss" (9:2) to afflict the human race. In Lk 8:31 the demons of the Gerasene demoniac beg Jesus not to send them back to "the abyss." In Rev 11:7 the beast which makes war with the two prophetic witnesses comes out of the abyss, and in 17:8 the beast which bears the harlot also comes out of the abyss. "The abyss" seems to be the *temporary* abode of the demons until the End, in contrast to "the lake of fire" (19:20; 20:10, 14, 15; 21:8), for at the End the dragon and all his hosts will be cast into "the lake of fire," which will be their *permanent* abode, where they will be tormented forever and ever (20:10).

The angel "closed" the abyss and "sealed [it] over him [the dragon]" (20:3). Seals were used to mark and guard an enclosure so that no one would enter or leave (e.g., Matt 27:66). Seals were also used to keep hidden or secret the contents of documents, and only the authorized person could break the seals and open the document (see Rev 5:1). Prisons also were sealed so that no one could enter or leave. So here in Rev 20:3 the abyss is closed and sealed. The dragon remains confined and cannot come out until the seal is broken and the cover of the abyss is removed. Only God, who authorized the closing and the sealing, can authorize the breaking of the seal and the uncovering of the abyss.

THE "THOUSAND YEARS"

The dragon is confined in the abyss for a "thousand years" (20:2–3). Only two other passages in the Bible mention a time period of a thousand years. In Ps 90:4 "a thousand years" are to God "like a day just gone past and like the watch of the night" (cf. Job 10:5). In 2 Pet 3:8 the apostle states "that a day with the Lord is like a thousand years and a thousand years like a day." Those two references suggest the hermeneutical method for interpreting the length of time represented by the "thousand years" that the dragon is confined. In both cases it is not a specific period of earthly history, exactly one thousand years long, that is in view. Rather, the "thousand years" is a general reference to a lengthy period of earthly time. God will bring his plans and purposes to completion according to his own time schedule.

While not referring to a time period, another illuminating reference to the number one thousand is found in Ps 50:10, where God says, "To me belongs all the wildlife of the forest, the beasts on a thousand hills." This is not a specific reference to exactly one thousand particular hills. Rather, it is *a number of completeness* designating all the hills of the earth. That a "thousand" can be used to signify *completeness* seems also to be evident in references such as Is 7:23, where "a thousand vines" represent abundant vines, vines in any and every place, whatever their exact number.

These biblical references indicate that a "thousand years" are not so much a literal chronological, period of time, but rather a period of time of completeness, a time when God will accomplish everything that he planned and set out to do. This indicates that this tradition of a thousand years in the sense of *the completeness and completion of all that God had planned to accomplish* was known in biblical times.

The stated purpose of the confinement of the dragon during the thousand years is "so that he could no longer deceive the nations" (Rev 20:3). In order for the church to fulfill her mission of proclaiming the Gospel to all peoples (cf. 10:11), the devil must not be permitted to ruin the church and thwart her efforts. Up to his imprisonment in the abyss, the devil could deceive and mislead people for the purpose of destroying them and any relationship they might have with God. This deception began in the Garden of Eden when the dragon, the ancient serpent (Rev 12:9), lied to and thus deceived Adam and Eve (Genesis 3). Ever since then he has been known as the liar and the father of lies (Jn 8:44; cf. 1 Jn 3:8). Before Christ's incarnation, death, resurrection, and ascension, Satan could even accuse and bad-mouth God's saints before God's heavenly throne (Job 1:6–11; 2:1–5; Zech 3:1–5). But at Christ's victory he was thrown out of heaven (Rev 12:7–12). Never again would Satan be able to accuse God's saints in his holy presence. Satan's exile from heaven was a direct result of Christ's saving ministry and death (cf. Lk 10:17–19; Jn 12:31–32), which exile was authorized and carried out at his ascension (Rev 12:5, 7–9).

When Satan was thrown out of heaven, was he also at that time bound and cast into the abyss? This seems to be so, for after his exile from heaven and his confinement to the earth he takes his wrath out on the woman in order to destroy her and her seed, the church (Rev 12:13–18). But he is restrained and hindered in his attempt to destroy her, for she is cared for and kept safe under God's protective hand (Rev 12:5–6, 14–16). *This restraint and holding back of Satan is depicted visually by his being bound and cast into the abyss. He was cast into the abyss "so that he could no longer deceive the nations," that is, so that he could not destroy the church (the woman) and her witness to Christ and her mission to the nations.* This interpretation agrees with what Jesus states in the synoptic gospels about his saving ministry, the result of which was the expulsion of Satan from heaven (Lk 10:18) and the binding of Satan as Christ set people free from slavery to the devil (Mt 12:22–29; Mk 3:20–27).

When the thousand years are completed, it will be necessary for the dragon to "be released for a short time" (20:3). Whatever the time period that the thousand years represents and whenever it takes place, what is certain (as implied by the number one thousand) is that *the divine purpose for which Satan had been bound will have been completed according to God's will.* During the season of time when Satan is bound and hindered, the church is able to carry out her mission of proclaiming Christ to the world (cf. Rev 11:3–13). After the appointed period of time, when God determines that the church's mission is completed, Satan will "be released for a short time." This short time is described in 20:7–10. No answer is given as to *why* he will be released, except that "it is necessary" (20:3) according to the sovereign will of God and his eternal plan for the consummation of all things.

This commentary's exposition of 20:1–3 is in harmony with the interpretation of many church fathers. Oecumenius (sixth century) in his Greek commentary on Revelation states that the binding of the devil took place "at the incarnation of the Lord." He cites as evidence Jesus' exorcisms (Mt 8:29) and the fact that Jesus, the "stronger one" (Lk 11:22), had come to bind the strong man (Mt 12:29; Mk 3:27).

Similarly Andreas of Caesarea (sixth century), who wrote a Greek commentary on Revelation a little later than Oecumenius, interpreted the purpose of the millennium to be "so that the Gospel can be preached everywhere in the whole world." He states that "the thousand years therefore are the time from the incarnation of the Lord until the coming of the Antichrist." Andreas credits a statement to Justin Martyr (ca. 100–ca. 165), who apparently considered both events, the binding of Satan in the abyss and his banishment into hell forever as having been determined by Christ's victory at his first advent, even if the final consignment of Satan to hell forever still lies in the future.

THE "FIRST RESURRECTION" (20:4–6)

Rev 20:4–6 describes those who come to life and rule with Christ during the period of the "thousand years" (20:2–7). Rev 20:4 says three things about those who are raised to life and reign with Christ during this time: (1) they sit on thrones and are given authority to execute judgment; (2) they suffer martyrdom because of their witness to Jesus; and (3) they do not worship the beast nor bear its mark. Does this threefold description refer to three different groups of people? Or does it refer to the same group, so that all of them sit on thrones, suffer martyrdom, and do not worship the beast?

John "saw thrones, and they sat upon them, and judgment was given to them" (20:4). This first description *could* refer to a select few among the entire company of people who are raised to live with Christ during the thousand years.

In 4:4 and 11:16 the twenty-four elders sit upon thrones around the throne of God in heaven. They represent the entire people of God of both testaments (twelve for the old covenant and twelve for the new). In Mt 19:28 Jesus said to the twelve disciples that when the Son Man would sit on his throne of glory, they "in the new age" would sit on twelve thrones, judging the twelve tribes of Israel (cf. Lk 22:30).

However, the picture in Rev 20:4 of those sitting upon thrones and judging might not be limited to just a select few. It *could also* include *all of God's saints*, who live, serve, and reign with Christ during the millennium. In 3:21 "the one who conquers" (that is, *all* the saints) will sit with Christ on his throne. In Dan 7:9 the prophet in a vision sees that "thrones were set in place, and the Ancient of Days was seated [enthroned]." Then "judgment was given to the saints of the Most High" (Dan 7:22), and later in the vision Daniel sees that all "the kingdom and the power and the greatness of the kingdoms under all the heavens will be given to the people of the saints of the Most High" (Dan 7:27). It is not entirely clear whether "judgment was given to the saints" in their favor (that is, they were judged favorably, justified), or whether the power of judgment was given to them to exercise on behalf of God. It could be the latter. In 1 Cor 6:2 Paul makes the statement "that the saints will judge the world." In Rom 5:17 Paul says that all those "having received the free gift of righteousness in life will rule through the one Jesus Christ." In Rom 5:17 there is a sense in which God's saints begin to rule with Christ *while still on earth,* and the saints before God's heavenly throne also rule.

Thus there is a biblical tradition that states that the people of God on earth already do rule and execute judgment on his behalf. What John saw here in Rev 20:4 in visionary form could well be this ruling and judging by God's saints on earth. Such a reigning with Christ is not limited only to the select few but is God's gift *to all in Christ.* Before God's throne in heaven this rule and judging, which belongs to all the saints, is represented by the twenty-four elders (4:4; 11:16). Such a ruling with Christ on earth and participating in the judgment of God over the nations may be difficult to understand, but it reflects the earthly ministry of Christ. As he rules everything (Mt 26:52–54, 63–64) and exercises all judgment on behalf of his heavenly Father (Jn 5:22–23; 12:31–33) despite appearances to the opposite, so also his church, in her ministry of witnessing for him to all the nations, does the same. This role of the church is also expressed in passages such as Mt 28:19–20, where Jesus authorizes the church—on the basis of all authority in heaven and on earth, which is given to Jesus—to carry out his ministry by baptizing and teaching on his behalf. *The way in which the church exercises judgment* may be seen, for example, in Mt 16:16–19 and Jn 20:21–23, where Jesus authorizes the church to open and shut heaven by forgiving the sins of the penitent and retaining the sins of the impenitent. These pronouncements by the church, of forgiveness or condemnation, are judgments proclaimed in the stead of Christ and on behalf of God.

Second, John saw those who participate in "the first resurrection" (Rev 20:5–6) as "the souls of the ones who had been beheaded on account of the witness of Jesus and on account of the Word of God" (20:4). Does this refer *only* to those who were *actually beheaded?* Does it have a wider reference to all those Christians who were martyred—put to death in any way—because of their Christian faith, as was Antipas, for example, in the church of Pergamum (2:13)? Or does it refer to *all Christians,* since all in Christ may, in one way or another, suffer for their Christian witness? If all Christians are in view here, then those martyrs who were beheaded serve as outstanding examples of the suffering that may come to all, in the same way that "the souls of those who had been slain because of the Word of God" underneath the altar in heaven represent *all* who have died in Christ (6:9–11).

The fact that a specific verb for beheading pointedly describes these martyrs *could* suggest that here it means *only* those who were *put to death in that particular way.* That John should use such a rare and gruesome word for beheading here in 20:4 could support the suggestion that he had in mind *only these* martyrs and not all Christians in their various sufferings. However, since crucifixion and martyrdom are used to represent the persecutions and sufferings that *all Christians do and will experience* (e.g., Mt 16:24–25), most likely the ones beheaded here in 20:4 represent *all Christians.* The deaths of the actual martyrs themselves would serve as epitomes or types of all sufferings and persecutions that all Christians experience because of their faith and witness. John's use of the verb "to behead with an ax" in 20:4 would then serve as *a violent reminder that all who live for and with Christ during the "thousand years"—the NT era, the church age—would suffer intense persecution of whatever sort it might be, such as was happening and had happened under Rome, for example, under Nero and Domitian.*

The words "martyr" or "witness," "to testify, witness," and "martyrdom" in the NT refer to *all Christians* in the sense that *all* are "witnesses" who give a "testimony" to the "witness" of Jesus and to the Word of God (cf. Lk 24:44–49; Jn 15:27; Acts 1:8). So also here in Rev 20:4 John sees those who had been beheaded because of their "witness" to Jesus. Rev 11:3–7 says that after the "two witnesses," who represent the entire Christian church, have finished "their witness," they were conquered and put to death. John himself on the island of Patmos suffered persecution because of the Word of God and his "witness" to Jesus (1:9). John did not suffer death as a martyr, yet he was still known as a martyr because of his witness and his suffering and persecution. *A martyr of Jesus, then, is a Christian who witnesses to the truth of Jesus and the Word of God,* for which he will suffer various forms of persecution. Whether he dies a martyr's death or not he is still a martyr of Jesus. *The biblical usage of "martyr"* and "martyrdom" supports an interpretation of beheading here in 20:4 as the epitome of the persecutions that all Christians experience. Christian witnesses (martyrs) back up and confirm their testimony with their lives, and if necessary, by the way they meet their death.

Third, John describes those who are raised to live with Christ during the thousands years as those "who did not worship the beast nor its image, and who had not received its mark upon the forehead and upon their hand" (20:4). While there may be some question as to who is represented by the ones on the thrones and the ones who were beheaded, *here it is clear that all Christians are meant.* All the faithful followers of Christ on earth do not worship the beast and its image, and they do not have the mark of the beast on their forehead and hand. All Christians have nothing to do with the beast.

The beast here in 20:4 is the same beast described in 13:1–10. It is the first beast, which comes from the sea and is an agent of the dragon (Satan, Revelation 12), and it represents all earthly and human powers (governmental, economic, societal, and so on) that the dragon manages to get under his control in his warfare against the woman, the church (12:13–18; cf. 20:10). An image is made for this first, political beast by the second beast (13:14–15), which is the beast from the earth; the second beast represents all false spirituality, in particular apostate Christianity. The second, religious beast evolves and later is identified as the false prophet (16:13; 19:20; 20:10) and as the harlot (17:1; 19:2). The religious beast makes an image of the political beast in order to encourage the human race to worship and serve this first monster which, under the dragon, dominates human affairs. In addition the second, religious monster places a "mark" (13:16) on the foreheads or hands of those who worship and serve the first beast (and its image) to identify its adherents. But the followers of Christ do not have such a mark, for they do not belong to the beast and the dragon. They have their own mark by which they are identified as saints of God in Christ. God has sealed them on their foreheads (7:3; cf. 9:4) with the seal of the name of the Lamb and the name of God the Father (14:1; 22:4). Those who bear the mark of the beast are destined for hell (19:19–21), while those who bear the mark of the name of Christ and his Father are destined for eternal life with God in the new heaven and earth (22:1–5).

Who are all these who live and reign with Christ during the thousand years? *They are the whole people of God, who follow his Christ, both those still on earth and those already in heaven.* The church militant on earth and the church triumphant in heaven, they rule with Christ on thrones (20:4; as represented by the twenty-four elders in 4:4; 11:16). Even those still on earth have in faith already died with Christ (Rom 6:3–4; Gal 2:20), and they also suffer persecution (Rev 20:4; as illustrated by the martyred saints under God's heavenly altar in 6:9), and they do not worship the beast nor bear its mark. While it is the whole people of God who live with Christ during the millennium, *the emphasis here in 20:1–6 is on those still on earth, the church militant* (cf. Rev 14:1–5). All Christians live and reign with Christ for a short time already while they live on earth during the thousand years (the NT or church age), and then upon their physical death they are brought before his heavenly throne where, at peace, they continue to live and reign with him and the heavenly Father (6:11).

THE TWO RESURRECTIONS

Those who come to life and live and reign with Christ *during the millennium* participate in "the first resurrection" (20:5–6). Some think that "came to life" in 20:4 and "did … come to life" in 20:5 refer to two physical resurrections, one (of the saints) at the beginning of the millennium and the other (of all people) at the present world's end. *The difficulty with that interpretation is that John does not speak of a second resurrection in 20:1–10.*

The scene in 20:1–10 is a unit to be interpreted first on its own merit and then related to what comes before and what follows. The relative independence of this unit is indicated by the words "and I saw" (20:1) which introduce the scene. These words are a formula that John often uses throughout Revelation to introduce *a new scene within a vision or a new vision itself,* or at times to introduce a particular thing within a scene (e.g., 5:6, 11; 8:13). John will also use the words "after these things/after this I saw" to introduce a new vision or scene (e.g., 4:1; 7:1; 15:5). *Here in Revelation 20* "and I saw" *is used in 20:1 and then again in 20:11. This indicates that 20:1–10 is a literary unit in its own right, and that it is followed by another literary unit, 20:11–15.*

In the first literary unit "the first resurrection" is mentioned (20:5–6), but not a second resurrection, though those who "come to life" *after* the millennium (20:5) are part of the second resurrection. In the following unit, 20:11–15, the second resurrection is described in fuller detail. It is the *physical* resurrection *of all bodies* at the End. This can be referred to as the second resurrection, in contrast to the one in 20:5–6, for it is the other resurrection that follows "the first resurrection" (20:5–6). *Since the two resurrections are in two different literary units and not in the same context* (except for the brief reference to the second resurrection in 20:5a) *they probably refer to two different kinds of resurrections. The first is the present, spiritual resurrection of all believers, and the second is the future, physical resurrection of all the dead on the Last Day.* To emphasize this difference, the two resurrections are presented differently. The first resurrection in 20:5–6 is presented only with the words "the resurrection, the first one." But the second resurrection in 20:13 is graphically described with these words: "and the sea gave up the dead which were in it, and death and the grave gave up the dead which were in them." While John does not speak of a second resurrection in 20:1–10, by mentioning a "first resurrection" (20:5–6), he seems to have in mind a second of *some* sort, for he knows that a universal physical resurrection will take place at the End (cf. Jn 11:24), as he will shortly view in Rev 20:11–15. But then what is this "first resurrection" mentioned in 20:5–6, and how is it to be related to the whole of the prophetic message of Revelation? Certainly the interpretation of this first resurrection plays an important part in attaining an understanding of what the millennium is all about. If the "first resurrection" is a *physical* one, then we have two bodily resurrections in Revelation 20 taking place at different times and in two different situations, the first one before the millennium and the second one after it at the End. If this were so, how could these two physical resurrections be reconciled with what is stated elsewhere in the NT concerning a bodily resurrection? Nowhere else in the entire Bible are two bodily resurrections referred to or described. For this reason many commentators refer to "the first resurrection" here in 20:5–6 as a *spiritual* resurrection.

Nowhere else does Scripture speak of two *physical* resurrections. Nor must one hear Revelation 20 as though it were speaking of two *physical* resurrections. Granted that this chapter does describe *two different resurrections*, the first one is spiritual and the second is one physical and bodily. This is consistent with the way in which the rest of the NT speaks. For example, in Jn 5:19–30, when Jesus spoke about his authority, he said (Jn 5:25) that the moment was then present when "the dead will hear the voice of the Son of God, and those who hear will come to life" (the verb is the same as is used in Rev 20:4–5). In Jn 5:25 the "dead" are unbelievers who, when they hear the Word of Jesus and believe, "come to life." Death and resurrection language is used to represent *conversion*, that is, the translation from *the spiritually dead state* of unbelief to the *resurrected* state of coming to life through believing in Jesus and his Word. At the end of his discourse concerning his authority, Jesus then spoke about the *bodily* resurrection at a future time when those in their "tombs will hear his voice and will come forth," either to the "resurrection of life" or to the "resurrection of judgment" (Jn 5:28–29). Here in the same context, the same discourse, *two different resurrections are described, one spiritual and one physical.* The spiritual resurrection takes place in the present time through conversion to faith in Christ, while the physical resurrection will occur at a future time, that is, at the consummation of the age.

In his writings the apostle Paul also refers to two resurrections, one *present* and *spiritual* and the other *future* and *physical.* The present, spiritual resurrection occurs through incorporation into Christ and as a result of Christ's bodily resurrection. In Eph 2:1–6 Paul reminds his hearers that formerly they were "dead" in their sins, but they are so now no longer, for in his grace God "*made [them] alive* with Christ" and he "*raised [them]* together in Christ Jesus." Similarly in Col 3:1–4 Paul reminds his readers that "if you *have been raised* with Christ, seek the things above." In Rom 6:1–5 Paul says that all of us who have been baptized into Christ Jesus "have been baptized into his death" (cf. Col 2:12). "We *were buried* with him through Baptism in his death, so that even as *Christ was raised* from the dead … so also we should walk in newness of life."As

John does in Jn 5:19–30, Paul also uses death to characterize the state of unbelief and separation from Christ, and resurrection language for conversion and newness of life in the state of faith as the result of being baptized into Christ, who has already been raised physically from the dead (Rom 6:1–5; Eph 2:1–6; cf. Col 3:1–4).

Those references in Paul with regard to the *spiritual resurrection of Christians in the present age* can be viewed in contrast to his references to *the physical resurrection at the end of the present age*. In 1 Cor 15:12–28 Paul relates Christ's bodily resurrection to the physical resurrection of all people at Christ's second coming (cf. 1 Thess 4:14–16). For this bodily resurrection he uses the words "to raise" and "to make alive" (1 Cor 15:22), which are used elsewhere for present, spiritual resurrection.

Is the "first resurrection" here in Rev 20:5–6 *spiritual* resurrection, that is, being raised to spiritual life in Christ? When viewed in contrast to John's graphic description of the *bodily* resurrection at the present world's end (20:13), it would certainly seem so. This would interpret John in Revelation in agreement with other parts of the NT which likewise refer to two resurrections, one spiritual, present now, and one physical, in the future at the End. Commentators who believe that John in Revelation 20 is speaking of two physical resurrections are creating a disagreement between Revelation 20 and the NT as a whole—a disagreement which would be difficult to reconcile. In Revelation 20 John is seeing *visually* what is presented verbally elsewhere in the NT, that a spiritual resurrection takes place in the present life when a person comes to faith in Christ, and a second resurrection, a physical one, will take place at the End.

A possible hindrance to interpreting "the first resurrection" as a spiritual one is the use of the word "resurrection" in 20:5–6. Almost every time this word occurs in the NT, it is in reference to *physical* resurrection. A possible exception would be Rev 20:5–6. In support of interpreting "resurrection" in a physical, bodily sense is Paul's reference in 2 Tim 2:18, in which he takes to task those who thought that the "resurrection"—that is, the bodily one—"had already taken place." Evidently some of Paul's hearers had understood his portrayal of Baptism and conversion as resurrection, a raising to life with Christ, as the *only* resurrection, and that there would not be another physical one at the End (cf. 1 Cor 15:12).

The use of "resurrection" here in Rev 20:5–6 might suggest that "the first resurrection" is a bodily resurrection, if John is using the word in the same sense as the other NT writers, especially Paul. However, before a final conclusion can be drawn, the use of the corresponding verb "raise" must be considered. When "raise" is used transitively in reference to "raising" the dead, most often its object is a physically dead person. When it is intransitive, it can likewise refer to a dead person miraculously rising up bodily. *But in Eph 5:14 it is used in reference to spiritual resurrection.* In this particular instance Paul quotes what appears to be either a combination of OT references or possibly a hymn verse, the source of which is unknown. It says, "Arise, O sleeping one, and rise up from the dead, and Christ will shine on you." Here the verb "rise" is used for spiritual resurrection from the death-like state of unbelief, or if the address is to people who are already Christians, the exhortation is to arise from a death-like state of apathetic indifference. Paul is urging his hearers who "have been raised from the dead" through faith in Christ increasingly day by day to live a new, resurrected kind of life. Thus *Christ's physical* resurrection is to be a constant reminder to them of their *spiritual* resurrection and the call to live accordingly as new creatures.

Similarly in Col 2:12 Paul voices the thought that "you were buried with him [Christ] in the Baptism, in which you have also been raised through faith of the working of God, who raised him [Christ] from the dead." Paul here uses the verb "to raise" to refer to God raising Christ bodily, and he uses a compound of that same verb to refer to the spiritual resurrection of Christians with Christ and its effect on the believers' lives. Paul also uses "to raise [Christians] together with [Christ]" in Col 3:1 and Eph 2:6 in reference to the *present, spiritual resurrection* of baptized believers in Christ. Eph 2:5 and Col 2:13 convey the same theological truth of the *present, spiritual resurrection* using the synonym "to make [Christians] alive together with [Christ]." Eph 2:6 even adds that God— already *now*, in a preliminary way—has also seated or enthroned Christians in heaven, even as those Christians (Paul, the Ephesians, and so on) still live on earth; the thought is the same as in Rev 20:4.

All these theologically parallel passages confirm that even though elsewhere in the NT "resurrection" most often is used for *physical* resurrection, in Rev 20:5–6 it may refer to the *present, spiritual resurrection* of Christians still on earth, in analogy with the use of the corresponding verb in Eph 5:14.

The relationship between Christ's physical resurrection and the new life of the Christian is an important thought throughout the NT. For example, in 1 Pet 1:3 the apostle gives thanks to God, "who according to his great mercy has given us new birth in a living hope through the *resurrection* of Jesus Christ." In Holy Baptism the Christian has died with Christ in order to be raised with Christ and to live now in "newness of life" (Rom 6:3–4). In Jn 11:23–26 Jesus said that because he is "the resurrection and the life," whoever believes in him will never again die (cf. Jn 8:51), and therefore the believer has "crossed over" or "been translated from" death into life (Jn 5:24). For that reason John can say here in Rev 20:6 that whoever participates in the first resurrection is blessed, because "over these the second death does not have authority."

THE TWO DEATHS

The "second death" is defined in 20:14 (see also 2:11; 21:8) as "the lake of fire." Those who have been spiritually resurrected with Christ will not be touched by the torments of hell. Christ has freed them from it, and it does not rule their thoughts and lives as they live with Christ here on earth (cf. Heb 2:14–15). "Rather they are and will be priests of God and of the Christ, and they rule and will continue to rule with him for [the] thousand years" (Rev 20:6). This recalls and reinforces what was said in 1:6, that Christ made God's people to be "a kingdom, priests to his God and Father," and in 5:9–10, that the victorious Lamb had "made them for our God a kingdom and priests, and they rule on the earth." This royal priesthood they exercise now and throughout the millennium (cf. 1 Pet 2:5, 9).

While there is no mention of the first death in 20:1–10 (or elsewhere in Scripture), if it were to be identified it would be a designation for the dead state of unbelief, as the word "death" is so used in Jn 5:24 and elsewhere (e.g., 1 Jn 3:14). The word "dead" is so used for the state of unbelief in Eph 2:1, 5. Thus John juxtaposes "the first resurrection" (Rev 20:5–6) and "the second death" (20:6). The relationship between these two ideas can be fully understood only if one keeps in mind that there also is a *second* resurrection and a *first* death. Because the Christian has experienced the first resurrection from the first death (conversion through faith), the second death has no hold on him, for he will participate in the second resurrection at the End—the bodily resurrection to life eternal, and not the bodily resurrection to eternal condemnation (Jn 5:28–29; Rom 6:3–5; Col 2:12–13; 3:3–4).

This then affirms that "the first resurrection" (Rev 20:5–6) is the spiritual coming to life by faith in Christ, for over those who have "a share in the first resurrection" (20:6) the second death (hell) has no power. If the first resurrection were the bodily resurrection to eternal life with Christ (e.g., 1 Corinthians 15), it would make little sense to say that the second death now has no authority over those already raised, body and soul, for they would be beyond the time when such a threat would pertain to them. But it does stand to reason to say that "the second death" (20:6; that is, "the lake of fire," 20:14) has no authority over believers in Christ who are still living here on earth, before the judgment at the End. On Judgment Day the second death *will* hold sway over all unbelievers, including those who fell away from the Christian faith back into the dead state of unbelief, and thus they will be thrown into the lake of fire (cf. 19:20). The dragon wars against the followers of Christ (that is, those who are participants in "the first resurrection"), as depicted in 12:13–17 (cf. also 1 Pet 5:8). Sadly in his war there are casualties: those who abandon the faith and forfeit God's gift of eternal life in Christ (cf. 1 Tim 1:19–20; Rev 3:1–3, 16). If the first resurrection were the physical one to eternal life and not the present, spiritual resurrection to faith, no such threats of hell could be hurled at those raised, for the bodily resurrected Christians will be beyond the realm in which such threats could still be applied to them. But Christians who have come to faith and by such faith live and rule with Christ here on earth during the millennium—to them such threats can still be hurled by the dragon, and the *possibility* of apostasy and damnation to hell is a reason for the Christian to continue to fear God during this earthly life (Lk 12:5). The purpose of the beatitude in Rev 20:6 is to instill hope and joyful confidence that God will preserve his people in the true faith until "the day of Christ Jesus" (his return) at the End (Phil 1:6). Like the other beatitudes in Revelation (1:3; 14:13; 16:15; 19:9; 22:7, 14), 20:6 has as its purpose the strengthening of the Christians' faith in God's grace in Christ by describing the joyful bliss of those who persevere in the faith until the End. "Blessed are the dead who are dying in the Lord from now on" (14:13).

"The rest of the dead did not come to life until the thousand years had come to an end" (20:5a). This first portion of 20:5 seems to be out of place or even redundant. Perhaps for those reasons many Greek manuscripts of Revelation omit it. But if this first sentence of 20:5 is genuine, *which it probably is,* a case can be made for its relevance both on the basis of what it says and on the basis of its position between the description of the millennium (20:4) and "the first resurrection" (20:5–6). Its content and its position certainly emphasize that *under no circumstances will those who are now spiritually dead, and who remain dead in the state of unbelief, live with Christ during the thousand years.* This sobering declaration is made after the description of those who do come to life and reign with Christ (20:4). Then and then only is the designation of "the first resurrection" presented (20:5–6), for the dead ones have already been excluded.

Who are "the dead" (20:5)? *In keeping with the understanding that "the first resurrection" is spiritual and the first death is the state of unbelief, "the rest of the dead" are all those throughout the thousand years who never come to faith in Jesus Christ.* They physically lived and died in impenitence and unbelief. Even while physically living on earth, they did not have true life (cf. Jn 10:10; 11:25; 14:6; 17:3) for they were dead in their sins and trespasses (cf. Eph 2:1; Col 2:13) and separated from God (cf. Eph 2:12; 4:18; Col 1:21). When they physically died and were buried, they remained "dead" (cf. Mt 8:22), separated from God and from his Christ as they wait for their eternal condemnation in the final judgment at the End. There is no state of blessedness for them. Only the bodily resurrection of the damned is in their future (cf. Jn 5:29). As mentioned above, John does not directly speak of a first death. However, his mention of "the rest of the dead" is a reference to the concept because "the dead" remain in the first state of death from their conception and birth (cf. Ps 51:5) up to the End. At the End they will come alive physically from the grave, only to be cast into "the second death," the lake of fire (Rev 20:6, 14). During the millennium, then, over these the second death *does* have authority, for sadly that is their future destiny (19:20; 20:10, 15).

SUMMARY OF 20:1–6

In summary, it is the view of this commentary that Tyconius and Augustine in the early church, and many interpreters who have agreed with them throughout church history down to the present day, are correct in interpreting the thousand years not as a literal, chronological period of time, but rather as a metaphor that symbolizes the completed era between Christ's first advent and his second coming at the end of this present world. The devil is bound so that he cannot destroy Christ's church nor prevent her godly task. Although Satan can cause the church much agony and suffering, he and the gates of hell cannot overcome her (cf. Mt 16:18).

This millennium began in the ministry, death, resurrection, and ascension of the Lord Christ. Satan was cast out of heaven at the ascension and enthronement of the Christ (the holy Child as portrayed in Rev 12:5–9), as a direct result of the victory of the Lamb, his death and resurrection (Revelation 4–5). Satan was also bound during Christ's earthly ministry (Mt 12:29; Mk 3:27; cf. Lk 11:21–22), which binding was completed by Christ's death and resurrection and demonstrated at his ascension, and Satan was cast into the abyss. Those who live and reign with Christ during the millennium because of "the first resurrection" (Rev 20:5–6) are the whole company of God's saints, the faithful followers of Christ, both the church militant on earth and the church triumphant in heavenly glory. The church militant reigns with Christ even now on earth (7:1–8; 14:1–5; 20:4); the church triumphant is with Christ in that heavenly peace before God's throne (7:9–17). The millennium, which is the present church age, will come to an end in God's own economy of time through the exalted reign of the Lamb, when the mission of the church is completed. At that time Christ will return to bring this present world to a close; all the dead will be raised bodily; and the judgment of all people will take place (20:11–15).

How "blessed and holy is the one who has a share in the first resurrection" (20:6), in this millennial reign of the Lord Christ! Those who rule with Christ during the thousand years are blessed, for "over these the second death ["the lake of fire," 20:14] does not have authority" (20:6). Even now while still on earth, Christians are and will continue to be priests of God and of the Christ, and their destiny is to reign with him now through the millennium and then forever in the new heaven and new earth (20:6; cf. 21:1–4).

In 1:6 the thought was first introduced that all those who have their sins forgiven through Christ's shed blood are as a result priests of God, royal priests (see also 5:9–10). Now here in 20:6 God's people are reminded that they are royal priests of God and the Christ. This is their blessing: they are privileged to serve their God and Lord throughout the millennium as his priests, as those who mediate the Christ and his redemptive work to an alienated world. This is their mission as they reign with Christ (cf. 1 Pet 2:9–10).

REVELATION 20:7–10

THE BATTLE OF GOG AND MAGOG AND THE FINAL DOOM OF SATAN

TRANSLATION

20 [7]And when the thousand years are finished, Satan will be let loose from his prison, [8]and he will go forth to deceive the nations which are in the four corners of the earth, Gog and Magog, to gather them for the war, the number of whom is as the sand of the sea. [9]And they went up over the expanse of the earth, and they encircled the encampment of the saints—the beloved city. And fire came down from heaven and devoured them. [10]And the devil, who was deceiving them, was cast into the lake of fire and brimstone, where also the beast and the false prophet are, and they will be tormented day and night forever and ever.

COMMENTARY

These verses describe the last battle in which the dragon desperately attempts once and for all to destroy the church and her mission of witness to Christ. This is the third and last view in which John sees this great battle. In the sixth scene (the sixth trumpet-angel, 9:13–21) of the second sevenfold vision of events on earth (8:6–11:19), John saw for the first time a glimpse of this battle. He saw a host gathered at the great river Euphrates, restrained and held back until the predetermined time when they would be released just before the End. In the sixth scene (the sixth censer-angel, 16:12–16) of the third sevenfold vision of events on earth (15:1–16:21), John saw a second view of this last battle. That time he saw the gathered host unleashed and engaged in actual battle at Armageddon. Now for a third and final time here in 20:7–10 John sees this terrible last battle—its conclusion.

At the conclusion of the thousand years, Satan is let loose from his prison, from the abyss (20:7). While in his temporary confinement during the thousand years, the dragon could not *directly* attack the woman (the church) in order to destroy her and her godly mission. He was hindered from doing so by God's care of the woman (12:6, 13–18; cf. 11:3–6). Through the two beasts (13:1–18), the beast and the harlot (17:1–18:24), the devil could cause all manner of suffering and agony and persecution for the people of the church. Now he is released to confront the church *directly,* and through devilish deceptions and force he attempts to keep the nations from hearing the witness of Christ as it is proclaimed by God's people. The limitations and restraints placed upon him by God during the millennium are now removed so that the world becomes increasingly hostile and violent toward the church and the message of Christ (cf. 20:3). Throughout the millennium, because of the warfare of the dragon through the beast and the harlot, the church always suffers opposition and persecution from the world—here and there and to a greater or lesser degree. Now that opposition and persecution will be worldwide and deadly.

The imagery that is used to portray this last great effort of the dragon to destroy the saints of God on earth is that of Gog and Magog. These two names represent the gathering of all the nations of the earth for this great war. The exact meaning of these names is not known. Possibly one or the other was the name of some ancient king of infamy and/or the name of an ancient and fierce people no longer known from historical records.

Whatever the source of the names, they eventually became terms which designated evil forces on earth opposed to God and godliness. In Ezekiel 38–39 they represent the enemies of God's people in a warfare in which they attempt to destroy the people of Israel. In this prophecy in Ezekiel, Gog is the prince and leader of the evil forces that are hurled against Israel (Ezek 38:7–9, 14–16). Gog comes from Magog, a land in the far north (Ezek 38:2, 15; 39:2). God promises to deliver his people from this onslaught just when they are about to be totally annihilated by striking the forces of Gog with fire from heaven (Ezek 39:3–6). So large in number would be the fallen hosts of Gog that their abandoned weapons would supply Israel with fuel for seven years (Ezek 39:9–10), and it would take the people of Israel seven months to bury their bodies (Ezek 39:12). God would invite the birds of prey and the wild animals to a celebration feast upon the fallen enemies, a feast furnished by God (Ezek 39:17–20). John saw this prophetic celebration banquet as a type of the great banquet of God which would celebrate the destruction of the beast and the false prophet in Rev 19:17–21. By the overthrow of Gog and his hosts, God would display his glory before all the nations of the world and to his own people (Ezek 39:21–29). Similarly in Rev 19:11–16 John saw the overthrow of the false prophet and the beast by the Lord Christ at his second coming at the End, and by such a judging of them Christ would display his own power and glory.

However the terms "Gog" and "Magog" were used to represent evil hosts, Augustine was correct when he rejected all narrow interpretations that tried to limit them to certain historical peoples or nations. He said in *The City of God* (20.11) that Gog and Magog symbolize *all the nations of the earth* which will rise up against the church in a final protest, "for this will be the last persecution …

which the holy church will endure from the whole world; just assuredly as the entire citizenry of Christ [is persecuted] by the entire citizenry of the devil, so much will it be everywhere over the earth."

Ezekiel 38–39 was for John the prophetic prototype of Gog and Magog as an illustration of the last great battle here in Rev 20:7–10. In Ezekiel (38:16) the hosts of Gog are hurled against the people of Israel in their own land. John sees the hosts of Gog and Magog covering "the expanse of the earth" as "they encircled the encampment of the saints—the beloved city" (Rev 20:9), that is, they attack the church of Christ wherever it is throughout the world. Prophetically speaking, the land and the people of Israel would typify the people of God in the church of Christ. The picture of "the encampment of the saints" (20:9) would also reflect the camp of the Israelites in the wilderness (Num 2:2), suggesting that the church of Christ is on her earthly pilgrimage, as were the people of God on a pilgrimage to the Promised Land (cf. Rev 12:14). The designation "the beloved city" (20:9) would also remind John of Mt. Zion, the city of God, which represents the heavenly Jerusalem (Ps 87:2; Heb 12:22; cf. Gal 4:24–26; Rev 21:2). Just as in Ezekiel (38:7–16) the evil hosts of Gog trampled underfoot the land of Israel and her people, so the church will be devastated by all the evil forces throughout the world (Rev 20:8; cf. 11:2). All the hosts of the devil, as represented by Gog and Magog, in this last great battle are singled-minded in their determination to destroy the people of God, the church of Christ, before the end of the present world comes.

The church would be totally annihilated were it not for God's direct intervention. In Mk 13:14–23 the Lord Jesus describes these last days of torment for the church. It will be "a tribulation" (Mk 13:19) of such magnitude that it is beyond comparing to any other since creation, and nothing comparable would ever happen again. In Mk 13:14 Jesus likens those days to "the abomination of desolation" mentioned in Daniel. But for the sake of his "elect, whom he has chosen," he will cut short those days (Mk 13:20). In Ezekiel 38–39 as Gog and his hosts, after having laid waste the land of Israel, were about to destroy God's people, God himself directly intervened to rescue them by sending fire on Magog (Ezek 39:6) and by striking the weapons from the hand of this host, whereupon the enemies would fall, never to rise again (Ezek 39:3–5). Here in Rev 20:9 John also sees that "fire came down from heaven." It devours the hosts of Gog and Magog, whereby God rescues his people.

"And the devil," who was the deceptive mastermind behind Gog and Magog, "was cast into the lake of fire and brimstone" (20:10) where also his henchmen, "the beast" and "the false prophet" (the harlot), had already been consigned (19:20). This is the final disgrace of the dragon, the ancient serpent. All through the millennium he had pursued the woman by means of the beast and the harlot, who is also the false prophet. He had caused her all manner of suffering (11:7–10). But now he is cast into hell, where he "will be tormented day and night forever and ever" (20:10). Even though he was let loose after the thousand years to manhandle the church in one last great effort to destroy her and her witness to Christ, he is now in total defeat and eternal shame. At the victory of the Lamb and at his ascension and coronation, Satan had been cast out of heaven (12:5–9). Now at the end of his last battle against the church (the woman of Revelation 12), at the end of Armageddon (16:16) and the battle of Gog and Magog, in total disgrace and defeat and utterly broken, he is consigned forever to the fires of hell. Never again can he speak against God's saints or pursue them or persecute and threaten them. The woman, the church, now stands victorious because of her bridegroom and Lord, the Christ (cf. 1 Jn 5:4–5; Rev 2:10). She now stands vindicated before God because of the victory of the Lamb, and she shall reign forever with her Lord and God in his peace and glory.

THE PURPOSE OF THE TRIBULATION

Why will the Lord God permit Satan to be unleashed after the thousand years (20:3)? What is the purpose the battle of Gog and Magog (20:8; called Armageddon in 16:16)? John is given an answer as to the purpose of the millennium: Satan's imprisonment is so that "he could no longer deceive the nations" (20:3), that is, so that Christ's church can carry out his mission to proclaim the Gospel to the whole world. But no such explicit answer is given as to why God will free Satan at the millennium's end to wage the last battle.

In Revelation 12 John was shown the reason why the dragon hunts down the woman in order to destroy her: because Satan, in his hatred of God, could not destroy the holy Child (12:3–5). So the devil takes his fury out on the woman and her seed, the church (Rev 12:6, 13–18). Even though the church suffers much, God protects her and cares for her (12:6, 14). *Through her sufferings and persecution the church now reflects the suffering of Christ on the cross as she witnesses to that event, and by her steadfast faith and hope she exhibits the resurrection and life of Christ as she proclaims the saving message of Christ's victory.*

All this is to the glory of God. As God provides for and protects his church in her warfare with the dragon (Revelation 12) and Satan's two beasts (Revelation 13), he shows forth his glory so that all might come to recognize him as the only God, who is the Creator of all life, and who alone is the Savior and Judge of the human race (Rev 15:3–4; cf. Jer 51:33–57).

Similarly, it may be that God will release Satan and permit him to ravage the church *so that he can glorify his name as he rescues her and then casts Satan into hell.* It may be that there is a prophetic type of such an interpretation in Ezekiel 38–39, concerning Gog and Magog. According to Ezekiel, it will be God who unleashes Gog upon Israel, his people (Ezek 38:3–16). But then God himself will also save the faithful remnant of Israel and judge Gog and his hosts (Ezek 38:22). The whole event of Gog and his hosts invading and plundering and nearly destroying Israel would happen under God's sovereign and gracious will *so that when he miraculously delivers his people and then judges Gog, he could show forth his greatness and make known his name among all the nations* (Ezek 38:23; 39:1–7). As a result *God would display his glory to all the peoples of the earth* (Ezek 39:21), and he would show especially to his own people, whom he has just delivered from Gog, that he is Yahweh, the Lord their God (Ezek 39:22). Thus all the nations of the world would then be encouraged to repent and come to recognize that Yahweh is also *their own God* (Ezek 39:23–29).

Since John in Rev 20:8 uses "Gog and Magog" from Ezekiel 38–39 as names of the combatants in the last great battle (which he also calls Armageddon in Rev 16:16), this imagery of the battle in which Gog would be let loose to tear into Israel could suggest why God will let Satan loose from his imprisonment in the abyss after the millennium. *God will permit Satan to assault and nearly destroy his people so that he can show his might and saving grace as he delivers his church and judges Satan and casts him into hell.* As God lets Satan have his way with the church, and as the church remains faithful despite all the terrifying sufferings and persecutions, *God will use this testing of the church and her fidelity to her Lord Christ as a way to demonstrate the power of the Gospel and to judge Satan visibly.* It is as if God were to say, "Satan, you had pillaged my saints on earth, but you could not take them from me. By their faithfulness they proclaimed my glory to all peoples, and because of your unjust attacks on them, I now damn you and all your hosts to the everlasting fires of hell." Thus God will show forth his glory as the only God and Savior and Judge of the entire human race. One biblical example of how God permits Satan to strike his saints for the purpose of revealing his grace and judging or showing up Satan is that of Job. God permitted Satan to strike Job for no justified reason (Job 2:3; cf. 1:1, 8). By this Job and his faith were severely tested (Job 1:6–12; 2:1–7; 23:10–12). But Job remained faithful and did not deny his Lord and Redeemer (Job 1:22; 2:10; 16:19–21; 19:23–27). It may be deduced that God not only tested Job to strengthen his faith through the ordeal, but also, through the testing, God displayed the enduring power of his grace by Satan's inability to destroy the faith and trust of one of God's saints. The end result of God permitting Satan to strike Job was not only the tested strengthening of Job's faith, but also the judgment of Satan—all for exhibiting the glory of God!

Certainly the ordeal that the church suffers now and will suffer in much greater degree as the last battle of Armageddon draws near will test her faith. This is testing by which her faith is and will be strengthened, to the glory of God in his Christ. But it is also a victorious testing by which God will display Satan's inability to destroy the church's faith, and thus God will demonstrate Christ's victory over Satan. This being the case, the church, the bride of Christ, will participate in the judgment of Satan—for she will be a witness against the dragon's arrogant (and ultimately futile) attempt to subvert her trust in her God, and she will be *a witness to the sustaining power of God's grace in his Christ, by which he holds his saints true to the End. That may well be the purpose for which God releases Satan.*

It is also often asked, when will the millennium end and Satan be let loose? When will the last great battle take place? Are we, perhaps, already in it? Though no timetable is given (for this is in the hidden wisdom of God, Mk 13:32–37), signs and events occur that alert the church that the battle of Armageddon and the End are close at hand (cf. Rev 1:3; 22:7). In Matthew 24 (cf. Mark 13; Luke 21) Jesus, shortly before his crucifixion, spoke about the "great tribulation" (Mt 24:21) and his second coming. He described certain signs and events that would take place—events that would reveal that the last sufferings and the End were very near (Mt 24:3–51). In particular, the sign of "the abomination of desolation" (Mt 24:15), that is, the great apostasy within visible Christendom, points to the imminent presence of the "great tribulation" (Mt 24:21). This "great tribulation" is the equivalent to the battle of Armageddon (Rev 16:16), which is also the battle of Gog and Magog (20:8), for both the "tribulation" and the great battle happen just before the End (cf. Mk 13:24–26; Rev 20:7–15).

There may be such terrifying days of evil and suffering for the church at any particular time, so that the Christians will be reminded of the last battle of Armageddon at the End, days of such evil that we think we might already be facing the assault by Gog and Magog. When such times of suffering happen in various places and at different times throughout the history of the church, they may be viewed as types of the final battle at the End, microcosms or miniatures of the bloodiest war (in terms of spiritual casualties) that will ever take place. Though "microcosmic Armageddons" are localized and limited in scope, so that only certain Christians at any given time would experience one, nevertheless, for them it would be as if it were *the* one at the End.

In Jesus' eschatological discourse (Matthew 24; Mark 13; Luke 21), the fearful days of suffering for the Jewish Christians that they would experience immediately before the destruction of Jerusalem would be for them their great affliction, after which the end of Jerusalem would come (Mt 24:15–22; Mk 13:14–24; cf. Lk 21:20–27). It was their Armageddon, in which Satan would sorely test them, and during which they probably would think that the End was at hand—and not just the end of Jerusalem. For the rest of Christendom and ever since then, each Armageddon in microcosm serves as a type of *the* Armageddon and as a warning to all Christians that such a microcosmic assault by Gog and Magog can happen at any time and in any place. Thus whenever the battle is joined, every such attack is a warning and a sign that the great battle of Armageddon will certainly come in God's own time—all to God's glory in his Christ.

REVELATION 20:11–15

THE BODILY RESURRECTION AND THE LAST JUDGMENT

TRANSLATION

20 ¹¹And I saw a large white throne and the One sitting on it, from whose face the earth and the heaven fled and a place was not found for them. ¹²And I saw the dead, the great and the small, standing before the throne. And books were opened, and another book was opened, which is [the book] of life, and the dead were judged by the things that had been written in the books according to their works. ¹³And the sea gave up the dead which were in it, and death and the grave gave up the dead which were in them, and they were judged, each according to their works. ¹⁴And death and the grave were thrown into the lake of fire. This is the second death: the lake of fire. ¹⁵And if anyone was not found written in the book of life, that one was thrown into the lake of fire.

COMMENTARY

The church has finished her mission. The *demonic* enemies who persecuted her have been banished to hell. She has been adorned as the bride of Christ (19:6–8). Now the moment has arrived for the last and final judgment of the *human race*.

John sees "a large white throne and the One sitting on it" (20:11). In the inaugural vision of heaven (4:1–5:14) which introduced the prophetic message of Revelation, John had seen this "throne" and "One sitting" on it (4:2). Here in 20:11 the throne is described as "large" and "white." In 4:2 the throne of God and his presence upon it are the *central and dominant* feature; around the throne are the twenty-four thrones of the elders (4:4) and the four winged creatures (4:6–7). Here in 20:11 the throne of God and his presence on it are the *only* feature, for now God on his throne is the supreme judge before whom the entire human race stands. Perhaps for this reason John notes the *large size* of the throne, for it alone is present, and the "throne and the One sitting on it" occupy and fill the entire scene. The whiteness of the throne would indicate the purity of the holy justice that will be dispensed. In Dan 7:9–10 the prophet sees a heavenly vision of God the Father, "the Ancient of Days," dressed in white. God was holding court and books of judgment were opened. Here in Rev 20:11 the whiteness of the throne is mentioned, for God's judgment will be righteous and no one can gainsay it or dispute its truth.

"The One sitting" on the throne is God the Father (as is clear in 5:6–7), and here he is the Judge at the End. Elsewhere in Scripture often the Son of God, Jesus Christ, is portrayed as the Judge. For example, in Jn 5:22–23 Jesus says that "the Father judges no one, but he has given all judgment to the Son, so that all should honor the Son just as they honor the Father." In Mt 25:31–46 Jesus, as the Son of Man on his throne of glory at the End, will judge the human race as a shepherd separates the sheep from the goats. In 2 Cor 5:10 Paul says that "it is necessary that we all appear before the judgment seat *of Christ.*" However, Paul also says in Rom 14:10 that "we all will stand at the judgment seat *of God.*" The ultimate judgment is under and by the authority of God the Father. But because Jesus Christ suffered and died in the stead of the human race, receiving God's judgment against all humanity's sin (Rom 5:16–19; 8:3–4; cf. Is 53:3–10), he earned the right to execute the judgment. God the Father and God the Son, Jesus Christ, are one in their relationship to the world (Jn 10:30) and act together (Jn 5:19), also in the judgment at the End (Rev 6:15–17). After the End the Father and the Son will be equally honored in occupying the same throne in the new heaven and earth (22:3).

So fearful is this judgment of God that "the earth and the heaven" attempt to flee from God's face (20:11). Already in 6:12–17, in the sixth scene (the sixth seal) of the first vision of events on earth (6:1–8:5), as John sees a scene of the End, the end of the present world, people of all classes try to hide themselves "from the face of the One sitting on the throne and from the wrath of the Lamb" (6:15–16). In the Garden of Eden Adam and Eve attempted to hide from God after they had disobeyed him (Gen 3:8). Here in Rev 20:11 it is "the earth and the heaven" that flee from the face of God. In 16:17–21, in the seventh scene of the third vision of events on earth (15:1–16:21), John saw that "every island passed out of sight, and mountains vanished from view" (16:20). This illustrates the terrifying impact that God's judgment will have even on the created earth.

The judgment of the earth and the heaven could be a poetic depiction of the fearful judgment of the human race. For example, in Zeph 3:8d God says, "By the fire of my jealous anger the whole world will be consumed." In Zephaniah "the whole world" includes all "nations" and "kingdoms" (Zeph 3:8b), which he will gather to pour out on them his wrath. In Rev 20:11 the fleeing of "the earth and the heaven" could thus be a pointed indication that all *human* life stands in fear of God's righteous judgment. However, it may also point to the *physical* world and thus suggest that in God's judgment the present earth and heaven will be dissolved and disappear—to be restored, recreated, as the new heaven and new earth. In 21:1 John will see "a new heaven and a new earth" which have taken the place of "the first heaven and the first earth," which have "passed away" (cf. 2 Pet 3:10–13), for God will "make all things new" (Rev 21:5; see also Ps 102:26; Is 51:6; Mk 13:31; 2 Pet 3:10).

But the chief focus of the judgment of God and his Christ will be the human race. All the dead stand before God's throne (Rev 20:12). The universal resurrection described in 20:13 is understood to have already taken place in 20:12. Now all the people of the earth stand before the awesome presence of God. As stated in Jn 5:28–29, the eternal destiny of each person will be declared—either eternal life or an eternal judgment of death. The people will be "judged by the things that had been written in the books" that "were opened" for the occasion (Rev 20:12). The opened books contain the complete record of "their works." In Dan 7:10, when the Ancient of Days took his seat in the midst of his "law court," "books were opened." Records are kept and deeds are recorded in scrolls or books (cf. Jer 32:8–14). God keeps his accurate record of each individual's life and deeds. The "books" are a visual representation of God's indelible and unerring mind and remembrance.

The last phrase of Rev 20:12 implies that all "the dead," both the wicked and God's own saints, are judged on the basis of what is recorded in the "books," for all stand before his judgment throne. But while the wicked are found guilty and sentenced because of their "works" recorded in the books (20:12–13), God's own people are acquitted—declared innocent and righteous—not on the basis of their works, but on the basis of "another book," because their names are recorded in the book of life (20:12, 15). While Christians also sin and thus could have had their sinful deeds recorded in the "books" of God's judgment in 20:12, other passages suggest that God keeps a record only of their good works, the deeds done out of faith and by the love of Christ (see Mt 25:34–40). So then John not only sees the books of judgment, but also "the book of life." All whose names are written in "the book of life" are recorded in the heart of God as ones who have been washed in the blood of the Lamb (Rev 3:5; 7:9–17). For this reason in the books of judgment only their good deeds are recorded and not their sins, for their sins and guilt have been blotted out of God's mind and so will not be the object of his righteous anger and judgment. God lists the good deeds of his saints, and they will be recalled as visible demonstrations of their saving faith in his grace, wrought for them by Christ, the victorious Lamb (cf. Mt 5:16; 7:15–20).

The idea of a "book of life" in which God records the names of all the people who belong to him reaches back into the OT. In Exodus 32, after the Israelites had committed idolatry by worshiping the golden calf, Moses again ascended Mt. Sinai and pleaded with God to forgive their sin. But Moses asked that if God would not do so, God should blot him out from "your book, which you have written" (Ex 32:32). God answered that whoever sinned against him would have his name removed from the book (Ex 32:33). Ps 69:28 refers to the "book of the living" in which the names of the righteous are written. In Dan 12:1 "everyone who is found written in the book" will be delivered at the End, for they will be raised to eternal life (Dan 12:2). In the NT outside of Revelation "the book of life" is mentioned only once, in Phil 4:3, where Paul reminds his hearers that his fellow workers together with him have their "names in the book of life." In Revelation it is mentioned in six verses. Christians who are victorious by grace will walk about in the white garments of Christ, and their names will not be erased from the book of life (3:5). The adherents and worshipers of the beast are not written in the book of life (13:8; 17:8). Those who are not written in the book of life will be judged for their sins (20:12) and thrown into hell (20:15). And those whose names are written in the book of life will be declared righteous (20:12) and will enter the new Jerusalem (21:27).

A vivid description is given of the *universal resurrection* at the End. The fact that John describes the resurrection (20:13) *after* he has seen the judgment (20:12) seems to be out of sequence. But events are not necessarily related in a strictly sequential order. Perhaps in 20:12–13 the judgment is shown first for the purpose of emphasis. All members of the human race will be raised from their graves in order to stand before the judgment seat of God, and so John sees the judgment first.

"And the sea gave up the dead" (20:13). How many have gone down to the sea in ships (Ps 107:23; Is 42:10) only to have the sea became their grave. The fact that in addition to death and the grave, John sees the sea giving up its dead suggests an emphasis on the bodily resurrection of the dead. It would be sufficient to refer to a resurrection by speaking only of "death" giving up its dead. But to say that "the sea gave up the dead which were in it," then to add the thought that also "the grave" would give up its dead, makes certain that John understood the resurrection to be a *bodily* and *physical* resurrection. The bones remaining from those who died on land would testify to their existence and could be raised to life (cf. Ezek 37:1–14). However, there would be no visible remains of those lost at sea. The reference to the retrieval of the dead from the sea (Rev 20:13) implies that even those without any known physical remains will be raised *bodily* on the Last Day.

John also sees "death and the grave" giving up their dead (20:13). "Death" would be the all-embracing term. All the bodies of the dead are released from "death" itself. A part of them come out of the sea, and others come out of graves in the earth. In Dan 12:2 all who "sleep in the dust of the earth will awake, some to everlasting life" and others "to shame and eternal contempt." In Ezekiel 37 the prophet sees in a vision a valley of dry bones which represent the people of Israel (Ezek 37:11). In the vision Ezekiel sees the bones take on flesh, and then the breath of life comes into the bodies and they come to life (Ezek 37:1–14). This vision in Ezekiel 37 promises the return and restoration of exiled Israel (Ezek 37:13) at the same time that it provides a typological picture of the physical resurrection of the dead, and it presents a graphic depiction of God's physical resurrection of dead bodies.

Nowhere else in the NT is there such an earthly and graphic picture of the bodily resurrection at the End as here in Rev 20:13. In 1 Corinthians 15 Paul describes the relationship between Christ's bodily resurrection and the general physical resurrection at the End, with the emphasis on the resurrection of the Christians. He speaks of how the dead are raised and that the mortal body will be changed into the immortal (1 Cor 15:16, 35–41, 53–55), but he gives no earthly description of the dead rising from the graves (cf. 1 Thess 4:13–16). There is the description of the bodily resurrection of Lazarus from the grave in Jn 11:38–44. This can serve as an illustration of the bodily resurrection of all the dead at the End, and thus it is akin to John's vivid description here in Rev 20:13.

Finally, at the End in the judgment of God "death and the grave were thrown into the lake of fire" (20:14). Already in 19:20 the beast and the false prophet (the harlot) were cast into the lake of fire. The devil (the mastermind behind them) was thrown there too in 20:10. Now here in Rev 20:14 John sees "death and the grave" join them. *The last enemy of mankind is now forever destroyed together with its terror and fear* (1 Cor 15:26; Heb 2:15). *Now the victorious reign of the exalted Lord Christ has been accomplished* (cf. 1 Cor 15:24–28). As Isaiah (25:8) had prophesied, the Lord has now swallowed up death forever and wiped away every tear from all faces. Paul proclaimed a loud amen in Christ to this when he said, "Death has been swallowed up into victory. Where, O death, is your victory? Where, O death, is your sting?" (1 Cor 15:54–55). This last enemy, death and the grave, has been swallowed up forever!

Rev 20:15 concludes the entire chapter. Those "not found written in the book of life" are then "thrown into the lake of fire." The "lake of fire" is the ultimate destination of all idolaters, all who love and do what is false (21:27; 22:15), all those not in Christ, who did not do the will of his Father, who did no kindness to the least of his brothers (Mt 7:21–23; 25:41, 46). "The lake of fire" is equivalent to Gehenna, which was the Hebrew name of a ravine just south and west of Jerusalem. This ravine or valley was the site of the abominable worship of burning children, which took place during the reigns of Ahaz and Manasseh. Thus "Gehenna" became a name for hell and its eternal fiery torment. Its fiery torments are never extinguished (Mk 9:47–48). "The breath of the Lord God like a flow of burning sulfur sets it on fire" (Is 30:33).

But those "written in the book of life" (Rev 20:15) shall inherit eternal life in righteousness forever with God and the victorious Lamb (21:27).

The New Heaven and New Earth Portrayed as the Heavenly City Jerusalem

REVELATION 21:1–8

THE NEW HEAVEN AND NEW EARTH

TRANSLATION

21 ¹And I saw a new heaven and a new earth. For the first heaven and the first earth had passed away, and the sea is no longer. ₂And the holy city, new Jerusalem, I saw coming down out of heaven from God, prepared like a bride adorned for her husband. ³And I heard a loud voice from the throne saying, "Behold, the tabernacle of God is with men, and he will dwell with them, and they themselves will be his people, and God himself will be with them [as their God]. ⁴And he will wipe away every tear from their eyes, and death shall no longer be, nor sorrow nor crying nor pain shall be ever again, because the first things have passed away." ⁵And the One sitting on the throne said, "Behold, I make all things new!" And he says, "Write, because these words are faithful and true." ⁶And he said to me, "It has come into being. I am the Alpha and the Omega, the Beginning and the End. To the one who is thirsty, I myself will give from the spring of the water of life freely. ⁷The one who conquers will inherit these things, and I will be his God and he will be my son. ⁸But as for the cowards and unfaithful persons and those who have made themselves vile, and murderers and sexually immoral persons and sorcerers and idolaters and all the liars, their portion [shall be] in the lake which burns with fire and brimstone, which is the second death."

COMMENTARY

THE NEW HEAVEN AND THE NEW EARTH
(21:1)

The conclusion to the entire prophetic message of Revelation is the vision of "a new heaven and a new earth" (21:1). At the end of the first world, John had seen the judgment of the harlot and the beast (17:1–18:24), the marriage feast of the Lamb and the second coming of the Lord Christ (19:1–21). Then he saw a flashback of the binding of the dragon at Christ's first advent, followed by the millennium (20:1–6), the loosing of the dragon for the battle of Gog and Magog just before the End (20:7–10), and the resurrection and the judgment of human race (20:11–15). John is now prepared to see *beyond* the end of the first world to the creation of "a new heaven and a new earth" (21:1).

In 20:11, as God on his throne held the last judgment, "the earth and the heaven fled" from his face "and a place was not found for them." This suggests that the present heaven and earth originally created by God (Gen 1:1) would not be a fit home for his resurrected and righteous saints. Under the judgment of God because of the sin of the human race, the earth was cursed and thus suffered decay and ruin. But as Isaiah had prophesied (65:17), God says, "Behold, I am creating a new heaven and a new earth," and "the former things," that is, the former heaven and earth and all the travail therein, "will not be remembered and will not arise in the mind." Then Isaiah (65:20–25) describes existence and life in the new heaven and new earth. His words seem to be an apt metaphorical description of the spiritual life on the present earth that God will bring about at the advent of the Messiah. But this description, in turn, by way of the messianic reign here on earth, is also a typological picture of life in the new heaven and new earth after the judgment and resurrection at this present world's end. According to Isaiah (66:22) this new heaven and new earth will endure forever before God as his own people will live forever.

God's promise of "a new heaven and a new earth" is found in 2 Pet 3:10–13, where the apostle reminds his hearers that the present heaven "will pass away," and the "elements" will burn and be destroyed, and the earth will be laid bare. The Lord Christ during his earthly ministry asserted that the present "heaven and earth will pass away" (Mt 24:35). Though he did not describe the new heaven and earth, he did refer to the transcendent quality of the life to come (e.g., Lk 20:34–36), which will be in "paradise" (Lk 23:43). The apostle Paul, while not speaking directly of a new heaven and earth, seems to imply such when in 1 Cor 15:35–42 he speaks of the differing bodies of earthly creatures and of the differing glory of the sun and moon and stars as indicative of the surpassing glory of human bodies that die and are raised in the resurrection.

Here in Rev 21:1 John sees "a new heaven and a new earth" which take the place of "the first heaven and the first earth." But he gives no description of the

passing away of the present heaven and earth (see 2 Pet 3:10–13) and no description of the new, except to say "the sea is no longer" (Rev 21:1). What is meant by
"the sea"? Does this refer to the physical bodies of waters on our present earth?
Or is "the sea" to be understood as the chaos that separates the human race from
God? While either interpretation could be received, the former might present
some difficulty, for it could suggest that in the new creation there will be no
bodies of water, such as oceans and lakes. For that reason "the sea" in 21:1 seems
to represent the chaos caused by sin and the fearful gulf that separates God
and humanity resulting from human sin and rebellion against God. In the OT
at times "the sea" is a terrifying embodiment of the violent tumult that exists
between people and God, and between humans. The sea lends itself toward such
a portrayal because to ancient people it held a terror, especially when its boiling
waves threatened and oftentimes destroyed human life (e.g., Ps 107:23–30). The
sea is home to the evil serpent (Amos 9:3), Leviathan. In the earthly ministry
of Jesus too, the sea was a threat to the apostles, a threat which Jesus conquered
(e.g., Mt 8:24–27; 14:24–33).

Certainly what is *not* present in the new heaven and earth is what the sea in
Scripture represents: its terrifying dread and the chaos and gulf that separates
mankind and God because of mankind's sin and rebellion. If the new heaven
and earth is the renewed and restored present heaven and earth and is thus
patterned after the original, there may well be waters collected together into
bodies of waters and seas, just as the first earth had (Gen 1:9–10; cf. Job 38:8; Ps
95:5). But the sea in its storm-tossed, boiling rage, and as the symbolical domain
of the primeval serpent, will no longer be present. That is, even if an ocean
were physically present in the new earth, it would not have its terror and fearful
character, for *that* sea has passed away. In the new heaven and earth the sea will
be calm and at peace (cf. Mk 4:35–41; 6:45–52). Thus calmed, such a sea will
never again remind God's people of the fearful gulf that once separated them
from God's holy presence.

Elsewhere in Revelation "the sea" does appear as a symbol which reminds
the saints of God still here on the present earth of the separation between God
and his fallen creation. As such a symbol it is also used to depict the arena of
the horrible warfare that the dragon and his minions wage against the church
militant. In Rev 4:6 John sees a "sea" before God's heavenly throne which in
appearance was like crystal clear glass. That sea was a gentle reminder to John
of his present separation: though a saint of God, he was still on his earthly
pilgrimage and not yet elevated to God's holy presence in heaven. John does *not*
see that glassy sea in the new heaven and earth, for in the recreated earth, he
and God's people will never again be separated from their Creator and Lord. In
13:1 one of the beasts called forth by Satan comes from the sea to terrorize the
woman of Revelation 12, the church. In 15:2 the "glassy sea mixed with fire"
depicts the field of warfare here on earth, upon which takes place the awesome

conflict between God's people and one of the beasts of the dragon—a warfare that continues throughout the entire NT era from Christ's ascension to his second coming. This "sea" John does *not* see in the new heaven and earth, for it is no longer present.

Isaiah uses a symbol of a quiet and peaceful sea when he prophetically describes the messianic age. In Is 11:9, when speaking of how the earth will be full of the knowledge of Yahweh and danger no longer will exist, he says that the fullness of divine knowledge will be like waters covering the sea. Similarly Hab 2:14 states that when the earth is "filled with the knowledge of the glory of Yahweh," it will be like waters covering the sea. Both prophets, by way of analogy, are saying that the knowledge of the Lord will cover the earth in the same way that waters cover or fill the sea, representing the righteousness and peace of God which according to Isaiah (11:1–10) the Branch of Jesse will bring. It might be conjectured that any physical bodies of water in the new heaven and earth would also be reminders that the righteousness and the glory of God in Christ will fill the newly recreated earth (cf. Rev 22:1), while at the same time the sea, which once reminded God's people of agony and suffering in the conflict with the old evil foe, is now gone forever.

THE NEW JERUSALEM (21:2)

Viewing the new heaven and new earth, John's attention immediately is drawn not to a physical description of the new heaven and earth but to "the holy city, new Jerusalem … coming down out of heaven from God" (21:2). This "new Jerusalem" is not the old historic city of the present earth restored. Rather it comes "from God," for God is its "architect and builder" (Heb 11:10), and it is the city where God dwells with his people (Heb 12:22), and it will remain forever (Heb 13:14). In the letter to the church of Philadelphia (Rev 3:7–13), a blessing is pronounced upon those who remain faithful, for the Son of Man is "coming quickly" (3:11) and he "will write upon [his faithful] the name of [his] God and the name of the city of [his] God—the new Jerusalem, which is coming down out of heaven from [his] God" (3:12). In Gal 4:25–26 Paul contrasts the earthly city Jerusalem of his day with "the new Jerusalem above," which is the heavenly city that is free (by grace) and that is the "mother" of Christians, who are the true heirs of Abraham by means of the covenant fulfilled in Christ (cf. Heb 12:22). The "new Jerusalem" here in Rev 21:2 is described as "prepared like a bride adorned for her husband." Similarly Isaiah speaks prophetically of Jerusalem or Zion as the bride of Yahweh. In chapters 54 and 60 he describes how the city of Jerusalem will be rebuilt (Is 54:11–12; 60:10–14) and thus will radiate the glory of God (Is 60:1–5). The city represents God's faithful people, who are identified as the bride of Yahweh (Is 54:4–8; 60:15–16, 21; cf. 62:1–12).

Already in Rev 19:7–8 John had seen the church, the bride of the Lamb, adorned and made ready to be received by her Lord. Now she is revealed to John in all her heavenly attire as the holy city, the new Jerusalem. In Ezek 16:1–14 the prophet graphically portrays how God adorned Jerusalem as his bride, and though she prostituted herself to alien gods (Ezek 16:15–58), God would make atonement for her and she again would belong to her rightful Lord (Ezek 16:59–63). Here in Revelation 21 John sees the end result of the redemption of the bride of God, now spoken of as the bride of Christ. In all her godly beauty, as portrayed by the holy city Jerusalem, she will forever remain in God's holy presence.

THE TABERNACLE OF GOD WITH HIS PEOPLE (21:3–4)

In the new heaven and earth God will tabernacle (dwell) with his bride, his people (21:3). In 21:3–4 John gives a description of what it will be like for them when God takes up his abode among them. To introduce this description John hears "a loud voice from the throne" (21:3). As often elsewhere in Revelation, the actual living source of the voice is not identified. Sometimes an object is named as the source or direction from which the voice comes: one of the corners of the heavenly incense altar (9:13); heaven itself (10:4; 12:10; 14:13; 18:4); the temple or sanctuary of God in heaven (16:1, 17); or God's heavenly throne (16:17; 19:5; 21:3). In 16:17 both the temple and the throne together are mentioned.

Whatever source might be named, the voice expresses the majesty and holiness and glory of the ultimate living source, God himself. When some object is named, such as the furnishings in the heavenly temple, that may emphasize that the source is not only God, *but the God who has bound himself to his people in an incarnational and sacramental way*—in Christ, who is the new temple, and in divine worship, when God comes to his people through his Word and Sacraments. Thus, naming the altar as the source of the voice would suggest that the one who provided atonement for sin and who hears and receives the prayers of his saints is the living source of the voice. Naming heaven as the source of the voice might suggest that the one who is adored by the heavenly hosts is the source, while naming the temple could suggest that the one who dwells among his people through his covenant of grace in Christ is the source. And naming the throne might suggest that the one who rules his people as their only King and Lord is the source. Because at times an angel speaks for God (5:2; 6:6–7; 7:2; 14:6–7; 18:1–2), it may be an angel who is speaking here, even though only "the throne" of God is mentioned. Even if it is an angel who is speaking, he is doing so for God and under God's authority, that is, by and under the authority of the royal Lord, who alone is the object of the worship of all creation in the new heaven and earth (see 19:4; cf. 19:10; 22:8–9).

The voice cries out, "Behold, the tabernacle of God is with men" (21:3). In 15:5 John saw in heaven "the sanctuary of the tabernacle of the testimony" of God. There the tabernacle was associated with the judgments of God upon the human race as portrayed in chapter 16. Here in 21:3 the tabernacle is associated with God's glorious and gracious presence with his people in the new heaven and earth. The OT tabernacle erected by Moses (Ex 26:1–37) was the visible location of God's covenantal presence with his people. But the tabernacle here in Rev 21:3 is not the restoration of the earthly tabernacle of Moses, for there is no material tabernacle or sanctuary in the new Jerusalem, since the Lord God himself and the Lamb are the sanctuary (21:22).

God's heavenly tabernacle here in 21:3 in the vision of the new heaven and earth *signifies* the actual presence of God with his people. When the new heaven and earth will actually be created, no visual tabernacle will be present. Its presence will not be necessary, *for God's actual and personal presence among his people, which was represented by the tabernacle in the OT and which the tabernacle represents here in John's vision of the new heaven and earth, will have become a permanent reality.* Here in 21:3 John sees the presence of God in the vision of the new heaven and earth still dwelling in the tabernacle, because it is still in the future and John is here on earth in the present age (cf. Heb 9:1–22). As the tabernacle, and later the temple, were typological, mediating structures that enabled the holy God to dwell among sinful people, and those structures were part of the sacrificial worship that provided typological atonement for sin, in eternity all that will remain of all this is the Lamb who once was slain (Rev 21:22).

As visually represented by the tabernacle God himself will dwell directly and personally with his people as a result of the covenant that he had made with them through the Lamb. The statement that "they themselves will be his people, and God himself will be with them [as their God]" (21:3) has its roots in the OT. Already in Lev 26:11–12 God promised that he would place his dwelling place with his people, and as a result he would walk among them as their God and they would be his people. The tabernacle served as an archetype of this dwelling of God. In Jer 31:33 the prophet declares that through Yahweh's covenant, he will be his people's God and they will be his people. In Ezek 37:27 God prophesied that he would place his dwelling with the people and he would be their God and they his people (cf. Jer 30:32; Hos 2:23; Zech 8:8).

The use of the future tense of the verb "to dwell, to tent" in Rev 21:3 is a pointed reminder of Jn 1:14, where the same verb is in the tense for *completed* action: "The Word became flesh and *dwelt* among us." Jesus Christ is the incarnation of the glory of Yahweh, in and through whom God dwells among his people. He is the new tabernacle, the new temple, the means of atonement and the place of the forgiveness of sins, the one who reconciles the holy God with sinful human beings (Mt 26:61; Jn 2:19; cf. Rev 21:22). This will be manifestly evident and realized in the new heaven and earth.

In Rev 21:4 the blessed benefits of God dwelling with his people in the new heaven and earth are described. Though given in negative terms, they are telling in their implications: the absence of sorrow, death, mourning, and pain. Perhaps the blessed state of life with God in the new heaven and earth is given in negative terms because it is easier for those still here in the present earth to understand what is being replaced, while the positive realities of heavenly existence transcend human comprehension. God "will wipe away every tear from [the] eyes" of the saints. No longer will weeping characterize the condition of God's people as in the present life of tribulation. As the psalmist (126:5–6) says, "Those who sow in tear[s] will reap with a song of joy, and he who now goes about weeping … will return with a song of joy" (cf. Is 35:10). God himself promised of old that when he would rejoice over Jerusalem and dwell in a state of happiness with his people, never again would they shed tears (Is 61:2–3; 65:19). God would destroy death and as a result would "wipe away the tear[s]" from all the faces of his people (Is 25:8). Already in Rev 7:17 John had seen the blessed state of the souls of the saints in heaven, the church triumphant, whose tears had been wiped away. Now here in 21:4 John hears this description of God's people *after* the resurrection in the state of eternal life in the new heaven and earth.

The awareness of sin against God and its attending sufferings is a major cause of tears in the condition of repentance (Is 22:12; Joel 2:12; Mk 14:72), and such tears flow openly in the face of death. But in the new heaven and earth all sin and its guilt are forever gone, and the last enemy, death, has been destroyed (Rev 20:14). So John hears the great voice saying, "And death shall no longer be, nor sorrow nor crying nor pain shall be ever again" (21:4). Then, as a confirming statement that death indeed has been forever destroyed, John hears the great voice saying, "because the first things have passed away" (Rev 21:4). All the things of the first creation are gone, gone because they were corrupted and twisted out of their original godly purpose (see Gen 3:14, 16–19; cf. Rom 8:18–22). Their corruption resulted in death (Gen 3:19), and because death is now gone forever, so also are all the "first things."

THE ONE ON THE THRONE SPEAKS (21:5–6)

In 21:5 for only the second time in Revelation God the Father (here "the One sitting on the throne") speaks in the first person. In the prologue (1:1–8) in 1:8 God the Father spoke directly in the first person. But since that time and hitherto throughout the prophetic message of Revelation the presence on the throne has spoken only through intermediaries. Now for the first time in the prophetic message proper God speaks directly. To whom does he speak? Since in 21:6 "and he said" appears with "to me," John is the one who is addressed.

God said, "Behold, I make all things new!" (21:5). By this word God creates. In Genesis 1 several times it is written, "And God said." After each "And God said" there follows the word he actually spoke: "Let there be light" (Gen 1:3); "Let there be a firmament" (Gen 1:6); and so on. By these words God created in each case what his words described. Here in Rev 21:5 after "And God said" there follows a word by which he creates, only this time it refers to the *new* creation, the heaven and earth being recreated, restored after "the first things have passed away" (21:4). It is quite fitting that the first time God speaks in the prophetic message of Revelation it should be his creative word by which he will make his original creation new.

The words "Behold, I make all things new" (21:5) are similar to those in the Greek text of Is 43:19, "behold, I make new things." In Isaiah these words have to do with the mercy that God will show to Israel (Is 43:14–21). Here in Rev 21:5 the words are spoken with regard to all things being restored, the final and end result of God's mercy in Christ. "New" points to the description of the "heaven" and "earth" in 21:1, for God's assertion that he will "make all things new" (21:5) refers to all that God had originally created, "the heavens and the earth" (Gen 1:1), which are transformed into the "new heaven" and "new earth" that John sees here in Revelation 21. The Lord God had promised long before the time of John through the prophet Isaiah (65:17; 66:22) that he would create "new heavens and a new earth." To "make all things new" (Rev 21:5) thus means that all things that God had originally created will be recreated and restored to their original pristine state. God will not annihilate the present creation, cast it out as some trash, but rather he will, by recreation, transform the old into the new.

"And he says, 'Write, because these words are faithful and true' " (21:5). Who is the speaker of these words? Some suggest that it is now an angel, and others say that it is still God himself. It is because of the change from "he said" to "he says" in 21:5 and then back again to "he said" in 21:6 that it is postulated that the speaker is an angel. This interpretation suggests that an angel (speaking on behalf of God) interposes with the word "write." Four other times with regard to the prophetic message of Revelation the command is given to John, "Write" (1:11, 19; 14:13; 19:9). In the first two instances (1:11, 19) it is the exalted Son of Man, Jesus Christ, who tells John to write. In 14:13 and in 19:9 an unidentified voice, though most likely an angel speaking on behalf of God, tells John to write. In 19:9 the voice tells John, "These are the true words of God." Here also in 21:5 John is told that the "words are ... true," but with the addition that they are also "faithful." This similarity in content to what the voice in 19:9 says could suggest that here also in 21:5 it is an angel who is speaking. But it is a little difficult to imagine that an angel would interrupt with his own voice while God is speaking directly to John. However, it could be that the same angel who has been attending John (17:1; 19:9–10; 22:8) throughout the conclusion (17:1–22:5) speaks to John while God is speaking to remind him that these are indeed the true and faithful words of God and that these words of God are to be written down for the sake of the church (as with the seven letters to the seven churches).

Whatever the actual source of the voice, John is explicitly told to "write," for "these words are faithful and true." In 19:9 the words that are "the true words of God" were the words that described the celebration at the marriage feast of the Lamb (19:5–10). The final time that John hears it said that "these words are faithful and true" is in 22:6, in the epilogue, where the "words" refer to the entire message of Revelation. Here in 21:5 they refer first of all to that which is said about the new heaven and the new earth and how God makes all things new. These words of God are certain and cannot be negated. *Without question* there will be a new heaven and earth. As was already prophesied by Isaiah (66:22), the new heaven and earth will last *forever*—as will God's people in them.

In Rev 21:6 God speaks again to John and tells him, "It has come into being." All that God has spoken of regarding the making of all things new and regarding the restoration of the new heaven and earth has come about. There is nothing to be added. As John sees it in this visionary prophetic message, the Lord Christ *has already come* (19:11–21), the resurrection and the final judgment *have taken place* (20:11–15), and the heavens and the earth *have been made new* and thus restored to their original pristine condition. Yet for John and God's saints still here on the present earth, this is still all in the future—even though John now in the prophetic vision sees it all as an accomplished fact. Nevertheless, in their regeneration through faith, God's people have the assurance of the fulfillment of what is yet to take place (cf. 2 Cor 3:18; 4:16–18; 5:16–17). God on his heavenly throne can now say that everything is accomplished because his Son, Jesus Christ, completed the work of restoring God's people by the shedding of his blood (Rev 5:9–10). The completion of the salvation of God's people was attested when Jesus cried out from the cross, "It is finished" (Jn 19:30). This work completed at his death was visibly demonstrated by his resurrection (Rev 1:17–18). Now in John's vision of the new heaven and earth he sees the final action of God, which is the result of Christ's completed work of redemption. Thus all is accomplished.

The One sitting on the throne, God the Father, continues to speak: "I am the Alpha and the Omega, the Beginning and the End" (21:6). The first time God called himself "the Alpha and the Omega" was in the prologue (1:8). Now for the second time, here in 21:6 he declares that he is such. Then God adds, "I am … the Beginning and the End." While this addition (which is not present in 1:8) may seem to be a definition and explanation of "the Alpha and the Omega," the two are not synonymous. "The Beginning and the End," while explaining the sense of "the Alpha and the Omega," does so *in reference to all creation*, that is, it declares that "the Alpha and the Omega" is also "the Beginning and the End" of all creation, of all life (cf. Col 1:13–20; Rev 3:14). While the phrase "the Beginning and the End" is not present with "the Alpha and the Omega" in the prologue (1:8), it is present here in 21:6 *because of the context of the new heaven and earth*. One more time the combination of "the Alpha and the Omega" and "the Beginning and the End" will appear, in 22:13, where *the Lord Christ* says this of himself. By sharing these titles, the full divinity of Christ and his equality with the Father are affirmed.

The eternal God assures John that he makes all things new. Therefore he can now say, "To the one who is thirsty I myself will give from the spring of the water of life freely" (Rev 21:6). These words are reminiscent of the gracious invitation spoken by God through Isaiah (55:1): "Come, all who are thirsty, to the waters ... come, buy wine and milk without money." The invitation prophetically spoken by Isaiah is now fulfilled in Jesus Christ, for in his earthly ministry he said, "If anyone is thirsty, let him come to me" (Jn 7:37; cf. Jn 4:10–14). Now at the conclusion of the prophetic message of Revelation and in reference to all things made new God reminds John of this invitation, an invitation that John and God's people heeded, and the fruition of which they now see in the new heaven and earth. In the epilogue (22:6–21) John will once again be reminded of this gracious call to the waters of life given freely (22:17).

THE BLESSED AND THE DAMNED (21:7–8)

Rev 21:7–8 gives a description of those who will inhabit the new heaven and earth and those who will not. "The one who conquers will inherit these things, and I will be his God and he will be my son" (21:7). In Revelation 2 and 3, the conclusion of each of the seven letters has a promise from the Lord Christ for "the one who conquers." "I will grant [to him] to eat from the tree of life, which is in the paradise of God" (2:7). He "will certainly never be harmed by the second death" (2:11). "I will give [to him] of the manna which has been hidden, and I will give to him a white stone [of innocence], and upon that stone a new name" (2:17). "I will give to him authority over the nations, and he will shepherd them with an iron rod" (2:26–27). He "will be clothed in white garments, and I will certainly not remove his name from the book of life, and I will confess his name before my Father and before his angels" (3:5). "I will place him as a pillar in the temple of my God ... and I will write upon him the name of my God and the name of the city of my God—the new Jerusalem, which is coming down out of heaven from my God—and my own new name" (3:12). "I will grant to him to sit with me on my throne" (3:21). Taken together, these conclusions of the seven letters to the seven churches are a sevenfold description of the blessed state of those who will live in the new heaven and earth. "The one who conquers" is an heir (21:7) of God's gift of eternal life in the new heaven and earth *because of the victory of the one who conquered,* for it was the Lamb who conquered and by his victory made a people for God (1:5–6; 5:5; 7:14–17)—and because of his victory the saints of God are also called victorious ones (12:11). As John says elsewhere, "Everyone who has been born of God conquers the world, and this is the victory which has conquered the world, our faith" (1 Jn 5:4).

The one who conquers "will inherit these things, and I will be his God and he will be my son" (Rev 21:7). To be an heir of God is to share in all the blessings that he confers upon his own son. The one who is in Christ, who has been clothed with Christ in Baptism and believes in him as the Savior, becomes such an heir of God, for it is through the righteousness of faith (Rom 4:13) in Christ that the sinner is adopted as a son of God and so an heir (Rom 4:13; Gal 3:26–29; Titus 3:5–7). Christ Jesus won this inheritance by his suffering and death, and as the heir of God he has made all who are in him children of God and heirs of his glory (Rom 8:17; Gal 3:29). The heir in Christ is acknowledged as God's son, for God is now his Father. Rev 21:3 promised that when the time comes that God will dwell with his people, "they themselves will be his people, and God himself will be with them [as their God]." Here in 21:7 the people of God are individualized as his heirs. As the Son of God is the heir of God, so each believer in Christ is a son of God as an individual heir (see Gal 4:7).

Only the heirs and sons of God in Christ will live in the new heaven and earth. All others will have as their eternal portion "the lake which burns with fire and brimstone, which is the second death" (Rev 21:8). They are described as "the cowards and unfaithful persons" (21:8). Jesus called his disciples "cowards" when their fear of a storm threatened to overpower their faith, but he allowed that they had some faith because he called them "of little faith" (Mt 8:26) and asked, "Do you not yet have faith?" (Mk 4:40). Here in Rev 21:8 "the cowards" are the "unfaithful persons"; they are unbelievers with *no* faith in Christ. They include apostate Christians who, because of fear and/or cares of this life and love of the world, have chosen self and earthly honor and security and riches over losing oneself in Christ. The following description of "those who have made themselves vile, and murderers and sexually immoral persons and sorcerers and idolaters and all the liars" (21:8) is meant to indicate all unbelievers and pagans. Apostate Christians are included, but also all those who never were followers of Christ. By such immoral living they demonstrate that they are not of Christ (cf. Mt 25:41–46; Rom 1:18–32; Eph 4:17–19).

Their "portion" is "the lake which burns with fire and brimstone, which is the second death" (Rev 21:8). This is a graphic portrayal of hell. In Mt 25:41 it is called "the eternal fire prepared for the devil and his angels." In Rev 20:10 John prophetically saw the devil thrown into "the lake of fire and brimstone," where also the beast and the false prophet (the harlot) had been cast (see also 19:20). In 20:15 John saw how anyone who was not found written in the book of life was thrown into "the lake of fire." This lake of fire is called "the second death" (20:14) in contrast to what could be called the first death, that is, the state of sin and unbelief in which all people are conceived and born.

REVELATION 21:9–27
THE NEW JERUSALEM

TRANSLATION

21 ⁹And one of the seven angels who had the seven
censers full of the seven last plagues came and
spoke with me saying, "Come, I will show to you
the bride, the wife of the Lamb." ¹⁰And he carried
me away in the Spirit to a large and high mountain,
and he showed to me the holy city Jerusalem coming
down out of heaven from God, ¹¹which has the
glory of God. Her radiance is like a most precious
stone, like a crystallized jasper stone. ¹²She has a
large and high wall, which has twelve gates, and
upon the gates are twelve angels and names which
have been inscribed, which are [the names] of the
twelve tribes of the sons of Israel. ¹³From the east
are three gates, and from the north are three gates,
and from the south are three gates, and from the
west are three gates. ¹⁴And the wall of the city
has twelve foundation stones, and upon them are
twelve names of the twelve apostles of the Lamb.
¹⁵And the one who was speaking with me had a golden
measuring rod, so that he might measure the city
and its gates and its wall. ¹⁶And the city was laid out
foursquare, and the length of it is as its width. And he
measured the city with the rod over twelve thousand
furlongs; the length and the width and the height of
it are equal. ¹⁷And he measured its wall: one hundred
forty-four cubits, the measure of a man, which is
[also that] of an angel. ¹⁸And the building material
of its wall was jasper, and the city was pure gold like
clear glass. ¹⁹The foundation stones of the wall of
the city were adorned with every kind of precious
stone. The first foundation stone was jasper, the
second sapphire, the third agate, the fourth emerald,

²⁰the fifth sardonyx, the sixth sardius, the seventh chrysolite, the eighth beryl, the ninth topaz, the tenth green quartz, the eleventh jacinth, the twelfth amethyst. ²¹And the twelve gates were twelve pearls, each one of the gates was of one pearl. And the main street of the city was pure gold, like transparent glass. ²²And I did not see a temple in it, for Yahweh, the [only] God, the Almighty, is its temple together with the Lamb. ²³And the city does not have need of the sun nor of the moon that they should give light to it, for the glory of God illuminated it, and her lamp is the Lamb. ²⁴And the nations will walk about by her light, and the kings of the earth bring their glory into her. ²⁵And her gates will never be closed by day, for night will not be there. ²⁶And they will bring the glory and the honor of the nations into her. ²⁷And never will there enter into her any unclean thing and the one doing an abominable thing and a lie, but only those who have been written in the book of life of the Lamb.

COMMENTARY

THE VISION OF THE BRIDE (21:9–14)

In these verses John is shown in detail the bride of Christ as she will live in the new heaven and earth. As stated above in 21:2, the bride is illustrated by and displayed as the holy city Jerusalem. Again an angel attends John and points out to him the bride of the Lamb in all her godly beauty. It is "one of the seven angels who had the seven censers full of the seven last plagues" (21:9), referring to the seven angels in 15:1, 7; 16:1–21. These seven angels had revealed to John the seven scenes in the third vision of events taking place on earth (16:1–21). One of these seven angels has been attending John throughout the conclusion of Revelation's prophecy (17:1–22:5). Most likely this angel remains the same. It seems that the seven censer-angels in 15:1–16:21 are the same as the seven trumpet-angels in 8:2–11:15, who in turn are the seven angels of the seven churches in chapters 1–3. Thus in Revelation there is one group of seven angels throughout. It is quite fitting that one of the angels of the seven churches (identified here in 21:9 as one of the censer-angels) should show to John the bride of the Lamb as she will appear in the new heaven and earth.

The angel says to John, "Come, I will show to you" (21:9). The same words were used in 17:1 when the same angel came to John to show him "the judgment of the great harlot." The harlot is the antichurch, which on earth is opposed to the true church of Christ. Christ's true church was portrayed by the woman in Revelation 12, who was adorned with the glory of God. That woman, who was the church militant in suffering (12:13–18), is now the bride of Christ (cf. 19:6–8). The harlot is gone forever, having been cast into hell (19:20; 20:10). Now the angel shows to John the true woman of God, the church triumphant, set forth here in Revelation 21 as the bride of the Lamb and portrayed as the holy city Jerusalem.

The angel carries John "in the Spirit to a large and high mountain" (21:10). This is the fourth and final time John is said to be "in the Spirit." In 1:10 John, on the Lord's day on Patmos, was "in the Spirit" when the exalted Son of Man commissioned him to write the revelation. In 4:2 John was "in the Spirit" when he was transported into heaven to see the vision of God's enthroned glory and of the elevation of the victorious Lamb. In 17:3, after the angel had said to him, "Come, I will show to you the judgment of the great harlot" (17:1), the angel carried John into the desert "in the Spirit." Now here in 21:10 John once again is "in the Spirit" as the angel carries him to a large mountain. "In the Spirit" indicates that it was by the Holy Spirit of God that John was transported to the mountain. This is an event in the Spirit (whether in the body or outside the body; cf. 2 Cor 12:2–4) by which John saw the bride of Christ visually, and possibly also experientially or empirically. Perhaps it was similar to the spiritual event in which Ezekiel was taken by the Spirit and lifted up between heaven and earth and then saw a vision in which he was taken by God from Babylon to Jerusalem (Ezek 8:1–4; cf. Ezek 3:12; 11:1).

In Rev 17:3 John was taken in the Spirit into "a desert" to see the harlot. Here in 21:10 he is taken in the Spirit to "a large and high mountain" to see the bride of the Lamb. Perhaps this mountaintop experience, on later reflection, may have reminded John of the mountaintop experience of the transfiguration (Lk 9:28–36), except that here it is not *Christ* who is transfigured, but Christ's *church,* adorned in the glory of the exalted Christ as it is displayed as the holy city Jerusalem.

Above in 21:2 the holy city Jerusalem was "prepared like a bride adorned for her husband." Here in 21:11 John sees that adornment as "the glory of God," which is her "radiance." The church on earth bears "the glory of God" because of Jesus Christ (2 Cor 3:18; Rev 12:1), but it is unseen to the human eye. Now, after the resurrection and the restoration of heaven and earth, the church is adorned with this glory for all to see. This "radiance" of the holy city appears like "a most precious stone, like a crystallized jasper" (Rev 21:11), a rare gem which is green in color but has the luster of crystal."

The holy city Jerusalem "has a large and high wall" (21:12). Usually a wall around a city was for protection and defense. Such physical protection would not be a necessity for the bride of Christ in the new heaven and earth because all her enemies will have been vanquished. (That is the theme of Revelation 17–19; 20:7–10.) For that reason the "wall" is most likely a symbol of God's care and protection, which insured that the peace and security of his people would last forever (see also Is 26:1; Zech 2:4–5). In Ezek 48:30–34 the prophet in a vision sees a restored and new Jerusalem in the end times, after the final battle of Gog from Magog (Ezekiel 38–39; cf. Rev 20:7–10), and in it Jerusalem has twelve gates in its wall. In Ezekiel's vision three gates are located in each of the four sides of the wall, three facing the north, three the east, three the south, and three the west. In Ezekiel's vision, the gates in the wall are named after the twelve tribes of the sons of Israel. In John's vision the gates in the wall are also named after the "twelve tribes of the sons of Israel" (Rev 21:12).

It was common for ancient Near Eastern cities to have only a single gate because the gate was more vulnerable to attack and was more difficult to defend than the wall. The *twelve* gates of the new Jerusalem bear witness to its security. More than that, the gates also emphasize that the entrance into the city is by the arrangement set by God himself.

The wall of the city rests on "twelve foundation stones," upon which are the "names of the twelve apostles" (21:14). As Paul describes it in Eph 2:19–22, citizens of God's household and family "were built on the foundation of the apostles and prophets," which foundation has as its cornerstone Christ Jesus. The twelve gates of the city, named after the twelve tribes, and the twelve foundation stones, named after Christ's twelve apostles, testify to the unity of the OT people of God with NT believers in a common faith that rests upon a shared gospel message. Thus by means of the wall with its twelve gates John is reminded that, as there has always been only one covenant of grace embracing the entire people of God, those of old by faith in the promise of the Messiah and those by faith in the fulfillment of that promise in Jesus Christ, so now the true Israel of God will be in the new heaven and earth as represented by the new Jerusalem (cf. Rom 4:13–25; Gal 4:21–28). John earlier had seen the twenty-four elders sitting around God and his throne in heaven; they too represent the entire people of God, of both the OT and the NT.

The twelve angels on the twelve gates are evidently guardians of the gates (cf. Pss 34:7; 91:11; Heb 1:14). In Is 62:6–7 the Lord tells the prophet that he will place "watchmen" or "sentries" on the wall of Jerusalem. These watchmen will continue to be vigilant until the Lord renews Jerusalem and establishes her as the praise of the whole earth. Perhaps on reflection that reference in Isaiah may have come to John's mind. Certainly these guardian angels would remind John (as did the wall) that no enemy will enter the city ever again to hurt God's people (see Rev 21:27 below). These twelve angels as a group are unique, for nowhere else in biblical literature is such a group mentioned. There are groups of seven angels (e.g., 1:20; 8:2; 15:1) but not of twelve. That twelve are mentioned here in 21:12 is not surprising (despite their uniqueness), for the city has twelve gates patterned after the twelve tribes, and each gate has its own angelic guardian. As the cherubim protected the Garden of Eden (Gen 3:24), though for a different purpose, so the guardian angels protect the holy city Jerusalem, the new Eden.

THE MEASURING OF THE CITY (21:15–21)

In these verses the dimensions of the holy city Jerusalem are given, together with a further description of the foundation stones as precious jewels. "The one who was speaking with" John (21:15) is most likely the same angel who has been attending him as a guide throughout this concluding vision (17:1–22:5). He has "a golden measuring rod, so that he might measure the city and its gates and its wall" (21:15). In Ezek 40:1–42:20 the prophet saw in a vision "a man whose appearance was like the appearance of bronze" (Ezek 40:3), who showed Ezekiel the new temple. The bronze-like man did this by measuring the temple, its courts and gates and various rooms. When the man whose appearance was like bronze had finished measuring the temple, the glory of God came into the temple and filled it (Ezek 43:1–5). The new temple would be God's dwelling place and throne, in which he would live forever with his people (Ezek 43:6–7). Probably the man with a bronze-like appearance was an angel, for he himself does not bear the splendor and glory of God, but rather acts on God's behalf.

In Ezekiel the angelic man measures the temple. The prophet Zechariah (2:1–5) in a vision saw an angel (2:1, 3) measuring the city Jerusalem. The measuring affirmed God's promise regarding the future Jerusalem, "I myself will be for her ... a wall of fire all around, and I will be [her] glory in her midst" (Zech 2:5). Here in Rev 21:15 the angel measures the holy city and its dimensions for a similar reason. It is to assure John of the certainty and concreteness of the new and restored Jerusalem, which will last forever and which will be God's holy dwelling place in the new heaven and earth. That which the measuring in both Ezekiel and Zechariah prophetically represented and which was confirmed by means of the coming messianic age (cf. Jn 2:19), John sees fulfilled and consummated in his vision here in Revelation 21 (cf. Ezek 37:24–28). Earlier in Revelation (11:1–2) in a vision there was a measuring of the temple. But that time John himself did the measuring. He measured the temple of God, its incense altar, and those worshiping in the temple. The temple and its worshipers represented the church on earth as it was prepared for mission (11:2–13). The measuring assured John that God would protect his church on earth as she carried out her mission.

The city Jerusalem "was laid out foursquare" (21:16). The "length and the width and the height of it are equal," that is, it is a perfect cube. Each side of the cube measured "twelve thousand furlongs/stadia" (21:16). A Greek "stade" measured 600 Greek feet (625 Roman feet), the equivalent of around 607 English feet. "Twelve thousand furlongs/stadia" would equal about 1,380 English miles or 2,200 kilometers. Thus the city would be about 1,380 miles long and wide

and high, a metropolis beyond imagination. Whatever one makes of these
measurements, the size and scope of the holy city Jerusalem in Revelation 21
certainly declares that it is all encompassing in its perfection and splendor. The
holy city has the glory of God because he dwells within her, and this glory is
Jerusalem's "radiance" (see 21:11 above). The fact that this is so is also attested
by its cubic dimensions, for a cube symbolizes perfection. This perfect cubic
shape of Jerusalem would certainly remind John of the perfect cubic shape and
dimensions of the Holy of Holies, the inner sanctuary of Solomon's temple (1 Ki
6:20; cf. Ezek 41:3–4; 45:1–2). This inner sanctuary was the place of God's holy
presence, for it housed the ark of the covenant. The holy city Jerusalem—that is,
the bride of Christ, the saints of God—will be the Holy of Holies, the holy place
of God's dwelling.

The angel then measured the wall of the city. It was "one hundred forty-
four cubits," the common "measure of a man" as well as that "of an angel" (Rev
21:17). That the measurement of a human person and of an angel are the same
suggests that, though the measurement was taken by an angel, it would have
been the same if a man had taken it—as John himself did in 11:1–2. The number
144 is the square of twelve and certainly is reminiscent of the 144,000 (which
is twelve times 12,000), the number of saints in 7:4–8. As the 144,000 in 14:1–5
represented the church militant on earth throughout the time between Christ's
ascension and his second coming at the End, so the measurement of the wall of
the holy city, 144 cubits, suggests that the church—now the church triumphant,
the bride of the Lamb—is this holy city, this Holy of Holies. God's people who
on earth had witnessed to the Christ and suffered because of that testimony
(11:7–10; cf. 12:13–18; 13:7) are now, in the new heaven and earth, his holy dwelling place, that new Holy of Holies in which God will dwell in the new heaven
and earth.

Rev 21:18–21 describes the building material and the composition and
adornment of the city, with its precious stones and gold. The color of the precious stones of "jasper" (21:18) and "sardius" (21:20) is akin to the description
of God on his heavenly throne in 4:3, for the presence on the throne was "like
in appearance to a jasper stone and a sardius." This suggests that the holy city
glows with and reflects the very glory of God himself, and so she reminds John
of God's splendid and glorious presence in the city. The city itself was "pure
gold like clear glass" (21:18), and its main street was "pure gold, like transparent
glass" (21:21). This gold indicates that the city and its main street convey the
supreme *royalty* of God's glory. "The foundation stones of the wall of the city
were adorned with every kind of precious stone," twelve kinds of stone in all
(21:19–20). The prophet Isaiah (54:11–12) prophetically proclaimed that the Lord
God would rebuild Zion, her walls and foundations and gates, with precious
stones. John may have been reminded of the breastplate of the high priest,
which was made of gold and inlaid with twelve precious stones, one for each of

the names of the twelve sons of Israel (Ex 28:15–17; 39:8–21). While the stones in the breastplate represented the twelve tribes of Israel, here in Rev 21:19–21 the twelve kinds of foundation stones represent the twelve apostles (see 21:14). Individually, the precious stones of the wall illustrate God's people as individuals who are precious in his sight. As represented by the twelve patriarchs of the tribes of Israel and by the twelve apostles, the saints in the holy city collectively reflect "the multicolored wisdom of God" (Eph 3:10). The church is the house and building of God (Eph 2:20–22), and she will ever be reminded as she lives with God in the new heaven and earth that she "was built on the foundation of the apostles and prophets with Jesus Christ as the capstone" (Eph 2:20).

One final description of the splendor of the city is that "the twelve gates were twelve pearls, each one of the gates was of one pearl" (Rev 21:21). In Is 54:12 God promises that the gates in the restored Jerusalem would be "precious jewels." Here in Rev 21:21 they are of "pearls." Jesus in a parable mentions how a merchant in seeking "pearls" found one so precious that he sold everything he possessed in order to purchase it (Mt 13:45–46; cf. Mt 7:6; 1 Tim 2:9). So precious is the entrance into the city that it is worth any cost—a price that only the Son of God could pay, but which now the Christian values as his one great possession, having abandoned everything else for its sake.

JERUSALEM'S TEMPLE AND LIGHT ARE GOD AND THE LAMB (21:22–27)

John says regarding the holy city Jerusalem, that is, the people of God living in the new heaven and earth, "I did not see a temple in it, for Yahweh, the [only] God, the Almighty, is its temple together with the Lamb" (21:22). The saints of God in their state of righteousness and holiness and perfection after the resurrection can now look directly into the face of God. No longer does God have to shield his people from the brilliance of his overpowering holiness and awesomeness (cf. Deut 31:17–18; Is 64:7). God can now directly and personally live in the midst of his saints with his glory. With sin and every evil having passed away, there is no longer a need for a tabernacle or temple to mediate and temper God's presence. God the Father himself together with the Lord Christ is now that temple. The city itself (that is, the people of God) is now the Holy of Holies in which God dwells. What Paul said in 2 Cor 6:16, that the believers in Christ living in the present age are "the temple of the living God," is now fulfilled in all its completeness and openness (cf. 1 Cor 3:16–17; 6:19–20).

"And the city does not have need of the sun nor of the moon" (Rev 21:23) for light. God himself by means of his "glory" will illuminate her, and "her lamp is the Lamb" (21:23). John is not referring to the physical sun and moon but rather is describing what it will be like for God's people, who are the new Jerusalem, the Holy of Holies, to live in God's holy presence. Will there be astrophysical luminaries in the new heaven and earth? If the physical universe of the new heaven and earth will be similar to that of the first created heaven and earth, the conjectured answer would be yes, but John does not deal with this mystery.

The prophet Isaiah used similar language when he spoke about the restored "city of Yahweh, Zion, the holy one of Israel" (Is 60:14). He says that "the sun will no longer be your light by day, nor will the moon by its brightness shine on you, for Yahweh will be your everlasting light" (Is 60:19). On this earth the physical sun and moon still fulfill the original function for which they were created and established by God: to govern the passage of time and to furnish light for the physical well-being of daily living (Gen 1:14–19). In the restored Jerusalem God would be the true light of his people. Similarly, Christians affirm that Jesus Christ is "the true light ... which is coming into the world" (Jn 1:9) and is "the light of the world" (Jn 8:12; cf. 3:19; 12:35). Jesus Christ is the light of the Christian's life, which illuminates his pilgrimage through this present earthly life. In the new heaven and earth, God in his glory and Jesus Christ as the lamp will be seen directly and experienced personally as the eternal light.

So wonderful is the light of the glory of God and of his Christ that John sees that "the nations will walk about by her light, and the kings of the earth bring their glory into her," the holy city (Rev 21:24). In eschatological terms, John here in 21:24 sees the consummation and final fulfillment of the prophecy in Is 60:1–6 concerning nations and kings who will see the glory of Yahweh coming to his people. A preview and type of this ultimate fulfillment occurred in the journey of the Magi from the east to worship the Christ Child (Mt 2:1–12). In Rev 21:24 "the nations" refer to believers in glory, and the term "the kings of the earth" denotes that Christ won many of them for himself. This is certainly indicated by John in Rev 5:9; 7:9; 10:11; 22:2, where the church's ministry extends to all nations and to kings and the church consists of people from all nations. Rev 21:24a is quoting Is 60:3, where the emphasis is the inclusion of all kinds of Gentiles, in addition to Israelites, in the kingdom of God. That the kings of the earth bring their glory into the new Jerusalem as tribute indicates the supreme royalty of Christ, who is "King of kings" (Rev 17:14; 19:16; cf. 1:5; 15:3). While "kings" in Revelation usually are unbelieving enemies of Christ and his church (e.g., 6:15; 16:12, 14; 18:3), the context of Is 60:3 suggests that the "kings" are Gentile rulers who join the true Israelites in turning to the God of Israel and believing in him (e.g., Is 60:9). That interpretation is reinforced by the fulfillment of Is 60:1–6 in the Magi and the gifts they brought to the Christ Child as tokens of their worship (Mt 2:1–12). "Kings" may also allude to the royal reign of *all Christians* with Christ (Rev 5:10; 20:4, 6; 22:5).

The "gates" of the city "will never be closed by day, for night will not be there" (Rev 21:25). As stated above in 21:12, 14, the city's wall represents God's surrounding, protective presence. Here in 21:25 the inability of any evil force or danger to threaten or hurt God's people is emphasized again, this time by the open "gates" which never are closed, and by the fact that "night" is totally absent. City gates were usually closed at night (e.g., Josh 2:5–7). "Night" here represents the spiritual darkness of sin and evil (cf. Jn 11:10; 12:35; 1 Thess 5:5). Because there is no darkness of sin and the suffering and terror of eternal death that sin generates, there is no need for the gates in the wall of the city to be closed. It will always be day because of the eternal light of God's presence (Rev 21:23–24). Rev 21:25 quotes Is 60:11, which promises the restored Jerusalem that "your gates will always be open; day and night they will never be shut." The purpose of them remaining open is so that through them the wealth of nations and their kings may be brought into the city in a worshipful procession. John sees that the nations and their kings (Rev 21:24) "will bring the glory and the honor of the nations into her" (21:26), that is, into the holy city. In the new heaven and earth, all peoples and all nations and all kings—yea, the entire creation and all the heavenly hosts—will honor and praise God and the Lamb (cf. 4:1–5:14).

Never again will "any unclean thing" or anyone "doing an abominable thing and a lie"—any evil whatsoever—be able to enter, to tarnish, to savage God's people and his creation (21:27). "Unclean" was a category in the OT laws of purity (Acts 10:14; Lev 11:4–8). While these purity laws were fulfilled and abolished in Christ (Mk 7:2, 5; Acts 10:28), in Rev 21:27 "unclean" has the theological sense of something abhorrent to God, as indicated by the synonyms "abominable" (as also in Rev 17:4–5; also Mt 24:15) and "a lie, falsehood" (as also in Rev 14:5; 22:15), which is characteristic of the devil (Jn 8:44; 2 Thess 2:9, 11). The short description in Rev 21:27 of those excluded will be expanded in 22:15 (see also 21:8).

Revelation has a number of descriptions of those who will enter the eternal abode of God. Here they are not described according to any of their own characteristics or actions; they are designated by God's own action for their sake: they are "those who have been written in the book of life of the Lamb" (21:27). Their names are engraved in the mind and heart of God and his Christ, the shepherd of his flock (cf. Jn 10:3, 11, 27–30; 20:11–16).

REVELATION 22:1–5

THE GARDEN RESTORED

TRANSLATION

22 ¹And he showed to me the river of the water of life,
clear as crystal, coming out from the throne of God
and of the Lamb. ²In between her [the city's] main
street and the river, on this side and on that, is the
tree of life producing twelve fruits, yielding its fruit
according to each month, and the leaves of the tree
are for the healing of the nations. ³And any curse
shall no longer exist. And the throne of God and
of the Lamb will be in her [the city], and his slaves
will serve him as worshipers, ⁴and they will see
his face, and his name will be on their foreheads.
⁵And night will no longer exist, and they do not
have need of the light of a lamp and of the light
of the sun, for Yahweh, the [only] God, will shine
upon them, and they will reign forever and ever.

COMMENTARY

THE RIVER OF LIFE AND
THE TREE OF LIFE

In Rev 22:1–5 John sees another depiction of the new heaven and earth,
this time reminiscent of the Garden of Eden. Though Eden itself is not explicitly
mentioned, "the river of the water of life" (22:1) and especially "the tree of life"
(22:2) are obvious allusions to the primeval paradise.

The one who "showed to" John "the river of the water of life" (22:1) is the
same angel who has been attending him throughout the vision of the End
(17:1–22:5). This angel is "one of the seven angels who had the seven censers"
(21:9; cf. 17:1). This commentary also identifies these seven angels (15:1, 6–7;
16:1–21) as the seven angels of the seven churches.

John is shown "the river of the water of life" which is so pure that it is "clear
as crystal" (22:1). This recalls that in the Garden of Eden a river flowed which
watered Eden and then became the source of four rivers which watered different
regions of the earth (Gen 2:10–14). Here in Rev 22:1 the river is called "the water
of life," which is best understood as a symbol of that life which God alone can

grant and sustain. In Jn 4:10–14 Jesus speaks of the "living water" which he gives and which, when received, becomes "a spring of water which wells up into eternal life." A similar use of a river as a symbol of life flowing from God is found in Ezekiel. After the prophet had seen in a vision a detailed description of the end-time temple (Ezek 40:1–46:24), he sees a renewed and transformed creation with a river of water flowing out from the temple, bringing life to creatures and furnishing food for people (Ezek 47:1–12). As the river flows it wells up, as it were, and becomes greater in depth (Ezek 47:3–5). When it empties into the Dead Sea, "the waters are healed" (Ezek 47:8); it rejuvenates that sea so that its waters sustain fish and other wildlife (Ezek 47:8–9). This river has such ability to create and sustain life because it flows from the temple of God (Ezek 47:12).

A brief reference is made to such a "river" in Zech 14:8. On the "day of Yahweh" (Zech 14:1) "living water will flow from Jerusalem" (Zech 14:8). Joel says that in the day that the Lord will judge the nations (Joel 3:2), "a spring will flow from the house of Yahweh" (Joel 3:18). While in Ezekiel and Joel the river flows from the temple and in Zechariah from Jerusalem, in Rev 22:1 it flows from "the throne of God and of the Lamb" in the new Jerusalem. The temple is no longer there, for God and the Lamb are the temple in the new heaven and earth (21:22).

Since pure physical water flowed freely in the Garden of Eden to water the earth and thus sustain and renew earthly life, such a river could easily be used pictorially for that spiritual force which flows from God to create and sustain the faith and spiritual life of his people. The fact that in Ezek 47:1–12 this water comes from the temple indicates that it is through God's covenantal presence in his Word and in the forgiveness of sins provided by divinely ordained sacrifice, which was fulfilled in Christ, that this saving power flows from God. That it also comes from Jerusalem (Zech 14:8) suggests that because of the salvation brought about in Zion, this spiritual power would go forth from the holy city. "The river of the water of life" here in Rev 22:1 refers to the spiritual power of God and of the Lamb that will sustain forever the communal life of God's people with him in the new heaven and earth. It also indicates that all physical life will also be richly supplied by pure natural water as in the first Eden.

"The tree of life" (Rev 22:2) first appears in Gen 2:9. Among the many trees God created, he made in the middle of the Garden of Eden "the tree of life" and "the tree of knowledge of good and evil." Because Adam and Eve ate of the tree of knowledge in disobedience to God's command (Gen 2:16–17; 3:2–11), they were driven from the garden (Gen 3:22–24). The Scriptures do not reveal exactly what role "the tree of life" would have played if Adam and Eve had not sinned. Most likely it represented the source and sustainer of true life, God the Creator. Perhaps if Adam had not sinned by eating of the tree of knowledge but instead had chosen to eat of "the tree of life," he would have lived forever by the power of

God. But once man sinned, God did not allow him to eat from "the tree of life," for death and not life was now his future (Gen 3:22).

Passages in the book of Proverbs (3:13, 18; 11:30; 13:12) refer to "the tree of life" as the one true source of life. In Ezek 47:1–12, after the vision of the end-time temple (Ezek 40:1–46:24), the prophet saw trees on each side of the river which flowed from the temple (Ezek 47:7). These trees never ceased bearing fruit; the leaves would never wither and would be for healing (Ezek 47:12) as are those in Rev 22:2. While Ezekiel does not call these trees "the tree of life," they have the same function as "the tree of life" here in Rev 22:2, and so they seem to serve as a prophetic illustration of it.

Because of the description of the tree being on both sides of the river or between the river and the main street, the references to "the tree of life" in Ezek 47:7, 12 and in Rev 22:1–2 suggest that "tree" is used in a collective sense. The Greek word used in Rev 22:2 (and also in 2:7; 22:14, 19) for the "tree" of life supports this collective understanding, for it literally means "wood" (cf. Lk 22:52; 1 Cor 3:12; Rev 18:12), while a different Greek term is the more common word for "tree." That "the tree of life" in both Ezekiel and Revelation is most likely collective could suggest the possibility that in Eden it was also collective. That is, it might have been a species of tree that served the purpose of pointing to God as the Creator and sustainer of life.

In the new heaven and earth, the new Eden, "the tree of life" will serve a similar function to that of "the tree of life" (Gen 2:9; 3:24) in the first Eden. John sees the tree "producing twelve fruits, yielding its fruit according to each month, and the leaves of the tree are for the healing of the nations" (Rev 22:2). As Ezekiel prophetically saw in the end-time temple, so John now sees fulfilled in the new Jerusalem "the tree of life" with its various fruits and the healing ability of its leaves. God will abundantly furnish all that is necessary for the sustaining of life in the new heaven and earth. Leaves for "healing" indicate a permanent state of complete physical and spiritual well-being. "The tree of life" is for all people of all nations who are written in the Lamb's "book of life" (Rev 20:12; 21:27), that is, all the redeemed people of God. Never again will God ever have to guard the tree with cherubim to keep it from people (cf. Gen 3:24).

Rev 22:1–5 does not use the designation "the Garden of Eden." Nevertheless, the description in these verses calls it to mind, especially the mention of "the tree of life" (22:2). The new heaven and earth will be the Garden of Eden restored for God's people to inhabit forever. The heavenly city Jerusalem in Revelation 21 represents the people of God, the bride and body of Christ, as a holy temple in the new heaven and earth, within whose midst God himself will dwell. The tree of life (and the entire Edenic paradise in 22:1–5) represents the abundant life and the lush surroundings that God will furnish and supply for his people throughout eternity.

In Gen 2:8 we are told that God "planted a garden in Eden in the east." The Hebrew word for "garden" was translated into Greek with the word that is the source of the English word "paradise." In biblical usage "paradise" came to be used as both in reference to the original Garden of Eden and also to the heavenly Garden of Eden in God's holy presence. The word appears three times in the NT. In Lk 23:42–43, when the thief on the cross petitioned Jesus to remember him when Jesus came into his kingdom, Jesus answered, "Of a truth I tell you, today you will be with me in paradise." In 2 Cor 12:2–4, Paul speaks of himself in the third person and mentions how he was "snatched up to the third heaven," which he identifies as "the paradise." In Rev 2:7 at the conclusion of the letter to the church at Ephesus, Christ promises "the one who conquers" that he will give to him "to eat from the tree of life, which is in the paradise of God." In Revelation "the tree of life" appears four times: 2:7; 22:2, 14, 19. Only in 2:7 is "the tree of life" mentioned in connection with "the paradise of God," the new Eden. In 2:7 in the blessing, at the conclusion of the first of the seven letters to the churches, it is spoken of in an eschatological context. Those who remain victorious to the End will "eat from the tree of life, which is in the paradise of God." Before they fell into sin, Adam and Eve could have eaten freely from this tree. But after their fall and consequent expulsion from the garden, they could not eat of it. In the new heaven and earth after the resurrection, those who are victorious in Christ will be able to eat from this tree, indicating that they have life forever with God.

While here in 22:2 only "the tree of life" is mentioned, it is to be understood that it is in the midst of paradise, the restored Garden of Eden. It renders its fruits and healing leaves forever for all "the nations," all the people of God in Christ. The third and fourth times that "the tree of life" is mentioned in Revelation are in the epilogue (22:6–21). Rev 22:14 affirms, "Blessed are those who wash their robes, so that their authority shall be over the tree of life, and by the gates they will enter into the city," and 22:19 warns that "if anyone should take away from the words of the book of this prophecy, God will remove his portion from the tree of life."

In the restored Garden of Eden, the paradise of God, there shall no longer be "any curse" (22:3). The original curse of God upon the earth because of Adam's sin (Gen 3:14–19) will be supplanted by God's eternal blessing. "Christ redeemed us from the curse of the Law, having become a curse on our behalf" (Gal 3:13; cf. Rom 8:3; Gal 4:4–5).

The curse is gone. Now "the throne of God and of the Lamb will be in her" (22:3), that is, in the city (21:2) now pictured as Eden, the paradise of God. In 22:1 "the river of the water of life" came "from the throne of God and of the Lamb"; this river flows through the city. Now in 22:3 attention is focused on the throne itself, the same throne of God and of the Lamb. The impression is given that the center and focus of the new Eden, the new heaven and earth, will be

"the throne." Previously in Revelation, John saw God the Father seated on the
throne. Twice the Lamb is seen by John *near* the throne (5:6; 7:17), but not *on* the
throne with God the Father. Now, as John is shown the new heaven and earth,
the restored Garden of Eden, *for the first time he sees the Lamb with the Father
sitting on the throne* (22:1; cf. 22:3). Jesus Christ, the incarnate Son, is now seen
together with God the Father because it was he who won the victory and reconciled to the Father his creation, and in particular his people as his kingdom (see
1:5–6; 5:10; cf. Col 1:13–20). Thus the full divinity of the Son and his equality
with the Father are emphasized by the fact that they share one single throne,
"the throne of God and of the Lamb" (22:1, 3). The *unity* of the Father and the
Son is stressed further by the *singular* pronouns whose antecedent is "God and
... the Lamb": "*his* [not *their*] slaves will serve *him* [not *them*]" (22:3).

"His slaves will serve him as worshipers" (22:3). God's people will live in
the new Eden as the slaves whose very actions and works will be a worship of
God and the Lamb. They are "slaves" in the sense of always being in the state of
righteousness given by their Lord. They are "slaves" who adore and glorify the
Author of their blessed state. No longer now, nor ever again will they be slaves of
sin and suffering and death (cf. Rom 6:12–23). Earlier John had seen and heard
the saints singing before God's throne (Rev 7:9–17), and he had seen and heard
the twenty-four elders, who represent all the saints, worshiping the Father and
the Lamb with the singing of the great Te Deum. Now he sees the people of God
in the new Eden after the resurrection, praising and worshiping God not only
with their voices but also in deeds, for their every action and work is also a great
Te Deum.

"And they will see his face, and his name will be on their foreheads" (22:4).
Since the fall no human being had ever seen God face to face, for to do so meant
death. Of old the promise had been given that God's people "in righteousness"
would one day see his "face" and his "likeness" (Ps 17:15). Now in the new
Eden that promise is fulfilled. In the letter to the church of Philadelphia Christ
promised the one who conquers, "I will write upon him the name of my God
and the name of the city of my God—the new Jerusalem, which is coming down
out of heaven from my God—and my own new name" (Rev 3:12). They belong
to God and to the Lamb as citizens of the new Jerusalem. Their entire lives are
consecrated to God as those who have been named and identified as his through
the redemption wrought by the Lamb.

In 21:22–25 John heard that in the holy city Jerusalem there would be no
night and no need for the sun and the moon, for God would be the city's light
and the Lamb her lamp. Here in 22:5 this blessed statement is given again, only
now in reference to the new Eden. The commentary on 21:22–25 suggested that
this does not necessarily mean there will be no *physical* sun and moon in the
new heaven and earth, but rather that God and the Lamb would be the true
spiritual light that would enlighten and inspire his people.

"And they will reign forever and ever" (22:5). Two passages in Revelation (5:10; 20:4–6) promise that God's people will and in fact do reign with Christ already now during their lives on earth. But only 22:5 says that the saints "will reign *forever.*" The reign of the saints on the present earth is temporary, and it continues during the time that God allots for his church to complete her mission in Christ (see 11:3–13), but the reign in the new heaven and earth will never end.

EXCURSUS

THE RESTORED
PHYSICAL CREATION

In the description of the new heaven and earth as the holy city Jerusalem (21:1–27) and as the new Eden (22:1–5), God did not reveal to John *how the newly restored creation in its geophysical dimensions and character will appear,* for such was not the Lord's purpose. In using the designations and descriptions of the holy city Jerusalem and the new Eden, God does give to John an awesome view of what it will mean for Christians to live with him in his holy presence (Jerusalem) under his perpetual care and blessings (Eden). Whatever the actual physical form of the restored earth, God and his Christ will dwell in the midst of his people, for they will be God's Holy of Holies, his holy Jerusalem. Whatever kind of physical life his people will live and experience in their resurrected bodies, God will richly supply their earthly needs as he did with Adam and Eve in the first paradise before the fall.

As the Lord gives this spiritual description of the new heaven and earth, using the illustrations of the holy city Jerusalem and the new Eden, does John receive any indication or hint as to what the restored geophysical earth might be like? Is it possible to see such an indication (despite the fact that this was not the primary intent) in the use of "the tree of life" (22:14, 19; cf. 2:7), which is an implicit reference to the Garden of Eden? The mention of the tree of life in the restored paradise could suggest that *the recreated physical earth under God's creative providence will forever supply people's every bodily need.*

That John receives, by way of the tree of life, the Garden of Eden, a theme with reference to the new heaven and earth could also suggest that the newly recreated physical earth will be like that of the original. The geophysical earth, in its pristine form with living creatures and plant life for the enjoyment and benefit of humanity (cf. Gen 1:28–30), and with bodies of water, as indicated by "the river of the water of life" (Rev 22:1), nourishing and refreshing the earth (Gen 1:9–10; 2:10), could be a type and model of the new earth. The solar system with its sun and moon and the heavens above with their stars in their original pristine form and function could well suggest that these or similar heavenly bodies will be present in the recreated heaven and earth, fulfilling similar functions (cf. Gen 1:14–18). All of this could be seen encompassed in God's assertion in Rev 21:5, "I make all things new!" Furthermore it may be that the *entire orb of the physical earth* in its restored condition will be a virtual Garden of Eden, and that the tree of life could be a particular species which is present over the entire orb of the earth—as suggested by the picture resulting if the tree of life in Rev 22:2 is a collective noun.

However and whatever one may surmise from these possible hints in the biblical text, God does not give to John a direct answer to the question as to what physical form or appearance the entire new heaven and earth will take. But his allusion to the Garden of Eden, with its suggestions as to what the recreated earth might look like, agrees with what Paul says in Rom 8:18–25. The apostle declares that the creation eagerly "awaits the unveiling of the sons of God" (Rom 8:19; cf. 8:22). Here "creation" refers to all that God created in addition to humanity, that is, the heavenly bodies, the earth, and its plant and animal life. Because the present creation was put under God's curse as a result of human sin, it "was subjected to futility" (Rom 8:20). It was subjected to ruin, decay, and atrophy, but also it was subjected "on the basis of hope, because creation itself will be set free from this slavery of destruction into the freedom of the glory of the children of God" (Rom 8:20–21). This is a clear biblical promise that the present earth, which is suffering God's judgment and thus is wasting away (as portrayed vividly in Revelation, for example, Rev 8:7–13), will be restored to its original state—even as God's people will have their bodies restored in the resurrection so that they will be like Christ's own glorious resurrection body (Phil 3:21). This renewal of the present decaying earth (as taught in Romans 8) agrees with Rev 21:5, where God promises, "I make all things new!"

The theology of the incarnation itself suggests that, as a result of Christ's redemptive activity and his own bodily resurrection, those in Christ in the resurrection will be restored to God's original design for humanity's bodily state, and so also will the present earth be restored to its original, divinely intended state as the home for God's resurrected people. Paul himself hints at such a connection between Christ's resurrection, the resurrection of all those in Christ, and the renewal of the present earth in 1 Corinthians 15. The Gospel of Christ's death and resurrection is the foundation upon which all Christian hope rests (1 Cor 15:1–8). The promise of "the resurrection of the body" (Apostles' Creed) is predicated upon Christ's own bodily resurrection (1 Cor 15:12–23). As for the question of "how are the dead raised?" (1 Cor 15:35), the apostle draws a series of analogies and comparisons. The comparison of the present mortal body to the Christian's resurrected body is analogous to the comparison of a seed to the full-grown plant into which it is transformed (1 Cor 15:36–38). Paul then uses in a comparison the sub-human bodies of earthly animate life and the heavenly inanimate bodies (1 Cor 15:39–41). His direct point of comparison is that the bodies of resurrected people and the earthly and heavenly bodies are not all of the same essence and they possess differing degrees of glory. While Scripture gives to the Christian such beautiful glimpses of the age to come, the fullness of its glory is beyond our ability to comprehend now, for "no eye has seen, no ear has heard, no mind has conceived what God has prepared for those who love him" (1 Cor 2:9 NIV). Nevertheless, it is a certainty that all creation, as a result of Christ's redemption and resurrection, will be restored and transformed to its original pattern of God's gracious creative activity.

22:6–21

EPILOGUE

REVELATION 22:6–21

EPILOGUE

TRANSLATION

22 ⁶And he said to me, "These words are faithful and true, and Yahweh, the God of the spirits of the prophets, sent his angel to show to his slaves what events are necessary to soon take place." ⁷"Behold, I am coming quickly. Blessed is the one who keeps the words of the prophecy of this book." ⁸And it is I, John, who was hearing and seeing these things. And when I heard and saw, I fell down to worship before the feet of the angel who was showing these things to me. ⁹And he says to me, "Beware, no! I am a fellow slave of yours and of your brothers— the prophets and those who are keeping the words of this book. Worship only God." ¹⁰And he says to me, "Do not seal the words of the prophecy of this book, for the time is near. ¹¹The one doing wrong, let him still continue to do wrong; and the one being filthy, let him continue to be filthy; and the righteous one, let him still continue to do righteousness; and the holy one, let him continue to be holy." ¹²"Behold, I am coming quickly, and my reward is with me to render to each as is his work. ¹³I am the Alpha and the Omega, the First and the Last, the Beginning and the End. ¹⁴Blessed are those who wash their robes, so that their authority shall be over the tree of life, and by the gates they will enter into the city. ¹⁵Outside are the wild dogs and the sorcerers and the sexually immoral and the murderers and the idolaters and everyone who loves and acts out a lie. ¹⁶I, Jesus, sent my angel to testify to you these things for the churches. I am the root and the descendant of David, the star, the bright morning one." ¹⁷And the Spirit and the bride say, "Come."

And the one who hears, let him say, "Come."
And he who thirsts, let him come; the one who
desires, let him receive the water of life freely.
[18]"I solemnly give witness to every person who hears
the words of the prophecy of this book: if anyone
should add to them, God will lay upon him the
plagues which have been written in this book, [19]and
if anyone should take away from the words of the
book of this prophecy, God will remove his portion
from the tree of life and from the holy city, about
which things have been written in this book."
[20]The One who is testifying to these things says, "Yes,
I am coming quickly." Amen, come now, Lord Jesus!
[21]The grace of the Lord Jesus be with all [of you].

COMMENTARY

THE FORM AND FUNCTION OF THE EPILOGUE

Rev 22:6–21 is the epilogue of this prophetic work of John. In the prologue (1:1–8) the source and purpose of the message were identified, and a trinitarian imprimatur was given. The epilogue serves not only as a farewell, but also as an affirming "amen" to the certainty that this prophetic message of Revelation is the last word from the Lord of the church until he comes. The epilogue, together with the prologue, declares the absolute authenticity of this work of John and the urgency for it to be heeded immediately by the church, "for the time is near" (22:10).

Similarities between the prologue and epilogue can be noted. In addition to the urgency expressed in the thought, "the time is near" (1:3; 22:6), there are, for example, the facts that the message of Revelation is a genuine prophecy (1:3; 22:6, 9), that the message is given to John through the angel of Jesus/God (1:1; 22:6, 16), and that John is mentioned as the human mediator to the churches (1:1–2; 22:8). Because of such similarities it is possible to surmise that the prologue might have been written after the epilogue and under its influence. The first thing that seems to have happened was the Son of Man's appearance to John to commission him to write the revelation (1:9–20), and the prologue (1:1–8) may have been composed later.

A FINAL ANGELIC AFFIRMATION (22:6)

The speaker ("he," 22:6) is most likely an angel, the same angel who has been attending John throughout the vision of the End (17:1–22:5; see the commentary above). He says to John that "these words" of the prophetic message of Revelation "are faithful and true" (22:6). This is a refrain, announced often in Revelation to describe the Son of Man (3:7, 14) as well as the ways (15:3), judgments (16:7), and words (19:9) of God.

These statements declare that there is an absolute truth, a truth that is righteous and so never changes, a truth that is faithful in its intent. God is the source of this truth and the Lord Christ is the faithful witness to it. Christ is also the "Amen" of this truth, that is, the confirmation that there is no truth except that which originates from God the Father and comes through Christ and his words. In the vision of the new heaven and earth (21:1–27), God himself says to John and his people, "these words [of mine] are faithful and true" (21:5). That applies, first of all, to the words that described the holy city Jerusalem. That statement that his words "are faithful and true" also affirms what God had said previously in the same verse, "Behold, I make all things new!" Now here in the epilogue, for a final time, the angel (on behalf of God) states the same absolute certainty, "These words are faithful and true" (22:6). Here they are an explicit affirmation *of the entire prophetic message of Revelation,* and like the other affirmations, these words also apply to *all of Scripture, with Revelation, the final book of the canon, serving as the amen to the entire Word of God* (cf. 22:18–19).

The words of the prophetic message of Revelation are faithful and true because "Yahweh, the God of the spirits of the prophets," is the one who sent his angel to transmit the words to John, and it is God himself who stands behind them (22:6). While a case can be made that the "prophets" of 22:6 are NT prophets, probably here the emphasis falls on the prophets of the OT. This seems to be so because of the sentence structure of 22:6, which makes a distinction between "the prophets" of God and God's "slaves," who now (at John's time) receive his words—the "slaves" being John himself and his audience, as stated in 1:1. The prophets of God seem to belong to the past while John and his fellow slaves of God are in the present.

God sent "his angel" to show to John and his hearers the message of Revelation (22:6). The definite article before this "angel" (literally "the angel of him") seems to identify him either as an angel who appeared earlier or as a particular, well-known angel—perhaps known even outside and beyond the book of Revelation. This is the only reference in Revelation to an angel as the angel of "Yahweh, the God" (22:6). In 1:1 we are told that Jesus Christ "through his angel" gave the message of Revelation to John. There too the definite article identifies this angel of Christ as a specific angel. In 22:16, in the epilogue, Jesus himself, referring to this same angel, says, "I ... sent my angel" to give to John and the churches the message. Again the definite article identifies this angel. The angel in 1:1 is the same as the one in 22:16.

Who is the angel of "Yahweh, the God" here in 22:6? Most likely it is the same angel whom Jesus Christ calls his own in 1:1 and 22:16. That this is evidently the case can be deduced when 1:1 is compared with 22:6 and 22:16. In 1:1 God gives the message to Jesus Christ, who in turn gives it *through his angel* to John. Rev 22:6 says that God gave his words through his angel. In 22:6 it may appear that the angel has taken the place of Jesus Christ as the mediator of the message. But that is not really the case, for 22:16 affirms again (as did 1:1) that Jesus gave it *through his angel*. The message originates with God the Father. It is then given by God to Jesus Christ, who through his angel (who is also the Father's angel) gives it to John. The apostle then mediates the revelation to the entire church (cf. 10:11).

This identification of the same angel being both the angel of God the Father and the angel of Jesus Christ becomes all the more apparent when the "mighty angel" of 10:1 is brought into consideration. In chapter 10 we have a picture of an angel who belongs to both God the Father (the cloud and the halo-like rainbow, 10:1) and to Jesus Christ (the sun, 10:1). This "mighty angel" in the place of God and Jesus Christ commissions John to take the message to all peoples (10:8–11). Thus the definite article here in 22:6, and also in 1:1 and 22:16, suggests that "the angel" of God and Jesus Christ is the same angel as the "mighty angel" of Revelation 10.

The angel in 22:6 was sent "to show to his [God's] slaves what events are necessary to soon take place." In both the prologue (1:1) and here in the epilogue the recipients of the message of Revelation, are called "slaves." Several times in Revelation, God's people, his saints on earth, are called his "slaves." John also calls himself a "slave" because he is the recipient who will give the message to the churches (1:1). In 10:7 the prophets of God to whom he had given the mystery of the Gospel are called "slaves" (cf. 11:18). In 15:3 Moses is called a "slave" of God. The saints of God and his prophets are called "slaves," because they are called to do his bidding. They belong to him and to no other *because they have been purchased by the blood of the Lamb and they bear his seal on their foreheads* (7:3). "Slave" is thus a term identifying those who have God's grace because of the redemption wrought by Christ and who belong to God's household for the purpose of a mission of service.

The words "what events are necessary to soon take place" (22:6) refer to the entire message of Revelation. The events described will certainly take place: human evil and the resulting sufferings under God's judgment, and the church of Christ completing her mission. It is *necessary* that these events take place— especially the completion of the witness of the church to Christ's redemption of the human race at his first advent and to his second coming in judgment. There is an *urgency* that the events prophesied be fulfilled, *for the time of Christ's return is near,* and the church only has so much time to complete her mission.

AN URGENT INTERRUPTION
FROM JESUS (22:7)

To impress upon John and his hearers that the time truly is near when all things will be quickly brought to their consummation, Christ's words ring out, "Behold, I am coming quickly" (22:7). Similar first person interjections that seemingly interrupt the words or the flow of thought of an angel have occurred earlier in Revelation (1:8; 21:5–6; cf. 16:15). *In this instance it is certainly the Lord Christ who is speaking, for he speaks of something that is applicable only to himself, namely, his second coming.* In Rev 2:16 and again in 3:11 the exalted Son of Man makes the same statement to individual churches in order to urge them to heed his message of warning and encouragement. Here in 22:7 these same words are spoken as an encouragement to everyone "who keeps the words of the prophecy of this book" (22:7), that is, the book of Revelation (cf. Mt 24:36–44). Here the words come *after* the entire prophetic message of Revelation has been heard and serve as an urgent reminder to heed the message in view of the imminence of the End.

Also in 16:15 the Lord Christ speaks in the first person and breaks into what John is seeing and hearing. Jesus says, "I am coming as a thief. Blessed is the one who stays awake and guards his garments, so that he might not walk about naked and so that they might not see his shame." Jesus says this in relation to what John sees concerning Armageddon, which is the final battle that will take place just before Christ's return to bring the present world to its end.

As in 16:15, so also here in 22:7, a beatitude is added: "Blessed is the one who keeps the words of the prophecy of this book." This is the sixth of the seven beatitudes in Revelation. The first beatitude (1:3) is addressed to both the lector (singular) and the people (plural) who are about to hear the prophecy: "Blessed is the one who reads and [blessed are] those who hear the words of this prophecy and who keep the things written in it." Here in the epilogue in 22:7 the beatitude is similar, but now in reference to the prophecy that has been revealed to John and heard by his audience.

AN ASSURANCE REGARDING HIS
TESTIMONY FROM JOHN (22:8–9)

As John does in the prologue (1:1–4), so also here in the epilogue, the apostle identifies himself as the human author of this prophetic work (22:8). As if by way of assuring his recipients, John tells them that he truly saw and heard these things. He was a witness who would vouch for and give testimony to the entire revelation (cf. 1:2). In 1 John he states that what he and the other witnesses had heard and seen with their own eyes and what their hands had touched, he has now announced and witnessed to his hearers (1 Jn 1:1–4). John claims this same eyewitness authenticity for this prophetic work of Revelation. His written work is truly the word and product of God, for this revelation was given to him from God the Father through Jesus Christ and by his angel (cf. Rev 1:1–3).

When John had heard and seen all that was revealed to him, he "fell down to worship before the feet of the angel" who had shown these things to him (22:8). This is the second time (the first was in 19:10) that John attempted to worship the angel who was attending him.

As was said in the commentary on 19:10, this action is difficult to understand. Certainly John did not attempt to worship the angel because of the status of the angel, for that would be a willful act of idolatry (cf. Col 2:18). And it is not the case that John supposed that the angel was God the Father or Christ and therefore was moved to worship him. Most likely (as in the case of 19:10) he knelt down because he was so overwhelmed by what he had heard and seen that he was moved to honor the angel who was guiding him through the visions. But this action was misplaced, for such honor and worship belong to God alone. And so the angel tells him not do so, for he (the angel) is also "a fellow slave" of God like John and his brothers the prophets and those who keep the words of this book (22:9). The angel who had shown these things to him was only acting as a slave of God and in so doing was a ministering angel in service to John (cf. Heb 1:14).

INSTRUCTION FOR THE PRESENT MOMENT (22:10–11)

The speaker in 22:10–11 is not directly identified, but it is most likely the same angel (cf. 22:6) that had been attending John throughout the vision of the End (17:1–22:5). He tells John not to "seal the words of the prophecy of this book, for the time is near." In Dan 8:26 just the opposite is said. Daniel *is* to "seal the vision" because it is about the distant future. Here in Rev 22:10 John is told *not* to seal the vision because the future events are imminent, that is, what John has seen and heard is about to be completed. The vision in Daniel was about the end time (Dan 8:17–19), and for Daniel the words describing that end time "were closed and sealed until the time of the end" (Dan 12:9). That is not so for John, for that end time was to arrive soon, almost immediately. For present-day hearers and readers, the time of the End is that much closer.

So near is the hour of fulfillment that the angel tells John people will have little time to change their manner of life. Earlier in Revelation, God's judgments had not evoked repentance in obdurate sinners (e.g., 9:20–21). So too here, despite the dire warnings, many will not heed the urgent call to repentance. Sinners will continue to "do wrong" and remain "filthy" (22:11). At the same time, God calls his people, "the righteous," to "continue to do righteousness" and to "continue to be holy" (22:11). The possibility is still present *right now* for change of status before God—from unrighteous and filthy to righteous and holy—through hearing the warnings of God and the gracious invitation of his mercy in Christ. But *now is the time,* not tomorrow, for the hour is late (cf. Rom 13:11–14; 1 Thess 5:6–7; 1 Jn 2:18). This passage underlines the extreme urgency of the church's mission to proclaim the Gospel and to persevere in the righteousness and holiness that are hers by grace.

A PROMISE FROM THE LORD CHRIST (22:12–13)

Again a voice speaks in the first person. As in Rev 22:7, it is the voice of the Lord Christ, who says, "Behold, I am coming quickly" (22:12). Then the exalted Christ adds, "And my reward is with me to render to each as is his work." In 22:7 he had said, "Blessed is the one who keeps the words of the prophecy of this book." Those who keep the words of Revelation will receive the "reward" from the Lord Christ himself. This word for "reward" in extrabiblical Greek usually refers to a monetary or material payment or recompense, "salary" or "wage." Most often in the NT the word is used not in that secular sense, but rather with the meaning of spiritual compensation. For example, in Mt 5:12 Jesus refers to the "reward" in heaven that belongs to those who are persecuted as were the prophets of old (cf. Mt 6:1). In Mt 10:40–42 those who belong to Jesus and who thus receive a prophet or who help Christ's disciples will not lose their "reward." In 1 Cor 9:17–18 Paul speaks of his "reward" as his call to proclaim the Gospel. His compensation is the sharing of Christ with his hearers. The word can also be used in a negative spiritual sense when, for example, Jesus refers to the "reward" of false piety: the hypocrites' false belief in their own self-righteousness is their only "reward" (Mt 6:2, 5).

Here in Rev 22:12 the "reward" is what Christ will give when he comes at the End. While the Lord Christ in judgment will render to each unbeliever that person's reward according to his works of evil (cf. Rom 2:6, 8–9), here in Rev 22:12 it is the "reward" that the Lord Jesus will give to his faithful followers. Their works do not earn the "reward," but rather their works demonstrate that by his grace and the power of the Spirit they keep "the words of the prophecy" of Revelation (22:7) and exhibit their faithfulness to their Lord (cf. Mt 25:31–40). Christ calls it *"my* reward" (Rev 22:12), *not their* reward; it is the reward *which Christ himself earned,* and which he freely gives to all believers by grace. *The "reward" itself is the gift of eternal life in God's holy presence, earned for God's people by the death and resurrection of the Lamb of God* (5:9–10; 7:13–17). *This "reward" is represented by the tree of life* (22:2, 14). A parallel OT theme is found in Isaiah. Yahweh will return to his people in power and glory, and "his reward is with him" (Is 40:10; 62:11). He will claim his redeemed people and shepherd them gently (Is 40:11; 62:12). Moreover, the Suffering Servant of Yahweh will share the victor's spoils, which *he himself* earned, with his many justified saints (Is 53:12).

THREE DIVINE TITLES (22:13)

The exalted Lord Christ continues in Rev 22:13 by saying, "I am the Alpha and the Omega, the First and the Last, the Beginning and the End." Here are three descriptive titles that point to the infinite and eternal magnitude of the presence of Jesus Christ. The first title, "the Alpha and the Omega," is applied to God the Father in 1:8 and 21:6. Here in 22:13 God the Son, the Lord Christ, identifies himself by this same title. Both the Father (21:1) and Jesus Christ (22:13) also claim the third title, "the Beginning and the End." However, the second title, "the First and the Last," is used only of Jesus Christ (1:17; 2:8; 22:13). (The Holy Spirit, the third person of the Trinity, is mentioned explicitly in the epilogue of Revelation in 22:17.)

While these three titles may seem to be synonymous, they certainly are not equivalents. Jesus Christ is called "the First and the Last" three times in Revelation (1:17; 2:8; 22:13), but the fact that God the Father is not so designated suggests that this title is not the exact equivalent of the other two. All three point to the infinite reality and the eternal presence of God; two are predicated of the Father and all three of the Son, Jesus. But each title has its own distinct and essential point.

THE THREE DIVINE NAMES IN REVELATION 22:13.

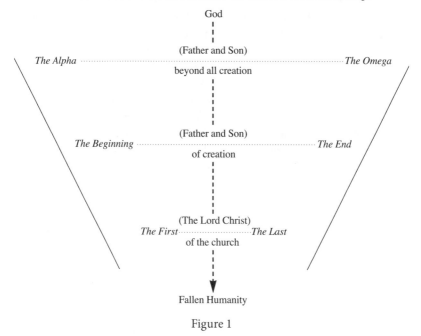

Figure 1

"THE ALPHA AND THE OMEGA"

Of the three, the first, "the Alpha and the Omega" (the first and the last letters of the Greek alphabet), is the most comprehensive, for it dominates and embraces the other two. It refers to the magnitude of the eternal presence of God far above and beyond *all creation*. Long before—forever before—he created the present universe, the triune God was and is. This title refers to God's eternal existence and presence *apart from and independent of his creative activity and the world he brought into existence*. Here in 22:13 Jesus Christ, as the exalted King of kings and Lord of lords (19:16), claims for himself this magnitude of the heavenly Father's eternal presence. He is the eternal God, together with the Father and the Spirit, but this title here in 22:13 is pertinent especially because, as the incarnate Son of God, he conquered the enemies of God's people. In claiming this title here in the epilogue, the victorious Lamb proclaims rightfully his divine equality with the heavenly Father. As true God from eternity, the Son always was present with the Father (Jn 1:1–2). But now the incarnate Son, the God-man, Jesus Christ, displays—in the personal union of his divine and human natures—this eternal magnitude which, as the victorious Lamb, he now shares with the Father.

"THE BEGINNING AND THE END"

Because both the Father and the Son, Jesus Christ, are "the Alpha and the Omega" (the first title in 22:13), far above and beyond *all creation*, the Father and the Son are also "the Beginning and the End" of creation (the third title). This *third* title appears in contexts that concern especially the *new creation*. In 21:5–6 the One sitting on the throne said, "Behold, I make all things new!" And then God the Father said, "I am the Alpha and the Omega, the Beginning and the End," that is, the beginning point and end point of what he had created and was now recreating, the new creation, the new heaven and earth. He who is "the Alpha and the Omega" above and beyond all creation is now also "the Beginning and the End" of all that he had created. Because he is "the Beginning and the End" of all creation, he will make it new and restore it to its original condition. "The Beginning and the End" points to the fact that God is the source and the beginning point of creation and that he is also its end and purpose. That is, all creation exists because of God's creative activity, and after the present order passes away, the new creation will continue to exist forever for his glory. Now here in 22:13 Jesus Christ, the victorious Lamb, also claims to be the source and beginning of all creation as well as its end point, its purpose and its goal, which will be consummated and demonstrated in the *new creation* (cf. 2 Cor 5:17; Gal 6:15; Eph 1:10).

In Rev 3:14, in the introduction to the letter to the seventh church, the exalted Son of Man calls himself "the source (the beginning) of the creation of God." Was the Lord Christ speaking more of the first or second creation? In Col 1:16–18 Paul states that in Christ Jesus "all things in the heavens and upon the earth were created," referring to the original creation (cf. Jn 1:1–3). But then Paul says that as "the head of the body, the church" Christ is "the beginning (the source)" and "the firstborn of the dead." Paul is saying that, because of the death and resurrection of Jesus Christ, he is the beginning (the source) of the resurrection of all the dead. Since he conquered death, the Lord Christ is able to be this beginning point and source by which all will be raised from their graves—and he was the first to be raised. Paul uses the word "beginning, source" in reference to the *new creation*, that is, *the resurrection of the dead* (the glorification of their bodies). This suggests that when Jesus Christ calls himself "the source of the creation of God" (Rev 3:14), he is referring not to the creation of the *original* heavens and earth (of which he was the agent, the Logos, Jn 1:1–3), for the Father was its source (Genesis 1). He is referring to the *new creation*, the new heaven and earth.

Christ will not only be the *agent* of the creation of the new heaven and earth (cf. "the Word," in Rev 19:13), but also, together with the Father, he will be the beginning point and source of it. Jesus Christ will share this honor with the Father because of his victory as the Lamb of God. And so here in 22:13, when the Lord Christ calls himself "the Beginning and the End" (the third title), he claims to be *the source of the new heaven and earth,* an honor he shares with the Father who makes all things new (21:5–6). He will also be the end point and purpose for its existence, and thus, together with the Father, its glory. *So what was said of the Father concerning the first creation is also true of the Son, the Lord Christ, concerning the new creation.* It will come into being because of Christ's creative activity, and it will exist for his glory.

"The First and the Last"

The second title suggests still another nuanced quality of the magnitude of the infinite and eternal presence of the Deity. But this second title is applied *only to Jesus Christ.* Three times in Revelation the Lord Christ calls himself "the First and the Last." In 1:17–18 the Son of Man, when he addresses John and tells him not to be afraid, says, "I am the First and the Last." He identifies himself with this title because he is "the Living One." Though he "was dead," he now is "alive forever and ever" and has "the keys of death and the grave." Because Jesus Christ died and came back to life, he is "the First and the Last."

Of what or of whom is Jesus "the First and the Last"? In Rev 2:8, at the beginning of the letter to the church of Smyrna, the Lord Christ identifies himself a second time with this second title. He says that he is "the First and the Last" again because he was dead but came back to life. It becomes clear that he is "the First and the Last" of all who die in him and together with him and are raised with him spiritually already now and will be raised physically and bodily in the resurrection at the End. He is the founder of the church and her end goal, her end purpose for living. He is her First and her Last as the eternally present one (Mt 28:20). Jesus Christ, who is "the Alpha and the Omega" beyond all creation from eternity and who is "the Beginning and the End" of the new creation, is also "the First and the Last" of God's people (cf. Col 1:17–20).

While Jesus Christ shares the first and the third titles with the Father, he alone bears the second title, "the First and the Last," because he died and rose again to rescue God's people in order to bring them back to life. *The incarnation, death, and resurrection are predicated only of God the Son, Jesus Christ.* In Is 44:6 Yahweh of hosts, "the King of Israel and his Redeemer," declared, "I am the First and I am the Last" (cf. Is 48:12, 20). Now here in Revelation (1:17; 2:8; 22:13) the exalted Lord Christ declares that he is that First and Last of God's people because he is their Redeemer.

Thus these three titles in 22:13 represent a compilation of the Christology in Revelation—in fact of the entire Bible. Jesus Christ is the everlasting God together with the Father and with the Holy Spirit, who is mentioned here in the epilogue in 22:17. From and throughout eternity he has been with the Father; the magnitude of this eternity is far above and beyond all creation and forever— long before there was this present universe. And so the title "the Alpha and the Omega" is applied to the Lord Christ. Since he is "the Alpha and the Omega," Christ is also, again together with the Father, the initial source and the end point, the goal, of all creation, in particular now of the new heaven and earth. And finally as "the Alpha and the Omega" and as "the Beginning and the End," the Lord Christ is "the First and the Last" of God's people, the church. He is this First and Last *apart from* God the Father *because he alone* died and rose again. This title "the First and the Last" is mentioned in between the other two because it is to be seen and understood in the forefront, for it is only through it that we can view the other two.

The three titles may be presented in a pyramid-like structure, but with the point facing down and not up—an inverse pyramid (see figure 5). The point is the title "the First and the Last." It is the smallest of the three in its scope (though not in its importance), for its scope and focus is the church because of the incarnation and death and resurrection of Jesus Christ. *It is only through this title and what it represents that God meets the human race* (cf. Jn 14:6–9; Heb 4:14–16; 10:19–25). Once one has seen Jesus Christ as the Savior, through him and the great mystery of his redemption one comes to recognize him together with his Father as the God of all creation—as represented by the title "the Beginning and the End." This title is larger in reference than that which points to Christ as the Savior of the human race, for it calls attention to the fact that Christ is also (together with the Father) the Lord of all creation, an entity that is larger in scope than the church. Once one has beheld Christ as the Lord of all creation, finally through Scripture's revelation of that truth one comes to recognize him, together with the Father (and the Spirit), as the God who is and exists far beyond and above and before the created universe, that is, "the Alpha and the Omega." This title is the largest of the three in scope, for it points to the awesome magnitude of the infinity and greatness of Christ as the eternal God, together with the Father and the Holy Spirit. Here in the epilogue, in 22:13, all this high Christology is also to be understood in relation to the new heaven and new earth.

A BEATITUDE AND AN EXCLUSION (22:14–15)

In 22:14 the seventh and last beatitude in Revelation is announced. "Blessed are those who wash their robes, so that their authority shall be over the tree of life." Who is the speaker, the angel mentioned in 21:9 and 22:8, or Christ himself? It seems to be the Lord Christ, as in 22:7. There Christ had said that he was coming quickly and then he announced a beatitude. So also here in 22:14, after Christ claims the three divine titles in 22:13, he speaks this last beatitude. Already in 7:14 John had seen those who had "washed their robes and made them white in the blood of the Lamb." They were standing before God's throne in heaven. Now here in the epilogue John is reminded by the Lord Christ himself how blessed they are. In their righteousness before God because of the blood of the Lamb, they have "authority … over the tree of life" (22:14). In the new Eden after the resurrection they shall be able to eat of this "tree of life" forever, and "they will enter into the city" (22:14). Because all evil as described in 22:15 will be "outside" the holy city, never again will God's people be tempted or injured by evil, nor will those who lived for the purpose of such evil ever again shame God or hurt his beloved saints.

AN ATTESTATION FROM JESUS HIMSELF (22:16)

The Lord Christ continues to address John in 22:16. The Lord Christ spoke directly to John in 1:9–20, when he commissioned him to write this prophetic message, and in chapters 2 and 3, when he instructed John to write to the seven churches. However, while his personal name, "Jesus" (Mt 1:21; Lk 1:31), appears fourteen times in Revelation, only here in 22:16 is it used by the Christ. Indeed, *this is the only time in the entire NT that the Lord uses his personal name to identify himself.* While the other names and titles by which he speaks of himself display or point to the majestic grandeur of who he is and what he has done for the salvation of humanity, his personal name, "Jesus," points to his humanity and to his intimate relationship with John and with all of God's people. He is John's personal and loving Savior and friend.

Jesus personally authenticates the prophetic message by saying, "I, Jesus, sent my angel to testify to you [plural] these things for the churches" (22:16). The plural "you" refers first to John and then to the other church leaders who will, in turn, proclaim the message to all the churches. The prologue states that the revelation was given to Jesus Christ by God, and in turn the Lord Christ gave it to John "through his angel" (1:1). This is most likely the same angel referred to in 22:6. A picture of this angel, called both the angel of God the Father and the angel of Jesus, appears in Revelation 10. Though the angel (together with the seven angels of the seven churches) mediates the message, it is God the Father and Jesus Christ who are the source, and John is to receive it as coming from the mouth of the Lord Christ himself.

Jesus continues, "I am the root and the descendant of David, the star, the bright morning one" (22:16). In 5:5 the Lamb of God is introduced to John as "the Lion who is from the tribe of Judah, the Root of David." Here in 22:16 Jesus calls himself "the root and the descendant of David." He is both David's Son and his Lord (Ps 110:1; Mk 12:35–37). In Is 11:1–10, the one who would come to dispense God's righteousness and justice (Is 11:4) and upon whom the Spirit of Yahweh would rest (Is 11:2; cf. Lk 4:17–21) would come as "a shoot" from "the stump of Jesse" and as "a branch from his roots" (Is 11:1). Jesus applies this designation of the "shoot" of "the stump of Jesse" (Is 11:1) to himself when he calls himself "the root and the descendant of David" (Rev 22:16).

In addition Jesus calls himself "the star, the bright morning one" (22:16). In 2:28, at the conclusion of the letter to the church of Thyatira, the exalted Son of Man says that to the one who conquers and remains faithful there will be given "the morning star," the same "star" that the heavenly Father has given to him, the Son. The seven stars in the hand of the Son of Man represent the angels of the seven churches (1:16, 20). While stars are associated with angels (see Job 38:7), the most brilliant star in the heavens, "the morning star," represents the brilliant glory of Christ. In Num 24:17 Balaam, in his fourth prophetic oracle, declared how "a star would come forth out of Jacob" who would become the ruling "scepter from Israel."

Jesus Christ now claims to be that "star" of Jacob (Rev 22:16). With this designation he promises that the day of salvation is about to dawn (cf. Mal 4:2). As the exalted Son of Man promised to the church of Thyatira (Rev 2:28), the faithful people of God will share in this glory of their "morning star."

THE RESPONSE: "COME" (22:17)

In a voice that responds to what Jesus had just said, the Holy Spirit prompts "the bride" of Christ—the church (Eph 5:23–32; Rev 21:2, 9)—to say, "Come" (22:17). Let everyone "who hears" the words of this prophecy likewise be moved by the Spirit, who works through the Word, and say, "Come." Anyone who thirsts is also invited to come and "receive the water of life freely." As the church calls out for her Lord to come, she also cries out to all people of the world to come and drink of the waters of salvation freely, by grace (Is 55:1). As his people "receive the water of life freely" (Rev 22:17), they are sustained in their faith and also motivated to pray, "Come." The Spirit also moves Christ's "bride" to invite others to come now and drink, for the time granted by God to do so is short.

A WARNING ABOUT THE PROPHETIC BOOK (22:18–19)

A sharp warning is given not to "add" (22:18) anything to the prophetic message of Revelation nor to "take away from the words of the book of this prophecy" (22:19). To do so will incur the wrath of God, in the form of "the plagues which have been written in this book" (22:18) and by the removal of one's "portion from the tree of life and from the holy city" (22:19). The speaker of these words of warning is Jesus Christ, who has been directly addressing John (22:7, 12–16). As the Lord Christ says in 22:16, "I, Jesus, sent my angel," so also here in 22:18, "I" is Jesus. His words "I solemnly give witness" point to his self-designation as "the witness, the faithful and true one" (3:14; also 1:5) and to his words with which the whole of Revelation ends: "The One who is testifying [bearing witness] to these things" (22:20). He is the witness who concludes the prophetic message of Revelation with this warning that no one dare alter the words of the book.

Such warnings to protect a literary writing were not uncommon in the ancient world, in particular with religious writings. Here the warning not to change the words of Revelation refers primarily to not changing its words in order to change its meaning. Elsewhere in the Bible such warnings are also given not to change or alter the words of God. For example, Moses in Deut 4:2 told the Israelites not to add or subtract from the commands of God (cf. Deut 12:32; Prov 30:6; Jer 26:2).

The warning that Jesus gives here in Rev 22:18–19, while directly applying to the book of Revelation, should also be applied by inference to the entire Bible, since Revelation is the climax and conclusion to the entire canon, both the OT and the NT. The writings of the entire Bible are also so to be received as the very words of God and thus not to be altered—as indicated by the warning of Moses (Deut 12:32). This extension to cover all Scripture is a necessity from the biblical point of view, for the apostle Paul himself said (Gal 1:6–9) of any person who would change the one received Gospel—even if that person would be Paul himself or an angel from heaven—"let him be cursed."

A Promise, a Prayer, and a Blessing (22:20–21)

The last word of the Lord Jesus, "Yes, I am coming quickly" (Rev 22:20), is a promise to his church, God's saints on earth. The same one who authenticates the prophetic message of Revelation also authenticates this promise, for it is spoken by the faithful witness of God, Jesus Christ (1:5), who solemnly testifies to everything that has been revealed to John and the churches. In Jn 14:1–3, after Jesus said that he was going away to prepare a place for his disciples in the house of his Father, he promised, "I come again and I will receive you unto myself" (Jn 14:3). Now here in Rev 22:20, in his last word spoken before he *does* come again, he says to John, "Yes, I am coming quickly." Did this promise, upon reflection, remind this "disciple whom Jesus loved" (Jn 21:20) of the word his Lord spoke to Peter about him in Jn 21:22, "If I wish him to remain until I come, what is that to you"? The aged John must have wondered often about that word. He knew that Jesus did not promise that he *would* remain on earth until the Lord came again, but *only that if the Lord wanted him to remain,* then he would remain (Jn 21:23). Now he who had lived so long as a witness to his Lord (cf. 1 Jn 1:1–4) hears this promise for the last time, "I am coming quickly" (Rev 22:20).

What is John's response? "Amen, come now, Lord Jesus" (22:20). The intent of this response is not to express the desire that the Lord should come *sometime*, but that he should "come *now*." After all that John had seen and experienced and heard as he was given the message of Revelation, now sealed by the promise of his Lord's impending return, he prays, "Come now, Lord Jesus." He had followed Jesus in his earthly pilgrimage to the cross, and then to his resurrection and ascension. How many times John must have prayed for his Lord's return! This disciple had been a faithful witness to his Lord over several decades since his Lord's earthly ministry. Now at this very moment, following the beatific vision he had just seen in Revelation, he prays again, "Come now, Lord Jesus."

This is also to be the prayer of every Christian individually, and of all Christians collectively, for it is the prayer of Christ's bride, the church. This prayer is lifted up elsewhere too. Paul in 1 Cor 16:22 voices the Aramaic equivalent of this prayer, "maranatha," "our Lord, come," in his conclusion of that epistle. In the Didache (early second century AD), the Aramaic form of the prayer comes at the close of liturgical instructions for the Eucharist in a prayer that was to be part of the congregation's Eucharistic celebration: "Let grace come and let this world pass away. ... If anyone is holy, let him come [to the Lord's Supper]; if anyone is not [holy], let him repent. Maranatha, amen" (Didache 10:6).

The voicing of this prayer heavenward is the end result of the reading and hearing the message of Revelation—in fact of the whole Bible. With the eyes of faith focused on the revelatory unveiling of Jesus Christ (1:1; cf. 1 Cor 1:7; Gal 1:12; 2 Thess 1:7; 1 Pet 1:13; 4:13) as presented and seen in Revelation, the church and each Christian are motivated to pray daily, "Amen, come *now*, Lord Jesus." This then is to be done in firm confidence that the Lord Jesus will keep his promise, "Yes, I am coming quickly" (Rev 22:20).

Until that glorious day, the epiphany of our great God and Savior, Jesus Christ (Titus 2:13), the closing benediction will sustain his church: "The grace of the Lord Jesus be with all" (Rev 22:21). That benediction highlights the truth that the Christian life is one of complete dependence upon God's grace in Christ, and a life of hope in the glory that will be revealed at his return. It also is an evangelistic prayer that the Lord's grace may indeed come to "all"—all people—through the proclaimed Gospel. Hence this blessing of grace, which opens so many of the NT epistles (e.g., Rom 1:7; 1 Cor 1:3; 2 Cor 1:2) and so many sermons is a most fitting conclusion for this final book of Scripture: "The grace of the Lord Jesus be with all [of you]."

EXCURSUS
SUMMARY OF THE CHRISTOLOGY OF REVELATION

In contrast to the Christology of the four gospels, that of Revelation presents Christ in glory. The gospels describe the life of Jesus on earth from his birth to his resurrection and ascension and thus present Christ in lowliness and humiliation, though their stories end with his entrance into his exalted glory. Where the gospels end, Revelation begins—at his ascension. It presents Christ in his state of exaltation (1:5, 13–20; 5:6–14) as Lord of lords and King of kings, from the time of his ascension until he comes again to judge the earth at the present world's end and to usher in the new creation.

The Christology of Revelation can be seen in the various roles Jesus Christ carries out in this prophetic message. He first appears to John in chapter 1 as the Son of Man (1:13). As such he is the mighty, exalted Lord of God's creation who will bring all history to an end when he comes in judgment of the human race (14:14; 19:11–21). As the Son of Man, Christ will be the Lord of the new creation, the new heaven and earth (3:14) under the authority of the Father and together with the heavenly Father (21:5–6; 22:13) and the Holy Spirit (22:17). And because Jesus Christ is the Son of Man, all creation will bow before him (1:5–7, 17; 19:11–16; cf. Phil 2:9–11).

In Revelation 5 Jesus Christ appears as the Lamb of God. Because of his victory by way of his death and resurrection, God's people have been redeemed and made into a kingdom for the heavenly Father (1:5–6; 5:10). It is by the blood of the Lamb that God's people are made righteous and holy in his sight and are thus presented to him for eternal life (7:14–17; 22:14). Because the Lamb of God won the victory for God's people over death and hell and over Satan, the dragon (12:5–12), Christ is honored and exalted as the Son of Man to rule all things in judgment and in life on behalf of the Father (5:6–14; 14:1–5, 14–20).

Another role that the exalted Christ plays in Revelation is that of the spokesman and Word of God, for he is the mediator and witness of the message of Revelation. While he himself does not appear in the guise of an angel (as did Yahweh in the OT, e.g., Ex 3:1–6; Judg 13:3–22), he fulfills such a role by the use of an angel who is arrayed in Christ's own heavenly glory and who acts on Christ's behalf, as vividly portrayed by the angel in Revelation 10. In such a role the Lord Christ presents himself to be "the angel/messenger of the covenant," (Mal 3:1), whom God promised to send to his people.

The high Christology of Revelation is brought to a climax and is compre-
hensively summarized in Rev 22:13, where the three divine titles describing
the eternal magnitude of the infinite God are applied to Jesus Christ. He is "the
First and the Last," the Lord of the church; "the Beginning and the End" of all
creation, and now also of the new creation; and "the Alpha and the Omega" of
all eternity. Together with the Father, Jesus of Nazareth, born of a woman, is
glorified and honored as God incarnate, through whom alone God deals with
the human race in creation and in redemption, in judgment and in mercy. To
him who reigns together with the Father and the Spirit be the glory, both now
and forever, amen!

Soli Deo Gloria

1